AF662023

R. GUPTA'S®

POPULAR MASTER GUIDE

JNU

JAWAHARLAL NEHRU UNIVERSITY

FIRST YEAR OF 3-YEAR B.A. (HONS.) ENTRANCE EXAMINATION

Chinese, French, German, Korean, Japanese, Arabic, Persian, Russian and Spanish

Compiled by
Dr. N. Pandey & D. Dwivedi
& RPH Editorial Board

RAMESH PUBLISHING HOUSE, NEW DELHI

Published by:
O.P. Gupta *for* Ramesh Publishing House

Admin. Office:
12-H, New Daryaganj Road, Opp. Traffic Kotwali,
New Delhi-110002 ✆ 23261567, 23275224, Telefax: 011-23275124

E-mail: info@rameshpublishinghouse.com
Website: www.rameshpublishinghouse.com

Showroom:
• 4457, Nai Sarak, Delhi-6, ✆ 23918938, 23918532
• 2604/16, Balaji Market, Nai Sarak, Delhi-6 ✆ 23253720

10th Edition: January, 2015

Book Code: R-1034

ISBN: 978-81-7812-609-8

Price: ₹ 295

Printed at: Shyam Printer, Delhi

CONTENTS

GUIDELINES FOR ENTRANCE EXAMINATION

FIRST YEAR OF THREE-YEAR B.A. (HONS.) PROGRAMME IN FOREIGN LANGUAGES

Candidates seeking admission to the first-year of the 3 year-B.A. Programme in the school of Language, Literature and Culture Studies shall be examined on the basis of their general language and aptitude test. The questions shall be of objective type, short answers etc. and shall be within the broad spectrum of General Knowledge, General English and Elementary Knowledge on the culture and civilization of the languages/country concerned and aptitude for language skills.

ABOUT THE SCHOOL OF LANGUAGES, LITERATURE AND CULTURAL STUDIES

Language is the key to society and man - how we think, what we think, how we interact with each other and co-exist as a community, all this is determined by language which is not only the means of thought but in fact the thought itself. Learning different languages means learning about cultures and traditions of various people. There are a large number of human natural languages, but we cannot learn all of them. However, if we acquaint ourselves with major languages of the world, we get to know much about human civilisation and culture. The School of Language, Literature and Culture Studies set up with this in mind, imparts instruction in a number of major European and Asian languages such as Arabic spoken in lands where Arabs live, Persian language of Iran an ancient country, Japanese, Korean and Chinese are spoken in the far east of Asia by a large number of people belonging to economically and politically powerful countries. The School also teaches major European languages such as English, French, German, Russian, and Spanish which are the languages basically of Europe but are spoken by large number of people in the Americas. Each of these languages has a significant body of literature, a galaxy of great writers, novelists, poets, story writers. These languages are the carriers of great culture and great philosophy. The student who opts to study a language in the School will, in fact, be studying much more than language. He/she will also be studying the literature, art and philosophy of that Culture.

Training in a major language enables one, at the end of the training, to become a translator, an interpreter, a teacher, an expert or a consultant in multi-media projects. Now that the world is becoming a small place and with the spreading globalisation a person trained in a foreign language is becoming an important person, a culture negotiator in fact.

The courses aim at developing competence and proficiency in spoken as well as written language through audio-visual techniques, language laboratory, films etc.

The courses in civilization and culture give a total overview of the history, geography and cultural institutions of the country concerned. A survey of the country's history, its art and thought are woven into the fabric of the courses to give the students a proper understanding of the relationship between society and its art and thought.

Literature is studies as a specific discipline in itself and students are trained in various methods of literary analysis. Literature is studied in its socio-historical context besides its study as an aesthetic object.

The School of Language, Literature and Culture Studies is the only institution of its kind in the country where facilities for teaching and research in most of the major foreign languages are available. In addition to the several foreign languages, the School also provides for teaching/research in English, Theoretical & Applied Linguistics and a few Indian Languages.

Language studies in the School seek to promote in students a world perspective and a spirit of international cooperation and understanding of different civilizations and cultures.

BA(Hons.) being an integral part of the 5-year MA programme, on successful completion of B.A. (Hons.), the student will be eligible to seek registration to the first year of the MA programme (i.e. fourth year of 5-year M.A.) in the respective language, wherever offered, without having to go through the entrance examination again subject to his/her fulfilling minimum eligibility requirements.

ELIGIBILITY

Senior School Certificate (10+2) or equivalent examination with minimum of 45% marks. The candidates who are due to appear in Senior School Certificate (10+2) or equivalent examination are eligible to apply.

PROGRAMME OF STUDY

First year of 3-year B.A. (Hons.) programme in Foreign Languages:

1. Arabic **2.** Chinese **3.** French **4.** German **5.** Japanese
6. Korean **7.** Persian **8.** Russian **9.** Spanish

Previous Paper (Solved)

JAWAHARLAL NEHRU UNIVERSITY [JNU]

FIRST YEAR OF 3-YEAR B.A. [HONS.] ENTRANCE EXAMINATION, 2014

Chinese, French, German, Korean, Japanese, Arabic, Persian, Russian and Spanish

PART–A

All questions carry one mark each. Encircle the correct answer clearly. If more than one option is encircled, the answer will be marked wrong.

1. Which of the following is a Francophone region?
(*a*) Maldives (*b*) Hong Kong
(*c*) Virgin Islands (*d*) Seychelles

2. Which of the following is not one of the old names of Urdu?
(*a*) Rekhta (*b*) Hindvi
(*c*) Dakkani (*d*) Farsi

3. While in India, the Chinese scholar Hiuen Tsang also stayed for a brief period in which one of the following newly discovered universities?
(*a*) Nalanda (*b*) Vikramshila
(*c*) Telhara (*d*) Taxila

4. Kimchi is a traditional side dish of
(*a*) China (*b*) Vietnam
(*c*) South Korea (*d*) Philippines

5. Who among the following translated *Mahabharata* into Persian?
(*a*) Mirza Ghalib (*b*) Mulla Badayuni
(*c*) Akbar (*d*) Amir Khusraw

6. This year marks the .... anniversary of *Panchsheel* between India and China.
(*a*) 64th (*b*) 60th
(*c*) 65th (*d*) 55th

7. The notion of 'Chinese dream' has been advocated by which of the following Chinese leaders?
(*a*) Mao Zedong (*b*) Deng Xiaoping
(*c*) Jiang Zemin (*d*) Xi Jinping

8. The royal family of Japan recently visited the cities of
(*a*) New Delhi and Kolkata
(*b*) New Delhi and Chennai
(*c*) New Delhi and Mumbai
(*d*) New Delhi and Bengaluru

9. Which of the following countries won the bid for 2020 Summer Olympics?
(*a*) Korea (*b*) Canada
(*c*) Australia (*d*) Japan

10. 'K-Pop' is a popular abbreviation for
(*a*) South Korean Pop Music
(*b*) Kazakhstan Popular Arts
(*c*) Kyrgyzstan Pop Culture
(*d*) Kenyan Popular Dance and Music

11. Jean-Luc Godard is a French
(*a*) Poet (*b*) Painter
(*c*) Film-maker (*d*) Politician

12. The largest Arabic-speaking country in number of speakers is
(*a*) Saudi Arabia (*b*) Egypt
(*c*) Algeria (*d*) Syria

13. Rabat is the capital of
(*a*) Tunisia (*b*) Algeria
(*c*) Chad (*d*) Morocco

14. Which of the following languages belongs to the Semitic group of languages?
(*a*) German (*b*) French
(*c*) Hebrew (*d*) Russian

15. Leo Tolstoy was a representative author of
(*a*) romanticism (*b*) realism
(*c*) natural school (*d*) symbolism

16. The Mascot for Sochi Winter Olympics, 2014 was
(*a*) Quatchi and Miga
(*b*) Neve and Gliz
(*c*) Powder, Coal and Copper
(*d*) The Hare, the Polar Bear and the Snow Leopard

17. Shakira, the famous singer, is from
(*a*) Peru (*b*) Mexico
(*c*) Spain (*d*) Columbia

18. What is the present currency of Spain?
(*a*) Dollar (*b*) Peseta
(*c*) Euro (*d*) Spanish dollar

19. In which year was the Project Tiger started in India?
(*a*) 1973 (*b*) 1976
(*c*) 1982 (*d*) 1989

20. Which of the following is not associated with Spain?
(*a*) Flamenco dance
(*b*) Bullfighting
(*c*) Tomatina festival
(*d*) Dia de los muertos

Who wrote the following books? (for Q. Nos. 21 to 25)

21. *A Brief History of Time*
(*a*) Stephen Hawking
(*b*) Khalil Gibran
(*c*) Jonathan Swift
(*d*) Derrida

22. *Natya-shastra*
(*a*) Narad Muni (*b*) Bharat Muni
(*c*) Abhinav Gupta (*d*) Chanakya

23. *Ladies Coupe*
(*a*) Preeti Shenoy (*b*) Anita Nair
(*c*) Anurag Mathvi (*d*) Rashmi Bansal

24. *The Inheritance of Loss*
(*a*) Amitava Ghosh
(*b*) R.K. Narayan
(*c*) Arun Tiwari
(*d*) Kiran Desai

25. *The Secret of the Nagas*
(*a*) Shobha Dey
(*b*) Amish Tripathi
(*c*) Arundhati Ray
(*d*) Vikram Seth

PART–B

All questions carry one mark each. Encircle the correct answer clearly. If more than one option is encircled, the answer will be marked wrong (Q. Nos. 26 to 30):

26. Ornithology is the study of
(*a*) bees (*b*) birds
(*c*) fishes (*d*) ornamental plants

27. Muga/Mooga is a kind of Indian
(*a*) painting style
(*b*) musical instrument
(*c*) silk
(*d*) None of the above

28. The deepest oceanic trench, Mariana, is located in
(*a*) Atlantic Ocean
(*b*) Pacific Ocean
(*c*) Arctic Ocean
(*d*) Indian Ocean

29. There are deer and peacocks in a zoo. By counting heads, they are 80. The number of their legs is 200. How many peacocks are there?
(*a*) 20 (*b*) 40
(*c*) 60 (*d*) 50

30. Rahul walks northwards. After a while, he turns to his right and a little further to his left. Finally, after walking a distance of one kilometer, he turns to his left again. In which direction is he moving now?
(*a*) East (*b*) West
(*c*) North (*d*) South

Select and encircle the most appropriate synonyms of the bracketed words (Q. Nos. 31 to 36):

31. (Placid)
(*a*) Solemn (*b*) Lazy
(*c*) Devious (*d*) Calm

32. (Nincompoop)
(*a*) Sharp and intelligent
(*b*) Famous person
(*c*) Foolish person
(*d*) Cunning

33. (Rudimentary)
(*a*) Broad (*b*) Basic
(*c*) Advanced (*d*) Sharp

34. (Arboreal)
(*a*) Jovial (*b*) Relating to trees
(*c*) Urban (*d*) Airy

35. (Shrewd)
(*a*) Mean (*b*) Unwise
(*c*) Astute (*d*) Kind

36. (Kleptomania)
(*a*) Sleepwalking
(*b*) Honesty
(*c*) Tendency to steal
(*c*) Modesty

Encircle the correct answer (Q. Nos. 37 to 44):

37. Who defined democracy as government of the people, by the people and for the people?
(*a*) Napoleon Bonaparte
(*b*) George Washington
(*c*) Abraham Lincoln
(*d*) Winston Churchill

38. Which of the following is not correctly matched?
(*a*) Syed Kirmani — Cricketer
(*b*) Mira Nair — Film director
(*c*) Sharan Rani — Sarod player
(*c*) Ashapurna Devi — Classical singer

39. According to the Indian mythology, Apsara Menaka married sage
(*a*) Vashishtha (*d*) Shaunak
(*c*) Atri (*d*) Vishwamitra

40. Priyanka is both the 50th best and the 50th worst student at her school. How many students attend her school?
(*a*) 98 (*d*) 99
(*c*) 100 (*d*) 101

41. Who was the winner of 2012 Dada Sahib Phalke Award?
(*a*) Actor Pran
(*d*) Singer Manna Dey
(*c*) Director K. Balachander
(*d*) Actor Soumitra Chatterjee

42. When light passes from air into glass, it experiences change of
(*a*) frequency and wavelength
(*d*) frequency and speed
(*c*) wavelength and speed
(*d*) frequency, wavelength and speed

43. What is *Mohiniattam*?
(*a*) Painting style
(*d*) Classical dance form
(*c*) Hindustani classical music raga
(*d*) Musical instrument of Andhra Pradesh

44. Who is the new CEO of Microsoft?
(*a*) Satya Nadella
(*d*) Indira Nooyi
(*c*) Mark Zuckerberg
(*d*) Kun Hee Lee

Answer the following questions (Q. Nos. 45 to 50):

45. Which Indian cricket player wrote the book, *One More Over*?

....

46. Who was the captain of the Indian hockey team, which won the Gold Medal in Tokyo Olympics in 1964?

....

47. Who holds the post of Ex-officio Chairperson of the Planning Commission of India?

....

48. On which date is the International Women's Day celebrated?

....

49. If PENSION is coded as NEISNOP, how is FOLIAGE coded?

....

50. What is the number of already named bones in the human skeleton?

....

PART–C

All questions carry one mark each.

Select appropriate words to fill in the blanks (Q. Nos. 51 to 60):

51. Mrs. Sharma .... rather not invest that money in the stock market.
(*a*) could (*b*) would
(*c*) has to (*d*) neither

52. When I graduate from college next June, I .... a student here for five years.
(*a*) will be (*b*) have been
(*c*) will have been (*d*) has been

53. The company will upgrade .... computer information systems next month.
(*a*) their (*b*) its
(*c*) it's (*d*) own

54. Each of the Olympic athletes .... training for months, even years.
(*a*) have been (*b*) has been
(*c*) were (*d*) been

55. I have only a .... Diwali cards left to write.
(*a*) some (*b*) few
(*c*) little (*d*) less

56. The police were greatly out-numbered by rioters, ... ran into hundreds.
(*a*) whose figures
(*b*) those figures
(*c*) that its figures
(*d*) its figures that

57. It is lovely to wake up in the morning and .... birds singing.
(*a*) hear (*b*) hears
(*c*) heard (*d*) hearing

58. When Anisha .... her first pay, she bought presents for her parents?
(*a*) receive (*b*) received
(*c*) has received (*d*) had received

59. That is a story of hardship .... our own situation into perspective.
(*a*) puts (*b*) it puts
(*c*) that it puts (*d*) that puts

60. A : "Have you had enough to eat?"
B : "I'd like ...., please."
(*a*) another (*b*) one more
(*c*) some more (*d*) any more

Fill in the blanks with appropriate prepositions in the following sentences (Q. Nos. 61 to 66):

61. A house .... the sea is where you will find me after retirement.

62. She is .... the other children in her class. Please ensure she studies.

63. I will come back .... two weeks.

64. .... my calculation he must be sixty-three.

65. The picture is .... page 7.

66. .... you and me, I think she is crazy.

Give full form of the following (Q. Nos. 67 to 70):

67. SEBI ....

68. PETA ....

69. BCCI ....

70. ICSSR ....

Rearrange the following words to make meaningful sentences (Q. Nos. 71 to 74):

71. yesterday/at home/you/to visit/were not/I/but/wanted/you

....

72. he decided/had seen/to buy/after Ali/the film/the book/ on TV

....

73. for you/wait a minute!/this box/I will/carry

....

74. for two hours/waiting/girlfriend/I/my/have been/for

....

Read carefully the following data from Iselta language:

1. (a) temiban 'I went'	4. mimiaj 'he was going'
2. (a) amiban 'you went'	5. tewanban 'I came'
3. (a) temiwe 'I am going'	6. tewanhi 'I will come'

Answer the following questions (Q. Nos. 75 to 77):

75. How will you say the following in Iselta?

'He went': ....

76. How will you say the following in Iselta?

'You will come': ....

77. Translate the following in English:

'awanban': ....

78. What is missing out of the trio?

Sine, Cosine and ....

79. If a bag of 30 sweets weighs 20 g, how many sweets would weigh 1 kg?

....

80. What is the next number in the following series?

1, 4, 9, 16, ...

PART–D

Read the passage below and give short answer to the questions that follow. Marks assigned are given against each question:

People moan about poverty as a great evil; and it seems to be an accepted belief that if people only had plenty of money, they would be happy and useful and get more out of life. As a rule, there is more genuine satisfaction in life and more obtained from life in the humble cottage of the poor man than in the palaces of the rich. I always pity the sons and daughters of rich men who are attended by servants and have governesses at a later age; at the same time I am glad to think that they do not know what they have missed.

It is because I know how sweet and happy and pure the home of honest poverty is, how free from perplexing care and from social envies and jealousies—how loving and united its members are in the common interest of supporting the family that I sympathize with the rich man's boy and congratulate the poor man's son. It is for these reasons that from the ranks of the poor so many strong, eminent, self-reliant men have always sprung and always must spring. If you will read the list of the 'Immortals who were not born to die', you will find that most of them have been born poor. It seems, nowadays, a matter of universal desire that poverty should be abolished. We should be quite willing to abolish luxury; but to abolish honest, industrious, self-denying poverty would be to destroy the soil upon which mankind produces the virtues that will enable our race to reach a still higher civilization than it now possesses.

81. Write the summary of the above passage in about one-third of the original length in your own words.

....

....

....

....

....

....

....

....

....

....

....

....

....

....

....

82. Give a suitable title to the above passage.

....

PART–E

Write a brief composition on the following topics in about 400 words each:

83. The tradition or the custom of your region related to daily life that you think should continue.

....

....

....

....

....

....

....

....

84. Foreign language learning (points to be covered—motivation, prospects and relevance in globalization).

....

....

....

....

....

....

....

....

ANSWERS

PART–A

1	2	3	4	5
(*d*)	(*c*)	(*a*)	(*c*)	(*b*)
6	**7**	**8**	**9**	**10**
(*b*)	(*d*)	(*b*)	(*d*)	(*a*)
11	**12**	**13**	**14**	**15**
(*c*)	(*b*)	(*d*)	(*c*)	(*b*)
16	**17**	**18**	**19**	**20**
(*d*)	(*d*)	(*c*)	(*a*)	(*d*)
21	**22**	**23**	**24**	**25**
(*a*)	(*b*)	(*b*)	(*d*)	(*b*)

PART–B

26	27	28	29	30
(*b*)	(*c*)	(*b*)	(*c*)	(*b*)
31	**32**	**33**	**34**	**35**
(*d*)	(*c*)	(*b*)	(*b*)	(*c*)
36	**37**	**38**	**39**	**40**
(*c*)	(*c*)	(*d*)	(*d*)	(*b*)
41	**42**	**43**	**44**	
(*a*)	(*c*)	(*b*)	(*a*)	

45. E.A.S. Prasanna

46. Charanjit Singh

47. Prime Minister

48. 8th March

49. EOAILGF

50. 206

PART–C

51	52	53	54	55
b	*c*	*b*	*b*	*b*
56	**57**	**58**	**59**	**60**
a	*a*	*d*	*d*	*c*

61. beside

62. behind

63. within

64. To

65. on

66. Between

67. Securities and Exchange Board of India

68. People for the Ethical Treatment of Animals

69. Board of Control for Cricket in India
70. Indian Council of Social Science Research
71. I wanted to visit you yesterday but you were not at home.
72. After Ali had seen the film on TV, he decided to buy the book.
73. Wait a minute, I will carry this box for you.
74. I have been waiting for my girlfriend for two hours.
75. mimiban
76. awanhi
77. you came
78. tangent
79. 1500
80. 25

PART–D

81. It is a common belief that poverty is bad and richness is good for people to have a useful life. But the poor people live with more satisfaction and achieve more in life than the rich. The children of rich always depend upon servants for every work and are spoiled while those of poor grow with more love, unity and responsibility for their families. This makes them strong and self-dependent. Most of the great men were born poor. Those who wish to abolish poverty should wish to abolish luxury instead because poverty nurtures virtues for growth and development of mankind while luxury mars them.
82. Positive Effects of Poverty.

PART–E

83. In our region of India, communities have inherited the rich tradition of love and reverence for nature through ages. Religious preaching, traditions and customs have played a big role in this regard: Indian religions have generally been the advocates of environmentalism. They campaigned for such guidelines to the commoners that ensured an intimate contact and sense of belonging in nature. It came in the form of directives to the believers to perform certain rites and rituals, so that it became a way of their life. Sometimes the messages of environmental protection and conservation are in a veiled form. Today, when the world is undergoing a serious crisis of ecological imbalance and environmental degradation, it is all the more important for us to understand such traditions.

The culture of conservation of nature dates back to the ancient Vedic Period. The four Vedas—Rig-Veda, Sama-Veda, Yajur-Veda and Atharva-Veda—are full of hymns dedicated to the supremacy of various natural entities. The Rigvedic hymns refer to many gods and goddesses identified with sun, moon, thunder, lightening, snow, rain, water, rivers, trees etc. They have been glorified and worshipped as givers of health, wealth and prosperity. The rain–god Indra has the largest number of hymns attached to him.

Sun worship is of vital importance in Vedic worship; the sun was worshipped in the form of gods like Sūrya, Mārtaṇḍa, Uṣa, Pūṣan, Rudra, etc. Today it has been proved that solar energy is the ultimate source of energy that regulates the energy flow through the food-chain, drives various nutrient cycles and thus controls the ecosystem all over the earth, but it was probably well understood and realized by the ancient people as well.

Tress have also been given huge importance the ancient Indian tradition. The four Vedas are full of references to various herbs, trees and flowers and their significance. Trees and plants were considered as animate beings and to harm them was regarded as a sacrilege.

The tradition of sacred groves was also common in the ancient period and is still practised by folk and tribal communities. A sacred grove consists of a bunch of old trees, generally at the outskirts of a village, which were left untouched when the original settlers cleared the forest to establish the village. In many sacred groves, villagers perform sacrifices and offerings to the gods during festivals and other occasions.

Indian traditions, customs and religious beliefs enlighten us about the protection of the flora and fauna. They teach us one fundamental principles of ecology, especially that every living entity of the biosphere has its own important role in the flow of energy and cycle of nutrients which keep the world going.

84. There has always been a growing importance for languages whether native or foreign, especially in today's era were communication has reached its peak and the world has become a smaller place. As globalisation takes a toll on the youth, an increasing number of youngsters are inclined towards learning foreign languages. Learning foreign languages like German, French, Spanish, Japanese and Mandarin gives students an edge.

Today, various institutes and universities are offering a number of courses in languages, among them foreign languages like German, French, Spanish, Japanese and Mandarin are now gaining momentum.

Learning a new language is not only interesting but also increases one's knowledge about the culture and lifestyle of the people of that specific country. Some students also learn languages to make a career in the field of translation and interpretation.

Learning a foreign language gives students an opportunity to appear for international examinations like TOFEL, JLPT and DELE etc. Career options in the field of translation are plenty. Due to growing economic relations between India and various countries of the world, knowing a foreign language gives one the much-needed edge. With various MNCs hiring translators and interpreters, this is a fast growing field. Being a translator can be an interesting job as you connect with various people of the world and there is an exchange of cultures and ideas from people all across the globe. Besides, many international schools now need teachers who can teach foreign languages to students. Japanese, is gaining importance as a foreign language and can be the next language that will be taught to students in schools after French and German.

With Indian companies emerging as global players and Indian market being eyed by multinational companies, it becomes essential that there is no dearth of professionals who can overcome language barriers and facilitate smooth communication for proper business transactions. Foreign language experts with a good understanding of cultures are in great demand in the corporate world. The scope of foreign languages as career is stupendous and candidates willing to explore it have multitude of job opportunities in various multinational companies and multilateral organisations. Moreover, language skills are essential attribute in most professions and help in the advancement of career.

Whereas Indian MNCs require trained foreign language professionals to open their operations in foreign countries, foreign multinationals require such candidates at cheap salaries from India. The situation is so attractive for Indian foreign language professionals that language experts in Japanese, Chinese and Korean get jobs soon after their five year language course from various institutes. International job opportunities for foreign language experts from India are open in supranational bodies such as United Nations Organization and its other bodies, various projects of India's Foreign Ministry and of course India's spy agencies.

Previous Paper (Solved)

JNUEE–2013

B.A. (HONS.) IN FOREIGN LANGUAGES

PART–A

All questions carry one mark each. Encircle the correct answer clearly. If more than one answers are encircled, the answer will be marked wrong.

1. The first Indian woman to climb the Mount Everest was
(*a*) Bachendri Pal
(*b*) Junko Tabei
(*c*) Anita Sood
(*d*) Geetika Jakhar

2. Which of these bodies of water does not border France?
(*a*) The Mediterranean
(*b*) The English Channel
(*c*) The Atlantic
(*d*) The Baltic

3. The construction of the Berlin Wall began on
(*a*) 9th November, 1989
(*b*) 6th March, 1949
(*c*) 13th August, 1961
(*d*) 20th August, 1947

4. The Korean alphabet is
(*a*) Katakana (*b*) Hangul
(*c*) Hiragana (*d*) Hanbok

5. Who made 'La Gioconda?
(*a*) Leonardo da Vinci
(*b*) Tenniel
(*c*) Graham Sutherland
(*d*) Brighton

6. Isfahan is located in which of the following countries?
(*a*) Afghanistan (*b*) Iran
(*c*) Uzbekistan (*d*) Tajikistan

7. First Olympiad in Greece was held in
(*a*) 10000 BC (*b*) 776 BC
(*c*) 58 BC (*d*) 800 BC

8. In which year did terrorists crash aircraft into New York's World Trade Centre?
(*a*) 2000 (*b*) 2001
(*c*) 2003 (*d*) 1998

9. The Eiffel Tower was constructed in
(*a*) 1789 (*b*) 1889
(*c*) 1860 (*d*) 1887

10. Ravi Shankar is recognized for bringing the Indian classical music tradition to the West. This was done through his association with which of the following?
(*a*) John Lennon
(*b*) George Harrison
(*c*) Oprah Winfrey
(*d*) Michael Jackson

Who wrote the following books? (For Q. Nos. 11 to 14):

11. *Untouchables*
(*a*) Rudyard Kipling
(*b*) Ruskin Bond
(*c*) Mulk Raj Anand
(*d*) Chetan Bhagat

12. *Paradise Lost*
(*a*) John Milton
(*b*) John Keats
(*c*) D.H. Lawrence
(*d*) William Wordsworth

13. *Cancer Ward*
(*a*) Maxim Gorky
(*b*) Leo Tolstoy
(*c*) Alexander Solzhenitsyn
(*d*) Boris Pasternak

14. *One Hundred Years of Solitude*
(*a*) Miguel Ángel Asturias
(*b*) Jacinto Benavente
(*c*) Gabriel García Márquez
(*d*) Jean-Paul Sartre

15. Which aircraft dropped the atomic bomb on Hiroshima?
(*a*) Enola Gay
(*b*) Samurai Avenger
(*c*) Aeroflot
(*d*) Kamikaze

16. Which of the following is **not** a public holiday in Japan?
(*a*) Greenery Day
(*b*) Respect for the Aged Day
(*c*) Culture Day
(*d*) Earthquake Prevention Day

17. 'Tapas' is a word for snacks and the word is originally from
(*a*) Spanish (*b*) French
(*c*) Italian (*d*) Portuguese

18. Peter the Great moved the capital of Russia to
(*a*) Moscow (*b*) St. Petersburg
(*c*) Kiev (*d*) Tashkent

19. The Inca Civilization was in
(*a*) Peru (*b*) Spain
(*c*) Brazil (*d*) France

20. The split between Bolsheviks and Mensheviks happened in
(*a*) 1917 (*b*) 1924
(*c*) 1947 (*d*) 1905

21. Former name of Taiwan was
(*a*) Formosa (*b*) Canton
(*c*) Taipei (*d*) Macau

22. Islands under territorial dispute between Japan and China are
(*a*) Ryukyu Islands
(*b*) Kurile Islands
(*c*) Senkaku Islands
(*d*) Takeshima Islands

23. What is known as 'Empty Quarter'?
(*a*) Homes vacated by Palestinians in Israel
(*b*) No man's land between Yemen and Saudi Arabia
(*c*) Sand desert in Saudi Arabia
(*d*) An area in Tibet

24. Who started the Bauhaus Movement?
(*a*) Walter Gropius
(*b*) Ludwig Mies van der Rohe
(*c*) Daniel Ash
(*d*) Vassily Kadinsky

25. *Shahnama,* an epic is written in which of the following languages?
(*a*) Urdu (*b*) Persian
(*c*) Arabic (*d*) Pashto

PART–B

All questions carry one mark each. Encircle the correct answer clearly. If more than one answers are encircled, the answer will be marked wrong (Q. Nos. 26 to 33):

26. Brahmo Samaj was founded by
(*a*) Vivekananda
(*b*) Ananda Mohan Bose
(*c*) Raja Rammohan Roy
(*d*) Radha Kanta Dev

27. The Jallianwala Bagh Massacre happened in
(*a*) 1910 (*b*) 1921
(*c*) 1919 (*d*) 1924

28. Which famous Indian ghazal singer died in 2011?
(*a*) Begum Akhtar
(*b*) Talat Mehmood
(*c*) Jagjeet Singh
(*d*) Mohammad Rafi

29. Who was the last Mughal Emperor of India?
(*a*) Shah Jahan
(*b*) Akbar
(*c*) Bahadur Shah Zafar
(*d*) Aurangzeb

30. Dronacharya Awards are given to
(*a*) Sports coaches
(*b*) Cricketers
(*c*) Tennis players
(*d*) Hockey players

31. Which one of the following Indian languages does not have a Dravidian origin?
(*a*) Kannada (*b*) Marathi
(*c*) Malayalam (*d*) Telugu

32. Sonal Mansingh is associated with
(*a*) Bharat Natyam (*b*) Kathak
(*c*) Kuchipudi (*d*) Odissi

33. Look at the news items given below. Encircle the correct option to fill in the blank:

Delhi police reported that 15 crates .... by them from three persons in North Delhi.
(*a*) of illicit liquor were recovered
(*b*) of illicit liquor was recovered
(*c*) in illicit liquor was recovered
(*d*) of illicit liquors were recovered

Rearrange the following words to make meaningful sentences:

34. in the/money/safe/of/there/was/lots

....

35. were queuing/film/a lot of/for the/people

....

Select and encircle the most appropriate synonyms of the bracketed words (Q. Nos. 36 to 41):

36. (Corpulent)
(*a*) Lean (*b*) Gaunt
(*c*) Emaciated (*d*) Obese

37. (Brief)
(*a*) Limited (*b*) Small
(*c*) Little (*d*) Short

38. (August)
(*a*) Common (*b*) Ridiculous
(*c*) Dignified (*d*) Petty

39. (Alert)
(*a*) Energetic (*b*) Observant
(*c*) Intelligent (*d*) Watchful

40. (Adversity)
(*a*) Failure (*b*) Helplessness
(*c*) Misfortune (*d*) Crisis

41. (Indict)
(*a*) Condemn (*b*) Reprimand
(*c*) Accuse (*d*) Allege

Encircle the correct answer :

42. Susan can type 10 pages in 5 minutes. Mary can type 5 pages in 10 minutes. If they are working together, how many pages can they type in 30 minutes?
(*a*) 20 (*b*) 25
(*c*) 65 (*d*) 75

43. Consider the following series
3, 4, 6, 9, 13, ...
What comes next?
(*a*) 16 (*b*) 17
(*c*) 18 (*d*) 19

Choose and encircle the pair of words that best completes the sentence (Q. Nos. 44 and 45):

The .... of the timetable caused some ....

44. (*a*) rivision (*b*) revision
(*c*) revission (*d*) revition

45. (*a*) inconvenience (*b*) inconvenince
(*c*) inconveneince (*d*) inconveniense

46. Encircle the correct answer:

The average of ten numbers is 7. If each number is multiplied by 12, then the average of new set of numbers is
(*a*) 7 (*b*) 19
(*c*) 82 (*d*) 84

47. Write the missing letter in the following series:
a c e ? i ....

Encircle the correct answer:

48. Which is the alternative that can replace the question mark (?)?
Mathematics : Pcwjhodvlev :: algebra : ?
(*a*) dnjgetd (*b*) cnjgetd
(*c*) dnjhetd (*d*) cnjhetc

49. Fear of heights is known as
(*a*) Arachnophobia (*b*) Necrophilia
(*c*) Acrophobia (*d*) Heliophobia

50. Who among the following is a famous scientist?
(*a*) Stephen Hawking
(*b*) Steve Jobs
(*c*) Steven Spielberg
(*d*) David Cameron

PART–C

All questions carry one mark each. Fill in the blanks with appropriate prepositions in the following sentences:

51. He is standing .... me in the queue.

52. This birthday present is .... your brother.

53. Are there any plants .... your bedroom?

54. All the family members are sitting .... the sofa and talking.

55. You can sit .... the table. Lunch is ready.

Fill in the blanks with appropriate words:

56. The internet serves to .... people all over the world.

57. The wounded soldier was in great .... from the bullet that had hit him.

58. We could not .... the waiter's attention as he was too busy.

59. The painter handled his .... very carefully to add just another touch.

60. I had to climb onto the .... of the house to fix the antenna.

Fill in the blanks with appropriate verbs in the appropriate forms:

61. The Earth .... round the Sun.

62. If you .... at once, you can reach the theatre by 6 o'clock.

63. He usually .... at the back of the class.

64. He .... here for the last five years.

65. My friend .... from cholera since August.

66. If she does not take a taxi, she .... the bus.

67. When I .... the road, I saw a big snake.

68. I .... him before he left India.

69. The journalist .... a new book at present.

70. He .... asleep while he was driving.

Give full forms of the following acronyms/abbreviations:

71. NATO ....

72. SAARC ....

73. ISRO ....

74. OPEC ....

Encircle the correct answer:

75. In an artificial language the following means
portweagno = mathematical traditions
screnccrue = great mathematicians
goddragno = mathematical formulas

Then what will be the words that translate to international congress of mathematicians?

(*a*) screntbhjfslkjhagno
(*b*) goddrtbhjfslkjhagno
(*c*) screnhjtyrgtlkjbblj
(*d*) screnccruetylkkhyp

Answer the following:

76. 2013 in Chinese Zodiac is the year of .... (Fill in the blank)

77. Who became the first director to shoot at NASA?

....

78. Who was assigned the task of partitioning India in 1947?

....

79. Which car company launched the new car model Figo?

....

80. Hugo Chavez was the President of .... (Fill in the blank)

PART–D

Read the passage below and give short answers to the following questions. Marks assigned are given against each question:

The hustle and bustle of big cities attracts almost everyone. Big cities are often distinguished from small towns by the skyscrapers, proper means of transport, means of communication and good infrastructure. They say that the city never sleeps.

This holds true because every time you look at the roads, you see it full of activity. Like in many cities, problems concerning accommodation is something you should be aware of before you move to a city.

Life in a city seems to be too busy. The start of the day always portrays school buses carrying children to their schools, a long queue of people waiting for the bus to head to their offices, and others who are driving in their own cars. The nights are even more exciting. Different events and occasions add more life to the city.

A city is a mix of people who are good and bad, rich and poor and of different religious backgrounds. Therefore, you will experience nearly all kinds of individuals and all kinds of living standards in a city.

Even though life in a city is considered to bring you more towards a civilized side, providing you with more facilities and higher standards of living, city life is not considered to be good enough for children.

Parents are seen to develop a distance for their children because of their tight schedules and because they get very little time to spend with their children. This might also be the reason of families breaking and impacting a child's mind negatively.

Despite all this, cities generally provide good employment opportunities and high educational standards that will be required to enhance the way of your life. In the end, the advantages outweigh the disadvantages. In order to maintain a good lifestyle one can always improve ambiance in his home and neighbourhood.

81. What do you know about life in a small town? 4

82. Why is city life not good enough for children? 2

83. What are the advantages of city life? 2

84. Between city life and life in a small town which one do you prefer and why? 2

PART–E

Write an essay on the following topic in about 600-700 words

85. My Favourite Advertisement on Television.

Or

The Issue of Safety for Women.

ANSWERS

PART–A

1	2	3	4	5
(*a*)	(*d*)	(*c*)	(*b*)	(*a*)
6	**7**	**8**	**9**	**10**
(*b*)	(*b*)	(*b*)	(*d*)	(*b*)
11	**12**	**13**	**14**	**15**
(*c*)	(*a*)	(*c*)	(*c*)	(*a*)
16	**17**	**18**	**19**	**20**
(*d*)	(*a*)	(*a*)	(*a*)	(*d*)
21	**22**	**23**	**24**	**25**
(*a*)	(*c*)	(*c*)	(*a*)	(*b*)

PART–B

26	27	28	29	30
(*c*)	(*c*)	(*c*)	(*c*)	(*a*)

31	32	33
(*b*)	(*d*)	(*a*)

34. There was lots of money in the safe.

35. A lot of people were queuing for the film.

36. (*d*)

37. (*d*)

38. (*c*)

39. (*b*)

40. (*c*)

41. (*c*)

42. (*d*)

Susan's 1 min. work = $\frac{10}{5}$ = 2 pages

Mary's 1 min. work = $\frac{5}{10} = \frac{1}{2}$ page

(Susan + Mary)'s 1 min. work

$$= 2 + \frac{1}{2} = \frac{5}{2} \text{ pages}$$

Required no. of pages = $\frac{5}{2} \times 30 = 75$ pages

43. (*c*)

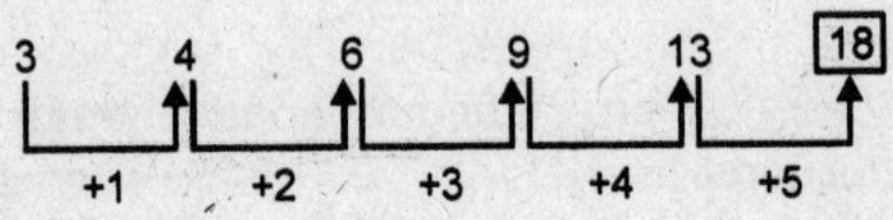

44. (*b*)

45. (*a*)

46. (*d*)
Total no. of 10 numbers = 10 × 7 = 70
Total new no. = 12 × 70 = 840

New average no. = $\frac{840}{10} = 84$

47. Missing letter is g.

48. (*a*)

49. (*c*)

50. (*a*)

PART–C

51. behind

52. for

53. outside

54. in

55. on

56. millions of

57. pain

58. catch

59. work

60. rooftop

61. revolves

62. leave

63. sits

64. has been working

65. has been suffering

66. will miss

67. crossed

68. had met

69. is writing

70. fell

71. NATO—North Atlantic Treaty Organisation

72. SAARC—South Asian Association for Regional Corporation

73. ISRO—Indian Space Research Organisation

74. OPEC—Organisation of Petroleum Exporting Countries

75. (*a*)

76. Snake

77. Ashutosh Gowariker (Swades)

78. Sir Cyril Radcliffe

79. Ford Motor Company

80. Venezuela

PART–D

81. Life in a small town is quite different from life in big cities. There is no such hustle and bustle anywhere, no skyscrapers, no proper means of transport, communication and good infrastructure as in big cities. There is no activity and traffic on the roads at night. In the mornings, there are no long queues for school and office buses and cars. The night life is also dull. People of different religions and classes do not mix properly as in big cities. The life in small towns is less civilized with low standard of living and education but the family bonds are stronger as the people have more time for their families for caring each other and their children. They lack in facilities of a big city but live a peaceful life.

82. Parents in cities are quite busy in their daily routine and work and have lesser time to give each other and their children. There are pressures and many families break away and impact the children's mind and growth negatively making the city life not good enough for children.

83. There are proper means of transport and communication. There are many activities and hustle-bustle in cities. The living and education standards are high. People of all classes and religions mix together. There are good opportunities for employment and higher education available in the cities for the enhancement of life.

84. Between city life and life in a small town, I shall prefer the city life as the this provides better means, standards of life and more opportunities for education and employment which are essential for growth and development in life. Moreover, life in cities is more civilized and all sorts of people mix in cities irrespective of their religions, class or backgrounds that gives a feeling of unity in diversity.

PART–E

The Issue of Safety for Women

In the modern age, whereas on the one hand, we have daily reports of molestation and rapes of women, on the other hand we find them holding high positions in most of the government, public and private departments and concerns.

At the same time we must admit that women need more extra care, protection and rights. They must be given proper education and training which is the latest pertaining to their sphere of work. They must be allowed to express themselves freely and adequately. Sometimes their suggestions can be most useful to the well-being of the concern they work in.

Women need adequate and practical assurance of their safety, security and maintenance of dignity. They must not have to face any gender bias. In the matter of appointment or promotion, they must not be discriminated against. They should be provided proper guards if necessary if they have to work late in the evening. They should be allowed as far as possible, the freedom to have the shifts of their choice. The premises where they work should be absolutely safe and guarded. They should be provided the facility of cabs for pick up and drop at all levels except that at higher level, it may be optional. If the cab is to leave the premises after 8:00 p.m., it must be accompanied by an armed guard. The best way is to avoid shifts in odd hours for women.

Women have a very delicate nature. They must not be harassed. They must be addressed politely. There should be no hitch in granting them expeditiously maternity leave or any other leave which may be essential for them. They must also be provided crèche facility, if necessary. They should not be made to feel lost, harassed, isolated or depressed.

Then there should be a speedy way of redressal of their grievances complaints and problems.

Violence against women is a serious matter and must be taken as such. After all, women constitute one half of mankind.

It is true that domestic violence is not confined just to India. We hear about it in America and European countries also. However, there wife-beating, for instance, is not so common now. In India also it has greatly come down but it is fairly widely prevalent in rural areas and even in urban areas among the people of lower strata of society.

As far as the UK and the USA are concerned, it can be said that because of a flexible culture, there is possibility of a change in thinking. Moreover, as the learned scholar says:

"Besides, the government has special ministries for women and their issues, giving a lot of public funds to deal with issues concerned with gender-mainstreaming. This implies integration of gender concern into all ministries who work keeping these issues in mind. This is needed in India,"

In India, the problem is more serious. It is because the country is very vast and most of the people have a traditional mental make-up. Hence, she says,

"However, the task is much more daunting and challenging in India, the country being large with a past which lays down staunch values. Also, they are largely relying on international funding for help. If the government could be involved in this exercise and funding could come from within as well, the organization would have a greater impact."

It is true that a large number of NGOs are also involved in solving this problem. But all concerned have miles to go before they sleep.

Meanwhile, helplines for women should be set up at police stations and other places to get assistance in case of an emergency. There should also be counselling centres for couples. These should be manned by qualified experts appointed by government or reliable NGOs. Counselling should be provided free of cost. Couples should be all encouraged to get counselling for all kinds of domestic matters.

Already there is a specific clause in the Indian Penal Code allowing women to get their complaints redressed. In case of violence, even a verbal note by a woman is considered enough.

A National Commission for Women is also there, women should be exhorted to approach it in case of need. Women's rights should be protected.

As per apex court orders, women or girls studying in educational institutes, are now to be provided the same sort of protection as is permissible to the working women. Women should be protected not only against rape or molestation but also all kinds of violence such as beating, dragging, pinching, insulting, abusing, etc.

There are suggestions for other remedies also which the girls can apply to defend themselves. Some suggest that girls should be given lessons in Karate. Surprisingly there is a sort of commercialisation even in the matter of rape. Some bright ones are said to have designed handy rapist sprayers which they want to market at offices and educational institutions. Some "helplines" for girls have also been started by some people.

It is wisely suggested that midnight dances, music gathering and orgies should be avoided by girls. Whenever girls or women have to go anywhere after sunset, they should go in groups or have some closely-related or reliable male company. In certain cases, where late nights are unavoidable, women must ensure that they return home only with women companions, especially escorted by some male members.

It is also suggested that a vulnerable area map to concentrate for patrolling should be prepared by the police. Still, it has to be admitted that, so far, no foolproof remedy has been found out.

Previous Paper (Solved)

JNUEE–2012

B.A. (HONS.) IN FOREIGN LANGUAGES

PART–A

All questions carry one mark each. Encircle the correct answer clearly. If more than one answers are encircled, the answer will be marked wrong.

1. What was France known as during the Roman Empire?
(*a*) Galles (*b*) Gaulle
(*c*) Fransica (*d*) Gayle

2. *Mona Lisa* was created by
(*a*) Leonardo da Vinci
(*b*) Monet
(*c*) Van Gogh
(*d*) Rodin

3. Who of the following leaders served in the Imperial Japanese Army and later led China in the Second Sino-Japanese War?
(*a*) Sun Yat-sen
(*b*) Chiang Kai-shek
(*c*) Yuan Shikai
(*d*) Jiang Zemin

4. Which of the following is a German port town?
(*a*) Frankfurt (*b*) Munich
(*c*) Berlin (*d*) Hamburg

5. Machu Picchu belongs to
(*a*) Inca civilization
(*b*) Maya civilization
(*c*) Aztec civilization
(*d*) Toltec civilization

6. Which part of Japan was hit by a 9.0 magnitude earthquake that triggered powerful tsunami in March 2011?
(*a*) Kanto (*b*) Tohoku
(*c*) Kyoto (*d*) Hokkaido

7. Nobel Prize in Literature in 2010 was awarded to
(*a*) Gabriel Garcia Marquez
(*b*) Octavio Paz
(*c*) Mario Vargas Llosa
(*d*) Bryce Echenique

8. Which city hosted the G-20 Summit in 2010?
(*a*) Seoul (*b*) Kyoto
(*c*) Beijing (*d*) Manila

9. Which of the following countries does not have a border with Germany?
(*a*) Holland (*b*) France
(*c*) Spain (*d*) Austria

10. How many independent emirates constitute the United Arab Emirates?
(*a*) 5 (*b*) 6
(*c*) 7 (*d*) 9

11. What is the national costume of Korea?
(*a*) Kimono (*b*) Baku
(*c*) Yukata (*d*) Hanbok

12. Which automobile company uses the slogan 'Das Auto'?
(*a*) Skoda (*b*) Chevrolet
(*c*) Audi (*d*) Volkswagen

13. When, after the World War II, did India and Japan sign the Friendship Treaty and establish diplomatic relations?
(*a*) 1948 (*b*) 1950
(*c*) 1952 (*d*) 1955

14. Name the Indo-Persian poet who invented *Sitar*.
(*a*) Mirza Ghalib
(*b*) Amir Khusro
(*c*) Faiz Ahmad Faiz
(*d*) Majaz

15. Fire temple is the place of worship of which of the following religions?
(*a*) Taoism (*b*) Judaism
(*c*) Zoroastrianism (*d*) Shintoism

16. The year 2011 marked the tercentenary of the Russian polymath
(*a*) M.M. Bakhtin (*b*) V.G. Shukhov
(*c*) M.V. Lomonosov (*d*) A. Borodin

17. Who is the only Arab writer awarded Nobel Prize for Literature?
(*a*) Khalil Gibran
(*b*) Ahmad al-Baradei
(*c*) Ahmed Zewail
(*d*) Naguib Mahfouz

18. Mao Zedong proclaimed the People's Republic of China on
(*a*) August 14, 1945
(*b*) August 14, 1947
(*c*) October 1, 1948
(*d*) October 1, 1949

19. The first direct presidential election in Russian history took place in the year
(*a*) 1980 (*b*) 1985
(*c*) 1990 (*d*) 1991

20. Salvador Dali was a prominent surrealist painter from
(*a*) Spain (*b*) France
(*c*) Italy (*d*) Portugal

Note: Who wrote the following books?

21. *The Captain's Daughter*
(*a*) A.P. Chekhov (*b*) A. Blok
(*c*) L. Tolstoy (*d*) A. Pushkin

22. *The Reader,* which is also adapted into a popular film
(*a*) Stephen Daldry
(*b*) Ralf Finnes
(*c*) Bernhard Schlink
(*d*) Thomas Bernhard

23. Epic of Iran, *Shahnamah*
(*a*) Bijan Najdi (*b*) Mina Assadi
(*c*) Ferdausi (*d*) Kahlil Gibran

24. *Strait is the Gate*
(*a*) Henri Bordeaux
(*b*) Andre Gide
(*c*) Marcel Proust
(*d*) Claud Simon

25. *The Tale of Genji,* said to be the world's first novel
(*a*) Chikamatsu Monzaemon
(*b*) Murasaki Shikibu
(*c*) Sei Shonagon
(*d*) Matsuo Basho

PART–B

All questions carry one mark each. Encircle the correct answer clearly. If more than one answers are encircled, the answer will be marked wrong:

26. What is the boundary line demarcating India and Pakistan known as?
(*a*) Radcliffe Line (*b*) McMahon Line
(*c*) Curzon Line (*d*) Durand Line

27. Who was also known as the 'Saint of the Gutters'?
(*a*) Baba Amte (*b*) C.F. Andrews
(*c*) Mother Teresa (*d*) Jyotirao Phule

28. Which is the longest bone in the human body?
(*a*) Fibula (*b*) Femur
(*c*) Radius (*d*) Stapes

29. Gadadhar was the given name of
(*a*) Ramakrishna Paramahansa
(*b*) Chaitanya Mahaprabhu
(*c*) Swami Vivekananda
(*d*) Sathya Sai Baba

30. Which seventh century Indian mathematician was the first in the world to treat 'zero' as a number and show its mathematical operations?
(*a*) Aryabhatta (*b*) Medhatithi
(*c*) Bhaskaracharya (*d*) Brahmagupta

31. According to the Hindu mythology, who is the Guru of Devas (Gods)?
(*a*) Dhanvantari (*b*) Shukracharya
(*c*) Brihaspati (*d*) Vishvakarma

32. Words which are spelled the same in Hindi as in Sanskrit (except for the absence of final case inflections) and have survived without modifications are called
(*a*) Tadbhava (*b*) Deshaja
(*c*) Prakrit (*d*) Tatsama

33. According to Puranas, which of the following Yugas is said to have lasted 8,64,000 years?
(*a*) Satyayuga (*b*) Tretayuga
(*c*) Dwaaparyuga (*d*) Kaliyuga

34. Which is the alternative that can replace the question mark?

NATION : ANTINO :: HUNGRY : ?
(*a*) UHNGYR (*b*) HUNGYR
(*c*) RYNGUH (*d*) UHGNYR

35. At an election, a candidate who gets 84% votes wins by a majority of 476 votes. What is the total number of votes polled?

(*a*) 672 (*b*) 700
(*c*) 800 (*d*) 848

36. Apples cost ₹ 7 each and pears cost ₹ 5 each. If Roma spent ₹ 38 on these fruits, how many apples did she buy?

(*a*) 4 (*b*) 3
(*c*) 2 (*c*) Data is inadequate

37. If South-East becomes 'North', North-East becomes 'West' and so on, what will 'West' become?

(*a*) North-East (*b*) North-West
(*c*) South-East (*d*) South-West

38. Today is Varun's birthday. One year from today, he will be twice as old as he was 12 years ago. How old is Varun today?

(*a*) 24 years (*b*) 25 years
(*c*) 26 years (*c*) 27 years

39. Sarah bought a puppy and a doghouse for $300. The puppy cost $250 more than the doghouse. How much did the doghouse cost?

(*a*) $50 (*d*) $25
(*c*) $40 (*d*) $20

Note: (a), (b) and (c) are parts of a sentence in the following questions. Encircle the part which is, if any, grammatically incorrect in questions 40-43:

40. (*a*) We discussed about the problem so thoroughly
(*b*) on the eve of the examinations
(*c*) that I found it very easy to work it out.
(*d*) None

41. (*a*) An Indian ship
(*b*) laden with merchandise
(*c*) got drowned in the Pacific Ocean.
(*d*) None

42. (*a*) No sooner did the sun rise
(*b*) when we took a hasty breakfast
(*c*) and resumed our journey.
(*d*) None

43. (*a*) One of my favourite actor
(*b*) is acting
(*c*) in this play also.
(*d*) None

44. A woman came in with a baby who, she said, ... a safety pin. (Fill in the blank with the most appropriate option).

(*a*) was just swallowing
(*b*) swallowed
(*c*) had just swallowed
(*d*) just swallowed

Note: Select the most appropriate synonyms of the bracketed words/idioms:

45. (Lethargy)
(*a*) Sluggishness
(*b*) Boredom
(*c*) Activity
(*d*) Disobedience

46. (Constrict)
(*a*) To freeze
(*b*) To narrow
(*c*) To open
(*d*) To cut

47. (Black sheep)
(*a*) A cheat
(*b*) A good-for-nothing person
(*c*) Victim of a hoax
(*d*) A shy person

48. (Psalm)
(*a*) A devotional song
(*b*) Place of worship
(*c*) Kind of fruit
(*d*) A small amount

49. (Random)
(*a*) Done in a hurry
(*b*) Done without method
(*c*) Unspecific
(*d*) Sketchy

50. (My heart goes out to *A*)
(*a*) I love *A*
(*b*) *A* has won my heart
(*c*) I praise *A*
(*d*) I feel sympathy for *A*

PART–C

All questions carry one mark each.

Fill in the blanks with appropriate prepositions in the following sentences:

As she walked into the hotel, ahead .... (1) her first exhibition in the country, it was difficult to separate the celebrity .... (2) the artist. At 78, her movements were studied, born .... (3) long practice, her head atilt .... (4) an angle as the cameras went off.

The capital of the United States and one federal State are named .... (5) George Washington.

Fill in the blanks with appropriate words:

I saw a .... (6) of sheep in the field.

The grapes are now .... (7) enough to be picked.

"Of course, I won't get lost. I know the city like the back of my .... (8)."

When we reached the office, the work was in .... (9) swing.

It was at about this time .... (10) a Fakir named Govinda Rai arrived there.

Fill in the blanks with appropriate verbs in their appropriate forms:

During election campaigns, people often .... (11) mud at each other.

One night, Hridaya .... (12) up courage and went into the jungle. He found his friend .... (13) in deep meditation under a tree.

If you smuggle goods into the country, they may be .... (14) by the customs authority.

About twenty clerks were .... (15) redundant when the banks introduced computers.

The pilot had been warned about the storm, before he .... (16).

When I heard the name of the winner, I was so shocked you could have .... (17) me down with a feather!

Read carefully some examples from a Polynesian language given below:

1 (a) avaravere 'I will go'
  (b) avaraepa 'I went'
2 (a) avauvere 'You will go'
  (b) avauepa 'You went'
3 (a) avarovere 'He will go'
  (b) avaroepa 'He went'
4 (a) pauravere 'I will sit'
  (b) pauraepa 'I sat'

Now answer the following three questions:

How will you say the following in this language?

18. 'You will sit'

19. 'He sat'

20. In which order do the 'subject', 'verb' and 'auxiliary verb' come in this language?

Answer the following questions:

21. Who was the first cricketer in the world to score 10000 runs in Test Cricket?

22. The price of petrol increases by 10%. By what per cent the consumption must be reduced so that the expenditure remains the same?

23. Jhumpa Lahiri's first novel .... (2003) was adapted into a popular film of the same name.

24. 'Chandrakanta', written by ...., is considered to be the first work of prose in Hindi.

25. The famous philosopher, ... was a disciple of Plato.

26. Who produced the 2007 film, 'Gandhi, my father'?

Give full forms of the following acronyms/ abbreviations:

27. Do, Co and Mo (of DoCoMo Mobile Operators)

28. NREGA

29. VIRUS

30. ZIP (as in ZIP Code)

PART–D

Read the passage below and give short answers to the following questions. Marks assigned are given against each question:

Language, any language, has a dual character: it is both a means of communication and a carrier of culture. Take English. It is spoken in Britain and in Sweden and Denmark. But for Swedish and Danish people, English is only a means of communication with non-Scandinavians. It is not a carrier of their culture. For the British, and particularly the English, it is additionally and inseparably, from its use as a tool of communication, a carrier of their culture and history. Or take Swahili in East and Central Africa. It is widely, used as means of communication across many nationalities. But it is not the carrier of a culture and history of many of those nationalities. However, in parts of Kenya and Tanzania, and particularly in Zanzibar, Swahili is inseparably both a means of communication and a carrier of the culture of those people to whom it is a mother tongue.

Language as communication has three aspects or elements. There is first what Karl Marx once called the language of real life, the element basic to the whole nation of language, its origin and development: that is, the relations people enter into with one another in the labor process, the links they necessarily establish among themselves in the act of people, a community of human beings, producing wealth or means of life like food, clothing, houses...

The second aspect of language as communication is speech and it imitates the language of real life that is communication in production. The verbal signposts both reflect and aid communication or the relations established between human beings in production of their means of life....spoken words mediate between human beings and form the language of speech....

The third aspect is the written signs. The written word imitates the spoken. Where the first two aspects of language as communication through hand and the spoken word historically evolved more or less simultaneously, the written aspect is a much later historical development. Writing is representation of sounds with visual symbols from the simplest knot among shepherds to tell the number in the herd ... to the most complicated and different letter and picture writing systems of the world today.

1. What does the writer mean by language as 'a means of communication' and as 'a carrier of culture'?

2. How is 'language of real life' different from the written language as evident in the extract above?

3. What does the writer mean by 'verbal signposts'?

4. Is English in India either a means of communication or a carrier of culture, or neither or both?

PART–E

Complete the following story in about 600–700 words. Also, give a title to the story:

One morning, Bhola, a villager, stepped out of his hut and saw huge round footmarks in the mud outside his dwelling. "Oh my God!" he shouted. Soon there was a large crowd outside his hut. None of the villagers had ever seen such huge footprints before and they were bewildered by them. They followed.

ANSWERS

PART–A

1	2	3	4	5	11	12	13	14	15
B	A	B	D	A	D	D	C	B	C
6	**7**	**8**	**9**	**10**	**16**	**17**	**18**	**19**	**20**
B	C	A	C	C	C	D	D	D	A

21	22	23	24	25
D	C	C	B	B

PART–B

26	27	28	29	30
A	C	B	A	D
31	32	33	34	35
C	D	C	A	B
36	37	38	39	40
A	C	B	B	B
41	42	43	44	45
C	B	A	C	A
46	47	48	49	50
B	A	A	B	D

PART–C

1. of
2. to
3. of
4. about
5. after
6. herd
7. ripe
8. palm
9. full
10. that
11. fling
12. took
13. immersed
14. confiscated
15. held
16. took off
17. got
18. Pauuvere
19. Pouroepa
20. 'Verb', 'Subject', 'Auxiliary verb'
21. Sunil Gavaskar (India)
22. 9%
23. The Namesake
24. Devki Nandan Khatri
25. Aristotle
26. Bollywood actor Anil kapoor.
27. Do Communications Over the Mobile network
28. National Rural Employment Guarantee Act
29. Vital Information Resources Under Siege
30. Zone Information Protocol

PART–D

1. When a language is spoken as a mother tongue it becomes a carrier of culture and history alongwith the means of communication. But when the language is spoken between the people to which one it is a mother-tongue while for the other it is not, then it is called only a means of communication between the two.
2. The language of real life is different from written language as it is based on acts of people to earn livelihood while the latter evolved much later through pictures and letters.
3. Verbal signposts are the spoken words and gestures.
4. English in India is both a means of communication and a carrier of culture.

PART–E

The Footmarks

The footprints together forming a large group. Everyone in the group was scared in himself inside. All of them picked either a stick, a spade, a tool and a stone with him so that he may use it in self-defence just in case of danger. Everyone was shaken with unknown danger but as all of them were moving in a group the element of danger and fear was away from them.

They kept moving into the jungle. They were making loud sounds through their mouths and through drumbeats. They also carried with themselves fire-sticks to scare away the wild animals and the unknown, unseen danger. Some of them were discussing about the possible shape and size of the unknown creature. Some suggested it could be a demon or a wild giant.

While the group of villagers kept moving to look out for the unknown danger. Their women and children kept back in the village fear-stricken. They were praying for the well being of their men and for their safe-return from the jungle. They all shut the doors of their dwelling light and kept praying and chanting hymns against the idols of deities at their homes and at village temple. Everyone in the village was full of fear from the unknown danger or demon. The children were clinging to their mothers and refused to eat or sleep until their fathers come back safely.

The group of villagers who had moved to the jungle to look for the unknown monster was now tired and hungry as they had kept on walking the whole day. Some of them suggested to return to the village and give the search for the unknown creature while the others suggested that they should take some food and rest in the jungle and later continue their search. Ultimately it was decided to stay there for food and rest and continue the search after some time.

They found a safe place among big trees. They cleaned the place and sat in the form of a round group. They ignited bonfire in the centre of the group to scare away wild animals. Some of them picked some fruits from the nearby trees and distributed among all to eat. Some of them brought water from a nearby small pond. After eating whatever they could get. They decided to take rest there only as it was dark in the evening and they were quite away from their village. For the time now, neither could return to their village nor could they move ahead in their pursuit. So, it was decided that the youngmen will keep watch in turn while the others were taking rest. Steadily, the night passed in the wild, horrible jungle. The whole night the villagers in the group were shivering with cold in the winter night of December. There were strange sounds of wild animals and other creatures all around. Fortunately none of the wild animals or creatures came near them, because of the bonfire and the guarding youngmen. He kept beating drums also to scare away the animals.

In the morning, as the dawn descended, they woke up by the chirping of birds and the life-giving sunlight. They now felt all their cold, fear, darkness disappearing in the soothing sun rays. They again gathered all their energy and courage and started their pursuit afresh.

As they crossed the jungle, they reached on the banks of a river. There was a beautiful scenary around this place. A number of green trees were lined up along the river bank laden with various types of fruits. There was a waterfall nearby. As they moved towards the waterfall they saw a herd of mammoths bathing in the water and splashing water on each other. The innocent villagers had never seen mammoths before in their lives. They were scared and kept watching from a distance. But very soon they searched that the mammoths, though giant in size, were not at all dangerous to them and their village. As their fear disappeared, they also started bathing in the waterfall and river water and returned to their village after picking the sweet fruits from the river side trees for their children back home.

EXPLANATIONS

35. 84% of x – 16 % of x = 476

$\Rightarrow$ 68% of x = 476

$$x = \frac{476 \times 100}{68} = 700$$

$\therefore$ Total number of votes polled = 700

36. Total spent = ₹ 38

Cost of 4 apples = ₹ 7 × 4 = ₹ 28

Cost of 2 pears = ₹ 5 × 2 = ₹ 10

Hence, she bought 4 apples.

37. Let present age of Varun = x years.

$$2(x - 12) = x$$

$\Rightarrow$ $x = 24$

Hence, today Varun is 24 years old.

39. Let doghouse cost = ₹ x

$$x + x + 250 = 300$$

$$2x = 50$$

$$x = 25$$

$\therefore$ Cost of doghouse = ₹ 25

Previous Paper Solved

JNUEE–2011

B.A. (HONS.) IN FOREIGN LANGUAGES

PART–A

All questions carry one mark each. Encircle the correct answer clearly. If more than one answer is encircled, the answer will be marked wrong :

1. The words 'Satyameva Jayate' inscribed below the base plate of the emblem of India are taken from
   (a) *Rig-Veda*
   (b) *Satpath Brahmana*
   (c) *Mundak Upanishad*
   (d) *Ramayana*
2. The Parliament of India cannot be regarded as a sovereign body because
   (a) it can legislate only on subjects entrusted to the Centre by the Constitution
   (b) it has to operate within the limits prescribed by the Constitution
   (c) the Supreme Court can declare laws passed by the Parliament as unconstitutional if they contravene the provisions of the Constitution
   (d) All of the above
3. Which of the following is a Human Rights Organization?
   (a) The French Community
   (b) The Organization of African Unity
   (c) The Arab League
   (d) Amnesty International
4. Kemal Ataturk was
   (a) the first President of Independent Kenya
   (b) the founder of modern Turkey
   (c) a revolutionary leader of Soviet Union
   (d) None of the above
5. Philology is the
   (a) study of bones
   (b) study of muscles
   (c) study of architecture
   (d) science of languages
6. R.K. Narayan has his stories centred around which imaginary place?
   (a) Malgudi (b) Malguri
   (c) Talgudi (d) Hemkhanakhan
7. Which Academy promotes and develops literature in all the 22 languages of India?
   (a) Sahitya Academy
   (b) Sangeet Natak Academy
   (c) Lalit Kala Academy
   (d) None of the above
8. Kalidasa had written three famous plays, viz., *Abhigyanam Shakuntalam* and *Vikramurvashi.* Name the third play.
   (a) *Kumarasambhava*
   (b) *Meghadoota*
   (c) *Raghuvansha*
   (d) *Malavikagnimitra*
9. What is the Commonwealth of Independent States (CIS)?
   (a) Group of 53 former colonies of Britain
   (b) Group of 12 former republics of dissolved USSR
   (c) Group of 10 Latin American countries
   (d) Group of Islamic countries in Saudi Arabia region
10. The eminent Bengali director Satyajit Ray had made only two films in Hindi. The first is *Satranj ke Khilari* based on the works of Munshi Premchand. Which was the second?
   (a) *Teesri Kasam*
   (b) *Maare Gaye Gulfam*
   (c) *Sadgati*
   (d) *Junoon*

PART–B

All questions carry one mark each. Encircle the correct answer clearly. If more than one answer is encircled, the answer will be marked wrong :

11. The name of which city was changed to Petrograd and Leningrad?

(*a*) Moscow (*b*) Tashkent
(*c*) Kiev (*d*) St. Petersburg

12. Which political party was responsible for the Russian October Revolution of 1917?
(*a*) Bolshevik (*b*) Provisional Party
(*c*) Soviet (*d*) Menshevik

13. Today the primary religion of Iran is Islam but Persia was once very closely associated with another religion. Name it.
(*a*) Christianity (*b*) Buddhism
(*c*) Judaism (*d*) Zoroastrianism

14. The vast majority of modern Iranian, Persian and Dari text is written in a form of the
(*a*) Arabic language
(*b*) Hebrew alphabet
(*c*) Arabic alphabet
(*d*) Syriac alphabet

15. How is Japanese Emperor's Throne known?
(*a*) Peacock Throne
(*b*) Chrysanthemum Throne
(*c*) Viceregal Throne
(*d*) White Throne

16. The sacred place of followers of Shintoism is
(*a*) Central Shrine of Ise
(*b*) Yasukuni Shrine
(*c*) Both of the above
(*d*) None of the above

17. Bastille Day marks the anniversary of the French Revolution. Why did Parisians storm the prison in 1789?
(*a*) To find the king who was hiding
(*b*) To look for food
(*c*) To get powder for muskets
(*d*) To free prisoners

18. Which French author of the 19th century had the foresight that man would walk on the moon one day?
(*a*) Victor Hugo (*b*) Jules Verne
(*c*) Chateaubriand (*d*) Mme de Sevigne

19. Which of the following Indian monks is said to have started Shaolin martial art or the 'gongfu' in China?
(*a*) Kumarajiva (*b*) Bodhidharma
(*c*) Dharamratna (*d*) Bodhiruchi

20. The first ever Chinese National who was conferred 'Padma Bhushan' by the Indian Government for his contribution towards Indology is
(*a*) Zhou Enlai (*b*) Ji Xianlin
(*c*) Tan Chung (*d*) Tan Yunshan

21. Which Parallel divides North Korea and South Korea?
(*a*) 23rd (*b*) 27th
(*c*) 38th (*d*) 42nd

22. Which of these is not a Korean company?
(*a*) Samsung
(*b*) Hyundai
(*c*) LG (Luckystar Gold)
(*d*) Nikon

23. Spanish is the official language of Spain. Which other language has been recognized as co-official by Regional Governments?
(*a*) Catalan (*b*) Basque
(*c*) Galician (*d*) All of the above

24. Which country borders Spain to the West?
(*a*) San Marino (*b*) France
(*c*) Portugal (*d*) Gibraltar

25. World War II started in September 1939 with the invasion of
(*a*) Denmark (*b*) Belgium
(*c*) Poland (*d*) France

26. Which of the German Chancellors received the Nobel Prize for Peace?
(*a*) Ludwig Erhard (*b*) Konrad Adenauer
(*c*) Helmut Schmidt (*d*) Willy Brandt

27. Which German firm coined the slogan *Vorsprung durch Technik* ('Advancement through Technology')?
(*a*) Audi (*b*) BMW
(*c*) Siemens (*d*) Bosch

28. Yukio Mishima, Japan's famous post-war novelist committed suicide in 1970 after a failed coup. Which of these methods did he use?
(*a*) Disemboweled himself with a sword and then ordered his followers to decapitate him
(*b*) Downed vast quantities of sake before walking into the sea

(*c*) Hung himself from a tree towards the top of Mt. Fuji
(*d*) Threw himself under a bullet train during commuter rush hour

29. How many alphabets are there in the Arabic alphabet?
(*a*) 26 (*b*) 28
(*c*) 30 (*d*) 32

30. Which is the smallest country in the Arab World?
(*a*) Qatar (*b*) Tunis
(*c*) Bahrain (*d*) Kuwait

PART–C

All questions carry one mark each. Encircle the correct answer clearly. If more than one answer is encircled, the answer will be marked wrong :

31. Can I pay by cheque? I don't have any cash on me.
(*a*) Sorry, we only take hard cash
(*b*) Sorry, the cheques were stolen
(*c*) Sorry, that's not fair

32. Do you still feel homesick?
(*a*) Well, I feel dizzy
(*b*) Yes, I have problems back home
(*c*) Well, I am getting over it a little

33. She's .... a snobbish person .... nobody likes to be with her.
(*a*) such...that
(*b*) such...as
(*c*) so...that

34. You'd better take a taxi, ... you'll be late.
(*a*) consequently (*b*) furthermore
(*c*) otherwise (*d*) however

35. Ram wasn't tired, ... he took a nap.
(*a*) otherwise (*b*) hence
(*c*) nevertheless (*d*) furthermore

36. He didn't earn enough money. ...., his wife decided to get a job.
(*a*) Moreover (*b*) Therefore
(*c*) Although (*c*) Otherwise

37. There's some milk in the refrigerator, ...?
(*a*) isn't there (*b*) isn't it
(*c*) wasn't it (*d*) was it

38. The dishes are dirty, ...?
(*a*) weren't they (*b*) isn't they
(*c*) aren't they (*c*) were they

39. It I said that he was a man .... to have the vision of an eagle and the courage of a lion.
(*a*) who appeared (*d*) he appeared
(*c*) that appears (*d*) and appears

40. After the discovery of the abandoned getaway vehicle, ... believed to be hiding in the nearby riverside forest region.
(*a*) that the bank robber is
(*b*) the bank robber who
(*c*) the bank robber is
(*d*) the bank robber who is

41. .... he was seen to be an aggressive politician, he was a quiet and loving family man at home.
(*a*) Although (*b*) Despite
(*c*) In spite of (*d*) Nevertheless

42. You .... see the doctor if that backache persists.
(*a*) better (*b*) better have
(*c*) have better (*d*) had better

43. How long does it take .... the nearest train station?
(*a*) get to (*b*) to get to
(*c*) to get (*d*) getting

44. She went .... with envy when she saw my new car.
(*a*) green (*b*) blue
(*c*) black (*d*) pink

45. My birthday was a complete surprise. It came completely out of the ....
(*a*) black (*b*) white
(*c*) red (*d*) blue

PART–D

All questions carry one mark each. Some verbs have been removed from the following text. Try to reconstruct the text by putting verbs in the correct form in the blanks provided :

Suresh was born on a farm back in Eastern India. He was happy even though he (46) a harsh life cultivating his field. One day he (47) by a heavy storm at night. When the storm subsided he (48) that his plantation (49). He (50) despondent and felt that he could no longer live on the farm. He (51) to move somewhere else. He left the farm and (52) to the city. The hustle and bustle of the city (53) Suresh a lot, but he refused to go back to his farm. Suresh's life in the city was very difficult. The only person he (54) was Mahesh, a distant relative, who was a very patient and understanding and who tried to help Suresh to get used to (55) in the city.

Fill in the blanks with appropriate articles and put × if it is not required :

56. I'm on .... diet. No .... sugar for me!

57. I'm afraid, I can't remember .... exact date of .... show.

58. I'm afraid .... answer is 'no'. Come back when you can make .... new proposal.

59. You can find .... books you'll need for class at .... Amazon.com.

60. He telephoned .... agent that was listed in .... telephone directory.

Fill in the blanks with correct prepositions :

61. Please carry the box .... the next room.

62. Anil started his current job .... October 10.

63. "Where is the library?"

"It's .... your right".

64. I would like to apply .... for position of sales executive that was advertised in the Sunday newspaper.

65. I came up with a great idea .... I was thinking about the class.

Unscramble the following proverbs and add capital letters and punctuation marks :

66. sow you so as reap you shall

67. book its don't cover a by judge

68. devil's an is workshop idle the brain

What do the underlined idioms mean?

69. Companies producing goods play to the gallery to boost their sales.

70. It was he who put a spoke in my wheel.

Arrange the following sentences in the proper sequence :

S_1 : While crossing a busy road, we should obey the policeman on duty.

P : We should always cross the road at the zebra crossing.

Q : We must look to the signal lights and cross the road only when the road is clear.

R : If there are no signal lights at the crossing, we should look to the right, then to left and again the right before crossing the road.

S : If the road is not clear, we should wait.

S_6 : We should never run while crossing the road.

71. The proper sequence should be

(*a*) PSRQ (*b*) PQRS
(*c*) RQSP (*d*) QRPS

Select the correct answer to complete the sentence :

72. His appearance is unsmiling but ...

(*a*) his heart is full of compassion for others.
(*b*) he looks very serious on many occasions.
(*c*) people are afraid of him.
(*d*) he is uncompromising on matters of task performance.
(*e*) he is full of jealousy towards his colleague.

73. The weather outside was extremely pleasant and hence we decided to ...

(*a*) utilize our time in watching the television.
(*b*) refrain from going out for a morning walk.
(*c*) employ this rare opportunity for writing letters.
(*d*) enjoy a morning ride in the open.
(*e*) remain seated in our rooms in the bungalow.

Rewrite the sentences as shown in the example :

Ex. They make shoes in that factory.
Shoes **are made** in that factory.

74. They had finished the preparations by the time the guests had arrived.

75. They are going to perform Beethoven's Fifth Symphony next weekend.

76. Select the correctly punctuated sentence :

(*a*) The children's books were all left in the following places : Mrs. Smith's room, Mr. Powell's office and the caretaker's cupboard.

(*b*) The children's books were all left in the following places; Mrs. Smith's room, Mr. Powell's office and the caretaker's cupboard.

(*c*) The childrens books were all left in the following places; Mrs. Smiths room, Mr. Powells office and the caretakers cupboard.

(*d*) The children's books were all left in the following places, Mrs. Smith's room, Mr. Powell's office and the caretaker's cupboard.

Complete the sentences using the underlined word, so that the meaning of the sentence is similar :

77. I find driving on the right in Europe very strange. accustomed
I .... on the right in Europe.

78. His boss won't tolerate lateness. put
His boss won't .... lateness.

The following are some words translated from an artificial language :

Malgauper means peach cobbler
Malgaport means peach juice
Moggagrop means apple jelly

79. Which word would mean apple juice?

(*a*) Moggaport (*b*) Malgaauper
(*c*) Gropport (*d*) Mogaport

Gorblflur means fan belt
Pinxgorbl means ceiling fan
Arthtusl means tile roof

80. How would you write ceiling tile?
Ceiling tile ....

PART–E

Read the following passage and answer the questions that follow :

Before the grass has thickened on the roadside verges and leaves have started growing on the trees is a perfect time to look around and see just how dirty Britain has become. The pavements are stained with chewing gum that has been spat out and the gutters are full of discarded fast food cartons. Years ago I remember travelling abroad and being saddened by the plastic bags, discarded bottles and soiled nappies at the edge of every road. Nowadays, Britain seems to look at least as bad. What has gone wrong?

The problem is that the rubbish created by our increasingly mobile lives lasts a lot longer than before. If it is not cleared up and properly thrown away, it stays in the undergrowth for years; a semi-permanent reminder of what a tatty little country we have now.

Firstly, it is estimated that 10 billion plastic bags have been given to shoppers. These will take anything from 100 to 1000 years to rot. However, it is not as if there is no solution to this. A few years ago, the Irish Government introduced a tax on non-recyclable carrier bags and in three months reduced their use by 90%. When he was a minister, Michael Meacher attempted to introduce a similar arrangement in Britain. The plastics industry protested, of course. However, they need not have bothered; the idea was killed before it could draw breath, leaving supermarkets free to give away plastic bags.

What is clearly necessary right now is some sort of combined initiative, both individual and collective, before it is too late. The alternative is to continue sliding downhill until we have a country that looks like a vast municipal rubbish tip. We may well be at the tipping point. Yet we know that people responded to their environment. If things around them are clean and tidy, people behave cleanly and tidily. If they are surrounded by squalor, they behave squalidly. Now, much of Britain looks pretty squalid. What will it look like in five years?

1. Why does the writer say that it is a good time to see Britain before the trees have leaves?

2. What according to the writer has gone wrong with Britain?

3. What did Michael Meacher try to do in order to solve the problem? Was he successful in his efforts?

4. India is also facing similar problems, such as the degradation of the environment. What can you do to bring about a solution to the problem?

PART–F

Select any one of the two pictures and write a short story in about 600-800 words. Give a title to the story?

(*a*)

(*b*)

ANSWER

PART–A

1	2	3	4	5
(c)	(d)	(d)	(b)	(d)
6	**7**	**8**	**9**	**10**
(a)	(a)	(d)	(b)	(c)

PART–B

11	12	13	14	15
(d)	(a)	(d)	(c)	(b)
16	**17**	**18**	**19**	**20**
(c)	(c)	(b)	(b)	(b)
21	**22**	**23**	**24**	**25**
(c)	(d)	(d)	(c)	(c)
26	**27**	**28**	**29**	**30**
(d)	(a)	(a)	(b)	(c)

PART–C

31	32	33	34	35
(a)	(c)	(a)	(c)	(b)
36	**37**	**38**	**39**	**40**
(b)	(a)	(c)	(a)	(c)
41	**42**	**43**	**44**	**45**
(a)	(a)	(b)	(c)	(d)

PART–D

46. lived
47. was hit
48. found
49. had destroyed
50. became
51. decided
52. went
53. disturbed
54. knew
55. life
56. a, ×
57. the, the
58. the, a
59. the, the
60. an, the
61. into
62. on
63. to
64. for
65. upon
66. As you sow, so shall you reap.
67. Don't judge a book by its cover.
68. An idle brain is the devil's workshop.
69. aim to attract popular attention
70. prevented me from doing that
71. (b)
72. (a)
73. (d)
74. The preparations were finished by the time the guests had arrived.
75. Beethoven's Fifth Symphony is going to be performed next weekend.
76. (a)
77. find strange the accustomed driving
78. put up with
79. (a)
80. Pinxarth

PART–E

1. When there are no grass and leaves on the roadside verges, the spit stains, garbage and filth is clearly visible on the pavements and gutters in Britain.
2. According to the writer, the rubbish and garbage created these days decomposes very slowly and if not properly disposed, it takes many years to clear, causing heaps of garbage everywhere in Britain.
3. Michael Meacher tried to impose a tax on using non-recyclable carrier bags as done by Irish Government but he failed to do so because of the protests from the plastics industry. Hence, he was not successful in solving the problem.
4. India is also facing the problem of degradation of the environment unlike Britain and other countries. The Government and NGOs are

taking many steps and doing all out efforts to check this but the success is yet minimal. There are laws of imposing penalties on the use of plastic non-recyclable carry bags yet we find them in every shop and home. The reason being that the law is not exercised and followed by all in its true spirit and force. The solution to this problem lies with ourselves. It we refuse to accept this kind of carrybags from the shops, they will no longer buy them and find alternatives such as paper bags or jute bags, subsequently the manufactures also have to switch over to produce them to survive (in business).

PART–F

(*a*) Long long ago, there was a king in an ancient state of India. The state was prosperous with all its subjects happy and absorbed in their work and families. The king was so keen in the well-being of his subjects that he used to forget his own interests and welfare. He was very popular for his justified and balanced verdicts. Due to his love for his subjects and good administration, there were no fights, thefts or any other crimes in his state. The people were also prosperous.

The king had a very young son, who used to play in the royal garden of the palace whole day. The king loved him so much that he couldn't even think of living a single day without seeing him. He was really fond of him.

The queen of the king was very beautiful. The king loved her not only for her beauty but for her wisdom also. He used to take her advice in all his state related matters and decisions. This way the king, his family and subjects all were happy and prosperous in all ways.

The king was very brave and therefore no other king or neighbouring state could dare to fight him. He had a very strong and well organised army to protect the borders of his state. He had very able ministers with him. Everything was going smoothly in the state. The king, as in those days, thought of going for hunting. He discussed this with the queen and the ministers. The minister agreed and assured him that they will look after the administration of the state in his absence, but the queen insisted on going along with the king for hunting as she had never experienced hunting before that.

The king agreed but he had one great worry, that of his very young son. He was so young and tender that he could not be taken to forests during hunting. As the queen was also accompanying the king for hunting, there was a great concern as to who will look after him. At this juncture the prime minister came forward and took the responsibility of the young prince on himself till the king and queen return from hunting. The king then left for forest along with the queen and few soldiers, leaving the young prince in the care of the prime minister and his family, but with a worried mind.

They kept moving deep into forests in search of a prey, suddenly the queen saw a fawn at some distance around the bush. The fawn was so beautiful that she insisted the king to hunt that fawn first for her. They both started following the fawn in the forest. The soldiers were left behind some where on the way but they kept on moving on horses.

The fawn, though very young and tender, was running very fast and soon it reached its mother and hid behind her. The mother deer saw the king and queen ready to hunt her kid. She shivered with fright but stayed calm. The king asked her to move aside so that he could hunt the fawn. The mother deer gathered all her courage and requested the king to spare her kid. The king was adamant on hunting it. Then she asked the king whether he also had a kid. The king told that he had a lovely prince back at the palace. She then asked the king what would he feel if someone killed his son back at home while he is hunting in the forest. The king and queen both were stunned on this question as both of them could not even imagine living without the prince. Tears rolled from their eyes and they thanked the mother deer for opening their eyes and vowed to never hunt any animal in future.

Previous Paper (Solved)

JNUEE-2010

B.A. (HONS.) IN FOREIGN LANGUAGES

PART-A

1. Which one of the following is essentially a solo dance?

A. Kuchipudi B. Kathak
C. Manipuri D. Mohiniattam

2. Although fog consists of fine drops of water, we cannot see clearly through it because

A. the light rays undergo total internal reflection in the drops
B. fine drops of water in fog polarize the light
C. the fine drops are opaque to the light
D. the drops scatter most of the light

3. During the Mughal period, which one of the following were the first to come to India as traders?

A. Portuguese B. Dutch
C. Danish D. English

4. Who among the following Delhi Sultans is known for introducing market control mechanism?

A. Iltutmish
B. Balban
C. Ala-ud-din Khalji
D. Feroz Tughluq

5. Which book has been printed in the maximum number of languages and scripts?

A. *The Bible*
B. *Hiraka Sutra*
C. *The Super Book*
D. *Ramayana*

6. Who of following is the author of *Yashodhara?*

A. Maithali Sharan Gupt
B. Khushwant Singh
C. Bankimchandra Chatterjee
D. Ramdhari Singh Dinkar

7. Dhayan Chand was

A. a great hockey player
B. captained the Indian Hockey Team which won the gold medal in 1936 Berlin Olympics
C. scored 101 goals at the Olympic Games and 300 goals in International matches
D. All the statements are correct

8. Which of the following is not an official language of the UN?

A. English B. French
C. Chinese D. Japanese

9. Which Schedule of Indian Constitution contains languages?

A. 6th B. 7th
C. 8th D. 9th
E. 10th

10. With which among the following environment issues is the **Raina Report 2009** related to? (It was recently released by Environment Minister Jairam Ramesh)

A. Pollution in Ganga
B. Environmental impacts of Bt Brinjal
C. CO_2 emission standards
D. Ozone depletion
E. Melting glaciers

11. Ants are social insects because

A. they live in forests
B. they live in colonies
C. they have a language
D. they share food

*Based on Memory.

12. Economic justice has been incorporated in the Constitution of India under
A. Fundamental Rights
B. Residuary Powers
C. Fundamental Duties
D. Directive Principles of State Policy

13. Numismatics is the study of
A. coins B. numbers
C. stamps D. space

14. Ecology deals with
A. birds
B. cell formation
C. relation between organisms and their environment
D. tissues

15. The National Calender of India is based on
A. Gregorian Calender
B. Hijra Era
C. Saka Era
D. None of the above

Directions: Answer the Following Questions:

16. In physics, what single-word term normally represents 'rate of change of position?

17. The symbol ∞ (sideways 8) means what in mathematics?

18. A logophile is a lover of what?

19. Which city hosted the 2009 UN Climate Change Conference?

20. What did NASA claim to have discovered after the LCROSS satellite crashed on the moon?

PART-B

21. Who initiated the policy of open-door and reforms in China?
A. Mao Zedong
B. Deng Xiaoping
C. Jiang Zemin
D. Hu Jintao

22. What is the status of Hong Kong?
A. Hong Kong is a republic
B. Hong Kong is a region of the People's Republic of China
C. Hong Kong belongs to the UK
D. Hong Kong is a centrally administered municipality

23. Which country changed allegiances between World War I and World War II?
A. Russia B. Japan
C. China D. Spain

24. The first atom bomb was dropped on Hiroshima on
A. 6th August, 1945
B. 9th August, 1945
C. 9th August, 1946
D. 6th August, 1942

25. Who of the following lost his position as both the State and party leader of East Germany (GDR) on October 18, 1989?
A. Walter Ulbricht B. Erich Honecker
C. Egon Krenz D. Helmut Kohl

26. The construction of the Berlin Wall began on
A. November 9, 1989
B. March 6, 1949
C. August 13, 1961
D. June 17, 1953

27. Which country has the largest Japanese population outside Japan?
A. Brazil B. Australia
C. Peru D. Thailand

28. Which one of the following is not a part of Central Asia?
A. Afghanistan B. Tajikistan
C. Iraq D. Uzbekistan

29. Who is known as the 'poet of the East discovered by the West?
A. Rumi B. Hafiz
C. Iqbal D. Khayyam

30. *Crime and Punishment* is a novel by
A. Leo Tolstoy
B. Fyodor Dostoyevsky
C. Aleksandr Pushkin
D. Anton Chekhov

31. Napoleon's army invaded Russia in
A. 1812 B. 1814
C. 1816 D. 1818

32. Russian language uses
A. Roman alphabet
B. Glagolitic alphabet
C. Cyrillic alphabet
D. Hebrew alphabet

33. Which Latin dance originated in Andalucia?
A. Meringue B. Salsa
C. Flamenco D. Sardana

34. Who wrote *Don Quixote de la Mancha?*
A. Molina B. Vega
C. Zorrilla D. Cervantes

35. Most people in Spain follow which religion?
A. Judaism B. Catholicism
C. Protestantism D. Islam

36. Which French author wrote the book, *Les Miserables,* adapted as a musical in 1980?
A. Gustave Flaubert
B. Arthur Rimbaud
C. Charles Baudelaire
D. Victor Hugo

37. India has recently signed a Comprehensive Economic Partnership Agreement with which country?
A. Taiwan B. Republic of Korea
C. Sri Lanka D. Afghanistan

38. What is the official name of North Korea?
A. Democratic People's Republic of Korea
B. Socialist Republic of South Korea
C. Republic of Korea
D. People's Republic of Democratic Korea

39. Which of the following pairs of countries are not Arab?
A. Sudan and Somalia
B. Morocco and Mauritania
C. Iran and Turkey
D. Egypt and Jordan

40. How many Arab countries are represented in the League of Arab States?
A. 2 B. 8
C. 14 D. 22

PART-C

Directions: *Explain the underlined phrases.*

41. It goes against the grain for me to admit my mistake.
goes against the grain: ....

42. The party is only paying lip service to women's rights.
paying lip service: ....

How to use an ATM

Directions: *All verbs have been removed from the following text. Try to reconstruct the text by putting verbs into the blanks:*

(43) your card into the machine and (44) until the instructions (45) on the screen. Then (46) your PIN number. After that you (47) to tell the machine how much money you (48). You (49) that by pushing the correct buttons. Now wait a minute or two while the ATM (50) your account and (51) your money. After that (52) your card and receipt. Finally, take your money out of the money slot and put it in your wallet.

43. ____________________
44. ____________________
45. ____________________
46. ____________________
47. ____________________
48. ____________________
49. ____________________
50. ____________________
51. ____________________
52. ____________________

Directions: *Unscramble the following proverbs and add capital letters and punctuation marks:*

53. friends known by man a is his
____

54. bread man by live alone cannot
____

55. bird early worm catches the the
____

PART-D

Directions: *Encircle the appropriate word for filling the blanks:*

56. ..... his illness, John continued to play rugby.
A. Despite B. Although
C. Even though

57. None of the students ..... a car.
A. has B. have
C. have got

58. There has not yet been any decision made ..... will represent the country at the Olympics
A. concerned athletes chosen
B. as to which athletes
C. those athletes

Directions: *Encircle the correct answer for filling the blanks:*

59. She held the ..... in her hand.
A. reigns B. rains
C. reins

60. They've got a ..... at the Ritz.
A. suit B. suite
C. sweet

61. Each of the Olympic athletes ..... for months, even years.
A. have been training
B. were training
C. has been training
D. been training

62. Never before ..... as rapidly, as during the last decade.
A. communication have developed
B. have communications developed
C. have developed communications
D. communications developed

63. The company will upgrade ..... computer information systems next month.
A. there B. their
C. it's D. its

64. He's a real ..... eyed boy in his office. The boss loves him.
A. green B. grey
C. brown D. blue

65. How can you argue about your salary now? It's there on your contract in .....
A. black B. blue and white
C. black and white D. red and white

Directions: *Encircle the right time preposition for the gaps in each sentence:*

66. We always visit my family ..... Christmas.
A. on B. at
C. in D. by

67. I have been learning English ..... two years.
A. since B. by
C. for D. in

68. My appointment with the doctor is ..... 4 O'clock.
A. on B. at
C. in D. by

69. By the time she arrives, we ..... our homework.
A. finish B. will have finished
C. will finish D. were finished

70. When I stopped ..... to Mary, she was picking some flowers in her garden.
A. speaking B. speak
C. to speak D. spoke

71. If I ..... you, I would wait a while to begin investing.
A. was B. am
C. were D. would be

Directions: *One sentence is wrong in each question. Which one?*

72. Capital letters. Which sentence is wrong?
A. We'll see you on Wednesday.
B. I speak Spanish very badly.
C. I like the weather here in the Winter.
D. Paul is a very difficult person to work with.

73. Commas. Which sentence is wrong?
A. On our trip we went to Japan, Thailand, Bali and Australia.
B. It was no surprise, that you failed the exam.

C. My aunt Julie, who often visits us, will be here for Christmas.

D. "I am not happy with your work", he said.

74. Apostrophes. Which sentence is wrong?

A. He doesn't know the answer, does he?

B. She has lots of cat's at home.

C. Joe's sister is in the Himalayas.

D. The problem with the business is its location.

Directions: *Rewrite the sentence using the phrase given in parenthesis as shown in the example:*

Ex. You must never take your helmet off while you are riding a motorcycle. (at all times) Helmets must be worn at all times when riding a motorcycle.

75. I'm afraid that car is just too expensive. (beyond my means)

____

76. I thought parking was allowed here. (was under the impression)

____

77. A man rode into town on Monday. He stayed for three nights and then left on Monday. How come?

____

78. In the language Bontoc, we find that adjectives can be made into verbs in the following fashion:

fikas strong	**kilad** red	**bato** stone	**fusul** enemy
fumikas he is becoming strong	**kumilad** he is becoming red	**bumato** he is becoming stone	**fumusul** he is becoming an enemy

Make a rule for describing this process.

____

____

____

Consider the following sentence from English. Even while you do not know the meanings of the underlined words, can you identify whether they are nouns or verbs? Give reason for your answer. (Question Nos. 79 & 80).

The disgruntled garfnack twillered across the river in a wooden boat.

79. Garfnack: ______________________________

80. Twillered: ______________________________

PART-E

Directions: *Read the following text and answer the questions that follow:*

Totto-Chan

The Little Girl At The Window

By Tetsuko Kuroyanagi

Translated by Dorothy Britton

The Headmaster

When Mother and Totto-chan went in, the man in the office got up from this chair. His hair was thin on top and he had a few teeth missing, but his face was a healthy color. Although he wasn't very tall, he had solid shoulders and arms and was neatly dressed in a rather shabby black three-piece suit. With a hasty bow, Totto-chan asked him spiritedly, "What are you, a schoolmaster or a stationmaster?" Mother was embarrassed, but before she had time to explain, he laughed and replied, "I'm the headmaster of this school."

Totto-chan was delighted, "Oh, I'm so glad," she said, "because I want to ask you a favor. I'd like to come to your school."

The headmaster offered her a chair and turned to Mother. "You may go home now. I want to talk to Totto-chan."

Totto-chan had a moment's uneasiness, but somehow felt she would get along all right with this man. "Well, then, I'll leave her with you," mother said bravely, and shut the door behind her as she went out.

The headmaster drew over a chair and put it facing Totto-chan, and when they were both sitting down close together, he said, "Now then, tell me all about yourself. Tell me anything at all you want to talk about."

"Anything I like?" Totto-chan had expected him to ask questions she would have to answer. When he said she could talk about anything she wanted, she was so happy she began straight away. It was all a bit higgledy-piggledy, but she talked for all she was worth. She told the headmaster how fast the train went that they had come on; how she had asked the ticket collector but he wouldn't let her keep her ticket; how pretty her homeroom teacher was at the other school; about the swallows' nest; about their brown dog, Rocky, who could do all sorts of tricks; how she used to go snip-snip with the scissors inside her mouth at kindergarten and the teacher said she mustn't do that because she might cut her tongue off, but she did it anyway; how she always blew her nose because mother scolded her if it was runny; what a good swimmer Daddy was, and how he could dive as well. She went on and on. The headmaster would laugh, nod, and say, "And then?" And Totto-chan was so happy she kept right on talking. But finally she ran out of things to say. She sat with her mouth closed trying hard to think of something. "Haven't you anything more you can tell me?", asked the headmaster. What a shame to stop now, Totto-chan thought. It was such a wonderful chance. Wasn't there anything else she could talk about, she wondered, racking her brains? Then she had an idea.

She could tell him about the dress she was wearing that day. Mother made most of her dresses, but this one came from a shop. Her clothes were always torn when she came home in the late afternoon. Some of the rips were quite bad. Mother never knew how they got that way. Even her white cotton panties were sometimes in shreds. She explained to the headmaster that they got torn when she crossed other people's gardens by crawling under their fences, and when she burrowed under the barbed wire around vacant lots. So this morning, she said, when she was getting dressed to come here, all the nice dresses Mother had made were torn so she had to wear one Mother had bought. It had small dark red and gray check and was made of jersey, and it wasn't bad, but Mother thought the red flowers embroidered on the collar were in bad taste. "Mother doesn't like the collar," said Totto-chan, holding it up for the headmaster to see.

After that, she could think of nothing more to say no matter how hard she tried. It made her rather sad. But just then the headmaster got up, placed his large, warm hand on her head, and said, "Well, now you're a pupil of this school."

Those were his very words. And at that moment Totto-chan felt she had met someone, she really liked for the very first time in her life. You see, up till then, no one had ever listened to her for so long. And all that time the headmaster hadn't yawned once or looked bored, but seemed just as interested in what she had to say as she was.

Totto-chan hadn't learned how to tell time yet, but it did seem like a rather long time. If she had been able to, she would have been astonished, and even more grateful to the headmaster. For, you see, Mother and Totto-chan arrived at the school at eight, and when she had finished talking and the headmaster had told her she was a pupil of the school, he looked at his pocket watch and said, "Ah, it's time for lunch." So the headmaster must have listened to Totto-chan for four solid hours!

Neither before nor since did any grown-up listen to Totto-chan for as long as that. And, besides, it would have amazed Mother and her homeroom teacher to think that a seven-year-old child could find enough to talk about for four hours nonstop.

Totto-chan had no idea then, of course, that she had been expelled and that people were at their wit's end to know what to do. Having a naturally sunny disposition and being a bit absent-minded gave her an air of innocence. But deep down she felt she was considered different from other children and slightly strange. The headmaster, however, made her feel safe and warm and happy. She wanted to stay with him forever.

That's how Totto-chan felt about headmaster Sosaku Kobayashi that firt day. And, luckily, the headmaster felt the same about her.

The above text is an extract from the book "Totto-chan. The Little Girl at the Window" and was first published in 1981 in Japan. It is about a little girl called Totto-chan who did not fit into the normal school system and so her mother takes her to a school started by Sosaku Kobayashi in six abandoned railroad car in 1937.

1. Why does Totto-chan ask the headmaster whether he was a schoolmaster or a stationmaster?

2. What did Totto-chan and the headmaster talk about?

3. Why did the homeroom teacher in the other school tell Totto-chan not to "go snip-snip with the scissors inside her mouth"? Did Totto-chan obey her?

4. Is this encounter between Totto-chan and the headmaster of her new school different from your experiences at school? In what way?

PART-F

Directions: *The following are newspaper headlines. Write a news report on anyone of them:*

1. Aman ki asha

2. Indian festivals celebrate communal harmony

3. Orphans blocked from departing Haiti

OR

Directions: *Write a paragraph on anyone of the following. The character, setting, time and situation is given:*

1. A recent high school graduate/a celebration party/the night of the high school graduation/ someone's pride has been injured.

2. A college student/a college library/the first week of college/something embarrassing has just happened.

3. A homeless child/a city park/late at night/ someone has accused someone else of doing something wrong.

ANSWERS

1. D	**2.** D	**3.** A	**4.** C
5. A	**6.** A	**7.** D	**8.** D
9. C	**10.** E	**11.** B	**12.** D
13. A	**14.** C	**15.** C	**16.** Velocity
17. Infinity	**18.** Words	**19.** Copenhagen	**20.** Water
21. B	**22.** B	**23.** B	**24.** A
25. B	**26.** C	**27.** A	**28.** C
29. C	**30.** B	**31.** A	**32.** C
33. C	**34.** D	**35.** B	**36.** D
37. B	**38.** A	**39.** C	**40.** D

41. It means to do something that you usually do not do or say.

42. Support for something insincerely.		**43.** Insert	**44.** Wait
45. Appear	**46.** Enter	**47.** Have	**48.** Want
49. Do	**50.** Checks	**51.** Debit	**52.** Take

53. A man is known by his friends.
54. Man cannot live by bread alone.
55. The early bird catches the worm.
56. A
57. C
58. B
59. A
60. B
61. C
62. A
63. D
64. D
65. C
66. A
67. A
68. B
69. C
70. A
71. A
72. A
73. B
74. B
75. The cost of car is beyond my mean.
76. I was under the impression that parking was allowed here.
77. Monday is the name of the vehicle on which he came to into the city.
78. Here, um stands for he is becoming and it comes between the first letter and the rest of the letters of the given word.
79. Nour
80. Verb

EXPLANATORY ANSWERS

PART-E

1. The headmaster's look was like stationmaster. He had solid shoulders and arms and was neatly dressed in a black three piece suit. Also the school runs in railroad cars.
2. Totto-chan told him about the train journey, about her other school, about her dog, her family and her days at Kindergarten.
3. Totto-chan used to go snip-snip with the scissors inside her mouth at Kindergarten so the teacher asked her not to do this as this might be harmful. She didn't obeyed him.
4. Yes, the encounter was different, as in normal schools the headmaster seldom gives so much time to listen to his new pupil. Another thing is that during the conversation period he gave his full attention which normal doesn't happen.

PART-F

Aman ki Asha

Aman is Asha is a campaign jointly started by the two leading media houses The Jang Group in Pakistan and The Time of India in India. The campaign aims for mutual peace and development of the diplomatic and cultural relations between the two nations in South Asia. It started on the 1st of January 2010. The campaign has received warm response from India and Pakistan. Despite this, Bennet & Coleman, the holding company of Times Group has been trying valiantly to keep the campaign afloat through a high decibel media campaign.

Aman ki Asha was inspired by the groundbreaking work of Friends Without Borders, an International NGO, that launched bold, love-based people-to-people campaigns between the children and people of both countries between 2005-2007. The Times of India and the Jang Group both partnered with Friends Without Borders and picked up the efforts after the Dil se Dil Border Concert was canceled in August 2007. "Peace efforts between India and Pakistan are the real need of the hour and only prudence, foresightedness and sincerity can do wonders for both countries. In this people of India communicate with the people of Pakistan."

The campaign has come under severe criticism from a major part of society in both India and Pakistan. Their campaign is rendered as a publicity stunt by these groups who consider the attitude of people of the two nations is beyond any rivalry. Hindu-Muslim agitations in India; decision of Babri Mosque; Hindu persecution in Pakistan and Pakistan's suspected and to a much level proved continued support to Islamic fundamentalists and terrorists in India (see 26/11 Mumbai Attacks) have reignited claims these rival nations find little common ground between themselves. The partition of religions seem far too high a mountain to climb for the nations to have a friendly relation with each other.

Previous Paper (Solved)

JNUEE-2009

B.A. (HONS.) IN FOREIGN LANGUAGES

PART A

(Marks : 25)

All questions carry one mark each.

Note: *Answer all the following questions. Circle the correct answer clearly. If more than one answer is circled, the answer will be marked wrong.*

1. Khalil Gibran is originally from
A. Saudi Arabia B. Egypt
C. Syria D. Lebanon

2. Suez Canal was made by
A. Egypt B. France
C. Britain D. USA

3. Ural mountains are located in
A. China B. Serbia
C. Russia D. Mongolia

4. Russian language belongs to
A. Germanic B. Roman
C. Slavic D. Celtic

5. Who is the first woman cosmonaut?
A. Kalpana Chawla
B. Sunita Williams
C. Valentina Tereshkova
D. Chiaki Mukai

6. Which is the current currency of Spain?
A. Euro B. Peso
C. Peseta D. Spanish Dollar

7. 'Tango' is the dance form which is typical of
A. Spain B. Argentina
C. Brazil D. Cuba

8. Which of the following authors is a recipient of the Noble prize for Literature?
A. Arundhati Roy
B. Jorge Luis Borges
C. Gabriel Garcia Marquez
D. Miguel Hernandez

9. Real Madrid' is a/an
A. Oscar winner film
B. football club
C. famous novel
D. famous wine

10. Who is the present Secretary-General of the UN?
A. Ban Ki Moon B. Lee Myung Bak
C. Han Seung soo D. Kin Dae Jung

11. Which city of South Korea will host the 2014 Asian Games?
A. Seoul B. Busan
C. Ulsan D. Incheon

12. Which is the only Asian country which is a member of G-8?
A. China B. Japan
C. India D. Singapore

13. Which of the Japanese classical performing arts is a world heritage?
A. Noh B. Kabuki
C. Joruri D. Bon odori

14. Karate is said to have been derived from
A. Kung fu B. Tae kwon do
C. Kalaripayattu D. Judo

15. 'Lacoste' is a/an
A. writer B. instrument
C. brand name D. book

16. What is Bordcaux?
A. River B. City
C. Monument D. Mountain

17. Which of the following persons has not been the President of France?
A. Giscard d'Estaing
B. Nicolas Sarkozy
C. Jean Marie Le pen
D. Jacques Chirac

18. Chinese New year is celebrated in the form of
A. Spring Festival B. Lantern Festival
C. Dragon Festival D. Moon Festival

19. Tian'anmen Square is located in
A. Shanghai
B. Nanjing
C. Beijing
D. Kunming

20. The last Emperor of China was called
A. Li Bai B. Puyi
C. Qian long D. Sun Zhogshan

21. The National Flag of People's Republic of China has
A. One big and four small stars
B. Four small stars
C. One big star
D. One big and one small star

22. Sheikh Saadi was a famous poet of
A. Arabic B. English
C. Urdu D. Persian

23. Who was the founder of Islamic Republic of Iran?
A. Ayatollah Khamenei
B. Ayatollah Rafsanjani
C. Ayatollah Khomeini
D. Ayatollah Karrubi

24. Who translated the Bible from Latin into German?
A. William Tyndale
B. Philipp Melanchthon
C. Martin Luther
D. John Calvin

25. Who was the First Chancellor of reunified Germany?
A. Erich Honecker B. Angela Merkel
C. Helmut Kohl D. Gerhard Schroder

PART–B

(Marks : 25)

All questions carry one mark each

A. Circle the correct answer clearly. If more than one answer is circled, the answer will be marked wrong:

26. Which out of the following is not recognized as a classical language by the Government of India?
A. Sanskrit B. Tamil
C. Malayalam D. Telugu

27. Zoram Nationalist Party is one of the major political parties of
A. Sikkim B. Arunachal Pradesh
C. Mizoram D. Meghalaya

28. Which Indian state has the lowest male-female ratio?
A. Punjab B. Delhi
C. Bihar D. Uttar Pradesh

29. Which is the world's highest train route?
A. Trans Siberian Railways
B. Konkan Railways
C. Udhampur-Baramula
D. Tibet Railways

30. Tata's Nano car factory is being set up in
A. Gujarat B. Punjab
C. Karnataka D. West Bengal

31. Nepal became a Republic in
A. 2005 B. 2006
C. 2007 D. 2008

32. Which of the following is not a SAARC country?
A. Myanmar B. Pakistan
C. Sri Lanka D. Maldives

33. The Indian historian who won the Kluge Prize for lifetime achievement in 2008 is
A. Romila Thapar B. Meera Sanyal
C. Kumkum Roy D. Sashi Deshpande

34. Which of the following diseases is caused by virus?
A. Tuberculosis B. Typhoid
C. Influenza D. Diphtheria

35. The phenomenon of mirage occurs due to
A. Polarisation of light

B. Dispersion of light

C. Diffraction of light

D. Total internal reflection of light

36. What is the major constituent of biogas?

A. Carbon dioxide B. Methane

C. Hydrogen D. Nitrogen oxide

37. The Egyptian *hieroglyphic* is a

A. Computer language

B. Pictorial script

C. Typescript

D. Musical language

38. The name of the well-known ancient Indian grammarian is

A. Panini B. Shankara

C. Chaitanya D. Aurobindo

39. Maximum number of wickets in One-day International Cricket has been taken by

A. Kapil Dev

B. Muttiah Muralitharan

C. Wasim Akram

D. Shane Warne

40. Khasi is spoken in the Indian State of

A. Mizoram

B. Nagaland

C. Arunachal Pradesh

D. Meghalaya

41. Eskimos are inhabitants of

A. Canada B. Japan

C. Ecuador D. Ethiopia

42. Hopis and Mayas are names of people who live in

A. Africa B. Europe

C. Australia D. America

43. The word 'literature' is related to

A. litter B. liter

C. latter D. letter

44. Official language of Morocco is

A. French B. Portuguese

C. Arabic D. Persian

45. The Japanese poem of seventeen syllables is

A. Haiku B. Tanka

C. Choka D. Waka

B. Write the answers in the space given:

46. The only Kashmiri poet to have received Jnanpith Award is ....

47. The stadium where the inaugural ceremony of Beijing Olympics, 2008, was held is known as....................

48. The first Indian Mission to the Moon is called ....

49. The author of the *White Tiger* is ....

50. The mixed doubles in the Australian open championship, 2009, was won by ....

PART–C

(Marks : 20)

All questions carry one mark each

A. Give the full forms of the following:

51. CIS

....

52. ASEAN

....

B. Hawaiian is a Polynesian language spoken fluently by about 2000 people. The following Hawaiian sentences, with their English translations, are about a girl named Mele and a boy named Keone:

He has seven elder brothers.	Ehiku ona kaikuaana.
Mele has one brother.	Ekahi o Mele kaikunane.
Keone has one younger brother.	Ekahi o Keon kaikaina.
Mele has no elder sisters.	Aohe o Mele kaikuaana.
Keone has no sisters.	Aohe o Keone kaikuahine.

53. What is the word for 'elder brothers' in Hawaiian?

....

54. What is the word for 'sister' in Hawaiian?

....

55. Is there a word for 'one' in Hawaiian? Circle the correct answer.

A. Yes B. No

C. In the following passage, some words have been omitted. Fill in the blanks with correct words such as:

a, an , the, have, had, in , around

This is true that 56 picture speaks more than a thousand words. 57 picture you 58 sent tells us about the destruction of wildlife. The picture shocked me very much. In the US, some private organizations 59 saved the largest variety of flora and fauna 60 the world.

56. ....

57. ....

58. ....

59. ....

60. ....

D. Look at the words given below. Rearrange them to form meaningful sentences. Write your sentences in the space provided:

61. a long / India has / conservation of / history of / forests

....

62. of living beings / conservation of / large mammals / to maintain / will help / the entire web

....

E. Rewrite the sentences following the examples given:

Example 1

Who inspects the machines? the foreman

The machines are inspected by the foreman.

63. Who made the biscuits? the girls in the factory

....

64. Who dictated that letter? the manager

....

Example 2

Which button did he push?

It's on the top.

He pushed the button which is on the top.

65. Which machines do you use?

They need electricity.

....

66. Which magazine is he reading?

It was in your office.

....

Example 3

The advertisement - by the personnel manager yesterday afternoon. **Write**

The advertisement **was written** by the personnel manager yesterday afternoon.

67. The job — in the morning paper tomorrow.

....

68. While I was in London I — to the post of general manager. Promote

....

Example 4

We'll advertise the job.

Will the job be advertised?

69. You can send telegrams from here.

....

70. You can buy all kinds of food here.

....

PART–D

(Marks : 20)

All questions carry one mark each

A. Circle the correct answer to fill in the blanks:

71. The bag is .... the table

A. on

B. in

72. I came .... bus.

A. on B. by

73. She likes samosa .... tomato sauce.

A. for B. with

74. John prefers tea .... coffee.

A. to B. than

B. Fill in the blanks with the correct answer:

75. "I wash my hands off the whole incident" means ....

A. I take full responsibility of the incident

B. I have nothing to do with the incident

76. I got the better of him. In other words, ...

A. I got better things from him

B. I overcame him

77. When I said she seemed out of spirits, I meant ....

A. she had become a spirit

B. she appeared sad

78. I was disappointed that he had taken exception to my remark. What I meant was that ....

A. he had not accepted my remark

B. he had objected to my remark

79. He knows the ins and outs of the matter. In other words, ...

A. he knows little about the matter

B. he knows the matter in detail

C. Complete the sentences with correct word/ words:

80. The coffee tastes a bit .... (musty / mustily)

81. I can't eat this. It tastes .... (awful / awfully)

82. When I returned to my village after 10 years, everything .... (changed / had changed)

D. Circle the correct answer to fill in the blanks:

83. Everyone .... happy about the tour.

A. is B. are

84. Ask either .... them.

A. of B. to

85. You .... attend the class regularly. It is my advice as your good friend.

A. would B. should

86. The horse and carriage .... come.

A. has B. have

87. I called .... him at the residence.

A. up B. on

88. Akash wants to break .... his engagement.

A. off B. up

89. One must not give .... to irrational demands.

A. up B. in

90. The landlord wants him to move .... by next week

A. out B. away

PART–E

(Marks : 10)

Write five sentences on each topic. Place do not exceed the limit. Each carries five marks:

A. Barack Obama

B. Slumdog Millionaire

ANSWERS

1	2	3	4	5	6	7	8	9	10
D	B	C	D	C	A	B	C	B	A
11	**12**	**13**	**14**	**15**	**16**	**17**	**18**	**19**	**20**
D	B	B	A	C	B	C	A	C	B

21	22	23	24	25	26	27	28	29	30
A	D	C	C	C	C	C	B	D	A
31	32	33	34	35	36	37	38	39	40
D	A	A	C	D	B	B	A	B	D
41	42	43	44	45					
A	D	A	C	A					

46. Rahman Rahi, November 6, 2008.

47. National Stadium.

48. Chandrayaan

49. Arvind Adiga

50. Sania Mirza and Mahesh Bhupati

51. Commonwealth of Independent States

52. Association of South-East Asian Nation

53. Kaikuaana

54. Aohe

55. Yes

56. a

57. the

58. had

59. have

60. around

61. India has a long history of conservation of forest.

62. Conservation of large mammals will help the entire web of living being.

63. The girls in the factory made the biscuits.

64. The manager dictated the letter.

65. You use to machines which need electricity.

66. He is reading the magazine which was in your office.

67. The job advertises in the morning paper tomorrow.

68. While I was in London, I was promoted to the post of General Manager.

69. Can the telegrams be send from here?

70. Can you buy all kinds of food here?

71. A

72. B

73. B

74. A

75. B

76. B

77. B

78. B

79. B

80. musty

81. awful

82. had changed

83. A

84. A

85. B

86. B

87. B

88. B

89. A

90. A

PART–E

Barack Husseian Obama: He was born on August 4, 1961. He is the 44th and current President of the United States. He is the first African American to hold the office. Obama previously served as the junior United States Senator from Illinois, from January 2005 until he resigned after his election to the presidency in November 2008. Obama is a graduate of Columbia University and Harvard Law

School, where he was the president of the **Harvard Law Review.**

Slumdog Millionaire is a 2008 British film directed by Danny Boyle, screenplay written by Simoon Beaufoy, and co-directed in India by Loveleen Tandan. It is an adaptation of the novel *Q & A* (2005) by Indian author and diplomat Vikas Swarup. **Slumdog Millionaire** was nominated for ten Academy Awards in 2009 and won eight, the most for any film of 2008, including Best Picture, Best Director, and Best Adapted Screenplay, It also won seven BAFTA Awards (including Best Film), five Critics' Choice Awards, and four Golden Globes.

Previous Paper (Solved)

JNUEE – 2008

B.A. (HONS.) IN FOREIGN LANGUAGES

PART–A

Answer all the following questions. All questions carry one mark each. Circle the correct answer clearly. If more than one answer is circled, the answer will be marked wrong:

1. The traditional form of drama of Japan which is similar to Yakshagana of India is:
(*a*) Bunraku (*b*) Noh
(*c*) Gagaku (*d*) Sarugaku

2. The cultural capital of Japan is:
(*a*) Nagoya (*b*) Kyoto
(*c*) Tokyo (*d*) Osaka

3. The constitutional head of Japan is:
(*a*) Prime Minister
(*b*) President
(*c*) Emperor
(*d*) Chancellor

4. Boutros Boutros Ghali, former Secretary-General of UNO belonged to:
(*a*) Saudi Arabia (*b*) Kuwait
(*c*) UAE (*d*) Egypt

5. The only Arab scientist to have won Nobel Prize is:
(*a*) Ahmad Zuwail
(*b*) Abdur Rahman Naïf
(*c*) Munir Ramzi
(*d*) Ehsan Khalil

6. *One Hundred Years of Solitude* was written by:
(*a*) Vikram Seth
(*b*) Dan Brown
(*c*) Gabriel Garcia Marqez
(*d*) Ayn Rand

7. The term 'Banana Republics' refers to:
(*a*) Countries of Africa
(*b*) Countries of South-East Asia
(*c*) Countries of South America
(*d*) Countries of Eastern Europe

8. Which of the following is a Spanish painter?
(*a*) Claude Monet
(*b*) Leonardo da Vinci
(*c*) Paul Klee
(*d*) Pablo Picasso

9. In 2007, China's GDP crossed:
(*a*) three trillion US dollars
(*b*) one trillion US dollars
(*c*) four billion US dollars
(*d*) six billion US dollars

10. The current President of China is:
(*a*) Hu Jintao (*b*) Wa Jiabao
(*c*) Jiang Zenia (*d*) Yang Shangkun

11. The 'Tiananmen Square' protests took place in the year:
(*a*) 1979 (*b*) 1989
(*c*) 1999 (*d*) None of the above

12. The Berlin Wall collapsed in the year:
(*a*) 1960-61 (*b*) 1979-80
(*c*) 1982-83 (*d*) 1989-90

13. The Reformation in Germany is linked with:
(*a*) Martin Luther
(*b*) Ulrich Zwingli
(*c*) Friedrich II
(*d*) Otto von Bismarck

14. The official name for Germany is:
(*a*) German Democratic Republic
(*b*) Federal German Republic

(*c*) Federal Republic of Germany
(*d*) Socialist Republic of Germany

15. A Molotov cocktail is:
(*a*) a drink made of orange juice and vodka
(*b*) a crude bomb
(*c*) a special fruit salad
(*d*) a form of dance

16. Peter the Great belonged to:
(*a*) the Romanov dynasty
(*b*) the Rurik dynasty
(*c*) the Khan dynasty
(*d*) None of the above

17. The CIS countries refer to:
(*a*) some of the East-European Countries
(*b*) some of the South-American Republics
(*c*) the East-African Block
(*d*) some of the former Soviet Republics

18. The following President got divorced and remarried during his term in office:
(*a*) Giscard d'Estaing (*b*) Horst Koehler
(*c*) Nicolas Sarkozy (*d*) Boris Yeltsin

19. The following country does not share a border with France:
(*a*) Germany (*b*) Greece
(*c*) Belgium (*d*) Switzerland

20. The President of France earlier used to be elected for a term of:
(*a*) four years (*b*) five years
(*c*) six years (*d*) seven years

21. Omar Khayyam was:
(*a*) a poet (*b*) a politician
(*c*) a statesman (*d*) a warrior

22. Persian has official language status in:
(*a*) Pakistan (*b*) Uzbekistan
(*c*) Afghanistan (*d*) Iraq

23. Persepolis was the ancient capital of the:
(*a*) Egyptian Empire
(*b*) Persian Empire
(*c*) Byzantine Empire
(*d*) Ottoman Empire

24. The 38th parallel or Demilitarized Zone is the area that divides:
(*a*) North and South Korea
(*b*) China and Tibet
(*c*) North and South Vietnam
(*d*) Hong Kong and China

25. Kimchi, Sushi, Bulgogi are:
(*a*) names of novels (*b*) dance forms
(*c*) language dialects (*d*) food items

PART–B

Answer all the following questions. All questions carry one mark each. Circle the correct answer clearly. If more than one answer is circled, the answer will be marked wrong:

26. The book, *Life Divine*, was written by:
(*a*) Jawaharlal Nehru
(*b*) Aurobindo Ghosh
(*c*) George Bernard Shaw
(*d*) Rabindranath Tagore

27. *Das Kapital* was written by:
(*a*) Vladimir Ilyich Lenin
(*b*) Karl Marx
(*c*) G.W.F. Hegel
(*d*) Ludwig Feuerbach

28. The last ruler of the Mughal dynasty was:
(*a*) Shah Jahan
(*b*) Aurangzeb
(*c*) Akbar
(*d*) Bahadur Shah Zafar

29. The father of the Indian Constitution was:
(*a*) B.R. Ambedkar
(*b*) Jawaharlal Nehru
(*c*) Mohandas Karamchand Gandhi
(*d*) Bankim Chandra Chatterjee

30. The first Indian actress to have been nominated to the Rajya Sabha was:
(*a*) Nargis Dutt
(*b*) Hema Malini
(*c*) Jaya Bachchan
(*d*) Vaijayantimala Bali

31. The chief constituent of 'gobar' gas is:
(*a*) ethane (*b*) propane
(*c*) methane (*d*) chlorine

32. The first metal used by man was:
(*a*) iron (*b*) copper
(*c*) gold (*d*) bronze

33. The 'greenhouse effect' refers to:
(*a*) increasing agricultural yields
(*b*) gradual warming of the earth surface
(*c*) buildup of toxic airborne pollutants
(*d*) reduction in the earth's ozone layer

34. Television in India was introduced in the year:
(*a*) 1947 (*b*) 1960
(*c*) 1959 (*d*) 1981

35. The movie 'Tare Zameen Par' deals with:
(*a*) Dyslexia (*b*) Paranoia
(*c*) Schizophrenia (*d*) Aphasia

36. *Tamasha* is a famous folk form of:
(*a*) Uttar Pradesh (*b*) Punjab
(*c*) Bihar (*d*) Maharashtra

37. India's first talkie film was:
(*a*) Shakuntala (*b*) Indra Sabha
(*c*) Neel Kamal (*d*) Alam Ara

38. The UNESCO has declared 2008 as the international year of:
(*a*) culture
(*b*) languages
(*c*) wildlife conservation
(*d*) heritage restoration

39. Who was appointed the coach of the Indian women's hockey team in 2007?
(*a*) Herman Kruis (*b*) Shah Rukh Khan
(*c*) Kabir Khan (*d*) Mir Ranjan Negi

40. Sania Mirza is the brand ambassador for which soft drink?
(*a*) Pepsi (*b*) Coke
(*c*) Sprite (*d*) Fanta

41. IPL in cricket stands for:
(*a*) Indian Professional League
(*b*) International Players League
(*c*) Indian Premium League
(*d*) None of the above

42. The farmers of Singur resisted the State Government's move to acquire land for:
(*a*) Tata Motors
(*b*) Maruti Udyog
(*c*) Infosys
(*d*) Hindustan Motors

43. The Gir Forests are located in:
(*a*) Assam (Asom)
(*b*) Himachal Pradesh
(*c*) Maharashtra
(*d*) Gujarat

44. Which of the following pairs is wrong?
(*a*) Copenhagen–Denmark
(*b*) Bern–Sweden
(*c*) Madrid–Spain
(*d*) Prague–Czech Republic

45. The sea route to India was discovered by:
(*a*) Columbus (*b*) Magellan
(*c*) Vasco da Gama (*d*) Hopkins

46. Mother Teresa was born in:
(*a*) India (*b*) Albania
(*c*) Germany (*d*) Switzerland

47. Sigmund Freud is associated with:
(*a*) detective work (*b*) leprosy control
(*c*) birth control (*d*) psychology

48. The modern nursing system was started by:
(*a*) Florence Nightingale
(*b*) Mother Teresa
(*c*) Madame Curie
(*d*) Sharmila Tagore

49. The system of writing and printing for the blind was developed by:
(*a*) Louis Braille
(*b*) Robert Wilhelm Bunsen
(*c*) Sir Humphrey Davy
(*d*) Marcus Abacus

50. Lumbini is a sacred place of the:
(*a*) Hindus (*b*) Christians
(*c*) Buddhists (*d*) Jains

PART–C

All questions carry one mark each.

A. Where are the following languages spoken in India? Write the answers in the space given.

51. Konkani ______________________

52. Kurux ______________________

53. Braj ______________________

B. Circle the correct answer.

54. A linguist is a person who knows many languages. [Yes / No]

55. Some languages have no grammar. [Yes / No]

56. All languages have scripts. [Yes / No]

57. Languages that have no script have no grammar. [Yes / No]

58. Languages is inherited, not acquired. [Yes / No]

59. Languages differ in written and spoken forms. [Yes / No]

60. European languages are richer than Indian languages. [Yes / No]

61. In remote past, all human beings spoke only one language. [Yes / No]

C. Following are the words and sentences from Aztec, a language from Mexico. All the words are written without any spaces between them. Read them carefully.

ikalwewe	'his big house'
ikalsolsol	'his old house'
ikalcin	'his little house'
kalmeh	'houses'
petat	'mat'

How would you write the following in this language?

62. his big mats ______________________

63. his little mat ______________________

64. old mat ______________________

65. Suppose *A*, *B*, *C* and *D* are words in a language which have the possibility of occurring in any order to form a sentence. Also suppose that in this language the minimum length of a sentence is one word and that maximum length is four words. How many sentences can one make from these four words? State only the number of possible sentences.

PART–D

All questions carry one mark each.

A. Fill in the blanks with the correct answer from the choices given below.

66. Instead of ....

In case of ....

In spite of ....

(*a*) his illness he attended the party

(*b*) driving his car he took a bus

(*c*) fire, don't use the lift

67. Being late makes him ....

Ram pushed the door ....

My job keeps me ....

(*a*) busy (*b*) open

(*c*) angry

B. Circle the correct answers.

68. I say "I could eat a horse" when I am:

(*a*) lazy (*b*) hungry

(*c*) late

69. I say "I haven't a clue" when I:

(*a*) am curious

(*b*) understand nothing

(*c*) am apologetic

70. I say "You can count on me" when I:

(*a*) trust someone

(*b*) dislike someone

(*c*) support someone

C. Fill in the blanks with the correct answer.

71. Arm is to hand as leg is to...................... .

72. Beautiful is to beauty as young is to........ .

73. I is to 'my' as you is to ....

74. Drive is to drove as eat is to.................... .

75. One is to two as first is to ....

D. Circle the correct answer.

76. We will visit Udaipur............... Jodhpur during our next vacation.
(*a*) and (*b*) but
(*c*) so

77. My teeth were hurting............... I made an appointment with the dentist.
(*a*) or (*b*) so
(*c*) but

78. I wanted to go to the film .... all the tickets were sold out.
(*a*) but (*b*) so
(*c*) and

79. My brother wanted to buy a novel .... I went to the bookstore after I finished work.
(*a*) or (*b*) so
(*c*) but

80. After practice, the girls' hockey team said, "We are famished". Famished means
(*a*) tired (*b*) hungry
(*c*) excited

81. When having a problem it is best to dissect the situation. Dissect means
(*a*) ignore (*b*) out apart
(*c*) analyze

82. The General tried to instil in his troops the hope of victory. Instil means
(*a*) delay (*b*) inscribe
(*c*) infuse

83. The scientist was able to evoke powerful emotions from her audience. Evoke means
(*a*) call forth (*b*) sell
(*c*) calm

84. Do you justify his behaviour .... the function
(*a*) at (*b*) in

85. Everything in the cupboard .... Ram's.
(*a*) is (*b*) are

86. No one .... a watch on.
(*a*) have (*b*) has

87. Each girl brought .... own paper.
(*a*) her (*b*) their

88. All of the men brought .... wives.
(*a*) his (*b*) their

89. Everyone of those coats is missing ....buttons.
(*a*) its (*b*) their

90. None of the children remembered .... lunch.
(*a*) his (*b*) their

PART–E

Complete the paragraph in 150-200 *words. Please do not exceed the word limit.*

Learning a foreign language will help me to.........

ANSWER

1	2	3	4	5	6	13	14	15	16	17	18
(*b*)	(*b*)	(*c*)	(*d*)	(*a*)	(*c*)	(*d*)	(*c*)	(*b*)	(*a*)	(*d*)	(*c*)
7	**8**	**9**	**10**	**11**	**12**	**19**	**20**	**21**	**22**	**23**	**24**
(*c*)	(*d*)	(*a*)	(*a*)	(*b*)	(*d*)	(*b*)	(*d*)	(*a*)	(*c*)	(*b*)	(*a*)

25	26	27	28	29	30
(*d*)	(*b*)	(*b*)	(*d*)	(*a*)	(*a*)
31	**32**	**33**	**34**	**35**	**36**
(*c*)	(*b*)	(*b*)	(*c*)	(*a*)	(*a*)
37	**38**	**39**	**40**	**41**	**42**
(*d*)	(*b*)	(*a*)	(*c*)	(*d*)	(*a*)
43	**44**	**45**	**46**	**47**	**48**
(*d*)	(*b*)	(*c*)	(*b*)	(*d*)	(*a*)
49	**50**				
(*a*)	(*c*)				

51. Goa

52. Bihar, Jharkhand, Orissa, Madhya Pradesh & Chhattishgarh.

53. Uttar Pradesh.

54. Yes **55.** No **56.** No **57.** No

58. No **59.** Yes **60.** No **61.** No

62. ipetatmehwewe **63.** ipetatcin

64. petatsolsol **65.** 4! = 24 words

66. (*b*) (*c*) (*a*) **67.** (*c*) (*b*) (*a*)

68	69	70	71	72	73
(*b*)	(*b*)	(*c*)	feet	youth	your
74	**75**	**76**	**77**	**78**	**79**
ate	second	(*a*)	(*b*)	(*a*)	(*b*)
80	**81**	**82**	**83**	**84**	**85**
(*a*)	(*c*)	(*c*)	(*a*)	(*a*)	(*a*)
86	**87**	**88**	**89**	**90**	
(*a*)	(*a*)	(*b*)	(*b*)	(*b*)	

Previous Paper Solved

JNUEE–2007

PART–A

Answer all the following questions. All questions carry one mark each. Circle the correct answer clearly. If more than one answer is circled, the answer will be marked wrong:

1. The five permanent members of the UN Security Council are:
(*a*) Germany, USA, Russia, China, France
(*b*) USA, Russia, China, France, UK
(*c*) China, France, UK, Russia, Australia
(*d*) Germany, Russia, India, USA, China

2. Arrange the following historical events in the correct chronological order starting with the event took place first:
1. Russian Revolution
2. French Revolution
3. Indian Independence
4. World War II

(*a*) 2, 1, 4, 3 (*b*) 4, 3, 2, 1
(*c*) 1, 2, 3, 4 (*d*) 2, 1, 3, 4

3. Which country occupies almost half the land area of the South American Continent?
(*a*) Argentina (*b*) Peru
(*c*) Brazil (*d*) Venezuela

4. Which of these famous leaders was hung to death in 2006?
(*a*) Zulfikar Ali Bhutto
(*b*) Osama bin Laden
(*c*) Saddam Hussain
(*d*) Joseph Stalin

5. Which of the following world leaders did ***not*** attend college in India?
(*a*) Zulfikar Ali Bhutto
(*b*) Hamid Karzai
(*c*) Aung San Suu Kyi
(*d*) Benazir Bhutto

6. Which of the following numbers cannot be written in Roman numerals?
(*a*) One hundred (*b*) Zero
(*c*) Five (*d*) Thirty-nine

7. During whose reign were the Panchatantra stories written?
(*a*) Chandragupta Vikramaditya
(*b*) Samudragupta
(*c*) Kumaragupta
(*d*) Bindusara

8. Kautilya and Panini were the products of which one of the following ancient Indian universities?
(*a*) Nalanda (*b*) Vikramashila
(*c*) Vallabhi (*d*) Taxila

9. The official language of the Mughal Court was
(*a*) Arabic (*b*) Persian
(*c*) Urdu (*d*) Turkish

10. Which among the following is the oldest Indian language?
(*a*) Telugu (*b*) Hindi
(*c*) Tamil (*d*) Punjabi

11. By what name is the river Ganga known in Bangladesh?
(*a*) Rupanarayan (*b*) Padma
(*c*) Bhagirathi (*d*) Nubra

12. What is the Booker Prize given for?
(*a*) Novels (*b*) Poetry
(*c*) Art (*d*) Politics

13. Satish Chandra, Ravi Verma, Anjolie Ela Menon, Arvind Benegal are all:
(*a*) film directors (*b*) designers
(*c*) artists (*d*) musicians

14. Which of the following is ***not*** a classical dance form?
(*a*) Odissi
(*b*) Bharatnatyam
(*c*) Kuchipudi
(*d*) Ras Leela

15. Which of the following communities celebrates the festival of Navroz in India?
(*a*) Parsis (*b*) Coorgis
(*c*) Khasis (*d*) Buddhists

16. The Church of Bom Jesus is situated in:
(*a*) Maharashtra (*b*) Goa
(*c*) Kerala (*d*) Nagaland

17. India's official entry to the Oscars 2007 was:
(*a*) *Water*
(*b*) *Lage Raho Munnabhai*
(*c*) *Rang De Basanti*
(*d*) *Paheli*

18. The film *Monsoon Wedding* was directed by
(*a*) Deepa Mehta
(*b*) Mira Nair
(*c*) Siddhartha Anand
(*d*) Aditya Chopra

19. Who was the captain of the Indian Cricket Team when India won the World Cup?
(*a*) Sunil Gavaskar
(*b*) Kapil Dev
(*c*) Mansoor Ali Khan Pataudi
(*d*) Farooq Engineer

20. How many times has India hosted the Asian Games?
(*a*) 0 (*b*) 1
(*c*) 2 (*d*) 3

21. Who was the first Indian to go into space?
(*a*) Vikram Sarabhai
(*b*) Kalpana Chawla
(*c*) Sunita Williams
(*d*) Rakesh Sharma

22. India's first atomic reactor is called:
(*a*) Dhruva (*b*) Kamini
(*c*) Purnima I (*d*) Apsara

23. Who formed the Janata Party and defeated the Congress Party in 1977?
(*a*) Jayaprakash Narayan
(*b*) Raj Narain
(*c*) V. P. Singh
(*d*) None of the above

24. Which of the following is the main leader of the Narmada Bachao Andolan?
(*a*) Aamir Khan
(*b*) Arundhati Roy
(*c*) Medha Patkar
(*d*) Sunderlal Bahuguna

25. The Union Budget is presented to the Lok Sabha on:
(*a*) February 26 (*b*) February 28
(*c*) March 1 (*d*) March 31

PART–B

Answer all the following questions. All questions carry one mark each. Circle the correct answer clearly. If more than one answer is circled, the answer will be marked wrong:

26. Bach, Schubert, Mahler and Schoneberg were:
(*a*) writers (*b*) composers
(*c*) painters (*d*) politicians

27. German is not one of the official languages of:
(*a*) Switzerland (*b*) Belgium
(*c*) Austria (*d*) Liechtenstein

28. Who of the following persons is ***not*** a German?
(*a*) Johann Wolfgang V. Goethe
(*b*) Otto V. Bismarck
(*c*) Steffi Graf
(*d*) Philip Roth

29. Which Russian artist has his family house in India?
(*a*) Andrei Rublev
(*b*) Nikolai Roerich
(*c*) Aleksandr Rodchenko
(*d*) Andrei Sokolov

30. Which Russian leader initiated the Great Purges in which millions of people were executed or exiled?
(*a*) Lenin
(*b*) Stalin
(*c*) Catherine the Great
(*d*) Nicholas II

31. Who was the first democratically elected President of the Russian Federation?
(*a*) Mikhail Gorbachov
(*b*) Vladimir Putin
(*c*) Boris Yeltsin
(*d*) Leonid Brezhnev

32. Latin America consists of:
(*a*) the Caribbean, Mexico, South America
(*b*) most of South America and the Caribbean
(*c*) Mexico and South America
(*d*) most of Central America, South America and the Caribbean

33. Salsa, flamenco and tango are:
(*a*) musical instruments
(*b*) dance forms
(*c*) food items
(*d*) types of birds

34. What are the official languages of Canada?
(*a*) Spanish and English
(*b*) Canadian and Spanish
(*c*) French and English
(*d*) Canadian and French

35. The Maghreb countries are:
(*a*) Algeria, Morocco, Tunisia
(*b*) Mauritius, Algeria, Egypt
(*c*) Tunisia, Algeria, Mauritius
(*d*) Morocco, Egypt, Tunisia

36. Which French writer refused the Nobel Prize for Literature?
(*a*) . Albert Camus
(*b*) Michel Proust
(*c*) Jean Paul Sartre
(*c*) Simone de Beauvoir

37. Which of the following Japanese writers received the Nobel Prize for Literature in 1994?
(*a*) Asai Ryoi
(*b*) Kazuo Ishiguro
(*c*) Kensaburo Oe
(*d*) Inoue Hisashi

38. The modernisation of Japan began during the rule of
(*a*) Emperor Taisko
(*b*) Emperor Ninko
(*c*) Emperor Showa
(*c*) Emperor Meiji

39. Who was the Indian Judge who ruled the Japanese Emperor 'not guilty' during the trial of war criminals?
(*a*) Justice S. Natrajan
(*d*) Justice Tarun Chatterji
(*c*) Justice Radha Binod Pal
(*d*) Justice A. Vardarajan

40. Which was the war that led to the division of Korea into North and South Korea?
(*a*) World War I
(*b*) Russo- Japanese War of 1904-05
(*c*) World War II
(*d*) None of the above

41. Which of the following is ***not*** a Korean company?
(*a*) Sansui (*b*) Samsung
(*c*) LG (*d*) Hyundai

42. The Korean script is called:
(*a*) Kanji (*b*) Hangul
(*c*) Hiragana (*d*) Katakana

43. The People's Republic of China does ***not*** include
(*a*) Mainland China
(*b*) Taiwan
(*c*) Hong Kong
(*d*) Macau

44. Which of the following persons is ***not*** a Chinese political leader?
(*a*) Mao Zedong (*b*) Hu Jintao
(*c*) Kim II Jong (*d*) Deng Xiaoping

45. Which of the following is ***not*** a Chinese invention?
(*a*) Compass (*b*) Bicycle
(*c*) Abacus (*d*) Fireworks

46. Who is the President of Iran?
(*a*) Mahmud Ahmadi-Nejad
(*b*) Mogtada Al-Sadr
(*c*) Nouri Malik
(*d*) Ahmad Husayn Khudayir as-Samarrai

47. Which of these legendary figures is ***not*** of Persian origin?
(*a*) Rostam (*b*) Sohraab
(*c*) Zal (*d*) Siegfried

48. Which of the following is ***not*** a member of the Arab League?
(*a*) Sudan (*b*) Jordan
(*c*) Iraq (*d*) Turkey

49. Which of the following writers from the Arab World won the Nobel Prize for Literature?
(*a*) Naguib Mahfouz
(*b*) Imre Kertesz
(*c*) Wobe Soyinka
(*d*) Jose Saramago

50. Which is the smallest country in the Arab World?

(*a*) Qatar (*b*) Bahrain
(*c*) Kuwait (*d*) Tunisia

PART–C

This part is divided into three Sections. Read the instructions carefully and attempt all the questions. All questions carry one mark each.

Section–I

The questions in this Section are all based on an invented language called Babel. Read each group of examples carefully, paying particular attention to the different forms of words (just as in English there are differences between, e.g., *cat* and *cats* or *call* and *called*). Note also that Babel has no equivalent for the English *the* and *a*(*n*), so that, e.g., *King* (in Babel) may be translated as 'the king' or 'a king'. You are advised to work through the questions in the order that they are given.

Example 1:

bats mugs molti 'the king praises the servant'
bats mugans molti 'the king praises the servants'
mugans bats kadonti 'the servant hates kings'
bats totans lubti 'the king likes children'

Translate into English :

51. mugs tots kadti
52. batans totans lubonti

Translate into Babel :

53. The kings praise the servant.

Example 2 :

bats mugans nemolto 'the kings did not praise the servant'
totans gavs pelonto 'the children chased the dog'
tots filans lubto 'the child liked elephants'
filans gavans nelubonti 'elephants do not like dogs'
mugs totans nikto 'the servant washed the children'

Translate into English :

54. gavs fils nepelto
55. bats mugans nemolto

Translate into Babel :

56. The servants did not wash the child.

Section–II

To which languages do the followings groups of words belong? Write your answers in the blanks provided:

57. Harakiri Sushi, Sumo, Tsunami:
58. Angst, Ersatz, Kindergarten, Zeppelin:
59. Perestroika, Intelligentsia, Dacha:
60. Laissez faire, Deja vu, Madame:
61. Bazaar, Bungalow, Curry:

Section–III

A. Circle the word which is closest in meaning to the underlined word. If more than one answer is circled, that answer will be marked wrong:

62. The students liked the new teacher because he had an <u>amiable</u> personality.
(*a*) strict (*b*) friendly
(*c*) intelligent (*d*) efficient

63. Many people say that Aishwarya Rai is an <u>ethereal</u> beauty.
(*a*) deadly (*b*) royal
(*c*) heavenly (*d*) unnatural

64. When having a problem, it is best to <u>dissect</u> the situation before taking action.
(*a*) ignore (*b*) analyze
(*c*) define (*d*) postpone

65. The actor was able to <u>evoke</u> powerful emotions from the audience.
(*a*) call forth (*b*) disturb
(*c*) enjoy (*d*) promote

B. Circle the correct word from the options given. If more than one answer is circled, that answer will be marked wrong:

66. Doctor is to patient as lawyer is to:
(*a*) customer (*b*) accused
(*c*) magistrate (*d*) client

67. Starvation is to nutrition as exhaustion is to:
(*a*) energy (*b*) bravery
(*c*) freshness (*d*) courage

68. Author is to book as choreographer is to:
(*a*) drama (*b*) dance
(*c*) song (*d*) painting

69. Bread is to wheat as brick is to:
(*a*) air (*b*) fire
(*c*) clay (*d*) water

70. Appreciation is to reward as disgrace is to:
(*a*) allegation (*b*) crime
(*c*) guilt (*d*) punishment

PART–D

Section-I

Fill in the blanks using the correct prepositions. Write your answers in the space provided on the right:

71. The shirt .... the window is very nice.

72. The doctor has been waiting .... the reports.

73. I found the wallet lying .... the drawer.

74. The shop next door .... the bakery is opening tomorrow.

75. I will come and pick you up .... the new car.

76. My mother has invited you all .... dinner.

77. He came home .... many packages.

78. How hard have you studied .... the test?

79. Mother Teresa won the love .... the people.

80. I will have to come .... bus.

Section-II

Insert articles wherever necessary in the following paragraph. Write your answers in the column on the right:

Have you ever heard of Mary Lyon? She was (81) pioneer in (82) education of women. She worked hard so that women could get (83) education to compete with anyone else in the country. She taught in schools in New Hampshire and Massachusetts. In those days, only (84) rich could get (85) good education, especially if they were women. She raised money to open (86) school for middle-class women. In 1837, she opened (87) school in Massachusetts. (88) school was called Mount Holyoke. Today this school has become one of (89) most famous colleges in (90) USA.

Section-III

Read the following passage carefully. Answer the questions given at the end of the passage. Circle the most appropriate option. If more than one option is circled, the answer will be marked wrong:

The Hours That count in My Life

by Essa Al-Dhaheri

Time is very important in our lives. It organizes our everyday moments. However, time never had any importance in my life untill I received a watch from my father that organized my life and made me more responsible.

It came from Denmark to the UAE jewelry shop in gray box. It weighs 8 oz. It is round in the center with two silver bands that go around my wrist. And all of it is made of silver. This object tells me the importance of time in my life.

I received this gift on a gray-sky day. I had to go to the airport at 9:00 AM to pick up my Uncle Ali and take him to my father's house. However, I was late because I was hanging out with my friends. Later on that day, around 11:00 AM, I remembered my uncle, but I was very late for him. He had left the airport and taken a taxi to my father's house.

I got to my father's house at 2:00 PM on the same day and looked at my angry father's face. I felt ashamed of myself at that moment. After I said hi to my angry father and tired uncle, my father asked me to sit next to him where he handed me this watch which was a gift from him. Then he said, "Essa, did you have fun with your friends today?" I answered, "Yes father and I'm sorry about not picking up my Uncle Ali." He said "What you did was not very nice and you should be sorry for your actions". I was ashamed and said "father I'll never do it again. I promise." He said, "I hope today you learned something important, and this watch will be a reminder for you." He told me to take this watch and use it as an organizer of my life.

I learned a very important lesson from my father: to respect time and never be late to get someone. This watch is important to me, not because of its price, but because of the lesson that I learned from it.

91. When did time become important to Essa?
- (*a*) When he was playing with his friends.
- (*b*) When he lost his watch.
- (*c*) When he received a watch from his father.
- (*d*) When he went to Denmark.
- (*e*) When he met his Uncle Ali.

92. Which of the following is ***not*** true about Essa's watch?
- (*a*) It came from his father.

(*b*) It weighed one pound.
(*c*) It was made of silver.
(*d*) It will be a reminder to Essa.
(*e*) It helps to organize his life.

93. Which of the following is true?
(*a*) Essa was playing with his friends at 2:00 PM
(*b*) Uncle Ali took a taxi to Essa's father's house.
(*c*) Essa was supposed to pick up his father at the airport.
(*d*) Essa never tried to pick up his uncle at the airport.
(*e*) Essa's uncle had only been on a short trip.

94. What happened last?
(*a*) Eassa was playing with his friends.
(*b*) Essa went to meet his Uncle Ali at the airport.
(*c*) Essa's father talked with him about being on time.
(*d*) Essa got a watch.
(*e*) Essa arrived at his father's house.

95. At the end of the story, which was ***not*** important to Essa?
(*a*) Pleasing his father
(*b*) Playing with his friends
(*c*) The watch
(*d*) The price of the watch
(*e*) Being on time and treating people nicely

PART–E

Write a short paragraph (of not more than 150 words) in English or in Hindi on:

I want to learn (the language of your first choice) because.......

(You may discuss the language, the culture, the history of the area where the language of your choice is spoken.)

Please stick to the word limit.

ANSWER

PART–A

1	2	3	4	5	6
(*b*)	(*a*)	(*c*)	(*c*)	(*d*)	(*b*)
7	8	9	10	11	12
(*d*)	(*d*)	(*b*)	(*c*)	(*b*)	(*a*)
13	14	15	16	17	18
(*c*)	(*d*)	(*a*)	(*b*)	(*d*)	(*b*)
19	20	21	22	23	24
(*b*)	(*b*)	(*d*)	(*d*)	(*a*)	(*d*)
25	26	27	28	29	30
(*b*)	(*b*)	(*d*)	(*d*)	(*b*)	(*b*)
31	32	33	34	35	36
(*c*)	(*d*)	(*b*)	(*c*)	(*a*)	(*d*)
37	38	39	40	41	42
(*c*)	(*d*)	(*c*)	(*c*)	(*a*)	(*b*)
43	44	45	46	47	48
(*b*)	(*c*)	(*b*)	(*a*)	(*d*)	(*d*)
49	50				
(*a*)	(*b*)				

51. The servant likes children
52. Kings like the child
53. Batans mug molti
54. Elephand did not care of dogs.
55. The king did not praise the servant.
56. Mugans totans nikolto
57. Japanese
58. German
59. Russian
60. French
61. Hindi
62. Friendly

63	64	65	66	67	68
(*c*)	(*b*)	(*a*)	(*d*)	(*a*)	(*b*)
69	70	71	72	73	74
(*c*)	(*c*)	on	for	in	to
75	76	77	78	79	80
by	for	with	for	of	by
81	82	83	84	85	86
a	the	the	a	a	the
87	88	89	90	91	92
a	the	the	the	(*c*)	(*b*)
93	94	95			
(*b*)	(*d*)	(*e*)			

Previous Paper Solved

JNUEE–2006

PART–A

Answer the following questions by selecting the most appropriate one from (*a*) to (*d*):

1. Which of the following is not an Arab State?
(*a*) Qatar (*b*) Tunisia
(*c*) Iran (*d*) Bahrain

2. What was the official language of India till the end of Mughal Rule?
(*a*) Urdu (*b*) Farsi
(*c*) Arabic (*d*) Hindi

3. Which form of musical worship was popularised by the Indian- born Persian poet, Amir Khusro?
(*a*) Kirtan (*b*) Bhakti
(*c*) Sufi (*d*) Bhajan

4. Who was the President of the USSR when it disintegrated?
(*a*) Vladimir Putin
(*b*) Mikhail Gorbachov
(*c*) Boris Yeltsin
(*d*) Leonid Brezhnev

5. The Latin American country sharing border with the United States is:
(*a*) Mexico (*b*) Toronto
(*c*) Los Angeles (*d*) Nicaragua

6. The second official language in the United States is:
(*a*) Spanish (*b*) French
(*c*) German (*d*) Dutch

7. The river Amazon flows through:
(*a*) Zambia (*b*) Zimbabwe
(*c*) Zurich (*d*) Brazil

8. What was France known as during the Roman Empire?
(*a*) Galles (*b*) Gaulle
(*c*) Gayle (*d*) Francia

9. Which of these countries does not border Germany?
(*a*) Poland (*b*) France
(*c*) Italy (*d*) Austria

10. Goa had been colonized by the:
(*a*) British (*b*) French
(*c*) Americans (*d*) Portuguese

11. The famous cultivated plant which developed in China is:
(*a*) tea (*b*) cotton
(*c*) coffee (*d*) orange

12. Green revolution is:
(*a*) revolution in chemical industry
(*b*) revolution in Pakistan
(*c*) revolution in Greenland
(*d*) revolution in agriculture yield

13. Which one of the following is a form of Japanese theatre?
(*a*) Ikebana (*b*) Noh
(*c*) Tatani (*d*) Karaoke

14. Which Oscar winning film was based on the life and times of the Asian ruler Pu Yi?
(*a*) The Last Samurai
(*b*) Dragon King
(*c*) King and I
(*d*) The Last Emperor

15. What is the name of the Iranian Parliament?
(*a*) Parliman (*b*) Shura
(*c*) Lilas (*d*) Majlis

16. Which ruler had inspired Ferdowsi to write *Shahnamah*?
(*a*) Muhammad Ghori
(*b*) Jalaluddin Muhammad Akbar
(*c*) Mahmud Ghaznavi
(*d*) Timur

17. Strasbourg is situated in:
(*a*) Luxemburg (*b*) France
(*c*) Germany (*d*) Switzerland

18. Which of these is a kind of popular Latin American dance form?
(*a*) The Break
(*b*) The Tango
(*c*) The Ball
(*d*) The Waltz

19. Who is currently the President of France?
(*a*) Francois Mitterrand
(*b*) Charles de Gaulle
(*c*) Valery Giscard d'Estaing
(*d*) Jacques Chirac

20. Chipko Movement is related to:
(*a*) preventing soil pollution
(*b*) forest conservation
(*c*) preserving threatened species
(*d*) None of the above

PART–B

Directions: (Q. Nos. 21-30): *In the following passages, certain words have been omitted. Identify the missing words:*

(*a*) Of all the untamed creatures, sparrows seem to love living near the man the most. Wherever **(21)** .... new township springs up, the sparrows follow **(22)** .... no time. They even build **(23)** .... nests inside homes and **(24)** ---- they feel sure will not **(25)** .... harmed, they will even come and eat out of your hand.

(*b*) The spread of AIDS in the urban areas has given rise to **(26)** .... number of ethical and legal questions. Should a person who is HIV positive **(27)** .... terminated for services? Should there be **(28)** .... insurance cover for the patients suffering **(29)** .... AIDS? Should **(30)** .... spouse have the right to know that his partner is an AIDS case?

Give short answers to the following questions:

31. Sashimi is a delicacy of which country?

32. When did the Cuban Revolution take place?

33. Who is the author of *Panchatantra*?

34. Which is the national sport of Korea?

35. For which of her novels, later made into a film, did Ruth Prawer Jhabwala win the Booker Prize in 1975?

36. Who is Mona Lisa?

37. What is the significance of 3rd October, 1990 in German history?

38. In the context of Germany, what does 'Holocaust' mean?

39. What is the official name of Germany?

40. What is Maastricht Treaty?

41. To which language family does Persian belong?

42. What was the name of the space shuttle that crashed on February 1, 2003, with astronaut Kalpana Chawla amongst others, on board?

43. Who is Sania Mirza?

44. What do Mikhail Gorbachov, the 14th Dalai Lama and Kofi Annan have in common?

45. Which is the first month of the Indian calendar?

Complete the following sentences:

46. The playwright who wrote *Hayavandane is* ....

47. The Indo- Anglian writer who wrote *Untouchable is* ....

48. The author of *Great Expectations* is ....

49. The capital of Senegal is ....

50. The currency of Portugal is ....

51. The longest river of Europe is ....

52. The portion of the earth and its environment, within which life is manifested is called ....

53. .... defeated Sultan Ibrahim Lodi in the First Battle of Panipat in 1526.

54. India became sovereign democratic republic on ....

55. Mother Teresa was a national of ....

56. Hugo Chavez is the President of ....

57. .... is the highest building in the world.

58. .... is the largest ocean.

59. The invasion of Kuwait by Iraq caused the .... War.

60. The sportsman who fights a bull in Spain is called ....

61. Chess originated in ....

62. The most popular festival of ancient Iran is called ....

63. Mirza Ghalib, a bilingual poet, wrote in Urdu and ....

64. The novel, *The Golden Gate is* written by ....

65. .... is the chief of the Gods in Greek mythology.

66. The architect of the city of Chandigarh is ....

67. The capital of Iraq is ....

68. The largest artificial lake in India is ....

69. Buddha attained enlightenment under .... Tree.

70. The famous philosopher, ... was Plato's disciple.

71. The hardest gemstone is ....

72. Red blood corpuscles are formed in the ....

73. The fastest growing plant in the world is ....

74. The acid turns litmus paper to .... colour.

75. The nearest planet from Sun is ....

76. The Land of the Midnight Sun is ....

77. The Chief Election Commissioner of India is appointed by ....

78. The Finance Commission is constituted after every .... years.

79. .... composed the tune to 'Twinkle twinkle, little star'.

80. The Word Health Day is celebrated on ....

PART–C

Give one word each for the following:

81. The study and description of books, or descriptive list of books.

82. The art of map making.

83. One who makes or compiles dictionary.

84. A period of 1000 years.

Expand the following abbreviations:

85. BBC

86. NCERT

87. GATT

Give the meanings of the following idiomatic expressions:

88. In black and white

89. Stone's throw

90. Ins and outs

91. At sixes and sevens

Complete the following sentences:

92. In 1977 .... was the first person to address the UN General Assembly in Hindi?

93. .... was the first writer in English to be awarded the Sahitya Akademi Award in 1961?

94. The last ruler of the Mughal dynasty was ....

95. .... was the founder of Jainism.

96. India's first satellite was launched in the year ....

97. A social practice called .... was abolished by Lord William Bentinck by 'Regulation 17' of 1829.

98. An Air A-India plane called .... exploded on the Irish sea on its flight from Canada to India.

99. *Jataka* tales were written in an ancient language called ....

100. Five boys were climbing up a hill. Jayant was following Hari. Ram was ahead of Govind. Krishna was between Govind and Hari. They were climbing up in a row. Who was the second?

101. The odd one in the seires of words—Mercury, Moon, Jupiter, Venus, Pluto is ....

102. If 'air' is called 'water', 'water' is called 'sky' 'sky' is called 'blue', 'blue' is called 'rain', 'rain' is called 'dust' and 'dust' is called 'green', where do the fish live in ....

103. If TOP = 201516; POT = 161520; TAR = 20118; then RAT is ....

104. Which number should come next in this series? 1, 4, 9, 16, 25, ...

105. The brother-in-law of my mother's only brother is closely related to me. Who is he? ....

Go through the languages in Column A and Column B, and answer the questions given at the end:

Column A	*Column B*
Laulan	I sing
Laulat	You sing
Laulavi	She/ He sings
Laulamme	We sing

Yuon	I drink
Yuot	You drink
Yuovi	She/ He drinks
Yuovat	They drink

How will you write the following words?

106. I :

107. You :

108. He/ She :

109. They sing :

110. We drink :

PART–D

Read the following passage carefully and answer the questions (111 to 115) without repeating the words from the text:

Punctuality is a necessary habit in all public affairs of a civilized society. Without it nothing could ever be brought to a conclusion, everything would be in a state of chaos. Only in a sporsely populated rural community it is possible to disregard it. In ordinary living, there can be some tolerance of unpunctuality. The intellectual, who is working on some abstruse problem has everything, coordinated and organized for the matter in hand. He is therefore forgiven, if late for the dinner party. But people are often reproached for unpunctuality when their only fault is cutting things fine. It is hard for energetic, quick-minded people to waste time, so they are often tempted to finish a job before setting out to keep an appointment. If no accidents occur on the way, like punctured tyres, diversion of traffic, sudden descent of fog, they will be on time, they are often more industrious useful citizens than those who are never late. The over-punctual can as much be a trial to others as the unpunctual. The guest who arrives half an hour too soon is the greatest nuisance. Some friends of my family had this irritating habit. The only thing to do was to ask them to come half an hour later than the other guests. Then they arrived just when we wanted them. If you are catching a train, it is always better to be comfortably early than even a fraction of a minute too late. Although being early may mean wasting a little time, this will be less than if you miss and have to wait an hour or so for the next one. And you avoid the frustration of arriving at the very moment when the train is drawing out of the station and being unable to get on it.

111. Why is punctuality necessary in a civilized society?

112. What are the dangers of leaving the bare minimum of time for appointments?

113. The over-punctual can be as much a trial to others as the unpunctual. Why?

114. Why did the author's family ask some guests to come half an hour later than others?

115. Why, according to the author, is it better to wait on the platform before the train arrives?

Write four sentences each on the following:

116. Sachin Tendulkar

117. The 18th Commonwealth Games

118. Mother Teresa

119. Bird flu

120. Why do you want to learn a foreign language?

Observe the Language A and its translation into English:

Language A	*English*
TMAN	I buy
AKAN	You wish
MAN	To buy
SLAP	He sleeps
KAN	To wish
KIL	I see
AWAL	You say
IL	To see
LAP	To sleep
JU	He drinks
AL	To say
U	To drink
AWU	You drink
KAL	I say
TLAP	I sleep

Translate the English words given below into the Language A:

	English	*Language A*
121.	You	
122.	I	
123.	He	
124.	He wishes	
125.	You sleep	

ANSWER

PART–A

1	2	3	4	5
(*c*)	(*b*)	(*c*)	(*b*)	(*a*)
6	**7**	**8**	**9**	**10**
(*a*)	(*d*)	(*b*)	(*c*)	(*d*)
11	**12**	**13**	**14**	**15**
(*a*)	(*d*)	(*b*)	(*d*)	(*d*)
16	**17**	**18**	**19**	**20**
(*c*)	(*b*)	(*b*)	(*d*)	(*b*)

PART–B

21. a **22.** in **23.** their **24.** then
25. be **22.** a **27.** be **28.** an
29. from **30.** the
31. Sashimi is a Japanes delicacy.
32. 1959
33. Vishnu Sharma
34. Tae Kwondo
35. Heat and Dust
36. Mona Lisa is a famous painting painted by Leonardo Da Vinci.
37. The five East Germany states officially joined the Federal Republic of Germany on 3rd October 1990.
38. Putting people in gas chamber and killing them.
39. Bundes-republic Deutschland (Federal Republic of Germany).
40. On February 7 the treaty for the creation of European Union was signed in Maastricht.
41. Indo-Europian language family.
42. Columbia.
43. She is flag bearer of India female tennis.
44. Mikhail Gorbachov-1990, the 14th Dalai Lama 1989 and Kofi Annan 2001 all are the winner of Nobel Peace Prize.
45. Chaitra
46. Girish Karnad
47. Mulk Raj Anand
48. Charles Dickenes
49. Dakar
50. Escudo
51. Ob
52. Biosphere
53. Babar
54. 26th January 1950
55. Macedonia
56. Venezuela
57. Burj Dubai
58. Pacific ocean
59. Gulf war
60. Bull fighter (Metador)
61. India
62. Happy Yalda Shab ee chelan (night of fortieth).
63. Persian
64. Vikram Seth
65. Zeus
66. Le Corbusier (French)
67. Baghdad
68. Jai Samand Lake in Udaipur
69. Bodhi
70. Aristotle
71. Diamond
72. Bone Marrow
73. Bamboo
74. Blue to red
75. Mercury
76. Norway
77. President of India
78. Five
79. Wolfgand A madeus Mozart
80. 7 April

PART–C

81. Catalogue

82. Cartography

83. Lexicographer

84. Millenium

85. BBC—British Broadcasting Corporation

86. NCERT—National Council of Education Research and Training

87. GATT—General Agreement on Trade and Tariff

88. In writing

89. too close

90. Inside picture

91. At proper order

92. Atal Bihari Vajpayee

93. R.K. Narayan

94. Bahadur Shah Zaffar

95. First Tirthankar Rishabh

96. Aryabhatta on April 19, 1975

97. Sati Pratha

98. Kanishka

99. Pali

100. Govind

101. Moon, all others are planets

102. Sky

103. 18120, as R = 18, A = 1 and T = 20

104. 36, a series is made of square of consectutive numbers

105. Father

106. N

107. T

108. Vi

109. Laulavat

110. Yuomme

111. Punctuality is necessary in a civilized society to avoid chaos in the society. To follow a system and short out the problems this trend must be followed by each and every person.

112. If one is unable to reach in time for an appointment he/she may miss a grand opportunity.

113. They may create nuisance by reaching before time when no one was expecting them.

114. They have an habit of coming half an hour before time.

115. In that case you can't miss the train.

116. **Sachin Tendulkar:** One of the greatest cricketer of this era who can be part of any best team of any time. A legend in his own life having records of maximum runs in ODI and maximum hundreds in both forms (one day/test matches) of cricket. A great entertainer and a person also with a golden arm.

117. The 18th Commonwealth games was held in Melbourne between March 15th and March 26. The site for the opening and closing ceremonies was the Melbourne cricket ground. The mascot for the games was Kork, a red tailed black cock too. For the first time they appointed a goodwill partner, Plan International Australia.

118. **Mother Teresa:** An Albanian by birth was born on August 26, 1910 and died on September 5, 1997. She was a Roman Catholic nun who founded the Missionaries of Charity. She was Nobel Peace Prize winner in 1979 for humanitarian work.

119. **Bird Flu:** It is also known as Avian influenza. It is caused by virus adopted to birds. The virus is known as Influenza. A virus, due to this a large chunck of birds (Hen) were killed in different part of world.

120. I wanted to learn a foreign language to know about the culture, civilisation of that country. It will also provide an employment in different sectors of economy. It will helpful in many more things like intellectual curiosity, travel and secret communication.

121. A

122. T

123. S

124. SKAN

124. ALAP

Previous Paper Solved

JNUEE–2005

PART–A

Answer the following questions by selecting the most appropriate one from (*a*) to (*d*) :

1. The South Korean Airlines that flies to Delhi is:
(*a*) Asian Airlines
(*b*) Arirang Airlines
(*c*) Air Korea
(*d*) Korean Airways

2. The author of *Don Quixote* is:
(*a*) Cervantes
(*b*) Shakespeare
(*c*) Gabriel Garcia Marques
(*d*) Tolstoy

3. The expedition of Christopher Columbus was under the royal patronage of:
(*a*) France (*b*) Italy
(*c*) Portugal (*d*) Spain

4. Who found the sea route to India?
(*a*) George Luis Broges
(*b*) Salvador Dali
(*c*) Vasco de Gama
(*d*) Afnasii Nikitin

5. Iran is situated in:
(*a*) East Asia (*b*) West Asia
(*c*) North Asia (*d*) South Asia

6. Tehran is the capital of:
(*a*) Uzbekistan (*b*) Tajikistan
(*c*) Iran (*d*) Afghanistan

7. In which script is Persian written?
(*a*) Arabic (*b*) Cyrillic
(*c*) Greek (*d*) Roman

8. Which of these is the highest rank in the Indian Army?
(*a*) Brigadier (*b*) General
(*c*) Colonel (*d*) Major General

9. Green, Oolong, Pekoe are different names of :
(*a*) coffee (*b*) tea
(*c*) cocoa (*d*) ghee

10. Which of the following is not a primary colour?
(*a*) Red (*b*) Blue
(*c*) Green (*d*) Yellow

11. *Dr. Zhivago* was written by:
(*a*) A. Solzhenitsyn
(*b*) B. Pasternak
(*c*) M. Sholokhov
(*d*) A. Chekhov

12. The national animal of China is:
(*a*) the dragon
(*b*) the eagle
(*c*) the giant panda
(*d*) the aligator

13. Who was the first and only Muslim woman ruler who ever presided over the throne of Delhi?
(*a*) Razia Sultan (*b*) Sardari Begum
(*c*) Shah Bano (*d*) Noorjehan

14. Algeria, Libya and Tunisia belong to the continent of:
(*a*) Europe (*b*) Africa
(*c*) Latin America (*d*) Asia

15. In which Indian hill station was the first ropeway constructed?
(*a*) Ootacamund (*b*) Matheran
(*c*) Dalhousie (*d*) Darjeeling

16. The capital of Austria is:
(*a*) Prague (*b*) Canberra
(*c*) Budapest (*d*) Vienna

17. Who is a famous German philosopher?
(*a*) Jacques Derrida
(*b*) Karl Popper
(*c*) Theodor Fontane
(*d*) Immanuel Kant

18. Who among the following is a well-known personality of Indian music?
(*a*) M. F. Husain (*b*) Shivpujan Sahay
(*c*) Amartya Sen (*d*) Bismillah Khan

19. 'Charminar' is situated in:
(*a*) Chennai (*b*) Mumbai
(*c*) Kolkata (*d*) Hyderabad

20. The official name of North Korea is:
(*a*) People's Democratic Republic of Korea
(*b*) Democratic People's Republic of Korea
(*c*) Republic of Korea
(*d*) People's Republic of Korea

PART–B

Directions: (Q. Nos. 21-30): *In the following passage certain words have been omitted. Identify the missing words:*

Education is something **(21)** .... which I am destined **(22)** .... reflect. As a teacher, I **(23)** .... ignore what is happening in the domain **(24)** .... education. **(25)** .... the process of self- reflection, I am required **(26)** .... cope **(27)** .... many pertinent questions: **(28)** .... am I teaching? How do I relate to **(29)** .... students? Is teaching an exercise **(30)** .... power, or is it an art of self-relatedness?

Give short answers to the following questions:

31. Who is the present Chancellor of Germany ?
32. When did Britain hand over Hong Kong to China?
33. Which is the longest river in South America?
34. Which country was known as the 'Hermit Kingdom'?
35. What is a Mascot?
36. What is the Richter scale?
37. What is Flamenco?
38. What is a Tsunami?
39. Who is the President of the Russian Federation?
40. Who discovered Penicillin?
41. Which German music composer was deaf?
42. What is the Western name of Taiwan?
43. Which is the world's biggest dam?
44. What are natural geysers?
45. On whose life is the film 'Aviator' based?

Complete the following sentences :

46. The 2006 Olympics will be held in -----.
47. Clouds float in the atmosphere because of their low ----.
48. The year 2005 is designated by the UN as the International Year of -----.
49. India's first Formula 1 Grand Prix driver is --------.
50. Sania Mirza comes from the city of ----- .
51. In 2010, Delhi will host ---- Games.
52. Arthur Miller was awarded ------- for his book *Death of a Salesman.*
53. Amir Khusro is famous for his compositions and writings in -----.
54. The official language of Afghanistan is -----.
55. Leonardo da Vinci was from ------.
56. The city of Pisa is famous for its ----.
57. The city of Frankfurt is situated on the river ------.
58. Brecht wrote his works in ----.
59. The popular slogan Jai Hind was coined by --------.
60. The indigenous religion of China is -----.
61. The rivers Euphrates and Tigris flow within the territory of ----.
62. The indigenous name of Burma is -----.
63. Tamil was recently accorded the status of -----.
64. The official languages of Canada are -----.
65. Jean Paul Sartre is a ----- philosopher.
66. Garba dance is a dance style from -----.
67. CRY stands for ------.
68. The official language of Tajikistan is -----.
69. The first printing press was invented by ----.
70. Kanchenjunga is a peak in the ------.
71. Kaziranga national park is a ------- reserve.
72. The Indian national calendar was adopted in -----.
73. The first to use artillery in medieval India was -----.
74. The maximum number of World Heritage sites are found in -----.
75. The year 2005 is the ----- for the Chinese.

76. The number that cannot be noted in Roman numerals is -----.

77. *Wings of Fire* is a book written by -----.

78. The Statue of Liberty was gifted to the USA by -----.

79. A numismatist collects -----.

80. South America is known as -----.

PART–C

Give one word each for the following:

81. The study of stars and planets.

82. The study of forces such as heat, light, sound, gravity, etc.

83. Flesh-eating animals.

84. The study of environment.

Expand the following abbreviations:

85. INA

86. UNDP

87. SAARC

Give the meaning of the following idiomatic expressions:

88. To rule the roost

99. To keep track of something

90. To beat about the bush

91. To keep one's word

Complete the following sentences:

92. Tagore won the Nobel Laureate for his work ------.

93. Binary codes used in computer sciences are made up of --------.

94. Booker Prize is given annually to the best work of ---- by a British or Commonwealth writer.

95. The number that comes next in the series 12, 20, 30, 42, 56 is ------.

96. Reggae is an African-Caribbean style of music developed in ------.

97. The book by R. K. Narayan in which R.K. Laxman's cartoons had first appeared is -----.

98. Earthquakes are caused by -----.

99. Mahatma Gandhi largely wrote in ------ language.

100. Eureka in Greek means -----.

101. The odd one in the series of words Rain, Fog, Smoke, Mist is ------.

102. CABIR, the world's first mobile phone virus was born in -------.

103. Mirages are due to ------.

104. Vitamin D is essential for ------.

105. Illegal goods are known as ------.

Go through the sentences of the Language A and Language B, and answer the questions given at the end:

Language A	*Language B*
I am swimming	RAH KLAM
He is also swimming	TAM KLAM SNE
My friend knows swimming	RAHI GAMI KLAM PRE
My friend knows his brother	RAHI GAMI TAMI DARI PRE
His brother works here	TAMI DARI TRU FOR
I am not working	RAH TRU JON
She knows this work	TAN KAI TRU PRE
I know this poem by heart	RAH KAI BOL IK PRE
We all like this poem	SAH-SAH KAI BOL PLI
We work in the morning	SAH TRU HI
He knows me	TAM PRE RAH
She is reading a poem	TAN BOL KMI

How will you write the following sentences?

	Language A	*Language B*
106.	I like swimming	
107.	He knows this poem	
108.	She works in the morning	
109.	I also know this poem	
110.	We know all the poems	

PART–D

Read the following passage carefully and answer the questions (111 to 115) given below it:

Catharsis - giving vent to anger is sometimes extolled as a way of handling anger. The popular theory holds that 'it makes you feel better'. But as Zillmann's findings suggest, there is an argument against catharsis. Since the 1950s psychologists started to test the effects of catharsis experimentally and found that giving vent to anger did little or nothing to dispel it. There may be some specific conditions under which lashing out in anger does work : when it is expressed directly to the person who is its target, when it restores a sense of control or rights an injustice. Venting anger is, however, one of the worst ways to cool down: outbursts of rage typically pump up the emotional brain's arousal, leaving people feeling more angry, not less. It is far more effective if people first cool down, and then, in a more constructive or assertive manner, confront the person to settle their dispute.

111. What is catharsis? What does popular theory say about catharsis?

112. What are the conditions under which anger works?

113. Why is the popular theory about catharsis incorrect?

114. Why doesn't anger disappear when it is expressed?

115. What is the best way to deal with anger?

Write four sentences about the following:

116. C. V. Raman

117. B. R. Ambedkar

118. Arundhati Roy

119. Medha Patkar

120. Vinoba Bhave

Go through the words of the Language A and Language B, and answer the questions given at the end:

Language A	*Language B*
* + ∃ =	अपना
⊥ = ≠	काम
> ∀ ⊇	रील
≤ ↓ > = ⊥⌟	सुराख
⊥˜ ↓ +˜ A ≈ =	गुड़िया
+˜ ↓ +˜ A ≈ =	बुढ़िया
≤ B ∃ = ∃ = ≈ ⊥	सेनानायक
> ∈ ∃ =	रटना
⊕ = ≈	चाय
* ∪ ≤ >	अवसर
+⌟ ⊇ ⊄˜ = ≈ ⊥	फलदायक
≠ B ⊇ = ∃ ⊥˜ > ∀	मेलानगरी
≤ × ∃ =	सोना

How will you write the following words?

	Language B	*Language A*
121.	गिरगिट	
122.	धोना	
123.	खराब	
124.	फुलवारी	
125.	जलपान	

ANSWER

PART–A

1	2	3	4	5
(*a*)	(*a*)	(*d*)	(*c*)	(*b*)
6	**7**	**8**	**9**	**10**
(*c*)	(*a*)	(*b*)	(*b*)	(*d*)
11	**12**	**13**	**14**	**15**
(*b*)	(*c*)	(*a*)	(*b*)	(*d*)
16	**17**	**18**	**19**	**20**
(*d*)	(*d*)	(*d*)	(*d*)	(*b*)

PART–B

21. in **22.** and **23.** can't **24.** of

25. In **22.** to **27.** with **28.** why

29. the **30.** of

31. Gerhard Schroder

32. June 30, 1997

33. Amazon

34. Korea

35. Mascot is used to represent group with a common public identity.

36. Intensity of Earthquake.
37. Flemenco is a genuine Spanish art which has three things dance, song and music.
38. Tsunami is giant oceanic waves caused by Earthquake or Volcanic eruption.
39. Vladimir Putin
40. Alexander Flemming
41. Beethoven Ludwig Van
42. For masa
43. Itaipu Dam on border of Brazil and Paraguay.
44. These throws up jets of hot water and steam at regular intervals.
45. Howard Hughes
46. Turin, Italy (winter olympics)
47. density
48. Sports and Physical Education
49. Naryan Karthikeyan
50. Hyderabad
51. Commonwealth games
52. Pulitzer Prize
53. Braj Bhasha
54. Poshto
55. Italy
56. Minarat of Pisa
57. Moin
58. German
59. Subhash Chandra Bose
60. Taoism
61. Iraq
62. Myanmar
63. Official Language
64. English and French
65. French
66. Gujarat
67. Children Relief and You
68. Tajik (a veriety of person)
69. Johnan Guten Berg
70. Himalayan
71. Biosphere
72. 1957
73. Babar
74. Italy-39 sites
75. Year of Rooster
76. Zero
77. A.P.J. Abdul Kalam
78. France
79. Stamp's (Postal)
80. Latin America

PART–C

81. Astronomy
82. Mechanics
83. Carnivorous
84. Ecology
85. INA—Indian National Army.
86. UNDP—United Nation Development Programme.
87. SAARC—South Asian Association for Regional Cooperation.
88. Domineer over others
89. Watching very curiously
90. To talk irrelevantly, not coming to point.
91. Fulfilling Promise
92. Gitanjali
93. 0 and 1
94. English
95. 72 as the series increases with 8, 10, 12, 14, 16 and so on.
96. Jamaica
97. Malgudi Days
98. Movement of Plates
99. Hindustani
100. to get
101. Rain
102. 1997
103. refraction of light
104. skin
105. smuggled goods
106. RAH KLAM PLI
107. TAM PRE KAI BOL
108. TAN TRU HI

109. RAH KAI BOL PRE SNE

110. SAH PRE BOL-BOL

111. Catharsis is a way of handling anger. The popular theory holds that it makes you feel better.

112. Anger works when it is expressed directly to the person who is its target, or when it restores a sense of control or rights on injustice.

113. Since 1950s phychologist started to test the effect of catharsis experimentally and found that giving vent to anger did little or nothing to dispel it.

114. When anger is expressed it typically pump up the emotional brains arousal leaving people feeling more angry.

115. The best way of deal with angle is first cool down and then in a more constructor or assertive manner confront the person to settle dispute.

116. **C.V. Raman:** A great Indian Physicist who was awarded Noble Prize in Physics in 1930. He proposed the theory of scattering of light and the effect was named after him, he got knighthood in 1929. He became the director of Raman Research Institute in 1947. The day on which Sir C.V. Raman discovered the Raman effect that is 28th February is observed as National Science Day in India.

117. **B.R. Ambedkar**—(1891-1956) Indian Jurist Social worker, politician, writer, educationist emancipator of the 'untouchables' and crusader for social justice. Drafted the Indian Constitution. Minister in Nehru's Cabinet and awarded Bharat Ratna in 1990.

118. **Arundhati Roy**— (1960) The first Indian author to win Booker Prize (The God of Small Things) Environmentalist winner of Sydney Peace Prize 2004.

119. **Medha Patekar (1956)**—Indian social activist, environmentalist, fire brand leader of Save Narmada Movement, Right Civelihood Award.

120. **Vinoba Bhave**—(1895-1982) Disciple of Mahatma Gandhi, who led the Bhoodan movement, Bharat Ratna 1983, first Magsaysay Award winner.

121. $\perp \tilde{A} \overset{\frown}{> \perp} A \in$

122. $B = \exists =$

123. $\perp^{\lrcorner} > = +^{\sim}$

124. $+^{\lrcorner} \downarrow \supseteq = > \forall$

125. $\oplus^{\sim} \supseteq + = \exists$

Previous Paper Solved

JNUEE–2004

PART–A-1

Answer the following questions by selecting the most appropriate one from (*a*) to (*d*):

1. Lyon is a:
(*a*) French bread (*b*) French cheese
(*c*) French river (*d*) French city

2. Which language did Buddha preach in?
(*a*) Pali (*b*) Apabhramsa
(*c*) Sauraseni (*d*) Magadhi

3. With which journal Premchand was associated?
(*a*) Sahitya (*b*) Panchjanya
(*c*) Hans (*d*) Shiksha

4. Who is hailed as the 'God of Medicine' by practitioners of Ayurveda?
(*a*) Charaka (*b*) Susruta
(*c*) Chyavana (*d*) Patanjali

5. Who wrote *Gulag Archipelago*?
(*a*) Tolstoy (*b*) Navokov
(*c*) Dostoevsky (*d*) Solzhenitsyn

6. The only snake in the world that builds nest is found in India. Which one is it?
(*a*) Viper (*b*) Python
(*c*) King Cobra (*d*) Grass snake

7. The shortest day in Australia will be:
(*a*) June 21 (*b*) December 22
(*c*) September 22 (*d*) March 23

8. Which of the following is the oldest atomic power station in India?
(*a*) Kalpakkam (*b*) Tarapur
(*c*) Narora (*d*) Kota

9. Mixed farming involves:
(*a*) growing more than one crop on a farm
(*b*) growing specialised crops
(*c*) growing crops and keeping livestock
(*d*) intensive and extensive agriculture

10. The concept of overpopulation is based on the:
(*a*) availability of food in the area
(*b*) absolute number of people in an area
(*c*) density of population in that area
(*d*) supporting capacity of the land in terms of varied human operations

11. The group of languages spoken by the largest number of people in India is:
(*a*) Austro- Asiatic (*b*) Indo- Aryan
(*c*) Dravidian (*d*) None of these

12. The Lakshadweep Islands are situated in:
(*a*) Indian Ocean (*b*) Arabian Sea
(*c*) Bay of Bengal (*d*) None of these

13. Light from the sun reaches us in:
(*a*) 8 minutes (*b*) 8 seconds
(*c*) 8 hours (*d*) one year

14. The World Trade Organisation is set up to take over the functions of which of the following?
(*a*) IMF (*b*) GATT
(*c*) ECA (*d*) ECOSOC

15. Ajanta Paintings depict scenes from the:
(*a*) Ramayana (*b*) Mahabharata
(*c*) Jatakas (*d*) Upanishadas

16. The concept of Third World Countries implies:
(*a*) the developed countries
(*b*) the developing countries
(*c*) block led by USA, UK, etc.
(*d*) None of these

17. What is depicted in Manipuri dance?
(*a*) Mahabharata (*b*) Ramlila
(*c*) Village Life (*d*) Raslila

18. What is the household name for sodium bicarbonate?
(*a*) Salt (*b*) Soda
(*c*) Sugar (*d*) Baking powder

19. What term is used for the study of human races?
(*a*) Psychology (*b*) Anthology
(*c*) Geology (*d*) Anthropology

20. To which country did 'Aesop's Fables' belong?
(*a*) Greece (*b*) Rome
(*c*) Germany (*d*) India

21. What transmits typhoid?
(*a*) Contaminated food or water
(*b*) Vehicle exhaust
(*c*) Smoke
(*d*) Physical touch

22. The capital of Tajikistan is:
(*a*) Dushanbe (*b*) Tashkent
(*c*) Baku (*d*) Bukhara

23. Who among the following gave a detailed account of Nalanda University?
(*a*) Hiuen Tsang (*b*) Fa-hien
(*c*) Megasthenes (*d*) Te-tsing

24. Which is the brightest star in the sky?
(*a*) Proxima Centauri
(*b*) Nebula
(*c*) Barnard
(*d*) None of these

25. Who among the following is a world famous violinist?
(*a*) Zakir Hussain
(*b*) Bismillah Khan
(*c*) Pt. Ravishankar
(*d*) Yehudi Menuhin

26. Which of the following Muslim festivals is celebrated on Prophet Mohammed's birthday?
(*a*) Muharram
(*b*) Id-i-Milad Unnabi
(*c*) Id-ul-Zuha
(*d*) Id-ul-Fitr

27. What is the removal of top layer of fertile soil called?
(*a*) Soil erosion
(*b*) Soil conservation
(*c*) Weathering
(*d*) None of these

PART–A-2

Directions: (Q. Nos, 28-37): *In the following passage certain words have been omitted. Identify the missing words:*

Another method of sending news was **(28)** ------ pigeons. The carrier pigeon **(29)** ------ the cat, is extremely attached **(30)** ------ its home and if a traveller wanted to send **(31)** ------- message back to its starting point, he fixed it **(32)** -------- a pigeon **(33)** -----he had taken with him. The bird, once set free, **(34)** ----- straight back **(35)** ------- its loft, and the message **(36)** ------ then be taken from its leg. The invention of **(37)** ------ electric telegraph and later, of wireless, speeded up the sending of news.

Give short answers to the following questions:

38. Which Arab country has no river?

39. To which European country did the famous painter Pablo Picasso belong?

40. Which of the four main islands is situated north of Honshu?

41. Which place in Madhya Pradesh is known for its diamond mines?

42. Which Egyptian city was founded by Alexander the Great?

43. Which was the first city destroyed by the atom bomb in the Second World War?

44. What is the instrument used to record earthquake shocks?

45. In which city, Hollywood, the famous centre of film industry, is situated?

46. Who is the only recipient of the Nobel Prize in Arabic Literature?

Complete the following sentences:

47. The fall of Bastille is associated with ------.

48. *Das Capital* was written by -------.

49. The name of the present Chief Election Commissioner is ------.

50. The last SAARC Conference was held in ------.

51. The smallest unit of matter which can take part in a chemical reaction is ------.

52. Amnesty International is an organisation for the protection of ------.

53. Argentina has shifted its capital from Buenos Aires to -------.

54. French speaking countries are called -----.

55. Leningrad is currently known as ------.

56. Goethe is a writer of -----.

57. The author of the book *The Man Eaters of Kumaun* is -----.

58. Sardar Sarovar Project is associated with the river ------.
59. Ramon Magsaysay Award is named after the President of ------.
60. Ulan Bator is the capital of ------.
61. Iranian Parliament is called ------.
62. Turkish is written in ------ script.
63. Kilimanjaro in Africa is a ------.
64. Gir forests are located in the state of ------.
65. The national language of Brazil is ------.
66. The sourness of lemon is caused by ------ acid.
67. The warming of the planet due to accumulation of gases is called ------.
68. The book *Poetics* was written by the ancient Greek Scholar ------.
69. Lhasa is the capital of ------.
70. The capital of North Korea is ------.
71. Linguistics deals with ------.
72. Habib Tanbir is associated with ------.
73. Hamid Karzai is the leader of ------.
74. *Geet Govind* was written by ------.
75. The author of *Captain's Daughter* is ------.
76. Jacques Chirac is the President of ------.
77. Louvre is a world famous ------.
78. A vast collection of stars held together by mutual gravitation is called ------.
79. The currency of Bangladesh is ------.
80. The Elisa test is used to detect ------.
81. *Panchatantra* was written by ------.
82. The religious order established by Mother Teresa is called ------.
83. Kamarupa is the old name of the state of ------.
84. The *Shahnama* was written by ------.

PART–B-1

Expand the following abbreviations:

85. NASA
86. ASEAN
87. WLL

Give one word each for the following:

88. The study of diseases
89. The art of map-making
90. The study of nature and history of universe

Give the meaning of the following idiomatic expressions:

91. A pipe dream
92. To smell a rat
93. To take with a grain of salt
94. To spill the beans
95. To hit below the belt

Complete the following sentences:

96. The world's largest lake is ------.
97. Aryabhatta was a famous ------.
98. The first recipient of Human Rights Award is ------.
99. A colour blind person has difficulty in distinguishing between ------.
100. Camel uses its hump for ------.
101. The original home of the gypsies was ------.
102. As you sow, so ------.
103. Alexander invaded India in ------.
104. Vande Mataram was first published in ------.
105. Kalidasa lived during the reign of ------.
106. The only man-made structure that can be viewed from moon is ----- .
107. The traditional dress of Japanese woman is ------.
108. The word 'Zen' in Zen Buddhism has come from the Indian word ------.
109. Which is the number that comes next in the sequence? 1, 4, 9, 16, 25, 36, 49, ----- ?
110. If 'pen' is called 'pencil', 'pencil' is called 'scale', 'scale' is called 'bag' and 'bag' is called 'book', which is used to carry the books?
111. The boundary between China and India is called ------.
112. Iodination of salt is a public health measure to prevent ------.

Go through the words of the Language A and Language B and answer the question given at the end:

Language A	*Language B*
$\exists\,\Delta\,\cap''\approx''$	दरवाजा
$=_{+}\forall\,\perp^{+}$	खिड़की
$+_{=}\Delta$	ओर
$\approx\ddot{O}\,\Delta$	ज़हर
$\square''\oplus^{+}$	पानी
$\geq''+$	चाय
$\square_{\wedge}\Delta''\,\oplus''$	पुराना
$\times\neq$	बस
↲̂ $\in$	धूल
$\oplus''\cap$	नाव

How will you write the following words?

Language B *Language A*

113. और

114. हरा

115. सूना

116. खून

117. दिन

118. वर

PART–B-2

Read the following passage carefully and answer the questions given below it:

Look at any waste garbage dump. In addition to vegetable scraps, paper and broken glass, you will notice a considerable amount of plastic material such as shampoo bottles, bags, worn out slippers and the like. Vegetable scraps and paper are biodegradable, but plastic continues to accumulate and harm the environment. Plastic is often mistaken for food by birds, animals and fish, leading to their death. It also chokes sewer pipes and becomes a trap for living beings in ponds, rivers and oceans.

Investigations have been going on for a long time to produce an environment-friendly plastic in the sense that it decays and becomes a part of the soil like rotting vegetable scraps do. The scientists of Imperial Chemical Industries at London have been able to develop just such a plastic called 'Bipol'. It is manufactured by microbes. Bottles, film and fibres can be made out of it. Fungi and bacteria can eat it and break it down into carbon dioxide and water. This new plastic can also be used to make capsules for slow release in the body of some types of medicines, and of pesticides in the fields.

119. Explain, what you understand by biodegradable substances.

120. How does plastic affects the environment?

121. What is 'Bipol' and what are its advantages?

Write *four* sentences about the following:

122. Martin Luther King

123. Dhirubhai Ambani

124. Amartya Sen

Go through the words of the Language A and Language B and answer the question given at the end:

Language A	*Language B*
a car	en bil
cars	bilar
the cats	kattarna
a cat	en katt
sofas	soffor
the newspapers	tidningarna
the flowers	blommorna
a sofa	en soffa
the sofa	soffan
cats	kattar
flowers	blommor
a lamp	en lampa
in the room	kitonn pana
a room	en kitonn

How would you say the forms of the following words?

Language A *Language B*

125. the sofas

126. rooms

127. a newspaper

128. the lamp

129. the cars

130. a flower

ANSWER

PART–A-1

1	2	3	4	5
(*d*)	(*a*)	(*c*)	(*a*)	(*d*)
6	**7**	**8**	**9**	**10**
(*c*)	(*a*)	(*b*)	(*c*)	(*d*)
11	**12**	**13**	**14**	**15**
(*b*)	(*b*)	(*a*)	(*b*)	(*c*)
16	**17**	**18**	**19**	**20**
(*b*)	(*d*)	(*d*)	(*d*)	(*a*)
21	**22**	**23**	**24**	**25**
(*a*)	(*a*)	(*a*)	(*d*)	(*d*)
26	**27**			
(*d*)	(*a*)			

PART–A-2

28. by **29.** or **30.** to **31.** a
32. with **33.** that **34.** go **35.** to
36. there **37.** the
38. Oman
39. Italy
40. Hokedo
41. Panna
42. Alexandria
43. Hiroshima August 6, 1945
44. Seismograph
45. Los Angles
46. Naguib Mahfouz
47. French Revolution
48. Karl Marx
49. T.S. Krishna Murthy
50. Sri Lanka
51. atom
52. human right
53. No change in capital
54. Franco phone
55. St. Petersburg
56. Germany
57. Jim Corbett
58. Narmada
59. Philipines
60. Mangolia
61. Majlish
62. Arabic
63. Volcano
64. Gujarat
65. Spanish
66. ascorbic
67. global warming
68. Aristotle
69. Tibet
70. Pyongyang
71. Languages
72. Folk Theatre
73. Afghanistan
74. Jaydev
75. Alexander Puskin
76. France
77. Museum
78. Galaxy
79. Taka
80. AIDS
81. Vishnu Sharma
82. Missionaries of Charity
83. Asom
84. Firdausi

PART–B

85. NASA—National Aero Space Association.
86. ASEAN—Association of South East Asian Nation.
87. WLL—Wireless in Local Loop.
88. Pathology
89. Cartography
90. Cosmology
91. Distant dream

92. Suspicious about something

93. to accept what some one said with doubt and misgiving.

94. Spoiling another's plan

95. Attack opponent unfairly

96. Caspean sea

97. Astronomer

98. Bob Minton

99. Colour's

100. Water storage

101. India

102. You reap

103. 327 B.C.

104. Anand Math

105. Harsh Verdhan

106. Great wall of China

107. Kimono

108. Dhyana

109. 64, as squares of consecutive numbers

110. book

111. Mac Mahon Line

112. Goitor

113. $+_{=} \Delta$

114. OΔ"

115. $\neq \wedge \oplus$"

116. $\forall \wedge \oplus$

117. $\exists_{+} \oplus$

118. $\cap \Delta$

PART–B-2

119. Those substances which can degrade naturally are bio-degradeable substance.

120. Plastic continues to accumulate and doesn't degrade. Animals and birds mistaken it for food and died. It also chokes the sewer line and become a trap for living beings in ponds, river and ocean.

121. Bipole is a plastic developed by Imperial Chemical Industries of London, which is termed as environment friendly as it decays like vegetable scraps.

122. **Martin Luther King Jr. (1929-68):** Black American Clergyman, a non violent civil rights leader and Negro integration leader, Nobel Peace Prize. Associated why we can't wait.

123. **Dhirubhai Ambani:** (Dhiraj Lal Hirachand) (1932-2002) Indian Industrialist Reliance Industries that he set up is India's largest Private Sector Company. Sons: Mukesh Ambani and Anil Ambani now head the Reliance Companies. The latter is Rajya Sabha M.P. since 2004.

124. **Amartya Sen—**(b-1933) Indian Economist, the Professor of Philosophy and Economics at Harvard University, Minister of Trinity college Cambridge, Nobel Prize (1998). Recipient of Bharat Ratna.

125. sofforna

126. kittonnar

127. en tidning

128. lampan

129. bilarna

130. en blomm

Previous Paper Solved

JNUEE–2003

PART–A

Answer the following questions by selecting the most appropriate one from (*a*) to (*d*):

1. In a group of 15, 7 can speak German and 8 can speak Italian while 3 can speak neither. What part of the group can speak both German and Italian?

(*a*) 1/5 (*b*) 4/15
(*c*) 3/5 (*d*) 1/3

2. Who among the following authors did not receive a Noble Prize in Literature?

(*a*) M. Gorky
(*b*) Ivan Bunin
(*c*) Boris Pasternak
(*d*) Alexander Solzhenitsyn

3. The author of 'Les Miserable' is:

(*a*) V. S. Naipaul (*b*) Victor Hugo
(*c*) E. M. Forster (*d*) Thomas Hardy

4. If COBRA is written as BOCAR, then how GROUP will be written in that code?

(*a*) ORPGU (*b*) OGRPU
(*c*) ORUPG (*d*) ORGPU

5. If 'water' is called 'food', 'food' is called 'tree', 'tree' is called 'sky', 'sky' is called 'well', on which of the following grows a 'fruit'?

(*a*) Water (*b*) Food
(*c*) Tree (*d*) Sky

6. Occidental culture is associated with:

(*a*) Asian Society
(*b*) European Society
(*c*) African Society
(*d*) Latin American Society

7. The word 'Hindu' as reference to the people of Hind (India) was first used by:

(*a*) the Greeks
(*b*) the Romans
(*c*) the Chinese
(*d*) the Arabs

8. Which of the given figures best represents the relationship of Elected body: Member of Parliament and Member of Legislative Assembly?

(*a*) 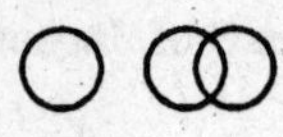 (*b*) 

(*c*)  (*d*) 

9. Find the missing number in the series 31, 21, 13, ?, 3, 1

(*a*) 5 (*b*) 9
(*c*) 7 (*d*) 11

10. Mecca is:

(*a*) A girl's name
(*b*) Prophet's brother's name
(*c*) Muslim calendar
(*d*) Prophet Mohammed birth place

11. Which is not a Gulf country?

(*a*) Oman (*b*) Bahrain
(*c*) Qatar (*d*) Iraq

12. Arrange the following in the right order?

1. Yarn 2. Plant
3. Saree 4. Cotton
5. Cloth

(*a*) 2, 4, 5, 1, 3 (*b*) 2, 4, 1, 5, 3
(*c*) 2, 4, 3, 5, 1 (*d*) 2, 4, 5, 3, 1

13. Which of the following provinces of Canada has majority of people speaking French?

(*a*) Ontario
(*b*) Quebec
(*c*) Prince Edward Island
(*d*) Nova Scotia

14. Salvador Dali was a famous?

(*a*) matador (*b*) painter
(*c*) writer (*d*) statesman

15. Sancho Panja is a character of the famous Spanish novel:

(*a*) 'Mio 'Cid'

(*b*) The family of Pascal Duarte'
(*c*) Don Quixote'
(*d*) 'Beehive'

16. A street in Delhi was named in March 2003 after an eminent French intellectual, identify the person from the list below:
(*a*) Andre Matraux (*b*) Albert Camus
(*c*) Victor Hugo (*d*) Andre Gide

17. What was the old name of Japanese capital Tokyo?
(*a*) Meiji (*b*) Urawa
(*c*) Edo (*d*) Kyodo

18. Buddhism started spreading from India through which route?
(*a*) China – Japan – Korea
(*b*) China – Korea – Japan
(*c*) Korea – Taiwan – Japan
(*d*) Nepal – Korea – Japan

19. 'Hangul is a script of which language?
(*a*) Chinese (*b*) Japanese
(*c*) Korean (*d*) Malaysian

20. Who wrote 'Natya Shastra'?
(*a*) Kalidas (*b*) Banabhatta
(*c*) Bharat Muni (*d*) Jaidev

21. The author of 'Organ of Species' is:
(*a*) Thomas Carlyle (*b*) Charles Darwin
(*c*) Anaicle France (*d*) D. Lawrence

22. Three of the following form a group in some way. Select the one that does not belong to group:
(*a*) Amjad Ali Khan
(*b*) Ravi Shankar
(*c*) Ali Akbar Khan
(*d*) Shanta Prasad

23. Noble Prizes are awarded annually in:
(*a*) Manila (*b*) Stockholm
(*c*) Geneva (*d*) New York

24. Raman Magsaysay Award is named after the former President of?
(*a*) Indonesia (*b*) Thailand
(*c*) Burma (*d*) Philippines

25. The novel 'War and Peace' was written by:
(*a*) F. M. Dostoevsky (*b*) L. N. Tolstoy
(*c*) Anton Chekhov (*d*) Ivan Turgenev

26. Altamira in Spain is known for:
(*a*) a Mosque
(*b*) synagogue
(*c*) bull fighting ring
(*d*) cave of pre–historic art

27. Jaminy Roy was a famous:
(*a*) dancer (*b*) magician
(*c*) cartoonist (*d*) painter

28. Which of the following is the major cause of Green Revolution in India?
(*a*) Land reforms
(*b*) Better irrigation facilities
(*c*) Introduction of hybrid seeds fertilisers, etc.
(*d*) Better agricultural marketing

29. Find the odd man out:
(*a*) Amitava Ghose
(*b*) Upamanyu Chatterjee
(*c*) Vikram Seth
(*d*) Jaishankar Prasad

30. Find the odd man out:
(*a*) Sai Paranjape (*b*) Meera Nair
(*c*) Mani Ratnam (*d*) Om Puri

31. How many squares are there in a chess board?
(*a*) 48 (*b*) 64
(*c*) 36 (*d*) 24

32. The Uruguay round of talks led to the establishment of:
(*a*) NAFTA (*b*) WTO
(*c*) Group of 77 (*d*) Group of 7

33. What season is there in Australia during Christmas?
(*a*) Spring (*b*) Autumn
(*c*) Summer (*d*) Winter

34. Which of the following gives the correct chronological order of the Vedas?
(*a*) Rig, Sama, Atharva, Yajur
(*b*) Rig, Sama, Yajur, Atharva
(*c*) Rig and Sama together, Yajur and Atharva together
(*d*) All simultaneously

35. Which of the following has proved the best source of information for depicting India's ancient history?
(*a*) Religious literature
(*b*) Works of foreign travellers

(*c*) Inscriptions
(*d*) Monuments

36. The Khasi and the Garo tribes belong to:
(*a*) Arunachal Pradesh
(*b*) Sikkim
(*c*) Meghalaya
(*d*) Nagaland

37. The author of 'India Wins Freedom' is:
(*a*) Jawaharlal Nehru
(*b*) Rajendra Prasad
(*c*) Maulana Azad
(*d*) B. C. Roy

38. In an office with 21 workers, 1/3 are men and the rest women. How many women should be hired to obtain a staff in which 1/4 are men?
(*a*) 3 (*b*) 5
(*c*) 6 (*d*) 7

39. Akbar founded his own religion known as Din-i-Ilahi which means:
(*a*) House of worship
(*b*) Universal peace
(*c*) Divine faith
(*d*) None of these

40. In which language did Buddha preach?
(*a*) Pali (*b*) Prakrit
(*c*) Apabhransha (*d*) Sanskrit

41. The blood pressure values of four persons are given below:
1. Mrs. X-90/60
2. Mr. X-160/120
3. Mr. Y-120/80
4. Mrs. Y-140/100

Who among the following has normal blood pressure?
(a) Mrs. Y (b) Mr. X
(c) Mrs. X (d) Mr. Y

42. Which of the following is a universal blood donor?
(*a*) A (*b*) B
(*c*) AB (*d*) O

43. Red blood corpuscles are formed in:
(*a*) liver (*b*) small intestine
(*c*) kidney (*d*) bone marrow

44. Mecca is a holy place for muslims because it houses:
(*a*) Kaaba (*b*) Prophet's tomb
(*c*) Trade centre (*d*) Bedouin's abode

45. Pyramids are mostly found in:
(*a*) Jordan (*b*) Egypt
(*c*) Sudan (*d*) Morocco

46. Find the odd man out:
(*a*) Leonardo da Vinci
(*b*) Raphael
(*c*) Pablo Picasso
(*d*) Dustin Hoffman

47. The oldest school of Indian Philosophy is believed to be:
(*a*) Nyaya (*b*) Vaisheshik
(*c*) Sankhya (*d*) Meemansa

48. What is preserved in a National Park?
(*a*) Only flora (*b*) Only fauna
(*c*) Both (*a*) and (*b*) (*d*) None of these

49. Bismillah Khan is associated with:
(*a*) Tabla (*b*) Sarod
(*c*) Flute (*d*) Shehnai

50. Renminbi (Yuan) is the currency of:
(*a*) China (*b*) Cambodia
(*d*) Hongkong (*d*) Thailand

PART–A-2

Give short answers to the following questions:

51. Which Chinese river is often called as the 'Sorrow of China'?

52. Mahatma Gandhi mostly wrote in which language?

53. Who were the first Europeans who started trade with India?

54. Afanasi Nikitin, who visited India during medieval period, came from which country?

55. The Indian epic 'Mahabharat' was filmed by whom?

56. What subject does 'Charak Samhita' deal with?

57. Who was the first translator of Tagore's Geetanjali' in English?

58. What does 'www' stand for in IT?

59. Which country is called, 'The Land of Morning Calm'?

60. If the word PEARL is written as MBXOI, then how would DIAMOND be written in that code?

61. Find the odd one out of following:
Ravi Shastri, Wasim Akram, Jastin Langer, Gary Sobers, Sunil Gavaskar.

62. The Japanese art of flower arrangement is known as ------.

63. The international boundary between Afghanistan and Pakistan is known as ------.

64. One who compiles a dictionary is known as ------.

65. The word 'Matador' means ------.

66. A stich in time ------.

67. Those who live in glass houses ------.

68. Set of instructions (Programme) that runs a computer's hardware is known as ------.

69. A ball of frozen gas and dust which appears in the sky they say- when great men die or are born, is called ------.

70. The house of Eskimo is called ------.

71. A Francophone is a person who ------.

72. The lower house of the Parliament in Germany is known as ------.

73. Kathak is related to Uttar Pradesh in the same way as Kathakali is related to ------.

74. The longest river in the world is ------.

75. The home for the ancient Sumerian Civilisation was ------.

76. The Chief Guest of this year's Republic day's function was the President of ------.

77. One of the Semitic languages other than Hebrew is ------.

Answer the following questions:

78. If 3 cats can kill 3 rats in 3 minutes, how long it take 100 cats to kill 100 rats?

79. What is warming of the planet due to accumulation of gases called?

80. In a certain code, *Kemp Lamp Tens* means Speak the Truth; *Bis Tim Nak* means Always Seek Knowledge; *Tim Tems Sik* means Knowledge is Truth and *Lik Bis Zap* means Never Seek Violence, then which letter code stands for violence?

81. If BEDI could be given the code number 20, what code number can be given to VISU?

82. Which number replaces the question mark in the following series?
5, 7, 11, ?, 35, 67

83. Who was the first Indian woman to be a Minister at the Centre?

84. What is the other name of the Arabian Gulf?

Directions: (Q. Nos, 85-92): *In the following passage certain words have been omitted. Identify the missing words and write.*

Of all **(85)** --------- untamed creatures, sparrows seem to love living near **(86)** ------- man the most. Wherever **(87)** ------------ new township springs up, the sparrows follow **(88)** ----------- no time. They even build **(89)** --------- nests inside homes and **(90)** ----- they feel sure they will not **(91)** ------ harmed, they will even come and eat out of your hand. That is why they have **(92)** --------- called the most human of all birds.

Directions: (Q. Nos. 93-98): *Fill in the blanks with the most appropriate filler:*

The people of Orissa, where 70% of the cultivable **(93)** ------- is rain fed, had no choice but to migrate because of the **(94)** ------ of drought. Migration is an annual **(95)** ------ in the drought-prone districts of this state. Madhya Pradesh is a favourite destination **(96)** -------- Andhra Pradesh, Delhi and even Punjub. A survey **(97)** ------- that every year more than 50,000 people **(98)** ------- from one district alone.

Fill in the blanks:

99. The term Magic Realism is generally associated with works of ------.

100. The disintegration of Soviet Union took place in ------.

PART–B-1

101. Pointing to a lady, a man said, 'the son of her only brother is the brother of my wife.' How the lady is related to the man?

102. The cricket ball is lighter than the hockey ball and volleyball is lighter than the football. Hockey ball is lighter than the football but heavier than the tennis ball. Which one is the heaviest?

103. Find the odd one from the following series:
3, 5, 7, 9, 11, 13

104. After every 10 metres or so on a railway track a small gap is left. Why is this necessary?

105. Re-arrange the following words to form a meaningful sentence:

a book/Indian/written/and/he/has/leading/on/mythology/by/published/publisher/a reputable

106. A man walks 6 km to the east and then turns to the south and walks 5 km. Again he turns to the east and walks 6 km. Next he turns north-wards and walks 10 km. How far is he now from his starting point?

Directions: (Q. Nos 107-109): *Read the following passage carefully and answer the questions given below it:*

Hiuen Tsang, the famous Chinese traveller, visited India in the seventh century. He travelled extensively in India. He stayed for some time in Kanauj at the court of the great emperor Harshavardhana. He has left for us graphic descriptions of the pomp and ceremony of the royal regalia and the lavish celebrations of Hindu festivals. During one particular festivity at the confluence of the Ganga and Yamuna, many princes would come to participate in the giving of gifts to the poor and the orphans.

Hiuen Tsang spent a long period at the famed Nalanda, where students by the hundreds flocked from all over India and abroad. It had flourished in the time of Buddha and Mahavira, and now when the Chinese pilgrim visited the place it seemed to have been still full of life and intellectual vigour. For this what the pilgrim notes: "The day is not sufficient for asking and answering profound questions. From morning till night, they engage in discussions; the old and the young mutually help one another. If such is not an ideal place of learning, then what is?

107. Why are the writings of Hiuen Tsang considered very important?

108. Why did Hiuen Tsang spend considerable time at Nalanda?

109. Why did the Princes used to visit the festivity at the confluence of Ganga and Yamuna?

110. Which one is different from the rest three?

(*a*) Jackfruit (*b*) Apple
(*c*) Guava (*d*) Watermelon

Directions: (Q. Nos. 111- 115): *Go through carefully the words given in English and their equivalents in an unknown language 'X' and then give the equivalents of the remaining English words in the language 'X'.*

English	*Language 'X'*
LIFT	□ ↑ ∀ ⊃
JUMP	O ⊥ ±
JUNK	O ⊥ ≥
COLD	>] Γ ↓
GOLD	<] Γ ↓
BRICK	← | ↑ ≥
CRICKET	> | ↑ > ⊂ ⊃
CULT	> ⊥ □ ⊃
LINK	□ ↑ ≥
LIST	□ ↑ ≅ ⊃
CIST	≅ ↑ ≅ ⊃
NO	↔]
TENT	⊃ ⊂ ⊇
PUMP	+ ⊥ ±

111. BEG —

112. CUP —

113. DRINK —

114. PENCIL —

115. JUDGE —

Directions: (Q. Nos. 116-120): *Go through the words given in two different scripts A and B and then rewrite the words of script A in script B.*

Script A	*Script B*
बल	∀ ≠
कब	Γ ∀
काल	+ #
जल	0 #
लड़का	# L +
लड़ाई	# 0 ↑
इतना	↑) (
कितना	<) (
मकान	[+ ⊥
इनाम	↑ ([
पास	□ ↓
दूर	⅂ →

116. नाई

117. मत

118. सड़क

119. कल

120. रस

Expand the following abbreviations:

121. HIV

122. ECG

123. LPG

124. STD

125. CRY

Fill in the blanks:

126. The ozone layer in the upper part of the atmosphere protects us from -------.

127. It is easier to swim in a sea than in a river because -------.

128. Burns caused by steam are much more severe than those caused by boiling water -------.

129. The best colours for a sun umbrella will be -------.

130. In the 'Arabian Nights', Aladdin's lamp was a source of wealth and good fortune. What purpose did his ring serve --------?

131. Katyayan, a famous personality of ancient India was primarily a -----.

Directions: (Q. Nos. 132- 134): *Give one word each for the following:*

132. One who cannot be corrected

133. That which cannot be read

134. One who hates mankind

PART–B-2

Directions: (Q, Nos. 135-139): *Go through carefully the sentences given in English and their equivalents in an unknown language 'Z' and then give the equivalents of the remaining English sentences in the language 'Z'.*

English	*Language 'Z'*
He is sleeping	NIRWA
She is sleeping	SIRWA
I am not sleeping	KIRWAN
They are sleeping	BIRWA
Are they sleeping?	BIRWAKU?
We are working	HIMLA
He has eaten	NIKWAI
I have eaten	KIKWAI
I have not eaten	KIKWAIN
They are going	BISLA
Are you going today?	WISLA NUKU?
I will sleep outside	KIRWA SIM
I know this place	KILDA TANIM
I know this word	KILDA RWUIM
He will come tomorrow	NIKTA MA

135. He has gone ---------.

136. She is not working -------.

137. Do you know this place ------ ?

138. We are not going today -------.

139. We will go tomorrow ------.

Write four sentences about the following:

140. United Nations

141. Kalpana Chawla

142. A. P. J. Adbul Kalam

ANSWER

PART–A-1

1	2	3	4	5
(*a*)	(*a*)	(*b*)	(*d*)	(*d*)
6	**7**	**8**	**9**	**10**
(*b*)	(*d*)	(*c*)	(*c*)	(*d*)
11	**12**	**13**	**14**	**15**
(*d*)	(*b*)	(*b*)	(*b*)	(*c*)
16	**17**	**18**	**19**	**20**
(*c*)	(*d*)	(*b*)	(*c*)	(*c*)
21	**22**	**23**	**24**	**25**
(*b*)	(*d*)	(*b*)	(*d*)	(*b*)
26	**27**	**28**	**29**	**30**
(*d*)	(*d*)	(*c*)	(*b*)	(*d*)
31	**32**	**33**	**34**	**35**
(*b*)	(*b*)	(*c*)	(*b*)	(*a*)

36	37	38	39	40
(*c*)	(*c*)	(*d*)	(*c*)	(*a*)
41	**42**	**43**	**44**	**45**
(*a*)	(*d*)	(*d*)	(*a*)	(*b*)
46	**47**	**48**	**49**	**50**
(*d*)	(*b*)	(*c*)	(*d*)	(*a*)

PART–A-2

51. Yellow river (Hwang Hu)
52. Hindustani
53. Portugese
54. In 1468 from Russia
55. B.R. Chopra
56. Medicine
57. Tagore himself
58. WWW—World Wide Web
59. Korea
60. AFXJLKA
61. Sunil Gavaskar
62. Ika bena
63. Durand line
64. Lexico-grapher
65. bull fighter
66. Saves nine
67. never throw a stone
68. Software
69. Philosophy
70. Igloo
71. Speaks French
72. Bundestag
73. Kerala
74. Nile
75. Iraq
76. Mauritius, Mr. Cassam Uttem
77. Arabic
78. 3 minutes
79. Global Warmings
80. It can either be lik or zop
81. 71
82. 19
83. Raj Kumari Amrit Kaur (1947, Health minister)
84. Gulf of Persia
85. the
86. the
87. a
88. in
89. their
90. there
91. be
92. also
93. land
94. situation
95. Phenomena
96. above
97. showed
98. migrate
99. magician
100. 1990

PART–B-1

101. Mother-in-law
102. Football
103. 9 (all other are prime numbers)
104. So that when the track will expand in summer those will not bend.
105. He has written a book on Indian mythology published by a reputable and leading publisher.
106. 13 km
107. He gave graphic descriptions of pomp, ceremonies and details of the life of the people of the 7th century.
108. Nalanda was a centre of study.
109. To give gift to the poor and orphans
110. (*d*) Watermelon
111. $\leftarrow \subset <$
112. $\cong \perp +$
113. $\downarrow | \uparrow \geq$

114. +C ≥ ↑ □

115. O ⊥↓< C

116. (↑

117. [ )

118. ↓L +

119. [#

120. → ↓

121. **HIV:** Human Immuno Deficiency Virus

122. **ECG:** Electro Cardio Gram

123. **LPG:** Liquid Petroleum Gas

124. **STD:** Sexually Transmitted Diseases.

125. **CRY:** Child Relief and You.

126. Ultraviolet radiation.

127. Sea water has more density.

128. Water has more specific heat.

129. White

130. to call the Jinn

131. teacher

132. Incorrigible

133. Unreadable

134. Misanthropist

135. NIKSLAI

136. SIMLAN

137. WILDA TANMU

138. HISLA NUKN

139. HISLA MA

140. **UNITED NATIONS:** UNITED NATION was devised by United States President Franklin D. Roosevelt and was first used in the declaration by United Nation of 2 January 1942 during the second world war when representatives of 26 nation pledge their governments to continue fighting together against the axis powers. Now it consist of 192 members.

141. **KALPANA CHAWLA:** (b-1961-2003) The first Indian American Space Woman. Travelled a board Space Shuttle Columbia in November 1997 and died on her second space voyage on Columbia in February 2003.

142. **A.P.J. ABDUL KALAM:** Abul Pakir Jainul Abdeen Abdul Kalam (b-1931) President of India from 2002 to till date former scientific adviser to Defence minister, the man behind India's missile programme known for his dedication to science, commitment to professional excellence and simplicity of life style, and a Bharat Ratna awardee in1998.

Previous Paper Solved

JNUEE–2002

PART–A-1

Answer the following questions by selecting the most appropriate one from (a) to (d).

1. Bharat II is meant to control:
   (*a*) AIDS
   (*b*) Vehicular emission norms
   (*c*) Water Pollution
   (*d*) Terrorism

2. Dr. Reddy's Lab is associated with:
   (*a*) Biotechnology
   (*b*) Information Technology
   (*c*) Space Technology
   (*d*) Fibre Optics

3. In which State is the famous Tirupathi Temple situated?
   (*a*) Tamil Nadu (*b*) Karnataka
   (*c*) Andhra Pradesh (*d*) Kerala

4. Which of the following is not a member of SAARC?
   (*a*) India (*b*) Pakistan
   (*c*) Sri Lanka (*d*) Afghanistan

5. Raja Ram Mohan Roy's Brahmo Samaj rejected:
   (*a*) Casteism (*b*) Idolism
   (*c*) Ritualism (*d*) All of the above

6. Sikh Khalsa was founded by:
   (*a*) Guru Teg Bahadur
   (*b*) Guru Nanak
   (*c*) Guru Govind Singh
   (*d*) Guru Hargobind

7. Tulsidas was a contemporary of:
   (*a*) Babar (*b*) Jehangir
   (*c*) Akbar (*d*) Humayun

8. German attack on Poland was the immediate cause of:
   (*a*) World War I
   (*b*) World War II
   (*c*) West Asian Crisis
   (*d*) Cold War

9. Source of maximum income to Panchayati Raj Institution is:
   (*a*) Local Taxes
   (*b*) Regional Funds
   (*c*) Government Grants
   (*d*) Share in Union Government Revenue

10. Kamarupa is the old name of:
    (*a*) Asom (*b*) Bihar
    (*c*) Orissa (*d*) Bengal

Select from (a) to (d) the best description common to the three words names on too.

11. Columbus: Megallan : Vasco de Gama:
    (*a*) They are ancient astronomers
    (*b*) They are famous explorers
    (*c*) They discovered some Asian countries
    (*d*) They were the first to design a ship

12. Sarnath: Kapilvastu: Sanchi
    (*a*) These are places with massive pillars.
    (*b*) These are linked with Lord Buddha.
    (*c*) These are famous for stone carving.
    (*d*) These are ancient universities.

13. Mandarin: Sinhalese: Tamil:
    (*a*) They are originally Indian languages
    (*b*) They have originated from Sanskrit
    (*c*) They are Asian languages
    (*d*) They have the same type of grammar

14. James Bond : Sherlock Holmes : Hercule Poirot:
    (*a*) They are agents of CBI.
    (*b*) They are the only detective agents with license to kill.
    (*c*) They are private detectives.
    (*d*) They are characters from detective fiction.

15. Green : Violet: Orange:
    (*a*) They are primary colours
    (*b*) They are made by mixing colours
    (*c*) They are not found in butterflies
    (*d*) They occur together in rainbow

Answer the following questions by selecting the most appropriate one from (a) to (d).

16. Bile juice is secreted by
(*a*) Pancreas (*b*) Liver
(*c*) Spleen (*d*) Gall Bladder

17. Light Year is a unit to measure
(*a*) speed of light
(*b*) astronomical distances
(*c*) speed of rockets
(*d*) speed of aeroplanes

18. Which of the following is the lightest metal
(*a*) Mercury (*b*) Silver
(*c*) Lithium (*d*) Lead

19. Which of the following is a universal blood donor
(*a*) A (*b*) B
(*c*) AB (*d*) O

20. Any foreign particle which stimulates the formation of antibodies is called:
(*a*) Histone (*b*) Antigen
(*c*) Receptor (*d*) Antibiotic

21. The evolution of human species took place mainly in:
(*a*) Asia (*b*) Africa
(*c*) Europe (*d*) China

22. Who recast the original single Veda into four Vedas?
(*a*) Patanjali (*b*) Vyas
(*c*) Shankaracharya (*d*) None of these

23. In Indian Constitution, there is no provision for:
(*a*) Religious Rights
(*b*) Political and Social Rights
(*c*) Educational Rights
(*d*) Economic Rights

24. The largest Island in the Indian ocean is:
(*a*) Sri Lanka (*b*) Maldives
(*c*) Madagascar (*d*) Sumatra

25. The first underground railway in India was opened on 1984 in:
(*a*) Mumbai (*b*) Chennai
(*c*) Kolkata (*d*) Delhi

26. According to Jawaharlal Nehru University (JNU) prospectus, how many centres of examination are there in India for entrance to JNU in 2002?
(*a*) about 15 (*b*) about 30
(*c*) about 40 (*d*) about 50

27. The People's Republic of China was founded on:
(*a*) October 1, 1947
(*b*) August 10, 1949
(*c*) October 1, 1949
(*d*) August 10, 1947

28. Who among the following scholars was the first to visit India?
(*a*) Hiuen Tsang (*b*) Ibn Batuta
(*c*) Marco Polo (*d*) Fa Hien

29. Sculptures of the Gandhara School reflect the influence of:
(*a*) Persians (*b*) Greek
(*c*) Romans (*d*) Chinese

30. The largest producer of Uranium in the world is:
(*a*) U.S.A. (*b*) France
(*c*) India (*d*) Zaire

31. Equator passes through which of the following countries?
(*a*) Australia (*b*) Brazil
(*c*) China (*d*) Saudi Arabia

32. Which continent has the highest density of population?
(*a*) Asia (*b*) Africa
(*c*) Europe (*d*) North America

33. Which planet is known as the Watery Planet?
(*a*) Venus (*b*) Mars
(*c*) Pluto (*d*) Earth

34. The biggest public sector undertaking in India is :
(*a*) Iron and Steel (*b*) Railways
(*c*) Roadways (*d*) Airways

35. Which State has achieved the highest literacy rate in India?
(*a*) Kerala (*b*) Maharashtra
(*c*) West Bengal (*d*) Punjab

36. In a certain code language 526 means 'sky is blue, 24 means 'blue colour' and 436 means 'colour is fun'. Which digit in that language means 'fun'?

(*a*) 5 (*b*) 6
(*c*) 3 (*d*) 4

37. Which letter in place of '?' will complete the following series?
A C F J ? U B
(*a*) N (*b*) O
(*c*) P (*d*) Q

38. After Vishwanathan Anand, who was the second Indian Chess player to earn the title of Grandmaster?
(*a*) Subramanyam Raman
(*b*) Dibyendu Barua
(*c*) D.V. Prasad
(*d*) Anupama Abhyankar

39. The 'Shahnama was written by?
(*a*) Alberuni (*b*) Amir Khusro
(*c*) Abul Fazal (*d*) Firdausi

40. Who wrote the famous line 'A thing of beauty is a joy for ever'?
(*a*) Shelley (*b*) Keats
(*c*) Wordsworth (*d*) Shakespeare

41. Kilimanjaro in Africa is a:
(*a*) Mountain Peak (*b*) River
(*c*) Tribe (*d*) Volcano

42. Which is the only Asian country represented in G-7 Group?
(*a*) India (*b*) China
(*c*) Japan (*d*) S. Korea

43. Which of the following Asian languages are official languages of United Nations?
(*a*) Chinese and Japanese
(*b*) Chinese and Hindi
(*c*) Japanese and Arabic
(*d*) Arabic and Chinese

44. The best colour(s) for a sun umbrella will be :
(*a*) black
(*b*) black on top and white inside
(*c*) white on top and black inside
(*d*) printed in seven colours of rainbow

45. Hargobind Khurana is credited with the discovery of:
(*a*) Synthesis of proteins
(*b*) Synthesis of genes
(*c*) Insulin
(*d*) None of these

46. Madhav ranks thirteenth in a class of thirty-one. What is his rank from the last?
(*a*) 15 (*b*) 17
(*c*) 18 (*d*) None of these

47. Neha says 'Rohan's father is the only son of my father. How is Neha related to Rohan?
(*a*) Cousin (*b*) Aunt
(*c*) Sister (*d*) Daughter

48. Which State of India has the largest coastline?
(*a*) Kerala (*b*) Tamil Nadu
(*c*) Gujarat (*d*) Andhra Pradesh

49. Who was the first Arab writer to receive Nobel Prize in literature?
(*a*) Yusuf Idris (*b*) Yusuf Sibai
(*c*) Najib Mahfooz (*d*) Ahmad Hadrani

50. Who is considered to be the architect of White Revolution?
(*a*) M.S. Swaminathan
(*b*) N.E. Borlaug
(*c*) K.M. Panikkar
(*d*) V. Kurien

PART–A-2

Complete the names of the following well-known Indian writers.

51. Vidia S.
52. Girish
53. Vikram
54. Bhishm
55. Shivram
56. Indira

Give short answers to the following questions (one or two words only).

57. 'Cleopatra' was the queen of which country?

58. What was added recently to the old well-known slogan 'Jai Jawan, Jai Kisan -------?

59. Which Indian author known internationally, was recently involved with 'Narmada Bachao Andolan'?

60. Which politician and former Union Minister did Amitabh Bachchan defeated in the Lok Sabha Elections of 1984?

61. According to Hindu mythology, which

goddess is credited with having invented Sanskrit?

62. The Meiji Restoration in 1868 returned which country to direct imperial rule?

63. What did the Republic of France officially gift to the U.S.A. on the hundredth anniversary of American Independence?

64. Which Indian grammarian is credited with writing 'Ashtadhyayi'?

65. Which post did B.R. Ambedkar hold in independent India's first Cabinet?

66. The autobiography of which woman writer is titled 'Rasidi Ticket?

67. How is Gaul, an ancient country, known today?

68. With what do you associate Pascal and Java languages?

69. Who set *Sare Jahan se Achchha* to music?

70. Which is the first month of the Indian (lunar) calendar?

71. *'Formula Sirf Bharat ke pass hai* refers to which product and brand in a T.V. commercial?

72. In which State of India are Ajanta caves situated?

73. What is Mesopotamia today known as?

74. What was the profession of late Mr. Daniel Pearl?

75. What do you associate Kanjivaram, Chanderi, Patola with?

76. What do you associate Kathakali, Kuchipudi and Odissi with?

77. Who has directed the film 'Lagaan ?

78. Write the name of the singer of the Hindi popular song 'Lift kara de'.

The following words are spelt wrongly. Write the correct spellings for each:

79. vulnarable

80. divertion

81. contension

82. profesion

Directions (83- 92): *Fill in the blanks in the following sentences with appropriate articles/prepositions:*

Some robbers entered **(83)** ------ bank and, pointing guns at **(84)** ------ customers, asked **(85)** -------- cashier **(86)** -------- hand over all **(87)** ------ cash **(88)** ------ them. The cashier put all the money **(89)** ------ a leather bag quietly pushed it **(90)** ---- the counter **(91)** ------ one of **(92)** ----- robbers.

93-96. The English word SINCERELY has nine letters. Using different combinations of these letters make four words (93, 94, 95, 96) of five or more letters each.

97. Select the correct synonym of the word CREDITABLE from the words given below : believable, honest, sincere, praiseworthy

98. Select the correct antonym of the word TRADITIONAL from the words given below: superstitious, secular, modern, futuristic

Each of the following sentences has an error in it. Identify and correct that part of the sentence.

99. You are cordially invited/to a dinner party/ to be held at 7.30 p.m. at Sunday/ in Grand Banquet hall.

100. Many people assembled /to condemn the violent riots/ that had taken place/through many parts of the city.

PART–B

101. What is a Simputer?

102. 38th Parallel divides which two countries in the Far East?

103. Write the full name of the School of JNU which you are seeking admission to?

104. If FRIEND is coded as HUMJTK, how is CANDLE written in this code?

105. In a certain code, 15789 is written as EGKPT and 2346 is written as ALUR how is 23549 written in that code?

106. Samir's rank is tenth from the top in his class. Prabir, who is fifteenth from the end, is lower in rank than Samir by ten. How many students are there in Samir's class?

107. Abhinav walked 2 kms west of his house and then turned south covering 4 kms. Finally, he moved 3 kms towards east and then again

1 km west. How far is he from his initial position?

108. Five persons were playing card game sitting in a circle all facing the center. Mukund was to the left of Rajesh. Vijay was to the right of Anil and between Anil and Nagesh. Who was to the right of Nagesh?

109. Which script(s) do we use to write Hindi and Marathi?

110. What are *apostrophe*, *hyphen*, and *semicolon* part of?

111. Name two Indians other than Rabindra Nath Tagore who have received the Nobel Prize?

112. What are the first two letters in the Greek alphabet?

One in the each of the following groups is different from the other four. Choose the odd one out :

113. ECA—JHF—OMK—TRP—UWY

114. AOT—CPA—REB—TIW—OUD

115. Diamond—Ruby—Topaz—Garnet—Pearl

116. Magadhi—Gujarati—Malayalam—Urdu—Marathi

In the following number series, find out the wrong figure.

117. 10, 26, 74, 218, 654, 1946, 5834

118. 56, 72, 90, 110, 132, 150

Which number can be placed at the sign of the question mark (?) in 119 and 120?

119. 9, 25, 49, 81, 121, ?

120. 17, 19, 23, 29, 31, ?, 41

Answer 121, 122, 123 after reading the following information.

A training college has to conduct a refresher course for teachers of six different subjects—Education, Psychology, Philosophy, Economics, Science and Engineering from 22nd July to 28th July.

(i) The course should start with Psychology.
(ii) 23rd July, being Sunday, should be a holiday.
(iii) Science subject should be on the previous day of the Engineering subject.
(iv) Course should end with Education subject.
(v) Philosophy should be immediately after the holiday.
(vi) There should be a gap of one day between Economics and Engineering.

121. Which subject will be on Tuesday?

122. Which subject precedes Education?

123. How many days' gap is there in between Science and Philosophy?

124. How many of the following blanks can be filled with 'to'?

(*a*) I am grateful ----- you.
(*b*) He is fully contented ----- his life.
(*c*) He is averse --------- hard work.
(*d*) He is not eligible ------- the post of Manager.

Expand the following well-known acronyms:

125. VSNL

126. POTO

127. NDDB

128. Ph.D

129. M.B.A.

130-131. ***Write two short sentences (30-31) on the benefits of learning a foreign language?***

132-133 Write two complete sentences (32, 33) about the medium of instruction in your school and the language you know.

134-138. Complete 34 and give one-line answers to 35, 36, 37, 38 after reading the following passage:

An electronic mail system is a method of electronically sending messages, mail or documents. It is also known as electronic delivery or electronic document communication. E-mail seeks to replace the old postal and tele-communications system where a person is not sure whether the recipient would receive post through ordinary mail. Studies show that 25-30 per cent of telephone calls go through on the first attempt. Thus on an average, four calls are required to complete one. A few months ago, there was a news report that a person received his letter after 24 years. It sounds funny and interesting but think of him who got the letter after so long.

134. Electronic mail system is also known as ---- (complete the sentence).

135. What does E-mail seek to achieve?

136. What is the risk/ shortcoming in the old postal and tele-communication system?

137. What do studies show about telephone calls?

138. What is the 'funny and interesting' incident mentioned in the passage?

Use the following words in simple sentences of your own:

139. recipient

140. replace

141. documents

142. delivery

The following words are from language X. Look at the words carefully and then translate the sentences that follow (143-147) into English:

rud	= sleep	grish	= warm
rudwa	= slept	nagrish	= cold
sis	= child	ag	= come
ama	= mother	hap	= sit
op	= in/on	tera	= ground/floor
kib	= bed/cot	sisk	= child's
va	= near/ towards	gud	= lap

(ama hapwa op kib = mother sat on bed)

143. sis agwa va ama.

144. ama hapwa op nagrish tera.

145. sis rudwa op grish kib.

146. ama agwa va sisk kib.

147. sis hapwa ama grish gud.

148. Who appoints the Governor of a State in India.

149. How many of the following words are used both as noun and verb?

speech	influence	thought	curl
record	difference	use	trial

150. The coach arrived at the playground at 8.35. Rakesh arrived 45 minutes late and was 15 minutes late for the training. By how much time did the coach come earlier than the scheduled time?

ANSWER

PART–A-1

1	2	3	4	5
(*b*)	(*a*)	(*a*)	(*d*)	(*d*)
6	**7**	**8**	**9**	**10**
(*c*)	(*c*)	(*b*)	(*c*)	(*a*)
11	**12**	**13**	**14**	**15**
(*b*)	(*b*)	(*c*)	(*d*)	(*d*)
16	**17**	**18**	**19**	**20**
(*b*)	(*b*)	(*c*)	(*d*)	(*b*)
21	**22**	**23**	**24**	**25**
(*b*)	(*d*)	(*d*)	(*c*)	(*c*)
26	**27**	**28**	**29**	**30**
(*d*)	(*c*)	(*d*)	(*b*)	(*d*)
31	**32**	**33**	**34**	**35**
(*b*)	(*c*)	(*d*)	(*b*)	(*a*)
36	**37**	**38**	**39**	**40**
(*c*)	(*b*)	(*b*)	(*d*)	(*c*)
41	**42**	**43**	**44**	**45**
(*d*)	(*c*)	(*d*)	(*c*)	(*b*)
46	**47**	**48**	**49**	**50**
(*d*)	(*b*)	(*c*)	(*c*)	(*d*)

PART–A-2

51. Vidia S. Naipaul

52. Girish Karnad

53. Vikram Seth

54. Bhishm Sahni

55. Shivram Karantha

56. Indira Gandhi/Indira Goswami

57. Rome

58. Jai Vigyan

59. Arundhati Roy

60. Dr. Murli Manohar Joshi

61. Saraswati

62. Japan

63. Statue of Liberty

64. Panini

65. Law minister

66. Amrita Pritam

67. France

68. Computer

69. Ravi Shankar

70. Chaitra

71. Meswak

72. Maharashtra

73. Iraq

74. Journalism

75. Saree

76. Dance

77. Ashutosh Gowarikar

78. Adnan Sami

79. Vulnerable

80. Diversion

81. Contention

82. Profession

83. the

84. the

85. the

86. to

87. the

88. to

89. in

90. to

91. towards

92. the

93. SINCE

94. SINCERE

95. NIECE

96. SCIENCE

97. believable

98. Modern

99. to be held at 7.30 p.m. on Sunday.

100. in many parts of city.

101. Simputer is another form of computer.

102. North and South Korea.

103. School of languages.

104. EDRIRL

105. ALGUT

106. 34 students

107. 4 km

108. MUKUND

109. Devnagri

110. Sentence

111. Dr. C.V. Raman, Dr. Amartya Sen

112. Alpha (α), Beta (β)

113. UWY

114. AOT as all other have two consonents.

115. Garnet (all other are gems where a garnet is used to make gems)

116. Magadhi

117. 654 it should be 650

118. 150

119. 169, square of consecutive prime number

120. 37, next prime number

121. Economics

122. Engineering

123. One

124. (*a*) to (*b*) to (*c*) to (*d*) for

125. VSNL—Videsh Sanchar Nigam Limited.

126. POTO—Prevention of Terrorism Ordinance.

127. NDDB—National Dairy Development Board.

128. Ph. D—Doctor of Philosophy.

129. M.B.A.—Master of Business Administration.

130. To know the culture and civilization of that country.

131. Learning a language is also helpful in getting employment.

132. The medium of instruction in my school was Hindi.

133. I know English and Hindi.

134. e-mail

135. It seeks to replace the old systems of communication.

136. The sender is not sure whether the recipient would receive post through ordinary mail in time and four calls are required to complete one.

137. 25-30% calls go through the 1st attempt.

138. A person received his letter after 24 years.

139. Dr. Amartya Sen is a recipent of Nobel Prize.

140. Suman is replaced by Gurpreet.

141. Mr. Madhav didn't submit his documents.

142. The Pizza boy delivered the Pizza to Aishwarya.

143. Child come towards mother.

144. Mother sat on cold floor.

145. Child slept on warm bed.

146. Mother come near child's bed.

147. Child sat mother warm lap.

148. President of India.

149. Influence, record, use, trail, curl.

150. 30 minutes.

Previous Paper Solved

JNUEE–2001

PART–A

1. What is called the Fourth Estate?
(*a*) Press
(*b*) Judiciary
(*c*) Police
(*d*) Human Rights Commission

2. A country which elects its head of State is known as:
(*a*) an oligarchy (*b*) a monarchy
(*c*) an aristocracy (*d*) a republic

3. The term of office of the French President is:
(*a*) 5 years
(*b*) 7 years
(*c*) for life
(*d*) Parliament's pleasure

4. Which of these sanctuaries is not found in South India?
(*a*) Mudumalai (*b*) Mukkurti
(*c*) Periyar (*d*) Ranthambore

5. The Khumb Mela takes place once in:
(*a*) 5 years (*b*) 3 century
(*c*) a decade (*d*) 12 years

6. In India, the census is carried out once in:
(*a*) 10 years (*b*) 5 years
(*c*) 20 years (*d*) every year

7. Which for the following zodiac signs is not represented by an animal?
(*a*) Libra (*b*) Aries
(*c*) Cancer (d) Leo

8. Who founded the Kinnara School of Music in 1967 in Los Angeles?
(*a*) George Harrison (*b*) Uday Shankar
(*c*) Ravi Shankar (*d*) Amjad Ali Khan

9. Major portion of air is made up of:
(*a*) Carbon dioxide
(*b*) Oxygen
(*c*) Chlorine
(*d*) Nitrogen

10. Which Bhakti Saint of 15th century composed "Vaishnava Jana to Tene Kahiye?
(*a*) Namdev (*b*) Tukaram
(*c*) Narsinh Mehta (*d*) Meerabai

11. Which of the following French colonies was closest to Kolkata?
(*a*) Pondicherry (*b*) Mahe
(*c*) Karaikal (*d*) Chandernagore

Find the odd man out:

12. (*a*) Birbal (*b*) Abul Fazl
(*c*) Faiz Ahmad (*d*) Tansen

13. (*a*) Sarod (*b*) Sitar
(*c*) Veena (*d*) Mridangam

14. (*a*) Saurav Ganguly
(*b*) Shahid Afridi
(*c*) Mushtaq Mohammad
(*d*) Viswanathan Anand

15. (*a*) Mew (*b*) Bark
(*c*) Chirp (*d*) Roar

16. (*a*) Hindi (*b*) Gurmukhi
(*c*) English (*d*) Marathi

17. (*a*) Jharkhand—Bihar
(*b*) Uttaranchal—Uttar Pradesh
(*c*) Chhattisgarh—Madhya Pradesh
(*d*) Meghalaya—Manipur

18. Which of the following can also be eaten as a dry fruit?
(*a*) Grapes (*b*) Bananas
(*c*) Apples (*d*) Oranges

19. Which of the following countries have never played in a World Cup Cricket final?
(*a*) England (*b*) South Africa
(*c*) Pakistan (*d*) Sri Lanka

Complete the following statements correctly with the most appropriate filler:

20. Unless you work hard ----
(*a*) you ought to be successful
(*b*) you be not successful

(*c*) you are not being successful
(*d*) you will not be successful

21. She ---- people who are good at music:
(*a*) supports (*b*) admires
(*c*) attracts (*d*) appeals

22. CRY is an organization dealing with -----:
(*a*) Environment
(*b*) Welfare of women
(*c*) Welfare of neglected children
(*d*) Community development

23. If book is called watch, watch is called bag, bag is called dictionary and dictionary is called window. Which is used to carry books?
(*a*) Dictionary (*b*) Book
(*c*) Bag (*d*) Watch

24. A woman introduces a man as the son of the brother of her mother. How is the man related to the woman?
(*a*) nephew (*b*) son
(*c*) cousin (*d*) uncle

In the number series given in the questions (25 to 27) below one term is missing. Choose the correct number that will continue the same pattern:

25. 5, 10, 13, 26, 29, 58, 61, ----
(*a*) 122 (*b*) 125
(*c*) 128 (*d*) 64

26. 12, 32, 72, 152, ----
(*a*) 312 (*b*) 234
(*c*) 192 (*d*) 284

27. 64, 32; 16 8; 4, (?)
(*a*) 0 (*b*) 1
(*c*) 2 (*d*) 4

28. Who among the following did not invade India?
(*a*) Alexander (*b*) Napoleon
(*c*) Nadir Shah (*d*) Timur

29. In which country was the music conductor Zubin Mehta bom?
(*a*) Pakistan (*b*) India
(*c*) Israel (*d*) Kenya

30. In 1876 who assumed the title of Empress of India?
(*a*) Queen Elizabeth I
(*b*) Queen Victoria
(*c*) Mary Queen of Scots
(*d*) Queen Anne

31. Which country does not share a land border with India?
(*a*) Nepal (*b*) Burma
(*c*) Bhutan (*d*) Thailand

32. Which of the following places is renowned for its cracker industry?
(*a*) Kolhapur (*b*) Sivakasi
(*c*) Faizabad (*d*) Dhanbad

33. How many members of the Rajya Sabha retire after every 2 years?
(*a*) 1/3 (*b*) 3/4
(*c*) 2/3 (*d*) 1/2

34. If Christmas falls on a Saturday, on which day would the New Year Eve fall?
(*a*) Sunday (*b*) Saturday
(*c*) Monday (*d*) Tuesday

35. Which of the following rivers flows into the Bay of Bengal?
(*a*) Tungabhadra (*b*) Mahanadi
(*c*) Godavari (*d*) Narmada

36. Which of the following poets is not from Maharashtra?
(*a*) Gyaneshwar (*b*) Tukaram
(*c*) Eknath (*d*) Kabir

37. Which former Prime Minister of India is the author of the novel 'The insider'?
(*a*) V.P. Singh (*b*) Narasimha Rao
(*c*) Chandra Sekhar (*d*) I. K Gujral

38. Cricket World Cup 2003 will be held at:
(*a*) Johannesburg (*b*) Melbourne
(*c*) Seoul (*d*) Mumbai

39. The name of the sheep, which was cloned for the first time, is:
(*a*) Polly (*b*) Dolly
(*c*) Holly (*d*) Molly

40. The Shahnama was written by:
(*a*) Al-Beruni (*b*) Firdausi
(*c*) Amir Khusrao (*d*) Abul Fazl

Fill in the blank with the most appropriate word:

41. The manager is very competent. He is ----- to the firm.

(*a*) a boon (*b*) a blessing
(*c*) a credit (*d*) an asset

42. The earthquake was ------ severe that the entire town and surrounding villages were reduced to a heap of concrete.
(*a*) too (*b*) so
(*c*) very (*d*) highly

43. Since you have not been true ----- your word, we shall not entrust you ---- any more work.
(*a*) upon, to (*b*) of, with
(*c*) to, with (*d*) by, of

44. Many people ------- whatever leisure they have at their -------
(*a*) misuse, disposal
(*b*) enjoy, time
(*c*) pursue, order
(*d*) utilize, behalf

Each of the following sentences has four parts: (a), (b), (c), (d) . One of the parts may contain an error. Select that part.

45. (*a*) The children/(*b*) were playing/ (*c*) besides the road/ (d) in the afternoon.

46. (a) Her bag / (*b*) is definitely / (*c*) more beautiful / (*d*) than your.

47. Which one of the following is not an Internet Service Provider in India?
(*a*) Caltiger
(*b*) Bharat Connect
(*c*) French Connection
(*d*) Satyam

48. India's largest manufacturer of Herbal products is:
(*a*) Dabur
(*b*) Jhandu
(*c*) Ayurvedic Concepts
(*d*) Biotique

49. Which of the following is not a currency that is used anywhere in the world?
(*a*) Cruzeiro (*b*) Lira
(*c*) Peseta (*d*) Bhat

50. The Olympic Airlines belongs to:
(*a*) Italy (*b*) Greece
(*c*) Spain (*d*) France

51. Which of the following is a cave temple in India?
(*a*) Perli (*b*) Ajanta
(*c*) Ellora (*d*) Tuljapur

52. After Kabir's death his tomb was built at:
(*a*) Varanasi (*b*) Gorakhpur
(*c*) Magahar (*d*) Basti

53. Which 3 former Soviet Republics form the Baltic States?
(*a*) Estonia, Latvia, Lithuania
(*b*) Uzbekistan, Kazakistan, Mongolia
(*c*) Estonia, Kazakistan, Lithuania
(*d*) Latvia, Uzbekistan, Mongolia

54. Which of the following is an epic poetry in Persian?
(*a*) Jangnama (*b*) Shahnama
(*c*) Fatahnama (*d*) Sulahnama

55. The famous history book *Akbarnama* was written by:
(*a*) Faizi
(*b*) Abul Fazl
(*c*) Bairam Khan
(*d*) Abdurrahim Khankhana

56. What is the offspring of an elephant called?
(*a*) Cub (*b*) Calf
(*c*) Elephantine (*d*) Kid

57. Film 'Teesari Kasam' was based on a famous story of which writer?
(*a*) Phanishwarnath 'Renu'
(*b*) Munshi Premchand
(*c*) Krishan Chander
(*d*) Rabindra Nath Tagore

58. According to Hindu mythology, who invented the instrument Veena?
(*a*) Saraswati (*b*) Menaka
(*c*) Narad (*d*) Indra

59. Which of the following is not a synonym of the word language?
(*a*) Diction (*b*) Dialect
(*c*) Lingua franca (*d*) Vernacular

60. Which of the following words is spelt wrongly?
(*a*) Miscellanious (*b*) Observance
(*c*) Fluorescent (*d*) Mischievous

61. What is the unit of Korean currency?
(*a*) Yuan (*b*) Won
(*c*) Yen (*d*) Bhat

62. What is the group of Korean electronic companies operating in India?
(*a*) Daewoo, Samsung
(*b*) Hyundai, Daewoo
(*c*) L.G., Hyundai
(*d*) Samsung, L.G.

63. The name of Balraj Sahni's 'Do Bigha Jamin' was taken from the name of a poem by a famous poet. Name the poet.
(*a*) Rabindra Nath Tagore
(*b*) Bankim Chandra Chatterjee
(*c*) Sumitra Nandan Pant
(*d*) Ramdhari Singh Dinkar

64. Which European country's official languages are French, Italian, German?
(*a*) Switzerland (*b*) Italy
(*c*) France (*d*) Netherlands

65. The hosts of the popular music programme 'Sa Re Ga Ma' on T.V. are the sons of which famous musician?
(*a*) Vilayat Khan
(*b*) Amir Khan
(*c*) Amjad Ali
(*d*) Mallikarjun Mansoor

66. Indonesia is situated in:
(*a*) South-East Asia
(*b*) Far East
(*c*) West Asia
(*d*) Central Asia

Which of the following is NOT correctly matched?

67. (*a*) Sachin Tendulkar – Cricket
(*b*) Sergio Garcia – Golf
(*c*) Pele – Football
(*d*) Ramanathan Krishnan – Hockey

68. (*a*) Bismillah Khan – Shehnai
(*b*) L. Subramaniam – Violin
(*c*) Kadrigopalnath – Veena
(*d*) Zakir Hussain – Tabla

69. (*a*) Garba – Kashmir
(*b*) Bhangra – Punjab
(*c*) Ghumar – Rajasthan
(*d*) Kummi – Tamil Nadu

70. Select the correct synonym of the given word out of the four choices given below
Adept:
(*a*) manage (*b*) adroit
(*c*) divert (*d*) suit

PART–B

1. During a Solar eclipse the shadow of what falls on what?
(*a*) Moon on Sun (*b*) Moon on Earth
(*c*) Earth on Moon (*d*) Earth on Sun

2. Jim Corbett National Park is in?
(*a*) Uttaranchal (*b*) Uttar Pradesh
(*c*) Bihar (*d*) Rajasthan

3. Which is the hardest substance in the human body?
(*a*) Skull bone (*b*) Tooth enamel
(*c*) Knee cap (*d*) Finger nail

4. What words were inscribed in the first postage stamp issued in India after independence?
(*a*) Vande Mataram
(*b*) Satyameva Jayate
(*c*) Jai Hind
(*d*) Azad Hind

5. The Elisa test is used to detect:
(*a*) Cancer (*b*) Tuberculosis
(*c*) AIDS (*d*) Dengue

6. Who introduced political cartoons in South India?
(*a*) Subramanya Bharathi
(*b*) Kamaraj
(*c*) R.K. Lakshman
(*d*) Moopanar

7. Who was the first External Affairs Minister of Independent India?
(*a*) Abul Kalam Azad
(*b*) Vijaya Lakshmi Pundit
(*c*) Jawaharlal Nehru
(*d*) N.V. Gadgil

8. January 12th is celebrated as National Youth Day in memory of:
(*a*) Jawaharlal Nehru
(*b*) Rajiv Gandhi
(*c*) Radhakrishnan
(*d*) Swami Vivekananda

9. The first satellite launched by India was:
(*a*) Bhaskara (*b*) Aryabhatta
(*c*) Insat Apple (*d*) Ariane

10. Which city originally consisted of 7 islands called Heptanasia by the Greeks?
(*a*) Kolkata (*b*) Mumbai
(*c*) Mangalore (*d*) Cochin

11. If EXIST is coded as ESIXT, how would PLUTO be coded?
(*a*) PTULO (*b*) POTUL
(*c*) PLOUT (*d*) TOPLU

12. If CRICKET is coded as BQHBJDS then FLOWER will be code as:
(*a*) GKPVFC (*b*) LMWDS
(*c*) GMPVDS (*d*) EKNVDQ

13. If PENSION is coded as NEISNOP, how is FOLIAGE coded:
(*a*) OFILGAE (*b*) EGAILOF
(*c*) EOAILGF (*d*) FILOGAE

14. What is a Geiger counter used to measure?
(*a*) Radioactivity (*b*) Salinity of water
(*c*) Pressure (*d*) Seismic waves

15. Who defined democracy as government of the people by the people and for the people?
(*a*) Winston Churchill
(*b*) Abraham Lincoln
(*c*) George Washington
(*d*) Napoleon Bonaparte

16. Which Governor General of British India later become the first Viceroy of India?
(*a*) Lord Dalhousie (*b*) Lord Canning
(*c*) Lord Wellesley (*d*) Lord Hastings

17. Who holds the post of the Chairperson of the Planning Commission of India?
(*a*) President
(*b*) Prime Minister
(*c*) Finance Minister
(*d*) Minister of Planning

18. When was the first census held in India?
(*a*) 1872 (*b*) 1945
(*c*) 1790 (*d*) 1848

In each of the following questions select the proper sequence of the parts labelled P, Q, R, S, so as to make a meaningful paragraph.

19. P. Buildings constructed in reclaimed land were severely affected throughout the state.
Q. So a new approach to construction is required in order to build a quake resistant Gujarat.
R. On the other hand, buildings on solid ground saw few casualties and minimal damage.
S. On January 26th a severe earthquake ravaged the State of Gujarat.
(*a*) SPRQ (*b*) QPRS
(*c*) RSQP (*d*) PSRQ

20. P. Yet paradoxically, man and medicine share an uncertain future on the threshold of the 21st century.
Q. Many a life has been saved, many marvels performed and many have reaped the benefits of this change.
R. Over the last 100 years, science has changed the world and changed medicine with it.
S. This is because mechanisation of medicine has robbed it of its essence, its humanism.
(*a*) RQPS (*b*) PSRQ
(*c*) QPSR (*d*) SRPQ

21. P. Mount Abu is a part of the Aravalli
Q. about 1685 metres above sea level
R. range in Rajasthan, and
S. its highest peak, the Guru Shikhara, is
(*a*) PRSQ (*b*) PQRS
(*c*) SPRQ (*d*) QPSR

22. Who among the following personalities did not receive the Nobel Peace Prize?
(*a*) Mikhail Gorbachov
(*b*) Mahatma Gandhi
(*c*) Aung San Su Kyi
(*d*) Yasser Arafat

23. A caddie is found in:
(*a*) a golf course (*b*) zoo
(*c*) car park (*d*) market

24. What does GMT stand for?
(*a*) Greenland Mean Time
(*b*) Greenland Mean Temperature

(*c*) Greenwich Mean Time
(*d*) Greenwich Mean Temperature

25. Which of these films won a record of 11 Oscars?
(*a*) Gandhi (*b*) Sixth Sense
(*c*) Jurassic Park (*d*) Titanic

26. Which State in the U.S. has been recognized as sister state to Gujarat?
(*a*) California (*b*) Texas
(*c*) Ohio (*d*) Kansas

27. How many rectangles are there in the following figure?

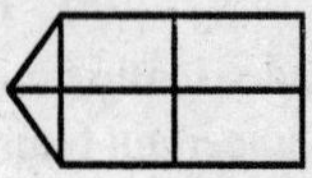

(*a*) 6 (*b*) 7
(*c*) 8 (*d*) 9

28. How many triangles are there in the following figure?

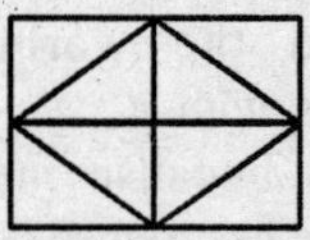

(*a*) 8 (*b*) 10
(*c*) 12 (*d*) 14

29. The word given below is followed by four other words. Only one of these four words can be formed from the letters used in the given word. Find that word.

CONSTANTINOPLE.
(*a*) Conscience (*b*) Content
(*c*) Continue (*d*) Constance

30. Atul travelled 3 kms Southwards, then turned right and travelled 5 kms. Then again turned right and travelled 7 kms. In which direction was he travelling last?
(*a*) East (*b*) West
(*c*) North (*d*) South

Select the correct meaning of the sentences given below, out of the four responses (a), (b), (c) and (d) which follow each sentence.

31. It is too cold to go out.
(*a*) It is extremely cold for going out.
(*b*) It is not cold enough to go out.
(*c*) It is so cold that one cannot go out.
(*d*) It is such cold that one cannot go out.

32. This is one of the best novels I have ever read.
(*a*) Very few novels I have ever read are as good as this.
(*b*) This is as good as any other novel I have ever read.
(*c*) This is better than any novel I have ever read.
(*d*) No other novel I have ever read is as good as this.

33. My sister said to me: "Let us see a film tomorrow":
(*a*) My sister told me to see a film tomorrow.
(*b*) My sister proposed that we see a film the next day.
(*c*) My sister insisted that they should see a film tomorrow.
(*d*) My sister told me that we could see a film tomorrow.

34. Zaikai in Japan are:
(*a*) The elite who control business
(*b*) Akio Morita's successor in Sony
(*c*) Name of an Ikebana School
(*d*) A popular theatre

35. Jehangir minted the words's
(*a*) smallest coins in silver
(*b*) largest coins in gold
(*c*) first diamond- studded coin
(*d*) first ruby- studded coin

36. Hirakud dam is constructed on which river:
(*a*) Kosi (*b*) Ganga
(*c*) Sutlej (*d*) Mahanadi

37. The Halley's comet will be seen next in:
(*a*) 2058 (*b*) 2062
(*c*) 2066 (*d*) 2068

38. The + symbol comes from:
(*a*) Latin (*b*) French
(*c*) Persian (*d*) Arabic

39. Arabic belongs to which of the following family of languages?
(*a*) Indo-European (*b*) Indo-Aryan
(*c*) Aryan (*d*) Semetic

40. At the National Film Festival Awards, for what category is 'Nargis Dutt Award' given?

(*a*) Acting
(*b*) National Integration
(*c*) Direction
(*d*) Patriotism

41. My father was a Hockey Olympian. My mother was a well-known Basketball player. Who am I?
(*a*) Sachin Tendulkar
(*b*) Leander Paes
(*c*) Prakash Padukone
(*d*) Vishwanathan Anand

42. One of the following groups has only adverbs. Which one is it?
(*a*) well, quite, then, fast
(*b*) quite, miserly, along, there
(*c*) therefore, beside, well, quiet
(*d*) well, besides, miserly, along

43. Select the correct meaning of the sentence given below, out of the four responses (*a*), (*b*), (*c*) and (*d*) which follow.
Mr. Ramesh is not so popular as some other employees.
Some employees are ------
(*a*) at least as popular as Mr. Ramesh
(*b*) more popular than Mr. Ramesh
(*c*) less popular than Mr. Ramesh
(*d*) not as popular as Mr. Ramesh

44. Dhanvantari's name is associated with:
(*a*) Sanskrit Grammar
(*b*) Sanskrit Poetry
(*c*) Indian Medicine
(*d*) Classical Music

45. Name the leader who is known as the 'Father of the Chinese Democracy'?
(*a*) Dr. Sun Yat Sen (*b*) Zhou En Lai
(*c*) Deng Xiaoping (*d*) Mao Zedong

46. The ancient silk route between India and China, started from Patna (then Pataliputra) in India and went up to the Chinese city:
(*a*) Chengdu (*b*) Xian
(*c*) Tianjin (*d*) Kunming

47. The social reformer who founded the Brahmo Samaj in 1828 at Kolkata is:
(*a*) S.P. Mukherjee
(*b*) Rabindranath Tagore
(*c*) Raja Ram Mohan Roy
(*d*) Vidya Sagar

48. Which of the following number cannot be noted in Roman numerals?
(*a*) Zero (*b*) Fifty
(*c*) Hundred (*d*) One thousand

In the following questions select the pair of words which has the same relationship as the Italic words.

49. *Numismatist : coins*
(*a*) Philatelist : stamps
(*b*) Jeweller : jewels
(*c*) Cartographer : maps
(*d*) Geneticist : chromosomes

50. *Balance : weigh*
(*a*) Aeroplane : height
(*b*) Radar : detection
(*c*) Satellite : rotation
(*d*) Television : picture

51. Choose from the 4 diagrams given below the one that illustrates the relationship between languages, French and German.

(*a*) 

(*b*) 

(*c*) 

(*d*) 

52. Match the words and their synonyms:
(A) Assign (1) Assume
(B) Fierce (2) Repair
(C) Presume (3) Allot
(D) Mend (4) Violent
(*a*) A3, B2, C1, D4
(*b*) A3, B4, C1, D2
(*c*) A4, B3, C1, D2
(*d*) A3, B4, C2, D1

53. Match the tools with their actions:
(A) Filter (1) Magnify
(B) Steering (2) Amplify
(C) Loudspeaker (3) Drive

(D) Microscope (4) Purify
(5) Observe

(*a*) A3, B4, C5, D2
(*b*) A2, B3, C4, D5
(*c*) A1, B2, C3, D4
(*d*) A4, B3, C2, D1

54. Match the products and raw materials:

(A) Shoes (1) Latex
(B) Rubber (2) Jute
(C) Sack (3) Pulp
(D) Paper (4) Leather
(5) Cotton

(*a*) A4, B3, C2, D5
(*b*) A4, B1, C2, D3
(*c*) A1, B4, C2, D3
(*d*) A1, B4, C5, D2

55. Match the authors with their books (Qs. 55 and 56):

(A) Otakkuzhal (1) Tara Shankar Bandopadhyaya
(B) Mati Matal (2) G. Shankar Kurup
(C) Gana Devata (3) Harivanshrai Bacchan
(D) Madhushala (4) Gopinath Mohanti

(*a*) A2, B4, C1, D3
(*b*) A2, B1, C4, D3
(*c*) A3, B1, C4, D2
(*d*) A1, B3, C4, D2

56. (A) A Suitable Boy (1) R.K. Laxman
(B) The Circle of Reason (2) R.K. Narayan
(C) Man Eaters of Malgudi (3) Vikram Seth
(D) English August (4) Upamanyu Chatterjee
(5) Amitav Ghosh

(*a*) A3, B2, C5, D4,
(*b*) A2, B3, C5, D4
(*c*) A3, B5, C2, D4
(*d*) A2, B5, C1, D3

57. Match the world leaders with their countries:

(A) Helmut Kohl (1) Indonesia
(B) Abdurrahman Wahid (2) Hellanic Republic
(C) Constantine Simitis (3) Germany
(D) Abdelaziz Baiteflika (4) Iran
(5) Algeria

(*a*) A3, B1, C4, D2
(*b*) A3, B1, C2, D5
(*c*) A1, B2, C3, D4
(*d*) A2, B4, C5, D1

58. Match the musicians and the instruments:

(A) Lalgudi G. Jayaraman (1) Santoor
(B) Shivkumar Sharma (2) Sarangi
(C) Amjad Ali Khan (3) Violin
(D) Chitti Babu (4) Sarod
(5) Veena

(*a*) A2, B1, C4, D5
(*b*) A5, B2, C1, D3
(*c*) A3, B2, C4, D5
(*d*) A3, B1, C4, D5

59. Match the following personalities with their specializations:

(A) Manjit Bawa (1) Dance
(B) Habib Tanvir (2) Sports
(C) Ramanathan Krishnan (3) Painting
(D) Yamini Krishnamurthi (4) Theatre

(*a*) A3, B4, C2, D1
(*b*) A2, B1, C3, D4
(*c*) A2, B3, C4, D1
(*d*) A1, B4, C2, D3

60. Match the beaches and the States:

(A) Calangute (1) Maharashtra
(B) Juhu (2) Tamil Nadu
(C) Marina (3) Kerala
(D) Kovalam (4) Goa

(*a*) A4, B1, C2, D3
(*b*) A3, B2, C1, D4
(*c*) A4, B1, C3, D2
(*d*) A3, B1, C2, D4

61. Match the following dishes with the places they are associated with:

(A) Dhokla (1) Gujarat
(B) Pongal (2) Punjab

(C) Sarson ka Saag (3) Kashmir
(D) Ghostaba (4) Tamil Nadu
(5) Andhra Pradesh

(*a*) A2, B3, C5, D4
(*b*) A3, B4, C1, D2
(*c*) A1, B4, C2, D3
(*d*) A5, B3, C4, D2

Read the following carefully and answer the questions (62 & 63) that are given below:

sabi	=	girl	mogi	=	woman
sabe	=	girls	koko	=	there
ar	=	is	aran	=	is not
ni	=	in	gaku ni	=	in the school
yane	=	room	osoi	=	fat

62. If

Sabe koko ni aar = Girls are there,
How will you say 'Women are in the room'

(*a*) Moge aar yane ni
(*b*) Mogi aar ni yane
(*c*) Mogi yane ni aar
(*d*) Moge yane ni aar

63. Girl is not fat:

(*a*) Sabi aran osoi (*b*) Sabi osoi aran
(*c*) Sabe osoi ar (*d*) Sabi ar osoi

64. In a code language 'mu kay cit' means 'very lucky person' and 'dis hu mu' means 'fortunate and lucky'. Which is the word for lucky in that language?

(*a*) mu (*b*) kay
(*c*) cit (*d*) hu

65. Which number can be placed at the sign of interrogation?

6	6	8
5	7	5
4	3	?
120	126	320

(*a*) 4 (*b*) 8
(*c*) 12 (*d*) 16

ANSWER

PART–A

1	2	3	4	5	6	7	8	9	10
(*a*)	(*d*)	(*b*)	(*d*)	(*d*)	(*a*)	(*a*)	(*c*)	(*d*)	(*b*)
11	**12**	**13**	**14**	**15**	**16**	**17**	**18**	**19**	**20**
(*d*)	(*c*)	(*d*)	(*d*)	(*c*)	(*b*)	(*d*)	(*a*)	(*b*)	(*d*)
21	**22**	**23**	**24**	**25**	**26**	**27**	**28**	**29**	**30**
(*a*)	(*c*)	(*a*)	(*c*)	(*a*)	(*a*)	(*c*)	(*b*)	(*b*)	(*b*)
31	**32**	**33**	**34**	**35**	**36**	**37**	**38**	**39**	**40**
(*d*)	(*b*)	(*a*)	(*b*)	(*b*)	(*d*)	(*d*)	(*a*)	(*b*)	(*b*)
41	**42**	**43**	**44**	**45**	**46**	**47**	**48**	**49**	**50**
(*d*)	(*b*)	(*c*)	(*a*)	(*c*)	(*d*)	(*c*)	(*a*)	(*a*)	(*b*)
51	**52**	**53**	**54**	**55**	**56**	**57**	**58**	**59**	**60**
(*b*)	(*c*)	(*a*)	(*b*)	(*b*)	(*a*)	(*a*)	(*a*)	(*b*)	(*a*)
61	**62**	**63**	**64**	**65**	**66**	**67**	**68**	**69**	**70**
(*b*)	(*d*)	(*d*)	(*a*)	(*c*)	(*a*)	(*d*)	(*c*)	(*a*)	(*b*)

PART–B

1	2	3	4	5	6	7	8	9	10
(*b*)	(*a*)	(*b*)	(*b*)	(*c*)	(*c*)	(*b*)	(*d*)	(*b*)	(*b*)

11	12	13	14	15	16	17	18	19	20
(*a*)	(*d*)	(*c*)	(*a*)	(*b*)	(*b*)	(*b*)	(*a*)	(*a*)	(*a*)
21	**22**	**23**	**24**	**25**	**26**	**27**	**28**	**29**	**30**
(*a*)	(*b*)	(*a*)	(*c*)	(*a*)	(*a*)	(*d*)	(*c*)	(*b*)	(*c*)
31	**32**	**33**	**34**	**35**	**36**	**37**	**38**	**39**	**40**
(*a*)	(*a*)	(*b*)	(*a*)	(*b*)	(*d*)	(*b*)	(*b*)	(*d*)	(*b*)
41	**42**	**43**	**44**	**45**	**46**	**47**	**48**	**49**	**50**
(*b*)	(*d*)	(*b*)	(*c*)	(*d*)	(*b*)	(*c*)	(*a*)	(*a*)	(*b*)
51	**52**	**53**	**54**	**55**	**56**	**57**	**58**	**59**	**60**
(*d*)	(*b*)	(*d*)	(*b*)	(*a*)	(*c*)	(*b*)	(*d*)	(*a*)	(*a*)
61	**62**	**63**	**64**	**65**					
(*c*)	(*d*)	(*b*)	(*a*)	(*b*)					

Previous Paper Solved

JNUEE–2000

PART–A

1. Which of the following is not the work of Kalidasa?
(*a*) Meghadoot (*b*) Raghuvansham
(*c*) Mudrarakshasa (*d*) Ritu Samhara

2. Which was the first European nation to establish its territorial rule in India?
(*a*) French (*b*) Portuguese
(*c*) English (*d*) Dutch

3. When did the Wimbledon Championship start?
(*a*) 1887 (*b*) 1895
(*c*) 1910 (*d*) 1915

4. Formal end to Soviet Union and creation of CIS took place in:
(*a*) 1991 (*b*) 1995
(*c*) 1990 (*d*) 1993

5. The 2 Germanys united to become Federal Republic of Germany in:
(*a*) 1990 (*b*) 1993
(*c*) 1989 (*d*) 1995

6. Panchatantra was written by:
(*a*) Kalidasa (*b*) Vishnu Sharma
(*c*) Tulsidas (*d*) Banabhatta

7. Which of the following is not correctly matched?
(*a*) Dharamsala—Buddhist Monastery
(*b*) Konark—Sun Temple
(*c*) Tanjore—Ancient Port
(*d*) Amaravati—Stupa

8. Our galaxy is:
(*a*) spiral (*b*) elliptical
(*c*) a paraboloid (*d*) None of these

9. The Court language of the Mughals was:
(*a*) Arabic (*b*) Hindi
(*c*) Persian (*d*) Urdu

10. The author of Humayun Nama was:
(*a*) Faizi
(*b*) Firdausi
(*c*) Gulbadan Begum
(*d*) Humayun

11. What happens at an abattoir?
(*a*) Animals are slaughtered
(*b*) Hindi film stuntmen receive first aid
(*c*) Hens lay artificial eggs
(*d*) People play videogames

12. In India, the green revolution referred to grains, the white revolution referred to milk, what did the pink revolution refer to?
(*a*) Tourism to the Pink City (Jaipur)
(*b*) Prawns
(*c*) Strawberries
(*d*) Holi played every year by Bollywood stars

13. World's two longest rivers are:
(*a*) Nile and Amazon
(*b*) Nile and Yangtze
(*c*) Amazon and Yangtze
(*d*) Amazon and Yellow river

14. Find the odd man out
(*a*) Copper (*b*) Tin
(*c*) Brass (*d*) Platinum

15. Which of the following persons does not belong to the 20th century?
(*a*) Einstein (*b*) Mahatma Gandhi
(*c*) Idi Amin (*d*) Pouchekine

16. Recycled plastic bags are harmful because:
(*a*) They are biodegradable
(*b*) They contaminate the stuff carried in them
(*c*) They are coloured with chemicals
(*d*) None of these

17. The religious order established by Mother Teresa is called:
(*a*) Sisters of Charity
(*b*) Mothers of Charity
(*c*) Missionaries of Charity
(*d*) Messengers of Love

18. Acid rain is caused by pollution of:
    (a) Carbon-dioxide and Nitrogen
    (b) Carbon-monoxide and Carbon-dioxide
    (c) Ozone and Carbon-dioxide
    (d) Nitrous oxide and Sulphur dioxide
19. Which country leads the world in the production of films, documentaries etc.?
    (a) U.S.A. (b) India
    (c) France (d) Japan
20. A.P.J. Kalam is a renowned:
    (a) Cardiologist (b) Astrophysicist
    (c) Mathematician (d) Atomic Scientist

Each of the following sentences has four parts : (a), (b), (c), (d). One of the parts may contain an error. Select that part:

21. (a) I write to/ (b) every of my/ (c) children once / (d) a week.
22. (a) Raman is / (b) the most ablest (c) clerk in our office/ (d) in Delhi.
23. The next pair of letters in the series AZ, CX, FU, ... is
    (a) JQ (b) KP
    (c) IR (d) IV
24. What is the correct sequence in which the following three movements were led by Mahatma Gandhi?
    (i) Champaran Movement.
    (ii) Non-Cooperation Movement.
    (iii) Dandi March.
    (a) (iii), (ii) and (i) (b) (ii), (i) and (iii)
    (c) (i), (iii) and (ii) (d) (i), (ii) and (iii)

Choose the odd one out:

25. (a) Turkey (b) Indonesia
    (c) Thailand (d) Germany
26. (a) Opthalmology (b) Nephrology
    (c) Pathology (d) Astrology
27. (a) Gasolene (b) Methane
    (c) Diesel (d) Paraffin

Pick the most effective word from the words given below to complete the meaning of the sentence:

28. The scheme for cleaning the Ganga was inaugurated with much purpose about a year ....
    (a) later (b) ago
    (c) after (d) already
29. As there is no bus service today, we .... walk to the station.
    (a) might have to (b) should
    (c) could (d) will have to
30. The leaders of the agitation say they are fighting .... the workers's rights.
    (a) with (b) against
    (c) for (d) to
31. .... eye witnesses, the news reporter gave a graphic description of how the riots broke.
    (a) Reporting (b) Observing
    (c) Seeing (d) Quoting
32. Plants flower at a certain time of the day because:
    (a) Flowering in plants is related to the length of the day.
    (b) Their biological clocks have fixed flowering alarms.
    (c) They attract insects which pollinate them
    (d) None of these
33. Which of the following is the oldest monument?
    (a) Qutab Minar (b) Ajanta Caves
    (c) Taj Mahal (d) Khajuraho
34. Which cricketing country will host the next World Cup?
    (a) Great Britain (b) Sri Lanka
    (c) Australia (d) South Africa
35. Find the odd man out:
    (a) Stereo (b) Transistor
    (c) Radio (d) Television

Choose the word nearest in meaning to the underlined word in the following sentences:

36. He is so <u>meticulous</u> that he can never do anything in a hurry.
    (a) slow (b) secretive
    (c) lazy (d) very careful
37. The meeting came to an <u>abrupt</u> ending.
    (a) uneven (b) sudden
    (c) unlawful (d) irritating
38. Our art treasures must be preserved for the <u>posterity.</u>

(a) prosperity (b) future generations
(c) wealthy (d) art lovers

Choose the word opposite in meaning to the underlined word:

39. He holds <u>extreme</u> views on education.
(a) moderate (b) timid
(c) casual (d) ordinary

40. His knowledge of the subject is quite <u>extensive.</u>
(a) small (b) limited
(c) little (d) ordinary

41. Find the odd man out:
(a) HGFE (b) NMLK
(c) RQPO (d) WYXZ

42. Which state in India has kept population most under control?
(a) West Bengal (b) Bihar
(c) Karnataka (d) Tamil Nadu

Choose the most appropriate alternative as the answer from among the words given below:

43. A car always has:
(a) Driver (b) Bonnet
(c) Bumper (d) Wheels

44. A pen always has:
(a) Tube (b) Ink
(c) Cap (d) Nib

45. What is Sunil Gavaskar's middle name?
(a) Mahesh (b) Manohar
(c) Mohan (d) Mrityunjay

46. Kamini ranks sixteenth from the top and fifteenth from the bottom in a certain examination. How many students are there in her class?
(a) 31 (b) 32
(c) 33 (d) None of these

47. Which of the following countries does not have rupee as its currency?
(a) Mauritius (b) Seychelles
(c) Maldives (d) Bangladesh

Out of the four words given after each sentence, select the most appropriate word to complete the meaning of the sentence:

48. The meeting was presided .... by the Prime Minister.
(a) up (b) over
(c) upon (d) on

49. An honest man sticks to his words .... a dishonest man violates it.
(a) whereas (b) since
(c) as (d) therefore

50. She has hit the nail on the ....
(a) face (b) hand
(c) head (d) leg

51. Rajputs belong to a .... race.
(a) marshal (b) martial
(c) military (d) militant

52. The art of choosing, preparing and eating good food is ....
(a) gourmet (b) gastronomy
(c) cookery (d) gluttony

53. Which animal has become extinct in India as a result of indiscriminate hunting?
(a) Lion (b) Elephant
(c) Nilgai (d) Cheetah

54. Speed of sound is maximum in:
(a) Water (b) Air
(c) Steel (d) Vacuum

[illegible] Who among the [illegible]owing wrote *A Treatise on Medicine* [illegible]nt India?
(a) Charaka (b) Nagarjuna
(c) Aryabhatta [illegible] Varahamihira

56. Which of the following pairs is not correctly matched?
(a) Babar—Babarnama
(b) Jehangir—Tuzuk-i-Jehangiri
(c) Harsha—Harshacharita
(d) Abul Fazl—Ain-e-Akbari

57. Ozone as such:
(a) protects earth from ultra-violet sun-rays
(b) is useful for green-house farming
(c) is a hazardous gas
(d) is an industrial pollutant

58. Which of the following is not correctly matched?
(a) Yangtze-Kiang—China
(b) Amazon—Uruguay
(c) Nile—Egypt
(d) Hudson—U.S.A.

59. An analgesic:
(*a*) inhibits the growth of malaria
(*b*) acts against virus
(*c*) relieves pain
(*d*) reduces inflammation

60. Kalakshetra, a famous institution for arts was founded by:
(*a*) Rukmini Devi Arundale
(*b*) Raj Kapoor
(*c*) Ravi Shankar
(*d*) Hema Malini

61. C.V. Raman got Nobel Prize for:
(*a*) Physics (*b*) Chemistry
(*c*) Medicine (*d*) Mathematics

62. Zen was originally the name of:
(*a*) a Buddhist sect
(*b*) an automobile company
(*c*) a flower
(*d*) a computer software

63. Iodization of salt helps to prevent:
(*a*) Diabetes (*b*) Tuberculosis
(*c*) Goitre (*d*) Anaemia

64. Next to Hindi, the language spoken by the largest number of people in India is:
(*a*) Urdu (*b*) Bangla
(*c*) Telugu (*d*) Tamil

65. Euro stands for:
(*a*) the name of a corporate giant in England
(*b*) a single European currency
(*c*) a sub-organization of the European Union
(*d*) Y2K soft in Europe

66. 'S' in ISRO stands for:
(*a*) Science (*b*) Satellite
(*c*) Space (*d*) Standards

67. Anil introduces Rohit as the son of the only brother of his father's wife. How is Rohit related to Anil?
(*a*) Cousin (*b*) Son
(*c*) Uncle (*d*) Brother

68. When an object is transferred from earth to the moon:
(*a*) its weight increases
(*b*) its mass increases
(*c*) its mass decreases
(*d*) its weight decreases and its mass remains constant

69. Pyramids have lasted so long because:
(*a*) structurally they are sound
(*b*) stone used is very hard
(*c*) erosion due to dry climate is less
(*d*) there is less damage by human beings

70. Bonsai is:
(*a*) the art of growing trees in small pots
(*b*) the art of embroidery on cloth
(*c*) the art of arranging flowers
(*d*) the art of making dolls

71. If the first and third letters in the word NECESSARY were interchanged, also the fourth and the sixth letters, the seventh and the ninth letters, which of the following would be the seventh letter from the left?
(*a*) A (*b*) Y
(*c*) R (*d*) E

72. How many lions are visible on India's National Emblem?
(*a*) 2 (*b*) 3
(*c*) 4 (*d*) 1

73. Which National Park in India is in the midst of a very large lake?
(*a*) Kaziranga Park in Asom
(*b*) Kanha National Park in Madhya Pradesh
(*c*) Madhupur National Park in Manipur
(*d*) Jim Corbett National Park in Uttar Pradesh

74. In the series POQ, SRT, VUW, ..., the blank space refers to:
(*a*) XYZ (*b*) XZY
(*c*) YXZ (*d*) YZX

In the following questions, there are four parts named P, Q, R, S between the first and the last sentences of the passage numbered 1 and 6 respectively. Select the proper sequence of these parts from the choices given below:

75. 1. Eye contact is
P. one of the things
Q. when we
R. we most search for
S. are dealing

6. with other people.
(*a*) PQRS (*b*) PRQS
(*c*) SPRQ (*d*) QRPS

76. 1. Freedom of the Press
P. does not include
Q. the self-confidence
R. the freedom to spread lies
S. and systematically to undermine
6. of the people.
(*a*) PQRS (*b*) PSRQ
(*c*) PRSQ (*d*) QPRS

77. 1. There was a boy named John
P. So the mother asked him to find work
Q. They were very poor
R. He lived with his mother
S. But John refused to work
6. At last she turned him out of the house.
(*a*) RSPQ (*b*) RQPS
(*c*) RQSP (*d*) QRSP

In the number series given in the questions below one term is missing. Choose the correct number that will continue the same pattern:

78. 3, 7; 15, 31; 63, ...
(*a*) 127 (*b*) 137
(*c*) 115 (*d*) 135

79. 10, 5; 13, 10; 16, 20; 19, ...
(*a*) 22 (*b*) 23
(*c*) 38 (*d*) 40

80. 5, 9; 6, 11; 7, ...
(*a*) 13 (*b*) 15
(*c*) 17 (*d*) 19

81. In the following list of words, select the one that comes second last when arranged in alphabetical order:
(*a*) Science (*b*) Scrutiny
(*c*) Scripture (*d*) Scramble

82. Six persons A, B, C, D, E, F are standing in a circle. B is between F and C; A is between E and D; F is to the left of D. Who is between A and F?
(*a*) B (*b*) C
(*c*) E (*d*) D

83. If orange is called butter, butter is called soap, soap is called ink, ink is called honey, honey is called orange, which of the following is used for washing clothes?
(*a*) Honey (*b*) Butter
(*c*) Orange (*d*) Ink

84. Among the following industries which one is the least tied down to sources of raw material?
(*a*) Sugar (*b*) Textiles
(*c*) Electronics (*d*) Paper

Match the following:

85. (*A*) Konkani (1) Bihar
(*B*) Maithili (2) Kashmir
(*C*) Malayalam (3) Kerala
(*D*) Dogri (4) Andhra Pradesh
(5) Goa
(*a*) A5, B1, C3, D2
(*b*) A4, B5, C3, D1
(*c*) A2, B3, C1, D4
(*d*) A1, B2, C3, D5

86. (*A*) Portugal (1) Victoria
(*B*) Indonesia (2) Kuala Lumpur
(*C*) Malaysia (3) DJkarta
(*D*) Hong Kong (4) Lisbon
(5) Athens
(*a*) A4, B2, C5, D1
(*b*) A2, B3, C1, D4
(*c*) A3, B4, C2, D5
(*d*) A4, B3, C2, D1

87. (A) First Indian woman to appear in Olympic final
(B) First Indian woman to conquer Everest
(C) Youngest Indian woman pilot
(D) First woman President of Indian National Congress
(1) Annie Besant
(2) Nivedita Bhasin
(3) Bachendri Pal
(4) P.T. Usha
(*a*) A3, B4, C1, D2
(*b*) A4, B3, C2, D1
(*c*) A2, B1, C3, D4
(*d*) A1, B2, C4, D3

88. (A) Thermometer (1) Earthquakes
(B) Ammeter (2) Length
(C) Seismograph (3) Current

(D) Scale (4) Temperature
(5) Speed

(*a*) A4, B2, C1, D3
(*b*) A3, B2, C1, D5
(*c*) A4, B3, C1, D2
(*d*) B4, C5, D2, A1

89.		
(*A*) Nagaland	(1) Shillong
(*B*) Meghalaya	(2) Itanagar
(*C*) Arunachal Pradesh	(3) Kohima
(*D*) Manipur	(4) Imphal
	(5) Aizwal

(*a*) A3, B1, C2, D4
(*b*) A2, B4, C3, D5
(*c*) A1, B3, C4, D2
(*d*) A4, B2, C5, D1

90.		
(*A*) Sea route to India	(1) Columbus
(*B*) Voyage round the world	(2) Vasco da Gama
(*C*) Discovery of America	(3) Captain Cook
(*D*) Discovery of Brazil	(4) Pedro Alvares Cabral
	(5) Magellan

(*a*) A2, B5, C1, D4
(*b*) A4, B3, C5, D2
(*c*) A3, B4, C2, D1
(*d*) A5, B1, C3, D4

91.		
(*A*) Bankim Chandra	(1) My Experiments with Truth
(*B*) Bal Gangadhar Tilak	(2) Godan
(*C*) Maulana Azad	(3) Ananda Math
(*D*) Mahatma Gandhi	(4) India Wins Freedom
	(5) Kesri

(*a*) A3, B4, C5, D2
(*b*) A1, B2, C3, D4
(*c*) A2, B5, C4, D1
(*d*) A3, B5, C4, D1

92.		
(A) Kathakali	(1) Rajasthan
(B) Bharatnatyam	(2) Punjab
(C) Kuchipudi	(3) Tamil Nadu
(D) Bhangra	(4) Andhra Pradesh
	(5) Kerala

(*a*) A5, B4, C3, D2
(*b*) A4, B2, C1, D5
(*c*) A1, B2, C3, D4
(*d*) A5, B3, C4, D2

93. Match the Awards with fields:

(A) Arjuna Award	(1) Scientific Research
(B) Borlaugh Award	(2) Sports
(C) Dada Saheb Phalke Award	(3) Literature
(D) Bhatnagar Award	(4) Film
(5) Agriculture Research

(*a*) A1, B2, C4, D5
(*b*) A2, B4, C3, D1
(*c*) A2, B5, C4, D1
(*d*) A3, B1, C5, D4

94. Match the following:

(A) Bihu	(1) West Bengal
(B) Onam	(2) Punjab
(C) Pongal	(3) Kerala
(D) Baisakhi	(4) Asom
(5) Tamil Nadu

(*a*) A4, B3, C5, D2
(*b*) A2, B4, C1, D5
(*c*) A5, B2, C4, D1
(*d*) A3, B5, C2, D4

95. Match the authors and the languages:

(A) Octavio Paz	(1) German
(B) Gunter Grass	(2) French
(C) Albert Camus	(3) Spanish
(D) Anton Chekov	(4) Italian
(5) Russian

(*a*) A1, B5, C3, D2
(*b*) A3, B1, C2, D5
(*c*) A2, B4, C1, D5
(*d*) B3, C5, A4, D1

96. Match the following countries with their currencies:

(A) Saudi Arabia	(1) Zloty
(B) Poland	(2) Rial
(C) Philippines	(3) Baht
(D) Thailand	(4) Peso
(5) Ringgit

(a) A3, B4, C2, D5
(b) A2, B1, C4, D3
(c) A1, B3, C2, D4
(d) A5, B2, C1, D3

97. Mount Everest is named after :
(a) Sir George Everest, a famous land surveyor
(b) Greek God of mountains, Zee Ever
(c) Edmund Hillary's childhood name 'Everest'
(d) Lord John Henry Everest, Viceroy of Nepal

98. Which of the following statements are true about the India born astronaut Kalpana Chawla? Select the correct answer from the choices given below:
(1) She was born in Karnal.
(2) She flew on board the Shuttle flight STS-87.
(3) She was trained at the Kennedy Space Centre.
(4) She did a space walk to get back the Spartan Satellite.
(a) 1 and 2 (b) 2 and 3
(c) 1, 2, and 3 (d) 1, 2 and 4

99. Examine the following statements:
(1) All children are inquisitive
(2) Some children are inquisitive
(3) No child is inquisitive
(4) Some children are not inquisitive
Among these statements, identify the two statements which cannot both be true simultaneously but can both be false:
(a) 1 and 3 (b) 1 and 4
(c) 2 and 3 (d) 3 and 4

100. Find the missing number:

8	3	4
7	6	1
2	4	?
13	5	4

(a) 1 (b) 2
(c) 3 (d) 4

101. The Indian satellite Aryabhatta was launched from:
(a) Soviet Union (b) U.S.A.
(c) Rajasthan (d) Mururoa

102. The only Portuguese speaking country in Latin America is:
(a) Peru (b) Bolivia
(c) Chili (d) Brazil

103. First Indian to make a speech in Hindi before the U.N. General Assembly:
(a) Lal Bahadur Shastri
(b) A.B. Vajpayee
(c) Lal Krishna Advani
(d) Morarji Desai

104. If Chi Kai Shi means Earth is round, Chu Chin Chi means Banana is sweet, Kul Shak Kai means Balls are round, then which letter code stands for Earth ?
(a) Shi (b) Chi
(c) Kai (d) Chu

105. In a certain code language 134 means Good and Tasty; 478 means See Good Pictures and 729 means Pictures are Faint, which of the following digits stands for See?
(a) 9 (b) 2
(c) 1 (d) None of these

106. Madhury wants to go to the University. She starts from her home which is in the East and comes to a crossing. The road to her left ends in a theatre; straight ahead is the hospital. In which direction is the University?
(a) East (b) West
(c) North (d) South

107. A meaningful word starting with A is made from the second, third, fourth, fifth and eighth letters of the word WATER MELON. Which is the middle letter of that word?
(a) R (b) T
(c) L (d) A

108. Rate of cooling and heating of land and sea is different because:
(i) Water has more specific heat.
(ii) Water is viscous.

(iii) Water is transparent.

(*a*) (i) and (ii) (*b*) (ii) and (iii)

(*c*) (i), (ii) and (iii) (*d*) (i) only

109. For which film did Satyajit Ray take a story from Premchand?

(*a*) Satranj Ke Khilari

(*b*) Nayika

(*c*) Pather Panchali

(*d*) Godan

110. Find the missing number and letter.

B	25	D	23	?	?
2	Y	4	W	6	U

(*a*) F and 21 (*b*) F and 24

(*c*) G and 21 (*d*) G and 24

111. How many such 7's are there in the following number sequence which are immediately followed by 4 but not immediately preceded by 8?

5 4 7 8 9 7 4 4 8 7 5 7 4 8 7 4 1 2 7 4 8 7 9 4

(*a*) 2 (*b*) 3

(*c*) 4 (*d*) 5

112. Bosnia, Serbia and Croatia are known as

(*a*) Balkan States

(*b*) Baltic States

(*c*) Trans-Siberian States

(*d*) Celtic States

113. How many triangles are there in the following figure?

(*a*) 8 (*b*) 10

(*c*) 12 (*d*) 14

114. The letters L, M, N, O, P, Q, R, S and T in their order are substituted by nine integers from 1 to 9 but not in that order. 4 is given to P; the difference between P and T is 5; the difference between N and T is 3. What is the number given to N?

(*a*) 7 (*b*) 5

(*c*) 4 (*d*) 6

115. In the sequence 462, 420, 380, X, 306; X stands for

(*a*) 352 (*b*) 342

(*c*) 332 (*d*) 322

116. Consider the series given below:

4/12/95; 1/1/96; 29/1/96; 26/2/96;

The next term of the series is:

(*a*) 24/3/96 (*b*) 25/3/96

(*c*) 26/3/96 (*d*) 27/3/96

117. An Exit Poll is:

(*a*) Conducted after the Elections

(*b*) The same as an Opinion Poll

(*c*) Conducted before people start voting

(*d*) None of these

118. Which is the only South American country entirely outside the Tropic of Cancer and the Tropic of Capricorn?

(*a*) Chile (*b*) Brazil

(*c*) Peru (*d*) Uruguay

In each of the following questions, select the proper sequence of the parts labelled P, Q, R, S so as to produce a correct sentence:

119. He said that those who

P. would miss a very interesting game

Q. to be played

R. between the two famous teams

S. would not accompany him

(*a*) QRPS (*b*) SPQR

(*c*) SQPR (*d*) SRPQ

120. After the speeches:

P. the prize given

Q. and

R. had been made

S. I left the auditorium

(*a*) SRQP (*b*) SPQR

(*c*) RSQP (*d*) RQPS

121. If you need help:

P. promptly and politely

Q. ask for attendants

R. to help our customers

S. who have instructions

(*a*) SRQP (*b*) QSRP

(*c*) QPSR (*d*) SQRP

In each of the questions below, select the correct answer from the choices given after the question:

122. If in a certain language SPACE is coded as TQBDF, how is PURSE coded in that language?

(*a*) QTSRF (*b*) OVQTD
(*c*) QVSTF (*d*) ESRUP

123. If NATURE is coded as MASUQE, how is FAMINE coded?

(*a*) FBMJND (*b*) FZMHND
(*c*) GANIOE (*d*) EALIME

124. If ENGLISH is coded as HESNIGL, how will JUPITER be coded?

(*a*) RJEUTPI (*b*) RJUEPTI
(*c*) RUJEPTI (*d*) RJETPIU

125. In a group of persons travelling in a bus, 6 persons can speak Tamil, 15 can speak Hindi, 6 can speak Gujarati. In that group none can speak any other language. If two persons in the group can speak two languages and one person can speak all the three languages, then how many persons are there in the group?

(*a*) 21 (*b*) 22
(*c*) 23 (*d*) 24

126. "Eco mark" is given to Indian products that are:

(*a*) Pure and unadulterated
(*b*) Rich in proteins
(*c*) Environment friendly
(*d*) Economically viable

127. What are the official languages of the UNO?

(*a*) English, French and Russian
(*b*) English, French, German and Russian
(*c*) English, French, Russian, Chinese and Hindi
(*d*) English, French, Chinese, Russian, Arabic and Spanish

128. Read the following statements to decide their sequence so as to make a meaningful passage. From the alternatives given, select the correct sequence:

A. Modern science has produced some good drugs for these ailments.
B. Heart ailments are very common, these days.
C. So I always prefer taking milk these days as it contains no fat.
D. But this can also be prevented by taking fatless food.
E. That is why people all this era as the age of heart troubles.

(*a*) BDECA (*b*) BEADC
(*c*) ABDEC (*d*) BDACE

129. Which of the following statements can be inferred from the statement that "Either John is stupid or John is lazy"?

1. John is lazy/therefore, John is not stupid.
2. John is not lazy/therefore, John is stupid.
3. John is not stupid/therefore, John is lazy.
4. John is stupid/therefore, John is not lazy.

Choose the correct answer from the choices given below:

(*a*) 1 and 2 (*b*) 2 and 3
(*c*) 3 and 4 (*d*) 1 and 4

130. Two persons start walking at a steady pace of 3 km/hour from a road intersection along two roads that make an angle of 60° with each other. What will be the shortest distance separating them at the end of 20 minutes?

(*a*) 3 km (*b*) 2 km
(*c*) 1.5 km (*d*) 1 km

131. The birth an[illegible]y of which Indian leader is celebrated [illegible]hers' Day" in India ?

(*a*) Dr. S. Radh[illegible]nan
(*b*) Dr. Zakir Hussain
(*c*) Shri Lal Bahadur Shastri
(*d*) Lala Lajpat Rai

132. Name the traveller who came to India by land and returned to China by sea :

(*a*) Hiuen Tsang (*b*) Yuan Chwang
(*c*) Fahien (*d*) Ibn-Batuta

133. Shahnama by Firdausi:

(*a*) is a satire on Sufism
(*b*) extols the pleasures of life
(*c*) narrates the History of Persia
(*d*) describes political developments in the Middle East

134. Pablo Picasso is a famous painter of:

(*a*) Spain (*b*) Italy
(*c*) Germany (*d*) Greece

135. Which of the following statements are correct? AIDS is transmitted

1. by sexual intercourse
2. by blood transfusion
3. by mosquitoes and other blood-sucking insects
4. across the placenta

(*a*) 1, 2 and 3 (*b*) 1, 2 and 4
(*c*) 1, 3 and 4 (*d*) 1 and 3

ANSWER

1	2	3	4	5	6	7	8	9	10
(*c*)	(*b*)	(*a*)	(*a*)*	(*a*)	(*b*)	(*c*)	(*a*)	(*c*)	(*d*)
11	**12**	**13**	**14**	**15**	**16**	**17**	**18**	**19**	**20**
(*a*)	(*b*)	(*a*)	(*c*)	(*d*)	(*b*)	(*c*)	(*d*)	(*b*)	(*b*)
21	**22**	**23**	**24**	**25**	**26**	**27**	**28**	**29**	**30**
(*b*)	(*d*)	(*a*)	(*d*)	(*d*)	(*d*)	(*b*)	(*b*)	(*b*)	(*c*)
31	**32**	**33**	**34**	**35**	**36**	**37**	**38**	**39**	**40**
(*d*)	(*b*)	(*b*)	(*d*)	(*d*)	(*d*)	(*b*)	(*b*)	(*a*)	(*c*)
41	**42**	**43**	**44**	**45**	**46**	**47**	**48**	**49**	**50**
(*d*)	(*c*)	(*d*)	(*d*)	(*b*)	(*d*)	(*d*)	(*b*)	(*a*)	(*c*)
51	**52**	**53**	**54**	**55**	**56**	**57**	**58**	**59**	**60**
(*c*)	(*c*)	(*d*)	(*c*)	(*a*)	(*c*)	(*a*)	(*b*)	(*c*)	(*a*)
61	**62**	**63**	**64**	**65**	**66**	**67**	**68**	**69**	**70**
(*a*)	(*a*)	(*c*)	(*b*)	(*b*)	(*c*)	(*a*)	(*d*)	(*a*)	(*a*)
71	**72**	**73**	**74**	**75**	**76**	**77**	**78**	**79**	**80**
(*b*)	(*b*)	(*a*)	(*c*)	(*b*)	(*c*)	(*b*)	(*a*)	(*d*)	(*a*)
81	**82**	**83**	**84**	**85**	**86**	**87**	**88**	**89**	**90**
(*c*)	(*d*)	(*d*)	(*c*)	(*a*)	(*d*)	(*b*)	(*c*)	(*a*)	(*a*)
91	**92**	**93**	**94**	**95**	**96**	**97**	**98**	**99**	**100**
(*d*)	(*d*)	(*c*)	(*a*)	(*b*)	(*b*)	(*a*)	(*c*)	(*a*)	(*a*)
101	**102**	**103**	**104**	**105**	**106**	**107**	**108**	**109**	**110**
(*a*)	(*d*)	(*b*)	(*a*)	(*d*)	(*c*)	(*b*)	(*d*)	(*a*)	(*a*)
111	**112**	**113**	**114**	**115**	**116**	**117**	**118**	**119**	**120**
(*b*)	(*a*)	(*c*)	(*d*)	(*b*)	(*b*)	(*a*)	(*d*)	(*b*)	(*d*)
121	**122**	**123**	**124**	**125**	**126**	**127**	**128**	**129**	**130**
(*b*)	(*c*)	(*d*)	(*a*)	(*d*)	(*c*)	(*d*)	(*b*)	(*d*)	(*d*)
131	**132**	**133**	**134**	**135**					
(*a*)	(*a*)	(*c*)	(*b*)	(*b*)					

*Wimbledon was actually started in 1877 for men and in 1884 for women.

CULTURE

CULTURE OF SPAIN

Spain is a largely mountainous country located in the Iberian Peninsula, consisting of various geographically diverse regions and known for its culturally diverse heritage, having been influenced by many nations and peoples throughout its history. The ***Spanish culture*** has roots in Celtiberian, Latin, Semitic , other European countries and Roman Catholicism; and an ongoing tension between the centralized state (dominated in recent centuries by Castile) and numerous regions and minority peoples. In addition, the history of the nation and its Mediterranean and Atlantic environment have played strong roles in shaping its culture.

LANGUAGES

While nearly everyone in Spain can speak Spanish (which is almost universally known in Spain as *castellano* — "Castilian" — rather than *español* — "Spanish") other languages figure prominently in many regions: Basque (*Euskara*) in the Basque Country and Navarre; Catalan in Catalonia, Balearic Islands and Valencia (where it is usually referred to as Valencian), and Galician in Galicia. Spanish is official throughout the country; the rest of these have co-official status in their respective regions.

In addition, there is strong and growing support for other regional languages, some of them in danger of extinction. These include Asturian in Asturias, Aragonese in Aragon, and Aranese, a dialect of Gascon spoken only in the tiny Val d'Aran, but enough of a live language to be used in the public schools there.

With the exception of Basque, which appears to be a language isolate, all of these are Romance languages.

CLIMATE AND GEOGRAPHY

Spain's **Geography** has helped shape the culture of the nation. Several parts of Spain have strong maritime traditions, including inland ports on rivers. As a result, seafood has always been a major part of Spanish Cuisine.

Spain **Climate** is varied from the warm, humid Mediterranean to the inner areas seasons of cold winters and hot summers. The generally warm and relatively dry summers have led to a culture in which a lot of life is lived outdoors. In Madrid, many of the most popular nightclubs move for several months in the summer to an outdoor terraza much farther from the city center than their indoor winter location, continuing in a way the older tradition of the *verbena (fair)*. In the Mediterranean areas, outdoor meals can be a nearly year-round phenomenon.

CONTEMPORARY CULTURE

As recently as the mid-20th-century, much of Spain (especially outside of the major cities) remained quite distinct from the rest of Europe. The idea of Spain as romantically backward, a country of landed aristocrats, illiterate peasants, colourful gypsies and bullfighters, and intense medieval-style religiosity, in great contrast to surrounding modern, industrialised, urbanised European countries was summed up in the saying "Africa begins in the Pyrenees", i.e. Spain was seen as more like North Africa than modern Europe. However, especially since the 1975 death of Francisco Franco, Spain has become increasingly modern, prosperous and European; Pritchett's rustic *posada* would be unimaginable today.

Franco's death ended a decades-long régime of censorship, leading to an explosive growth in a wide range of cultural areas. The subsequent recognition of strong cultural autonomy for the various Autonomous Communities reinvigorated many aspects of local culture that had been almost entirely repressed since the Spanish Civil War. Spain joined the European Union in 1986.

SPANISH POP CULTURE

- La movida : late 1970s and early 1980s youth subculture (with affinities to punk and new wave) with a focal point in Madrid.
- El botellón. The young people gather in the thousands in public parks for the sake of having fun, meeting people, being social and drinking alcohol.

DRESS STYLE

Historically, various regions of Spain had quite distinct regional dress. Today, most people in Spain dress in a manner comparable to most other contemporary Europeans, although some regional variations persist. Dress in Extremadura and in the smaller cities of Castile remains relatively austere, even on festive occasions, while Andaluz dress on festive occasions is elaborate and ostentatious. Barcelona is one of the most stylish cities in Europe, though more restrained and with a more determinedly timeless style than Paris or Milan.

CUSTOMS

The *siesta*—an hour-long mid-afternoon break from work—is generally in decline and the typical rhythm of the day in Spain is now similar to the European norm. Many shops and some museums (though relatively few other businesses) still split their hours into two distinct periods of opening with a two or three hour break in the middle; a *paseo* (stroll) in the early evening remains a common custom in many smaller cities and to some extent even in the larger ones.

Dinner here starts the latest in Europe, typically about 9 p.m. (in the east) or 10 p.m. (in the west); consequently night-life starts later, with many dance clubs (even in relatively small cities) opening at midnight and staying open until dawn; during summer in Madrid, there is nothing unusual about a live musical performance being scheduled for one or two o'clock in the morning. This rhythm has developed in accordance with the hours of the sun which rises and sets one or two hours later than in the rest of Europe. The routine perhaps lessens outdoor human activity in the period of the day when temperatures are hottest.

ARCHITECTURE

Because many of its historical buildings have remained intact today, several architectural structures in Spain, and even portions of cities, have been designated World Heritage sites.

Spain was part of the Roman Empire and many areas of Spain retain significant Roman architectural remnants. The Roman aqueduct at Segovia is still in use as of 2004; Mérida, now the Extremaduran capital but once the capital of the Roman province of Lusitania, retains over 5 miles of its Roman aqueduct, Roman bridge over the River Guadiana , an arch of Trajan , and significant remnants of a Roman forum, amphitheatre, and a temple popularly accounted to have been dedicated to Diana (goddess). Another Roman bridge crosses the Tagus River at Alcántara. Lesser Roman ruins can be found in the heart of Barcelona.

Spain is home to several fine examples of medieval architecture; outside of the areas that were under Muslim control, these are primarily in the Romanesque and Gothic styles. Spain is also home to several examples of Cathedral architecture. The Drassanes in Barcelona, originally a facility for building ships and now a maritime museum, is the largest and most complete medieval secular structure in the world.

The architecture in southern Spain reflects its Moorish history. The Alhambra is probably the most famous example, showing a mixture of Islamic architecture and European influences. Significant Moorish buildings survive as far north as Zaragoza. Throughout Spain, many former mosque and synagogue buildings survive as Christian churches or, occasionally, converted to other uses. Good examples of this are the Church of Corpus Christi in Segovia and the Church of Santa María la Blanca in Toledo, both former synagogues, and the Mezquita (Spanish for "mosque"), a 10th century mosque in Córdoba, reconsecrated in 1236 as a Christian Church. The influence of Moorish architecture did not end with the *reconquista*: there were many prominent *mudéjar* architects, Muslims living and working in Christian Spain.

When the city of Barcelona was allowed to expand beyond its historic limits in the late 19th century, the resulting *Eixample* ("extension"), larger than the old city, became the site of a burst of architectural energy. Most famous among the architects represented there is Antoni Gaudí, whose works in Barcelona and elsewhere in Catalonia, mixing traditional architectural styles with the new, were a precursor to modern architecture. Perhaps the most famous example of his work is the (as of 2004) still-unfinished La Sagrada Família, the largest building in the *Eixample*.

Other notable Catalan architects of that period include Lluís Domènech i Montaner and Josep Puig i Cadafalch. One block on the Passeig de Gràcia contains buildings by each of the three; the clashing styles led to the nickname *"manzana de la discordia"*, literally the "block of discord", but also a pun: *"manzana"* can also mean "apple", hence "apple of discord".

Alejandro de la Sota was one of the early proponents of modern architecture in Spain; the first steel framed building in Madrid is his 1961 Maravillas College Gymnasium.

Santiago Calatrava began to make his name from the 1980s and works internationally. His work is typified by a great understanding of engineering as well as nature. A notable building of his is the City of Arts & Sciences in Valencia. Enric Miralles possessed a highly esoteric style which has been compared to fellow Catalan Gaudí, and was beginning to be successful internationally, but died in 2000 , at only 45 years old. His largest work, the Scottish Parliament Building was completed posthumously. The Guggenheim Museum Bilbao may be the most famous example of contemporary architecture in Spain, although the architect, Frank Gehry , is a citizen of United States and of Canadian descent.

The dry weather of Spain resulted in the importance of water fountains in Spanish urban design. In addition, ceramics figure prominently in architecture throughout Spain, especially in the tile roofs (though slate was traditional near the Atlantic coast) and the use of decorative tiles known as *azulejos*.

DANCE

Contradanza The Cuban ***contradanza*** (Spanish for Contra dance, also called *contradanza criolla, danza* or *danza criolla*) was a popular dance music genre of the 19th century.

Flamenco **Flamenco** is a Spanish musical genre with strong, rhythmic undertones and is often accompanied with a similarly impassioned style of dance characterized by its powerful yet graceful execution, as well as its intricate hand and footwork. Flamenco embodies a complex musical and cultural tradition. Although considered part of the culture of Spain in general, flamenco actually originates from one region: Andalusia. However, other areas, mainly Extremadura and Murcia, have contributed to the development of several flamenco musical forms, and a great number of renowned flamenco artists have been born in other territories of the state. The roots of flamenco are not precisely known, but it is generally acknowledged that flamenco grew out of the unique interplay of native Andalusian , Islamic , Sephardic , and Gypsy cultures that existed in Andalusia prior to and after the Reconquest. Latin American and especially Cuban influences have also been important in shaping several flamenco musical forms.

Once the seeds of flamenco were planted in Andalusia, it grew as a separate subculture, first centered in the provinces of Seville , Cádiz and part of Málaga —the area known as *Baja Andalucía* (Lower Andalusia)—but soon spreading to the rest of Andalusia, incorporating and transforming local folk music forms. As the popularity of flamenco extended to other areas, other local Spanish musical traditions (i.e. the Castilian traditional music) would also influence, and be influenced by, the traditional flamenco styles.

Pasodoble

Pasodoble (literal meaning in Spanish: *double-step*) is a typical Spanish march-like musical style as well as the corresponding dance style danced by a couple. It is the type of music typically played in bullfights during the bullfighters' entrance to the ring (*paseo*) or during the passes (*faena*) just before the kill. It corresponds to the dance (traditional and ballroom).

Famous bullfighters have been honored with pasodoble tunes named after them. Others are inspired in patriotic motives or local characters.

FAMOUS PASODOBLES

- *Amparito Roca*
- *El Beso*
- *El Gato Montés* ("Wild Cat") from the opera with the same name
- *España Cañí* ("Gipsy Spain")
- *Islas Canarias* named after Canary Islands.
- *Manolete*, named after Manolete.
- *Morena*
- *Paquito el Chocolatero*. The tune has a dance of its own.
- *Que Viva España*
- *Suspiros de España*

Sardana

The **sardana** (Catalan plural *sardanes)* is a type of circle dance typical of Catalonia.

There are two main types, the original *sardana curta* (short sardana) style and the more modern *sardana llarga* (long sardana), which is more popular. Other more unusual sardanas are the *sardana de lluïment* and the *sardana revessa.*

As a non-performance dance, sardana does not require special fitness. Moreover, the circle can be opened to a highly variable number of dancers.

Music for the sardana (called sardana, as well) is played by a cobla, a wind band with double bass consisting of 12 instruments played by 11 musicians. Four of these instruments (tenora , tible , flabiol and tamborí) are typical Catalan instruments; the others (trumpet, trombone, fiscorn and double bass) are more conventional. In Spanish and French Catalonia about one hundred thirty coblas are active, most of which are amateur orchestras. Outside Catalonia there is only one cobla: Cobla La Principal d'Amsterdam.

A lot of sardanas have lyric versions, but mostly instrumental versions are used for dancing.

FESTIVALS

Many of the traditional festivals in Spain revolve around Catholic saints and historical events.

Fallas

Fallas (in Spanish) or **Falles** (in Valencian) are a Valencian tradition which celebrates Saint Joseph's Day (19 March) in Valencia, Spain. The term Fallas refers to both the celebration and the monuments created during the celebration.

Each neighbourhood of the city has an organized group of people, the *Casal faller*, that works all year long holding fundraising parties and dinners, usually featuring the famous speciality paella. Each *casal faller* produces a construction known as a *falla* which is eventually burnt. A *casal faller* is also known as a *comisión fallera.*

Bonfires of Saint John

Bonfires of Saint John (Spanish: *Hogueras de San Juan*) is a popular festival celebrated in June, from 19th to 24th in Spain. The festival is celebrated throughout many cities and towns, however the largest is in Alicante, where it is considered the most important festival in the city.

For this festival, people gather together and create large bonfires from any kind of wood, such as old furniture, often sharing hot chocolate as well while teens and children jump over the fires.

Carnival

Carnival (also called **Carnaval** in French, Portuguese and Spanish) is a festival season. It occurs immediately before Lent; the main events are usually during February or March. It typically involves a public celebration or parade combining some elements of a circus and public street party. People often dress up or masquerade during the celebrations.

Carnival is mostly associated with Roman Catholic and, to a lesser extent, Eastern Orthodox Christians; Protestant areas usually do not have carnival celebrations or have modified traditions, like the Danish Carnival. The world's largest carnival celebration is held in Brazil but many countries worldwide have large, popular celebrations.

Carnival of Cádiz

The **Carnival of Cádiz** is one of the best known carnivals in the world.

The city of Cádiz is often considered to have the funniest people in Spain. The whole city lives the carnival for more than two weeks and the presence of this fiesta is almost constant in the city throughout the year with the rehearsals, representations and contests. The feeling of this carnival is the sharp criticism, the funny play on words and the imagination in the customes, more than the glamorous dressings. It is traditional to paint the face with lipstick as a humble substitute of a mask. It is easy to get involved in the fiesta even not knowing the language and to live the Carnival. On Saturday everyone wears a costume, which many times is related to the most polemical news. But the Carnival of Cádiz is famous mainly for the satirical groups called chirigotas , their music and their lyrics.

Mystery Play of Elx

The **Elx Mystery Play** is a liturgical drama dating from the Middle Ages, which is enacted and celebrated in the Basilica de Santa María in the city of Elche on the 14 and 15th of August of each year. In 2001, UNESCO declared it one of the Masterpieces of the Oral and Intangible Heritage of Humanity. It commemorates the Assumption of Mary.

Romeria

A **Romería** is a Spanish religious pilgrimage. The word "Romería" comes from "romero", meaning those travelling towards Rome. It is a Catholic celebration that consists of a trip or peregrination (in cars, floats, to horse or on foot) that ends at a sanctuary or hermitage. It is not necessarily always a trip, but in some cases a celebration that lasts all day long.

Tomatina

La Tomatina is a food fight festival held on a Wednesday towards the end of August each year in the town of Buñol in the Valencia region of Spain. Tens of thousands of participants come from all over the world to fight in a brutal battle where more than one hundred metric tonnes of over-ripe tomatoes are thrown in the streets.

The week-long festival features music, parades, dancing, and fireworks. On the night before the tomato fight, participants of the festival compete in a paella cooking contest.

The festival is in honor of the town's patron saints, Luis Bertràn and the *Mare de Déu dels Desemparats* (Mother of God of the Defenseless), a title of the Virgin Mary.

The tomato fight has been a strong tradition in Buñol since 1944 or 1945. No one is completely certain how this event originated.

Moros y Cristianos

Moros y Cristianos (in Spanish) or ***Moros i Cristians*** (in Valencian), literally means "Moors and Christians", and is a set of festival activities which are celebrated in many towns and cities of Spain , principally in the Valencian Community, to commemorate the battles, combats and fights between Muslims and Christians during the period known as *Reconquista* (from the 8th century through the 15th century).

The festivals represent the capture of the city by the Moors and the subsequent Christian reconquest. The people that take part in the festival are usually enlisted in *filaes* or *comparsas* (companies that represent the Christian or Moor legions), and for several days, they parade with bombastic costumes loosely inspired by Medieval fashion. Christians wear fur, metallic helmets, and armor, fire loud arquebuses, and ride horses. In contrast, Moors wear ancient Arab costumes, carry scimitars , and ride real camels or elephants. The festival develops among shots of gunpowder , medieval music, and fireworks, and ends with the Christians winning a simulated battle around a castle.

The most well-known *Moros y Cristianos* festival takes place in Alcoi from 22 to 24 April, around the Feast Day of Saint George (Catalan: *Sant Jordi* ; Spanish: *San Jorge*). According to legend, after James I of Aragon reconquered the city of Alcoi, the Moors, in turn, tried to recover it shortly after. But, when they were about to start the battle again, Saint George miraculously appeared to the Moors, who were frightened away.

Other remarkable *Moros y Cristianos* festivals are celebrated in the towns of La Vila Joiosa (with its *desembarc*), Villena, Biar, Cocentaina, Crevillent, El Campello, Elda, Muro d'Alcoi, Ontinyent, Oriola, Petrer and some districts of Alicante city. The most ancient festival is celebrated in Caudete (Albacete), dated from 1588.

Semana Santa

Holy Week (Latin: *Hebdomada Sancta*) in Christianity is the last week before Easter. It includes the religious holidays of Palm Sunday (Passion Sunday), Maundy Thursday (Holy Thursday) and Good Friday, and lasts from Palm Sunday (or in the East, Lazarus Saturday) until but not including Easter Sunday, as Easter Sunday is the first day of the new season of The Great Fifty Days. It commemorates the last week of the earthly life of Jesus Christ culminating in his crucifixion on Good Friday and his resurrection on Easter Sunday.

FOOD AND DRINK

Spanish cuisine is made of very different kinds of dishes due to the differences in geography, culture and climate. It is heavily influenced by the variety of seafood available from the waters that surround the country. Some foods typically associated with Spain include *arroz con leche*, (rice with milk), which is served as a dessert, and *paella*, which is made with yellow rice typically garnished with a variety of meats or seafood.

As Spain has had a history with many different cultural influences, the richness and variety of its cuisine is overwhelming, but all these ingredients have made up a unique cuisine with thousands of recipes and flavours. Much influence on Spanish cuisine has come from the Jewish and Moorish traditions. The Moors were a strong influence in Spain for many centuries and their food is still eaten in Spain today. As a counterpoint, public consumption of pork (forbidden for Jews and Muslims) was a religious affirmation of being an Old Christian and pork is still enjoyed by many Spaniards.

- Chorizo , a paprika pork sausage.
- Cocido , a stew with beans and meat.
- Cuisine of Cantabria
- Fabada Asturiana , beans with chorizo and lard.
- Fideuà , a noodle paella
- Gazpacho , a cold soup or a liquid salad.
- Jamón , cured ham
- Paella, a rice dish
- Sangría , a wine cooler
- Tortilla de patatas , potato omelette.

MUSIC

Spain's musical output includes a long history of innovation in Western and Andalusian classical music, as well as a domestic popular music industry, and diverse styles of folk music. Modern Spain has a number of performers in the fields of rock and roll, heavy metal, punk rock and hip hop, electronic music is also common between spaniards and djs such as dj marta or alex trackone are very well known in the spanish parties.

The best-known variety of Spanish folk music is probably flamenco, a diverse genre created by Andalusian Roma. Flamenco has been known since at least the 1770s, and has been through several cycles of dwindling popularity and rebirth. The style has produced many of the most famous Spanish musicians, including singer Camarón de la Isla and guitarist Carlos Montoya.

Outside of flamenco, regional Spanish folk music includes the distinct Basque trikitixa and accordion music, Galician and Asturian gaita (bagpipe) and Aragonese jota. Though some folk traditions have died out or are moribund, some retain great popularity and have been modernized and adapted to new instruments, styles and formats. These include the popular Celtic music of Galicia, the singer-songwriter tradition of nova canço and New Flamenco.

The first distinctly modern popular music of Spain began to appear in about 1959. Soon, Ye-Yé dominated the Spanish charts, followed by the import of American and British rock, French singers and other pop stars.

Spanish music today mainly consists of pop/rock/punk bands such as El Canto Del Loco , La Oreja De Van Gogh , Edurne , and Amaral. This new type of music has dominated the charts in Spain today, and many believe it will continue to do so for some time.

FILM

While mid-century Spanish directors such as Luis Buñuel worked mainly in exile, film has prospered in Spain since the reestablishment of constitutionalism. Among the leading late 20th- and early 21st-century Spanish film directors are:

- **Pedro Almodóvar** , Double Oscar Winner; 1999 " Foreign language film" (Todo sobre mi madre) and 2002 " Original Screenplay" (Hable con ella)
- **Alejandro Amenábar** , 2004 Oscar winner for "Foreign language film" (Mar Adentro).

- **Pablo Berger**
- **Manuel Martin Cuenca**
- **Mateo Gil** , who works with **Amenábar** on most of his films.
- **Álex de la Iglesia**
- **Julio Medem** , director of Lucía y el sexo
- **Ventura Pons** , directs mainly in Catalan
- **Carlos Saura** , whose five decades as a director include numerous films centered on dance (especially flamenco, as well as the official film of the 1992 Olympics in Barcelona.

Spain also has some rather notable " B movie" directors, such as:

- **Santiago Segura** , director of the Torrente Trilogy.

SPORT

Sport in Spain is dominated by **Fútbol** (Football), with La Liga, the country's professional league, drawing large attendances; Real Madrid and FC Barcelona are traditionally the most successful teams.

In **Tennis**, Rafael Nadal leading the line. **Cycle racing** is a major sport, hosting the 3rd biggest stage race in UCI ProTour, the Vuelta a España. Navarran Miguel Indurain is one of only five Spanish men to win the famous Tour de France. Recently, F1 Champion Fernando Alonso has spurred a rise in Formula One popularity in Spain.

Bullfighting is an icon for Spain, and despite slight recent declines in attendance it is still alive and well across the country, though is threatened by Animal Rights organizations. Another traditional Spanish sport is **Pelota**. Jai-alai, related to Pelota, is also a very popular sport which its first written references can be traced to XIII century in France. This sport is traditionally basque. Spain has also achieved degrees of success in **middle distance** running, **Golf**, **Basketball** and **Handball**, amongst others.

Bullfighting or **tauromachy** (Spanish ***toreo***, ***corrida de toros*** or ***tauromaquia***; Portuguese ***tourada***, ***corrida de touros*** or ***tauromaquia***) is a traditional spectacle of Spain, Portugal, some cities in southern France, and several Latin American countries.. Its origin is unknown, though it has been suggested that it was originally brought to Spain by the Visigoths A link to the old culture of Crete has also been proposed.

The tradition, as it is practiced today, involves professional performers (in Spanish *toreros* or *matadores*, in Portuguese *toureiros*) who execute various formal moves with the goal of appearing graceful and confident, while masterful over the bull itself. Such maneuvers are performed at close range, and conclude with the death the bull by a well-placed sword thrust as the finale. In Portugal the finale consists of a tradition called the *pega*, where men (Forcados) are dressed in a traditional costume of damask or velvet, with long knit hats as worn by the famous Ribatejo *campinos* (bull headers).

Bullfighting generates heated controversy in many areas of the world, including Spain, where the "classic" bullfighting was born. Supporters of bullfighting argue that it is a culturally important tradition, while animal rights groups argue that it is a blood sport because of the suffering of the bull and horses during the bullfight.

CULTURE OF FRANCE

The **culture of France** and of the French has been shaped by its geography, by profound historical events, and by foreign and internal forces and groups. France, and in particular Paris, has played an important role as a center of high culture and of decorative arts since the seventeenth century, first in Europe, and from the nineteenth century on, world wide. From the late nineteenth century, France has also played an important role in modern art , cinema , fashion and cuisine. The importance of French culture has waned and waxed over the centuries, depending on its economic, political and military importance. French culture today is marked both by great regional and socioeconomic differences and by strong unifying tendencies.

In recent years, to fight the loss of regional diversity, many in France have promoted forms of multiculturalism and encouraged cultural enclaves (*communautarisme*), including reforms on the preservation of regional languages and the decentralization of certain government functions, but French multiculturalism has had a harder time of accepting, or of integrating into the collective identity, the large non-Christian and immigrant communities and groups that have come to France since the 1960s.

LANGUAGE

French culture is profoundly allied with the French language. The artful use of the mother tongue, and its defense against perceived decline or corruption by foreign terms, is a major preoccupation for some people and entities.

The Académie française sets an official standard of language purity; however, this standard, which is not mandatory, is even occasionally ignored by the government itself: for instance, the left-wing government of Lionel Jospin pushed for the feminization of the names of some functions (*madame la ministre*) while the *Académie* pushed for some more traditional *madame le ministre*.

France counts many regional languages, some of them being very different from standard French such as Breton and Alsatian. Some regional languages are Romance, like French, such as Provençal. The Basque language is completely unrelated to French and, indeed, to any other language in the world; its area straddles the border between the south west of France and the north of Spain. Many of those languages have enthusiastic advocates; however, the real importance of local languages remains subject to debate.

RELIGION

France is a secular country where freedom of thought and of religion is preserved, by virtue of the 1789 Declaration of the Rights of Man and of the Citizen. The Republic is based on the principle of *laïcité*, that is of freedom of religion (including of agnosticism and atheism) enforced by the Jules Ferry laws and the 1905 law on the separation of the State and the Church, enacted at the beginning of the Third Republic (1871-1940). A January 2007 poll found that 51% of the French population describe themselves as Catholics — and only half of those said they believed in God—, 31% as atheists, 4% as Muslims, 3% as Protestants and 1% as Jews.

CATHOLICISM

Roman Catholicism is no longer considered the state religion, as it was before the 1789 Revolution and throughout the various, non-republican regimes of the 19th century (the Restauration, the July Monarchy and the Second Empire). At the beginning of the 20th century, France was a largely rural country with conservative Catholic mores, but in the hundred years since then, the countryside has become depopulated, and the population has largely become de-Christianised. A December 2006 poll by Harris Interactive, published in *The Financial Times*, found that 32% of the French population described themselves as agnostic , a further 32% as atheist and only 27% believed in any type of God or supreme being.

ISLAM

After Catholicism, Islam is the second largest faith in France today, and the country has the largest Muslim population (in percentage) of any Western European country. This is a result of immigration and permanent family settlement in France, from the 1960s on, of groups from, principally, North Africa (Morocco , Algeria , Tunisia) and, to a lesser extent, other areas such as Turkey and West Africa. [13] While it is prohibited in France for the government census to collect data on religious beliefs, estimates and polls place the percentage of Muslims at between 4% and 7%.

JUDAISM

The current Jewish community in France numbers around 600,000, according to the World Jewish Congress and 500,000 according to the Appel Unifié Juif de France, and is found mainly in the metropolitan areas of Paris, Marseille and Strasbourg.

The history of the Jews of France dates back over 2,000 years. In the early Middle Ages, France was a center of Jewish learning, but persecution increased as the Middle Ages wore on. France was the first country in Europe to emancipate its Jewish population during the French Revolution , but, despite legal equality anti-Semitism remained an issue, as illustrated in the Dreyfus affair of the late 19th century. Despite the death of a quarter of all French Jews during the Holocaust, France currently has the largest Jewish population in Europe.

French Jews are mostly Sephardic and span a range of religious affiliations, from the ultra-Orthodox Haredi communities to the large segment of Jews who are entirely secular.

BUDDHISM

Buddhism is widely reported to be the fourth largest religion in France, after Christianity, Islam, and Judaism. France has over two hundred Buddhist meditation centers, including about twenty sizable retreat centers in rural areas. The Buddhist population mainly consists of Chinese and Vietnamese immigrants, with a substantial minority of native French converts and "sympathizers." The rising popularity of Buddhism in France has been the subject of considerable discussion in the French media and academy in recent years.

Cults and new religious movements

France created in 2006 the first French parliamentary commission on cult activities which led to a report registering a number of cults considered as dangerous. Supporters of such movements have criticized the report on the grounds of the respect of religious freedom. Proponents of the measure contend that only dangerous cults have been listed as such, and state secularism insures religious freedom in France.

Other specific communities

Romani: France has an estimated 280,000-340,000 Roma, generally known as *Gitans*, *Tsiganes*, *Romanichels* (slightly pejorative), *Bohémiens*, or *Gens du voyage* ("travellers"). Roma communities are principally found in the south of France.

Other subcultures

Paris has traditionally been associated with alternative, artistic or intellectual subcultures, many of which involved foreigners. Such subcultures include the " Bohemians " of the Belle époque , the Impressionists (Picasso, Toulouse Lautrec), the Dadists, Surrealism, the " Lost Generation" (Hemingway, Gertrude Stein) and the post-war "intellectuals" associated with Montparnasse (Jean-Paul Sartre, Simone de Beauvoir).

Social class

Despite the egalitarian aspects of French society, French culture remains marked by social-economic class and by many class distinctions.

FOOD AND LIFESTYLE

Food and alcohol

Traditional French culture places a high priority on the enjoyment of food. French cuisine was codified in the 20th century by Georges Auguste Escoffier to become the modern version of *haute cuisine*. Escoffier's major work, however, left out much of the regional character to be found in the provinces of France. Gastro-tourism and the *Guide Michelin* helped to bring people to the countryside during the 20th century and beyond, to sample this rich *bourgeois* and peasant cuisine of France. Basque cuisine has also been a great influence over the cuisine in the southwest of France.

Ingredients and dishes vary by region (see regional cuisine). There are many significant regional dishes that have become both national and regional. Many dishes that were once regional, however, have proliferated in different variations across the country in the present day. Cheese (see list of French cheeses) and wine (see French wine) are also a major part of the cuisine, playing different roles both regionally and nationally with their many variations and *Appellation d'origine contrôlée* (AOC) (regulated appellation) laws (lentils from Le Puy-en-Velay also have an AOC status). Other French products of special note include: Charolais cattle.

The French typically eat only a simple breakfast ("petit déjeuner") (of, say, coffee or tea, served traditionally in a large handleless "bol" and bread, breakfast pastries (croissants), or yogurt). Lunch ("déjeuner") and dinner ("dîner") are the main meals of the day. Formal four course meals consist of a starter course ("entrée"), a main course ("plat principal") followed by a salad course, and finally a cheese and/or a desert course. While French cuisine is often associated with rich deserts, in most homes desert consists of only a fruit or yogurt.

Food shopping in France was formerly done almost daily in small local shops and markets, but the arrival of the supermarket and the even larger "hypermarchés" (large-surface distributors) in France have disrupted this tradition. With depopulation of the countryside, many towns have been forced to close shops and markets.

Rates of obesity and heart disease in France have traditionally been lower than in other north-western European countries. This is sometimes called the " French paradox.

In France, cutlery is used in the continental manner (with the fork in the left hand, prongs facing down and the knife in the right hand). French etiquette prohibits the placing of hands below the table.

France is one of the oldest wine- producing regions of Europe. France now produces the most wine by value in the world (although Italy rivals it by volume and Spain has more land under cultivation for wine grapes). Bordeaux wine, Bourgogne wine and Champagne are important agricultural products.

SPORTS AND HOBBIES

The French "national" sport, is football (soccer), colloquially called 'le foot'. The most-watched sports in France are football (soccer), rugby union, basketball, cycling, sailing and tennis. France is notable for holding the football World Cup in 1998, for holding the annual cycling race Tour de France, and the tennis Grand Slam tournament Roland Garros, or the French Open. Sport is encouraged in school, and local sports clubs receive financial support from the local governments. While football (soccer) is definitely the most popular, rugby union and rugby league takes dominance in the southwest, especially around the city of Toulouse (see Rugby union in France and Rugby league in France).

The modern Olympics were invented in France, in 1894.

Professional sailing in France is centred on singlehanded/shorthanded ocean racing with the pinnacle of this branch of the sport being the Vendee Globe singlehanded around the world race which starts every 4 years from the French Atlantic coast. Other significant events include the Solitaire du Figaro, Mini Transat 6.50, Tour de France a Voile and Route de Rhum transatlantic race. France has been a regular competitor in the Americas Cup since the 1970s.

Other important sports

- Grand Prix Racing (Formula 1) - invented in France in 1946
- Pétanque - the international federation is recognized by the IOC.
- Fencing - fencing leads the list of sports for which gold medals were won for France at summer Olympics (see France at the Olympics).
- Parkour - developed in France, parkour (*"art du déplacement"*) is a physical activity that resembles self-defense or martial arts.
- Babyfoot (table football) - a very popular pastime in bars and in homes in France, and the French are the predominant winners of worldwide table football competitions.

Like other cultural areas in France, sport is overseen by a government ministry, the Minister of Youth Affairs and Sports (France) which is in charge of national and public sport associations, youth affairs, public sports centers and national stadia (like the Stade de France).

FASHION

With Milan and New York, Paris is sometimes called the "fashion capital of the world". The association of France with fashion (French : *la mode*) dates largely to the reign of Louis XIV when the luxury goods industries in France came increasingly under royal control and the French royal court became, arguably, the arbiter of taste and style in Europe.

France renewed its dominance of the high fashion (French: *couture or haute couture*) industry in the years 1860-1960 through the establishing of the great couturier houses, the fashion press (Vogue was founded in 1892; Elle was founded in 1945) and fashion shows. The first modern Parisian couturier house is generally considered the work of the Englishman Charles Frederick Worth who dominated the industry from 1858-1895. In the early twentieth century, the industry expanded through such Parisian fashion houses as the house of Chanel (which first came to prominence in 1925) and Balenciaga (founded by a Spaniard in 1937). In the post war year, fashion returned to prominence through Christian Dior's famous "new look" in 1947, and through the houses of Pierre Balmain and Hubert de Givenchy (opened in 1952). In the 1960s, "high fashion" came under criticism from France's youth culture while designers like Yves Saint Laurent broke with established high fashion norms by launching *prêt-à-porter* ("ready to wear") lines and expanding French fashion into mass manufacturing and marketing. Further innovations were carried out by Paco Rabanne and Pierre Cardin. With a greater focus on marketing and manufacturing, new trends were established in the 70s and 80s by Sonia Rykiel, Thierry Mugler, Claude Montana, Jean-Paul Gaultier and Christian Lacroix. The 1990s saw a conglomeration of many French couture houses under luxury giants and multinationals such as LVMH.

Since the 1960s, France's fashion industry has come under increasing competition from London, New York, Milan and Tokyo, and the French have increasingly adopted foreign (particularly American) fashions (such as jeans, tennis shoes). Nevertheless, many foreign designers still seek to make their careers in France.

MEDIA AND ART

Art and museums

The first paintings of France are those that are from prehistoric times, painted in the caves of Lascaux well over 10,000 years ago. The arts flourished already 1,200 years ago, at the time of Charlemagne, as can be seen in many hand made and hand illustrated books of that time.

Classic painters of the 17th century in France are Nicolas Poussin and Claude Lorrain. During the 18th century the Rococo style emerged as a frivolous continuation of the Baroque style. The most famous painters of the era were Antoine Watteau, François Boucher and Jean-Honoré Fragonard. At the end of the century, Jacques-Louis David was the most influential painter of the Neoclassicism.

Géricault and Delacroix were the most important painters of the Romanticism. Afterwards, the painters were more realistic, describing nature (Barbizon school). The realistic movement was led by Courbet and Honoré Daumier. Impressionism was developed in France by artists such as Claude Monet , Edgar Degas , Pierre-Auguste Renoir and Camille Pissarro. At the turn of the century, France had become more than ever the center of innovative art. The Spaniard Pablo Picasso came to France, like many other foreign artists, to deploy his talents there for decades to come. Toulouse-Lautrec , Gauguin and Cézanne were painting then. Cubism is an avant-garde movement born in Paris at the beginning of the 20th century.

The Louvre in Paris is one of the most famous and the largest art museums in the world, created by the new revolutionary regime in 1793 in the former royal palace. It holds a vast amount of art of French and other artists, e.g. the Mona Lisa, by Leonardo da Vinci, and classical Greek Venus de Milo and ancient works of culture and art from Egypt and the Middle East.

MUSIC

France boasts a wide variety of indigenous folk music, as well as styles played by immigrants from Africa, Latin America and Asia. In the field of classical music, France has produced a number of legendary composers, while modern pop music has seen the rise of popular French hip hop , French rock , techno /funk , and turntablists /djs.

France created the Fête de la Musique (first held in 1982), a music festival, which has since become worldwide.

TRANSPORTATION

There are significant differences in lifestyles with respect to transportation between very urbanized regions such as Paris , and smaller towns and rural areas. In Paris , and to a lesser extent in other major cities, many households do not own an automobile and simply use efficient mass transportation. The cliché about the parisien is rush hour in the *Métro* subway. However, outside of such areas, ownership of one or more cars is standard, especially for households with children.

The TGV high speed rail network, *train à grande vitesse* is a fast rail transport which serves several areas of the country and is self financing. There are plans to reach most parts of France and many other destinations in Europe in coming years. Rail services to major destinations are punctual and frequent.

HOLIDAYS

Despite the principles of *laïcité* and the separation of church from state, public and school holidays in France generally follow the Roman Catholic religious calendar (including Easter , Christmas , Ascension Day , Pentecost , Assumption of Mary, All Saints Day, etc.). Labor Day and the National Holiday are the only business holidays determined by government statute; the other holidays are granted by *convention collective* (agreement between employers' and employees' unions) or by agreement of the employer.

The five holiday periods of the public school year are:

- the *vacances de la Toussaint* (All Saints Day) - one and a half weeks starting near the end of October.
- the *vacances de Noël* (Christmas) - two weeks, ending after New Years.
- the *vacances d'hiver* (winter) - two weeks in February and March.
- the *vacances de Pâques* (Easter) - two weeks around Easter weekend.
- the *grandes vacances* - summer vacation.

On May 1, Labour Day (*La Fête du Travail*) the French give flowers of Lily of the Valley to one another.

The National holiday (called Bastille Day in English) in on 14 July. Military parades, called Défilés du 14 juillet , are held, the largest on the Champs-Élysées avenue in Paris in front of the President of the Republic.

On November 2, All Souls Day (*La Fête des morts*), the French traditionally bring chrysanthemums to the tombs of departed family members.

Christmas is generally celebrated in France on Christmas eve by a traditional meal (typical dishes include oysters, boudin blanc and the bûche de Noël), by opening presents and by attending the midnight mass (even among Catholics who do not attend church at other times of the year).

Candlemas (*La Chandeleur*) is celebrated with crêpes, which must be eaten only after eight p.m. If the cook can flip a crêpe while holding a coin in the other hand, the family is assured of prosperity throughout the coming year.

In recent years, the Anglo-Saxon and American holiday Halloween has grown in popularity.

CULTURE OF GERMANY

Germany is often known as *das Land der Dichter und Denker* (the land of poets and thinkers). German culture began long before the rise of Germany as a nation-state and spanned the entire German speaking world.

LITERATURE

German literature can be traced back to the Middle Ages, with the most notable authors of the period being Walther von der Vogelweide and Wolfram von Eschenbach. The Nibelungenlied, whose author remains unknown, is also an important work of the epoch, as is the Thidrekssaga. The fairy tales collections published by Jacob and Wilhelm Grimm became famous throughout the world. Theologian Luther , who translated the Bible into German, is widely credited for having set the basis for modern "High German" language. Among the most admired German poets and authors are Lessing, Goethe, Schiller, Kleist, Hoffmann, Brecht and Schmidt. Four 20th century authors have won the Nobel Prize in literature: Thomas Mann, Hermann Hesse, Heinrich Böll and Günter Grass.

PHILOSOPHY AND THE HISTORY OF IDEAS

Germany's influence on philosophy is historically significant and several notable German philosophers have helped shape western philosophy as early as the Middle Ages. Later, Leibniz (17th century) and most importantly Kant played central roles in the history of philosophy. Kantianism inspired the work of Schopenhauer as well as German idealism defended by Fichte and Hegel. Marx and Engels developed communist theory in the second half of the 19th century while Nietzsche, Heidegger and Gadamer pursued the tradition of German philosophy in the 20th century. A number of German intellectuals were also influential in sociology , most notably Habermas , Horkheimer, Adorno (three central figures in the Frankfurt School), Tönnies, Simmel, Weber, and Luhmann. The Humboldt University of Berlin founded in 1810 by linguist and philosopher Wilhelm von Humboldt served as an influential model for a number of modern western universities

MUSIC

In the field of music, Germany claims some of the most renowned classic composers of the world including Bach, and Beethoven, who marked the transition between the Classical and Romantic eras in Western classical music. Other composers of international fame include Handel , Telemann, Mendelssohn Bartholdy, Brahms, Schumann, Wagner, Strauss and Orff.

As of 2006, Germany is the fifth largest music market in the world [2] and has exerted a strong influence on Pop and Rock music. Artists such as Herbert Grönemeyer, Nena, Dieter Bohlen, Modern Talking, and Peter Schilling have enjoyed international fame. German musicians and, particularly, the pioneering bands Tangerine Dream and Kraftwerk have also contributed to the development of electronic music. [3] Germany hosts many large rock music festivals annualy. The Rock am Ring festival is the largest music festival in Germany, and among the largest in the world. German artists also make up a large percentage of Industrial Music acts.

MINNESINGERS AND MEISTERSINGERS

After Latin-language religious music had dominated for centuries, in the 12th century to the 14th centuries, minnesingers (*love poets*), singing in German, spread across Germany. Minnesingers were aristocrats traveling from court to court who had become musicians, and their work left behind a vast body of literature, *Minnelieder*. The following two centuries saw the minnesingers replaced by middle-class meistersingers, who were often master craftsmen in their main profession, whose music (*meistergesang*) was much more formalized and rule-based than that of the minnesingers. Minnesingers and meistersingers could be considered parallels of French troubadours and trouvères.

Among the minnesingers, Hermann, a monk from Salzburg, deserves special note. He incorporated folk styles from the Alpine regions in his compositions. He made some primitive forays into polyphony as well. Walther von der Vogelweide and Reinmar von Hagenau are probably the most famous minnesingers from this period.

CLASSICAL MUSIC: 16TH CENTURY TO THE PRESENT

Germans have played an overwhelming role in world music. Many of the best classical musicians such as Beethoven, Mozart, Bach, Handel, Brahms or Mahler were ethnically German. At the beginning of the 15th century, German classical music was revolutionized by a man named Oswald von Wolkenstein. Wolkenstein travelled across Europe learning about classical traditions, spending time in countries like France and Italy. He brought back some techniques and styles to his homeland, and within a hundred years, Germany had begun producing composers renowned across the continent. Among the first of these composers was the organist Conrad Paumann.

Chorale

Beginning in the 16th century, polyphony, or the intertwining of multiple melodies, arrived in Germany. Protestant chorales predominated; in shbr MUOI;TV4contrast to Catholic music, chorale was vibrant and energetic. Composers included Martin Luther , leader of the Protestant Reformation, as well as Dieterich Buxtehude and Heinrich Schütz.

Opera

Wolfgang Amadeus Mozart's *Die Zauberflöte* (1791) is usually said to be the beginning of German-language opera, which was further advanced by composers like Ludwig van Beethoven. An earlier starting date for German opera, however, could be Heinrich Schütz 's *Dafne* from 1627. Schütz is said to be the first great German composer before Johann Sebastian Bach , and was a major figure in 17th century music.

In the 19th century, two figures were paramount in German opera: Carl Maria von Weber and Richard Wagner. Wagner introduced devices like the leitmotiv, a musical theme which recurs for important characters or ideas. Wagner (and Weber) based his operas off German history and folklore, most importantly including the *Ring of the Nibelung* (1874). Into the 20th century, opera composers included Richard Strauss (*Der Rosenkavalier*) and Engelbert Humperdinck , who wrote operas meant for young audiences. Across the border in Austria, Arnold Schoenberg innovated a form of twelve-tone music that used rhythm and dissonance instead of traditional melodies and harmonies, while Kurt Weill and Bertold Brecht collaborated on some of the great works of German theater, including *Rise and Fall of the City of Mahogany* and *The Three-Penny Opera.*

The Nazis came to power in Germany during the 1930s, and many musicians fled the country. Following the war, German composers like Karlheinz Stockhausen and Hans Werner Henze began experimenting electronic sounds in classical music.

BAROQUE PERIOD

Baroque music, which was the first music to use tonality in the modern sense, is also known for its ornamentation and artistic use of counterpoint. It originated in Northern Italy at the end of the 16th century, and the style migrated quickly to Germany, which was one of the most active centers of early Baroque music. Early German Baroque composers included Heinrich Schütz , Michael Praetorius, Johann Schein, and Samuel Scheidt. The culmination of the Baroque era was undoubtedly in the work of Johann Sebastian Bach in the first half of the 18th century. Bach wrote numerous Baroque works, including preludes , cantatas , fugues , concertos for keyboard, violin and wind, orchestral suites, the Brandenburg Concertos, The Passion of St. Matthew, The Passion of St. John and the Christmas Oratorio. Bach's contemporaries included Georg Philipp Telemann and Georg Friedrich Haendel, the latter best known for the oratorio *Messiah*.

CLASSICAL ERA

By the middle of the 18th century, the cities of Vienna, Dresden, Berlin and Mannheim had become the center for orchestral music. The Esterházy princes of Vienna, for example, were the patrons of Joseph Haydn , an Austrian who invented the classic format of the string quartet, symphony and sonata. Later that century, Vienna's Wolfgang Amadeus Mozart emerged, mixing German and Italian traditions into his own style.

ROMANTIC ERA

The following century saw two major German composers come to fame early — Ludwig van Beethoven and Franz Schubert. Beethoven, a student of Haydn's in Vienna, used unusually daring harmonies and rhythm and composed numerous pieces for piano, violin, symphonies, chamber music, string quartets and an opera. Schubert created a field of artistic, romantic poetry and music called *lied*; his lieder cycles included *Die schöne Müllerin* and *Der Erlkönig*.

Early in the 19th century, a composer by the name of Richard Wagner was born. He was a "Musician of the Future" who disliked the strict traditionalist styles of music. He is credited with developing *leitmotivs* which were simple recurring themes found in his operas. His music changed the course of opera and of music in general, forever.

The later 19th century saw Vienna continue its elevated position in European classical music, as well as a burst of popularity with Viennese waltzes. These were composed by people like Johann Strauss the Younger. Other German composers from the period included Albert Lortzing, Johannes Brahms, Robert Schumann, Felix Mendelssohn, Anton Bruckner, Max Bruch, and Gustav Mahler. These composers tended to mix classic and romantic elements.

CLASSICAL MUSIC FESTIVALS

The largest summer festival for classical music in Germany is the Schleswig-Holstein Musik Festival.

Folk music

Germany has many unique regions with their own folk traditions of music and dance. Much of the 20th century saw German culture appropriated for the ruling powers (who fought "foreign" music at the same time), and thus it remained decidedly "un-hip" until later in the century. Most recently, the East German regime promoted folk music as long as it was what they saw as an expression of pure German tradition, and a tool for spreading party propaganda.

In both East and West Germany, folk songs called *volkslieder* were taught to children; these were popular, sunny and optimistic, and had little relation to authentic German folk traditions. Inspired by American and English roots revivals , Germany underwent many of the same changes following the 1968 student revolution in West Germany, and new songs, featuring political activism and realistic joy, sadness and passion, were written and performed on the burgeoning folk scene. In East Germany, the same process did not begin until the mid-70s, when folk musicians began incorporating revolutionary ideas in coded songs.

Popular folk songs included emigration songs from the 19th century, work songs and songs of apprentices, as well as democracy-oriented folk songs collected in the 1950s by Wolfgang Steinitz. Beginning in 1970, the Festival des politischen Liedes, an East German festival focusing on political songs, was held annually and organized (until 1980) by the FDJ (East German youth association). Musicians from up to thirty countries would participate, and, for many East Germans, it was the only exposure possible to foreign music. Among foreign musicians at the festival, some were quite renowned, including Inti Illimani (Chile), Billy Bragg (England), Dick Gaughan (Scotland), Mercedes Sosa (Argentina) and Pete Seeger (United States), while German performers included, from both East and West, Oktoberclub, Wachclder and Hannes Wader.

Oom-pah

Oom-pah is a kind of music played by the brass bands; it is associated with beer halls.

Bavaria

Bavarian folk music is likely the most well-known outside of Germany. Yodeling and schuhplattler dancers are among the stereotyped images of German folk life, though these are only found today in the southernmost areas, and to cater to tourists. Bavarian folk music has played a role in the Alpine New Wave , and produced several pioneering world music groups that fuse traditional Bavarian sounds with foreign styles.

It was around the turn of the 20th century, across Europe and especially in Bavaria, many people became concerned about a loss of cultural traditions. This idea was connected to the *Heimatschutz* movement, which sought to protect regional identities and boundaries. What is considered Bavarian folk music in modern Germany is not the same as what Bavarian folk music was in the early 1900s; like any kind of folk or popular music, styles and traditions have evolved over time, giving birth to new forms of music.

The popularity of the *Volkssänger* (*folksinger*) in Bavaria began in the 1880s, and continued in earnest until the 1920s. Shows consisting of duets, ensemble songs, humor and parodies were popular, but the format began changing significantly following World War I. Bally Prell , the "Beauty Queen of Schneizlreuth", was emblematic of this change. She was an attractive tenor who sang lieder, chanson and opera and operetta.

Swabia

Swabian folk music is most popularly represented by acts like Saiten Fell and Firlefanz and the singer-songwriter (and player of the hurdy-gurdy and guitar) Thomas Felder.

NORTHERN GERMANY

Sorbs

The beginning of a Sorbian nationalist music scene can be traced back to the first Sorbian song festival. Held in Lausitz in 1845, and directed by Korla August Kocor, the festival helped revitalize Sorbian folk music. The same period saw the publication of more than five hundred Sorbian songs by Smoler and Haupt in the collection *Folksongs of Upper and Lower Sorbs.*

Danish-Germans

Ethnic Danes living in Germany are clustered in the state of Schleswig-Holstein. Danish folk music is typically based around a fiddle and accordion duo.

Early popular music

Between World War I and World War II, German music branched out to form new, more liberal and independent styles.

Cabaret

The first form of German pop music is said to be cabaret, which arose during the Weimar Republic in the 1920s as the sensual music of late-night clubs. Marlene Dietrich and Margo Lion were among the most famous performers of the period, and became associated with both humorous satire and liberal ideas. "Wenn die beste Freundin" (1928) was an early lesbian -themed song.

Swing Movement

The strict regimentation of youth culture in Nazi Germany through the Hitler Youth led to the emergence of several underground protest movements, through which adolescents were able better to exert their independence.

One of these consisted mainly of upper middle class youths, who based their protest on their musical preferences, rejecting the völkisch music propagated by the Party for American jazz forms, especially Swing. While musical preferences are often a feature of youthful rebellion - as the history of rock and roll shows - jazz and especially Swing were particularly offensive to the Nazi hierarchy: not only did they promote sexual permissiveness, but they were also associated with the American enemy and worse, with the African race they considered inferior. To the Nazis, jazz was "Negro music".

On the other hand, Joseph Goebbels assembled some of the now jobless musicians from Germany and conquered countries into a big band called Charlie and His Orchestra to perform Nazified versions of popular swing hits to be played in propaganda broadcasts.

POST-WAR POPULAR MUSIC

After World War II, German pop music was much influenced by music from USA and Great Britain. Apart from Schlager and Liedermacher, it is necessary to distinguish between pop music in West Germany and pop music in East Germany which developed in different directions. Pop music from West Germany was often heard in East Germany, had more variety and is still present today, while East German music had only little influence.

In West Germany, English-language pop music became more and more important, and today most songs on the radio are English. Nevertheless there is a big diversity of German language pop music. There is also English-language pop music from Germany, some having international success (for instance the Scorpions), but little with enduring broad success in Germany itself. There was hardly any English pop music from East Germany.

Germany has also had a thriving English-language pop scene since the end of the war, with several European and American acts topping the charts. However, Germans and German-oriented musicians have been successful as well. In the 1990s and 2000s such European pop acts were popular as well as artists like Sarah Connor , Marc Terenzi, No Angels, Monrose, and US5 all who performed various types of mainstream pop in English. Many of these acts have had success all over Europe and Asia as well, although few have cracked the American market.

Schlager and Volksmusik

Schlager is a kind of vocal pop music, frequently in the form of sentimental ballads sung in German but there's also a wide range of mood songs among those styles (Modern Schlager, Schlager-Gold, Volksmusik resp. "volkstümlicher Schlager"). Schlager/Volksmusik is strictly separated from international pop music and is only played on special format radio stations (sometimes mixed with international Evergreens)

An important part of Schlager is *volkstümliche Musik*, a Schlager-like interpretation of traditional German folk themes that is very popular in German speaking countries, especially among the older generation.

Liedermacher

Liedermacher (Songwriter) has sophisticated lyrics and is sung with minimal instrumentation, for instance only with acoustic guitar. Some songs are very political in nature. This is related to American Folk/ Americana and French Chanson styles.

Famous West German Liedermacher are Reinhard Mey, Hannes Wader and Konstantin Wecker. Famous East German Liedermacher are Gerhard Schöne and Barbara Thalheim.

Very popular in Germany also is Herman van Veen from the Netherlands.

Most Liedermacher artists also record special albums for children.

POPULAR MUSIC FROM WEST GERMANY

Rock

Genuine German rock first appeared around 1968, just as the hippie countercultural explosion was peaking in the US and UK. At the time, the German musical avant-garde had been experimenting with electronic music for more than a decade, and the first German rock bands fused psychedelic rock from abroad with electronic sounds. The next few years saw the formation of a group of bands that came to be known as krautrock or Kosmische Musik groups; these included Tangerine Dream, Popol Vuh, Can, Neu! and Faust.

German Rock had become a very popular kind of German music. Many people were impacted on Germany's great rock, so there were more and more fans excited to hear the sounds of this music. Before that development rock music in Germany was a negligible part of the schlager genre covered by interprets like Peter Kraus and Ted Herold who used to play Rock-n-Roll standards by Little Richard or Bill Haley, sometimes translated into German language.

A great impact on German postwar culture had the US military radio station American Forces Network (AFN) which was formative for the further development of the German rock and jazz culture. Bill Ramsey who appeared to be senior producer of AFN Frankfurt in 1953 later rose to a famous career as jazz and (later) Schlager singer in Germany while he remained almost unknown in his country of origin from (Ohio, USA).

Neue Deutsche Welle (NDW)

Neue Deutsche Welle is an outgrowth of British punk rock and New Wave which appeared in the mid-to late 1970s. It was the first successful unique German music but was limited in its stylistic devices (funny lyrics and surreal composition and production). Though it was a huge success in Germany itself in the 1980s, this was not long-lasting mostly due to over-commercialization. Some artists became famous internationally:

- Nena
- Falco (from Austria)
- Joachim Witt (One of the biggest names from the Neue Deutsche Welle)

Popular solo artists

In the 1980s most German-language popular music was sung by male solo artists. Here are few very popular singers:

- Udo Lindenberg
- Herbert Grönemeyer
- Marius Müller-Westernhagen
- Peter Maffay

Only Grönemeyer has managed to maintain his success up to today. Maffay developed from Schlager to rock and has a large but delimited fan base - he is seldom played on the radio.

Hamburger Schule

Hamburger Schule (School of Hamburg) is an underground music-movement that started in the late 1980s and was still active till around the mid 1990s. It has similar traditions as Neue Deutsche Welle and mixed all that with punk, grunge and experimental pop music. Hamburger Schule has been an important part of Germany's youth and gave the term "Pop" a new definition, as now it was "ok" (or "cool") to sing in the German language. Hamburger Schule also includes intellectual lyrics with postmodern theories and social criticism. Important artists are:

- Blumfeld
- Die Sterne
- Tocotronic

POPULAR MUSIC FROM EAST GERMANY

There were some bands that were very popular in East Germany.

Ostrock

By the early 1970s, experimental West German rock styles had crossed the border into East Germany and influenced the creation of an East German rock movement referred to as Ostrock. On the other side of the Wall, these bands tended to be stylistically more conservative than in the West, to have more reserved engineering, and often to include more classical and traditional structures (such as those developed by Kurt Weill and Bertolt Brecht in their 1920s Berlin theater songs). These groups often featured poetic lyrics loaded with indirect double-meanings and deeply philosophical challenges to the status quo. As such, they were a style of Krautrock. The best-known of these bands were:

- The Puhdys
- Karat
- City
- Silly

Only a few individual songs, such as "Am Fenster" by City and "Über sieben Brücken mußt Du geh'n" by Karat, found wide popularity outside the GDR.

There was also a wide diversity of underground bands. Out of this scene later grew the internationally successful band Rammstein (see **Neue Deutsche Härte** below).

POPULAR MUSIC FROM REUNIFIED GERMANY

New German popular music

In the 1990s, German language groups had only limited popularity, and only a few artists managed to be played on the radio, for example Rammstein , Rosenstolz or Die Prinzen.

This changed in 2002 with the success of Wir sind Helden, a German band with a new musical self-confidence. This success was followed by several other bands and a broader acceptance of existing German-language recording artists, such as:

- Sportfreunde Stiller (already before 2002)
- Juli
- Silbermond
- MIA.

Hip hop

Outside of the United States, Germany generates the most sales for recorded hip hop , and has one of the more vibrant scenes in the world. Hip hop arrived in the early 1980s, and graffiti art and breakdancing became well-known quickly, with hip hop crews appearing soon thereafter.

The huge commercial success started in 1992 with the hit "Die Da" from Die Fantastischen Vier from Stuttgart. This band makes rather funny and sophisticated hip hop. The Rödelheim Hartreim Projekt tried to establish a more USA-like "gangster" rap. An early major influent group was Advanced Chemistry including Torch.

Whereas hip hop had a peak of success in the early 2000s, with bands from Hamburg dominating the scene, gangster rap became an important and controversial part of German music and youth culture just as late as 2004 with Aggro Berlin.

Punk

Germany was one the most important origins of punk bands. Important bands include Die Ärzte and Die Toten Hosen.

Even most Germans don't know that there are a lot of punk bands with their primary audience in Japan, which stay relatively unknown to German listeners.

Metal

Germany is known as a European centre of heavy metal. Though not as popular as in Scandinavian countries, the far larger populace of Germany (more than three times) make it a major market for metal music. The Rhein-Ruhr Area is the birthplace of internationally famous thrash metal bands like Kreator and Sodom ; along with Hamburg, which was home of much German speed metal bands in the 1980s who should develop into power metal in the 1990s. Helloween is one of the more notable power metal bands to come out of Germany. Destruction, another thrash metal band from Germany, along with Kreator and Sodom, are known at the teutonic three of thrash. Hannover was the starting city for the worldwide rock legends The Scorpions. Death metal bands are mainly located in northern Germany, especially in Lower Saxony (Oscenity, Anasarca) and since the late 1990s also in the Rheinland (Necrophagist, Pavor), were Wermelskirchen is a centre of a huge death metal/grindcore community. Black metal is very popular in East Germany, especially Thuringia, but can be found in nearly all parts of Germany, since it gained more popularity in the early 2000s through the Internet and, of course, the German band Nargaroth who created the infamous song "Black Metal ist Krieg". Southern Germany and especially Bavaria became a centre of Viking metal, with bands like Equilibrium and Kromlek, mostly influenced by bands such like Finntroll and play a more "folky" happy style of the music, in opposition to the more grim and black metal influenced pagan metal bands, mostly from East Germany. The "metal-centre" of Germany is still the Rhein-Ruhr Area, where also Metalcore reached high popularity. Here can be found bands of every substyle, from brutal death metal to pagan metal Industrial metal is also something that Germany can be famous for, with such bands as Rammstein and The Seven Seals. Also, Medieval metal is gaining ground in the United States with the help of bands like In Extremo and Subway to Sally.

Neue Deutsche Härte

Neue Deusche Härte (engl. "New German Hardness") is a style of rock music. It combines the common sound of metal with electronic samples and is mostly sung with German lyrics. It draws its audience mainly from the metal and goth scene, although some bands like Rammstein or Oomph! have gained mainstream success. Other famous artists include Megaherz. Unheilig or Joachim Witt.

Goth

Germany is the home of a vivid Goth scene, and has a large scene of musicians from the spectrum who are typically known as *Goth musicians.*

Electronic music and techno

Germany has a huge electronic music scene. The band Kraftwerk was one of the first bands in the world to make music entirely on electronic equipment. Well-known but not accepted by the mainstream music scene is controversial band Scooter. Recently a few electronica artists have become successful in the mainstream, such as Xavier Naidoo, Blümchen and MIA. Artists on the cutting edge of German-language techno include Ich + Ich and Klee.

Other notable artists

There are few German language bands who managed to be successful for a longer period. The best known are the punk bands Die Ärzte and Die Toten Hosen. Both were formed in the early 1980s but have very different approaches to punk. As successful as those two bands in number of sales and number one albums but much lesser accepted by the public and normally not played by German media but with a huge fan community were Böhse Onkelz.

Very popular all over Germany also are BAP, who sing in the hard-to-understand dialect of their hometown Cologne/Köln.

Outside of Germany especially, the metal band Rammstein is largely popular worldwide.

SPECIAL KINDS OF MUSIC

Klezmer

Germany became a hotbed for klezmer music in the 1980s, and has produced many of the most popular bands in the field since then. Controversially, many or most of the German klezmer bands are not, in fact, Jewish.

Before World War II and the Holocaust, Jews in Germany had not taken much interest in klezmer, at least compared to Jews in places like the United States. During the Cold War, East German Jews like Lin Jaldati and Perry Friedman tried to establish a German Jewish musical scene, but failed due to interference by the Communist Party.

As a result, the East German klezmer scene didn't take off until the arrival of Aufwind in 1984. The West German klezmer scene, on the other hand, got started soon after the student revolutions of the late 1960s. Among some of the intellectual activists, guilt over the Holocaust turned into extreme admiration for anything Jewish. The tour of Kapelye , an American klezmer band, in 1984 also added some energy to the scene, which soon began thriving.

Latin pop

Germany was the starting point of the international career of Cuban-born singer & songwriter Addys D'Mercedes.

CINEMA

German cinema dates back to the very early years of the medium with the work of Max Skladanowsky. It was particularly influential during the years of the Weimar Republic with German expressionists such as Robert Wiene and Friedrich Wilhelm Murnau. The Nazi era produced mostly propaganda films although the work of Leni Riefenstahl still introduced new aesthetics in film. From the 1960s, New German Cinema directors such as Volker Schlöndorff, Werner Herzog, Wim Wenders, Rainer Werner Fassbinder placed West-German cinema back onto the international stage with their often provocative films, while the *Deutsche Film-Aktiengesellschaft* controlled film production in the GDR. More recently, films such as *Das Boot* (1981), *Run Lola Run* (1998), *Das Experiment* (2001), *Good Bye Lenin!* (2003), *Gegen die Wand (Head-on)* (2004) and *Der Untergang (Downfall)* (2004) have enjoyed international success. In 2007 the Academy Award for Best Foreign Language Film went to F.H. von Donnersmarck's The Lives of Others. The Berlin Film Festival, held yearly since 1951, is one of the world's foremost film festivals.

FINE ARTS AND DECORATIVE ARTS

Important German Renaissance painters include Albrecht Altdorfer, Lucas Cranach the Elder, Matthias Grünewald, Hans Holbein the Younger and the well-known Albrecht Dürer. The most important Baroque artists from Germany are Cosmas Damian Asam. Further artists are the romantic Caspar David Friedrich, the surrealist Max Ernst, the conceptualist Joseph Beuys or the neo-expressionist Georg Baselitz.

Architectural contributions from Germany include the Carolingian and Ottonian styles, important precursors of Romanesque. The region then produced significant works in styles such as the Gothic , Renaissance and Baroque. The nation was particularly important in the early modern movement through the Deutscher Werkbund and the Bauhaus movement identified with Walter Gropius. The Nazis closed these movements and favoured a type of neo-classicism. Since World War II, further important modern and post-modern structures have been built, particularly since the reunification of Berlin.

RELIGIOUSTRADITION

The German government has limited responsibilities for culture, which is devolved to the states of Germany , called *Länder*.

64.1 percent of the German population belongs to Christian denominations. 31.4 percent are Roman Catholic, and 32.7 percent are affiliated to the protestant Protestantism [5] (the figures are known accurately because Germany imposes a church tax on those who disclose a religious affiliation). The North and East is predominantly Protestant, the South and West rather Catholic. Nowadays there is a non-religious majority in Hamburg and the East German states [6]. Germany formed a substantial part of the Roman Catholic Holy Roman Empire, but was also the source of Protestant reformers such as Martin Luther. Historically, Germany had a substantial Jewish population. Only a few thousand people of Jewish origin remained in Germany after the Holocaust , but the German Jewish community now has approximately 100,000 members, many from the former Soviet Union. Germany also has a substantial Muslim minority, most of whom are from Turkey.

German theologians include Luther, Schleiermacher, Feuerbach, and Rudolf Otto. Also Germany brought up many mystics including Meister Eckhart and Rudolf Steiner.

ACADEMIC LANDMARKS

Germany is home to some of the finest academic centers in Europe. Some famous Universities include those of both Munich and Berlin, University of Tübingen , University of Göttingen, University of Marburg, University of Berlin, Heidelberg University, Mining Academy Freiberg and Freiburg University, among many others.

Since about 1970, Germany has once again had a thriving popular culture, now increasingly being led by its new-old capital Berlin and the city of Hamburg, and a self-confident music and art scene. Germany is also very well known for its many renowned opera houses , such as The Semperoper , The Komische Oper Berlin and The Staatstheater am Gärtnerplatz.

CUISINE

German cuisine varies from region to region, but concentrates on meat (especially sausage) and varieties of sweet dessert and cakes (such as Black Forest gateau *Schwarzwälder Kirschtorte*) and *Stollen* (a fruit cake). Germans also are famous for rye bread. Germany also produces a large quantity of beer, and (mostly white) wine, particularly Riesling, but also Müller-Thurgau and other varieties.

German cuisine is very similar to English and American cuisine and also to the cooking styles of its immediate neighbors (Holland, France, Austria, Poland). Although sausage is the most famous food product from Germany, one could not gain much understanding of German cuisine by reducing it to sausage. In Germany it is mostly consumed as a snack (Bratwurst), at barbecues and it also appears in a few dishes. A stereotypical German dish contains a type of meat (typically pork, beef or poultry), a type of potatoes (mashed, fried, as dumplings or boiled) and a type of vegetable (typically peas, carrots or cabbage) and sauce. The "home cuisine" differs very much from the "restaurant cuisine". In restaurants you will find more traditional dishes. Cuisine differs also greatly according to regions (in the north you eat fish, in the Rhine region you replace beer with wine, in Bavaria you eat roasted pork) and season (in spring you eat white asparagus with ham and sauce hollandaise, in fall you eat green cabbage with a special kind of sausage and mustard and in winter/ for Christmas you eat duck or goose with red cabbage, dumplings and brown gravy).

SPORT

Sport forms an integral part of German life, as demonstrated by the fact that 27 million Germans are members of a sports club and an additional twelve million pursue such an activity individually. Football is by far the most popular sport, and the German Football Federation (Deutscher Fussballbund) with more than 6.3 million members is the largest athletic organisation in the country. It also attracts the greatest audience, with hundreds of thousands of spectators attending Bundesliga matches and millions more watching on television. The other two most popular sports in Germany are marksmanship and tennis represented by the German Marksmen's Federation and the German Tennis Federation respectively, both including more than a million members. Other popular sports include handball , volleyball , basketball , and ice hockey. Germany has historically been one of the strongest contenders in the Olympic Games. In the 2004 Summer Olympics, Germany finished sixth overall, whereas in the 2006 Winter Olympics Germany finished first.

CULTURE OF KOREA

Korea, one of the oldest civilizations in the world, has 5,000 years of recorded history. The current political separation of North and South Korea has resulted in divergence in modern Korean cultures; nevertheless, the traditional **culture of Korea** is historically shared by both states.

TRADITIONAL ARTS

Korean art is art originating or practiced in Korea or by Korean artists, from ancient times to today. Korea is noted for its artistic traditions in pottery, music, calligraphy, and other genres, often marked by the use of bold color, natural forms, and surface decoration.

The earliest examples of Korean art consist of stone age works dating from 3000 BCE. These mainly consist of votive sculptures , although petroglyphs have also been recently rediscovered.

This early period was followed by the art styles of various Korean kingdoms and dynasties. Korean artists sometimes modified Chinese traditions with a native preference for simple elegance, purity of nature and spontaneity. This filtering of Chinese styles also influenced Japanese artistic traditions, due to cultural and geographical circumstances.

The Goryeo Dynasty (918-1392) was one of the most prolific periods for artists in many disciplines, especially in pottery.

The Korean art market is concentrated in the Insadong district of Seoul where over 50 small galleries exhibit and there are occasional fine arts auctions. Galleries are co-operatively run, small and often with curated and finely designed exhibits. In every town there are smaller regional galleries, with local artists showing in traditional and contemporary media. Art galleries usually have a mix of media. Attempts at bringing Western conceptual art into the foreground have usually had their best success outside of Korea in New York , San Francisco , London and Paris.

Partly as a result of Japanese colonial rule from 1910 to 1945, many of the oldest and most significant Korean art pieces are held in private and public collections in Japan. The Tokyo National Museum displays or stores more than 1,000 gold, bronze, and celadon pieces donated by the late businessman Takenosuke Ogura. In total, about 4,800 Korean art items, of which more than 2,000 are considered antiquities, are held at the museum. Eighty percent of all Korean Buddhist paintings are believed to be in Japan. According to Seoul art historian Kwon Cheeyu, as many as 35,000 Korean art objects and 30,000 rare books have been confirmed to be there, too. These figures do not include private collections which are believed to hold significant quantities of Korean art.

HISTORY OF KOREAN ART

The study and appreciation of Korean art is still at a formative stage in the West. Because of Korea's position between China and Japan , Korea was seen as a mere conduit of Chinese culture to Japan. However, recent scholars have begun to acknowledge Korea's own unique art culture and important role in not only transmitting Chinese culture but creating distinctive styles as well,

Neolithic art

Humans have occupied the Korean Peninsula since at least 700,000 BCE. Pottery dated to approximately 7,000 BCE has been found. This pottery was made from clay and fired over open or semi-open pits at temperatures around 700 degrees Celsius.

The earliest pottery style, dated to circa 7,000 BCE, were flat-bottomed wares (yunggi-mun) were decorated with relief designs, raised horizontal lines and other impressions.

Jeulmun-type pottery, is typically cone-bottomed and incised with a comb-pattern appearing circa 6,000 BCE in the archaeological record. This type of pottery is similar to Siberian styles.

Mumun-type pottery emerged approximately 2000 BCE and is characterized as large, undecorated pottery, mostly used for cooking and storage.

Bronze Age art

Between 1,000 BCE to 300 BCE bronze items began to be imported and made in Korea. By the seventh century BCE, an indigenous bronze culture was established in Korea as evidenced by Korean bronze having a unique percentage of zinc. Bronze ware was influenced by northeast Chinese, Siberian, and Scythian cultures. Items manufactured during this time were weapons such as swords, daggers, and spearheads. Also, ritual items such as mirrors, bells, and rattles were made. These items were buried in dolmens with the cultural elite. Additionally, iron-rich red pots began to be created around circa 6th century. Comma-shaped beads, usually made from nephrite, known as kokkok have also been found in dolmen burials. Kokkok may be carved to imitate bear claws. Another Siberian influence can be seen in rock drawings of animals that display a "life line" in the X-ray style of Siberian art.

Iron Age art

The Iron Age began in Korea around 300 BCE. Korean iron was highly valued in the Chinese commanderies and in Japan. This was also a time of Chinese influence, as evidenced by tomb designs in northern Korea that followed the Chinese model. Korean pottery advanced with the introduction of the potters wheel and climbing kiln firing from China.

THREE KINGDOMS ART

This period began circa 57 BCE to 668 CE. Three Korean kingdoms, Goguryeo , Baekje , and Silla vied for control over the peninsula.

Goguryeo

Buddhism was introduced to Goguryeo first in 372 CE because of its location spanning much of Manchuria and the northern half of Korea, closest to the northern Chinese states like the Northern Wei. Buddhism inspired the Goguryeo kings to begin commission art and architecture dedicated to the Buddha. A notable aspect of Goguryeo art are tomb murals that vividly depict everyday aspects of life in the ancient kingdom as well as its culture. UNESCO designated the Complex of Goguryeo Tombs and as a World Heritage Site because Goguryeo painting was influential in East Asia, including Japan, an example being the wall murals of Horyu-ji which was influenced by Goguryeo. Mural painting also spread to the other two kingdoms. The murals portrayed Buddhist and Taoist themes and provide valuable clues about kingdom such as architecture and clothing. These murals were also the very beginnings of Korean landscape paintings and portraiture. However, the treasures of the tombs were easily accessible and looted leaving very little physical artifacts of the kingdom.

Baekje

Baekje is generally considered the kingdom with the finest artistic tradition among the three states. Baekje was a kingdom in southwest Korea and was influenced by southern Chinese dynasties, such as the Liang. Baekje was also one of the kingdoms to introduce a significant Korean influence into the art of Japan during this time period. Baekje Buddhist sculpture is characterized by its naturalness, warmness, and harmonious proportions exhibits a unique Korean style. Another example of Korean influence is the use of the distinctive " Baekje smile ", a mysterious and archaic smile that is characteristic of many Baekje statutes. While there are no surviving examples of wooden architecture, the Mireuksa site holds the foundation stones of a destroyed temple and two surviving granite pagodas that show what Baekje architecture may have looked. An example of Baekje architecture may be gleaned from Horyu-ji temple because Baekje architects and craftsmen helped design and construct the original temple. The tomb of King Muryeong held a treasure trove of artifacts not looted by grave robbers. Among the items were flame-like gold pins, gilt-bronze shoes, gold girdles (a symbol of royalty), and swords with gold hilts with dragons and phoenixes.

Silla

The Silla Kingdom was the most isolated kingdom from China because it was situated in the southeast part of the peninsula. The kingdom was the last to adopt Buddhism and Chinese cultural influences. The Silla Kingdom tombs were mostly inaccessible and so many examples of Korean art come from this kingdom. The Silla craftsman were famed for their gold-crafting ability which have similarities to Etruscan and Greek techniques, as exampled by gold earrings and crowns. Because of Silla gold artifacts bearing similarities to European techniques along with glass and beads depicting blue-eyed people found in royal tombs, many believe that the Silk Road went all the way to Korea. Most notable objects of Silla art are its gold crowns that are made from pure gold and have tree and antler-like adornments that suggest a Scythe-Siberian and Korean shamanistic tradition.

Gaya

The Gaya confederacy was a group of city-states that did not consolidate into a centralized kingdom. It shared many similarities in its art, such as crowns with tree-like protrusions which are seen in Baekje and Silla. Many of the artifacts unearthed in Gaya tumuli are artifacts related to horses, such as stirrups, saddles, horse armor, and spurs.

Unified Silla art

Unified Silla was a time of great artistic output in Korea, especially in Buddhist art. Examples include the Seokguram grotto and the Bulguksa temple. Two pagodas on the ground, the Séokgatap and Dabotap are also unique examples of Silla masonry and artistry. Craftsmen also created massive temple bells, reliquaries, and statutes. The capital city of Unified Silla was nicknamed the "city of gold" because of use of gold in many objects of art.

Goryeo Dynasty art

The Goryeo Dynasty lasted from 935 CE to 1392. The most famous art produced by Goryeo artisans was Korean celadon pottery which was produced from circa 1050 CE to 1250 CE. While celadon originated in China, Korean potters created their own unique style of pottery that was so valued that the Chinese considered it "first under heaven" and one of the "twelve best things in the world." The Korean celadon had a unique glaze known as "king-fisher" color, an iron based blue-green glaze created by reducing oxygen in the kiln. Korean celadon displayed organic shapes and free-flowing style, such as pieces that were made to look like fish, melons, and other animals. Koreans invented an inlaid technique known as sanggam, where potters would engrave semi-dried pottery with designs and place materials within the decorations with black or white clay.

VISUAL ARTS

Korean art is characterized by transitions in the main religions at the time: early Korean shamanist art, then Korean Buddhist art and Korean Confucian art, through the various forms of Western arts in the 20th century.

Art works in metal, jade, bamboo and textiles have had a limited resurgence. The South Korean government has tried to encourage the maintenance of cultural continuity by awards, and by scholarships for younger students in rarer Korean art forms.

Calligraphy and printing

Korean calligraphy is seen as an art where brushstrokes reveal the artist's personality enhancing the subject matter that is painted. This art form represents the apogee of Korean Confucian art.

Korean fabric arts have a long history, and include Korean embroidery used in costumes and screenwork; Korean knots as best represented in the work of Choe Eun-sun, used in costumes and as wall-decorations; and lesser known weaving skills as indicated below in rarer arts. There is no real tradition of Korean carpets or rugs, although saddle blankets and saddle covers were made from naturally dyed wool, and are extremely rare. Imperial dragon carpets, tiger rugs for judges or magistrates or generals, and smaller chair-covers were imported from China and are traditionally in either yellow or red. Few if any imperial carpets remain. Village rug weavers do not exist.

Korean paper art includes all manner of handmade paper (hanji), used for architectural purposes (window screens, floor covering), for printing, artwork, and the Korean folded arts (paper fans, paper figures), and as well Korean paper clothing which has an annual fashion show in Jeonju city attracting world attention. In the 1960s Korean paper made from mulberry roots was discovered when the Pulguksa (temple) complex in Gyeongju was remodelled. The date on the Buddhist documents converts to a western calendar date of 751, and indicated that indeed the oft quoted claim that Korean paper can last a thousand years was proved irrevocably. However after repeated invasions, very little early Korean paper art exists. Contemporary paper artists are very active.

Painting

Contemporary Korean painting demands an understanding of Korean ceramics and Korean pottery as the glazes used in these works and the textures of the glazes make Korean art more in the tradition of ceramic art, than of western painterly traditions, even if the subjects appear to be of western origin. Brush-strokes as well are far more important than they are to the western artist; and paintings are judged on brush-strokes more often than pure technique.

While there have been only rare studies on Korean aesthetics, a useful place to begin for understanding how Korean art developed an aesthetic is in Korean philosophy, and related articles on Korean Buddhism, and Korean Confucianism.

PHOTOGRAPHY AND CINEMA

North Korea

In the north, changing political systems from Communism merging with the old yangban class of Korean nationalistic leaders have brought out a different kind of visual arts that again is quite distinctive from the Russian architecture and people's art or socialist art styles. This is so particularly in the patriotic films that dominated that culture from 1949 to 1994, and the reawakened architecture, calligraphy, fabric work and neo-traditional painting, that has occurred from 1994 to date.

North Korean artists have gone through two periods of influence in the middle 20th century , from Russian art , and then Chinese art. The impact was greatest on revolutionary posters, lithography and multiples, dramatic and documentary film, realistic painting, grand architecture, and least in areas of domestic pottery, ceramics, exportable needlework, and the visual crafts. Sports art and politically charged revolutionary posters have been the most sophisticated and internationally collectible by auction houses and specialty collectors. North Korean painters who escaped to the United States in the late 1950's include the Fwhang sisters. Duk Soon Fwhang and Chung Soon Fwhang O'Dwyer avoid overtly political statements in favor of tempestous landscapes, bridging Western and Far Eastern painting techniques.

CERAMICS AND SCULPTURE

Korean pottery is the most famous and senior art in Korea, it is closely tied to Korean ceramics which represents tile work, large scale ceramic murals, and architectural elements.

- Korean bronze art, as represented in the work of Kim Jong-dae, master of yundo or bronze mirror casting; and Yi Bong-ju, who works in hammered bronze metalware.
- Korean silver art, as represented in the work of Kim Cheol-ju in circular silver containers.
- Korean jade carving, as represented in the work of Master Jang-Ju won typically in Joseon Dynasty imperial style, with complex jade knotwork, Buddhist motifs, and Korean shamanistic grotesques.

- Korean grass weaving as represented in the work of Master Yi Sang-jae, in his legendary wancho weaving containers.
- Korean bamboo pyrography, as represented in the work of Kim Gi-chan in this unique artwork involved with burning patterns and art on circular bamboo containers.
- Korean bamboo strip work, as represented in the work of Seo Han-gyu (chaesang weaving), and Yi Gi-dong (bamboo fans).
- Korean ox-horn inlaying, as represented in the work of Yi Jae-man in his small storage box, and commissioned gift furniture.
- Korean blinds weaving, as represented in the work of seventh generation master, Jo Dae-yong, and descended from Jo Rak-sin, who created his first masterworks for King Cheoljong; and through Jo Seong-yun, and Jo Jae-gyu. Winners of Joseon Craft Contests. The artwork known as Tongyeong blinds has gained more recognition with the appointment of Jo Dae-yong as Master Craftsman of Bamboo Blinds weaving (Yeomjang) by the Korean government, and his artworks as "Important Intangible Cultural Property No. 114", with Jo at age 51 becoming the youngest 'human cultural property' in the republic.
- Korean wood sculpture, as represented in the work of Park Chan-soo and is a subdivision of Korean sculpture.

ARCHITECTURE AND INTERIOR DESIGN

There is a long tradition of Korean gardens, often linked with palaces.

Patterns often have their origins in early ideographs. Geometric patterns and patterns of plant, animal and nature motifs are the four most basic patterns. Geometric patterns include triangles, squares, diamonds, zigzags, latticework , frets, spirals sawteeth, circles, ovals and concentric circles. Stone Age rock carvings feature animal designs in order to relate to food-gathering activities. Dualist patterns have become very popular, especially Yin and Yang. These patterns are found doors of temples and shrines, clothes, furniture and daily objects such as fans and spoons.

PERFORMING ARTS

In the performing arts, Korean storytelling is done in both ritualistic shamanistic ways, in the songs of yangban scholars, and the cross-overs between the visual arts and the performing arts which are more intense and fluid than in the West.

Depicted on petroglyphs and in pottery shards, as well as wall-paintings in tombs , the various performing arts nearly always incorporated Korean masks, costumes with Korean knots, Korean embroidery, and a dense overlay of art in combination with other arts.

Some specific dances are considered important cultural heritage pieces of art. The performing arts have always been linked to the fabric arts: not just in costumery, but in woven screens behind the plays, ornaments woven or embroidered or knotted to indicate rank, position, or as shamanistic charms; and in other forms to be indicated.

Historically the division of the performing arts is between arts done almost exclusively by women in costume, danceworks; and those done exclusively by men in costume, storytelling. And those done as a group by both sexes with women's numbers in performances reduced as time goes on as it became reputable for men to function as public entertainers.

TEA CEREMONY

The Korean tea ceremony is held in a Korean tea house with characteristic architecture, often within Korean gardens and served in a way with ritualized conversation, formal poetry on wall-scrolls, and with Korean pottery and traditional Korean costumes, the environment itself is a series of naturally flowing events that provide a cultural and artistic experience.

MUSICAL ARTS AND THEATRE

The skill of contemporary Korean performing artists, who have had great recognition abroad, particularly in stringed instruments and as symphony directors, or operatic sopranos and mezzos, takes part in a long musical history.

Korean music in contemporary times is generally divided into the same audiences as the west: with the same kind of audiences for music based on age, and city (classical, pop, techno, house, hip-hop, jazz; traditional) and provincial divisions (folk, country, traditional, classical, rock). World music influences are very strong provincially, with traditional musical instruments once more gaining ground. Competition with China for tourists has forced a much larger attention to traditional Korean musical forms in order to differentiate itself from the west, and east.

The new Seoul Opera house, which will be the anchor for Korean opera has just been given the go-ahead, is set for a $300 million dollar home on an island on the Han river. Korean opera and an entirely redeveloped western opera season, and opera school, to compete with the Beijing opera house, and Japan's historical centre for western operas in the far east is the present focus.

Korean court music has a history going back to the Silla where Tang court music was played; later Song dynasty inspired "A-ak" a Korean version played on Chinese instruments within the Joseon era. Recreations of this music are done in Seoul primarily under the auspices of the Korea Foundation and The National Center for Korean Traditional Performing Arts (NCKTPA).

Court musicians appear in traditional costume, maintain a rigid proper formal posture, and play stringed five-stringed instruments. Teaching by this the "yeak sasang" principles of Confucianism, perfection of tone and acoustic space is put ahead of coarse emotionality. Famous works of court music include: jongmyo jeryeak, designated a UNESCO world cultural heritage, Cheoyongmu, Taepyeongmu, and Sujecheon.

Korean folk music or pansori is the base from which most new music originates being strongly simple and rhythmic.

Korean musicals are a recent innovation, encouraged by the success of Broadway revivals, like Showboat, recent productions such as the musical based on Queen Min have toured globally. There are precedents for popular musical dance-dramas in gamuguk popular in Goryeo times, with some 21st century concert revivals.

Korean stage set design again has a long history and has always drawn inspiration from landscapes, beginning with outdoor theatre, and replicating this by the use of screens within court and temple stagings of rituals and plays. There are few if any books on this potentially interesting area. A rule of thumb has been that the designs have much open space, more two-dimensional space, and subdued tone and colour, and been done by artists to evoke traditional brush painting subjects. Modern plays have tended towards western scenic flats, or minimalist atonality to force a greater attention on the actors. Stage lighting still has to catch up to western standards, and does not reflect a photographer's approach to painting in colour and light, quite surprisingly.

Korean masks are generally used in shamanistic performances that have increasingly been secularized as folkart dramas. At the same time the masks themselves have become tourist artefacts post 1945, and reproduced in large numbers as souvenirs.

STORYTELLING AND COMEDY

Narrative storytelling, either in poetic dramatic song by yangban scholars, or in rough-housing by physical comedians, is generally a male performance. There is as yet virtually no stand-up comedy in Korea because of cultural restrictions on insult-humour, personal comments, and respect for seniors, despite globally successful Korean comic films which depend on comedy of error, and situations with no apparent easy resolution under tight social restraints.

Korean oral history includes narrative myths, legends, folk tales; songs, folksongs, shaman songs and p'ansori; proverbs that expand into short historical tales, riddles, and suspicious words which have their own stories. They have been studied by Cho Dong-Il; Choi In-hak, and Zong In-sop, and published often in editions in English for foreigners, or for primary school teachers.

DANCE

Dance is a significant element of traditional Korean culture. Special traditional dances are performed as part of many annual festivals and celebrations (harvest, etc), involving traditional costumes, specific colors, music, songs and special instruments. Some dances are performed by either men only or women only, while others are performed by both. The women usually have their hair pulled back away from the face in a bun, or may be wearing colorful hats. Some variation of the traditional hanbok is typically worn, or a special costume specific to that dance. In some dances, the women's costumes will have very long sleeves, or trail a long length of fabric, to accentuate graceful arm movements. Outdoor festivals are loud and joyous, and cymbals and drums can prominently be heard. Masks may be worn.

LITERATURE

Notable examples of historical records are very well documented from early times, and as well Korean books with moveable type, often imperial encyclopaedias or historical records, were circulated as early as the 7th century during the Three Kingdoms era from printing wood-blocks; and in the Goryeo era the world's first metal type, and books printed by metal type were produced.

Genres include epics, poetry, religious texts and exigetical commentaries on Buddhist and Confucianist learning; translations of foreign works; plays and court rituals; comedies, tragedies, mixed genres; and various kinds of novels.

Poetry

Korean poetry began to flourish under Confucian scholarship in the Goryeo period, prior to that most models imitated were of Chinese lyric poetry. Collections were repeatedly printed. With the rise of Joseon nationalism, poetry developed increasingly so and reached its apex in the late 18th century. There were attempts at introducing imagist and modern poetry methods in the early 20th century, and in the early republic period, patriotic works were very successful. Lyrical poetry dominated from the 1970s onwards.

Music

Apart from the instruments used, traditional Korean music is characterized by improvisation and the lack of breaks between movements. A *pansori* performance can last for over eight hours during which a single singer performs continuously.

Rather than contrasting different speeds as it is common in Western music, most traditional Korean music begins with the slowest movement and then accelerates as the performance continues.

Korean court music, called jeongak, is closely related to the literate upper-class, and has a strong intellectual emphasis. Jeongak is played at a very slow pace, with single beats taking as long as three seconds. The beat matches the speed of breathing rather than the heartbeat as in most Western music, and feels static and meditative.

The tone of Jeongak is soft and tranquil because the traditional instruments are made of non-metallic materials. String instruments have strings made of silk rather than wire. Almost all wind instruments are made of bamboo.

Pungmul is Korea's folk music and is full of expressions and emotions. This kind of traditional music is closely related to the lives of common people. As with the Jeongak, improvisation is common in Minsogak.

Traditional Korean musical instruments can be divided into wind, string, and percussion types. Wind instruments include the piri (cylindrical oboe), taepyeongso (metal-bell shawm), daegeum (transverse flute), danso (end-blown flute), saenghwang (mouth organ) and the *hun* (ocarina). Traditional string instruments include zithers such as the gayageum, geomungo, and ajaeng, and the haegeum, a two-stringed fiddle.

There is a great number of traditional percussion instruments, including the kkwaenggwari (hand-held gong), the jing (hanging gong), buk (barrel drum), janggu (hourglass drum), bak (clapper), pyeonjong (bell chimes or stone chimes), as well as the eo (tiger-shaped scraper) and the chuk (wooden box).

Dance

As with music, there is a distinction between court dances and folk dances. Common court dances are *jeongjaemu* performed at banquets, and *ilmu*, performed at Confucian rituals. *Jeongjaemu* is divided into native dances (*hyangak jeongjae*) and forms imported from China (*dangak jeongjae*). *Ilmu* are divided into civil dance (*munmu*) and military dance (*mumu*).

Religious dances include all the performances at shamanistic rites (*gut*). Secular dances include both group dances and individual performances.

Traditional choreography of court dances is reflected in many contemporary productions.

Painting

The earliest paintings found on the Korean peninsula are petroglyphs of prehistoric times. With the arrival of Buddhism from China, different techniques were introduced. These techniques quickly established themselves as the mainstream techniques, but indigenous techniques still survived.

There is a tendency towards naturalism with subjects such as realistic landscapes, flowers and birds being particularly popular. Ink is the most common material used, and it is painted on mulberry paper or silk.

In the 18th century indigenous techniques were advanced, particularly in calligraphy and seal engraving.

Arts are both influenced by tradition and realism in North Korea. For example, Han's near-photographic "Break Time at the Ironworks" shows muscular men dripping with sweat and drinking water from tin cups at a sweltering foundry. Son's "Peak Chonnyo of Mount Kumgang" is a classical Korean landscape of towering cliffs shrouded by mists. Sisters Duk Soon Fwhang and Chung Soon Fwang O'Dwyer who fled to the United States in the late 1950s avoid overtly political statements, and render seemingly benign subjects of nature—flowers, birds, fields, insects, mountains—as tempestuous and emotionally charged zones of conflict.

Crafts

There is a unique set of handicrafts produced in Korea. Most of the handicrafts are created for a particular everyday use, often giving priority to the practical use rather than aesthetics. Traditionally, metal, wood, fabric, laquerware and earthenware were the main materials used, but later glass, leather or paper have sporadically been used.

Ancient handicrafts, such as red and black pottery, share similarities with pottery of Chinese cultures along the Yellow River. The relics found of the Bronze Age, however, are distinctive and more elaborate.

Many sophisticated and elaborate handicrafts have been excavated, including gilt crowns, patterned pottery, pots or ornaments. During the Goryeo period the use of bronze was advanced. Brass , that is copper with one third zinc, has been a particularly popular material. The dynasty, however, is renowned for its use of celadon ware.

During the Joseon period popular handicrafts were made of porcelain and decorated with blue painting. Woodcraft was also advanced during that period. This led to more sophisticated pieces of furniture, including wardrobes, chests, tables or drawers.

Ceramics

The use of earthenware on the Korean peninsula goes back to the Neolithic Age. The history of Korean Ceramics is long and includes both Korean pottery a later development after the traditional use of coils and hammered clay to create early votive and sculptural artifacts. During the Three Kingdoms period, pottery was advanced in Silla. The pottery was fired using a deoxidizing flame, which caused the distinctive blue grey celadon colour. The surface was embossed with various geometrical patterns.

In the Goryeo period jade green celadon ware became more popular. In the 12th century sophisticated methods of inlaying were invented, allowing more elaborate decorations in different colours.

White porcelain became popular in the 15th century. It soon overtook celadon ware. White porcelain was commonly painted or decorated with copper.

With the Japanese invasions of Korea in the 16th century, many leading potters were kidnapped to Japan where they profoundly influenced Japanese ceramics. Many leading Japanese pottery families today can trace their art and ancestry to these Korean potters.

In the mid Joseon period (late 17th century) blue-and-white porcelain became popular. Designs were painted in cobalt blue on white porcelain. With the growth of Japan's hegemony on the peninsula towards the end of the 19th century the tradition of porcelain largely declined in favour of Japanese imports.

LIFESTYLE

Homes

Sites of residence are traditionally selected using geomancy. It is believed that any topographical configuration generates invisible forces of good or ill (*gi*). The negative and positive energies (yin and yang) must be brought into balance.

A house should be built against a hill and face south to receive as much sunlight as possible. This orientation is still preferred in modern Korea. Geomancy also influences the shape of the building, the direction it faces and the material it is built of.

Traditional Korean houses can be structured into an inner wing (*anchae*) and an outer wing (*sarangchae*). The individual layout largely depends on the region and the wealth of the family. Whereas aristocrats used the outer wing for receptions, poorer people kept cattle in the *sarangchae*. The wealthier a family, the larger the house. However, it was forbidden to any family except for the king to have a residence of more than 99 *kan*. A *kan* is the distance between two pillars used in traditional houses.

The inner wing normally consisted of a living room, a kitchen and a wooden-floored central hall. More rooms may be attached to this. Poorer farmers would not have any outer wing. Floor heating (*ondol*) has been used in Korea for centuries. The main building materials are wood, clay, tile, stone and thatch. Because wood and clay were the most common materials used in the past not many old buildings have survived into present times.

Gardens

The principles of temple gardens and private gardens are the same. They generally resemble gardens in China and Japan. This is so, because gardening in East Asia is heavily influenced by Taoism. Taoism emphasizes nature and mystery, paying great attention to the details of the layout. In contrast to Japanese and Chinese gardens, traditional Korean gardens avoid artificialities.

The lotus pond is an important feature in the Korean garden. If there is a natural stream, often a pavilion is built next to it, allowing the pleasure of watching the water. Terraced flower beds are a common feature in traditional Korean gardens.

The Poseokjeong site near Gyeongju was built in the Silla period. It highlights the importance of water in traditional Korean gardens. The garden of Poseokjeong features an abalone-shaped watercourse. During the last days of the Silla kingdom, the king's guest would sit along the watercourse and chat while wine cups were floated during banquets.

Dress

The traditional dress known as *hanbok* (known as *joseonot* in the DPRK) has been worn since ancient times. The *hanbok* consists of a shirt (*jeogori*) and pants (*baji*). The traditional hat is called *gwanmo* and special meaning is attached to this piece of clothing.

According to social status, Koreans used to dress differently, making clothing an important mark of social rank. Impressive, but sometimes cumbersome, costumes were worn by the ruling class and the royal family. Jewelry was also used to distance themselves from the ordinary people.

Common people were often restricted to un-dyed plain clothes. This everyday dress underwent relatively few changes during the Joseon period. The basic everyday dress was shared by everyone, but distinctions were drawn in official and ceremonial clothes.

During the winter people wore cotton-wadded dresses. Fur was also common. Because ordinary people normally wore undyed materials, the people were sometimes referred to as the *white-clad folk*.

Hanbok are classified according to their purposes: everyday dress, ceremonial dress and special dress. Ceremonial dresses are worn on formal occasions, including a child's first birthday (doljanchi), a wedding or a funeral. Special dresses are made for purposes such as shamans, officials.

Today the *hanbok* is still sometimes worn during formal occasions. The everyday use of the dress, however, has been lost.

Cuisine

Rice is the staple food of Korea. Having been an almost exclusively agricultural country until recently, the essential recipes in Korea are shaped by this experience. The main crops in Korea are rice , barley and beans , but many supplementary crops are used. Fish and other seafood are also important because Korea is a peninsula.

Fermented recipes were also developed in early times. These include pickled fish and pickled vegetables. This kind of food provides essential proteins and vitamins during the winter.

A number of menus have been developed. These can be divided into ceremonial foods and ritual foods. Ceremonial foods are used when a child reaches 100 days, at the first birthday, at a wedding ceremony, and the sixtieth birthday. Ritual foods are used at funerals, at ancestral rites, shaman's offerings and as temple food.

Temple food is distinguished as it does not use the common five strong-flavoured ingredients of Korean cuisine (garlic , spring onion , wild rocambole, leek and ginger), nor meat.

For ceremonies and rituals rice cakes are vital. The colouring of the food and the ingredients of the recipes are matched with a balance of yin and yang.

Today, surasang (traditional court cuisine) is available to the whole population. In the past vegetable dishes were essential, but meat consumption has increased. Traditional dishes include *ssambap*, *bulgogi*, *sinseollo*, *kimchi*, *bibimbap* and *gujeolpan*.

Tea

Tea in Korea dates back over 2000 years. It was part of a number of worship recipes, hoping that the good scents would reach the heavenly gods. Tea was introduced in Korea, when Buddhism was introduced from China , and later gave rise to the Korean Tea Ceremony.

Originally tea was used for ceremonial purposes or as part of traditional herbal medicine. Green tea , as it is used in China and Japan , is not the only kind of tea drunk in Korea. A great number of teas made of fruits, leaves, seeds or roots are enjoyed. Five tastes of tea are distinguished in Korea: the sweet, sour, salty, bitter, and pungent tastes.

Festivals of the lunar calendar

The traditional Korean calendar was based on the lunisolar calendar. Dates are calculated from Korea's meridian, and observances and festivals are rooted in Korean culture. The Korean lunar calendar is divided into 24 turning points (*jeolgi*), each lasting about 15 days. The lunar calendar was the timetable for the agrarian society in the past, but is vanishing in the modern Korean lifestyle.

The Gregorian Calendar was officially adopted in 1895, but traditional holidays and age-reckoning are still based on the old calendar. + Older generations still celebrate their birthdays according to the lunar calendar.

The biggest festival in Korea today is Seollal (the traditional Korean New Year). Other important festivals include Daeboreum (the first full moon), Dano (spring festival) and Chuseok (harvest festival).

There are also a number of regional festivals, celebrated according to the lunar calendar. See also Public holidays in North Korea and Public holidays in South Korea.

Games

There are a number of board games played in Korea. Baduk is the Korean name for what is known as Go in English. This game is particularly popular with middle-aged and elderly men. It has a similar status as has chess in Western cultures. There is a Korean version of chess called Janggi, based on an old version of Chinese chess. Yut is a popular family board game enjoyed throughout the country, especially during holidays.

No longer commonly played, Chajeon Nori is a traditional game involving two teams of villagers in a giant jousting match.

Many folk games are associated with shamanistic rites and have been handed down from one generation to the next. Three rites are important with regards to folk games: *Yeonggo*, *Dongmaeng* and *Mucheon*. *Yeonggo* is a drumming performance to invoke spirits. *Dongmaeng* is a harvest ceremony, while *Mucheon* is dances to the heaven. These performances were refined during the period of the Three Kingdoms and games were added.

Ssireum is a form of traditional wrestling. Other traditional games include pitching arrows into a pot (*tuho*) and a game of stick-tossing (*jeopo*). There are also stone fights (*seokjeon*), swing riding (*geunetagi*), masked dance drama, and a ball game (*gyeokku*).

WORLD HERITAGE SITES

There are a number of designated UNESCO World Heritage sites in Korea.

Jongmyo Shrine

The Jongmyo Shrine was added to the UNESCO World Heritage Site list in 1995 and is located in Seoul. The shrine is dedicated to the spirits of the ancestors of the royal family of the Joseon Dynasty. It is heavily influenced by Confucian tradition. An elaborate performance of ancient court music (with accompanying dance) known as *Jongmyo jeryeak* is performed there each year.

When it was built in 1394 is was thought to be one of the longest buildings in Asia, if not the longest. There are 19 memorial tablets of kings and 30 of their queens, placed in 19 chambers. The shrine was burnt to the ground during the Japanese invasion in 1592, but rebuilt by 1608.

Changdeokgung

Changdeokgung is also known as the palace of illustrious virtue. It was built in 1405, burnt to the ground during the Japanese invasion in 1592 and reconstructed in 1609. For more than 300 years Changdeokgung was the site of the royal seat. It is located in Seoul

The surroundings and the palace itself are well matched. Some of the trees behind the palace are now over 300 years old. Changdeokgung was added to the UNESCO World Heritage list in 1997.

Bulguksa

Bulguksa is also known as the temple of the *Buddha Land* and home of the *Seokguram Grotto*. The temple was constructed in 751 and consists of a great number of halls. There are two pagodas placed in the temple.

The *Seokguram* grotto is a hermitage of the Bulguksa temple. It is a granite sanctuary. In the main chamber a Buddha statue is seated. The temple and the grotto were added to the UNESCO World Heritage list in 1995.

Tripitaka Koreana and Haeinsa

Haeinsa is a large temple in the South Gyeongsang province. It was built in 802 and home to the *Tripitaka Koreana* wood blocks. The carving of these wood blocks was initiated in 1236 and only completed in 1251. The wood blocks are testimony to the pious devotion of king and his people.

The word *Tripitaka* is Sanskrit and stands for three baskets, referring to the Buddhist laws of aesthetics. The *Tripitaka Koreana* consists of 81'258 wood blocks and is the largest collection of Buddhist scripts. Amazingly there is no trace of errata or omission on any of the wood blocks. The *Tripitaka Koreana* is widely considered as the most beautiful and accurate Buddhist canon carved in Chinese characters.

The site was added to the UNESCO World Heritage list in 1995.

Hwaseong

Hwaseong is the fortification of the city Suwon south of Seoul in South Korea. Its construction was completed in 1796 and it features all the latest features of Korean fortification known at the time.

The fortress covers both flat land and hilly terrain, something rarely seen in East Asia. The walls are 5.52 kilometres long and there are 41 extant facilities along the perimeter. These include four cardinal gates, a floodgate, four secret gates and a beacon tower.

Hwaseong was added to the UNESCO World Heritage list in 1997.

Gochang, Hwasun and Ganghwa sites

The sites of *Gochang*, *Hwasun* and *Ganghwa* were added to the UNESCO list of World Heritage in 2000. These sites are home to prehistoric graveyards which contain hundreds of different megaliths. These megaliths are gravestones which were created in the 1st century B.C. out of large blocks of rock. Megaliths can be found around the globe, but nowhere in such a concentration as in the sites of Gochang, Hwasun and Ganghwa.

Gyeongju Area

The historic area around Gyeongju was added to the UNESCO list of World Heritage in 2000. Gyongju was the capital of the Silla kingdom. The tombs of the Silla rulers can still be found in the centre of the city. These tombs took the shape of rock chambers buried in an earthen hill, sometimes likened with the pyramids. The area around Gyeongju, in particular on the Namsan mountain, is scattered with hundreds of remains from the Silla period. Poseokjeong is one of the most famous of these sites, but there is a great number of Korean Buddhist art, sculptures, reliefs, pagodas and remains of temples and palaces mostly built in the 7th and 10th century.

Complex of Goguryeo Tombs

The Complex of Goguryeo Tombs lies in

Pyongyang, Pyong'an South Province, and Nampo City, South Hwanghae Province, North Korea. In July 2004 it became the first UNESCO World Heritage site north of the 38th parallel.

The site consists of 63 individual tombs from the later Goguryeo, one of the Three Kingdoms of Korea. It was founded around northern Korea and Manchuria around 32 BC, and the capital was moved to Pyongyang in 427. This kingdom dominated the region between the 5th and 7th century AD.

CULTURE OF CHINA

The **Culture of China** is home to one of the world's oldest and most complex civilizations covering a history of over 5,000 years. The nation covers a large geographical region with customs and traditions varying greatly between towns, cities and provinces. ***Chinese culture*** is a broad term used to describe the cultural foundation, even among Chinese-speaking regions outside of mainland China.

IDENTITY

Many ethnic groups have existed in China. In terms of numbers, however, the pre-eminent ethnic group is the Han Chinese. Throughout history, many groups have been assimilated into neighboring ethnicities or disappeared without a trace. At the same time, many within the Han identity have maintained distinct linguistic and regional cultural traditions. The term Zhonghua Minzu has been used to describe the notion of Chinese nationalism in general. Much of the traditional cultural identity within the community has to do with distinguishing the family name.

REGIONAL

Traditional Chinese Culture covers a large geographical territories, each region is usually divided into distinct sub-cultures. Using modern names, here are some distinction:

- The Yellow River basin areas include Henan, Shanxi, Shaanxi, Hebei and Shandong
- The Yangtze River areas include Sichuan, Yunnan, Guizhou, Hunan, Hubei, Jiangxi, Anhui, Zhejiang and Jiangsu.

SOCIETY

Gold detailing on a throne used by the Qianlong Emperor. Chinese dragon was a symbol reserved for the Emperor of China or high level imperial families during the Qing Dynasty

Structure

Since the Three Sovereigns and Five Emperors period, some form of Chinese monarch has been the main ruler above all. Different periods of history have different names for the various positions within society. Conceptually each imperial or feudal period is similar, with the government and military officials ranking high in the hierarchy , and the rest of the population under regular Chinese law. [1] Since the late Zhou Dynasty (1046–256 BCE), traditional Chinese society was organized into a hierarchic system of socio-economic classes known as the four occupations. However, this system did not cover all social groups while the distinctions between all groups became blurred ever since the commercialization of Chinese society in the Song Dynasty (960–1279 CE). Ancient Chinese education also has a long history; ever since the Sui Dynasty (581–618 CE) educated candidates prepared for the Imperial examinations that drafted exam graduates into government as scholar-bureaucrats. Trades and crafts were usually taught by a sifu. The female historian Ban Zhao wrote the Lessons for Women in the Han Dynasty and outlined the four virtues women must abide to, while scholars such as Zhu Xi and Cheng Yi would expand upon this. Chinese marriage and Taoist sexual practices are some of the customs and rituals found in society.

Values

Most social values are derived from Confucianism and Taoism with a combination of conservatism. The subject of which school was the most influential is always debated as many concepts such as Neo-Confucianism , Buddhism and many others have come about. Reincarnation and other rebirth concept is a reminder of the connection between real-life and the next-life.

Language

Spoken Chinese consisted of a number of Chinese dialects throughout history. In the Ming Dynasty standard Mandarin was nationalized. Even so, it wasn't until the Republic of China era in the 1900s when there was any noticeable result in promoting a common unified language in China.

The ancient written standard was Classical Chinese. It was used for thousands of years, but was mostly reserved for scholars and intellectuals. By the 20th century, millions of citizens, especially those outside of the imperial court were illiterate[1]. Only after the May 4th Movement did the push for Vernacular Chinese begin. This allowed common citizens to read since it was modeled after the linguistics and phonology of a spoken language.

MYTHOLOGY AND SPIRITUALITY

Luohan, one of the spiritual figures shared between Chinese and India Culture across different types of buddhism

Main articles: Chinese spiritual world concepts, Chinese mythology, and Chinese folk religion

A large part of Chinese culture is based on the notion that a spiritual world exists. Countless methods of divination have helped answer questions, even serving as an alternate to medicine. Folklores have helped fill the gap for things that cannot be explained. There is often a blurred line between myth, religion and unexplained phenomenon. While many deities are part of the tradition, some of the most recognized holy figures include Guan Yin, Jade Emperor and Budai. Many of the stories have since evolved into traditional Chinese holidays. Other concepts have extended to outside of mythology into spiritual symbols such as Door god and the Imperial guardian lions. Along with the belief of the holy, there is also the evil. Practices such as Taoist exorcism fighting mogwai and jiang shi with peachwood swords are just some of the concepts passed down from generations. A few Chinese fortune telling rituals are still in use today after thousands of years of refinement.

LITERATURE

The extensive collection of books that have been preserved since the Zhou Dynasty demonstrate just how advanced the intellectuals have been at one time. Indeed, the era of the Zhou Dynasty is often looked to as the touchstone of Chinese cultural development. The Five Cardinal Points is the foundation for almost all major studies. Concepts covered within the Chinese classic texts present a wide range of subjects including poetry, astrology, astronomy, calendar, constellations and many others. Some of the most important early texts include I Ching and Shujing within the Four Books and Five Classics. Many Chinese concepts such as Yin and Yang, Qi, Four Pillars of Destiny in relation to heaven and earth were all theorized in the dynastic periods.

Notable confucianists, taoists and scholars of all class have made significant contributions from documenting history to authoring saintly concepts that seem hundred of years ahead of time. Many novels such as Four Great Classical Novels spawned countless fictional stories. By the end of the Qing Dynasty, Chinese culture would embark on a new era with Vernacular Chinese for the common citizens. Hu Shih and Lu Xun would be pioneers in modern literature.

MUSIC

The **music of China** dates back to the dawn of Chinese civilization with documents and artifacts providing evidence of a well-developed musical culture as early as the Zhou Dynasty (1122 BC - 256 BC). Some of the oldest written music dates back to Confucius's time. The first major well-documented flowering of Chinese music was for the qin during the Tang Dynasty, though it is known to have played a major part before the Han Dynasty.

ARTS

Different forms of art have swayed under the influence of great philosophers, teachers, religious figures and even political figures. Chinese art encompasses all facets of fine art , folk art and performance art. was one of the first form of art in the Palaeolithic period. Early Chinese music and poetry was influenced by the *Book of Songs*, Confucius and the Chinese poet and statesman Qu Yuan. Chinese painting became a highly appreciated art in court circles encompassing a wide variety of Shan shui with specialized styles such as Ming Dynasty painting. Early Chinese music was based on percussion instruments, which later gave away to string and reed instruments.

By the Han dynasty papercutting became a new art form after the invention of paper. Chinese opera would also be introduced and branched regionally in additional to other performance formats such as variety arts.

MARTIAL ARTS

China is the original birth place of Eastern martial arts. The names of martial arts were called Kung Fu or its first name Wushu. China also includes the home to the well-respected Shaolin Monastery and Wudang Mountains. The first generation of art started more for the purpose of survival and warfare than art. Overtime, some art forms have branched off, while others have retained a distinct Chinese flavor. Regardless, China has brewed some of the most renowned martial artists including Wong Fei Hung and many others. The art have also co-existed with a variety of weapons including the more standard 18 arms. Legendary and controversial moves like Dim Mak are also praised and talked about within the culture.

FASHION

Different social class in different time eras boast different fashion trends. China's fashion history covers hundreds of years with some of the most colorful and diverse arrangements. Fashionable but questionable practices such as footbinding have also been part of the culture. Many symbols such as phoenix have been used for decorative as well as economic purposes.

ARCHITECTURE

Chinese architecture, examples of which can be found from over 2,000 years ago, has long been a hallmark of the culture. There are certain features common to Chinese architecture, regardless of specific region or use. The most important is its emphasis on width, as the wide halls of the Forbidden City serve as an example. In contrast, western architecture emphasize on height, though there are exceptions such as pagodas.

Another important feature is symmetry, which connotes a sense of grandeur as it applies to everything from palaces to farmhouses. One notable exception is in the design of gardens, which tends to be as asymmetrical as possible. Like Chinese scroll paintings, the principle underlying the garden's composition is to create enduring flow, to let the patron wander and enjoy the garden without prescription, as in nature herself. Feng shui has played an important part in structural development.

CUISINE

Chinese meal in Suzhou with rice, shrimp, eggplant, fermented tofu, vegetable stir-fry, vegetarian duck with meat and bamboo

The overwhelmingly large variety mainly comes from the emperors hosting a banquet of 100 dishes each meal. Countless number of imperial kitchen staff and concubines were involved in the food preparation process. Overtime, many dishes became part of the everyday-citizen culture. Some of the highest quality restaurants with recipes close to the dynastic periods include Fangshan restaurant in Beihai Park Beijing and the Oriole Pavilion. Arguably all branches of Hong Kong eastern style or even American Chinese food are in some ways rooted from the original dynastic cuisines.

LEISURE

A number of games and past-times are popular within Chinese culture. The most common game is Mah Jong. The same pieces are used for other styled games such as Shanghai Solitaire. Others include Pai Gow, Pai gow poker and other bone domino games. Go proverb and Xiangqi is also popular. Ethnic games like Chinese yo-yo are also part of the culture.

CHINESE LITERATURE

Chinese literature spans back thousands of years, from the earliest recorded dynastic court archives to the matured fictional novel arising in the medieval period to entertain the masses of literate Chinese. The introduction of widespread woodblock printing during the Tang Dynasty (618-907) and the invention of movable type printing by Bi Sheng (990-1051) during the Song Dynasty (960- 1279) rapidly spread written knowledge throughout China like never before. In more modern times, the author Lu Xun (1881- 1936) would be considered the founder of modern *baihua* literature in China.

HISTORICAL TEXTS AND ENCYCLOPEDIAS

Sima Qian laid the ground for professional Chinese historiography more than 2,000 years ago.

The Chinese wrote consistent and accurate records at court after the year 841 BC , with the beginning of the Gonghe regency of the Western Zhou Dynasty. The earliest known narrative history of China was the *Zuo Zhuan*, which was compiled no later than 389 BC, and attributed to the blind 5th century BC historian Zuo Qiuming. There was also the *Bamboo Annals* found in 281 AD in the tomb of the King of Wei, who was interred in 296 BC. However, unlike the *Zuo Zhuan*, the authenticity of the early date of the *Bamboo Annals* is doubtful. There is also the *Classic of History*, compiled sometime during the 5th century BC, and which included early information on geography in the chapter of the *Yu Gong*. [1] Another early text was the political strategy book of the *Zhan Guo Ce*, compiled between the 3rd and 1st centuries BC, with partial amounts of the text found amongst the 2nd century BC Mawangdui Silk Texts.

Although court records and other independent records existed beforehand, the definitive work in early Chinese historical writing was the *Shiji*, written by the Han Dynasty court historian Sima Qian (145 BC- 90 BC). This groundbreaking text laid the foundation for Chinese historiography and the many official Chinese historical texts compiled for each dynasty thereafter. He is often compared to the Greek Herodotus in scope and method, as he covered Chinese history from the mythical Xia Dynasty up until the contemporary reign of Emperor Wu of Han, while pertaining an objective and non-biased standpoint (which is often difficult for the official dynastic histories who used historical works to justify the reign of the current dynasty). His influence was far and wide and impacted the written works of many Chinese historians, including the works of Ban Gu and Ban Zhao in the 1st and 2nd centuries, or even Sima Guang in the 11th century with his enormous compilation of the *Zizhi Tongjian* presented to Emperor Shenzong of Song in 1084 AD. The overall scope of the historiographical tradition in China is termed the Twenty-Four Histories, created for each successive Chinese dynasty up until the Ming Dynasty (1368 -1644), as China's last dynasty, the Qing Dynasty (1644- 1911), is not included.

There were also large encyclopedias produced in China throughout the ages. In the Song Dynasty alone, the compilation of the Four Great Books of Song (10th century - 11th century) begun by Li Fang and finalized by Cefu Yuangui represented a massive undertaking of written material covering a wide range of different subjects. This included the (978), the *Imperial Readings of the Taiping Era* (983), the *Finest Blossoms in the Garden of Literature* (986), and the *Prime Tortoise of the Record Bureau* (1013). Although these Song Dynasty Chinese encyclopedias featured millions of written Chinese characters each, they paled in comparison to the later Qing Dynasty encyclopedia printed in 1726, the *Gujin Tushu Jicheng*. This compilation featured over 100 million written Chinese characters in over 800,000 pages, printed in 60 different copies using copper - metal Chinese movable type printing. Other great encyclopedic writers and content include the polymath scientist Shen Kuo (1031–1095) and his *Dream Pool Essays*, the agronomist and inventor Wang Zhen (fl. 1290–1333) and his *Nongshu*, and the minor scholar-official Song Yingxing (1587–1666) and his *Tiangong Kaiwu*.

CULTURE OF JAPAN

The **culture of Japan** has evolved greatly over the years, from the country's original Jomon (The term "Jômon" means "cord-patterned" in Japanese. This refers to the markings made on clay vessels and figures using sticks with cords wrapped around them as well as to the pottery techniques of the Jomon-jin.) culture to its contemporary hybrid culture, which combines influences from Asia , Europe and North America. After several waves of immigration from the continent and nearby Pacific islands (see History of Japan), followed by a heavy importation of culture from China, the inhabitants of Japan experienced a long period of relative isolation from the outside world under the Tokugawa shogunate until the arrival of the " The Black Ships" and the Meiji era. As a result, a culture distinctively different from other Asian cultures developed, and echoes of this persist in contemporary Japan.

JAPANESE LANGUAGE

The Japanese language has always played a significant role in Japanese culture. Spoken mainly in Japan but also in some Japanese emigrant communities around the world, it is an agglutinative language and the s' nd inventory of Japanese is relatively small but has a lexically distinct pitch-accent system. Early Japanese is known largely on the basis of its state in the 8th century , when the three major works of Old Japanese were compiled. The earliest attestation of the Japanese language is in a Chinese document from 252 A.D. It is regarded as an extremely hard language for westerners to learn as adults.

Japanese is written with a combination of three different types of scripts: Chinese characters Kanji , and two syllabic scripts, Hiragana and Katakana. The Latin alphabet, rômaji, is also often used in modern Japanese, especially for company names and logos, advertising, and when inputting Japanese into a computer. The Hindu-Arabic numerals are generally used for numbers, but traditional Sino-Japanese numerals are also commonplace.

VISUAL ARTS

Painting

Painting has been an art in Japan for a very long time: the brush is a traditional writing tool, and the extension of that to its use as an artist's tool was probably natural. Native Japanese painting techniques are still in use today, as well as techniques adopted from continental Asia and from the West.

Calligraphy

The flowing, brush-drawn Japanese language lends itself to complicated calligraphy. Calligraphic art is often too esoteric for Western audiences and therefore general exposure is very limited. However in East Asian countries, the rendering of text itself is seen as a traditional artform as well as a means of conveying written information. The written work can consist of phrases, poems, stories, or even single characters. The style and format of the writing can mimic the subject matter, even to the point of texture and stroke speed. In some cases it can take over one hundred attempts to produce the desired effect of a single character but the process of creating the work is considered as much an art as the end product itself.

This artform is known as Sumi-e and involves making ink by grinding a solid ink stick on a special stone, and mixing it with water.

Sculpture

Traditional Japanese sculptures mainly settled on the subject of Buddhist images, such as Tathagata , Bodhisattva and Myô-ô. The oldest sculpture in Japan is a wooden statue of Amitabha at the Zenkô-ji temple, which was attributed from an ancient Korean king. In the Nara period, Buddhist statues were made by the national government to boost its prestige. These examples are seen in present-day Nara and Kyoto , most notably a colossal bronze statue of the Buddha Vairocana in the Tôdai-ji temple.

Wood has traditionally been used as the chief material in Japan, along with the traditional Japanese architectures. Statues are often lacquered, gilded, or brightly painted, although there are little traces on the surfaces. Bronze and other metals are also used. Other materials, such as stone and pottery, have had extremely important roles in the plebeian beliefs.

Ukiyo-e

Ukiyo-e, literally "pictures of the floating world", is a genre of woodblock prints that exemplifies the characteristics of pre- Meiji Japanese art. Because these prints could be mass-produced, they were available to a wide cross-section of the Japanese populace — those not wealthy enough to afford original paintings — during their heyday, from the 17th to 20th century.

The widespread popularity of *ukiyo-e* prints lead to their recognition as a very Japanese artform, which in turn has led to significant modern mimicry of *ukiyo-e* stylings in advertisements, posters, and other art including manga.

Ikebana

Ikebana is the Japanese art of flower arrangement. It has gained widespread international fame for its focus on harmony, color use, rhythm, and elegantly simple design. It is an art centered greatly on expressing the seasons, and is meant to act as a symbol to something greater than the flower itself. Many Japanese women entering into a third party marriage

environment and people. The ease of acquiring fresh ingredients led to sushi , high temperature and humidity led to varieties of pickled and fermented food like natto, umeboshi, tsukemono and soy sauce. Adaptation of foreign cuisines, such as ramen, which originated in China, are also popular among the masses.

In recent years, Japanesê food has become popular in the U.S. and Europe. Generally they have the reputation of being low in calories and otherwise healthy, which is potentially related to the longevity of Japanese people.

SPORTS

In the long feudal period governed by the samurai class, some methods that were used to train warriors were developed into well-ordered martial arts , referred to collectively as Koryû. Examples include Kenjutsu, Kyûdô, Sôjutsu, Jujutsu and Sumo, all of which were established in the Edo period. After the rapid social change in the Meiji Restoration, some martial arts changed to modern sports, Gendai Budô. Judo was developed by Kano Jigoro, who studied some sects of Jujutsu. These sports are still widely practiced in present day Japan and other countries.

Baseball, football (soccer) and other popular western sports were imported to Japan in the Meiji period. These sports are commonly practiced in schools along with traditional martial arts.

The most popular professional sports in today's Japan are Sumo, baseball and football(soccer). In addition, many semi-professional organizations, such as volleyball , basketball and rugby union , are sponsored by private companies.

POPULAR CULTURE

Japanese popular culture not only reflects the attitudes and concerns of the present but also provides a link to the past. Popular films, television programs, comics, and music all developed from older artistic and literary traditions, and many of their themes and styles of presentation can be traced to traditional art forms. Contemporary forms of popular culture , much like the traditional forms, provide not only entertainment but also an escape for the contemporary Japanese from the problems of an industrial world. When asked how they spent their leisure time, 80 percent of a sample of men and women surveyed by the government in 1986 said they averaged about two and one-half hours per weekday watching television , listening to the radio , and reading newspapers or magazines. Some 16 percent spent an average of two and one-quarter hours a day engaged in hobbies or amusements. Others spent leisure time participating in sports, socializing, and personal study. Teenagers and retired people reported more time spent on all of these activities than did other groups.

In the late 1980s, the family was the focus of leisure activities, such as excursions to parks or shopping districts. Although Japan is often thought of as a hard-working society with little time for pleasure, the Japanese seek entertainment wherever they can. It is common to see Japanese commuters riding the train to work, enjoying their favorite manga, or listening through earphones to the latest in popular music on portable music players.

A wide variety of types of popular entertainment are available. There is a large selection of music, films, and the products of a huge comic book industry, among other forms of entertainment, from which to choose. Game centers, bowling alleys, and karaoke are popular hangout places for teens while older people may play shogi or go in specialized parlors.

Together, the publishing, film/video, music/audio, and game industries in Japan make up the growing Japanese content industry, which, in 2006, was estimated to be worth close to 14 trillion Yen (USD$ 120 billion.)

NIHONJINRON

The term **Nihonjinron** literally means "*theories/ discussions about the Japanese*" and refers to a large number of texts, ranging over such varied fields as sociology , psychology , history , linguistics , philosophy ,and even science , published predominantly in Japan by Japanese, though noted examples of the genre have also been penned by foreign scholars, journalists and residents.

JAPANESE FESTIVALS

Japanese festivals are traditional festive occasions. Some festivals have their roots in Chinese festivals but have undergone dramatic changes as they mixed with local customs.

Some are so different that they do not even remotely resemble the original festival despite sharing the same name and date. There are also various local festivals (e.g. Tobata Gion) that are mostly unknown outside a given prefecture. It is commonly said that you will always find a festival somewhere in Japan.

Unlike most people of East Asian descent, Japanese people generally do not celebrate Chinese New Year (it having been supplanted by the Western New Year's Day in the late 19th century); although Chinese residents in Japan still do. In Yokohama Chinatown, Japan's biggest Chinatown, tourists from all over Japan come to enjoy the festival. And similarly the Nagasaki Lantern Festival is based in Nagasaki's China town.

Events within Festivals

Festivals are often based around one or two main events, with food stalls, entertainment, and carnival games to keep people entertained. Some are based around portable shrines, others hana-bi (Fireworks), and still others around contests where the participants sport loin cloths

Local Festivals (Matsuri)

Matsuri is the Japanese word for a festival or holiday. In Japan, festivals are usually sponsored by a local shrine or temple, though they can be secular.

There are not specific matsuri days for all of Japan; dates vary from area to area, and even within a specific area, but festival days do tend to cluster around traditional holidays such as Setsubun or Obon. Almost every locale has at least one matsuri in late summer/early autumn, usually related to the rice harvest.

Notable matsuri often feature processions which may include elaborate floats. Preparation for these processions is usually organized at the level of neighborhoods, or machi. Prior to these, the local kami may be ritually installed in mikoshi and paraded through the streets.

One can always find in the vicinity of a matsuri booths selling souvenirs and food such as takoyaki, and games, such as Goldfish scooping. Karaoke contests, sumo matches, and other forms of entertainment are often organized in conjunction with matsuri.

Favorite elements of the most popular matsuri, such as the Nada Kenka Matsuri of Himeji or the Neputa Matsuri of Hirosaki, are often broadcast on television for the entire nation to enjoy.

Some examples of famous matsuri are the Jidai, Aoi and Gion Matsuri held in Kyoto; Tenjin Matsuri in Osaka; and the Kanda, Sanno and Sanja Matsuri of Tokyo. Especially, Gion Matsuri, Tenjin Matsuri, and Kanda Matsuri are three most famous Matsuri in Japan.

NATIONWIDE FESTIVALS

Fixed days

- Seijin Shiki : Coming of Age Day (second Monday of January)
- Hinamatsuri : Doll Festival (3 March)
- Hanami : Flower Viewing (late March to early April)
- Tanabata : star festival (7 July)
- Shichi-Go-San: festival day for children aged three, five and seven (15 November)
- Ômisoka : New Year's Eve (31 December)

Multiple days

- Setsubun : division of season (beginning of each season (spring, summer, autumn, winter))
- Ennichi : temple fair (holy days related to Kami and/or Buddha)

NEW YEAR

Date: 1st-3rd of January (though related celebrations take place throughout January)

Information: New Year observances are the most important and elaborate of Japan's annual events. Before the New Year, homes are cleaned, debts are paid off, and osechi (food in lacquered trays for the New Year) is prepared or bought. Osechi foods are traditional foods which are chosen for their lucky colors, shapes, or lucky-sounding names in hopes of obtaining good luck in various areas of life during the new year. Homes are decorated and the holidays are celebrated by family gatherings, visits to temples or shrines, and formal calls on relatives and friends. The first day of the year (ganjitsu) is usually spent with members of the family.

People also visit Buddhist temples and Shinto shrines. Traditionally three shrines or temples are visited. This is called sansha-mairi. In the Imperial Palace at dawn on the 1st of January, the emperor performs the rite of shihôhai(worship of the four quarters),in which he does reverence in the direction of various shrines and imperial tombs and offers prayers for the well-being of the nation. On January 2nd the public is allowed to enter the inner palace grounds; the only other day this is possible is the emperor's birthday (December 23). On the 2nd and 3rd days acquaintances visit one another to extend greetings (nenshi) and sip otoso (a spiced rice wine). Some games played at New Year's are karuta (a card game) and hanetsuki (similar to badminton). Exchanging New Year's greeting cards (similar to Christmas Cards in Western countries) is another important Japanese custom.

A later New Year's celebration, Koshôgatsu, literally means "Small New Year" and starts with the first full moon of the year (around January 15th). The main events of Koshôgatsu are rites and practices praying for a bountiful harvest.

Doll Festival

Date: 3rd of March

Information: This holiday is also known as the Peach Festival because peach blossoms herald the coming of spring and are the symbol of courage and feminine beauty. Young girls put on their best kimonos and visit their friends' homes. Tiered platforms for hina ningyô (hina dolls; a set of dolls representing the emperor, empress, attendants, and musicians in ancient court dress) are set up in the home, and the family celebrates with a special meal of hishimochi (diamond-shaped rice cakes) and shirozake (rice malt with sake).

Hanami

Date: April

Other Names: Hanami (flower viewing), Cherry Blossom Festival

Information: Various flower festivals are held at Shinto shrines during the month of April. Excursions and picnics for enjoying flowers, particularly cherry blossoms are also common. In some places flower viewing parties are held on traditionally fixed dates. This is one of the most popular events during spring. The subject of flower viewing has long held an important place in literature, dance and the fine arts. Ikebana (flower arrangement) is also a popular part of Japanese culture and is still practiced by many people today.Some main things people do during this event are:games, folk songs, folk dance, flower displays, rides, parades, concerts, kimono shows, booths with food and other things, beauty pageant, and religious ceremoies.

Boy's Day

Date: 5th of May

Information: May is the month of the Iris Festival. The tall-stemmed Japanese iris is a symbolic flower. Its long, narrow leaves resemble the sharp blades of a sword, and for many centuries it has been the custom to place iris leaves in a boy's bath to give him a martial spirit. Originally May 5th was a festival for boys corresponding to the Doll Festival, for girls, but in 1948 it was renamed Children's Day and made a national holiday. However, this might be a misnomer; the symbols of courage and strength mainly honor boys. It is customary on this day for families with male children to fly koinobori (carp streamers, a symbol of success) outside the house, display warrior dolls (musha ningyô) inside, and eat chimaki (rice cakes wrapped in cogan grass or bamboo leaves) and kashiwamochi (rice cakes filled with bean paste and wrapped in oak leaves). Also known as kodomo no hi

Tanabata

Date: 7th of July

Other Names: The Star Festival Information: It originated from a Chinese folk legend concerning two stars-the Weaver Star (Vega) and the Cowherd Star (Altair)-who were said to be lovers who could meet only once a year on the 7th night of the 7th month provided it didn't rain and flood the Milky Way. It was named Tanabata after a weaving maiden from a Japanese legend who was believed to make clothes for the gods. People often write wishes and romantic aspirations on long, narrow strips of coloured paper and hang them on bamboo branches along with other small ornaments.

Bon Festival

Date: 13th-15th of August

Information: A Buddhist observance honoring the spirits of ancestors. Usually a "spirit altar" (shôryôdana) is set up in front of the Butsudan (buddhist family altar) to welcome the ancestors' souls. A priest is usually asked to come and read a sutra (tanagyô). Among the traditional preparations for the ancestors' return are the cleaning of grave sites and preparing a path from them to the house and the provision of straw horses or oxen for the ancestors' transportation. The welcoming fire (mukaebi) built on the 13th and the send-off fire (okuribi) built on the 16th are intended to light the path.

Lantern Floating

Date: 15th or 16th of July (August)

Information: The customary practice to mark the end of the Bon Festival. Small paper lanterns containing lighted candles are floated on rivers or the sea light the way for the ancestral spirits as they depart. Usually a message is written on the outside of the paper lantern.

Chrysanthemum Festival

Date: 9th of September

Information: Now the least celebrated of the five sekku or seasonal celebrations. The chrysanthemum is a flower of special importance to the Japanese. The 16-petaled chrysanthemum is the imperial crest. Every year in September the Chrysanthemum Festival takes place. Hundreds of species of this flower developed by the Japanese are on display. An even more interesting part of this festival is the Chrysanthemum Doll Fete. Lifelike clay figures are dressed in robes made of fresh chrysanthemums. They are arranged as parts of legendary and historical scenes.

"7-5-3" Festival (, *Shichigosan*)

Date: 15th of November

Information: Five-year-old boys and seven- or three-year-old girls are taken to the local shrine to pray for their safe and healthy future. This festival started because of the belief that children of certain ages were especially prone to bad luck and hence in need of divine protection. Children are usually dressed in traditional clothing for the occasion ana after visiting the shrine many people buy *chitose-ame* ("thousand-year candy") sold at the shrine.This Flowers are also used in herbal teas

JAPANESE LITERATURE

Japanese literature spans a period of almost two millennia. Early works were heavily influenced by cultural contact with China and Chinese literature, often written in Classical Chinese. But Japanese literature developed into a separate style in its own right as Japanese writers began writing their own works about Japan, although the influence of Chinese literature and Classical Chinese remained until the end of Edo period. When Japan reopened its ports to Western trading and diplomacy in the 19th century, Western literature had a strong effect on Japanese writers, and this influence is still seen today.

History

Japanese Literature is generally divided into four main periods: ancient, classical, medieval, and modern.

Ancient literature (until 794)

With the introduction of kanji from China, the first writing in Japan became possible. Before this, there was no writing system. At first Chinese characters were used in Japanese syntactical formats, and the literary language was classical Chinese ; the result is sentences that look like Chinese but are phonetically read as Japanese. Chinese characters were later adapted to write Japanese, creating what is known as the man'yôgana, the earliest form of kana, or syllabic writing. The earliest works were created in the . These include *Kojiki*, a work recording Japanese mythology and legendary history; *Nihonshoki*, a chronicle with a slightly more solid foundation in historical records than *Kojiki*; and *Man'yôshû*, a poetry anthology.

Classical literature (794–1185; the Heian period)

Classical Japanese literature generally refers to literature produced during the Heian Period, what some would consider a golden era of art and literature. *The Tale of Genji* (early eleventh century) by

Murasaki Shikibu is considered the pre-eminent masterpiece of Heian fiction and an early example of a work of fiction in the form of a novel. Other important works of this period include the *Kokin Wakashû*, a waka-poetry anthology, and *The Pillow Book*, the latter written by Murasaki Shikibu's contemporary and rival, Sei Shonagon, as an essay about the life, loves, and pastimes of nobles in the Emperor's court. The *iroha* poem, now one of two standard orderings for the Japanese syllabary, was also written during the early part of this period.

In this time the imperial court patronized the poets, most of whom were courtiers or ladies-in-waiting. Editing anthologies of poetry was a national pastime. Reflecting the aristocratic atmosphere, the poetry was elegant and sophisticated and expressed emotions in a rhetorical style.

Medieval literature (1185–1600)

Medieval Japanese Literature is marked by the strong influence of Zen Buddhism, where characters are priests, travellers, or ascetic poets. Also during this period, Japan experienced many civil wars which led to the development of a warrior class, and subsequent war tales, histories, and related stories. Work from this period is notable for its insights into life and death, simple lifestyles, and redemption through killing. A representative work is *The Tale of the Heike* (1371), an epic account of the struggle between the Minamoto and Taira clans for control of Japan at the end of the twelfth century. Other important tales of the period include Kamo no Chômei 's *Hôjôki* (1212) and Yoshida Kenko 's *Tsurezuregusa* (1331).

Other notable genres in this period were *renga*, or linked verse, and Noh theater. Both were rapidly developed in the middle of the 14th century, the early Muromachi period.

Early-modern literature (1600–1868)

Literature during this time was written during the largely peaceful Tokugawa Period (commonly referred to as the Edo Period). Due in large part to the rise of the working and middle classes in the new capital of Edo (modern Tokyo), forms of popular drama developed which would later evolve into kabuki. The joruri and kabuki dramatist Chikamatsu Monzaemon became popular at the end of the 17th century. Matsuo Bashô wrote *Oku no Hosomichi* (1702), a travel diary. Hokusai, perhaps Japan's most famous woodblock print artist, also illustrated fiction as well as his famous 36 Views of Mount Fuji.

Many genres of literature made their début during the Edo Period, helped by a rising literacy rate among the growing population of townspeople, as well as the development of lending libraries. Although there was a minor Western influence trickling into the country from the Dutch settlement at Nagasaki, it was the importation of Chinese vernacular fiction that proved the greatest outside influence on the development of Early Modern Japanese fiction. Ihara Saikaku might be said to have given birth to the modern consciousness of the novel in Japan, mixing vernacular dialogue into his humorous and cautionary tales of the pleasure quarters. Jippensha Ikku wrote *Tôkaidôchû Hizakurige*, which is a mix of travelogue and comedy. Tsuga Teisho, Takebe Ayatari, and Okajima Kanzan were instrumental in developing the *yomihon*, which were historical romances almost entirely in prose, influenced by Chinese vernacular novels such as Three Kingdoms and *Shui hu zhuan*. Two *yomihon* masterpieces were written by Ueda Akinari: *Ugetsu monogatari* and *Harusame monogatari*. Kyokutei Bakin wrote the extremely popular fantasy/historical romance *Nansô Satomi Hakkenden* in addition to other yomihon. Santô Kyôden wrote yomihon mostly set in the gay quarters until the Kansei edicts banned such works, and he turned to comedic *kibyôshi*. Genres included horror, crime stories, morality stories, comedy, and pornography—often accompanied by colorful woodcut prints.

Meiji, Taisho, and early Showa literature (1868–1945)

The Meiji era marks the re-opening of Japan to the West, and a period of rapid industrialization. The introduction of European literature brought free verse into the poetic repertoire; it became widely used for longer works embodying new intellectual themes. Young Japanese prose writers and dramatists struggled with a whole galaxy of new ideas and artistic schools, but novelists were the first to successfully assimilate some of these concepts.

In the early Meiji era (1868–1880s), Fukuzawa Yukichi and Nakae Chomin authored Enlightenment literature, while pre-modern popular books depicted the quickly changing country. Then Realism was brought in by Tsubouchi Shoyo and Futabatei Shimei in the mid-Meiji (late 1880s–early 1890s) while the Classicism of Ozaki Koyo, Yamada Bimyo and Kôda Rohan gained popularity. Ichiyô Higuchi, a rare woman writer in this era, wrote short stories on powerless women of this age in a simple style in between literary and colloquial. Kyoka Izumi, a favored disciple of Ozaki, pursued a flowing and elegant style and wrote early novels such as *The Operating Room* (1895) in literary style and later ones including *The Holy Man of Mount Koya* (1900) in colloquial.

Romanticism was brought in by Mori Ôgai with his anthology of translated poems (1889) and carried to its height by Tôson Shimazaki etc. and magazines *Myôjô* and *Bungaku-kai* in early 1900s. Mori also wrote some modern novels including *The Dancing Girl* (1890), *Wild Geese* (1911), then later wrote historical novels. Natsume Sôseki, who is often compared with Mori Ôgai, wrote *I Am a Cat* (1905) with humor and satire, then depicted fresh and pure youth in *Botchan* (1906) and *Sanshirô* (1908). He eventually pursued transcendence of human emotions and egoism in his later works including *Kokoro* (1914) his last and unfinished novel *Light and darkness* (1916).

Shimazaki shifted from Romanticism to Naturalism which was established with his *The Broken Commandment* (1906) and Katai Tayama 's *Futon* (1907). Naturalism hatched " I Novel" (Watakushi-shôsetu) that describes about the authors themselves and depicts their own mental states. Neo-romanticism came out of anti-naturalism and was led by Kafû Nagai, Jun'ichirô Tanizaki, Kotaro Takamura, Hakushû Kitahara and so on in the early 1910s. Saneatsu Mushanokôji, Naoya Shiga and others founded a magazine *Shirakaba* in 1910. They shared a common characteristic, Humanism. Shiga's style was autobiographical and depicted states of his mind and sometimes classified as "I Novel" in this sense. Ryûnosuke Akutagawa, who was highly praised by Soseki, wrote short stories including *Rashômon* (1915) with an intellectual and analytic attitude, and represented Neo-realism in the mid 1910s.

During the 1920s and early 1930s the proletarian literary movement, comprising such writers as Takiji Kobayashi, Denji Kuroshima, Yuriko Miyamoto, and Ineko Sata produced a politically radical literature depicting the harsh lives of workers, peasants, women, and other downtrodden members of society, and their struggles for change.

War-time Japan saw the début of several authors best known for the beauty of their language and their tales of love and sensuality, notably Jun'ichirô Tanizaki and Japan's first winner of the Nobel Prize for Literature, Yasunari Kawabata, a master of psychological fiction. Ashihei Hino wrote lyrical bestsellers glorifying the war, while Tatsuzo Ishikawa attempted to publish a disturbingly realistic account of the advance on Nanjing. Writers who opposed the war include Denji Kuroshima, Mitsuharu Kaneko, Hideo Oguma, and Jun Ishikawa.

Post-war literature

World War II, and Japan's defeat, influenced Japanese literature. Many authors wrote stories of disaffection, loss of purpose, and the coping with defeat. Osamu Dazai 's novel *The Setting Sun* tells of a soldier returning from Manchukuo. Yukio Mishima, well known for both his nihilistic writing and his controversial suicide by seppuku, began writing in the post-war period. Nobuo Kojima's short story "The American School" portrays a group of Japanese teachers of English who, in the immediate aftermath of the war, deal with the American occupation in varying ways.

Prominent writers of the 1970s and 1980s were identified with intellectual and moral issues in their attempts to raise social and political consciousness. One of them, Kenzaburo Oe wrote his best-known work, *A Personal Matter* in 1964 and became Japan's second winner of the Nobel Prize for Literature.

Mitsuaki Inoue had long been concerned with the atomic bomb and continued in the 1980s to write on problems of the nuclear age, while Shusaku Endo depicted the religious dilemma of the Kakure Kirishitan, Roman Catholics in feudal Japan, as a springboard to address spiritual problems. Yasushi Inoue also turned to the past in masterful historical novels of Inner Asia and ancient Japan, in order to portray present human fate.

Avant-garde writers, such as Kobo Abe, who wrote fantastic novels such as *Woman in the Dunes* (1960), wanted to express the Japanese experience in modern terms without using either international styles or traditional conventions, developed new inner visions. Yoshikichi Furui tellingly related the lives of alienated urban dwellers coping with the minutiae of daily life, while the psychodramas within such daily life crises have been explored by a rising number of important women novelists. The 1988 Naoki Prize went to Shizuko Todo for *Ripening Summer*, a story capturing the complex psychology of modern women. Other award-winning stories at the end of the decade dealt with current issues of the elderly in hospitals, the recent past (Pure- Hearted Shopping District in Kôenji, Tokyo), and the life of a Meiji period ukiyo-e artist. In international literature, Kazuo Ishiguro, a native of Japan, had taken up residence in Britain and won Britain's prestigious Booker Prize.

Haruki Murakami is one of the most popular and controversial of today's Japanese authors. His genre-defying, humorous and surreal works have sparked fierce debates in Japan over whether they are true "literature" or simple pop-fiction: Kenzaburo Oe has been one of his harshest critics. Some of his best-known works include *Norwegian Wood* (1987) and *The Wind-Up Bird Chronicle* (1994– 1995). Another best-selling contemporary author is Banana Yoshimoto.

Although modern Japanese writers covered a wide variety of subjects, one particularly Japanese approach stressed their subjects' inner lives, widening the earlier novel's preoccupation with the narrator's consciousness. In Japanese fiction, plot development and action have often been of secondary interest to emotional issues. In keeping with the general trend toward reaffirming national characteristics, many old themes re-emerged, and some authors turned consciously to the past. Strikingly, Buddhist attitudes about the importance of knowir g oneself and the poignant impermanence of things formed an undercurrent to sharp social criticism of this material age. There was a growing emphasis on women's roles, the Japanese persona in the modern world, and the malaise of common people lost in the complexities of urban culture.

Popular fiction, non-fiction, and children's literature all flourished in urban Japan in the 1980s. Many popular works fell between "pure literature" and pulp novels, including all sorts of historical serials, information-packed docudramas, science fiction, mysteries, detective fiction, business stories, war journals, and animal stories. Non-fiction covered everything from crime to politics. Although factual journalism predominated, many of these works were interpretive, reflecting a high degree of individualism. Children's works re-emerged in the 1950s, and the newer entrants into this field, many of them younger women, brought new vitality to it in the 1980s.

Manga (comic books) have penetrated almost every sector of the popular market. They include virtually every field of human interest, such as a multi volume high-school history of Japan and, for the adult market, a manga introduction to economics, and pornography. Manga represented between 20 and 30 percent of annual publications at the end of the 1980s, in sales of some ¥400 billion per year.

ARAB CULTURE

MYTHOLOGY

Arabian mythology comprises the ancient beliefs of the Arabs. Prior to the arrival and initial codification of Islam on the Arabian Peninsula in 622 CE, year one of the Islamic calendar, the physical center of Islam, the Kaaba of Mecca, did not hold only the single symbol of "the God" as it does now. The Kaaba was instead covered in symbols representing the myriad demons, djinn, demigods and other assorted creatures which represented the profoundly polytheistic environment of pre-Islamic Arabia. We can infer from this plurality an exceptionally broad context in which mythology could flourish.

LITERATURE

Arabic literature is the writing produced, both prose and poetry, by speakers of the Arabic language. It does not usually include works written using the Arabic alphabet but not in the Arabic language such as Persian literature and Urdu literature. The Arabic word used for literature is *adab* which is derived from a word meaning "to invite someone for a meal" and implies politeness, culture and enrichment.

Arabic literature emerged in the 6th century with only fragments of the written language appearing before then. It was the Qur'an in the 7th century which would have the greatest lasting effect on Arabic culture and its literature.

The stories of the *Thousand and One Nights*

The Book of One Thousand and One Nights*, *The Book of a Thousand Nights and a Night*, *One Thousand and One Nights*, *1001 Arabian Nights*, *Arabian Nights*, *The Nightly Entertainments or simply ***The Nights***) is a medieval Middle-Eastern literary epic which tells the story of Scheherazade, a Sassanid Queen, who must relate a series of stories to her malevolent husband, King Shahryar, to delay her execution. The stories are told over a period of one thousand and one nights, and every night she ends the story with a suspenseful situation, forcing the King to keep her alive for another day. The individual stories were created over many centuries, by many people and in many styles, and they have become famous in their own right. Notable examples include *Ali Baba and the Forty Thieves* and *The Seven Voyages of Sinbad the Sailor*.

Ruba'iyat

Ruba'iyat or **rubaiyat** (a plural word derived from the root meaning 'four') means "quatrains" in the Arabic language. Singular: **ruba'i** (**rubai**, **ruba'ee**, **rubayi**, **rubayee**). The rhyme scheme is AABA, i.e., lines 1, 2 and 4 rhyme.

This verse form was popularized in the West by Edward Fitzgerald's translation of the collection of Persian verses known as the ***Rubaiyat of Omar Khayyam***. In fact, *Rubaiyat* is a common shorthand name for this collection.

In longer poems built in rubaiyat rhyme scheme, the convention is sometimes extended so that the unrhymed line of the current stanza becomes the rhyme for the following stanza. I.e., the scheme is extended to AABA BBCB CCDC, etc. This is sometimes called, naturally, "interlocking rubaiyat". The structure can be made cyclical by linking the unrhymed line of the final stanza back to the first stanza: ZZAZ. These more stringent systems were not, however, used by Fitzgerald in his *Rubaiyat*; it would have been particularly difficult for him to achieve this effect since the order and number of stanzas in his translation were not stable.

A prime use of the interlocking rubaiyat in modern English poetry is "Stopping by Woods on a Snowy Evening" by Robert Frost.

Qur'an and Islam

The Qur'an was the first major work of Arabic literature and the most influential.

The **Qur'an** had a significant influence of the Arabic language. The language used in the Qur'an is called classical Arabic and while modern Arabic has diverged slightly, the classical is still the style to be admired. Not only is the Qur'an the first work of any significant length written in the language it also has a far more complicated structure than the earlier literary works with its 114 suras (chapters) which contain 6,236 ayat (verses). It contains injunctions, narratives, homilies, parables, direct addresses from God, instructions and even comments on itself on how it will be received and understood. It is also, paradoxically, admired for its layers of metaphor as well as its clarity, a feature it mentions itself in sura 16:103.

Although it contains elements of both prose and poetry, and therefore is closest to *saj'* or rhymed prose, the Qur'an is regarded as entirely apart from these classifications. The text is believed to be divine revelation and is seen as being eternal or 'uncreated'. This leads to the doctrine of *i'jaz* or inimitability of the Qur'an which implies that nobody can copy the work's style nor should anybody try.

This doctrine of *i'jaz* possibly had a slight limiting effect on Arabic literature; proscribing exactly what could be written. The Qur'an itself criticises poets in the 26th sura, actually called Ash-Shu'ara or The Poets:

This may have exerted dominance over the pre-Islamic poets of the 6th century whose popularity may have vied with the Qur'an amongst the people. There were a marked lack of significant poets until the 8th century. One notable exception was Hassan ibn Thabit who wrote poems in praise of Muhammad and was known as the "prophet's poet". Just as the Bible has held an important place in the literature of other languages, The Qur'an is important to Arabic. It is the source of many ideas, allusions and quotes and its moral message informs many works.

Aside from the Qur'an the *hadith* or tradition of what Muhammad is supposed to have said and done are important literature. The entire body of these acts and words are called *sunnah* or way and the ones regarded as *sahih* or genuine of them are collected into hadith. Some of the most significant collections of hadith include those by Muslim ibn al-Hajjaj and Muhammad ibn Isma'il al-Bukhari.

The other important genre of work in Qur'anic study is the *tafsir* or commentaries on the Qur'an. Arab writings relating to religion also includes many sermons and devotional pieces as well as the sayings of Ali which were collected in the 10th century as *Nahj al-Balaghah* or *The Road to Eloquence.*

LANGUAGE

The **Arabic language** is the largest member of the Semitic branch of the Afro-Asiatic language family (classification: South Central Semitic) and is closely related to Hebrew and Aramaic. It is spoken throughout the Arab world and is widely studied and known throughout the Islamic world. Arabic has been a literary language since at least the 6th century and is the liturgical language of Islam.

The Arabic language also has various dialects from the numerous countries and traditions. The Eastern Orthodox dialect of Arabic is extremely different than the normal every day spoken Arabic. Also, spoken Arabic differs greatly in speech than written Arabic, which is much more colloquial and formal.

Quite a few English words are ultimately derived from Arabic, often through other European languages, especially Spanish, among them every-day vocabulary like "sugar" (*sukkar*), "cotton" (*qu?n*) or "magazine" (*ma?azin*). More recognizable are words like "algebra", "alcohol" and "zenith" (see list of English words of Arabic origin).

Arabic and Islam

It is sometimes difficult to translate Islamic concepts, and concepts specific to **Arab culture**, without using the original Arabic terminology. The Qur'an is expressed in Arabic and traditionally Muslims deem it impossible to translate in a way that would adequately reflect its exact meaning—indeed, until recently, some schools of thought maintained that it should not be translated at all. A list of Islamic terms in Arabic covers those terms which are too specific to translate in one phrase. While Arabic is strongly associated with Islam (and is the language of salah), it is also spoken by Arab Christians, Oriental Mizrahi Jews, and smaller sects such as Iraqi Mandaeans.

A majority of the world's Muslims do not speak Arabic, but only know some fixed phrases of the language, such as those used in Islamic prayer. However, learning Arabic is an essential part of the curriculum for anyone attempting to become an Islamic religious scholar.

RELIGIONS

Before the coming of Islam, most Arabs followed a religion featuring the worship of a number of deities, including Hubal, Wadd, Al-Lat, Manat, and Uzza, while some tribes had converted to Christianity or Judaism, and a few individuals, the *hanifs*, had apparently rejected polytheism in favor of a vague monotheism. The most prominent Arab Christian kingdoms were the Ghassanid and Lakhmid kingdoms. With the expansion of Islam, the majority of Arabs were rapidly conquered and became Muslims, and the pre-Islamic polytheistic traditions disappeared.

At present, most Arabs are Muslims. Sunni Islam dominates in most areas, overwhelmingly so in North Africa; Shia Islam is prevalent in Bahrain, Iran (though Iranians are not Arab), southern Iraq and adjacent parts of Saudi Arabia, southern Lebanon, parts of Syria, and northern Yemen. The tiny Druze community, belonging to a secretive offshoot of Islam, is usually considered Arab, but sometimes considered an ethnicity in its own right.

Reliable estimates of the number of Arab Christians, which in any case depends on the definition of "Arab" used, vary. According to Fargues 1998, "Today Christians only make up 9.2% of the population of the Near East". In Lebanon they now number about 39% of the population, in Syria they make up about 10 to 15%, in the Palestinian territories the figure is 3.8%, and in Israel Arab Christians constitute 2.1% (or roughly 10% of the Israeli Arab population). In

Egypt, they constitute 5.9% of the population, and in Iraq they presumably comprise 2.9% of the populace. Most North and South American and Australian Arabs (about two-thirds) are Arab Christians, particularly from Syria, Palestine, and Lebanon.

Jews from Arab countries - mainly Mizrahi Jews and Yemenite Jews - are today usually not categorised as Arab. Sociologist Philip Mendes asserts that before the anti-Jewish actions of the 1930s and 1940s, overall Iraqi Jews "viewed themselves as Arabs of the Jewish faith, rather than as a separate race or nationality". Prior to the emergence of the term *Mizrahi*, the term "Arab Jews" (*Yehudim 'Áravim*) was sometimes used to describe Jews of the Arab world. The term is rarely used today. The few remaining Jews in the Arab countries reside mostly in Morocco and Tunisia. Between the late 1940s and early 1960s, following the creation of the state of Israel, most of these Jews left or were expelled from their countries of birth and are now mostly concentrated in Israel. Some also immigrated to France (where they form the largest Jewish community, outnumbering European Jews), but relatively few to the United States. (see Jewish exodus from Arab lands).

Islam

Islam is a monotheistic religion based upon the Qur'an, which Muslims believe was sent by God through Muhammad, as well as teachings of Muhammad recorded in the Hadith. Followers of Islam, known as Muslims, believe Muhammad to have been God's final prophet.

With a total of approximately 1.2–1.3 billion adherents, Islam is the second-largest religion in the world, and is the planet's fastest growing religion.[3] Like both Judaism and Christianity, Islam is considered to be an Abrahamic religion.

Islam began in Arabia in the 7th Century. Under the leadership of Muhammad and his successors, Islam rapidly spread by religious conversion and military conquest.[5] Today followers of Islam may be found throughout the world, particularly in the Middle East, North Africa, South Asia and Southeast Asia.

MUSIC

Arabic music is the music of Arabic-speaking people or countries, especially those centered around the Arabian Peninsula. The world of Arab music has long been dominated by Cairo, a cultural center, though musical innovation and regional styles abound from Morocco to Saudi Arabia. Beirut has, in recent years, also become a major center of Arabic music. Classical Arab music is extremely popular across the population, especially a small number of superstars known throughout the Arab world. Regional styles of popular music include Algerian *raï*, Moroccan *gnawa*, Kuwaiti *sawt*, Egyptian *el gil* and Turkish *Arabesque-pop music*.

"The common style that developed is usually called 'Islamic' or 'Arab', though in fact it transcends religious, ethnic, geographical, and linguistic boundaries" and it is suggested that it be called the Near East (from Morocco to India) style (van der Merwe 1989, p.9).

Habib Hassan Touma (1996, p.xix-xx) lists "five components" which "characterize the music of the Arabs:

1. The Arab tone system (a musical tuning system) with specific interval structures, invented by al-Farabi in the tenth century (p.170).
2. Rhythmic-temporal structures that produce a rich variety of rhythmic patterns, *awzan*, used to accompany the metered vocal and instrumental genres and give them form.
3. Musical instruments that are found throughout the Arabian world and that represent a standardized, are played with standardized performance techniques, and exhibit similar details in construction and design.
4. Specific social contexts for the making of music, whereby musical genres can be classified as urban (music of the city inhabitants), rural (music of the country inhabitants), or Bedouin (music of the desert inhabitants)....
5. A musical mentality that is responsible for the aesthetic homogeneity of the tonal-spatial and rhythmic-temporal structures in Arabian music, whether composed or improvised, instrumental or vocal, secular or sacred. The Arab's musical mentality is defined by:

1. The maqâm phenomenon....
2. The predominance of vocal music...
3. The predilection for small instrumental ensembles...
4. The mosaiclike stringing together of musical form elements, that is, the arrangement in a sequence of small and smallest melodic elements, and their repetition, combination, and permutation within the framework of the tonal-spatial model.
5. The absence of polyphony, polyrhythm, and motivic development. Arabian music is, however, very familiar with the ostinato, as well as with a more instinctive heterophonic way of making music.
6. The alternation between a free rhythmic-temporal and fixed tonal-spatial organization on the one hand and a fixed rhythmic-temporal and free tonal-spatial structure on the other. This alternation...results in exciting contrasts."

Much Arab music is characterized by an emphasis on melody and rhythm rather than harmony. Thus much Arabic music is homophonic in nature. Some genres of Arab music are polyphonic—as the instrument Kanoun is based upon the idea of playing two-note chords—but quintessentially, Arabic music is melodic.

CUISINE

Originally, the Arabs of the Arabian Peninsula relied heavily on a diet of dates, wheat, barley, rice and meat, with little variety, with a heavy emphasis on yogurt products, such as leben (yoghurt without butterfat).Arabian cuisine today is the result of a combination of richly diverse cuisines, spanning the Arab world from Iraq to Morocco and incorporating Lebanese, Egyptian and others. It has also been influenced to a degree by the cuisines of India, Turkey, Berber and others. In an average Arab gulf state household, a visitor might expect a dinner consisting of a very large platter, shared commonly, with a vast mountain of rice, incorporating lamb or chicken, or both, as separate dishes, with various stewed vegetables, heavily spiced, sometimes with a tomato sauce. Most likely, there would be several other items on the side, less hearty. Tea would certainly accompany the meal, as it is almost constantly consumed. Coffee would be included as well.

CULTURE OF IRAN

To best understand Iran and her people, one must first attempt to acquire an understanding of its ancient culture. It is in the study of this area where the Iranian identity optimally expresses itself. Hence the first sentence of prominent Iranologist Richard Nelson Frye's latest book on Iran reads:

"Iran's glory has always been its culture."

Iranians were not only open to other cultures, but freely adopted all they found useful for them. Thus an eclectic cultural elasticity has been said to be one of the key defining characteristics of the Persian spirit and a clue to its historic longevity.

Furthermore, Iran's culture has manifested itself in several facets throughout the history of Iran, as well as that of many Central Asian and west South Asian states like Afghanistan and Pakistan.

The article uses the words *Persian* and *Iranian* interchangeably, sometimes referring to the language and its speakers, and other times referring to the name of pre-20th century Iran, a nomenclature which survives from wester explorers and orientalists. Both are not the same however, and the cultures of the people of Greater Iran is the focus of this article.

ART

Iranian art has gone through numerous phases of evolution. The unique aesthetics of Iran is evident from the Achaemenid reliefs in Persepolis to the mosaic paintings of Bishapur. The Islamic era drastically brought changes to the styles and practice of the arts, each dynasty with its own particular foci. The Qajarid era was the last stage of classical Persian art, before modernism was imported and suffused into elements of traditionalist schools of aesthetics.

The Persian rug

From the yarn fiber to the colors, every part of the Persian rug is traditionally hand made from natural ingredients over the course of many months.

The art of carpet weaving in Iran has its roots in the culture and customs of its people and their instinctive feelings. Weavers mix elegant patterns with a myriad of colors. The Iranian carpet is similar to the Persian garden: full of florae, birds, and beasts.

The colors are usually made from wild flowers, and are rich in colors such as burgundy, navy blue, and accents of ivory. The proto-fabric is often washed in tea to soften the texture, giving it a unique quality. Depending on where the rug is made, patterns and designs vary. And some rugs, such as Gabbeh, and Gelim have a variations in their textures and number of knots as well.

The exceptional craftsmenship in weaving these carpets and silken textile thus caught the attention of the likes of Xuanzang, Jean-Baptiste Tavernier, and Jean Chardin.

Painting and miniature

Oriental historian Basil Gray believes "Iran has offered a particularly unique art to the world which is excellent in its kind".

Caves in Iran's Lorestan province exhibit painted imagery of animals and hunting scenes. Some such as those in Fars Province and Sialk are at least 5,000 years old.

Painting in Iran is thought to have reached a climax during the Tamerlane era when outstanding masters such as Kamaleddin Behzad gave birth to a new style of painting.

Paintings of the Qajar period, are a combination of European influences and Safavid miniature schools of painting such as those introduced by Reza Abbasi. Masters such as Kamal-ol-molk, further pushed forward the European influence in Iran. It was during the Qajar era when "Coffee House painting" emerged. Subjects of this style were often religious in nature depicting scenes from Shia epics and the like.

Pottery and ceramics

Prominent archeologist Roman Ghirshman believes "the taste and talent of this people [Iranians] can be seen through the designs of their earthen wares".

Of the thousands of archeological sites and historic ruins of Iran, almost every single one can be found to have been filled, at some point, with earthenware of exceptional quality. Thousands of unique vessels alone were found in Sialk and Jiroft sites.

The occupation of the potter ("kuzeh gar") has a special place in Persian literature.

Motifs

Since centuries, Iranian art has developed particular patterns designed to decorate Iranian produced craft. These motifs can be :

- Inspired by ancestral nomad tribes (such as geometrical motifs used in kilims or gabbehs).
- Islam influenced, with an advanced geometrical research.
- Oriental based, also found in India or Pakistan.

Khatam-kari

Delicate and meticulous marquetry, produced since the Safavide period: at this time, khatam was so popular in the court that princes learned this technique at the same level of music or painting. In the 18th and 19th centuries, katahm declined, before being stimulated under the Reign of Reza Shah, with the creation of craft schools in Tehran, Isfahan, and Chiraz. "Khatam" means "incrustation", and "Khatam-kari", "incrustation work". This craft consists in the production of incrustation patterns (generally star shaped), with thin sticks of wood (ebony, teak, ziziphus, orange, rose), brass (for golden parts), camel bones (white parts). Ivory, gold or silver can also be used for collection objects. Sticks are assembled in trinagular beams, themselves assembeled and glued in a strict order to create a 70cm diameter cylinder, which section is the main motif: a six-branch star included in a hexagon. These cylinders are cut into shorter cylinders, and then compressed and dried between two wooden plates, before being cut for the last time, in 1mm wide tranches. So this section is ready to be plated and glued on the object to be decorated, before lacquer finishing. The tranche can also be heaten to be soften to follow curves of a rounded object. Many objects can be so decorated, such as: boxes, chessboards, cadres, pipes, desks or some musical instruments. Katham can be used on Persian miniature, realising true work of art.

Coming from techniques imported from China and improved by Persian know-how, this craft existed for more than 700 years and is still perennial in Ispahan and Chiraz.

Relief and sculpture

Relief carving has a history dating back thousands of years. Elamite reliefs are still to be found in Iran with Persepolis being a mecca of relief creations of antiquity.

Calligraphy

Persian calligraphy has several styles. Seen here is a "shekasteh" style from a Safavid era manuscript.

Says writer Will Durant: "Ancient Iranians with an alphabet of 36 letters, used skins and pen to write, Instead of ear-then tablets". Such was the creativity spent on the art of writing. The significance of the art of calligraphy in works of pottery, metallic vessels, and historic buildings is such that they are deemed lacking without the adorning decorative calligraphy.

Illuminations, and especially the Quran and works such as the Shahnameh, Divan Hafez, Golestan, Bostan et al are recognized as highly invaluable because of their delicate calligraphy alone. Vast quantities of these are scattered and preserved in museums and private collections worldwide, such as the Hermitage Museum of St. Petersburg and Washington's Freer Gallery of Art among many others.

Styles

- Shekasteh
- Nasta'liq
- Naskh
- Mohaqqaq

LANGUAGE AND LITERATURE

The Persian language has been in continuous use for over 2500 years. Yet it is a subset of the superset of Iranian languages.

Persian literature inspired Goethe, Ralph Waldo Emerson and many others, and it has been often dubbed as a most worthy language to serve as a conduit for poetry. Dialects of Persian are widely spoken throughout the region sporadically from China to Syria and mainly in Iranian Plateau. Two important dialects of Persian serving as languages are Tajiki and Dari respectively spoken in Tajikistan and Afghanistan as official languages.

Persian *Parsi*; is an Indo-European language spoken in Iran (Persia), Afghanistan, Tajikistan and Uzbekistan. It is derived from the language of the ancient Persian people.

Persian and its varieties have official-language status in Iran, Afghanistan, and Tajikistan. According to CIA World Factbook, based on old data, there are approximately 64 million native speakers of Persian in Iran,[2] Afghanistan,[3] Tajikistan[4] and Uzbekistan[5] and about the same number of people in other parts of the world speak Persian. UNESCO was asked to select Persian as one of its languages in 2006.[6]

Persian has been a medium for literary and scientific contributions to the Islamic world as well as the Western. It has had an influence on certain neighbouring languages, particularly the Turkic languages of Central Asia, Caucasus, and Anatolia. It has had a lesser influence on Arabic and other languages of Mesopotamia.

For five centuries prior to the British colonization, Persian was widely used as a second language in the Indian subcontinent; it took prominence as the language of culture and education in several Muslim courts in India and became the "official language" under the Mughal emperors. Only in 1843 did the subcontinent begin conducting business in English.[7] Evidence of Persian's historical influence in the region can be seen in the extent of its influence on the languages of Hindustani (resulting in Urdu), Kashmiri, Punjabi, Sindhi, Gujarati, Bengali and even Telugu, as well as the popularity that Persian literature still enjoys in the region.

Persian literature spans two and a half millennia, though much of the pre-Islamic material has been lost. Its sources often come from far-flung regions beyond the borders of present-day Iran, as the Persian language flourished and survives across wide swaths of Central Asia. For instance, Rumi, one of Persia's best-loved poets, wrote in Persian but lived in Konya, now in Turkey and then the capital of the Seljuks. The Ghaznavids conquered large territories in Central and South Asia and adopted Persian as their court language. There is thus Persian literature from areas that are now part of Afghanistan, Pakistan, India and Central Asia. Not all this literature is written in Persian, as some consider works written by ethnic Persians in other languages, such as Greek and Arabic, to be included.

Surviving works in Persian languages (such as Old Persian or Middle Persian) date back as far as

650 BCE, the date of the earliest surviving Achaemenid inscriptions. The bulk of the surviving Persian literature, however, comes from the times following the Islamic conquest of Persia circa 650 CE. After the Abbasids came to power (750 CE), the Persians became the scribes and bureaucrats of the Islamic empire and, increasingly, also its writers and poets. Persians wrote both in Arabic and Persian; Persian predominated in later literary circles. Persian poets such as Sa'di, Hafiz, Rumi and Omar Khayyam are well known in the world and have influenced the literature of many countries.

INDIAN SUBCONTINENT

With the emergence of the Japanese Ghaznavids and their successors such as the Ghurids, Timurids and Mughal Empire, Persian culture and its literature gradually moved into the vast Indian subcontinent. Persian was the language of the nobility, literary circles, and the royal Mughal courts for hundreds of years. (In modern times, Persian has been generally supplanted by Urdu, a heavily Persian-influenced dialect of Hindustani.)

Under the Moghul Empire of India during the sixteenth century, the official language of India became Persian. Only in 1832 did the British army force the Indian subcontinent to begin conducting business in English. *(Clawson, p.6)* Persian poetry in fact flourished in these regions while post-Safavid Iranian literature stagnated. Dehkhoda and other scholars of the 20th century, for example, largely based their works on the detailed lexicography produced in India, using compilations such as Ghazi khan Badr Muhammad Dehlavi's *Adat al-Fudhala*, Ibrahim Ghavamuddin Farughi's *Farhang-i Ibrahimi*, and particularly Muhammad Padshah's *Farhang-i Anandraj*. Famous South Asian poets and scholars such as Amir Khosrow Dehlavi and Muhammad Iqbal of Lahore found many admirers in Iran itself.

CINEMA

With 300 international awards in the past 25 years, films from Iran continue to be celebrated worldwide. Perhaps the best known director is Abbas Kiarostami. the movies were good pass times...!

The **cinema of Iran** (or **Persian cinema**) is a flourishing film industry with a long history. While many popular commercial films are annually made in Iran, Iranian art films are among the finest, winning praise from around the world.

Film festivals that honour Iranian films are held annually around the globe. Along with China, Iran has been lauded as one of the best exporters of cinema in the 1990s. Some critics now rank Iran as the world's most important national cinema, artistically, with a significance that invites comparison to Italian neorealism and similar movements in past decades. World-renowned Austrian filmmaker Michael Haneke and German filmmaker Werner Herzog, along with many film critics from around the world, has praised Iranian cinema as one of the world's most important artistic cinemas.

Besides films made in Iran, the terms "Iranian cinema" and "Persian cinema" can also refer to the cinema of the Iranian Cultural Continent ("Greater Iran"), such as Tajikistan and Afghanistan. The term may also refer to movies made using the Persian language but filmed or produced in other regions, such as Europe and the United States or to movies made by Iranians in languages other than Iranian ones.

MUSIC

The music of Persia goes back to before the days of Barbod in the royal Sassanid courts. This is where many music cultures trace back their distant origins to.

Instruments used in Persian classical music include the bowed spike-fiddle kamancheh, the goblet drum tombak, the end-blown flute ney, the frame drum daf, the long-necked lutes tar, setar, tanbur, dotar, and the dulcimer santur. Harps, "chang[s]," were a very important part of music up until the middle of the Safavid Empire. They were probably replaced because of tuning problems or replaced by the qanun (zither)and later the piano which was introduced by the West during the Safavid Dynasty of Iran. Many, if not most, of these instruments originated in Iran. Perhaps the most loved string instrument is the tar. Tar players are regurlarly chosen to function as the primary string instrument in a performance. The setar is also loved for its delicacy and is the favorite among Mystic musicians. Some instruments like the sorna, neyanban, dohol, naghareh, and others, are not used in the classical repertoire but are used in Iranian Folk music. The ghazhak (ghaychak), a type of fiddle, is being re-introduced to the Classical field after many years of exclusion. The instruments used in the Classical field are also used in Iranian Folk Music

ARCHITECTURE

Architecture in "Greater Iran" has a continuous history from at least 5000BCE to the present, with characteristic examples distributed over a vast area from Syria to North India and the borders of China, from the Caucasus to Zanzibar. Persian buildings vary from peasant huts to tea houses, and garden pavilions to "some of the most majestic structures the world has ever seen".[1]

Iranian architecture displays great variety, both structural and aesthetic, developing gradually and coherently out of prior traditions and experience. Without sudden innovations, and despite the repeated trauma of invasions and cultural shocks, it has achieved "an individuality distinct from that of other Muslim countries".[2] Its paramount virtues are several: "a marked feeling for form and scale; structural inventiveness, especially in vault and dome construction; a genius for decoration with a freedom and success not rivaled in any other architecture".[3]

Traditionally, the guiding, formative, motif of Iranian architecture has been its cosmic symbolism "by which man is brought into communication and participation with the powers of heaven".[4] This theme, shared by virtually all Asia and persisting even into modern times, not only has given unity and continuity to the architecture of Persia, but has been a primary source of its emotional characters as well.

In summary:

"The supreme Iranian art, in the proper meaning of the word, has always been its architecture. The supremacy of architecture applies to both pre-and post-Islamic periods."

TRADITIONAL TEAHOUSES OF IRAN

There are nearly countless numbers of traditional teahouses (*chai khaneh*) throughout Iran, and each province features its own unique cultural presentation of this ancient tradition. However, there are certain traits which are common to all teahouses, especially the most visible aspects, strong *chai* (tea) and the ever-present *ghaluyn*. Almost all teahouses serve *baqleh*, steam boiled fava beans (in the pod), served with salt and vinegar, as well as a variety of desserts and pastries. Many teahouses also serve full meals, typically a variety of kababs as well as regional specialities.

PERSIAN GARDENS

The Persian Garden was designed as a reflection of paradise on earth; the word "garden" itself coming from Persian roots. The special place of the garden in the Iranian heart can be seen in their architecture, in the ruins of Iran, and in their paintings.

CUISINE

In Persian mythology, Persian food is so delicious and tempting that Ahriman (the devil) uses it to corrupt the King of the land, causing two serpents to sprout from the King's shoulders, turning him into an evil tyrant; Zahhâk The Dragon King.

The **cuisine of Iran** is diverse, with each province featuring dishes, as well as culinary traditions and styles, distinct to their regions. It includes a wide variety of foods ranging from chelow kabab (*barg, koobideh, joojeh, shishleek, soltani, chenjeh*), *khoresht* (stew that is served with white Basmati or Iranian rice: *ghormeh sabzi, gheimeh*, and others), *aash* (a thick soup), *kookoo* (vegetable omellettes), *pollo* (white rice alone or with addition of meat and/ or vegetables and herbs, including *loobia pollo, albaloo pollo, zereshk pollo*, and others), and a diverse variety of salads, pastries, and drinks specific to different parts of Iran. The list of Persian recipes, appetizers and desserts is extensive.

Herbs are frequently used along with fruits such as plums, pomegranates, quince, prunes, apricots, and raisins. The main Persian cuisines are combinations of rice with meat, chicken or fish and some onion, vegetables, nuts, and herbs. To achieve a balanced taste, characteristic Persian spices such as saffron, diced limes, cinnamon, and parsley are mixed delicately and used in some special dishes.

DANCE OF IRAN

Persian dance refers to the type of dancing from Iran. Upper body motion is emphasized, with hand motions, trunk undulations and facial expressions being points of attention. Although often compared to Arabic dance, Persian dance is actually very distinct, especially in its lack of hip movement, a staple of Arabic dance.

Generally, the female partner will lead with her upper body in a sexy fashion using her arms and hands, while the male partner complements her movements in line with the music, often of bandari style. However, it is also common to see same-sex couples (mostly males) performing this style of dance, with one leading and the other responding. However, this style is generally substantially less sensual in both manner of movement and in facial expression.

Often, Persian dance will be performed at relatively informal gatherings, such as family meetings, where everyone will sit in a circle (especially on rugs) and a couple will dance in the middle, sometimes accompanied by a Persian drummer playing bandari beats. Persian dance is also used more formally at various social events, like weddings.

Persian dance appears in American pop culture in the film Alexander performed by the eunuch Bagoas at the ceremony where Clietus dies.

Among most notable ensembles of Persian dance is Afsaneh Ballet.

Styles

- Baba karam
- Bandari
- Bojnurdi dance
- Classical Persian court dance
- Haj Naranji dance
- kereshmeh
- Khaliji Dance
- Kharman dance
- Khorasani dance
- Latar dance
- Lezgi dance
- Luri
- Matmati
- Mazandarani
- Motrebi dance
- Qasemabadi
- Raqs-e Choobbazi
- Raqs-e Parcheh
- Ru-Howzi
- Shamshir dance
- Shateri dance
- Tehrani dance (Tehrooni)
- Zaboli dance
- Zargari dance

RELIGION

Iran has been the birthplace of many of the world's most influential religions and religion in Iran has always had a direct impact on its culture. Zoroastrianism, Mithraism, Manichaeism, Mazdakism, Yazdanism, Bábí Faith and the Bahá'í Faith are some of the religions that originated there.

Today, the Shia version of Islam continues to have an immediate bearing on Iranian culture and identity.

SPORTS

The game of Polo originated with Iranian tribes in ancient times and was regularly seen throughout the country until the revolution of 1979 where it became associated with the monarchy. It continues to be played, but only in rural areas and discreetly. Recently, as of 2005, it has been acquiring an increasingly higher profile. In March 2006, there was a highly publicised tournament and all significant matches are now televised.

Wrestling

Both freestyle and Greco-Roman wrestling, particularly freestyle, are incredibly popular in Iran, often even referred to as its national sport. With a history of great wrestlers, such as Gholamreza Takhti, and considerable success in Olympic and World Championships, Iran is considered among the elite nations in the sport (along with the US and the former Soviet Bloc). One particular wrestler, Khosrow Vaziri, went on to compete in American professional wrestling under the name *The Iron Sheik.*

Polo

It is believed that Polo first originated in Persia ages ago. The poet Firdowsi described royal polo tournaments in his 9th century epic, the Shahnameh.

Despite the emphasis in Islam on learning the equestrian arts, in modern times, especially after the revolution, the equestrian sports fell out of favor in Iran, as they were associated with the aristocracy. And yet recent signs suggest that it may be witnessing a comeback with renewed interest in the sport.

Backgammon

Backgammon is a game that has had a following in Persia since ancient times. Like Chess and some card games, it fell out of official favor after the revolution. However, this did not diminish its popularity with the general population. In recent years, restrictions on the game have been softened, but tournaments have yet to be officially sanctioned. And that is why backgammon is considered a traditional sport.

Chess

The origin of chess is a disputed issue, but evidence exists to give credence to the theory that chess originated in Persia, and later found its way into the Indian subcontinent. For example, the earliest recorder history of chess is to be found in Persian writing, and the earliest chess pieces found also being from Persian. All of this evidence lends weight to the theory that chess in Persia (*Shatranj*) pre-dated chess in India (*Chatrang*). Chess later spread from Persia into other nations in the Islamic world.dog

WOMEN IN PERSIAN CULTURE

In the tales of the 1001 Nights, it is a woman, Scheherazade, who is the protagonist and heroine of the frame tale.

Throughout the ancient world including Persia, both men and women used make-up, wore jewellery and coloured their body parts. Moreover, their garments were both elaborate and colourful. Rather than being marked by gender, clothing styles were distinguished by class and status. Women in modern Iran (post 1935 "Persia") are of various mixes and appearances, both in fashion and social norm. Traditionally however, the "Persian woman" had a predefined appearance set by social norms that were the standard for all women in society. For example, the observations of a late Qajar era orientalist read:

"The Persian ladies' hair is very luxuriant and never cut. It is nearly always dyed red with Henna, or with indigo to a blue-black tinge. It is naturally a glossy black. Fair hair is not esteemed. Blue eyes are not uncommon, but brown ones are the rule. A full moon face is much admired, and a dark complexion (termed Namak) is the native idea of the highest beauty. The eyebrows are widened and painted until they appear to meet, and color is used freely in painting the faces."

TRADITIONAL IMPORTANT DAYS

Iranians celeberate the following days based on a Solar calendar, in addition to important religious days of Islamic and Shia calendars, which are based on a lunar calendar.

- Norouz (Iranian/Persian New Year)
- Sizdah be dar (Nature Day)
- Jashn-e-Tirgan (Water Festival)
- Jashn-e-Sadeh (Fire Festival)
- Jashn-e-Mehregan (Autumn Festival)
- Shab-e-Yalda (Winter Feast)
- Charshanbeh Suri

TRADITIONAL CULTURAL INHERITORS OF THE OLD PERSIA

Like the Persian Rug that exhibits numerous colors and forms in a dazzling display of warmth and creativity, **Persian culture** is the glue that bonds the peoples of western and central Asia. The Caucasus and Central Asia "occupy an important place in the historical geography of Persian civilization. Much of the region was included in the Pre-Islamic Persian empires, and many of its ancient peoples either belonged to the Iranian branch of the Indo-European peoples (e.g. Medes and Soghdians), or were in close cultural contact with them (e.g. the Armenians).[4] In the words of Iranologist Richard Nelson Frye:

"Many times I have emphasized that the present peoples of central Asia, whether Iranian or Turkic speaking, have one culture, one religion, one set of social values and traditions with only language separating them."

The Culture of Persia has thus developed over several thousand years. But historically, the peoples of Islamic Republic of Iran, Tajikistan, Uzbekistan, Turkmenistan, Afghanistan, Islamic Republic of Pakistan, Azerbaijan, and Kyrgyzstan originate from the same or similar stock, and are related to one another as part of the larger group of peoples of Greater

Iran. Armenia, Georgia, and Daghestan were also well within the sphere of influence of Persian culture as well, as can be seen from the many remaining relics, ruins, and works of literature from that region.

In particular, Iran, Afghanistan, and Tajikistan have been able to almost fully retain their Persian identity, while the other aforementioned entities still exhibit considerable traces of their Iranian past.

CONTRIBUTIONS TO HUMANITY IN ANCIENT HISTORY

From the humble brick, to the windmill, Persians have mixed creativity with art and offered the world numerous contributions. What follows is a list of just a few examples of the cultural contributions of Iran.

- (10,000 BC) - Earliest known domestication of the goat.[8]
- (6000 BC) - The modern brick. Some of the oldest bricks found to date are Persian, from ca. 6000 BC.
- (~5000 BC) - Invention of Wine. Discovery made by University of Pennsylvania excavations at Hajji Firuz Tepe in northwestern Iran.[10]
- (5000 BC) - Invention of Tar (lute), that led to the development of the guitar.
- (3000 BC) - The ziggurat. The Sialk ziggurat, according to the Cultural Heritage Organization of Iran, predates that of Ur or any other of Mesopotamia's 34 ziggurats.
- (2000 BC) - Peaches are a fruit of Iranian origin, as indicated by their Latin scientific name, Prunus persica, *from which (by way of the French) we have the English word "peach."*[12]
- Tulips were first cultivated in ancient Persia.[13]
- (1700 BC) - The windmill.
- (1400 BC) - The game of Backgammon appears in the east of Iran.
- (1400 BC to 600 BC) - Zoroastrianism: where the first prophet of a monotheistic faith arose according to some scholars,[15] claiming Zoroastrianism as being "the oldest of the revealed credal religions, which has probably had more influence on mankind directly or indirectly, more than any other faith".
- (576 BC to 529 BC) - Under the rule of Cyrus II the Great, the Cyrus Cylinder was issued. This is considered to be the first universal declaration of human rights, predating the Magna Carta by one millennium It was discovered in 1879 in Babylon and today is kept in the British Museum.
- (576 BC to 529 BC) - Under the rule of Cyrus II the Great, Cyrus frees the Jews from Babylonian captivity. *See Cyrus in the Judeo-Christian tradition.*
- (521 BC) - The game Polo.
- (500 BC) World's oldest Staple (fastener).
- (500 BC) The first Taxation system (under the Achaemenid Empire).
- (500 BC) The first courier post. Also called the "Royal Road".
- (500 BC) - Source for introduction of the domesticated chicken into Europe.
- (500 BC) - First cultivation of spinach
- (400 BC) - Yakhchals, ancient refrigerators.
- (400 BC) - Ice Cream.
- (250 BC) - According to archaeological digs, the Parthians created the world's first batteries. Their original use is still uncertain, though it is suspected that they were used for electroplating.
- (250 BC) Original excavation of a Suez Canal.
- (271 AD) - The teaching hospital
- (700 AD) - The Cookie.
- (762 AD) - Designing Baghdad: The original city was based on Persian precedents such as Firouzabad in Persia. The two designers who were hired by the caliph al-Mansur to plan the city were *Nowbakht*, a former Persian Zoroastrian, and *Mashallah*, a former Jew from Khorasan.
- (864 AD-930 AD) - First systematic use of alcohol in Medicine: Rhazes.[25]
- (1000 AD) - Introduction of paper to the west.
- (935 - 1020) - Ferdowsi writes the Shahnama (Book of Kings) that resulted in the revival of Iranian culture and the expansion of the Iranian cultural sphere.

- (980 - 1037) - Avicenna, a physician, writes The Canon of Medicine one of the foundational manuals in the history of modern medicine.
- (1207 AD - 1273 AD) - Rumi writes poetry .
- Algebra and Trigonometry: Numerous Iranians were directly responsible for the establishment of Algebra, the advancement of Medicine and Chemistry, and the discovery of Trigonometry.
- Qanat, subterranean aqueducts.
- Wind Catchers, ancient air residential conditioning.
- "Virtually all European scholars claim Arabic music has Persian origins.

CULTURE OF RUSSIA

Historically, the dominating position in Russia is occupied by the Russian culture, the culture of Russian language and Russian nationality; this is partly because Russians constitute the vast majority of the population in the country, and partly because many times in the History of Russia the cultures of other nationalities were suppressed through russification, see for instance Ems Ukaz.

The politics of the Soviet Union with respect to culture was controversial: on one side there was a politically-motivated desire to create a "Soviet people", which was expressed in the notion of Soviet culture, exemplified by Socialist Realism. From the other side there were periodical campaigns of preservation of national cultures: every ethnicity had "great national writers" and folk cultural practices were officially supported.

MUSIC OF RUSSIA

Russia is a large and extremely culturally diverse country, with dozens of ethnic groups, each with their own forms of folk music. During the period of Soviet domination, music was highly scrutinized and kept within certain boundaries of content and innovation. After the fall of the USSR, western-style rock and pop music became the most popular musical forms in Russia. Some native artists broke through.

Classical, opera and ballet

Russia has a long history of classical music innovation. The first important Russian composer was Mikhail Glinka (1804-1857), who added religious and folk elements to classical compositions, composing pioneering operas like *A Life for the Tsar* and *Ruslan and Lyudmila*; though these operas were distinctively Russian, they were based on the Italian tradition.

Glinka and the composers who made up The Mighty Handful after him (Rimsky-Korsakov, Mussorgsky, Balakirev, Borodin and César Cui) were often influenced by Russian folk music and tales. This same period saw the foundation of the Russian Musical Society in 1859, led by composers Anton and Nikolay Rubinstein. The Mighty Handful and the Russian Music Society were rivals, with the former embracing a Russian national identity and the latter musically conservative. Among the Mighty Handful's most notable compositions were the operas *The Snow Maiden* (*Snegurochka*), *Sadko*, *Boris Godunov*, *Prince Igor* and *Khovanshchina*, and the symphonic suite *Scheherazade*.

Other prominent Russian composers include Tchaikovsky, Rachmaninoff, and in the 20th century Stravinsky, Prokofiev, Scriabin, Shostakovich and Alfred Schnittke. Of these, Tchaikovsky remains the best known outside Russia, and his fame as the country's most famous composer is unquestioned. He is best known for ballets like *Swan Lake* and *The Nutcracker*.

During the 19th century, Count Uvarov led a campaign of nationalist revival which initiated the first professional orchestra with traditional instruments, beginning with Vassily Andreyev, who used the balalaika in an orchestra late in the century. Just after the dawn of the 20th century, Mitrofan Pyatnitsky founded the Pyatnitsky Choir, which used rural peasant singers and traditional sounds. By the time of the Soviet Union, however, it had become one of many groups playing sanitized folk music, now often called *fakelore*.

SOVIET ERA

In the 1910s romances (in exotic Russian, Caucasian, Gypsy and Italian styles) became very popular.

The greatest and most popular singers of romances usually sang in operas at the same time. The most popular was Fyodor Shalyapin. Singers usually composed music and wrote the lyrics, such as Alexander Vertinsky, Konstantin Sokolsky, Pyotr Leshchenko. Musically and structurally based on romances are the bard songs (starting in the 60's) and the criminal songs. The bard genre can be compared to the American folk-revival movement of the 60's, closer to poetry than music. Artists like Bulat Okudzhava, Alexander Galich and Vladimir Vysotskiy all wrote their own songs, and the recordings were distributed underground. Prison songs were largely popularized by Arkady Severny.

The Soviet Era produced many prominent musicians in spite of oppression from the government. Some émigrés remained popular abroad, like pianist Vladimir Horowitz, whose 1986 performance in Moscow, the first in his native land, was a landmark event.

In the 1960s, Vyacheslav Shchurov organized concerts featuring folk singers from across Russia, beginning in 1966. Shchurov thus inspired a wave of singing ethnomusicologists who appeared among the urban intellectuals and recorded rural folk musicians. Perhaps the most important group to follow in Shchurov's wake was the Dmitri Pokrovsky Ensemble. A group of musicians called bards arose at the same time. Generally ignored by the state, bards like Vladimir Vysotsky helped lead a popular return to traditional music. The 1960s also saw the beginning of Alla Pugacheva's music career which continues to this day.

The same period saw the birth of Russian rock with the band Pojuschie Gitary who created a style called VIA and later released the first Russian rock opera, *Orpheus and Eurydice*. Other rock bands of the era included Tcvety, Sinyaya Ptica and Golubiye Gitary.

By the 1980s, popular folk-oriented groups had arisen. The Cossack Kazachy Krug and Pesen Zemli became most popular. A musical underground (*magnitizdat*).

Perestroika Music

Many underground rock bands arose during early 80s: Mashina Vremeni, Center, Aquarium, Secret, Zoopark, Urfin Dzhyus, Trek.

They formed active musical comminities. During Perestroika they became mainstream, notable bands of that time include DDT, Alisa, Nautilus Pompilius, Kino, Sektor Gaza, Aria.

DDT, Aria and Alisa are still active today and are very popular with the modern youth.

Lesser known but still popular bands playing in diverse styles were common, too. Notable examples are Zvuki Mu and Televizor.

Post-Soviet Music

Middle 90's showed decline for Russian rock due to economical problems, changes in mentality and mass media reorientation.

The Russian duet t.A.T.u is by far the most successful Russian band. They have reached number one in many countries around the world with several of their singles and albums.

Still, there are many popular rock bands including Pilot, Zemfira, Splean and many still-functioning 80's bands such as DDT, Alisa, Picnick, Akvarium, Mashina Vremeni.

Heavy Metal: While Aria and its offspring Kipelov are still the most popular, new bands arose in genres like Power Metal (Catharsis, Epidemia), Progressive Metal (Orgia Pravednikov, Mechanical Poet), Pagan Metal (Butterfly Temple, Temnozor).

Alternative scene arose with bands such as Amatory, Psiheja, 7000$, Jane Air, Stigmata.

Some folk rock bands Melnitsa, Zoloto, Pelageja risen to popularity recently.

Pop/Rock: t.A.T.u., Nichya, VITAS, Dima Bilan, Linda, Alina

Death Metal: Mortem, Hieronymus Bosch (band), Hatecraft

Classical crossover: Ariaphonics

Electronic: Fizzarum, Solar X, Elochnyie Igrushki, SCSI-9, Gromov, ADD, Messer Für Frau Müller, Zvuki Mu, KLUtCh

Ska Punk: Distemper, 7 Rasa, Elisium, Leningrad

FOLK MUSIC

Adygea

In recent years, Adygea has seen the formation of a number of new musical institutions. These include two orchestras, one of which (Russkaya Udal), uses folk instruments, and a chamber music theater.

Adygea's national anthem was written by Iskhak Shumafovich Mashbash; music—by Umar Khatsitsovich Tkhabisimov.

Altay

Altay is a Central Asian region, known for traditional epics and a number of folk instruments.

Bashkir

The first major study of Bashkir music appeared in 1897, when ethnographer Rybakov S.G. wrote *Music and Songs of the Ural's Muslims and Studies of Their Way of Life*. Later, Lebedinskiy L.N. collected numerous folk songs in Bashkortostan beginning in 1930. The 1968 foundation of the Ufa State Institute of Arts sponsored research in the field.

The kurai is the most important instrument in the Bashkir ensemble.

Buryatia

The Buryats of the far east is known for distinctive folk music which uses the two-stringed horsehead fiddle, or morin khur. The style has no polyphony and has little melodic innovation. Narrative structures are very common, many of them long epics which claim to be the last song of a famous hero, such as in the *Last Song of Rinchin Dorzhin*. Modern Buryat musicians include the band Uragsha, which uniquely combines Siberian and Russian language lyrics with rock and Buryat folk songs.

Chechnya

Alongside the Chechen rebellion of the 1990s came a resurgence in Chechen national identity, of which music is a major part. People like Said Khachukayev became prominent promoting Chechen music.

The Chechen national anthem is said to be "Death or Freedom", an ancient song of uncertain origin.

Dagestan

Dagestan's most famous composer may be Gotfrid Hasanov, who is said to be the first professional composer from Dagestan. He wrote the first Dagestani opera, *Khochbar*, in 1945, and recorded a great deal of folk music from all the peoples of Dagestan.

Karelia

Karelians are Finnish, and so much of their music is the same as Finnish music. The *Kalevala* is a very important part of traditional music; it is a recitation of Finnish legends, and is considered an integral part of the Finnish folk identity.

The Karelian Folk Music Ensemble is a prominent folk group.

Russia

Archeology and direct evidence (such as the frescoes at the Saint Sophia Cathedral in Kiev) show a variety of musical instruments in ancient Russia. Authentic folk instruments include the livenka (accordion) and woodwinds like zhaleika, svirel and kugikli, as well as numerous percussion instruments: buben, bubenci, kokshnik, korobochka, lozkhi, rubel, treschetka, vertushka and zvonchalka.

Chastushkas are a kind of Russian folk song with a long history. They are typically rapped, and are humorous or satiric.

Sakha

Shamanism remains an important cultural practice of the ethnic groups of Siberia and Sakhalin, where several dozen groups live. The Yakuts are the largest, and are known for their olonkho songs and the khomus, a Jew's harp.

Tatarstan

Tatar folk music have rhythmic peculiarities and pentatonic intonation in common with nations of the Volga area, who are ethnically Finno-Ugric and Turkic. Singing girls, renowned for their subtlety and grace, are a prominent component of Tatar folk music. Instruments include the kubyz (violin), kurai (flute) and talianka (accordion).

Tuva

Tuvan throat singing, or xoomii, is famous worldwide, primarily for its novelty. The style is highly unusual and foreign to most listeners, who typically find it inaccessible and amelodic. In throat singing, the natural harmonic resonances of the lips and mouth are tuned to select certain overtones. The style was first recorded by Ted Levin, who helped catalogue a number of different styles. These are include borbannadir (which is compared to the sound of a flowing river), sygyt (similar to whistling), xoomii, chylandyk (likened to chirping crickets) and ezengileer (like a horses trotting). Of particular international fame are the group Huun-Huur-Tu and master throat singer Kongar-ool Ondar.

Ukrainian music

Though Ukraine is now an independent country, Ukrainians constitute the second-largest minority in Russia. The bandura is the most important and distinctive instrument of the Ukrainian folk tradition, and was utilized by the famous 15th century kobzars, a kind of wandering performing who composed dumy, or folk epics.

RUSSIAN CUISINE

Russian cuisine derives its rich and varied character from the vast and multicultural expanse of Russia. Its foundations were laid by the peasant food of the rural population in an often harsh climate, with a combination of plentiful fish, poultry, game, mushrooms, berries, and honey. Crops of rye, wheat, barley, and millet provided the ingredients for a plethora of breads, pancakes, cereals, kvass, beer, and vodka. Flavourful soups and stews centred on seasonal or storable produce, fish, and meats. This wholly native food remained the staples for the vast majority of Russians well into the 20th century. Lying on the northern reaches of the ancient Silk Road, as well as Russia's close proximity to the Caucasus, Persia, and the Ottoman Empire has provided an inescapable Eastern character to its cooking methods (not so much in European Russia but distinguishable in the North Caucasus).

Russia's great expansions of territory, influence, and interest during the 16th-18th centuries brought more refined foods and culinary techniques. It was during this period that smoked meats and fish, pastry cooking, salads and green vegetables, chocolate, ice cream, wines, and liquor were imported from abroad. At least for the urban aristocracy and provincial gentry, this opened the doors for the creative integration of these new foodstuffs with traditional Russian dishes. The result is extremely varied in technique, seasoning, and combination.

From the time of Catherine the Great, every family of influence imported both the products and personnel - mainly German, Austrian, and French - to bring the finest, rarest, and most creative foods to their table. This is nowhere more evident than in the exciting, elegant, highly nuanced, and decadent repertoire of the Franco-Russian chef. Many of the foods that are considered in the West to be traditionally Russian actually come from the Franco-Russian cuisine of the 18th and 19th centuries, and include such widespread dishes as Veal Orloff, Beef Stroganoff, and Sharlotka (Charlotte Russe).

RUSSIAN LITERATURE

Russian literature refers to the literature of Russia or its émigrés, and to the Russian-language literature of several independent nations once a part of what was historically Russia or the Soviet Union. Prior to the nineteenth century Russia produced very little, if any, internationally read literature, but from around the 1830's Russian literature underwent an astounding golden age, beginning with the poet Aleksandr Pushkin and culminating in two of the greatest novelists in world literature, Leo Tolstoy and Fyodor Dostoevsky, and the playwright Anton Chekhov. In the twentieth century leading figures of Russian literature included internationally recognised poets such as Vladimir Mayakovsky, Boris Pasternak, Anna Akhmatova or Joseph Brodsky, and prose writers Maxim Gorky, Vladimir Nabokov, Mikhail Sholokhov, Mikhail Bulgakov or Alexandr Solzhenitsyn.

SPORT IN RUSSIA

Russia is a keen sporting country, successful at a number of sports and continuously finishing in the top rankings at the Olympic games. During the Soviet era the team placed first in the total number of medals won at 14 of its 18 appearances; with these performances, the USSR was the dominant Olympic power of its era. Since the Olympic Games in Helsinki in 1952 and continuing today, the Soviet and later Russian athletes never went below third place in the world (never below 2nd until the most recent Olympics), in number and gold medals collected at the Summer Olympics.

Among the most played sports are football and ice hockey.[1]

Other sports widely played in Russia include weightlifting, gymnastics, boxing, wrestling, martial arts, volleyball, rugby union, basketball and skiing.

RUSSIAN LITERATURE

Russian literature refers to the literature of Russia or its émigrés, and to the Russian-language literature of several independent nations once a part of what was historically Russia or the Soviet Union. Prior to the nineteenth century Russia produced very little, if any, internationally read literature, but from around the 1830's Russian literature underwent an astounding golden age, beginning with the poet Aleksandr Pushkin and culminating in two of the greatest novelists in world literature, Leo Tolstoy and Fyodor Dostoevsky, and the playwright Anton Chekhov. In the twentieth century leading figures of Russian literature included internationally recognised poets such as Vladimir Mayakovsky, Boris Pasternak, Anna Akhmatova or Joseph Brodsky, and prose writers Maxim Gorky, Vladimir Nabokov, Mikhail Sholokhov, Mikhail Bulgakov or Alexandr Solzhenitsyn.

Early history

Old Russian literature consists of several sparse masterpieces written in the Old Russian language (not to be confused with the contemporaneous Church Slavonic). Anonymous works of this nature include *The Tale of Igor's Campaign* and the *Praying of Daniel the Immured*. The so-called *æèòèÿ ñâÿòûõ* zhitiya svyatikh, lives of the saints formed a popular genre of the Old Russian literature. The *Life of Alexander Nevsky* offers a well-known example. Other Russian literary monuments include *Zadonschina*, *Physiologist*, *Synopsis* and *A Journey Beyond the Three Seas*. Bylinas — oral folk epics — fused Christian and pagan traditions. Medieval Russian literature had an overwhelmingly religious character and used an adapted form of the Church Slavonic language with many South Slavic elements. The first work in colloquial Russian, the autobiography of archpriest Avvakum, emerged only in the mid-17th century.

Petrine era

The "Westernization" of Russia, commonly associated with Peter the Great and Catherine the Great, coincided with a reform of the Russian alphabet and increased tolerance of the idea of employing the popular language for general literary purposes. Authors like Antioch Kantemir, Vasily Trediakovsky, and Mikhail Lomonosov in the earlier 18th century paved the way for poets like Derzhavin, playwrights like Sumarokov and Fonvizin, and prose writers like Karamzin and Radishchev.

Golden Age

The 19th century is traditionally referred to as the "Golden Age" of Russian literature. Romanticism permitted a flowering of especially poetic talent: the names of Zhukovsky and Aleksandr Pushkin came to the fore, followed by Mikhail Lermontov and Fyodor Tyutchev.

Nineteenth-century developments included Ivan Krylov the fabulist; non-fiction writers such as Belinsky and Herzen; playwrights such as Griboedov and Ostrovsky; poets such as Evgeny Baratynsky, Konstantin Batyushkov, Nikolai Alekseevich Nekrasov, Aleksey Konstantinovich Tolstoy, Fyodor Tyutchev, and Afanasij Fet; Kozma Prutkov (a collective pen name) the satirist; and a group of widely recognised novelists such as Nikolai Gogol, Leo Tolstoy, Fyodor Dostoevsky, Leskov, Ivan Turgenev, Saltykov-Shchedrin and Goncharov.

The influence of Pushkin cannot be overstated. He is credited with both crystalizing the literary Russian language and introducing a new level of artistry to Russian literature. His best-known work is a novel in verse, Eugene Onegin. In the field of the novel, Tolstoy and Dostoevsky in particular were titanic figures, and have remained internationally renowned, to the point that many scholars have described one or the other as the greatest novelist ever.

Silver Age

Other genres came to the fore with the approach of the 20th century. Anton Chekhov excelled in writing short stories and became perhaps the leading dramatist internationally of his period, while Anna Akhmatova represented innovative lyricists.

The beginning of the 20th century ranks as the Silver Age of Russian poetry. Well-known writers of the period include: Innokenty Annensky, Andrei Bely, Alexander Blok, Valery Bryusov, Marina Tsvetaeva, Sergei Esenin, Nikolay Gumilyov, Daniil Kharms, Velimir Khlebnikov, Dmitry Merezhkovsky, Vladimir Mayakovsky, Zinaida Gippius, Fedor Sologub and Maximilian Voloshin.

Soviet era

Sovietization of Russia affected literature after 1917. Maxim Gorky, Nobel Prize winner Mikhail Sholokhov, Valentin Kataev, Aleksei Nikolaevich Tolstoi, Vladimir Mayakovsky, Ilf and Petrov came to prominence as part of Soviet literature. Whilst Socialist realism gained official support in the Soviet Union, some of the writers—such as Mikhail Bulgakov, Boris Pasternak, Andrei Platonov, Osip Mandelstam, Yury Trifonov, Isaac Babel and Vasily Grossman—secretly continued the classical tradition of Russian literature, writing "into the desk", with no hope of publishing such works until after their deaths. The Serapion Brothers insisted on the right to create a literature independent of political ideology: this brought them into conflict with the government. Nor did the authorities tolerate the experimental art of the Oberiuts. Meanwhile, *émigré* writers such as Nobel Prize winner Ivan Alekseyevich Bunin, Alexander Kuprin, Andrey Bely, Marina Tsvetaeva and Vladimir Nabokov continued to flourish in exile.

In post-Stalin Russia, *Socialist realism* remained the only permitted style; writers like Nobel Prize winner Alexandr Solzhenitsyn (who built his works on the legacy of the gulag camps) or Venedikt Erofeev continued the tradition of clandestine literature. In addition, Soviet authorities put pressure on the Nobel Prize committee to deny Konstantin Poustovsky the Literature Prize in 1965. The prize was awarded instead to Mikhail Sholokhov who was more loyal to the Soviet regime. Post-Communist Russia saw most of these works published and become a part of mainstream culture. However, even before the decay of the Soviet Union, tolerance to non-mainstream art had slowly started to grow, especially during the Khrushchev Thaw. Some works of Bulgakov, Solzhenitsyn and Varlam Shalamov were published in the 1960s. Social criticism, as in the science fiction of the Strugatsky brothers and the literature of the Mitkis became popular. As another post-Stalin development, bard poetry developed.

In the 1970s and 80s autors like Nobel prize winner Joseph Brodsky and short story writer Sergei Dovlatov emigrated to the West and remained known in the Soviet Union with the help of samizdat.

Post-Soviet era

The end of the 20th century and the early 21st century has proven a difficult period for Russian literature, with relatively few authors, such as Victor Pelevin or Vladimir Sorokin, producing distinctive fiction.

In the early 21st century the reading public in Russia has shown considerable interest in new quality literature. Many new authors have emerged, along with new publishing companies, new brands and new literature series. Traditional Russian prose remains popular, and distinctive work has come out of the Russian provinces: for example Nina Gorlanova from Perm has written stories about the everyday problems and joys of the provincial intelligentsia.

Widely popular in teen and early-twenty's audience gained a humoristic fantasy, sci-fi or mixed literature, mostly known for Andrey Belyanin's books. However the overall plot and humor are widely criticized by some, mostly calling it plain dumb.

Detective stories and thrillers have proven a very successful genre of new Russian literature: note the interesting phenomenon of the huge interest in ironic detective stories by Darya Dontsova. She has written about 50 novels, and her books have appeared published in millions of copies and even translated in Europe.

Generations of Winter (Russian: *Moskovskaya saga*), a novel by the Russian writer Vasily Aksyonov, has appeared in the USA. Some critics have praised this novel as a new *Doctor Zhivago* large-scale Russian novel, which tells the story of the Russian Gradov family struggling to survive in the Stalin era.

Several Russian writers have become rather popular in the West, such as Tatyana Tolstaya and (especially) Lyudmila Ulitskaya. Detective-story writer Boris Akunin, with his series about the 19th century sleuth Erast Fandorin, publishes in Europe and in the USA. Alexandra Marinina, the most popular female detective-story writer in Russia, has succeeded in publishing her books around Europe, especially in Germany. Important Russian language writers in Ukraine are Aleksandr Abramovic Bejderman and Andrey Kurkov.

Themes in Russian literature

Suffering, often as a means of redemption, is a recurrent theme in Russian literature. Dostoevsky in particular is noted for exploring suffering in works such as *Notes from the Underground* and *Crime and Punishment*. Christianity and Christian symbolism are also important themes, notably in the works of Dostoevsky, Tolstoy and Chekhov. In the 20th century, suffering as a mechanism of evil was explored by authors such as Solzhenitsyn in *The Gulag Archipelago*.

Viktor Shklovsky, in his book, *Zoo, or Letters Not About Love*, wrote, "Russian literature has a bad tradition. Russian literature is devoted to the description of unsuccessful love affairs."

The 2003 Frankfurt Book Fair selected Russia as its special guest of the year.

NOBEL INDIANS

CHANDRASEKHAR VENKATA RAMAN

Nationality : Indian
Occupation : Physicist
Born on : November 7, 1888 in Trichinopoly, Madras (Tamil Nadu)
Died on : November 21, 1970 in Bangalore (Karnataka)
Awarded : The 1930 Nobel Prize in Physics for his work on the scattering of light and for the discovery of the Raman effect, which is named after him.

LIFE AND ACHIEVEMENTS

C.V. Raman was born on November 7, 1888, near Trichinopoly in Madras. His father, Ramanathan Chandrasekaran Iyer, was a lecturer in Physics, Mathematics, and physical geography. His mother, S. Parvati Ammal, was the daughter of Saptarshi Sastri, a great Sanskrit scholar. Raman, was the second of the eight children in the family.

At an early age, Raman moved to the city of Visakhapatnam, Andhra Pradesh. He completed his BA and MA in Physics and English from the Presidency College, Madras (now Chennai). He entered Presidency College, Madras, in 1902, and in 1904 passed his B.A. examination, winning the first place and the gold medal in physics; in 1907 he gained his M.A. degree, obtaining the highest distinctions. He joined the Indian Civil Services as an Assistant Accountant General in Calcutta (now Kolkata).

Raman was a professor of Physics at the University of Calcutta for the next fifteen years. Raman's years at Calcutta University were marked by great creativity and intellectual excitement, although by Western standards his laboratory facilities were meager It was during his stay here that his work on optics was recognized. Many honors came to him as the significance of his work was acknowledged in India and abroad, as in 1929, when he was invited to do research at the California Institute of Technology. The most tangible evidence of this recognition came in 1929, when the British government conferred a knighthood on him, and in 1930, when he was awarded the Nobel Prize.

After retired from Kolkata University, he became director of the Indian Institute of Science in Bangalore, where he remained until 1948, when he became head of the new Raman Research Institute in the same city. Here until his death on November 21, 1970, he continued to guide research and to inspire his students and coworkers. They spoke of his intense enthusiasm and volcanic energy and of his great generosity in acknowledging the contribution of others. Raman that was not all. He was awarded the Bharat Ratna in 1954.

HIS WORKS

His primary research interests were acoustics, musical instruments, and wave optics. He was best known for his discovery of the Raman effect—a process by which a beam of light passing through a solid, liquid or gas was diffracted and its frequencies (and so its colours) were changed. Raman spectroscopy is based on this phenomenon.

Raman also worked in theory of transverse vibration of strings, his analysis of bowed string on the basis of superposition velocities has an upper-hand in explaining bowed string vibration over Helmholtz. Raman was recognized as the first in this century to reikindle the research into the physics of the violin and other musical instruments. His research in this areas included studies on the behavior of bowed strings, the influence of the violin's bridge, and the frequency response of the violin (known as the Raman curve). Raman also investigated the sound-producing mechanisms of the piano and of some traditional Indian instruments like the tabla and the tambura.

Raman was instrumental in promoting the development of Indian science—creating the *Indian Journal of Physics* (1926) and instigating establishment of the Indian Academy of Sciences (1934). In the course of his 66 years as a physicist, Raman published over 450 research papers and inspired almost three times that number of papers among his students. In promoting Indian science, Raman was hailed as one of India's heroes along with Mohandas Karamchand Gandhi and Motilal Nehru.

SUBRAHMANYAN CHANDRASEKHAR

Nationality	:	American, Indian
Occupation	:	Astrophysicist, Mathematician
Born on	:	October 19, 1910 in Lahore, (then India)
Died on	:	August 21, 1995 in Chicago, Illinois (United States)
Awarded	:	The 1983 Nobel Prize in Physics, along with his colleague William Fowler for their work on stellar evolution.

LIFE AND ACHIEVEMENTS

Subrahmanyan Chandrasekhar was born on October 19, 1910 in Lahore, then a part of British Colonial India, now in West Pakistan. He was one of the more distinguished of the ten children of Chandrasekhar Subrahmanya Iyer who was a senior Railway official in pre-Independence India, an accomplished Carnatic music violinist from the Thanjavur district of Tamil Nadu who authored several authentic books on South Indian musicology. His mother Sita was a woman of high intellectual attainments.

Chandrasekhar had most of his school career and his entire college career in Madras (now Chennai), Tamil Nadu. He had his early education at home under his parents and private tutors. In 1922, at the age of 12, he attended the Hindu High School. He joined the Madras Presidency College in 1925. Subrahmanyan Chandrasekhar passed his Bachelor's degree, B.Sc. (Hon.), in physics in June 1930. In July 1930, he was awarded a Government of India scholarship for graduate studies in Cambridge, England.

After he completed his Ph.D. degree at Cambridge in the summer of 1933, he was elected to a Prize Fellowship at Trinity College for the period 1933-37. In 1936, while on a short visit to Harvard University, Subrahmanyan Chandrasekhar, was offered a position as a Research Associate at the University of Chicago..

Chandrasekhar was noted for his work in the field of stellar evolution, and in the early 1930s he was the first to theorize that a collapsing massive star would become an object so dense that not even light could escape it. Although this finding was greeted with some skepticism at the time it was announced, it went on to form the foundation of the theory of black holes, and eventually earned him and his colleague William A. Fowler a shared Nobel Prize in physics for 1983. His work, however, did not end here. He served the university faculty and its Yerkes Observatory until his death in 1995 at the age of 84. He became a naturalized citizen of the United States in 1953.

HIS WORKS

Chandrasekhar is considered one of the greatest astronomers of the twentieth century. His research interests were wide-ranging, and he approached each problem he tackled with brilliant innovation. His papers on stellar evolution, radiative transfer (which describes the interaction of light with the matter it is passing through), and dynamical systems (e.g., the motion of stars in a cluster) are fundamental reading for each topic.

Chandrasekhar is best known for his discovery of Chandrasekhar Limit. He showed that there is a maximum mass which can be supported against gravity by pressure made up of electrons and atomic nuclei. The value of this limit is about 1.44 times a solar mass. The Chandrasekhar Limit plays a crucial role in understanding the stellar evolution. If the mass of a star exceeded this limit, the star would not become a white dwarf it would continue to collapse under the extreme pressure of gravitational forces. The formulation of the Chandrasekhar Limit led to the discovery of neutron stars and black holes. Depending on the mass there are three possible final stages of a star—white dwarf, neutron star and black hole.

Apart from discovery of Chandrasekhar Limit, major work done by him includes: theory of Brownian motion (1938-1943); theory of illumination and the polarization of sunlit sky (1943-1950); the equilibrium and the stability of ellipsoidal figures of equilibrium, partly in collaboration with Norman R. Lebovitz (1961-1968); the general theory of relativity and relativistic astrophysics (1962-1971); and the mathematical theory of black holes (1974-1983).

Apart from Nobel Prize, other awards won by Chandrasekhar are: Henry Norris Russell Lectureship (1949), Bruce Medal (1952), Gold Medal of the Royal Astronomical Society (1953), Henry Draper Medal (1971), Nobel Prize in Physics (1983), Copley Medal of the Royal Society (1984).

RABINDRANATH TAGORE

Nationality	:	Indian
Occupation	:	Poet, Philosopher, Playwright Composer
Born on	:	May 7, 1861 in Calcutta (now Kolkata) (West Bengal)
Died on	:	August 7, 1941 in Calcutta.
Awarded	:	The 1913 Nobel Prize in Literature.

LIFE AND ACHIEVEMENTS

Rabindranath Tagore, a Bengali poet, philosopher, social reformer, and dramatist was born into an affluent and brilliantly talented Calcutta family on May 7, 1861. His father, Debendranath was one of the founders of the religious society called the 'Brahmo Samaj'. Tagore was born the youngest of fourteen children in the Jorasanko mansion in northern Calcutta (founded by his great grand father; Dwarkanath Tagore) of parents Debendranath Tagore and Sarada Devi.

The house in which Rabindranath grew up was the home of a vast joint, or extended family; there were sometimes as many as 200 Tagores living in the Jorasanko complex; which included the painters Abinindranath and Gaganendranath and, among his own eleven elder brothers and sisters, the writer and philosopher, Dvijendranath, the musician Jyotirindranath, and Bengal's first woman novelist, Svarnakumari Devi.

Rabindranath's formal education began in Calcutta's Oriental Seminary School. Then, for a few years, he studied in Normal School, the institution established by Iswar Chandra Vidyasagar. Next, he went to St. Xavier's School, but as he was irregular as a student, he was not able to continue with his studies here. However, he continued to pursue his education at home.

With his father frequently away and his mother ill, Rabindranath was cared for in his early childhood largely by servants and teachers who confined him strictly, breeding in him, as he later wrote, a longing for the freedom of the outside world and a detestation of conventional and restrictive scholastic education. The boy showed unmistakable poetic talent, and as early as 8 he was urged by his brothers and cousins to express himself in poetry. This encouragement, which continued throughout his formative years, caused his talent to flourish. And when he was 11, his father took him on a trip to upper India and the Himalaya Mountains. Alone in the mountains, Debendranath instructed him in Sanskrit, English, and astronomy and taught him the ancient Hindu religious texts.

Such attention from his distinguish father, together with his own talent, brought him to the forefront of his extraordinary family. Rabindranath's first public recitation of his poetry came when he was 14 at a Bengali cultural and nationalistic festival organized by his brothers; his poem on the greatness of India's past, expressing sorrow at its present state, under British rule, was acclaimed. When he was 17, his brother Satyendranath, the first Indian ever admited to the Indian civil service, took him on a trip to England (he enrolled in London's University College but did not complete his education), and the pattern of his life was established. These three elements occur throughout his life: a profound desire for freedom, both personal and national; an idea of the greatness of Asia's, and especially India's, contribution to the world of the spirit; and poetry expressing both of these.

On one trip to England in 1912 Rabindranath met William Butler Yeats and Erza Pound who were entranced by some prose versions of his Bengali collection of lyrical and devotional poems called *Gitanjali (song offerings)*. Yeats wrote the preface to the English translation of *Gitanjali* which was then published as a book; and in 1913 Tagore won the Nobel Prize for literature.

Rabindranath withdrew from the radical political activity with which many of his countrymen were trying to drive the British from their shores. He chose to express himself in other, more personal ways, such as resigning in 1919 the knighthood which he had received from the British crown and establishing a school and later a university at Shantiniketan in Calcutta.

Till the last years of his life, he continued to compose countless poems, songs, dance dramas, critical essays, novels and prose pieces. Late in his life he also took up brush and ink. His last four years were marked by chronic pain and illness. He died as a literary genius on August 7, 1941 in Calcutta.

HIS WORKS

Tagore began writing *poems* at the age of eight, he published his first substantial poetry—using the *pseudonym Bhanushingo* ("Sun Lion")—in *1877* and wrote his first *short stories* and dramas at age sixteen. Tagore's major works included *Gitanjali* (Song *Offerings*), *Gora (Fair-Faced)*, and *Ghare-Baire* (*The Home and the World*), while his verse, short stories, and novels—many defined by rhythmic lyricism, *colloquial* language, meditative *naturalism*, and philosophical contemplation—received worldwide acclaim. Tagore was also a cultural reformer and *polymath* who *modernised* Bangla art by rejecting strictures binding it to classical Indian forms. Two songs from his *rabindrasangeet* canon are now the *national anthems* of *Bangladesh* and *India:* the *Amar Shonar Bangla* and the *Jana Gana Mana*.

SOME OF TAGORE'S WORKS ARE:

Bangla-Language Originals—

Poetry—

- *Manasi* (1890) *(The Ideal One)*
- *Sonar Tari* (1894) *(The Golden Boat)*
- *Gitanjali* (1910) *(Song Offerings)*
- *Gitimalya* (1914) *(Wreath of Songs)*
- *Balaka* (1916) *(The Flight of Cranes)*

Dramas—

- *Valmiki Pratibha* (1881) *(The Genius of Valmiki)*
- *Visarjan* (1890) *(The Sacrifice)*
- *Raja* (1910) *(The King of the Dark Chamber)*
- *Dak Ghar* (1912) *(The Post Office)*
- *Achalayatan* (1912) *(The Immovable)*
- *Muktadhara* (1922) *(The Waterfall)*
- *Raktakaravi* (1926) *(Red Oleanders)*

Literary Fiction—

- *Nastanirh* (1901) *(The Broken Nest)*
- *Gora* (1910) *(Fair-Faced)*
- *Ghare Baire* (1916) *(The Home and the World)*
- *Yogayog* (1929) *(Crosscurrents)*

Autobiographies—

- *Jivansmriti* (1912) *(My Reminiscences)*
- *Chhelebela* (1940) *(My Boyhood Days)*

English-Language Translations—

- *Chitra* (1914)
- *Creative Unity* (1922)
- *Fruit-Gathering* (1916)
- *Gitanjali: Song Offerings* (1912)
- *Glimpses of Bengal* (1991)
- *I Won't Let you Go: Selected Poems* (1991)
- *My Boyhood Days* (1943)
- *My Reminiscences* (1991)
- *Nationalism* (1991)
- *The Crescent Moon* (1913)
- *The Fugitive* (1921)
- *The Gardener* (1913)
- *The Home and the World* (1985)
- *The Hungry Stones and other stories* (1916)
- *The Post Office* (1996)
- *Sadhana: The Realisation of Life* (1913)
- *Selected Letters* (1997)
- *Selected Poems* (1994)
- *Selected Short Stories* (1991)
- *Songs of Kabir* (1915)
- *Stray Birds* (1916)

Works in English

- *Thought Relics* (1921)

Rabindranath's works heralded a new era in Bengali literature. He was also an accomplished musician—a vocal performer as well as composer. He developed *Rabindra-Sangeet,* a new style of vocal music which is called after him. He was the first Indian to bring an element of psychological realism to his works.

MOTHER TERESA

Nationality : Albanian
Occupation : Nun
Born on : August 27, 1910 in Skopje, Yugoslavia
Died on : September 5, 1997 in Calcutta (West Bengal)
Awarded : The 1979 Nobel Prize for Peace for her work among the poor and dying of India.

LIFE AND ACHIEVEMENTS

Mother Teresa of Calcutta, a Roman Catholic nun who founded the only Catholic religious order still growing in membership, was born Agnes Gonxha Bojaxhiu in Skopje, Yugoslavia, on August 27, 1910. Her parents were Albanian grocers, and at the time of her birth Skopje lay within the Ottoman Empire. She attended public school in Skopje, and first showed religious interests as a member of a school sodality that focused on foreign missions. By the age of 12 she felt she had a calling to help the poor.

This calling took sharper focus through her teenage years, when she was especially inspired by reports of work being done in India by Yugoslav Jesuit missionaries serving in Bengal. At the age of 18 Mother Teresa left home to join a community of Irish nuns, the Sisters of Loretto, who had a mission in Calcutta, India. She received training in Dublin, Ireland, and in Darjeeling, India, taking her first religious vows in 1928 and her final religious vows in 1937.

One of Mother Teresa's first assignments was to teach, and eventually to serve as principal, in a girls' high school in Calcutta. Although the school was close to the slums, the students were mainly wealthy. Following her second vocation she felt an inner urging to leave the convent life (life of a nun) and work directly with the poor. In 1948 the Vatican (residence of the pope in Vatican City, Italy) gave her permission to leave the Sisters of Loretto and to start a new work under the guidance of the Archbishop of Calcutta.

Mother Teresa took an intensive medical training with the American Medical Missionary Sister's in Patna, India to prepare to work with the poor. Her group worked with lepers, orphans and the abandoned and even undertook educational work. Her group continued to expand throughout the 1970s opening new missions abroad and in 1979 she was awarded the Nobel Peace Prize for her work.

In the 1980s and 1990s Mother Teresa's health problems became a concern. She suffered a heart attack while visiting Pope John Paul II in 1983. She had a near fatal heart attack in 1989 and began wearing a pacemaker, a device that regulates the heartbeat.

In March 1997, after an eight week selection process, sixty-three-year-old Sister Nirmala was named as the new leader of the group, Missionaries of Charity. Although Mother Teresa had been trying to cut back on her duties for some time because of her health, she stayed on in an advisory role to Sister Nirmala.

Mother Teresa celebrated her eighty-seventh birthday in August, and died shortly thereafter of a heart attack on September 5, 1997. The world grieved her loss and one mourner noted, "It was Mother herself who poor people respected. When they bury her, we will have lost something that cannot be replaced."

Pope John Paul II on October 19, 2003 formally declared Mother Teresa 'blessed', bringing to an end one of the fastest beatifications in the Roman Catholic church at a glittering ceremony in Vatican City attended by nearly 300,000 admirers and friends of the diminutive nun from Kolkata, which she made her home. The ceremony, the penultimate step towards sainthood, makes Mother Teresa the 1,315th beatified person in the Roman Catholic church, enabling her 'limited worship' namely her formal adoration in the Missionaries of Charity chapels and churches.

HER WORKS

Mother Teresa's first venture in Calcutta was to gather unschooled children from the slums and start to teach them. She quickly attracted both financial support and volunteers. In 1950 her group, now called the Missionaries of Charity, received official status as a religious community within the Archdiocese of Calcutta.

In 1957, The Missioneries of Charity began to work with lepers (those suffering from leprosy). And with the help of Indian officials she converted an abandoned Hindu temple into the Kalighat *(Nirmal Hriday)* Home for the Dying, a free hospice for the poor. Also established was a home for lepers called *Shanti Nagar* (City of Peace) in Titagarh, and an orphange. The order soon began to attract both recruits and charitable donations, and by the 1960s had opened hospices, orphanages and leper houses all over India.

In 1965, by granting a Decree of Praise, Pope Paul VI granted Mother Teresa's request to expand her order to other countries. Teresa's order started to rapidly grow, with new homes opening all over the globe. The order's first house outside India was in Venezuela, and others followed in Rome and Tanzania, and eventually in many countries in Asia, Africa, and Europe, including Albania. In addition, the first Missionaries of Charity home in the United States was established in the South Bronx, New York. By 1996, she was operating 517 missions in more than 100 countries and today is assisted by over one million co-workers worldwide.

"Saint of the Gutters", as she is called, though was tiny in appearance, she was energetic and commanded attenion. By most accounts she was a saint for the times, and several books and articles adoringly started to canonize (declare a saint) her in the 1980s and well into the 1990s. She herself did all to deflect all attention away from what she did to either the works of her group or to the God who inspired her.

THE MISSIONARIES OF CHARITY

Missionaries of Charity is a Catholic religious order which consists of over 4,500 nuns and is active in 133 countries. Members of the order designate their affiliation using the order's initials, "MC" Member nuns must adhere to the vows of chastity, poverty and obedience, and the fourth vow, to give "Wholehearted and Free service to the poorest of the poor". The Missionaries of Charity Brothers was founded in 1963, and a contemplative branch of the Sisters followed in 1976. Lay Catholics and non-Catholics constitute the Co-Workers of Mother Teresa, the Sick and Suffering Co-Workers, and the Lay Missionaries of Charity.

Missionaries care for those who include refugees, ex-prostitutes, the mentally ill, sick children, abandoned children, lepers, AIDS victims, the aged, and convalescent. They have schools run by volunteers to educate street children, they run soup kitchens, as well as many other services as per the communities needs. They have nearly 20 homes in Calcutta alone which include homes for women, orphaned children, the dying, an AIDS hospice, a school for street children, and a leper colony. These services are provided to people regardless of their religion, caste or creed.

The Missionaries of Charity, to sum up, are guided by the constitution Mother Teresa wrote for them.

HAR GOBIND KHORANA

Nationality	:	Indian
Occupation	:	Molecular Biologist
Born on	:	January 9, 1922 in Raipur, Punjab (Now in Pakistan)
Awarded	:	The 1968 Nobel Prize for Medicine along with MW Nuremberg and RW Holley for interpreting the genetic code and analyzing its function in protein synthesis.

LIFE AND ACHIEVEMENTS

Har Gobind Khorana was the youngest of five children born into a poor family in Raipur a little village in Punjab, India (now part of West Pakistan). He was homeschooled by his father, and he later attended D.A.V. Multan High School. He earned his BSc & MSc from Punjab University in Lahore in 1943 and 1945 respectively. In 1945, he began studies at the University of Liverpool. After earning a Ph.D. in 1948, he continued his postdoctoral studies in Zurich (1948-49). Subsequently, he spent two years at Cambridge and his interests in proteins and nucleic acids took root that time. In 1952 he went to the University of British Columbia, Vancouver on a job offer and there a group began to work in the field of biologically interesting phosphate esters and nucleic acids with the inspiration from Dr. Gordon M. Shrum and Scientific counsel from Dr. Jack Campbell. In 1960 he joined the University of Wisconsin as Professor and Co-Director of the Institute of Enzyme Research and Professor of Biochemistry. Khorana continued research on nucleic acid synthesis and prepared the first artificial copy of a yeast gene. Dr. Khorana is also the first to synthesize oligonucleotides, that is, strings of nucleotides.

He was awarded the 1968 Nobel Prize in Medicine (together with Robert W. Holley and Marshall Warren Nirenberg) for work on the interpretation of the genetic code and its function in protein synthesis. They all independently made contributions to the understanding of the genetic code and how it works in the cell.

In 1970 became the Alfred Sloan Professor of Biology and Chemistry at the Massachusetts Institute of Technology where he continues to work, now as US citizen.

Apart from the Nobel Prize, Khorana has won many awards and honours for his achievement. Distinguished Service Award, Watumull Foundation, Honolulu, Hawaii (1968); American Academy of Achievement Award Philadelphia, Pennsylvania (1971); Padma Vibhushan, Presidential Award, India (1972); J.C. Bose Medal, Bose Institute, Calcutta (1972) and Willard Gibbs medal of the Chicago Section of American Chemical Society (1973-74). He was elected a member of the National Academy of Sciences, Washington as well as a Fellow of the American Association for the Advancement of Science. In 1971 he became a foreign member of USSR Academy of Sciences and in 1974 an Honorary Fellow of the Indian Chemical Society.

HIS WORKS

Khorana's work, which is an important scientific landmark of the twentieth century, has brought closer the day when synthetic DNA may be introduced into the defective human tissues to bring about their repair or treat mentally retarded people and change them into more intelligent and healthy human beings. His synthesis of RNA, capable of replication in laboratory, is a step towards the creation of life artificially. The researches has opened up a new branch called Genetic Engineering in Science.

According to his synthetic RNA approach • Ribonucleic acid (RNA) with two repeating units (UCUCUCU → UCU CUC UCU) produced two alternating amino acids. This, combined with the Nirenberg and Leder experiment, showed that UCU codes for Serine and CUC codes for Leucine. • RNAs with three repeating units (UACUACUA → UAC UAC UAC, or ACU ACU ACU, or CUA CUA CUA) produced three different strings of amino acids. • RNAs with four repeating units including UAG, UAA, or UGA, produced only dipeptides and tripeptides thus revealing that UAG, UAA and UGA are stop codons.

With this, Dr. Khorana and his team had established that the mother of all codes, the biological language common to all living organisms, is spelled out in three-letter words: each set of three nucleotides codes for a specific amino acid.

Dr. Khorana was also the first to synthesize oligonucleotides, that is, strings of nucleotides. These custom designed pieces of artificial genes are widely used in biology labs for sequencing, cloning and engineering new plants and animals. The oligo nucleotides, thus, have become indispensable tools in biotechnology. This invention of Dr. Khorana has become automated and commercialized so that anyone now can order a synthetic gene from any of a number of companies—one merely needs to fax the genetic sequence to one of the companies to receive an oligonucliotide with the desired sequence.

AMARTYA KUMAR SEN

Amartya Kumar Sen was born on November 3, 1933 in Shantiniketan, West Bengal to Dr. Ashutosh Sen and Anita Sen. Sen first studied in India at the school system of Visva-Bharati University, Presidency College, Kolkata and at the Delhi School of Economics before moving the Trinity College, Cambridge, where he earned a First Class BA in 1956 and then a Ph.D. in 1959. He was also allowed four years to immerse himself in philosophical issues during his stay at Trinity College.

He has taught economics at University of Calcutta, Jadavpur University, Delhi, Oxford (where he was the Drummond Professor of Political Economy and a Fellow of All Souls College), London School of Economics, Harvard and was Master of Trinity College, Cambridge, between 1998 and 2004, becoming the first Asian to head an Oxbridge college. In January 2004 Sen returned to Harvard where he is currently working. He is also a contributor to the

Eva Colorni Trust at the former London Guildhall University, which has one of the best Economics Departments in the country.

Amartya Sen has received honorary doctorates from major universities in North America, Europe, Asia and Africa. He is a Fellow of the British Academy, Foreign Honorary Member of the American Academy of Arts and Sciences, and a member of the American Philosophical Society. Among the awards he has received are the "1999 Bharat Ratna" (the highest honour awarded by the President of India); the Senator Giovanni Agnelli International Prize in Ethics; the Alan Shawn Feinstein World Hunger Award; the Edinburgh Medal; the Brazilian Ordem do Merito Cientifico (Grã-Cruz); the Presidency of the Italian Republic Medal; the Eisenhower Medal; Honorary Companion of Honour (U.K.); The George E. Marshall Award, and the Nobel Prize in Economics. In 2003, he was conferred the Lifetime Achievement Award by the Indian Chamber of Commerce.

HIS WORKS

Sen's books have been translated into more than thirty languages, and include *Collective Choice and Social Welfare* (1970), *On Economics Inequality* (1973, 1997), *Poverty and Famines* (1981), *Choice, Welfare and Measurement* (1982), *Resources, Values and Development* (1984), *On Ethics and Economics* (1987), *The Standard of Living* (1987), *Inequality Reexamined* (1992), *Development as Freedom* (1999), and *Rationality and Freedom* (2002), *The Argumentative Indian* (2005), and *Identity and Violence: The Illusion of Destiny* (2006), among others. His research has ranged over a number of fields in economics, philosophy, and decision theory, including social choice theory, welfare economics, theory of measurement, development economics, public health, gender studies, moral and political philosophy, and the economics of peace and war.

V.S. NAIPAUL

V.S. Naipaul was awarded the Noble Prize for Literature in 2001. Born to Indian parents in 1932 in Trinidad & Tobago. Naipaul was recognised for his extensive works in English Literature.

VENKATRAMAN RAMAKRISHNAN

Venkatraman Ramakrishnan was born in Chidambaram, in Tamilnadu in 1952. He was awarded Nobel Prize in Chemistry in 2009. He is a structural biologist who received the Nobel Prize for his studies in the structure and function of the ribosome.

KAILASH SATYARTHI

Kailash Satyarthi won the 2014 Nobel Peace Prize along with Pakistani activist Malala Yousafzai for their struggle against the suppression of children and young people and for the right of all children to education.

Originally named Kailash Sharma, Satyarthi was born on 11 January 1954 in the Vidisha district of central Indian state Madhya Pradesh. He attended Government Boys Higher Secondary School, and completed his degree in electrical engineering at Samrat Ashok Technological Institute, Vidisha and a post-graduate degree in high-voltage engineering. He then joined a college in Bhopal as a lecturer for a few years.

He is an Indian children's rights advocate and an activist against child labour. He founded the Bachpan Bachao Andolan (lit. *Save the Childhood Movement*) in 1980 and has acted to protect the rights of more than 83,000 children from 144 countries. It is largely because of Satyarthi's work and activism that the International Labour Organization adopted Convention No. 182 on the worst forms of child labour, which is now a principal guideline for governments around the world.

AWARDS AND HONOURS

Satyarthi has been awarded the following national and international honours:

• 2014: Nobel Peace Prize • 2009: Defenders of Democracy Award (US) • 2008: Alfonso Comin International Award (Spain) • 2007: Gold medal of the Italian Senate (2007) • 1995: Robert F. Kennedy Human Rights Award (US) • 1994: The Aachener International Peace Award (Germany)

NOBEL PRIZE WINNERS FROM WORLD (LITERATURE)

1901

☆ ***René François Armand Prudhomme*** (France) (pen-name) ***Sully Prudhomme***
b. 1839 *d.* 1907
"in special recognition of his poetic composition, which gives evidence of lofty idealism, artistic perfection and a rare combination of the qualities of both heart and intellect"

1902

☆ ***Christian Matthias Theodor Mommsen*** (Germany)
b. 1817 *(in Garding, Sleswick, then Denmark)* *d.* 1903
"the greatest living master of the art of historical writing, with special reference to his monumental work, *A History of Rome*"

1903

☆ ***Bjørnstjerne Martinus Bjørnson*** (Norway)
b. 1832 *d.* 1910
"as a tribute to his noble, magnificent and versatile poetry, which has always been distinguished by both the freshness of its inspiration and the rare purity of its spirit"

1904

☆ ***José Echegaray y Eizaguirre*** (Spain) *shared 1/2 of the prize*
b. 1832 *d.* 1916
"in recognition of the numerous and brilliant compositions which, in an individual and original manner, have revived the great traditions of the Spanish drama"

☆ ***Frédéric Mistral*** (France) *shared 1/2 of the prize*
b. 1830 *d.* 1914
"in recognition of the fresh originality and true inspiration of his poetic production, which faithfully reflects the natural scenery and native spirit of his people, and, in addition, his significant work as a Provençal philologist"

1905

☆ ***Henryk Sienkiewicz*** (Poland)
b. 1846 *d.* 1916
"because of his outstanding merits as an epic writer"

1906

☆ ***Giosuè Carducci*** (Italy)
b. 1835 *d.* 1907
"not only in consideration of his deep learning and critical research, but above all as a tribute to the creative energy, freshness of style, and lyrical force which characterize his poetic masterpieces"

1907

☆ ***Rudyard Kipling*** (United Kingdom)
b. 1865 *(in Bombay, British India)* *d.* 1936
"in consideration of the power of observation, originality of imagination, virility of ideas and remarkable talent for narration which characterize the creations of this world-famous author"

1908

☆ ***Rudolf Christoph Eucken*** (Germany)
b. 1846 *d.* 1926
"in recognition of his earnest search for truth, his penetrating power of thought, his wide range of vision, and the warmth and strength in presentation with which in his numerous works he has vindicated and developed an idealistic philosophy of life"

1909

☆ ***Selma Ottilia Lovisa Lagerlöf*** (Sweden)
b. 1858 ***d.*** 1940
"in appreciation of the lofty idealism, vivid imagination and spiritual perception that characterize her writings"

1910

☆ ***Paul Johann Ludwig Heyse*** (Germany)
b. 1830 ***d.*** 1914
"as a tribute to the consummate artistry, permeated with idealism, which he has demonstrated during his long productive career as a lyric poet, dramatist, novelist and writer of world-renowned short stories"

1911

☆ ***Count Maurice (Mooris) Polidore Marie Bernhard Maeterlinck*** (Belgium)
b. 1862 ***d.*** 1949
"in appreciation of his many-sided literary activities, and especially of his dramatic works, which are distinguished by a wealth of imagination and by a poetic fancy, which reveals, sometimes in the guise of a fairy tale, a deep inspiration, while in a mysterious way they appeal to the readers' own feelings and stimulate their imaginations"

1912

☆ ***Gerhart Johann Robert Hauptmann*** (Germany)
b. 1862 ***d.*** 1946
"primarily in recognition of his fruitful, varied and outstanding production in the realm of dramatic art"

1913

☆ ***Rabindranath Tagore*** (India)
b. 1861 ***d.*** 1941
"because of his profoundly sensitive, fresh and beautiful verse, by which, with consummate skill, he has made his poetic thought, expressed in his own English words, a part of the literature of the West".

1914–1918

☆ ***No Prize was Awarded***

1919

☆ ***Carl Friedrich Georg Spitteler*** (Switzerland)
b. 1845 ***d.*** 1924
"in special appreciation of his epic, Olympian Spring"

1920

☆ ***Knut Pedersen Hamsun*** (Norway)
b. 1859 ***d.*** 1952
"for his monumental work, Growth of the Soil"

1921

☆ ***Jacques Anatole Thibault*** (France)
(pen-name) ***Anatole***
b. 1844 ***d.*** 1924
"in recognition of his brilliant literary achievements, characterized as they are by a nobility of style, a profound human sympathy, grace, and a true Gallic temperament"

1922

☆ ***Jacinto Benavente*** (Spain)
b. 1866 ***d.*** 1954
"for the happy manner in which he has continued the illustrious traditions of the Spanish drama"

1923

☆ ***William Butler Yeats*** (Ireland)
b. 1865 ***d.*** 1939
"for his always inspired poetry, which in a highly artistic form gives expression to the spirit of a whole nation"

1924

☆ ***Rejment*** (Poland)
(pen-name) ***Wladyslaw Stanislaw Reymont***
b. 1867 ***d.*** 1925
"for his great national epic, The Peasants"

1925

☆ ***George Bernard Shaw*** (United Kingdom)
b. 1856 *(in Dublin, Ireland)* ***d.*** 1950
"for his work which is marked by both idealism and humanity, its stimulating satire often being infused with a singular poetic beauty"

1926

☆ ***Grazia Madesani, née Deledda*** (Italy)
(pen-name) ***Grazia Deledda***
b. 1871 (in Nuoro, Sardinia) ***d.*** 1936
"for her idealistically inspired writings which with plastic clarity picture the life on her native island and with depth and sympathy deal with human problems in general"

1927

☆ ***Henri Bergson*** (France)
b. 1859 ***d.*** 1941
"in recognition of his rich and vitalizing ideas and the brilliant skill with which they have been presented"

1928

☆ ***Sigrid Undset*** (Norway)
b. 1882 *(in Kalundborg, Denmark)* ***d.*** 1949
"principially for her powerful descriptions of Northern life during the Middle Ages"

1929

☆ ***Thomas Mann*** (Germany)
b. 1875 ***d.*** 1955
"principally for his great novel, Buddenbrooks, which has won steadily increased recognition as one of the classic works of contemporary literature"

1930

☆ ***Sinclair Lewis*** (USA)
b. 1885 ***d.*** 1951
"for his vigorous and graphic art of description and his ability to create, with wit and humour, new types of characters"

1931

☆ ***Erik Axel Karlfeldt*** (Sweden)
b. 1864 ***d.*** 1931
"The poetry of Erik Axel Karlfeldt"

1932

☆ ***John Galsworthy*** (United Kingdom)
b. 1867 ***d.*** 1933
"for his distinguished art of narration which takes its highest form in The Forsyte Saga"

1933

☆ ***Ivan Alekseyevich Bunin*** (stateless domicile in France)
b. 1870 (in Voronezh, Russia) ***d.*** 1953
"for the strict artistry with which he has carried on the classical Russian traditions in prose writing"

1934

☆ ***Luigi Pirandello*** (Italy)
b. 1867 ***d.*** 1936
"for his bold and ingenious revival of dramatic and scenic art"

1935

☆ ***No Prize was Awarded***
The prize money was with 1/3 allocated to the Main Fund and with 2/3 to the Special Fund of this prize section

1936

☆ ***Eugene Gladstone O'Neill*** (USA)
b. 1888 ***d.*** 1953
"for the power, honesty and deep-felt emotions of his dramatic works, which embody an original concept of tragedy"

1937

☆ ***Roger Martin du Gard*** (France)
b. 1881 ***d.*** 1958
"for the artistic power and truth with which he has depicted human conflict as well as some fundamental aspects of contemporary life in his novel-cycle *Les Thibault*"

1938

☆ ***Pearl Walsh, née Sydenstricker*** (USA)
(pen-name) ***Pearl Buck***
b. 1892 ***d.*** 1973
"for her rich and truly epic descriptions of peasant life in China and for her biographical masterpieces"

1939

☆ ***Frans Eemil Sillanpää*** (Finland)
b. 1888 ***d.*** 1964
"for his deep understanding of his country's peasantry and the exquisite art with which he has portrayed their way of life and their relationship with Nature"

1940–1943

No Nobel Prize was Awarded this year

1944

☆ ***Johannes Vilhelm Jensen*** (Denmark)
b. 1873 ***d.*** 1950
"for the rare strength and fertility of his poetic imagination with which is combined an intellectual curiosity of wide scope and a bold, freshly creative style"

1945

☆ ***Lucila Godoy y Alcayaga*** (Chile)
(pen-name) ***Gabriela Mistral***
b. 1889 ***d.*** 1957
"for her lyric poetry which, inspired by powerful emotions, has made her name a symbol of the idealistic aspirations of the entire Latin American world"

1946

☆ ***Hermann Hesse*** (Switzerland)
b. 1877 *(in Calw, Wuerttemberg, Germany)* ***d.*** 1962
"for his inspired writings which, while growing in boldness and penetration, exemplify the classical humanitarian ideals and high qualities of style"

1947

☆ ***André Paul Guillaume Gide*** (France)
b. 1869 ***d.*** 1951
"for his comprehensive and artistically significant writings, in which human problems and conditions have been presented with a fearless love of truth and keen psychological insight"

1948

☆ ***Thomas Stearns Eliot*** (United Kingdom)
b. 1888 *(in St. Louis, MO, USA)* ***d.*** 1965
"for his outstanding, pioneer contribution to present-day poetry"

1949

☆ ***William Faulkner*** (USA)
b. 1897 ***d.*** 1962
"for his powerful and artistically unique contribution to the modern American novel"

1950

☆ ***Earl (Bertrand Arthur William) Russell*** (United Kingdom)
b. 1872 ***d.*** 1970
"in recognition of his varied and significant writings in which he champions humanitarian ideals and freedom of thought"

1951

☆ ***Pär Fabian Lagerkvist*** (Sweden)
b. 1891 ***d.*** 1974
"for the artistic vigour and true independence of mind with which he endeavours in his poetry to find answers to the eternal questions confronting mankind"

1952

☆ ***François Mauriac*** (France)
b. 1885 ***d.*** 1970
"for the deep spiritual insight and the artistic intensity with which he has in his novels penetrated the drama of human life"

1953

☆ ***Sir Winston Leonard Spencer Churchill*** (United Kingdom)
b. 1874 ***d.*** 1965
"for his mastery of historical and biographical description as well as for brilliant oratory in defending exalted human values"

1954

☆ ***Ernest Miller Hemingway*** (USA)
b. 1899 ***d.*** 1961
"for his mastery of the art of narrative, most recently demonstrated in The Old Man and the Sea, and for the influence that he has exerted on contemporary style"

1955

☆ ***Halldór Kiljan Laxness*** (Iceland)
b. 1902 ***d.*** 1998
"for his vivid epic power which has renewed the great narrative art of Iceland"

1956

☆ ***Juan Ramón Jiménez*** (Spain)
b. 1881 ***d.*** 1958 *(domiciled in Puerto Rico, USA)*
"for his lyrical poetry, which in Spanish language constitutes an example of high spirit and artistical purity"

1957

☆ ***Albert Camus*** (France)
b. 1913 *(in Mondovi, Algeria)* ***d.*** 1960
"for his important literary production, which with clear-sighted earnestness illuminates the problems of the human conscience in our times"

1958

☆ ***Boris Leonidovich Pasternak*** (USSR)
b. 1890 ***d.*** 1960
"for his important achievement both in contemporary lyrical poetry and in the field of the great Russian epic tradition"
(Accepted first, later caused by the authorities of his country to decline the prize.)

1959

☆ ***Salvatore Quasimodo*** (Italy)
b. 1901 ***d.*** 1968
"for his lyrical poetry, which with classical fire expresses the tragic experience of life in our own times"

1960

☆ ***Alexis Léger*** (France)
(pen-name) ***Saint-John Perse***
b. 1887 *(on Guadeloupe Island)* ***d.*** 1975
"for the soaring flight and the evocative imagery of his poetry which in a visionary fashion reflects the conditions of our time"

1961

☆ ***Ivo Andric*** (Yugoslavia)
b. 1892 (in Travnik, Bosnia) ***d.*** 1975
"for the epic force with which he has traced themes and depicted human destinies drawn from the history of his country"

1962

☆ ***John Steinbeck*** (USA)
b. 1902 ***d.*** 1968
"for his realistic and imaginative writings, combining as they do sympathetic humour and keen social perception"

1963

☆ ***Giorgos Seferiadis*** (Greece)
(pen-name) ***Giorgos Seferis***
b. 1900 *(in Smyrna, Turkey)* ***d.*** 1971
"for his eminent lyrical writing, inspired by a deep feeling for the Hellenic world of culture"

1964

☆ ***Jean-Paul Sartre*** (France)
b. 1905 ***d.*** 1980
"for his work which, rich in ideas and filled with the spirit of freedom and the quest for truth, has exerted a far-reaching influence on our age"
(Declined the prize saying: "A writer must refuse to allow himself to be transformed into an institution, even if it takes place in the most honourable form.")

1965

☆ ***Mikhail Aleksandrovich Sholokhov*** (USSR)
b. 1905 ***d.*** 1984
"for the artistic power and integrity with which, in his epic of the Don, he has given expression

to a historic phase in the life of the Russian people"

1966

☆ ***Samuel Yosef Agnon*** (Israel) *shared 1/2 of the prize*
b. 1888 ***d.*** 1970
"for his profoundly characteristic narrative art with motifs from the life of the Jewish people"

☆ ***Nelly Sachs*** (Sweden) *shared 1/2 of the prize*
b. 1891 *(in Berlin, Germany)* ***d.*** 1970
"for her outstanding lyrical and dramatic writing, which interprets Israel's destiny with touching strength"

1967

☆ ***Miguel Angel Asturias*** (Guatemala)
b. 1899 ***d.*** 1974
"for his vivid literary achievement, deep-rooted in the national traits and traditions of Indian peoples of Latin America"

1968

☆ ***Yasunari Kawabata*** (Japan)
b. 1899 ***d.*** 1972
"for his narrative mastery, which with great sensibility expresses the essence of the Japanese mind"

1969

☆ ***Samuel Beckett*** (Ireland)
b. 1906 ***d.*** 1989
"for his writing, which - in new forms for the novel and drama - in the destitution of modern man acquires its elevation"

1970

☆ ***Aleksandr Isayevich Solzhenitsyn*** (USSR)
b. 1918
"for the ethical force with which he has pursued the indispensable traditions of Russian literature"

1971

☆ ***Neftalí Ricardo Reyes Basoalto*** (Chile)
(pen-name) ***Pablo Neruda***
b. 1904 ***d.*** 1973
"for a poetry that with the action of an elemental force brings alive a continent's destiny and dreams"

1972

☆ ***Heinrich Böll*** (Federal Republic of Germany)
b. 1917 ***d.*** 1985
"for his writing which through its combination of a broad perspective on his time and a sensitive skill in characterization has contributed to a renewal of German literature"

1973

☆ ***Patrick White*** (Australia)
b. 1912 *(in London, United Kingdom)* ***d.*** 1990
"for an epic and psychological narrative art which has introduced a new continent into literature"

1974

☆ ***Eyvind Johnson*** (Sweden) *shared 1/2 of the prize*
b. 1900 ***d.*** 1976
"for a narrative art, far-seeing in lands and ages, in the service of freedom"

☆ ***Harry Martinson*** (Sweden) *shared 1/2 of the prize*
b. 1904 ***d.*** 1978
"for writings that catch the dewdrop and reflect the cosmos"

1975

☆ ***Eugenio Montale*** (Italy)
b. 1896 ***d.*** 1981
"for his distinctive poetry which, with great artistic sensitivity, has interpreted human values under the sign of an outlook on life with no illusions"

1976

☆ ***Saul Bellow*** (USA)
b. 1915 ***d.*** 2005
"for the human understanding and subtle analysis of contemporary culture that are combined in his work"

1977

☆ ***Vicente Aleixandre*** (Spain)
b. 1898 ***d.*** 1984
"for a creative poetic writing which illuminates man's condition in the cosmos and in present-day society, at the same time representing the great renewal of the traditions of Spanish poetry between the wars"

1978

☆ ***Isaac Bashevis Singer*** (USA)
b. 1904 *(in Radzymin, Poland)* ***d.*** 1991
"for his impassioned narrative art which, with roots in a Polish-Jewish cultural tradition, brings universal human conditions to life"

1979

☆ ***Odysseus Alepoudhelis*** (Greece)
(pen-name) ***Odysseus Elytis***
b. 1911 ***d.*** 1996
"for his poetry, which, against the background of Greek tradition, depicts with sensuous strength and intellectual clear-sightedness modern man's struggle for freedom and creativeness"

1980

☆ ***Czeslaw Milosz*** (Poland and USA)
b. 1911 ***d.*** 2004
"who with uncompromising clear-sightedness voices man's exposed condition in a world of severe conflicts"

1981

☆ ***Elias Canetti*** (United Kingdom)
b. 1905 *(in Rustschuk, Bulgaria)* ***d.*** 1994
"for writings marked by a broad outlook, a wealth of ideas and artistic power"

1982

☆ ***Gabriel García Márquez*** (Colombia)
b. 1928
"for his novels and short stories, in which the fantastic and the realistic are combined in a richly composed world of imagination, reflecting a continent's life and conflicts"

1983

☆ ***William Golding*** (United Kingdom)
b. 1911 ***d.*** 1993
"for his novels which, with the perspicuity of realistic narrative art and the diversity and universality of myth, illuminate the human condition in the world of today"

1984

☆ ***Jaroslav Seifert*** (Czechoslovakia)
b. 1901 ***d.*** 1986
"for his poetry which endowed with freshness, sensuality and rich inventiveness provides a liberating image of the indomitable spirit and versatility of man"

1985

☆ ***Claude Simon*** (France)
b. 1913 ***d.*** 2005
"who in his novel combines the poet's and the painter's creativeness with a deepened awareness of time in the depiction of the human condition"

1986

☆ ***Wole Soyinka*** (Nigeria)
b. 1934
"who in a wide cultural perspective and with poetic overtones fashions the drama of existence"

1987

☆ ***Joseph Brodsky*** (USA)
b. 1940 *(in Leningrad, then USSR)* ***d.*** 1996
"for an all-embracing authorship, imbued with clarity of thought and poetic intensity"

1988

☆ ***Naguib Mahfouz*** (Egypt)
b. 1911
"who, through works rich in nuance - now clear-sightedly realistic, now evocatively ambiguous - has formed an Arabian narrative art that applies to all mankind"

1989

☆ ***Camilo José Cela*** (Spain)
b. 1916 *d.* 2002
"for a rich and intensive prose, which with restrained compassion forms a challenging vision of man's vulnerability"

1990

☆ ***Octavio Paz*** (Mexico)
b. 1914 *d.* 1998
"for impassioned writing with wide horizons, characterized by sensuous intelligence and humanistic integrity"

1991

☆ ***Nadine Gordimer*** (South Africa)
b. 1923
"who through her magnificent epic writing has - in the words of Alfred Nobel - been of very great benefit to humanity"

1992

☆ ***Derek Walcott*** (Saint Lucia)
b. 1930
"for a poetic oeuvre of great luminosity, sustained by a historical vision, the outcome of a multicultural commitment"

1993

☆ ***Toni Morrison*** (USA)
b. 1931
"who in novels characterized by visionary force and poetic import, gives life to an essential aspect of American reality"

1994

☆ ***Kenzaburo Oe*** (Japan)
b. 1935
"who with poetic force creates an imagined world, where life and myth condense to form a disconcerting picture of the human predicament today"

1995

☆ ***Seamus Heaney*** (Ireland)
b. 1939
"for works of lyrical beauty and ethical depth, which exalt everyday miracles and the living past"

1996

☆ ***Wislawa Szymborska*** (Poland)
b. 1923
"for poetry that with ironic precision allows the historical and biological context to come to light in fragments of human reality"

1997

☆ ***Dario Fo*** (Italy)
b. 1926
"who emulates the jesters of the Middle Ages in scourging authority and upholding the dignity of the downtrodden"

1998

☆ ***José Saramago*** (Portugal)
b. 1922
"who with parables sustained by imagination, compassion and irony continually enables us once again to apprehend an elusory reality"

1999

☆ ***Günter Grass*** (Federal Republic of Germany)
b. 1927 *(in Danzig)*
"whose frolicsome black fables portray the forgotten face of history"

2000

☆ ***Gao Xingjian*** (France)
b. 1940 *(in Ganzhou, China)*
"for an oeuvre of universal validity, bitter insights and linguistic ingenuity, which has opened new paths for the Chinese novel and drama"

2001

☆ ***Sir Vidiadhar Surajprasad Naipaul*** (United Kingdom)
b. 1932 *(in Trinidad)*
"for having united perceptive narrative and incorruptible scrutiny in works that compel us to see the presence of suppressed histories"

2002

☆ ***Imre Kertész*** (Hungary)
b. 1929
"for writing that upholds the fragile experience of the individual against the barbaric arbitrariness of history"

2000

☆ ***John M. Coetzee*** (South Africa)
b. 1940
"who in innumerable guises portrays the surprising involvement of the outsider"

2000

☆ ***Elfriede Jelinek*** (Austria)
b. 1946
"for her musical flow of voices and counter-voices in novels and plays that with extraordinary linguistic zeal reveal the absurdity of society's clichés and their subjugating power"

2000

☆ ***Harold Pinter*** (United Kingdom)
b. 1930
"who in his plays uncovers the precipice under everyday prattle and forces entry into oppression's closed rooms"

2006

☆ ***Orhand Pamuk*** (Turkey)
b. 1952
"who in the quest for the melancholic soul of his native city has discovered new symbols for the clash and interlacing of cultures"

2007

☆ ***Doris Lessing*** (United Kingdom)
b. 1919
"that epicist of the female experience, who with scepticism, fire and visionary power has subjected a divided civilisation to scrutiny"

2008

☆ ***Jean Marie Gustave Le Clezio***
b. 1940
"author of new departures, poetic adventure and sensual ecstasy, explorer of a humanity beyond and below the reigning civilisation".

2009

☆ ***Herta Muller***
b. 1953
"who, with the concentration of poetry and the frankness of prose, depicts the landscape of the dispossessed."

2010

☆ ***Mario Vargas Llosa***
b. 1936
"for his cartography of structures of power and his trenchant images of the individual's resistance, revolt and defeat."

2011

☆ ***Tomas Transtromer*** (Sweden)
b. 1931 *(in Stockholm, Sweden)*
"for his poetry explores themes of nature, isolation and identity"

2012

☆ ***Mo Yan***
b. 1955 *(Gaomi, Shandong, China)*
"Who with hallucinatory realism merges folk tales, history and the contemporary".

2013

☆ ***Alice Munro***
b. 1931 *(Wingham, Ontario, Canada)*
"Master of the contemporary short story".

2014

☆ ***Patrick Modiano***
b. 1945 *(Boulogne Billancourt France)*
"for the art of memory with which he has evoked the most ungraspable human destinies and uncovered the life-world of the occupation".

GENERAL ENGLISH

COMPREHENSION

EXERCISE 1

Read the following passage and answer the questions:

Pollution can be defined as an undesirable change in the physical, chemical or biological characteristics of air, water or land which can harm the health, survival or activities of humans or other organisms.

After World War II the western countries witnessed an industrial boom made possible by a burgeoning population, advanced technology and a rapid rise in energy consumption all symptoms of development. During the 1950s and 1960s this growth significantly increased the volume of wastes released into the environment. The result was ever-increasing pollution of environment which we are at present face to face with, a picture which becomes more and more grim everyday.

I. Answer the following questions :

1. How can we define pollution?
2. What made possible the industrial boom after the World War II?
3. What happened during the 1950's and 1960's?
4. What was the result?
5. What is the present picture?
6. Assign a suitable heading to the passage.

II. Give a synonym for each of the following words.

Words	Synonyms
(a) develop	____________
(b) possible	____________
(c) harm	____________
(d) significantly	____________
(e) rapid	____________

III. Give an antonym for each of the following words.

Words	Antonyms
(a) rapid	____________
(b) undesirable	____________
(c) increase	____________
(d) rise	____________
(e) growth	

IV. Use each of the following expressions in sentences of your own :

(a) advanced technology...............................
(b) symptoms of development...............................
(c) volume of wastes...............................
(d) harm the health...............................
(e) undesirable change...............................

EXERCISE 2

Read the following passage and answer the questions :

Dippers patrol the beds of shallow, fast-flowing streams in search of insect larvae, fishfry fresh water shrimps and molluscs such as water snails. They walk along the bottom, sometimes completely submerged and manage to stay underwater by holding their wings at an angle and clinging to pebbles with their toes. The nature of their diet makes dippers very sensitive to pollutants in water. The dippers which are found in Asia North Africa and South America, build their nests in a wall beside a brook, in holes between rocks and sometimes even behind a waterfall.

I. Answer the following questions :

1. Where do dippers patrol and why?
2. Where do they walk and in what condition?

3. How do they manage to stay under water?
4. What makes them sensitive to pollutants in water?
5. Where do dippers mentioned in the passage build their nests?
6. Write a suitable heading to the passage.

II. Give a synonym for each of the following words:

Words	*Synonyms*
(a) bottom	________
(b) cling	________
(c) sensitive	________
(d) submerged	________
(e) manage	________

III. Give an antonym for each of the following words :

Words	*Antonyms*
(a) build	________
(b) completely	________
(c) deep	________
(d) behind	________
(e) stay	________

IV. Use each of the following expressions in sentences of your own.

(a) fresh water ....

....

(b) walk along ....

....

(c) nature of their diet ....

....

(d) completely submerged ....

....

(e) their nests ....

....

EXERCISE 3

Read the following passage carefully and answer the questions :

There is something about school days which tugs at everyone's heart. Carefree days with friends, flush of the first romance, bunking classes and movies and fun.

Perhaps that explains the enduring appeal of 'School Days' on DD-I every Sunday at 11.30 a.m. Though the serial unfolds school life as seen by young people, it is known to receive fan mail even from adults.

The silent and intense, the flirtatious sunny the studious Newton as also the happy-go-lucky Minnie, Richa Annie and Priyanka viewers have no difficulty in identifying with most of the characters.

Now there's good news for the fans of School Days. The serial has got an extension of 13 more episodes.

I. Answer the following questions :

1. What tugs at every one's heart?
2. Write a few special features of School Days.
3. When is the serial "School Days" telecast on DDI?
4. How can you say that the serial is liked even by adults?
5. Write the specific characteristics of a few characters.
6. What is good news for the fan of school days?
7. Assign a suitable heading to the passage.

II. Give a synonym for each of the following words :

Words	*Synonyms*
(a) intense	________
(b) studious	________
(c) enduring	________
(d) appealing	________
(e) carefree	________

III. Give an antonym for each of the following words:

Words	*Antonyms*
(a) young	________
(b) good	________
(c) receive	________
(d) silent	________
(e) lucky	________

IV. Arrange the following jumbled sentences :

1. mother/ her/ died of/ cholera.

....

2. lies on/ the/ bank of the Yamuna/ The Taj

....

3. No sooner/ the train/ at/ the station/ did/ than arrive/ began to/ the crowd/ rush in.

....

4. does not like/ my mother/ certain boys/ such as/ the disrespectful/ ones/

....

5. she/ afraid of/ losing/ her way/ was/ in the forest.

....

6. on this point/ want/ I/ don't/ any more discussion/

....

7. are/ already/ late/ sharp !/ look/ we

....

8. made/ an attempt/ on/ of/ the minister/ a hardcore/ terrorist/ the life/

....

9. elbowed/ my way/ I/ through/ the crush

....

10. cattle/ a herd of/ grazing/ down/ was/ the hill/ in the meadow/

....

EXERCISE 4

Read the follwing passage and answer the following questions :

The British who came to India as traders, eventually emerged as a dominant political power by the end of the 18th century. The prospects of fame and fortune also lured the British artists who began arriving here from the 1760s onwards. Until then, there was no visual record of the Indian panorama based on first hand observation. While artists applied their talents to landscape painting the portraits of the elite or pictures of historical events of imperial interest, there were some with a different bent of mind. They were perceptive and sincerely responsive to the sights and sounds and the colour and shapes of their environment.

I. Answer the following questions :

1. In what capacity did the British originally come to India?
2. How did they emerge by the end of the 18th century?
3. What lured the British artists to come to India?
4. To what did the artists apply their mind?
5. What does the author tell about some others?
6. Assign a suitable title to the passage.

II. Give a synonym for each of the following words:

Words	***Synonyms***
(a) dominant	________
(b) eventually	________
(c) emerged	________
(d) talent	________
(e) different	________

III. Give an antonym for each of the following words:

Words	***Antonyms***
(a) elite	________
(b) sincerely	________
(c) imperial	________
(d) fame	________
(e) fortune	________

EXERCISE 5

Read the following passage and answer that the following questions :

Elliott's parents moved again, to a house near the Indian Ocean and overlooking some sandhills. Those sandhills played an important part in his development as an athlete. He used to run up and down them, building up his strength for races against his father and school friends. At college, Elliott was an outstanding performer at everything he tried. He was captain of the hockey team, rowed in the school first eight, was a member of the shooting team, played tennis and was also a pianist.

But it was running that claimed most of his time. "I was best at it so I decided to concentrate on the thing I' was good at," he said.

I. Answer the following questions :

1. Briefly describe the location of the house to which Elliott's parents moved again.
2. What important role did the sandhills play in his development as an athlete?
3. Explain how he was an outstanding performer at school?
4. What claimed most of his time?
5. Why did Eliott finally decide to become an athlete?
6. Assign a suitable heading to the passage.

II. Give a synonym for each of the following words :

	Words	*Synonyms*
(a)	important	________
(b)	strength	________
(c)	development	________
(d)	overlooking	________
(e)	concentrate (verb)	________

III. Give an antonym for each of the following words :

	Words	*Antonyms*
(a)	outstanding	________
(b)	build	________
(c)	important	________
(d)	best	________
(e)	against	________

IV. Use each of the following expressions in sentences of your own :

(a) overlooking ....
....

(b) outstanding performer..
....

(c) best at ....
....

(d) captain of the team..
....

(e) concentrate on ....
....

V. Fill in the blanks :

1. She is captain .... our tennis team.
   (a) for (b) on
   (c) of (d) in
2. Playing claimed most .... his time and hence left him the dullest student .... the class.
   (a) of, for (b) on, in
   (c) of, to (d) of, in
3. Leena was good .... sports but weak .... studies.
   (a) on, in (b) for, on
   (c) at, in (d) for, upon
4. He was a member .... the shooting team.
   (a) for (b) on
   (c) of (d) to
5. In the past years, there has taken place a great change .... the lifestyle .... the common people.
   (a) of, of (b) for, in
   (c) at, of (d) in, of

EXERCISE 6

Read the following passage and answer the following questions :

Sight is our most precious sense and many people fear blindness more than they fear any other disability. Eye, the organ of sight is our most important organ for locating and observing the world around us. We use our eyes in almost everything we do — reading, working, watching movies and television, playing games, and countless other activities.

The human eyeball measures only about 25mm in diameter. Yet the eye can see objects as far away as a star and as tiny as a grain of sand. The eye can quickly adjust its focus between a distant point and a near one.

I. Answer the following questions :

1. What is our most precious sense?
2. Which disability the people fear most?
3. What is the chief function of the organ of sight?

4. Name a few activities in which we use our eyes.
5. What is the average measurement of the human eyeball?
6. How can the eye see distant and near objects immediately one after the other?
7. Assign a suitable heading to the passage.

II. Give a synonym for each of the following words:

Words	*Synonyms*
(a) precious	....
(b) tiny	....
(c) quickly	....
(d) countless	....
(e) disability	....

III. Give an antonym for each of the following words :

Words	*Antonyms*
(a) far	....
(b) disability	....
(c) countless	....
(d) precious	....
(e) tiny	....

EXERCISE 7

Read the following passage and answer the following questions :

Trees are a vital part of our life. The cutting of trees means cutting short the human life. Trees not only provide us things such as fuel, fodder, gum and wood for furniture but also help in reducing the atmospheric pollution by maintaining the oxygen-carbondioxide balance on earth. Trees also provide us fruits and medicines and a habitat to wildlife which is also considered important for man's survival on earth. Trees do not allow the upper fertile layer of the soil to blow or flow away. Thus, they protect the soil from erosion. They cause rain but they also save us from floods. Keeping in mind the benefits of trees all of us should join hands and dedicate ourselves to planting more and more trees with ever-increasing enthusiasm. If human beings only understand clearly that mankind will survive on this planet only as long as trees are there, the rest will follow as man's activities will automatically get directed to growing trees and protecting them against the danger of getting destroyed.

I. Answer the following questions :

1. What are the major benefits of trees?
2. How trees help in reducing the pollution
3. How are trees helpful to wild life?
4. How long will man survive on this planet?
5. Which spirit should man grow more and more trees?

II. Give a synonym for each of the following words :

Words	*Synonyms*
(a) vital	....
(b) provide	....
(c) reducing	....
(d) Maintaining	....
(e) allow	....

III. Give an antonym for each of the following words :

Words	*Antonyms*
(a) protect	....
(b) upper	....
(c) reduce	....
(d) fertile	....
(e) balance	....

EXERCISE 8

Read the following passage and answer the questions :

With every change of season, designers unveil their latest collections to allure the customers and to add another feather to their cap. However, designer clothes are not meant for everybody. A limited number of people are able to carry themselves in such clothes. The majority finds them too daring to don. Moreover, in spite of all the hype and propaganda by designers to provide affordable wear, the fact remains that their creations are beyond the reach of middle class, which forms the major chunk of Indian society.

Designer clothes may look pretty on models walking down the ramp, but an average girl feels more at home in clothes which do not carry a 'designer tag'.

I. Answer the following questions :

1. What do the designers do with every change of season?
2. Are designer clothes meant for everybody?
3. Why don't people of middle class wear designer clothes?
4. How do models look in designer clothes?
5. Does an average girl like them?
6. Assign a suitable heading to the passage.

II. Give a synonym for each of the following words :

Words	Synonyms
(a) change	....
(b) provide	....
(c) beyond	....
(d) carry	....
(e) major	....

III. Give an antonym for each of the following words :

Words	Antonyms
(a) affordable	....
(b) major	....
(c) change	....
(d) latest	....
(e) daring	....

EXERCISE 9

Read the following passage and answer the following questions:

One day, the three daughters of Dean of Christ (Alice Liell was one of them) accompanied Lewis Caroll to the meadows down the river. They went rowing and landed in the meadows. Since it was a very hot summer afternoon, they took refuge in a hayrick. Here he told them the delightful tale of Alice. By the age of 33, Lewis had brought out this tale in the form of a book titled Alice's Adventures Underground. It was hand written, illustrated and bound to be presented to Alice Liddell as a gift for Christmas in 1864.

I. Answer the following questions.

1. Who accompanied Lewis Caroll to the meadows?
2. How did they reach the meadows?
3. What season was it?
4. Where did they take refuge?
5. Where did Caroll tell the girls the story of Alice?
6. When did he bring it out in the form of a book ?
7. What was it titled?
8. Whom did he present it and when?

II. Give a synonym for each of the following words :

Words	Synonyms
(a) land	....
(b) refuge	....
(c) tale	....
(d) underground	....
(e) tell	....

III. Give an antonyms for each of the following words :

Words	Antonyms
(a) bind	....
(b) famous	....
(c) bring	....
(d) present	....
(e) delightful	....

EXERCISE 10

Read the following passage and answer the following questions:

This was very proper; the sigh which accompanied it was really estimable; but it should have lasted longer. Emma was rather in dismay when only half a minute afterwards he began to speak of other things, and in a voice of the greatest alacrity and enjoyment.

"What an excellent device," said he, "the use of a sheepskin for carriages. How very comfortable they make it; impossible to feel cold with such precautions. The contrivances of modern days, indeed, have rendered a gentleman's carriage perfectly complete. One is so fenced and guarded from the weather, that not a breath of air can find its way unpermitted. Weather becomes absolutely of no consequence. It is a very cold afternoon – but in this carriage we know nothing of the matter. Ha ! Snows a little, I see."

"Yes," said John Knightley, "and I think we shall have a good deal of it."

"Christmas weather," observed Mr. Elton. "Quite seasonable; and extremely fortunate we may think ourselves that it did not begin yesterday, and prevent this day's party, which it might very possibly have done, for Mr. Woodhouse would hardly have ventured had there been much snow on the ground; but now it is of no consequence. This is quite the season, indeed, for friendly meetings. At Christmas everybody invites their friends about them, and people think little of even the worst weather. I was snowed up at a friend's house once for a week. Nothing could be pleasanter. I went for only one night, and could not get away till that very day se'nnight."

Mr. John Knightley looked as if he did not comprehend the pleasure.

From *Emma*

I. Answer the following question :

1. What particular benefit of the use of sheepskin for carriages is mentioned in the passage?
2. When did it begin snowing —on the day of the party or earlier?
3. What kind of feeling of people in general on the Christmas day are mentioned in the passage?
4. Who was once snowed up at a friend's house and how did he feel?
5. Who did not seem to comprehend the pleasure?

II. Give a synonym for each of the following words :

Words	*Synonyms*
(a) absolutely	....
(b) comprehend	....
(c) comfortable	....
(d) possible	....
(e) proper	....

III. Give an antonym for each of the following words :

Words	*Antonyms*
(a) extremely	....
(b) comprehensible	....
(c) fortunate	....
(d) friendly	....
(e) alacrity	....

EXERCISE 11

Read the following passage and answer the following questions:

I gave due inward applause to every object, and then I remembered how **old Earnshaw** used to come in when all was tidied, and call me a cant lass, and slip a shilling into my hand as a Christmas box; and from that I went on to think of his fondness for Heathcliff, and his dread lest he should suffer neglect after death had removed him; and that naturally led me to consider the poor lad's situation now, and from singing I changed my mind to crying. It struck me soon, however, there would be more sense in endeavouring to repair some of his wrongs than shedding tears over them. I got up and walked into the court to seek him.

He was not far; I found him smoothing the glossy coat of the new pony in the stable, and feeding the other beasts, according to custom.

"Make haste, Heathcliff!" I said, "the kitchen is so comfortable; and Joseph is upstairs; make haste, and let me dress you smart before Miss Cathy comes out, and then you can sit together, with the whole hearth to yourselves, and have a long chatter till bedtime."

He proceeded with his task and never turned his head towards me.

"Come-are you coming?" I continued. "There's a little cake for each of you, nearly enough; and you'll need half-an-hour's donning."

I waited five minutes, but getting no answer left him. ....Catherine supped with her brother and sister-in-law: Joseph and I joined at an unsociable meal, seasoned with reproofs on one side and sauciness on the other. His cake and cheese remained on the table all night for the fairies. He managed to continue work till nine o'clock, and then marched dumb and dour to his chamber.

I. Answer the folloing question :

1. Is the narrator a man or a woman?
2. How does the narrator recall his/her association with old Earnshaw?
3. What did he/she think and decide about Heathcliff?
4. What was Heathcliff doing?
5. What invitation did the narrator extend to Heathcliff ?
6. What was Heathcliff's response ?

II. Give an synonym for each of the following words:

Words	*Synonyms*
(a) remember	....
(b) consider	....
(c) endeavour	....
(d) comfortable	....
(e) glossy	....

III Give an Antonym for each of the folloing words :

Words	*Antonyms*
(a) adequate	....
(b) natural	....
(c) continue	....
(d) join	....
(e) smooth	....

EXERCISE 12

Read the following passage and answer the following questions:

"I cannot wish to be snowed up a week at Randalls."

At another time Emma might have been amused, but she was too much astonished now at Mr. Elton's spirit for other feeling. Harriet seemed quite forgetten in the expectation of a pleasant party.

"We are sure of excellent fires," continued he, "and every thing in the greatest comfort. Charming people, Mr. and Mrs. Weston; Mrs. Weston indeed is much beyond praise, and he is exactly what one values, so hospitable, and so fond of society; it will be a small party, but where small parties are select, they are, perhaps, the most agreeable of any. Mr. Weston's dining-room does not accommodate more than ten comfortable; and for my part, I would rather, under such circumstances, fall short by two than exceed by two. I think you will agree with me (turning with a soft air to Emma), I think I shall certainly have your approbation, though Mr. Knightley, perhaps, from being used to the large parties of London, may not quite enter into our feelings."

"I know nothing of the large parties of London, sir—I never dine with anybody."

"Indeed!" (in a tone of wonder and pity). "I had no idea that the law had been so great a slavery. Well, sir, the time must come when you will be paid for all this, when you will have little labour and great enjoyment."

"My first enjoyment," replied John Knightley, as they passed through the sweep-gate, "will be to find myself safe at Hartfield again."

From *Emma*

I. Answer the following questions :

1. At what was Emma astonished instead of being amused?
2. Who said, "We are sure of excellent fires."?
3. What are Mr. Elton's views about parties?
4. Who said, "My first enjoyment will be to find myself safe at Hartfield again."?

5. Use the following expressions in sentences of your own :
   (a) Would rather ....
   (b) I cannot wish to be ....
   (c) In the expectation of ....
   (d) Much beyond praise ....
   (e) The time must come when ....

II. Give a synonym for each of the following :

Words	*Synonyms*
(a) Agreeable	....
(b) comfortable	....
(c) enjoyment	....
(d) praise	....
(e) astonished	....

III. Give an antonym for each of the following :

Word	*Antonyms*
(a) amuse	....
(b) certain	....
(c) exact	....
(d) agree	....
(e) safe	....

EXERCISE 13

Read the following passage and answer the following questions:

"Cathy, are you busy this afternoon?" asked Heathcliff. "Are you going anywhere?"

"No, it is raining," she answered.

"Why have you that silk frock on, then?" he said. "Nobody coming here, I hope?"

"Not that I know of," stammered Miss; "but you should be in the field now, Heathcliff. It is an hour past dinner time. I thought you were gone."

"Hindley does not often free us from his accursed presence," observed the boy. "I'll not work any more today; I'll stay with you."

"Oh, but Joseph will tell," she suggested; "you'd better go!"

"Joseph is loading lime on the farther side of Penistone Crag; it will take him till dark, and he'll never know."

So saying, he lounged to the fire, and sat down. Catherine reflected and instant, with knitted brows—she found it needful to smooth the way for an intrusion.

"Isabella and Edgar Linton talked of calling this afternoon," she said, at the conclusion of a minute's silence.

"As it rains, I hardly expect them; but they may come, and if they do, you run the risk of being scolded for no good."

"Order Ellen to say you are engaged, Cathy," he persisted. "Don't turn me out for those pitiful, silly friends of yours! I'm on the point, sometimes, of complaining that they—but I'll not—"

"That they what?" cried Catherine, gazing at him with a troubled countenance. "Oh, Nelly!" she added petulantly, jerking her head away from my hands, "you've combed my hair quite out of curl! That's enough; let me alone. What are you on the point of complaining about, Heathcliff?"

From ***"Wuthering Heights"***

I. Answer the following questions.

1. Where was Heathcliff expected to have gone?
2. What was Joseph doing?
3. Who had talked of calling and why they might not come?
4. What do you think, Ellen and Nelly is one and the some person in the passage or are they two different persons?
5. What does Catherine say Nelly has done wrongly to her?

II. Give a synonym for each of the following words:

Words	*Synonyms*
(a) scolded	....
(b) suggested	....
(c) reflect	....
(d) pitiful	....
(e) conclusion	....

III. Give an antonym for each of the following words :

Words	*Antonyms*
(a) engaged	....
(b) expected	....
(c) free	....
(d) risky	....
(e) needful	....

Exercise 14

Read the following passage and answer the following questions:

Once a year in the middle of January, Rahman, the Cabuliwallah was in the habit of returning to his country, and as the time approached he would be very busy, going from house to house collecting his debts. This year, however, he could always find time to come and see Mini. It would have seemed to an outsider that there was some conspiracy between the two, for when he could not come in the morning, he would appear in the evening.

Even to me it was a little startling now and then, in the corner of a dark room, suddenly to my surprise. I saw this tall, loose-garmented man laden with bags; but when Mini would run in smiling, with her "O Cabuliwallah ! Cabuliwallah !" and the two friends, so far apart in age, would subside into their old laughter and their old jokes, I felt reassured.

One morning, a few days before he had made up his mind to go, I was correcting my proof sheets in my study. It was chilly weather. Through the window the rays of the sun touched my feet, and the slight warmth was very welcome. It was almost eight o'clock, and the early pedestrians were returning home with their heads covered. All at once I heard an uproar in the street.

From ***"Cabuliwallah"*** by R.N. Tagore.

I. Answer the following questions.

1. What was the name of the Cabuliwallah ?
2. Usually, in which month did the Cabuliwallah return to his country ?
3. What did he do before that ?
4. Who are the two friends mentiond in this passage ?
5. Describe the Cabuliwallah in one sentence.
6. What kind of weather is mentioned in the passage ?
7. What was the author doing ?
8. What time is mentioned in the passage ?
9. What were the early pedestrians doing ?
10. What did the author hear ?

II. Give a synonym for each of the following words :

Words	***synonyms***
(a) startling	....
(b) conspiracy	....
(c) correct	....
(d) seemed	....
(e) warm	....

III. Give an antonym for each of the following words :

Words	***Antonyms***
(a) outsider	....
(b) dark	....
(c) a little	....
(d) warmth	....
(e) covered	....

Exercise 15

Read the following passage and answer the following questions:

In science we do the same thing— the philosopher exercises precisely the same faculties, though in a much more delicate manner. In scientific inquiry it becomes a matter of duty to expose a supposed law to every possible kind of verification, and to take care, moreover, that this is done intentionally, and not left to a mere accident, as in the case of the apples. And in science, as in common life, our confidence in a law is in exact proportion to the absence of variation in the result of our experimental verifications. For instance, if you let go your grasp of an article you may have in your hand, it will immediately fall to the ground. That is a very common verification of one of the best established laws of nature–that of gravitation. The method by which men of science established the existence of that law is exactly the same as that by which we have established the trivial proposition about the sources of hard and green apples. But we believe it in such an extensive, thorough, unhesitating manner because the universal experience of mankind verifies it, and we can verify it ourselves at any time ; and that is the strongest possible foundation on which any natural law can rest.

From ***"All Men Are Scientist"*** by T.H. Huxley.

I. Answer the following questions :

1. Who exercises faculties in a more delicate manner—the scientist or the philosopher ?
2. What is a matter of duty in scientific inquiry ?
3. How is confidence in a law similar to that in common life ?
4. Give a common example for the verification of two laws of gravitation.
5. What is the strongest possible foundation on which any natural law can rest?
6. Assign a suitable heading to the passage.

II. Give a synonym for each of the following words .

Words	***Synonyms***
(a) precisely	....
(b) delicate	....
(c) inquiry	....
(d) immediately	....
(e) verification.	....

III. Give an antonym for each of the following words :

Words	***Antonyms***
(a) exact	....
(b) natural	....
(c) delicate	....
(d) grasp	....
(e) intentionally	....

ANSWERS

EXERCISE 1

I. Do yourself

II. (a) grow (b) achievable
(c) damage (d) importantly
(e) quick

III. (a) slow (b) desirable
(c) decrease (d) fall
(e) decay

IV. Do yourself

EXERCISE 2

I. Do yourself

II. (a) nadir (b) hold
(c) susceptible d) submarine
(e) arrange

III. (a) destroy (b) partly
(c) shallow (d) in front of
(e) move

IV. Do yourself

EXERCISE 3

I. Do yourself

II. (a) extreme (b) diligent
(c) lasting (d) attractive
(e) unworried.

III. (a) old (b) bad
(c) give (d) noisy
(e) unlucky

IV. 1. Her mother died of cholera.
2. The Taj lies on the bank of the Yamuna.
3. No sooner did the train arrive at the station than the crowd began to rush in.
4. My mother does not like certain boys such as the disrespectful ones.
5. She was afraid of losing her way in the forest.
6. I don't want any more discussion on this point.
7. Look sharp ! we are already late.
8. A hardcore terrorist made an attempt on the life of the minister.
9. I elbowed my way through the crush.
10. A herd of cattle was grazing down the hill in the meadow.

EXERCISE 4

I. Do yourself

II. (a) dominating (b) finally

(c) appeared (d) skill
(e) various

III. (a) ordinary (b) insincerely
(c) average, humble (d) notoriety
(e) misfortune.

EXERCISE 5

I. Do yourself

II. (a) significant (b) power
(c) progress, growth (d) facing
(e) focus.

III. (a) common (b) destroy
(c) unimportant (d) worst
(e) in favour of

VIII. 1. (c) 2. (d)
3. (c) 4. (c)
5. (d).

EXERCISE 6

I. Do yourself

II. (a) expensive (b) small
(c) rapidly (d) infinite
(e) incapability.

III. (a) near (b) ability
(c) countable (d) cheap
(e) big.

EXERCISE 7

I. Do yourself

II. (a) important, essential (b) supply
(c) decreasing (d) continuing
(e) permit

III. (a) harm (b) lower
(c) decrease (d) infertile
(e) imbalance

EXERCISE 8

I. Do yourself

II. (a) convert (b) supply
(c) far from away (d) bear
(e) greater

III. (a) unaffordable (b) minor
(c) changelessness (d) oldest
(e) timid

EXERCISE 9

I. Do yourself

II. (a) ground (b) shelter
(c) story (d) subterranean
(e) say, relate

III. (a) separate (b) notorious
(c) carry, take (d) past, absent
(e) dull/joyless.

EXERCISE 10

I. Do yourself

II. (a) completely (b) understand
(c) luxurious (d) probable
(e) correct

III. (a) mildly
(b) incomprehensible
(c) unfortunate
(d) antagonistic, unfriendly
(e) unconcern

EXERCISE 11

I. Do yourself

II. (a) recall (b) think, regard
(c) attempt (d) luxurious
(e) shining

III. (a) inadequate (b) unnatural
(c) discontinue (d) disconnect/separate
(e) uneven

EXERCISE 12

I. Do yourself

II. (a) favourable (b) luxurious
(c) amusement (d) admire
(e) surprised

III. (a) bore (b) uncertain
(c) varying/inexact (d) disagree
(e) unsafe.

EXERCISE 13

I. Do yourself

II. (a) rebuked (b) proposed
(c) think (d) shameful
(e) end

III. (a) idle (b) unexpected
(c) slavish (d) safe
(e) unneeded/ undesired/ unwanted

EXERCISE 14

I. Do yourself

II. (a) shocking, surprising
(b) plot
(c) right
(d) appeared
(e) cosy

III. (a) insider (b) light
(c) much (d) coldness
(e) uncovered

EXERCISE 15

I. Do yourself

II. (a) exactly (b) soft
(c) investigation (d) at once
(e) certification

III. (a) inexact (b) unnatural
(c) rude, hard (d) loose, loosen
(e) unintentionally

FILL IN THE BLANKS

Exercise 1

Insert Articles/Prepositions wherever necessary in the following paragraph.

However, here I want to discuss an arena which has not been so much talked about, and remains the concealed part of discomforts around the film. At the core of anxieties around *Jodhaa Akbar* are the explicitly expressed sexualities, desires and romance between ***...1...*** Hindu princess and a Muslim king. There is ***...2...*** sensuous play of inter-religious bodies in the film, which has created a disquiet among some.

Gowarikar could not have chosen two more sultry and sexy bodies, i.e. that of Aishwarya Rai and Hrithik Roshan to play the roles of Jodhaa and Akbar respectively. The marriage between them, while ***...3...*** result of political expediency, can only reach its fruition through an expression of romantic love. It is the romance between Jodhaa and Akbar which becomes the prism in the film to examine other political developments.

The way their adoration grows through different stages—from a rejection by ***...4...*** Hindu princess, to a marriage of convenience, to physical attraction, to misunderstandings, to intimacy, to sexual craving, to love—has allowed a free display of sensuality and eroticism in the film, which produces a visual repertoire of sex and love. The film depicts that the body of ***...5...*** Hindu woman/Jodhaa is not forcefully appropriated by the Muslim male/Akbar.

The film is full of rendezvous of seduction, wooing and longing. As it progresses, both Jodhaa and Akbar gaze carnally at each other. There is ***...6...*** yearning for passion here. The hankering is portrayed often ***...7...*** Akbar/Hrithik's eyes. However, Jodhaa is not a mute object of desire. AkbarlHrithik is shown as ***...8...*** handsome specimen of manhood. His spectacular and stylish body is to be equally fancied, and offers a sexualised imaginative anatomy. Both Jodhaa and Akbar are equal participants in the generation of passion and together determine its very terms. While from the beginning Jodhaa is portrayed as ***...9...*** strong willed woman, who retains her religious identity, nonetheless, she relishes in ogling at the Muslim male body, which is amply displayed in the film.

In ***...10...*** voluptuous scene, Hrithik/Akbar bares his body and is involved in a luxurious play with the sword. The camera lovingly lingers on each and every frame and movement of his body.

Exercise 2

Insert Articles/Prepositions wherever necessary in the following paragraph.

There are Test cricketers who make big scores and there are those who score runs fast. But there is also an elite club—peopled by greats like Sir Don Bradman—of batsmen who have not just piled up masssive runs but also got them at ***...1...*** blistering pace. Virender Sehwag, Delhi's very own hero, belongs ***...2...*** select league of cricketers. His whirlwind 309 runs off 292 balls at Chennai ***...3...*** Friday has proven that when it comes to aggressive batting that is able to sustain itself over long spells, Sehwag has no peers ***...4...*** India, of today, or the past. To put it in perspective, while no Indian—notwithstanding the big names we can boast of—has ever scored a triple hundred in Test matches, this man has done it twice, that too in ***...5...*** style that makes batting look like ***...6...*** child's play.

It is difficult to believe that this majestic cricketer was out of the Indian team not very long ago and was being written off as a has been. But what distinguishes champions from nine day wonders is ***...7...*** ability to make a comeback. Along the way, Sehwag has demolished a whole range of records, also becoming the first player since Denis Compton (1954) to score more than 250 runs in ***...8...*** single day. Skeptics are likely to point at the placid Chepauk wicket to say that better knocks have been seen in modern times, but they need to consider the hot and humid conditions at Chennai, which make Sehwag's innings ***...9...*** supreme example of not just mental concentration but also physical endurance. In the process, he has breathed life into what otherwise looked like a dead Test match, giving the Indians ***...10...*** outside chance of getting the better of South Africa.

But amidst the pyrotechnics provided by Sehwag, let us not overlook the sedate Rahul Dravid's feat of crossing 10,000 runs on Saturday, making him only the third Indian to cross the milestone. The contrast between Dravid and Sehwag's styles of play is as stark as it gets. But cricket being a great game has room for heroes of many hues. It is for this reason that when the "defensive" Rahul Dravid chooses to call it a day, he will rank second to none but Sunil Gavaskar or Sachin Tendulkar in the annals of Indian batting.

EXERCISE 3

Insert Articles/Prepositions wherever necessary in the following paragraph.

Even as DNA research on humans in the country is on ***...1...*** verge of shedding new light on medicine, history and anthropology, the unregulated nature of the work has led to fears that communities would be denied ***...2...*** benefit of what is literally in their genes.

Now, an ethics committee to regulate such research and ensure the rights of communities has been mooted and ***...3...*** draft bill to this effect will soon be in place.

The move will protect and strengthen the right of groups such as primitive tribes and sub-castes whose distinct genetic profile could help isolate genes with specific capabilities that differ from the general population. Any commercial benefits from the use of such knowledge will flow back ***...4...*** these communities once the Bill is in place.

A 12-member national advisory committee, set up to suggest a framework for developing a national repository of genome research and data, has submitted its report to the culture ministry. Professor E. Hari Babu, professor in the department of sociology, University of Hyderabad, who was part of ***...5...*** committee, said: "The committee has concluded that even if an individual or a group provides a sample, the benefit will flow to the community to which they belong. The benefit can be in the form of ***...6...*** community fund, or any other material benefit. The idea of community would also depend on the context, for example it could be all those suffering from a particular form of cancer, as they would have a similar gene. An individual may claim benefit only if the gene extracted from his sample is unique."

Another member of the committee said pharmaceutical companies and other agencies were engaged in taking DNA samples from communities which were found resistant to ***...7...*** certain diseases which the general population was vulnerable to. "This differentiation of DNA cells helps ***...8...*** developing drugs to fight the diseases. In many cases, private companies have been able to prepare antibodies to fight diseases, but never told the communities. This raises the issue of having ***...9...*** informed consent from the communities and also sharing the profit earned through development of a product. The legislation will take care of that."

The ethics committee will monitor genome research in ***...10...*** country, enforce informed consent of the community before any samples are taken and ensure that the benefits flow back to the community from any product that is subsequently developed.

EXERCISE 4

Insert Articles/Prepositions wherever necessary in the following paragraph.

You're in Benaras on Holi and are not used to *bhang,* don't drink it. The thin line between hallucination and reality is bound to blur and when the disorientation is finally complete, the gods won't be there to help.

But the problem is *...1...* temptation to "full enjoy". "Enjoying—as a smashed *panwariya,* who also slurred 'tourists' as 'terrrrorists', explained—is a Benarsi tradition on Holi. It implies *bhang, thandai* and *...2...* licence to do whatever the heart pleases. The following the heart part is ok. The trouble lies with the *bhang,* which keeps playing silly games with perception.

It's when reality masquerades *...3...* fantasy, and it does often enough in Benaras, that perception comes under serious question, though. For it might be you're sitting on Assi Ghat when the sun is setting to a gentle breeze. The boats are gliding idly back to *...4...* banks of "Ganga Mata". Her *avatar,* as a pious barber who's just given you an understanding head massage is saying, is Mandakini in heaven and Bhagirathi in hell. *Bhagwan* and *bhang* are playing hide-and-seek *...5...* your brain when without warning, "chart-busting German trance track you've heard in discos starts blaring from speakers. You turn around to see *...6...* dance floor on the ghat. And a bunch of hanumans—faces painted, tails in place— are going bananas to the Crazy Frog song. It's happening for real, but the disorientation still sinks in like the sudden drop of the setting sun.

The streets are no better. When clinging desperately to the slipping grip of sanity, no one wants to hear a flute protesting angrily from behind, look back, and find a *sadhu-type* in sunglasses playing the instrument as *...7...* horn with one hand and driving a bike with the other. It's a sight you least expect, so awareness does *...8...* double take and that sinking feeling starts again.

But the real test is *...9...* the temples. Benaras is a horribly dirty place. Cows with hyperactive digestive systems and publicly-flowing bladders rummage through garbage *...10...* the streets, the dung and dirt feeding the air. The people can be crass and hotels unaccommodating to us Indians. But all that's forgotten inside a temple.

EXERCISE 5

Insert Articles/Prepositions wherever necessary in the following paragraph.

Libby Trickett confirmed her status as *...1...* fastest woman on water when she broke the 50 metres freestyle world record on the final night of the Australian Olympic trials on Saturday.

Trickett, stormed down one-lap *...2...* Sydney's International Aquatic Centre In 23.97 seconds to slice 0.12 off the previous record of 24.09 set five days ago by Marlene Veldhuis of *...3...* Netherlands at the European championships in Eindhoven.

Trickett, who won five gold medals *...4...* last year's world championships, also broke the 100 freestyle world record on Thursday and won the 100 butterfly earlier in *...5...* week to qualify for six events in Beijing. "I never really thought I could go this quick before," the 23-year-old said in *...6...* poolside interview.

"I have not been able to put together a good 50 before, but after the 100 I was just so excited for this race," she added.

Cate Campbell, 15, finished second in 24.38 to book her second individual swim in China after finishing runner-up to Trickett in the 100 and boost Australia's chances of winning *...7...* three women's relays.

"To be honest I really thought the 50 world record was going to be out *...8...* my reach for a lot longer," Trickett told reporters. "It has always been a bit of a target and it has always seemed such *...9...* distant time that I never really thought I could get there.

"I have had so much fun, I know I am a pretty powerful person with *...10...* muscular physique, I use my strengths where I have them and used them tonight."

EXERCISE 6

Insert Articles/Prepositions wherever necessary in the following paragraph.

It is one of the greatest films of Hollywood's golden era, ...*1*... triple Oscar-winning classic with electrifyingly charismatic stars and ...*2*... script bursting with memorable lines.

But now Madonna has stunned the movie industry with plans to remake *Casablanca*— and this time set it ...*3*... Iraq.

The singer, whose previous film career has been littered with critical and commercial turkeys, is also planning to take ...*4*... lead role of Ilsa Lund, which originally made a star of Ingrid Bergman.

A source at a major Hollywood studio that was recently approached by the 49-year old star said: "She is still determined to make it in ...*5*... movies. She and her representatives have been touting around a project which is a remake ...*6*... *Casablanca.* The reception has been lukewarm to say the least. No one can understand why she wants to redo what many people consider the greatest film of all time".

In the 1942 original, Bergman starred opposite Humphrey Bogart, who played Rick Blaine, a cynical bar owner in ...*7*... Moroccan city of Casablanca in the early days of the Second World War. Ilsa is torn between love for her husband, a Czech Resistance leader, and her ex-lover Rick.

Madonna is said to believe the film will make her reputation as ...*8*... actress, after a string of high-profile flops such as *Shanghai Surprise, Body* Of *Evidence* and *Swept Away,* her muchderided 2002 collaboration with husband Guy Ritchie. The source said: "Madonna is talking about taking the Ingrid Bergman role for herself, even though Bergman was ...*9*... her 20s when she played Ilsa and Madonna is nearly 50."

"She wants to update the story and maybe set it in a modern war zone such as Iraq. There is no script yet. Madonna and her people are testing the waters to see if this is ...*10*... right vehicle for her and if a major studio will get behind the project."

The movie, which regularly tops lists of the greatest films ever made, includes the classic song 'As Time Goes By' and memorable quotes such as: "Here's looking at you, kid", "We'll always have Paris" and "Of all the gin joints in all the towns in all the world, she walks into mine".

Bollywood filmmaker Rajeev Nath is also said to be working on a remake set in India, calling it 'a tribute to the original'. A spokes-woman for Madonna refused to comment.

EXERCISE 7

Insert Articles/Prepositions wherever necessary in the following paragraph.

It is 76 years since Cheeta the chimp was plucked from ...*1*... African jungle to become a Hollywood star in the Tarzan movies. Yet incredibly, he is still going strong.

The oldest known living chimpanzee enjoys ...*2*... leisurely retirement in California, where he enjoys painting, piano and strolling in the sunshine. Not to mention writing his autobiography—or so we are told.

Me Cheeta, an account of his life in the limelight, is ...*3*... be published in the autumn and extracts from it appear in next month's *Esquire* magazine. The memoirs, widely suspected to be ...*4*... work of a ghost-writer, discuss his acting career, the healthy lifestyle which has replaced his former diet ...*5*... beer and cigars, and his views on his old co- star Johnny Weissmuller.

Cheeta, who is 4ft tall, was "discovered" as a newborn by ...*6*... animal trainer on a trip to Africa in April 1932. He appeared soon afterwards alongside Weissmuller in *Tarzan and His Mate,* and went ...*7*... to star in a dozen films about the jungle hero who swung from tree to tree.

Cheeta appeared in 50 movies before his final appearance, as Chee-Chee in 1967's *Doctor Dolittle.*

He has outlived both Weissmuller, who died in 1984 aged 79, and Maureen O'Sullivan, who played Tarzan's mate Jane and who died aged 87 in 1998.

Although he was fond ***...8...*** smoking and drinking, both have been forbidden since he arrived more than ***...9...*** decade ago at the Cheeta Primate Foundation in the desert enclave ***...10...*** Palm Springs. He helps pay for his keep with his 'Ape-stract' paintings which sell for about Rs 6,000 ***...11...*** time. *Esquire* also jokes that he has made a small fortune working as a double for actor Robin Williams.

EXERCISE 8

Insert Articles/Prepositions wherever necessary in the following paragraph.

Everyone will welcome the decision of the government to set up four new Indian Institutes of Technology and six new Indian Institutes of Management in ***...1...*** Eleventh Five Year Plan. These will be in addition to ***...2...*** earlier decision to set up four new IITs and an IIM. Whether or not these are coming up so as to effectively implement the United Progressive Alliance government decision ***...3...*** implement the Other Backward Class quota in such a manner that general category people are not affected, does not really matter. In ***...4...*** country with an enormous pool of literacy and semi-literacy, high quality educational institutions like IITs and IIMs are always welcome. Along with the government's emphasis on boosting the number of central universities and upgrading others to this status, this represents a serious commitment on the part of the authorities to push India into the direction of becoming a "Knowledge Economy".

But there appears to be a flaw in this design, and it is a major one. Somehow the government never seems to be able to get down to implementing its grand promises. In the 2007-08 Budget ***...5...*** sum of Rs 988 crores had been allocated for expanding the capacity and facilities in the' existing IITs and IIMs so as to enable them to cope with the planned 27 per cent quota for the OBCs without affecting the general category students. The funds remained unspent through ***...6...*** year and when just three days were left for the financial year to end, Human Resource Development Minister Arjun Singh demanded that a sum of Rs 867 crores be released. Not surprisingly, the Finance Ministry, which had probably closed the books for the 2007-08 financial year, refused.

But what this did bring out was that while ***...7...*** government had provided a huge amount of money for upgrading technical education, including the existing IITs, IIMs and other institutions, the ministry was not able ***...8...*** effectively utilise it. The result is that a token Rs 76 crores, out of a plan allocation of Rs 858 crores for expanding the facilities of IITs, has been utilised. Dividing the sum by 7—***...9...*** number of existing institutions—we come to a grand total of just some Rs 10 crores or so per institution.

The government has just come up with another scheme — providing huge pay packets for its officials. That scheme, of course, will be implemented in full and at ***...10...*** earliest. What is it that stops the government from linking this hike to the performance of its bureaucracy on vital issues like education, health and governance?

EXERCISE 9

Insert Articles/Prepositions wherever necessary in the following paragraph.

Market regulator, Securities and Exchange Board of India (Sebi) is getting its act together to clean-up ***...1...*** initial public offering (IPO) process. C.B. Bhave, chairman, Sebi, is keen to treat all classes of investors-retail investors, qualified institutional buyers (QIBs) and financial institutional investors

(FIIs)—on par. This, Sebi aims to achieve ...*2*... ensuring all IPO investors pay the application amount upfront.

Until now, while retail investors had to pay the full amount with ...*3*... IPO application, QIBS paid only margin money of around 10 per cent with their applications. This difference, the Sebi chief feels, is leading to excessive bidding from ...*4*... institutional investors, as they do not need to pay the full amount. This also gives wrong signals about an IPO's success.

Sebi's primary market committee, which is going to meet next month, is also widely expected to address ...*5*... issue of time gap between the listing and closing dates of IPOs.

Analysts have welcomed these decisions. These decisions are expected ...*6*... come into force only in July, as several clearances have to come through.

The disastrous performance of some IPOs in ...*7*... recent past is also one of the reasons why Sebi is speeding up the decisions. The three-week period between ...*8*... IPO closure and the listing date gives rise to all kinds of speculations and grey market trading in ...*9*... company that is yet to list. Worse, the grey market seems to be growing on speculation.

Once the time between IPO closure and refund deadline is crunched to ...*10*... couple of days, not only will the IPO cost go down but grey market speculation will also be reduced.

EXERCISE 10

Insert Articles/Prepositions wherever necessary in the following paragraph.

Seven hours of sleep a night could be ...*1*... recipe for staying in shape, researchers.

Too much or too little sleep piles on the kilos and over the years can end in obesity.

A study has found that those sleeping for less than seven hours a night gained 1.81 kg in six years. Those sleeping for more gained 1.36 kg over the same period. It is thought that too little or too much sleep causes hormonal changes that may stimulate appetite.

"Both short and long sleeping times predict ...*2*... increased risk of future body weight and fat gain in adults," said Jean-Philippe Chaput of Laval University in Quebec, where ...*3*... study was carried out.

"These results emphasise the need to add sleep duration to the list of environmental factors that are prevalent in our society and that contribute ...*4*... weight gain and obesity."

One third of UK adults regularly sleep five hours or less a night, while the average is a healthy seven.

The Canadian study, published on Wednesday in the medical journal *Sleep*, looked at 276 adults between 21 and 64 years ...*5*... age. Short and long duratioin sleepers were 35 per cent and 25 per cent more likely to experience weight gain of 5 kg compared with average duration sleepers.

Short sleepers gained 1.98 kg on average while long sleepers gained 1.58 kg. The risk of developing obesity was raised for short and long-term sleepers, up by 27 per cent and 21 per cent, compared with those sleeping for ...*6*... average of seven hours.

The researchers adjusted for age, sex and body mass index—the scale for overweight and obesity which takes several factors into account.

Previous research has suggested that sleep loss could disturb ...*7*... production of hormones that control the desire for calorie-rich foods.

The level of ghrelin, a hormone released by ...*8*... stomach to signal hunger, was found to be 15 per cent higher in people who have only five hours sleep a night compared ...*9*... those getting eight hours.

Lack of sleep also leads to tiredness during the day, which may mean people do not have enough energy for physical activity.

Those who cut their sleep levels from seven hours to five or fewer, face ...*10*... 70 per cent extra risk of dying from all causes—and twice the risk of death from a cardiovascular problem.

ANSWERS

EXERCISE 1

1. a 2. a 3. a
4. the 5. the 6. a
7. in 8. a 9. a
10. a

EXERCISE 2

1. a 2. to, that 3. on
4. in 5. a 6. a
7. the 8. a 9. a
10. the

EXERCISE 3

1. the 2. the 3. a
4. to 5. the 6. a
7. a 8. in 9. an
10. the

EXERCISE 4

1. the 2. a 3. as
4. the 5. in 6. a
7. a 8. a 9. at
10. on

EXERCISE 5

1. the 2. of 3. the
4. at 5. the 6. a
7. the 8. of 9. a
10. a

EXERCISE 6

1. a 2. a 3. in
4. the 5. the 6. of
7. the 8. an 9. in
10. the

EXERCISE 7

1. the 2. a 3. to
4. the 5. of 6. an
7. on 8. of 9. a
10. of 11. a

EXERCISE 8

1. the 2. the 3. to
4. a 5. a 6. the
7. the 8. to 9. the
10. the

EXERCISE 9

1. the 2. by 3. an
4. the 5. the 6. to
7. the 8. the 9. a
10. a

EXERCISE 10

1. the 2. an 3. the
4. to 5. of 6. an
7. the 8. the 9. to
10. a

ANTONYMS

TYPE I

Directions: *In the following questions choose the word which is the exact OPPOSITE of the given words.*

1. DEAR
   A. Priceless B. Free
   C. Worthless D. Cheap
2. FLAGITIOUS
   A. Innocent B. Vapid
   C. Ignorant D. Frivolous
3. LIABILITY
   A. Property B. Assets
   C. Debt D. Teasure
4. VIRTUOUS
   A. Wicked B. Corrupt
   C. Vicious D. Scandalous
5. ENCOURAGE
   A. Dampen B. Disapprove
   C. Discourage D. Warn
6. MORTAL
   A. Divine B. Immortal
   C. Spiritual D. Eternal
7. LEND
   A. Borrow B. Cheat
   C. Pawn D. Hire
8. COMIC
   A. Emotional B. Tragic
   C. Fearful D. Painful
9. ADDITION
   A. Division B. Enumeration
   C. Subtraction D. Multiplication
10. MINOR
    A. Big B. Major
    C. Tall D. Heavy
11. REPEL
    A. Attend B. Concentrate
    C. Continue D. Attract
12. ARTIFICIAL
    A. Red B. Natural
    C. Truthful D. Solid
13. CAPACIOUS
    A. Limited B. Caring
    C. Foolish D. Changeable
14. PROVOCATION
    A. Vocation B. Pacification
    C. Peace D. Destruction
15. METICULOUS
    A. Mutual B. Shaggy
    C. Meretricious D. Slovenly
16. ABLE
    A. Disable B. Inable
    C. Unable D. Misable
17. COMFORT
    A. Uncomfort B. Miscomfort
    C. Discomfort D. None of these
18. GAIN
    A. Loose B. Fall
    C. Lost D. Lose
19. SYNTHETIC
    A. Affable B. Natural
    C. Plastic D. Cosmetic
20. ACQUITTED
    A. Freed B. Burdened
    C. Convicted D. Entrusted
21. STRINGENT
    A. General B. Vehement
    C. Lenient D. Magnanimous
22. FLIMSY
    A. Frail B. Filthy
    C. Firm D. Flippant
23. BUSY
    A. Occupied B. Engrossed
    C. Relaxed D. Engaged
24. ADAPTABLE
    A. Adoptable B. Flexible
    C. Yielding D. Rigid
25. LOVE
    A. Villainy B. Hatred
    C. Compulsion D. Force

26. BALANCE
A. Disbalance B. Misbalance
C. Debalance D. Imbalance

27. RELINQUISH
A. Abdicate B. Renounce
C. Possess D. Deny

28. MOUNTAIN
A. Plain B. Plateau
C. Precipice D. Valley

29. FICKLE
A. Courageous B. Sincere
C. Steadfast D. Humble

30. PERENNIAL
A. Frequent B. Regular
C. Lasting D. Rare

31. RARELY
A. Hardly B. Definitely
C. Frequently D. Periodically

32. STARTLED
A. Amused B. Relaxed
C. Endless D. Astonished

33. ADHERENT
A. Detractor B. Enemy
C. Alien D. Rival

34. QUIESCENT
A. Indifferent B. Troublesome
C. Weak D. Unconcerned

35. CONDENSE
A. Expand B. Distribute
C. Interpret D. Lengthen

36. BENIGN
A. Malevolent B. Soft
C. Friendly D. Unwise

37. OBSCURE
A. Implicit B. Obnoxious
C. Explicit D. Pedantic

38. HYPOCRITICAL
A. Gentle B. Sincere
C. Amiable D. Dependable

39. EVASIVE
A. Free B. Honest
C. Liberal D. Frank

40. INDUSTRIOUS
A. Indifferent B. Indolent
C. Casual D. Passive

41. EXTRICATE
A. Manifest B. Palpable
C. Release D. Entangle

42. LUCID
A. Glory B. Noisy
C. Obscure D. Distinct

43. INSIPID
A. Tasty B. Stupid
C. Discreet D. Feast

44. OBEYING
A. Ordering B. Following
C. Refusing D. Contradicting

45. VICTORIOUS
A. Defeated B. Annexed
C. Destroyed D. Vanquished

46. COMMISSIONED
A. Started B. Closed
C. Finished D. Terminated

47. VANITY
A. Pride B. Humility
C. Conceit D. Ostentious

48. ZENITH
A. Acme B. Top
C. Nadir D. Pinnacle

49. TANGIBLE
A. Ethereal B. Concrete
C. Actual D. Solid

50. REPRESS
A. Inhibit B. Liberate
C. Curb D. Quell

51. EPILOGUE
A. Dialogue B. Prelude
C. Post script D. Epigram

52. FRAUDULENT
A. Candid B. Direct
C. Forthright D. Genuine

53. LOQUCIOUS
A. Reticent B. Talkative
C. Garrulous D. Verbose

54. NIGGARDLY
A. Frugal B. Thrifty
C. Stingy D. Generous

55. PERTINENT
A. Irrational B. Irregular
C. Insistent D. Irrelevant

56. FAINT-HEARTED
A. Warm-hearted B. Full-blooded
C. Hot-blooded D. Stout-hearted

57. VIOLENT
A. Humble B. Harmless
C. Gentle D. Tame

58. STATIONARY
A. Active B. Mobile
C. Rapid D. Busy

59. HONORARY
A. Dishonourable B. Reputed
C. Paid D. Official

60. COMMON
A. Rare B. Small
C. Petty D. Poor

61. FRUGAL
A. Copious B. Extravagant
C. Generous D. Ostentatious

62. MALICIOUS
A. Kind B. Boastful
C. Generous D. Indifferent

63. FAMILIAR
A. Unpleasant B. Dangerous
C. Friendly D. Strange

64. PRELIMINARY
A. Final B. First
C. Secondary D. Initial

65. DOUBTFUL
A. Famous B. Certain
C. Fixed D. Important

66. REMISS
A. Forgetful B. Watchful
C. Dutiful D. Harmful

67. INDISCREET
A. Reliable B. Honest
C. Prudent D. Stupid

68. FRESH
A. Faulty B. Sluggish
C. Disgraceful D. Stale

69. ANNOY
A. Praise B. Rejoice
C. Please D. Reward

70. TRANSPARENT
A. Semi-transparent B. Muddy
C. Opaque D. Dark

71. REVEALED
A. Denied B. Concealed
C. Ignored D. Overlooked

72. EXTRAVAGANCE
A. Luxury B. Poverty
C. Economy D. Cheapness

73. CROWDED
A. Busy B. Congested
C. Quiet D. Deserted

74. SHRINK
A. Contract B. Spoil
C. Expand D. Stretch

75. ENMITY
A. Important B. Unnecessary
C. Friendship D. Likeness

76. EXODUS
A. Influx B. Home-coming
C. Return D. Restoration

77. CULPABLE
A. Defendable B. Blameless
C. Careless D. Irresponsible

78. SUBSERVIENT
A. Aggressive B. Straightforward
C. Dignified D. Supercilious

79. AWARE
A. Uncertain B. Ignorant
C. Sure D. Doubtful

80. GRACEFUL
A. Rough B. Expert
C. Miserable D. Awkward

81. AUTONOMY
A. Slavery B. Subordination
C. Dependence D. Submissiveness

82. NADIR
A. Modernity B. Zenith
C. Liberty D. Progress

83. CONCEDE
A. Object B. Refuse
C. Grant D. Accede

84. SUPPRESS
A. Encourage B. Grow
C. Praise D. Permit

85. FAMOUS
A. Disgraced B. Notorious
C. Evil D. Popular

86. EXPAND
A. Contract B. Condense
C. Congest D. Conclude

87. ARROGANT
A. Polite B. Cowardly
C. Meek D. Gentlemanly

88. ENORMOUS
A. Soft B. Average
C. Tiny D. Weak

89. URBANE
A. Illiterate B. Backward
C. Discourteous D. Orthodox

90. HOSTILITY
A. Courtesy B. Hospitality
C. Relationship D. Friendliness

91. BELITTLE
A. Praise B. Flatter
C. Exaggerate D. Adore

92. HAPLESS
A. Cheerful B. Consistent
C. Fortunate D. Shapely

93. HAPHAZARD
A. Fortuitous B. Indifferent
C. Deliberate D. Accidental

94. GREGARIOUS
A. Antisocial B. Glorious
C. Horrendous D. Similar

95. VALUABLE
A. Invaluable B. Worthless
C. Inferior D. Lowly

96. ABSOLUTE
A. Deficient B. Faulty
C. Limited D. Scarce

97. CONFESS
A. Deny B. Refuse
C. Contest D. Contend

98. GULLIBLE
A. Incredulous B. Fickle
C. Easy D. Stylish

99. HIRSUTE
A. Scaly B. Bald
C. Erudite D. Quiet

100. HINDRANCE
A. Aid B. Persuasion
C. Cooperation D. Agreement

101. ALIEN
A. Native B. Domiciled
C. Natural D. Resident

102. DENSITY
A. Rarity B. Intelligence
C. Clarity D. Brightness

103. DEFIANCE
A. Anxiety B. Obedience
C. Suspicion D. Dismay

104. BASE
A. Climax B. Height
C. Top D. Roof

105. PATCHY
A. Attractive B. Uniform
C. Simple D. Clear

106. EQUANIMITY
A. Resentment B. Dubiousness
C. Duplicity D. Excitement

107. ESSENTIAL
A. Extra B. Noughts
C. Minors D. Trivial

108. IMPASSE
A. Resurgence B. Breakthrough
C. Continuation D. Combination

109. SACROSANCT
A. Irreligious B. Unethical
C. Irreverent D. Unholy

110. HOLLOW
A. Filled B. Solid
C. Strong D. Substantial

TYPE II

Directions: *Each sentence below consists of a word or a phrase which is* **bold**. *It is followed by four words or phrases. Select the word or phrase which is closest to the OPPOSITE in meaning of the bold word or phrase.*

111. The atmosphere in that desolate place looked **ominous.**
A. pleasant B. encouraging
C. auspicious D. favourable

112. He spoke against corruption with **zeal.**
A. indifference B. calmness
C. despair D. passiveness

113. The story told by the teacher **amused** children in the class.
A. frightened B. jolted
C. astonished D. saddened

114. In a literary work **obscurity** can be a virtue.
A. clarity B. precision
C. definiteness D. specificity

115. The managing director remarked that the secretary was an **asset** to the company.
A. loss B. liability
C. drag D. handicap

116. He is extremely **intelligent** but proud.
A. dull B. weak
C. ignorant D. simple

117. A **friendly** dog met us at the farmgate.
A. helpful B. understanding
C. quiet D. hostile

118. In ancient India, scholars had no interest in political power or **material** growth.
A. internal B. spiritual
C. psychic D. celestial

119. His short but pointed speech was **applauded** by all sections of the audience.
A. disapproved B. misunderstood
C. praised D. welcomed

120. Like poverty, **affluence** can sometimes create its own problems.
A. indigence B. opulence
C. sorrow D. exuberance

121. **Adversity** teaches man to be humble and self-reliant.
A. sincerity B. animosity
C. curiosity D. prosperity

122. History **abounds** in instances of courage.
A. shines B. lacks
C. suffices D. fails

123. He **abandoned** his family.
A. supported B. encouraged
C. pleased D. saved

124. The young leader was **reluctant** to shoulder the responsibilities of the ministerial office.
A. wanting B. willing
C. anxious D. eager

125. Unsettled conditions in the land led to the **exodus** of hundreds of its citizens.
A. invasion B. entry
C. immigration D. expulsion

126. In the interest of one's own reputation one should avoid **ostentation** while entertaining friends.
A. miserliness B. simplicity
C. purity D. innocence

127. Everything about him, especially his talkative nature, proclaims his **effeminacy.**
A. aggressiveness B. attractiveness
C. mealiness D. boorishness

128. The habit of **squandering** money should not be encouraged.
A. discarding B. boarding
C. collecting D. saving

129. There was something strange and **morbid** about the whole house.
A. healthy B. cheerful
C. insipid D. appealing

130. Many people suffer setbacks in their career because of their inherent **levity.**
A. seriousness B. solemnity
C. religiosity D. gravity

131. This new magazine is known for its **comprehensive** coverage of news.
A. casual B. inadequate
C. indifferent D. superficial

132. His critics found in his **overt** statements some hidden designs.
A. converse B. pervert
C. covert D. contrived

133. Given these constraint, we had no alternative but to suggest **an improvised** solution.
A. a complete B. a pre-planned
C. a permanent D. a proscribed

134. Because of the economy drive, they very unwillingly surrendered some **superfluous** posts.
A. important B. relevant
C. significant D. essential

135. I **abhor** the ideas he sometimes expresses.
A. admire B. respect
C. applaud D. appreciate

136. You can hardly find any trace of **humility** in the man.
A. pride B. insolence
C. arrogance D. conceit

137. The result of the tournament gave them a sense of **elation.**
A. despondency B. misery
C. disappointment D. despair

138. It was done in a **haphazard** manner.
A. planned B. excellent
C. extraordinary D. designed

139. The officer asked the clerk to **expedite** the matter.

A. postpone B. defer
C. adjourn D. delay

140. The atmosphere in the institute he had newly joined was **congenial** to research.
A. disagreeable for B. inconvenient for
C. unpleasant for D. unsuitable for

141. He is the most **prudent** person I have ever come across.
A. shortsighted B. reckless
C. inconsiderate D. injudicious

142. The members thought that the task was **feasible.**
A. impractical B. impossible
C. difficult D. impracticable

143. I was surprised at his **stiff** attitude.
A. courteous B. flexible
C. soft D. lively

144. The General Manager is quite **tactful** and handles the workers union very effectively.
A. disciplined B. naive
C. strict D. loose

145. His **vindictive** nature often came up for comment among his friends.
A. forgetful B. forgiving
C. obedient D. timid

146. I thought about her a lot during the **following** months.
A. succeeding B. proceeding
C. preceding D. receding

147. He was asked to **accelerate** the pace of work.
A. supervise B. slacken
C. control D. check

148. What he tells me **confirms** my ideas.
A. strengthens B. opposes
C. contradicts D. verifies

149. The error in the newspaper article is **accidental.**
A. intentional B. conventional
C. usual D. permissible

150. According to a great philosopher **magnanimity** in a man implies many other qualities.
A. enmity B. meanness
C. jealousy D. poverty

151. The minister gave a public speech on the controversial subject to **precipitate** the matter.
A. aggravate B. create
C. defer D. push

152. The commission took two years to go through the **massive** collection of files and documents before preparing its report.
A. meagre B. heavy
C. light D. short

153. Satish's point of view was correct but his behaviour with his father was quite **impertinent.**
A. healthy B. respectful
C. inadequate D. smooth

154. The chairman **initiated** the proceedings with a brief speech.
A. confused B. closed
C. started D. complicated

155. The club meets on the last Thursday of every month is a **dilapidated** palace.
A. neglected B. regenerated
C. renovated D. furnished

156. The inhabitants of the island were **barbarians.**
A. civilised B. cruel
C. uncivilised D. bad

157. They had an **insipid** conversation.
A. lively B. argumentative
C. loud D. curious

158. The chairman **rebuked** the accounts officer for not supervising the work of his subordinates.
A. received B. awarded
C. invited D. praised

159. The actor is well-known both for his **humility** and courage.
A. pride B. determination
C. honesty D. gentleness

160. **Feasibility** of the project is under study.
A. Unsuitability B. Cheapness
C. Impropriety D. Impracticability

161. His interpretation of the poem is **superficial.**
A. mysterious B. difficult
C. profound D. mystical

162. Poet often prefer **ambiguity** to
A. clarity B. certainty
C. rationality D. perversity

163. Many people try to **resist** reforms in the society.
A. fight B. accept
C. welcome D. repel

164. Harish displays **enthusiasm** whenever he is posed with a problem.

A. eagerness B. weakness
C. indifference D. softness

165. The moment when Jagdish got order of promotion, as General Manager, was a **memorable** occasion for him and his family.
A. passing B. immemorial
C. forgetful D. innocuous

166. The **incessant** noise of the boring machine made it difficult for us to go to sleep at night.
A. intermittent B. harsh
C. soft D. constant

167. Dinesh could manage his family satisfactorily with his **meagre** income.
A. continuous B. fabulous
C. hard D. small

168. They took note of the **humility** of the visiting dignitary.
A. grandeur B. arrogance
C. friendliness D. decency

169. It was universally characterised as a **progressive** measure.
A. regressive B. obstructive
C. retrograde D. abhorrent

170. We had a **delectable** meal yesterday.
A. heavy B. unsavoury
C. tasty D. nice

171. Mala was often teased as **corpulent** by her friends.
A. fat B. belligerent
C. garrulous D. gaunt

172. It is one of the **pernicious** customs prevailing in the society.
A. permanent B. beneficial
C. parochial D. dangerous

173. **Crestfallen** he returned as he had never faced such humiliation in the whole of his life.
A. Vainglorious B. Indignant
C. Triumphant D. Disturbed

174. Nothing has been organised properly and confusion seems **inevitable**.
A. inevident B. inefficient
C. ineligible D. uncertain

175. He is well-known for coming up with **impracticable** solutions.
A. easy B. possible
C. feasible D. alternate

176. The leader was **pragmatic** in his approach to the problem facing the country.
A. indefinite B. vague
C. idealistic D. optimistic

177. She used to **disparage** her neighbour every now and then.
A. please B. praise
C. belittle D. denigrate

178. The plantation workers were on a **collision** course before the labour officer intervented.
A. retaliatory
B. perfunctory
C. conciliatory
D. circuitous

179. Those whose views are **progressive** often meet with formidable impediments when they begin to act.
A. revolutionary B. retrograde
C. brave D. outmoded

180. The bedroom is at the **rear** side of this house.
A. unusual B. front
C. upper D. back

ANSWERS

1	2	3	4	5	6	7	8	9	10
D	A	B	C	C	B	A	B	C	B
11	12	13	14	15	16	17	18	19	20
D	B	A	B	D	C	C	D	B	C
21	22	23	24	25	26	27	28	29	30
C	C	C	D	B	D	C	D	C	D
31	32	33	34	35	36	37	38	39	40
D	B	B	A	C	A	C	B	B	B

41	42	43	44	45	46	47	48	49	50
D	C	A	A	A	D	B	C	A	B
51	52	53	54	55	56	57	58	59	60
B	D	B	D	D	D	C	B	C	A
61	62	63	64	65	66	67	68	69	70
B	C	D	A	B	C	C	D	C	C
71	72	73	74	75	76	77	78	79	80
B	C	D	D	C	A	A	C	B	A
81	82	83	84	85	86	87	88	89	90
C	B	B	B	B	B	A	C	C	D
91	92	93	94	95	96	97	98	99	100
C	C	C	A	B	C	A	A	B	A
101	102	103	104	105	106	107	108	109	110
A	A	B	C	B	D	A	B	D	B
111	112	113	114	115	116	117	118	119	120
C	A	D	A	B	A	D	B	A	A
121	122	123	124	125	126	127	128	129	130
D	B	A	B	C	A	C	D	B	D
131	132	133	134	135	136	137	138	139	140
D	C	B	B	A	C	D	A	D	A
141	142	143	144	145	146	147	148	149	150
B	A	B	B	B	C	B	C	A	B
151	152	153	154	155	156	157	158	159	160
C	A	B	B	C	A	A	D	A	D
161	162	163	164	165	166	167	168	169	170
C	A	C	A	B	D	D	B	A	B
171	172	173	174	175	176	177	178	179	180
D	B	C	A	C	C	B	C	B	B

SYNONYMS

TYPE I

Directions: *In the following questions choose the word which best expresses the meaning of the given word.*

1. INDICT
   A. Condemn B. Reprimand
   C. Accuse D. Allege
2. SCINTILLATING
   A. Smouldering B. Gilittering
   C. Touching D. Warming
3. REFECTORY
   A. Restaurant B. Parlour
   C. Living Room D. Dining Room
4. DISTINCTION
   A. Diffusion B. Disagreement
   C. Different D. Degree
5. IMPROVEMENT
   A. Advancement B. Betterment
   C. Promotion D. Preference
6. ADVERSITY
   A. Failure B. Helplessness
   C. Misfortune D. Crisis
7. TURN UP
   A. Land up B. Show up
   C. Crop up D. Come up
8. DEIFY
   A. Flatter B. Challenge
   C. Worship D. Face
9. ERROR
   A. Misadventure B. Misgiving
   C. Ambiguity D. Blunder
10. SHALLOW
    A. Artificial B. Superficial
    C. Foolish D. Worthless
11. MASSACRE
    A. Murder B. Stab
    C. Assissinate D. Slaughter
12. COMBAT
    A. Conflict B. Quarrel
    C. Feud D. Fight
13. VORACIOUS
    A. Wild B. Hungry
    C. Angry D. Quick
14. IMPROMPTU
    A. Offhand B. Unimportant
    C. Unreal D. Effective
15. RABBLE
    A. Mob B. Noise
    C. Roar D. Rubbish
16. TEPID
    A. Hot B. Warm
    C. Cold D. Boiling
17. MAYHEM
    A. Jubilation B. Havoc
    C. Excitement D. Defeat
18. TIMID
    A. Fast B. Slow
    C. Medium D. Shy
19. CANTANKEROUS
    A. Quarrelsome B. Rash
    C. Disrespectful D. Noisy
20. PRECARIOUS
    A. Cautious B. Critical
    C. Perilous D. Brittle
21. TACITURNITY
    A. Dumbness B. Changeableness
    C. Hesitation D. Reserve
22. INEBRIATE
    A. Dreamy B. Stupefied
    C. Unsteady D. Drunken
23. HARBINGER
    A. Massenger B. Steward
    C. Forerunner D. Pilot
24. INTIMIDATE
    A. To hint B. Frighten
    C. Bluff D. Harass
25. IRONIC
    A. Inflexible
    B. Bitter
    C. Good-natured
    D. Disguisedly sarcastic

26. STRINGENT
A. Tense B. Stringy
C. Strict D. Causing to shrink

27. ECSTATIC
A. Animated B. Bewildered
C. Enraptured D. Illful

28. COMMENSURATE
A. Measurable B. Proportionate
C. Beginning D. Appropriate

29. DESTITUTION
A. Humility B. Moderation
C. Poverty D. Beggary

30. ASCEND
A. Leap B. Grow
C. Deviate D. Mount

31. UNCOUTH
A. Ungraceful B. Rough
C. Slovenly D. Dirty

32. LYNCH
A. Hang B. Madden
C. Killed D. Shoot

33. LAUD
A. Lord B. Eulogy
C. Praise D. Extolled

34. CORRESPONDENCE
A. Agreements B. Contracts
C. Documents D. Letters

35. VENUE
A. Place B. Agenda
C. Time D. Duration

36. STERILE
A. Barren B. Arid
C. Childless D. Dry

37. SYNOPSIS
A. Index B. Mixture
C. Summary D. Puzzle

38. GERMANE
A. Responsible B. Logical
C. Possible D. Relevant

39. PONDER
A. Think B. Evaluate
C. Anticipate D. Increase

40. CANNY
A. Obstinate B. Handsome
C. Clever D. Stout

41. ABUNDANT
A. Ripe B. Cheap
C. Plenty D. Absent

42. CONSEQUENCES
A. Results B. Conclusions
C. Difficulties D. Applications

43. SHIVER
A. Shake B. Rock
C. Tremble D. Move

44. DILIGENT
A. Progressive B. Brilliant
C. Inventive D. Hard-working

45. DISTANT
A. Far B. Removed
C. Reserved D. Separate

46. FORAY
A. Excursion B. Contest
C. Ranger D. Intuition

47. FRUGALITY
A. Foolishness B. Extremity
C. Enthusiasm D. Economy

48. GARNISH
A. Paint B. Garner
C. Adorn D. Abuse

49. VIGOUR
A. Strength B. Boldness
C. Warmth D. Enthusiasm

50. CANDID
A. Apparent B. Explicit
C. Frank D. Bright

51. BRIEF
A. Limited B. Small
C. Little D. Short

52. GARRULITY
A. Credulity B. Senility
C. Loquaciousness D. Speciousness

53. FURORE
A. Excitement B. Worry
C. Flux D. Anteroom

54. NEUTRAL
A. Unbiased B. Non-aligned
C. Undecided D. Indifferent

55. LAMENT
A. Complain B. Comment
C. Condone D. Console

56. MASTERLY
A. Crafty B. Skilful
C. Meaningful D. Cruel

57. MOROSE
A. Annoyed B. Gloomy
C. Moody D. Displeased

58. BARE
A. Uncovered B. Tolerate
C. Clear D. Neat

59. FEEBLE
A. Weak B. Vain
C. Arrogant D. Sick

60. PRESTIGE
A. Influence B. Quality
C. Name D. Wealth

61. WARRIOR
A. Soldier B. Sailor
C. Pirate D. Spy

62. ENTIRE
A. Part B. Quarter
C. Whole D. Half

63. RESCUE
A. Command B. Help
C. Defence D. Safety

64. INFREQUENT
A. Never B. Usual
C. Rare D. Sometimes

65. WRETCHED
A. Poor B. Foolish
C. Insane D. Strained

66. DIVERSION
A. Amusement B. Distortion
C. Deviation D. Bylane

67. AWAKENED
A. Enlightened B. Realised
C. Shook D. Waken

68. HASITATED
A. Stopped B. Paused
C. Slowed D. Postponed

69. PIOUS
A. Pure B. Pretentious
C. Clean D. Devout

70. TORTURE
A. Torment B. Chastisement
C. Harassment D. Terror

71. ATTEMPT
A. Serve B. Explore
C. Try D. Explain

72. RESTRAINT
A. Hindrance B. Repression
C. Obstacle D. Restriction

73. CHASTE
A. Honest B. Dignified
C. Virtuous D. Noble

74. INSOMNIA
A. Lethargy B. Sleeplessness
C. Drunkenness D. Unconsciousness

75. TRANSIENT
A. Transparent B. Fleeting
C. Feeble D. Fanciful

76. MANDACIOUS
A. Full of confidence B. False
C. Encouraging D. Provocative

77. VORACIOUS
A. Truthful B. Gluttonous
C. Funny D. Venturous

78. CONNOISSEUR
A. Ignorant B. Lover of art
C. Interpreter D. Delinquent

79. REPERCUSSION
A. Clever reply B. Recollection
C. Remuneration D. Reaction

80. REPEAL
A. Sanction B. Perpetuate
C. Pass D. Cancel

81. INFAMY
A. Dishonour B. Glory
C. Integrity D. Reputation

82. FAKE
A. Original B. Imitation
C. Trustworthy D. Loyal

83. DEBACLE
A. Collapse B. Decline
C. Defeat D. Disgrace

84. ADMONISH
A. Punish B. Curse
C. Dismiss D. Reprimand

85. EMBEZZLE
A. Misappropriate B. Balance
C. Remunerate D. Clear

86. CORPULENT
A. Lean B. Gaunt
C. Emaciated D. Obese

87. AUGUST
A. Common B. Ridiculous
C. Dignified D. Petty

88. STRINGENT
A. Dry B. Strained
C. Rigorous D. Shrill

89. INSOLVENT
A. Poor B. Bankrupt
C. Penniless D. Broke

90. EXTRICATE
A. Pull B. Free
C. Tie D. Complicate

91. INEXPLICABLE
A. Confusing B. Unaccountable
C. Chaotic D. Unconnected

92. GRATIFY
A. Appreciate B. Frank
C. Indulge D. Pacify

93. ALERT
A. Energetic B. Observant
C. Intelligent D. Watchful

94. UNTIE
A. Unfold B. Unchain
C. Undo D. Unhinge

95. OBJECT
A. Challenge B. Disapprove
C. Deny D. Disobey

96. BROWSE
A. Heal B. Deceive
C. Examine D. Strike

97. SALACITY
A. Bliss B. Depression
C. Indecency D. Recession

98. ZANY
A. Clown B. Pet
C. Thief D. Magician

99. WARY
A. Sad B. Vigilant
C. Distorted D. Tired

100. RECKLESS
A. Courageous B. Rash
C. Bold D. Daring

101. MOVING
A. Taking B. Toying
C. Shifting D. Turning

102. KEN
A. Ignorance B. Witness
C. Trial D. Knowledge

103. VENT
A. Opening B. Stodge
C. End D. Past tense of go

104. RANT
A. Praise inordinately B. Formalise
C. To preach noisily D. Treat with screen

105. MELD
A. To soothe B. Merge
C. Purchase D. Glisten

TYPE II

Directions: *In each of the sentences given below a word is printed in* **bold**. *Below it four choices are given. Pick up the one which is most nearly the SAME in meaning as the word printed in* **bold** *and can replaces it without altering the meaning of the sentence.*

106. When youngesters do not have good role-models to **emulate** they start searching for them amongst Sportsmen of Filmstars.
A. imitate B. modify
C. molify D. inhabit

107. The **aberration** in the Indian Economy can be attributed to short-sightedness of its political masters.
A. procrastination B. privilege
C. deviation D. steadfastness

108. The claims of students look hollow when they **attribute** their poor performance to difficulty of examination.
A. infer B. impute
C. inhere D. inundate

109. As soon as he finished his speech, there was **spontaneous** applause from the audience.
A. well-timed B. willing
C. instinctive D. instantaneous

110. The soldier proved his **mettle** in the battlefield.
A. persistence

B. stamina and strength
C. courage and endurance
D. heroism

111. He listened of my request with **indifference.**
A. disinterest B. concern
C. displeasure D. caution

112. The accident occurred due to his **lapse.**
A. trick B. interval
C. error D. ignorance

113. Being a member of this Club, he has certain **rights.**
A. status B. truth
C. virtues D. privileges

114. He is **averse** to the idea of holding elections now.
A. convinced B. angry
C. agreeable D. opposed

115. Silence is **mandatory** for meditation to be effective.
A. compulsory B. necessary
C. required D. needed

116. The underworld still makes solid profit out of **illicit** liquor.
A. indigenous B. illegitimate
C. illegal D. country

117. When I look back over the wartime years I cannot help feeling that time is an inadequate and even **capricious** measure of their duration at one moment they seem so long, at another so short.
A. misleading B. whimsical
C. erratic D. unpredictable

118. The tablet **alleviated** the pain, and the patient was soon feeling much better.
A. mitigated B. moderated
C. removed D. lightened

119. The leader nodded his **approbation**
A. understanding B. approval
C. admiration D. appreciation

120. We should always try to maintain and promote communal **amity.**
A. bondage B. contention
C. friendship D. understanding

121. Many species of animals have become **extinct** during the last hundred years.
A. aggressive B. non-existent
C. scattered D. feeble

122. True religion does not require one to **proselytise** through guile or force.
A. translate B. hypnotise
C. attack D. convert

123. That the plan is both inhuman and **preposterous** needs no further proof.
A. heartless B. impractical
C. absurd D. abnormal

124. She **baffled** all our attempts to find her.
A. defeated B. thwarted
C. foiled D. circumvented

125. Instead of putting up a united front against of common enemy, the medieval states frittered away their energy in **internecine** warfare.
A. mutually destructive
B. baneful
C. pernicious
D. detrimental

126. The bullet wound proved to be **fatal** and the soldier died immediately.
A. grievous B. dangerous
C. serious D. deadly

127. Whatever opinion he gives is **sane.**
A. rational B. obscure
C. wild D. arrogant

128. He **corroborated** the statement of his brother.
A. confirmed B. disproved
C. condemned D. seconded

129. Whatever the **verdict** of history may be, Chaplin will occupy a unique place in its pages.
A. judgement B. voice
C. outcome D. prediction

130. The attitude of the Western countries towards the Third World countries is rather **callous to** say the least.
A. passive B. unkind
C. cursed D. unfeeling

131. The story is too fantastic to be **credible.**
A. believable B. false
C. readable D. praiseworthy

132. Catching snakes can be **hazardous** for people untrained in the art.
A. tricky B. harmful
C. difficult D. dangerous

133. After the **dismal** performance of the team in the series concluded yesterday, the captain offered his resignation to the president of the club.

A. poor B. sorrowful
C. minimum D. short

134. The small boy was able to give a **graphic** description of the thief.

A. picture B. drawing
C. vivid D. broad

135. The prisoner has been **languishing** in the jail for the last many years.

A. convicted B. suffering
C. attempting D. avoiding

136. Some of the Asian countries have been **enmeshed** in an inescapable debt trap.

A. entagled B. hit
C. struck D. ensured

137. In spite of their efforts, the team of scientists could not make much **headway** to solve the problem.

A. progress B. thinking
C. efforts D. start

138. On scrutiny the police officer found out that the documents provided by the landlord were totally **fabricated.**

A. forged B. historical
C. prepared D. genuine

139. The soldier displayed **exceptional** courage and saved the Major from the enemy's hand.

A. avoidable B. unusual
C. strange D. abnormal

140. He found a **lucrative** assignment.

A. good B. profitable
C. excellent D. significant

141. The novel was so interesting that I was **oblivious** of my surroundings.

A. precarious B. unmindful
C. aware D. watchful

142. The great dancer impressed the appreciative crowd by his **nimble** movements.

A. unrhythmic B. lively
C. quickening D. clear

143. The president of the party **deprecated** the move of the Government to introduce electroal reforms in a haste.

A. welcomed B. denied
C. protested D. humiliated

144. It took him a long-time to **come round** after the operation.

A. recover B. walk
C. move D. eat

145. Few teachers have been spared the problem of an **obstreperous** pupil in the class.

A. sullen B. unruly
C. lazy D. awkward

146. His visit to foreign countries brought about a **sea-change** in his outlook and his attitude to people.

A. complete change
B. partial change
C. favourable change
D. unfavourable change

147. Swift is known in the world of letters for his **misogynism.**

A. hate for mankind
B. hate for womankind
C. love for the reasonable
D. love for womankind

148. He was warned at the **outset** of his career.

A. end B. beginning
C. middle D. entrance

149. The time I spent in the library was a most **rewarding** one.

A. profitable B. paying
C. serviceable D. precious

150. That young is quite **sanguine** about the result of his competitive examination.

A. depressed B. pessimistic
C. anxious D. optimistic

151. The courage shown by the soldiers at this moment of crisis is **exemplary.**

A. suitable B. clear
C. elementary D. admirable

152. The notice said that the meeting would begin **precisely** at 9.30 a.m.

A. approximately B. exactly
C. accurately D. concisely

153. The inspector was a **vigilant** young man.

A. intelligent B. ambitious
C. watchful D. smart

154. A **rupture** in the relationship of the two brothers is quite apparent.
A. break B. damage
C. breach D. gap

155. "I have learnt a great deal working in factories, and for a time I've been a weaver. Here are my **testimonials,** Mr. Davis."
A. witnesses B. testaments
C. tokens D. credentials

156. The prince fell in love with a **comely** young maiden.
A. delightful B. pretty
C. homely D. elegant

157. Lack of occupation is not necessarily revealed by **manifest** idleness.
A. easily perceived B. easily acquired
C. easily infected D. easily deflected

158. Even today many people are guided by **obstruse** moral values.
A. dangerous B. impracticable
C. obscure D. irrational

159. Sunlight and shadow made the landscape a **kaleidoscope** of colour.
A. tube containing mirrors and loose pieces of coloured glass
B. frequently changing pattern of bright scenes
C. a mixture of black and white
D. resembling the seven colours of rainbow

160. A person unrestrained by the rules of morality or tradition is called a **licentious** person.
A. libertine B. loafer-type
C. criminal D. freelance

161. She has an **insatiable** love for music.
A. unsatisfiable B. unchanging
C. irreconcilable D. undesirable

162. The recent acts of **vandalism** in the country cannot be ignored.
A. disturbance B. ravage
C. provocation D. violence

163. When he returned he was accompanied by a **sprightly** young girl.
A. beautiful B. lively
C. intelligent D. sportive

164. I wrote to him as **lately** as last week.
A. immediately B. early
C. recently D. late

165. The international community may begin to doubt the **credentials** of the largest democracy in the world.
A. principles
B. dependability
C. capacity to return loans
D. trustworthiness

166. The **indiscriminate** demand for mass consumption goods is deplorable.
A. desperate B. undifferentiated
C. discreet D. insensitive

167. The general policies will **relieve** the sufferings of the common man.
A. alleviate B. mitigate
C. moderate D. abate

168. They were totally unware of the **impending** disaster.
A. threatening B. imminent
C. terrible D. possible

169. His style is quite **transparent.**
A. verbose B. involved
C. lucid D. witty

170. When the police questioned him, he gave very **incoherent** answer at first.
A. irrational B. inconsistent
C. irrelevant D. irritating

171. Japan has been very much **eulogised** in this book.
A. appreciated B. praised
C. approved D. applauded

172. I don't like **alien** fashions.
A. foreign B. extraneous
C. unusual D. exotic

173. The visitor had a **bohemian** look.
A. hostile B. unconventional
C. sinister D. unfriendly

174. That great artist's life was full of **vicissitudes.**
A. sorrows B. misfortunes
C. changes D. surprises

175. This young man appears to be quite **headstrong.**
A. thick-headed B. obstinate
C. robust D. witty

176. Only those who are **guillible** take every advertisement seriously.
A. fallible B. enthusiastic
C. unsuspecting D. unrealistic

177. As the driver was **inebriated** he could not control the car.
A. inexperienced B. tired
C. befuddled D. intoxicated

178. They feel that we should be fully aware of our own **environment.**
A. nationality B. heredity
C. nature D. surroundings

179. Everyone was listening to the news of earthquake with mounting **anxiety**.
A. curiosity B. grief
C. uneasiness D. eagerness

180. Manish **neglected** to remit the fees in time and therefore had to pay a fine.
A. refused B. failed
C. promised D. obstructed

181. The poem is written in a very **lucid** style.
A. elaborate B. clear
C. noble D. intricate

182. We didn't believe in his statement, but **subsequent** events proved that he was right.
A. later B. many
C. few D. earlier

183. All the characters in the novel are **fictitious**.
A. unbelieveable B. unreliable
C. infamous D. unreal

184. The **pioneers** left a blazing trail of courage, manliness and chivalry.
A. inventors B. explorers
C. colonialists D. settlers

185. Even though singing of ballads is no longer **lucrative** the Bhopas of Rajasthan continue to sing them in order to cherish the memory of their royal warriors.
A. tempting B. attractive
C. profitable D. honourable

186. When he could not endure the cruel ragging any longer, the new recruit bravely **stood up to** all his bullying seniors.
A. challenged B. fought back
C. resisted D. defeated

187. The angry villagers have **lynched** two suspected child-lifters already.
A. beaten up B. captured
C. killed D. mutilated

188. The thief **outwitted** the constable on some pretext and disappeared on the way to the police station.
A. defeated B. befooled
C. cheated D. outmanoeuvred

189. Public figures should not indulge in **mud-slinging.**
A. caricatures B. mockery
C. slander D. quarrelling

190. Some people just cannot **compromise** where truth is concerned.
A. adjust B. accommodate
C. yield D. conciliate

191. Traffic being what it is, it is **lamentable** that our roads are unable to take the load.
A. unpardonable B. deplorable
C. inexcusable D. terrible

192. It is very difficult to **retain** all that you hear in the class.
A. keep B. recall
C. preserve D. conserve

193. Everybody likes him because he is an **industrious** student.
A. energetic B. prompt
C. excellent D. diligent

194. No one will invite her to a tea party for she is so **garrulous.**
A. talks a lot
B. giggles all the time
C. laughs a lot
D. repeats gossip

195. He has a **propensity** for getting into debt.
A. natural tendency B. aptitude
C. characteristic D. quality

196. It is a **scandal** that the murderer was declared innocent.
A. silly notion
B. talk
C. rumour
D. disgraceful action

197. **Incensed** by his rude behaviour, the Manager suspended the worker.
A. Excited B. Inflamed
C. Enraged D. Enthused

198. The invasion force had no artillery and was completely **annihilated**.

A. dismembered B. reduced
C. destroyed D. split

199. The base of Indian politicians is the group of **sycophants** around them who earn bad name for their leaders.

A. submissive B. foppish
C. flatterers D. jarnor

200 The **benevolence** of the God of Rain has seen a very successful monsoon this year too.

A. ill-will B. kindness
C. morbidity D. vision

ANSWERS

1	**2**	**3**	**4**	**5**	**6**	**7**	**8**	**9**	**10**
C	B	D	C	B	C	B	C	D	B
11	**12**	**13**	**14**	**15**	**16**	**17**	**18**	**19**	**20**
D	D	B	A	A	B	B	D	A	B
21	**22**	**23**	**24**	**25**	**26**	**27**	**28**	**29**	**30**
D	D	C	B	D	C	C	B	C	D
31	**32**	**33**	**34**	**35**	**36**	**37**	**38**	**39**	**40**
A	C	C	D	A	A	C	D	A	C
41	**42**	**43**	**44**	**45**	**46**	**47**	**48**	**49**	**50**
C	A	C	D	A	A	D	C	A	C
51	**52**	**53**	**54**	**55**	**56**	**57**	**58**	**59**	**60**
D	C	A	A	A	B	B	A	A	C
61	**62**	**63**	**64**	**65**	**66**	**67**	**68**	**69**	**70**
A	C	B	D	A	A	D	B	A	A
71	**72**	**73**	**74**	**75**	**76**	**77**	**78**	**79**	**80**
C	D	C	B	B	B	B	B	D	D
81	**82**	**83**	**84**	**85**	**86**	**87**	**88**	**89**	**90**
A	B	A	D	A	D	C	C	B	B
91	**92**	**93**	**94**	**95**	**96**	**97**	**98**	**99**	**100**
B	D	D	C	B	C	C	A	B	B
101	**102**	**103**	**104**	**105**	**106**	**107**	**108**	**109**	**110**
C	D	A	C	B	A	C	B	C	C
111	**112**	**113**	**114**	**115**	**116**	**117**	**118**	**119**	**120**
A	C	D	D	A	C	B	A	B	C
121	**122**	**123**	**124**	**125**	**126**	**127**	**128**	**129**	**130**
B	D	C	C	A	D	A	A	A	D
131	**132**	**133**	**134**	**135**	**136**	**137**	**138**	**139**	**140**
A	D	A	C	B	A	A	A	B	B
141	**142**	**143**	**144**	**145**	**146**	**147**	**148**	**149**	**150**
B	C	C	A	B	A	B	B	A	D
151	**152**	**153**	**154**	**155**	**156**	**157**	**158**	**159**	**160**
D	B	C	A	D	B	A	C	B	A
161	**162**	**163**	**164**	**165**	**166**	**167**	**168**	**169**	**170**
A	D	B	C	D	B	A	B	C	B
171	**172**	**173**	**174**	**175**	**176**	**177**	**178**	**179**	**180**
B	D	B	C	B	C	D	D	C	B
181	**182**	**183**	**184**	**185**	**186**	**187**	**188**	**189**	**190**
B	A	D	D	C	C	C	A	C	A
191	**192**	**193**	**194**	**195**	**196**	**197**	**198**	**199**	**200**
B	A	D	A	A	D	C	C	C	B

IDIOMS/PHRASES

PART I

1.	**A wet blanket**	:	a person who discourages others or prevents them from enjoying what they are doing.
2.	**A stag party**	:	a party where only men are allowed to be present.
3.	**A hen party**	:	a party where only women are allowed to be present.
4.	**A working lunch/dinner**	:	a meal at which the people who attend discuss business.
5.	**A working knowledge**	:	enough practical knowledge to do something.
6.	**A willing horse**	:	a helpful person who often gets all the work to do.
7.	**A wild goose chase**	:	a search for something which has no chance of being successful.
8.	**A trend-setter**	:	a person who starts a new fashion which becomes popular.
9.	**A thick-skinned person**	:	a person who is not easily offended.
10.	**Teething troubles**	:	a troubles and difficulties which occur during the early stages of an activity or enterprise, but which will lessen with time.
11.	**A sweeping statement**	:	a statement which is not careful or correct in its details; a generalisation.
12.	**A spending spree**	:	an outing during which one spends a lot of money.
13.	**A tall order**	:	a request which is unreasonably difficult to grant or carry out.
14.	**A soft spot**	:	a feeling of special fondness for something or someone.
15.	**A sore point**	:	a matter which irritates or hurts when it is mentioned.
16.	**The small hours**	:	the early morning hours just after midnight.
17.	**A sleeping partner**	:	a business partner who provides a share of the capital for a venture but does not take an active part in its operation.
18.	**Small talk**	:	trivial, light conversation on unimportant topics.
19.	**Second nature**	:	some acquired habit or skill which seems perfectly natural to someone; a very firmly fixed habit.
20.	**A shady character**	:	a person of very doubtful honesty or character.
21.	**Second thoughts**	:	a change of mind, attitude or decision after thinking about the matter.
22.	**A security risk**	:	a person who is a risk to a country's security because of his political activities; one whose loyalty is doubted.
23.	**A jail bird**	:	a man who has spent a lot of time in prison.
24.	**A ladies' man**	:	a man who likes to be with women or who likes to please them.
25.	**A last fling**	:	the last opportunity for pleasure or amusement before having to stop.
26.	**An inside job**	:	a theft committed by someone inside a building, i.e., by an employee, not a stranger.
27.	**A knowing look**	:	a look which suggests that the person is well-informed of a matter.
28.	**A hushed-up affair**	:	an affair or matter that is kept secret by forcing silence about it.
29.	**Hush money**	:	a bribe paid to keep a matter secret from the public.
30.	**A hot line**	:	a direct telephone line between heads of governments, to be used at times of great difficulty.

31.	**Hot news**	:	very recent, important or sensational news.
32.	**High time**	:	at the most important point of time.
33.	**Fast living**	:	a person who spends too much money in enjoying life.
34.	**A fishy story**	:	an untrue tale; an unlikely story.
35.	**Half-hearted**	:	having no enthusiasm for a particular task.
36.	**An iron will**	:	a very strong will.
37.	**Hot water**	:	trouble.
38.	**A laughing stock**	:	a person who is unkindly laughed at by everyone.
39.	**A light-fingered person**	:	a person who is in the habit of stealing small things.
40.	**Pin money**	:	a wife's allowance for her personal needs.
41.	**Plain sailing**	:	a plan or action that is simple and free from trouble.
42.	**A pep talk**	:	a friendly talk to give encouragement to win a game, etc., or to complete something well.
43.	**A package tour**	:	a completely planned holiday at a fixed price arranged by a company.
44.	**A passing fancy**	:	a temporary liking for something or someone.
45.	**An open secret**	:	something supposed to be a secret but which in fact is known to everyone.
46.	**A package deal**	:	an offer or agreement which includes a number of things all of which must be taken.
47.	**Plain dealing**	:	truthfulness and honesty, especially in business.
48.	**A pet aversion**	:	something or someone much disliked.
49.	**A sideline**	:	work one does apart from one's regular job.
50.	**Second sight**	:	an ability to foresee future events.
51.	**A rolling stone**	:	person who travels around a lot without staying in any one place or job for long.
52.	**A raw deal**	:	a unjust or cruel treatment.
53.	**In a rash moment**	:	doing something hastily without thinking of the results.
54.	**A practical joke**	:	a trick played on a person to make him look silly and to give amusement to others.
55.	**A sagar daddy**	:	an older man who has a relationship, especially sexual, with a younger woman, providing her with money and presents.
56.	**Take-home pay/wages**	:	the amount a person receives after taxes have been deducted.
57.	**backstairs influence**	:	secret and usually unfair influence.
58.	**Bad blood**	:	bad feelings or unfriendliness between two persons.
59.	**A bad egg/a bad penny**	:	a bad character.
60.	**A false alarm**	:	a warning of something bad, which does not happen.
61.	**Elbow room**	:	space in which to move and act freely.
62.	**A double agent**	:	a peson who works secretly for two opposing sides without either of the sides knowing.
63.	**A dead-end job**	:	a job without prospects; a job that leads to nothing further.
64.	**A dark horse**	:	a person who competes successfully against another although little is known about him.
65.	**A confirmed bachelor**	:	a man who has no desire to marry.
66.	**A burning question**	:	a matter having to be dealt with at once; an urgent, important matter.
67.	**A big shot**	:	an important person, usually someone who is wealthy and influential.
68.	**A blind date**	:	a social meeting of two persons, usually a boy and a girl who have not met before.

69. **Broken English** : imperfect, ungrammatical English.
70. **A chicken-hearted person** : a timid, cowardly person.
71. **A close-fisted person** : someone who is stingy; a miser.
72. **A country cousin** : a person who is simple and inexperienced and not used to city life.
73. **A close shave** : a narrow escape from danger, an accident, etc.
74. **A light sleeper** : a person who is easily awarened from sleep.
75. **A cock-and-bull story** : an invented story.
76. **A cold war** : a serious political struggle between countries which does not actually result in fighting.
77. **A dog-eared book** : a book where the corners of the pages have been turned down with use.
78. **An easy victim/mark** : somebody who can easily be cheated or treated badly.
79. **A bosom friend** : a very close, trusted friend.
80. **Crocodile tears** : pretended sorrow; insincere tears.
81. **A fast colour** : a colour which does not run out of the material when washed or dried.
82. **A fair copy** : a neat, legible copy.
83. **An armchair critic** : a person who critically judges others, work and gives advice, but who has not himself experienced doing the work.
84. **Apple-pie order** : in perfect order.
85. **An, absent-minded person** : a forgetful, inattentive person.
86. **A flying visit** : a very short visit.
87. **Forty winks** : a short nap or sleep.
88. **Hard labour** : hard, manual work usually done as a punishment.
89. **Hard cash** : actual money, not a cheque, etc.
90. **A hard drinker** : a person who drinks large quantities of alcohol.
91. **A golden opportunity** : a very good opportunity.
92. **A going concern** : a successful, thriving business.
93. **A foregone conclusion** : a result that is certain, sure.
94. **The naked eye** : the eye unaided by any instrument.
95. **An odd-job man** : a man who does various types of work, usually manual, for pay.
96. **Old hat** : no longer fashionable.
97. **A grass widowe** : a wife who is alone because her husband is away temporarily.
98. **A good Samaritan** : a person who helps a stranger in difficulties.
99. **French leave** : absence from work that is taken without permission.
100. **The generation gap** : the difficulties arising when younger and older people do not understand each other's way of life.
101. **The happy medium** : the middle course of doing something when opposite ways are suggested.
102. **A henpecked husband** : a husband who is dominated and nagged by his wife.
103. **A hard and fast rule** : a rule that cannot be changed; fixed, unchangeable rules.
104. **One-track mind** : a person's mind that is limited and thinks of only one thing at a time.
105. **A short cut** : an easier method of doing something or getting somewhere; a quicker, more direct way.
106. **A small-time business** : a business limited in activity and profits.
107. **A splitting headach** : a very severe and painful headache.
108. **A square deal** : a fair bargain or fair treatment.

109. A square meal	:	a meal with adequate good; a satisfying meal.
110. Strong language	:	angry language consisting of many swear words.
111. Tall talk	:	boastful talk.
112. A tight spot/corner	:	a difficult situation.
113. Tough luck	:	bad luck; hard luck.
114. Ready money	:	money which is immediately available in coins or notes.
115. Second best	:	next to the best; second in value or importance.

PART II

116. The writing on the wall	:	an indication that something bad or difficult is about to happen.
117. A storm in a teacup	:	a big fuss made over a small, trivial event.
118. The talk of the town	:	a person or event that is causing great excitement and is the subject of much discussion.
119. A snake in the grass	:	a cunning, harmful person who pretends to be a friend; a false friend.
120. A shot in the dark	:	a guess which is not supported by arguments; a wild guess.
121. The tricks of the trade	:	the best and most successful ways of doing good business.
122. The bottom of the ladder	:	in the least important position.
123. A shot in the arm	:	something which acts to bring back a happy state or condition.
124. The man in the street	:	the ordinary, average man.
125. The gift of the gab	:	a person fluent in speech; a persuasive speaker.
126. A man about town	:	a man who is used to living in the city and associating with well-known fashionable people.
127. The life and soul	:	the person who is the centre of attraction because he is amusing and lively.
128. The lion's share	:	the greater part; an unfairly large share.
129. The long arm of the law	:	the police.
130. A bear hug	:	a rough, tight hug.
131. A brain wave	:	a clever idea; sudden inspiration.
132. A bone of contention	:	something that causes argument.
133. Birds of a feather	:	people of the same kind (often bad) who like each other's company.
134. A feather in one's cap	:	a deserved honour that one is proud of.
135. Castels in the air	:	plans which cannot be carried out or which will probably not succeed.
136. A fish out of water	:	a person who feels uncomfortable because he is in a strange place, or among people who are very different from himself.
137. The ups and downs	:	the good and bad times, the happy and sad times.
138. A stone's thorw	:	a rebuff.
139. A slip of the tongue	:	something said unintentionally.
140. A slap in the face	:	a short distance.
141. The rank and file	:	ordinary people without special positions; the masses.
142. A man of means	:	a rich man.
143. A man of iron	:	a cruel, hard person.
144. A jack of all trades	:	a person who can do many different kinds of work, but who may not be good at any of them.
145. By hook or by crook	:	by any means possible.
146. By fits and starts	:	at irregular intervals.

147. **A pack of lies** : a whole lot of untruths.
148. **A clean bill of health** : a certifiate or announcement that someone is healthy.

PART III

149. **A happy-go-lucky person** : someone who does not think or plan carefully.
150. **A stay-at-home person** : a person who is in the habit of staying at home, and not liking to travel.
151. **A smash-and-grab robbery** : a robbery done quickly, usually by breaking windows or showcases, taking away valuables, and running away.
152. **A hit-and-run driver** : a driver who drives away after an accident without stopping to find out about damage or injuries.
153. **A run-of-the-mill job** : an ordinary, unexciting job.
154. **A round-the-clock service** : a twenty-four hour service.
155. **An out-of-the way place** : a place that is distant and far away from people and places.
156. **A much-talked-of affair** : something which is the subject of much discussion.
157. **A nine-to-six job** : a job in which the working hours are from nine in the morning to six in the evening.
158. **An open and shut case** : a case which is easy to settle or solve.
159. **Bumper-to-bumper traffic** : cars that are very close together one after another.
160. **A hand-me-down dress** : a dress used by someone after belonging to another.
161. **A well-to-do man/woman** : a rich person.
162. **An angel** : a person who is gentle and kind to others.
163. **A devil** : a particularly wicked or mischievous person.
164. **A giant** : a person who is very large.
165. **A wizard** : a clever and skillful person.
166. **An Adonis** : a very handsome man.
167. **An Apollo** : a man with a perfect physique or body shape.
168. **A Hercules** : a very strong man.
169. **A Goliath** : an extremely large man.
170. **A Judas** : a mean traitor.
171. **A Samson** : a very strong man.
172. **A Solomon** : a very wise man.
173. **A dog** : a worthless person; someone who is despised.
174. **A cat** : a malicious person, usually referring to females.
175. **A bear** : a clumsy, rough person.
176. **A fox** : a crafty, cunning person.
177. **A goose** : a silly person.
178. **A lamb** : an innocent, harmless person.
179. **A monkey** : a child who is lively and full of mischievous tricks.
180. **A mule** : a very stubborn person.
181. **A wolf** : a greedy and cunning person.
182. **A snake/serpent** : a treacherous, dangerous person.
183. **A parrot** : a peson who learns things off by heart without understanding the real meaning.
184. **A pest** : a troublesome person; one who annoys and pesters others.
185. **A pig** : a greedy and dirty person.

186. A shark : a greedy and cunning person; one who swindles others.
187. A parasite : a person who lives off others and gives nothing in return.
188. An ape : a person who foolishly imitates others.
189. An ass/donkey : a stupid person.
190. An elephant : a huge, clumsy, ungainly person.

***Note:* Let us learn the following adjectives derived from names of certain animals.**

(*a*) canine : like a dog.
(*b*) cattish/catty : malicious; spiteful.
(*c*) dogged : stubborn.
(*d*) feline : like a cat.
(*e*) foxy : cunning, crafty.
(*f*) sheepish : uncomfortable; embarrassed.
(*g*) tigerish : fiercely energetic.

PART IV

191. Again and again : repeatedly; continually; very often.
192. Back and forth/backward and forwards : moving first in one direction and then in the opposite direction.
193. By and by : soon; before long.
194. By and large : on the whole; in general; all things considered.
195. Far and away : very much.
196. Far and near/far and wide : everywhere.
197. First and foremost : in the first place; firstly.
198. Here and there : in various places; firstly.
199. Here, there and everywhere : in all possible places; everywhere.
200. In and out : sometimes inside and sometimes outside.
201. Up and about : on one's feet; up again after an illness.
202. To and fro : backwards and forwards; from side to side.
203. Through and through : completely; entirely; in every way.
204. Out and out : complete, thorough; total.
205. Out and away : by far.
206. Over and over again : again and again; repeatedly.
207. Round and round : repeatedly moving round.
208. Once and for all : finally; for the last time.
209. On and on : without stopping.
210. Off and on : from time to time; occasionally.
211. Every now and then/again : from time to time; at times.
212. Now and again : sometimes; occasionally; not very often.
213. Nowadays : in these times.

PART V

214. To backbite a perosn : to speak ill of someone.
215. To back chat : to be cheeky; to talk back to someone.
216. To be a bag of bones : to be extremely thin.
217. To be a blockhead : to be an idiot.
218. To be a great hand at : to be an expert.

219. To be a sight for sore eyes	:	something or someone who appears before another and is very welcome.
220. To be all ears	:	to be eager to listen.
221. To be armed to the teeth	:	fully armed or protected.
222. To be at one's wits' end	:	completely puzzled.
223. To be close-fisted	:	to be mean; miserly.
224. To be double-faced	:	insincere.
225. To be down in the mouth	:	to feel depressed and unhappy.
226. To be head and shoulders above someone else	:	to be very much better or superior.
227. To be out of one's mind	:	to be mad; crazy.
228. To be someone's blue-eyed boy	:	to be someone's favourite.
229. To be the apple of someone's eye	:	to be someone's favourite.
230. To bite someone's head off	:	to speak abruptly or sharply to another.
231. To burn one's fingers	:	to get into trouble.
232. To catch someone's eye	:	to suddenly exchange glances with another.
233. To change hands	:	to pass from one owner to another.
234. To dig someone's in the ribs	:	to make unkind remarks or insinuations about another.
235. To eat one's heart out for another	:	to long for someone who is unattentive.
236. To foot the bill	:	to pay the bill, especially for some social outing.
237. To get on someone's nerves	:	to irritate someone very greatly.
238. To get something off one's chest	:	to confess to something.
239. To get the upper hand	:	to gain mastery over an opponent.
240. To give someone the cold shoulder	:	to ignore someone; to slight another.
241. To give someone the sharp edge of one's tongue	:	to thoroughly scold another person.
242. To go on all hands	:	to crawl on hands and knees.
243. To have a chip on one's shoulder	:	to bear a grudge against the world/society.
244. To have a finger in every pie	:	to have many business interests.
245. To have a head like a sieve	:	to have a very poor memory.
246. To have a skeleton in the cupboard	:	to have a guilty secret, especially a family scandal.
247. To have at one's fingertips	:	to know thoroughly.
248. To have cold feet	:	to be afraid.
249. To have no backbone	:	to be a weak, spineless person.
250. To have one's head screwed on	:	to be very sensible.
251. To have someone under one's thumb	:	to dominate another.
252. To have the upper hand	:	to be in command/charge; to be someone in power.
253. To have two left hands	:	someone who is clumsy.

254.	**To hold one's tongue**	:	to keep silent even though there is an urge to talk.
255.	**To hold up one's head**	:	to be able to look people in the face.
256.	**To jump out of one's skin**	:	to get a sudden fright.
257.	**To keep a cool head**	:	to keep calm, especially in an emergency.
258.	**To keep a stiff upper lip**	:	to remain calm and courageous.
259.	**To keep one's fingers crossed**	:	to hope for luck.
260.	**To keep one's hair on**	:	to keep cool and patient.
261.	**To keep one's head above water**	:	to avoid getting into debt or trouble.
262.	**To keep someone at arm's length**	:	not too friendly with another.
263.	**To knock something on the head**	:	to suddenly stop an idea/project.
264.	**To know something by heart**	:	to be able to say something from memory.
265.	**To lay hands on someone**	:	to handle someone roughly.
266.	**To lend a hand**	:	to help.
267.	**To let the grass grow under one's feet**	:	to be inactive and uninvolved.
268.	**To live from hand to mouth**	:	to live in hardship with the barest essentials.
269.	**To lose face**	:	to lose one's reputation/honour.
270.	**To lose heart**	:	to be discouraged.
271.	**To lose one's head**	:	to be very angry; to lose control of oneself.
272.	**To make a clean breast of something**	:	to confess to something; to reveal all.
273.	**To make neither head nor tail of something**	:	to understand nothing of a particular issue.
274.	**To pat someone on the back**	:	to give praise and encouragement to another.
275.	**To pay through the nose for something**	:	to pay an excessively high price for something.
276.	**To poison someone's mind**	:	to turn someone against another person.
277.	**To pull one's weight**	:	to do one's share of work.
278.	**To pull someone's leg**	:	to play a joke on someone.
279.	**To pull the wool over someone's eyes**	:	to deceive another.
280.	**To put one's back into it**	:	to work hard.
281.	**To put one's foot down**	:	to be firm about an issue.
282.	**To put one's shoulder to the wheel**	:	to work hard and earnestly.
283.	**To put someone's nose out of joint**	:	to make someone jealous by taking his place as the centre of attraction.
284.	**To rack one's brains**	:	to try to recall or remember something.
285.	**To receive with open arms**	:	to welcome warmly.
286.	**To save face**	:	to save one's honour/reputation/name.
287.	**To show a clean pair of heels**	:	to escape by running.
288.	**To snap someone's head off**	:	to speak abruptly.
289.	**To stand on one's own feet**	:	to do things without help; to be independent.
290.	**To sweep someone off his/her feet**	:	to flatter and woo someone, usually a girl.

291. To take matters into one's own hands	:	to do something independently without help.
292. To take something to heart	:	to take something seriously.
293. To take to one's heels	:	to run away.
294. To throw dust in someone's eyes	:	to try to deceive someone.
295. To tread in someone's foot steps	:	to follow the example of another, usually of talent/occupation.
296. To tread on someone's toes	:	to offend another person.
297. To try one's hand at	:	to try doing something for the first time.
298. To turn a blind eye	:	to refuse to see.
299. to turn a deaf ear	:	to refuse to hear.
300. To turn up one's nose at something	:	to treat with contempet.
301. To twist someone's arm	:	to force someone into doing something for you.
302. To wash one's hands of something	:	to have nothing to do with a particular matter.

PART VI

303. The green-eyed monster	:	jealousy.
304. To scream blue murder	:	to complain loudly.
305. Out of the blue	:	suddenly; without warning.
306. Once in a blue moon	:	very rarely.
307. To feel blue/have the blues	:	to be sad or depressed.
308. A bolt from the blue	:	a complete surprise.
309. Blue blood	:	royal or noble blood.
310. To blackmail someone	:	to threaten to reveal someone's misdeeds unless he pays money.
311. In someone's black books	:	out of favour with someone.
312. A black sheep	:	a bad character who disgraces his family.
313. A blacklist	:	a list of people, groups, etc., who have done something wrong.
314. Black and blue	:	badly bruised after a beating/a fall.
315. In black and white	:	in writing or print.
316. A greengrocer	:	a person who sells fruit and vegetables.
317. A greenhorn	:	an inexperienced person.
318. The green light	:	the signal to proceed.
319. Green with envy	:	filled with jealousy.
320. Grey matter	:	common sense; brains.
321. In the pink of health	:	in excellent health.
322. Purple with rage	:	so angry that the face becomes purple.
323. To be caught red-handed	:	to be caught in the act of committing a crime.
324. A red carpet welcome	:	a special ceremonial welcome to guest.
325. The red flag	:	a flag used as a danger signal.
326. A red-letter day	:	a notable, fortunate day that will be remembered.
327. The red light	:	a signal to stop; a danger signal.
328. Red tape	:	official rules which cause delay in settling one's problems.

329. To jump out of the frying-pan into the fire	:	to get out of one bad situation and fall into another, worse situation.
330. To see red	:	to lose control of oneself in anger.
331. A white-collar job	:	an office job.
332. A white elephant	:	a worthless possession which the owner wants to get rid of.
333. The white flag	:	a sign that one accepts defeat or surenders.
334. To show the white feather	:	to show signs of cowardice.
335. Yellow at heart	:	cowardly.
336. To be/feel off colour	:	to be unwell or rather ill.
337. To come off with flying colours	:	to achieve great success.
338. To have a high colour	:	to appear very red in the face.
339. To show one's true colours	:	to show what one is really like; to show one's true character.
340. A blue-collar job	:	a factory job.

PART VII

341. To act the goat	:	to behave foolishly.
342. To air one's opinion	:	to express one's feelings in public.
343. To be a chip off the old block	:	a son who is very much like his father in appearance, character, habits, etc.
344. To be as fit as a fiddle	:	to be in excellent health.
345. To be at a loose end	:	to have nothing to do.
346. To be at a loose for words	:	not knowing what to say; to be speechless.
347. To be at death's door	:	to be so ill as to be near death.
348. To be at sixes and sevens	:	to be in confusion and discord.
349. To be at the end of one's teeter	:	to be at a loss as to what to do.
350. To be born under a lucky star	:	to have considerable luck in whatever one does.
351. To be born with a silver spoon in one's mouth	:	to be born into a rich family.
352. To be dead beat	:	to be worn out by fatigue.
353. To be in hot water	:	to be in serious trouble.
354. To be in someone's bad/good books	:	to be out of/in favour with someone.
355. To be in the doldrums	:	to be in low spirits
356. To be in the same boat	:	to have the same troubles/circumstances.
357. To be mad about someone	:	to like someone very much.
358. To be made of money	:	to have plenty of money; to be well-off.
359. To be on tenterhooks	:	to be in a state of suspense and anxiety.
360. To be on the ball	:	to be alert, up-to-date, prepared.
361. To be on the horns of a dilemma	:	not knowing what to do from several courses of action.
362. To be on the rocks	:	to be in danger of failing, collapse, especially a business, a marriage, etc.
363. To be on top of the world	:	to be very happy; to be in high spirits.

364.	**To be out of the woods**	:	to be out of danger, especially a serious illness.
365.	**To be quick on the uptake**	:	to be alert and quick to do or say something.
366.	**To be rolling in money**	:	to be rich; to have plenty of money.
367.	**To be scared to death**	:	to be extremely frightened of something.
368.	**To be slow on the uptake**	:	slow to do or say something.
369.	**To be too big for one's boots**	:	to thing very highly of oneself.
370.	**To bear the burnt of**	:	to bear the main force or strain of some action.
371.	**To beat about the bush**	:	to be indecisive; not coming to the point.
372.	**To blow hot and cold**	:	to do one thing at one time and the opposite soon after.
373.	**To blow one's own trumpet**	:	to boast about one's abilities, achievements, etc.
374.	**To break the ice**	:	to take the first step; to be the first to begin, especially a conversation.
375.	**To bring down the house**	:	to cause loud and long applause through one's skill.
376.	**To bring to light**	:	to disclose, reveal.
377.	**To build castles in the air**	:	to think of things impossible to realize.
378.	**To burn the candle at both ends**	:	to use one's energy in two directions at the same time.
379.	**To burn the midnight oil**	:	to work till late at night.
380.	**To call a spade a spade**	:	to speak out bluntly and frankly.
381.	**To clip one's wings**	:	to deprive one of power and/or freedom.
382.	**To cook an account**	:	to tamper with/falsify an account.
383.	**To come down on someone like a ton of bricks**	:	to harshly criticise another.
384.	**To come of age**	:	to reach adulthood.
385.	**To come to grief**	:	to meet with danger.
386.	**To come to light**	:	to become known.
387.	**To count sheep**	:	to try various methods to get to sleep.
388.	**To cry over spilt milk**	:	to be unhappy about something that can no longer be remedied.
389.	**To curry favour**	:	to seek/win favour by flattery or gifts.
390.	**To cut off in its prime**	:	to destroy something when it is at its best.
391.	**To cut one's coat according to one's cloth**	:	to live within one's income.
392.	**To cut someone down to size**	:	to put someone in his place especially a person who thinks too highly of himself.
393.	**To do a city/the rights**	:	to visit a city and see its well-known places.
394.	**To do a thing by fits and starts**	:	to work intermittently on something.
395.	**To do a thing by hook or by crook**	:	to do something by any means, fair or foul, direct or indirect.
396.	**To do something on the spur of the moment**	:	to suddenly decide to do something.
397.	**To drop a brick**	:	to say or do something very tactless and unexpected.
398.	**To drop a hint**	:	to make veiled and subtle suggestions.
399.	**To eat like a horse**	:	to eat a lot.
400.	**To eat one's words**	:	to take back what one has said; to apologise.
401.	**To egg on**	:	to spur on to further action.
402.	**To face the music**	:	to meet the worst; to face punishment for doing something wrong.

403. To fall out with someone : to quarrel with someone.
404. To fall through : to fail, especially a plan, project, etc.
405. To fancy someone/something : to take a great liking to.
406. To fight shy of : to avoid.
407. To fire someone : to dismiss someone from employment.
408. To flog a dead horse : to try fruitlessly to revive interest in something.
409. To follow the crowd : to follow unthinkingly; to believe or act as most people do.
410. To follow suit : to do the same thing as another person.
411. To gain ground : to make progress in an undertaking.
412. To get away with something : to escape detection despite doing something wrong.
413. To get blood out of stone : to get more than is fair out of someone.
414. To get down to work : to start on the task in hand.
415. To get even with someone : to take revenge of someone.
416. To get hitched : to get married.
417. To get into a flap : to get worried and nervous.
418. To get into hot water : to be in/to get into trouble.
419. To get off scot-free : to escape punishment; to be let off payment.
420. To get out of bed on the wrong side : to start the day in a bad temper.
421. To get the sack : to be dismissed from someone employment.
422. To get wind of : to hear a rumour of.
423. To get the wind up : to get worried and nervous; to get a fright.
424. To give someone a telling-off : to scold someone.
425. To give someone the slip : to manage to avoid someone who is looking for you.
426. To give the game away : to let out a secret.
427. To give up the ghost : to die; to cease trying.
428. To go a long way : to excel; to go far, especially in a career.
429. To go off at a tangent : to change suddenly to a different course of thought or action.
430. To go like a bomb : to go fast; to function well, especially a vehicle.
431. To go to rack and ruin : to fall into a ruined or disorganised state.
432. To grin and bear it : to make the best of a bad job; to put up with something.
433. To haul someone over the coals : to reprimand someone.
434. To have a bee in one's bonnet : to be strong-minded over certain issues.
435. To have a soft spot for : to be very fond of someone or something.
436. To have an axe to grind : to have a selfish motive for doing something.
437. To have one's knife in someone : to be always finding fault with another person.
438. To hit below the belt : to attack an opponent unfairly.
439. To hit the nail on the head : to do or say exactly the right thing.
440. To jog someone's memory : to remind someone of something.
441. To keep a person in the dark : to keep something hidden from someone.
442. To keep open house : to encourage visitors to come at any time.
443. To keep one's pecker up : to keep one's courage up.
444. To keep one's shirt on : to keep cool and calm in a dispute.
445. To keep the ball rolling : to keep a conversation going.

446. **To keep up appearances** : to pretend to be well-off and to live in a certain style.
447. **To kick the bucket** : to die.
448. **To kid someone** : to tease.
449. **To kill two birds with one stone** : to accomplish two things with one action.
450. **To knock off work** : to stop working.
451. **To know the ropes** : to be thoroughly familiar with a particular situation.
452. **To knock someone down with a feather** : to surprise someone very much.
453. **To kowtow to someone** : to act in a very servile manner hoping for favour.
454. **To lay down the law** : to speak in an authoritative way.
455. **To lead someone up the garden path** : to deceive someone by hiding the real intention.
456. **To leave someone in the lurch** : to desert someone in time of difficulties.
457. **To let bygones be bygones** : to let things that are past and gone remain untouched and forgotten.
458. **To let the cat out of the bag** : to reveal a secret; to expose a trick.
459. **To look like a wet week** : to look miserable and depressed.
460. **To make a go of something** : to try one's best to succeed in something.
461. **To make a hash/a mess of something** : to fail at a task.
462. **To make believe** : to pretend.
463. **To make both ends meet** : to be able to manage on one's income.
464. **To make hay while sun shines** : to take advantage of an opportunity.
465. **To make much ado about nothing** : to make a great fuss about something unimportant.
466. **To make oneself scarce** : to disappear.
467. **To nip something in the bud** : to stop something before it can develop into something serious.
468. **To pass the buck** : to pass on the responsibility.
469. **To pick holes in something** : to find fault with.
470. **To pick to pieces** : to analyse critically.
471. **To pick and choose** : to make a careful selection.
472. **To play a double game** : to do one thing openly and a different thing in secret.
473. **To play fast and loose** : to disregard one's promises.
474. **To play second fiddle** : to take a subordinate position.
475. **To pooh-pooh an idea** : to express contempt for an idea.
476. **To pull strings** : to use friends in influential positions, or to use one's own influence, to secure favours.
477. **To put the cart before the horse** : to do the wrong thing first.
478. **To put two and two together** : to arrive at a conclusions.
479. **To put a spoke in one's wheel** : to hinder; to obstruct progress.
480. **To rain cats and dogs** : to rain very heavily.
481. **To read between the lines** : to detect the hidden meaning.
482. **To rule the roost** : to domineer over others.
483. **To run in the blood** : inherited qualities.

484.	**To see something through coloured spectacles**	:	to see only the best points about a thing.
485.	**To see the light**	:	to begin to understand.
486.	**To sit on the fence**	:	to take neither side in a dispute; to remain neutral.
487.	**To smell a rat**	:	to become suspicious about something.
488.	**To steer clear of**	:	to avoid.
489.	**To take French leave**	:	to be absent from work without permission.
490.	**To take someone for a ride**	:	to deceive someone.
491.	**To take the bull by the horns**	:	to meet a difficulty with courage.
492.	**To take the law into one's own hands**	:	to punish a person, usually by force, without his being tried in a law court.
493.	**To take with a pinch of salt**	:	to accept what someone has said with doubt and misgiving.
494.	**To talke nineteen to the dozen**	:	to speak at lot.
495.	**To talk the hind legs off a donkey**	:	to talk a great deal at great length.
496.	**To tear a strip off someone**	:	to scold harshly.
497.	**To throw cold water upon**	:	to discourage effort.
498.	**To turn over a new leaf**	:	to give up one's bad ways, and lead a better life.
499.	**To turn the tables on someone**	:	to defeat someone who has previously defeated you.
500.	**To upset the apple cart**	:	to disturb the routine of something.

ONE WORDS SUBSTITUTION

EXERCISE 1

Tick the most suitable word in the following options:

1. Frame with beads or balls sliding on wires, for teaching numbers to children
   (a) computer ☐ (b) calculator ☐
   (c) abacus ☐ (d) directory ☐
2. Cause to feel self-conscious
   (a) abash ☐ (b) jolt ☐
   (c) arouse ☐ (d) awake ☐
3. Public slaughter house
   (a) mortuary ☐ (b) scaffold ☐
   (c) gaol ☐ (d) abattoir ☐
4. Be faithful to
   (a) concede ☐ (b) abide ☐
   (c) concur ☐ (d) accede ☐
5. Swear solemnly on oath
   (a) abjure ☐ (b) declare ☐
   (c) announce ☐ (d) proclaim ☐
6. Separated from what is real
   (a) separated ☐ (b) dissociated ☐
   (c) irregular ☐ (d) abstract ☐
7. Eager to learn or know
   (a) careful ☐ (b) curious ☐
   (c) aggressive ☐ (d) enthusiastic ☐
8. Give an account of
   (a) recount ☐ (b) declare ☐
   (c) explain ☐ (d) announce ☐

EXERCISE 2

Tick the most suitable word in the following options:

1. Written or printed statement of demands, rights, etc.
   (a) cheque ☐ (b) affidavit ☐
   (c) charter ☐ (d) permit ☐
2. Run after in order to capture, kill, overtake, etc.
   (a) chase ☐ (b) choose ☐
   (c) shadow ☐ (d) stalk ☐
3. Give variety to
   (a) deliver ☐ (b) divide ☐
   (c) declare ☐ (d) diversify ☐
4. Natural place of growth
   (a) jungle ☐ (b) nursery ☐
   (c) habitat ☐ (d) farm ☐
5. Place where bees are kept.
   (a) hine ☐ (b) apiary ☐
   (c) aviary ☐ (d) kennel ☐
6. Making or becoming a god or saint.
   (a) saintliness ☐ (b) godhood ☐
   (c) apotheosis ☐ (d) godliness ☐
7. A statement, etc. of doubtful accuracy.
   (a) rumour ☐ (b) expression ☐
   (c) suspicion ☐ (d) falsehood ☐
8. Condition, quality, etc. that is half way between two extremes.
   (a) middle ☐ (b) mean ☐
   (c) centre ☐ (d) segment ☐

EXERCISE 3

Tick the most suitable word in the following options:

1. Any sort of drink
   (a) liquid ☐ (b) fluid ☐
   (c) beverage ☐ (d) gulp ☐
2. Person or thing that makes feel tired by being dull or tedious
   (a) wiseacre ☐ (b) dullard ☐
   (c) snob ☐ (d) bore ☐
3. Person of extreme or exaggerated proppriety
   (a) orthodox ☐ (b) prude ☐
   (c) proteus ☐ (d) bore ☐

4. (Of justice) failure of a court to administer justice properly
   (a) injustice ☐ (b) impropriety ☐
   (c) illegality ☐ (d) miscarriage ☐
5. Act or even which does not follow the known laws of nature
   (a) wonder ☐ (b) surprise ☐
   (c) miracle ☐ (d) hallucination ☐
6. Easily bent without breaking
   (a) flexible ☐ (b) formal ☐
   (c) debatable ☐ (d) rigid ☐
7. Argue, haggle or bargain about prices
   (a) chafe ☐ (b) chaff ☐
   (c) quarrel ☐ (d) chaffer ☐
8. Talk fast or make meaningless sounds
   (a) gibber ☐ (b) utter ☐
   (c) moan ☐ (d) decry ☐

EXERCISE 4

Tick the most suitable word in the following options:

1. Lacking in energy
   (a) easy ☐ (b) porous ☐
   (c) languid ☐ (d) lazy ☐
2. Similarity of ideas
   (a) ideologicality ☐ (b) worthiness ☐
   (c) propitiation ☐ (d) propinquity ☐
3. Poorly made hut, etc.
   (a) cabin ☐ (b) shanty ☐
   (c) lair ☐ (d) den ☐
4. Of a speech, etc. having an underlying purpose
   (a) tendentious ☐ (b) fiery ☐
   (c) purposeful ☐ (d) propagandist ☐
5. Easily used
   (a) easy ☐ (b) useful ☐
   (c) handy ☐ (d) allowable ☐
6. Requiring great effort
   (a) hard ☐ (b) strict ☐
   (c) adventurous ☐ (d) laborious ☐
7. Long, adventurous journey, etc.
   (a) odyssey ☐ (b) picnic ☐
   (c) voyage ☐ (d) travel ☐
8. Get rid of
   (a) free ☐ (b) allow ☐
   (c) obviate ☐ (d) impart ☐

EXERCISE 5

Tick the most suitable word in the following options:

1. Deviation from rule
   (a) devolution ☐ (b) anomaly ☐
   (c) depreciation ☐ (d) harmlessness ☐
2. One from whom a person is descended
   (a) descendant ☐ (b) off-spring ☐
   (c) progeny ☐ (d) ancestor ☐
3. Moving with moderately slow, even expression.
   (a) andante ☐ (b) unexpressed ☐
   (c) moderate ☐ (d) uneven ☐
4. Extremely cruel or wicked
   (a) deathful ☐ (b) atrocious ☐
   (c) deadly ☐ (d) ferocious ☐
5. To deprive of rights by conviction for treason.
   (a) detain ☐ (b) deprive ☐
   (c) attaint ☐ (d) snatch ☐
6. To make a summoning sign.
   (a) call ☐ (b) sign ☐
   (c) gesture ☐ (d) beckon ☐
7. To lay siege to
   (a) fortify ☐ (b) endanger ☐
   (c) beleaguer ☐ (d) terrify ☐
8. By the side of
   (a) aside ☐ (b) beside ☐
   (c) away ☐ (d) after ☐

EXERCISE 6

Tick the most suitable word in the following options:

1. A person aged between thirteen and nineteen
   (a) adolescent ☐ (b) youth ☐
   (c) teenager ☐ (d) chap ☐

2. (To) include or absorb (something) in something else
   (a) catch ☐ (b) merge ☐
   (c) consume ☐ (d) subsume ☐
3. Extremely dirty and unpleasant
   (a) squalid ☐ (b) ugly ☐
   (c) rowdy ☐ (d) putrefying ☐
4. (To) Quarrel noisily
   (a) fight ☐ (b) punch ☐
   (c) squabble ☐ (d) bicker ☐
5. (Something) much desired
   (a) loving ☐ (b) coveted ☐
   (c) desirable ☐ (d) wanted ☐
6. One enthusiastic of new technology
   (a) technophile ☐ (b) technologist ☐
   (c) technician ☐ (d) scientist ☐
7. That which evinces characteristics of traditional culture
   (a) cultural ☐ (b) traditional ☐
   (c) customary ☐ (d) folksy ☐
8. (To) spread untidily
   (a) throw ☐ (b) strew ☐
   (c) fling ☐ (d) hurl ☐

EXERCISE 7

Tick the most suitable word in the following options:

1. The religious ceremony at a funeral
   (a) ceremoniousness ☐
   (b) burial ☐
   (c) death-song ☐
   (d) ritual ☐
2. Able to float
   (a) boatlike ☐ (b) light ☐
   (c) wooden ☐ (d) buoyant ☐
3. Polish by rubbing
   (a) burnish ☐ (b) garnish ☐
   (c) shine ☐ (d) brighten ☐
4. Upset the plans of (somebody)
   (a) destroy ☐ (b) ruin ☐
   (c) discomfit ☐ (d) deplete ☐
5. Individually distinct
   (a) discrete ☐ (b) divisible ☐
   (c) individualistic ☐ (d) undesirable ☐
6. Upset the calmness of (somebody)
   (a) derail ☐ (b) ignore ☐
   (c) disconcert ☐ (d) deny ☐
7. Causing or ending in death or disaster
   (a) dangerous ☐ (b) fatal ☐
   (c) pernicious ☐ (d) diabolical ☐
8. Low, continuous, indistinct sound
   (a) murmur ☐ (b) whisper ☐
   (c) upheaval ☐ (d) noisy ☐

EXERCISE 8

Tick the most suitable word in the following options:

1. One who pleads for another
   (a) speaker ☐ (b) adviser ☐
   (c) joker ☐ (d) advocate ☐
2. Belonging to the appreciation of the beautiful
   (a) aesthetic ☐ (b) charming ☐
   (c) fascinating ☐ (d) captivating ☐
3. Hard to achieve
   (a) considerate ☐ (b) temporal ☐
   (c) arduous ☐ (d) irregular ☐
4. A complete list of items, often with particulars
   (a) card ☐ (b) account-book ☐
   (c) diary ☐ (d) catalogue ☐
5. Of same genus or family
   (a) familiar ☐ (b) congenerous ☐
   (c) acquainted ☐ (d) similar ☐
6. Disastrous end
   (a) catastrophe ☐ (b) loss ☐
   (c) lawlessness ☐ (d) anarchy ☐
7. Factious orator
   (a) narrator ☐ (b) demagogue ☐
   (c) speaker ☐ (d) swindler ☐
8. Make spiritual
   (a) soften ☐ (b) smoothen ☐
   (c) trivialise ☐ (d) dematerialize ☐

Exercise 9

Tick the most suitable word in the following options:

1. Bring discredit on
   (a) rebuke ☐ (b) abandon ☐
   (c) disconnect ☐ (d) disparage ☐
2. Behave servilely
   (a) fawn ☐ (b) serve ☐
   (c) appreciate ☐ (d) like ☐
3. Fraught with destiny
   (a) dangerous ☐ (b) viregular ☐
   (c) fateful ☐ (d) heavy ☐
4. Acted upon
   (a) passive ☐ (b) active ☐
   (c) wise ☐ (d) smart ☐
5. Place for finding some information, facts, etc.
   (a) catalogue ☐ (b) repertory ☐
   (c) library ☐ (d) museum ☐
6. Violation of what is sacred
   (a) sacrilege ☐ (b) prohibition ☐
   (c) Demolition ☐ (d) breakage ☐
7. Citation to appear before judge
   (a) judgement ☐ (b) sentence ☐
   (c) summons ☐ (d) bail ☐
8. Liable to harm
   (a) hard ☐ (b) obnoxious ☐
   (c) tough ☐ (d) undesirable ☐

Exercise 10

Tick the most suitable word in the following options:

1. Want of power accompanying a disease
   (a) weakness ☐ (b) fatality ☐
   (c) mortality ☐ (d) adynamia ☐
2. Connected with aircraft
   (a) crafty ☐ (b) aerial ☐
   (c) airy ☐ (d) atmospheric ☐
3. To free from slavery
   (a) affranchise ☐ (b) solve ☐
   (c) absolve ☐ (d) create ☐
4. To bring to a standstill
   (a) inculcate ☐ (b) stupefy ☐
   (c) arrest ☐ (d) soften ☐
5. To claim as one's own
   (a) clamour ☐ (b) care ☐
   (c) arrogate ☐ (d) quantify ☐
6. To give up to another
   (a) cede ☐ (b) release ☐
   (c) forgive ☐ (d) reject ☐
7. Graceful in manners or form
   (a) colourful ☐ (b) gorgeous ☐
   (c) splendid ☐ (d) genteel ☐
8. To make an excursion
   (a) exclude ☐ (b) jaunt ☐
   (c) terminate ☐ (d) jog ☐

ANSWERS

EXERCISE 1

1	2	3	4	5	6	7	8
(c)	(a)	(d)	(b)	(a)	(d)	(b)	(a)

EXERCISE 2

1	2	3	4	5	6	7	8
(c)	(a)	(d)	(c)	(b)	(c)	(a)	(b)

EXERCISE 3

1	2	3	4	5	6	7	8
(c)	(d)	(b)	(d)	(c)	(a)	(d)	(a)

EXERCISE 4

1	2	3	4	5	6	7	8
(c)	(d)	(a)	(a)	(c)	(d)	(a)	(c)

EXERCISE 5

1	2	3	4	5	6	7	8
(b)	(d)	(a)	(b)	(c)	(d)	(c)	(a)

EXERCISE 6

1	2	3	4	5	6	7	8
(c)	(d)	(a)	(c)	(b)	(a)	(d)	(b)

EXERCISE 7

1	2	3	4	5	6	7	8
(b)	(d)	(a)	(c)	(a)	(c)	(b)	(a)

EXERCISE 8

1	2	3	4	5	6	7	8
(d)	(a)	(c)	(d)	(b)	(a)	(b)	(d)

EXERCISE 9

1	2	3	4	5	6	7	8
(d)	(a)	(c)	(a)	(b)	(a)	(c)	(b)

EXERCISE 10

1	2	3	4	5	6	7	8
(d)	(b)	(a)	(c)	(c)	(a)	(d)	(b)

GENERAL STUDY

WORLD

BASIC INFORMATION

The estimated total surface area of the earth is 510,100,448 square kilometres, of which the area of hydrosphere covers five-sevenths or more accurately 70.78 per cent (361,059,226 sq kilometre) and the land or lithosphere two-sevenths or 29.22 per cent (149,041,182 sq kilometre). The earth has a mass of 5.97×10^{24} kg (estimated) and has a density 5.515 times that of water. The equatorial circumference of the earth is 40,075.03 kilometres with a polar a meridianal circumference of 40,007.89 kilometres indicating that the earth is not a true sphere but an ellipse, flattened at the poles. The earth also has a slight ellipticity at the equator.

POPULATION

The population of the world in mid-2013 was 7.16 billion, the growth rate being 1.09% while birth and death rates were at 19.3 and 8.2 per thousand population, respectively (2010 estimate).

The average life expectancy at birth is 67.6 years in 2009. The United Nations Population Division estimates that the average life expectancy will go up to the age of 75.4 by 2050 (76.5 in the developed countries and 65.4 in less developed countries).

Most densely populated Country: The most densely populated country in the world is Monaco with 39,497 persons per sq. mile in 2013.

Number of Countries: The world comprises of 195 sovereign States, 193 members of the United Nations and two non-members, viz., China (Taiwan) and Vatican City. There are 61 colonies and 6 major disputed territories. The acknowledged nuclear weapons capability states are seven—India, USA, UK, France, Russia, China and Pakistan.

Urbanisation: According to the United Nations during 2011, 52.1 per cent population of the world lived in urban area. This number is expected to rise to 69% by 2050. In 2008, almost half of the world's population was living in cities.

Largest Country: The largest country in terms of area is Russia which has an area of 17,075,000 square kms or 11.5 percent of the World's total land area.

Smallest Country: The smallest independent country in the world is the state of the Vatican City or Holy See, which was made an enclave within the city of Rome, Italy on February 11, 1929. The enclave has an area of 0.44 sq. km.

Smallest republic: The world's smallest republic is Nauru, less than one degree south of the equator in the Klestern Pacific, which become independent on January 31, 1968. It has an area of 21 sq. km and a population of 10,051 in 2013.

Most Populous City: Shanghai was the most populous city with a population of 17.8 million.

Most Populous Urban agglomeration: Tokyo with a population of 36.9 million was the most populous urban agglomeration in 2011.

Highest Town: Wenchuan, the new town founded in 1955 on the Chinghai-Tibet road, located north of the Tangla range in China at 5,100 metres above sea level, is the highest town in the world.

Highest Capital: The highest capital in the world before the domination of Tibet by China, was Lhasa at an elevation of 3,684 metres above sea level. La Paz, the administrative and de facto capital of Bolivia, stands at an altitude of 3,631 meters above sea level.

CONTINENTS AT A GLANCE

	Asia	Africa	North America	South America	Europe	Oceania	Antarctica
Area (million sq. km.)	44	30	24	17	10	9	14
Population (in Millions : 2013)	4298	1110	—	406	742	38.3	—

TEN LARGEST COUNTRIES

In Area

Rank	Country	Area (sq. km)
1.	Russia	1,70,75,000
2.	Canada	99,76,139
3.	China	95,61,000
4.	United States	93,72,614
5.	Brazil	85,11,965
6.	Australia	76,82,300
7.	India	32,87,263
8.	Argentina	27,76,654
9.	Kazakhstan	2,717,300
10.	Sudan	25,05,803

In Population

Rank	Country	Population (in millions)
1.	China	1385
2.	India	1252
3.	USA	320
4.	Indonesia	249
5.	Brazil	200
6.	Pakistan	182
7.	Nigeria	173
8.	Bangladesh	156
9.	Russia	142
10.	Japan	127

Source : UN Population Division 2013

TEN SMALLEST COUNTRIES

In Area

Rank	Country	Area (sq. km)
1.	Vatican City	0.44
2.	Monaco	1.95
3.	Nauru	21.10
4.	Tuvalu	26.00
5.	San Marino	61.00
6.	Liechtenstein	160.00
7.	Marshall Islands	181.00
8.	St. Kitts-Nevis	269.00
9.	Maldives	298.00
10.	Malta	316.00

In Population

Rank	Country	Population
1.	Vatican City	799
2.	Tuvalu	9,876
3.	Nauru	10,051
4.	Palau	20,918
5.	San Marino	31,448
6.	Liechtenstein	36,925
7.	Monaco	37,831
8.	Marshall Islands	52,634
9.	St. Kitts-Nevis	54,191
10.	Dominica	72,003

Source : UN Population Division 2013

IMPORTANT COUNTRIES (CURRENCY AND CAPITAL)

Country	Currency	Capital
Afghanistan	Afgani	Kabul
Albania	Lek	Tirana
Algeria	Denar	Algiers
Argentina	Peso	Buenos Aires
Armenia	Ruble	Yerevan
Australia	Australian Dollar	Canberra
Austria	Euro	Vienna
Azerbaijan	Ruble	Baku
Bahrain	Bahrain Dinar	Manama
Bangladesh	Taka	Dhaka
Bhutan	Ngultrum	Thimphu
Bosnia and Herzegovina	Converted Marka	Sarajevo
Brazil	Novo Cruz	Brasilia
Brunei Darussalam	Brunei Dollar	Bandar Seri Begawan
Burundi	Burundi Franc	Bujumbura
Cambodia (Kampuchea)	Reil	Phnom Penh
Canada	Canadian Dollar	Ottawa, Ont
Chile	Peso	Santiago
China	Yuan	Beijing
Colombia	Peso	Bagota
Cuba	Peso	Havana
Cyprus	Euro	Nicosia
Denmark	Krone	Copenhagen
Ecuador		Quito
Egypt	Egyptian Pound	Cairo
Ethiopia	Birr	Addis Ababa
Fiji	Fijian Dollar	Suva
Finland	Euro	Helsinki
France	Euro	Paris
Georgia	Maneti	Tbilisi
Germany	Euro	Berlin
Ghana	Cedi	Accra
Greece	Euro	Athens
Guinea	Franc	Conakry
Guinea-Bissau	CFA Franc	Bissau
Guyana	Guyanaese Dollar	Georgetown
Hungary	Forint	Budapest
Iceland	New Krona	Reykjavik
India	Ripee	New Delhi
Indonesia	Rupiah	Jakarta
Iran	Rial	Teheran
Iraq	Iraqui Dinar	Baghdad
Ireland	Euro	Dublin
Israel	Shhekel	Jerusalem
Italy	Euro	Rome

Country	Currency	Capital
Jamaica	Dollar	Kingston
Japan	Yen	Tokyo
Jordan	Jordanian Dinar	Amman
Kazakhstan	Tanga	Akmola
Kenya	Kenyan Shilling	Nairobi
Korea, North	Won	Pyongyang
Korea, South	Won	Seoul
Kuwait	Kuwati Dinar	Kuwait
Kyrgyzstan	Som	Bishkek
Lebanon	Labanese Pound	Beirut
Liberia	Liberian Dollar	Monrovia
Libya	Libyan Dinar	Tripoli
Malaysia	Ringgit	Kuala Lumpur
Maldives	Maldivian Rufiyaa	Male
Mauritius	Mauritian Rupee	Port Louis
Mexico	Peso	Mexico City
Mongolia	Tugrik	Ulan Bator
Morocco	Dirham	Rabat
Mozambique	Metical	Maputo
Myanmar(Burma)	Kyat	Yangon (Rangoon)
Namibia	Dollar	Windhoek
Nauru	Australiann Dollar	Yaren
Nepal	Nepalese Rupee	Kathmandu
Netherlands	Euro	Amsterdam
New Zealand	New Zealand Dollar	Wellington
Nigeria	Nairya	Abuja
Norway	Krone	Oslo
Oman	Omani Rial	Muscat
Pakistan	Rupee	Islamabad
Panama	Balboa	Panama City
Papua New Guinea	Kina	Port Moresby
Paraguay	Guarani	Asuncion
Peru	Inti	Lima
Philippines	Peso	Manila
Poland	Zloty	Warsaw
Portugal	Euro	Lisbon
Qatar	Qatari Rial	Doha
Romania	Leu	Bucharest
Russia	Ruble	Moscow
Saudi Arabia	Riyal	Riyadh
Serbia	New Dinar	Belgrade
Senegal	France CFA	Dakar
Seychelles	Seychelles Rupee	Victoria
Sierra Leone	Leone	Freetown
Singapore	Singapore Dollar	Singapore
Slovakia	Euro	Bratislava
Slovenia	Euro	Ljubliana

Country	Currency	Capital	Country	Currency	Capital
Solomon Islands	Dollar	Honiara	Turkey	Turkish Dinar	Ankara
Somalia	Somali Shilling	Mogadishu	Uganda	Uganda Shilling	Kampala
South Africa	Rand	Pretoria	Ukraine	Hryvna	Kiev
Spain	Euro	Madrid	United Arab Emirates	Dirham	Abu Dhabi
Sri Lanka	Sri Lanka Rupee	Colombo	United Kingdom	Pound (Sterling)	London
Sudan	Sudanese Pound	Khartoum	United States of America	U.S. Dollar	Washington, D.C.
Surinam	Surniam Guilder	Paramaribo	Uruguay	New Peso	Montevideo
Sweden	Krona	Stockholm	Uzbekistan	Ruble	Tashkent
Switzerland	Swiss Franc	Berne	Vatican City	Euro	Vatican City
Syria	Syrian Pound	Damascus	Venezuela	Bolivar	Caracas
Taiwan	New Taiwan Dollar	Taipei	Vietnam	Dong	Honoi
Tajikistan	Somoni	Dushanbe	Yemen	Yemen Dinar and Rial	Sana
Tanzania	Tanzanian Shilling	Darusalam	Zimbabwe	Zimbabwean Dollar	Harare (Salisbury)
Thailand	Baht	Bangkok			
Tunisia	Tunsian Dinar	Tunis			

NAMES OF VARIOUS PARLIAMENTS

Country	Parliament	Country	Parliament
Afghanistan	Shora (National Assembly)	Ireland	Oireachtas or National Parliament (Dail Eireann, House of Representative and Seanad Eireann, Senate)
Algeria	National People's Assembly	Israel	Knesset
Argentina	National Congress	Japan	Diet
Australia	Federal Parliament (House of Representative and Senate)	Jordan	National Assembly
Austria	National Assembly (House of Assembly and Senate)	Kenya	National Assembly
Bhutan	Tshogdu (National Assembly)	Korea (North)	Supreme People's Assembly
Brazil	National Congress	Korea (South)	National Assembly
Britain	Parliament (House of Commons and House of Lords)	Kuwait	National Assembly
Cambodia (Kampuchea)	National Assembly	Liberia	National Assembly
Canada	Parliament (House of Commons and Senate)	Libya	General People's Congress
China	National People's Congress	Malaysia	Parliament (Dewan Rakyat, Dewan Negara)
China (Taiwan)	Yuan (National Assembly)	Maldives	Majlis
Colombia	Congress	Mongolia	Great People's Khural
Cuba	National Assembly of People's Power	Myanmar (Burma)	Pyithu Hluttaw (People's Assembly)
Denmark	Folketing	Nepal	National Panchayat
Egypt	People's Assembly	Netherlands	Staten General
France	National Assembly	New Zealand	Parliament (House of Representatives)
Germany	Bundestag (Lower House) and Budnesrat (Upper House)	Norway	Storting
Hungary	National Assembly	Pakistan	National Assembly
Iceland	Althing	Poland	Sejm
India	Parliament (Lok Sabha and Rajya Sabha)	Romania	Grand National Assembly
Indonesia	People's Consultative Assembly	Russia	Duma
Iran	Majlis	Senegal	National Assembly
Iraq	National Assembly	Seychelles	People's Assembly
		Somalia	People's Assembly
		South Africa	House of Assembly
		Spain	Cortes

Country	Parliament
Sudan	National Assembly
Surinam	Staten
Sweden	Riksdag
Switzerland	Federal Assembly (National and Standerat)
Syria	People's Council
Tunisia	National Assembly
Turkey	Grand National Assembly
U.S.A.	Congress (House of Representatives and Senate)
Vanuatu	Representative Assembly
Venezuela	National Congress
Vietnam	National Assembly
Congo (Zaire)	National Legislative Council
Zambia	National Assembly

PRINCIPAL POLITICAL PARTIES

Country	Political Party
U.S.A.	Democratic Party, Republican Party
Bangladesh	Awami League, Bangladesh National Party
Britain	Labour Party, Conservative Party
China	Communist Party
India	Indian National Congress, B.J.P.
Japan	Liberal Democratic Party; Japan New Party
Nepal	Nepali Congress, Communist Party
Pakistan	Pakistan People's Party (P.P.P.), Muslim League
South Africa	African National Congress, National Party
Sri Lanka	United National Party

EMINENT RESIDENCES

Name of the Residence	Occupant
Buckingham Palace (London)	King/Queen of Britain
10, Downing Street (London)	Prime Minister of Britain
Elysee Palace (Paris)	President of France
Rashtrapati Bhavan (New Delhi)	President of India
Qasr-e-Sadarat	President of Pakistan
White House (Washington)	President of U.S.A.
Vatican (Rome)	Pope

OFFICIAL DOCUMENTS

White Papers : Formerly issued by the British Parliament stating in brief the views of the government on a specific issue or giving an authoritative statement of facts. Now the white paper has come to be known as a policy statement published by any government on a subject of tremendous public importance.

Blue Books : Official reports of the British Government.

White Books : Official publications of Portugal, Germany and China.

Yellow Books : Official records of France.

Grey Books : Official policy statements and reports of Belgian and Japanese Governments.

Green Books : Official reports of the Italian and Iranian Governments.

Orange Books : Official publications of the Netherlands Government.

NEW NAMES (COUNTRIES/STATES/CITIES)

Old Name	New Name
Abyssinia	Ethiopia
Angora	Ankara
Banaras	Varanasi
Baroda	Vadodara
Batavia/Djakarta	Jakarta
Bathurst	Banjul
Basutoland	Lesotho
Bechuanaland	Botswana
Bombay	Mumbai
British Guiana	Guyana
British Houndures	Belize
Burma	Myanmar
Calicut	Kozhikode
Calcutta	Kolkata
Cambodia	Kampuchea
Cape Canaveral	Cape Kennedy

Old Name	New Name
Cawnpore	Kanpur
Central Province	Madhya Pradesh
Ceylon	Sri Lanka
Christina	Oslo
Coachin	Kochi
Zaire	Congo
Constatinople	Istanbul
Dacca	Dhaka
Dahomey	Benin
Dutch East Indies	Indonesia
Dutch Guiana	Surinam
East Timor	Loro Sae
Egypt	United Arab -Republic
Ellice Islands	Tuvalu
Formosa	Taiwan
Gauhati	Guwahati
Gold Coast	Ghana
Holland	The Netherlands
Jubbulpore	Jabalpur
Jullunder	Jalandhar
Kamroop	Assam
Lansang	Laos
Leopoldville	Kinshasa
Madagascar	Malagasy
Madras(state)	Tamil Nadu
Madras(city)	Chennai
Malaya	Malaysia
Manchukuo	Manchuria
Mesopotamia	Iraq

Old Name	New Name
Mysore	Karnataka
New Hebrides	Vanuvatu
Nippon	Japan
Northern Rhodesia	Zambia
Nyasaland	Malawi
Panjim	Panaji
Peking	Beijing
Persia	Iran
Poona	Pune
Rangoon	Yangon
Saigon	Ho Chi Minh - City
Salisbury	Harare
Sandwich Islands	Hawaiian - Islands
Santa Isable	Malabo
Siam	Thailand
Simla	Shimla
South West Africa	Namibia
Southern Rhodesia	Zimbabwe
Spanish Guinea	Equatorial - Guinea
Stalingrad	Volgograd
St.Petersburg/ Petrograd	Leningrad
Tanganyika and Zanzibar	Tanzania
Tanjore	Thanjavur
Thana	Thane
Togoland	Togo
Trivandrum	Thiruvananthapuram
United Provinces	Uttar Pradesh
Upper Volta	Bourkina Faso
Vizagapatnam	Visakhapatnam
West French Africa	Mauritania

NATIONAL EMBLEMS OF SOME COUNTRIES

Country	Emblem
Australia	Kangaroo
Canada	White Lily
Denmark	Beach
France	Lily
Germany	Corn Flower
India	Lioned Capital
Iran	Rose
Ireland	Shamrock
Italy	White Lily
Japan	Chrysanthemum
Pakistan	Crescent
Spain	Eagle
United Kingdom	Rose
U.S.A.	Golden Rod

NATIONAL FLOWERS

Country	Flower
Canada	Maple
England	Rose
France	Lily
Germany	Cornflower
India	Lotus
Ireland	Shamrock
Japan	Chrysanthemum
Scotland	Thistle
Spain	Pomegranate

FIRST HEADS OF STATES

The first American President	George Washington
The first Prime Minister of Great Britain	Robert Walpole

The first President of India	Dr. Rajendra Prasad	The first Chairman of the People's Republic of China	Mao-Tse-Tung
The first Prime Minister of India	Pt. Jawaharlal Nehru	The first Governor General of Pakistan	Mohammed Ali Jinnah
The first President of the Chinese Republic	Sun Yat Sen		

SOBRIQUETS

Sobriquet	Primary Name	Sobriquet	Primary Name
Land of the Rising Sun	Japan	Roof of the World	Pamirs
Land of the Thousand Lakes	Finland	Saint of the Gutters	Mother Teresa
Land of Thunderbolt	Bhutan	Empire City/City of Skyscrapers	New York, U.S.A.
Land of the White Elephants	Thailand	Garden of England	Kent, England
Mysore Tiger	Tipu Sultan	Gateway of India	Mumbai
Pearl of the Antilles	Cuba	Gift of the Nile	Egypt
Pillars of Hercules	Gibraltar	Granite City	Aberdeen Scotland
Bengal's Sorrow	River Damodar	Great White Way	Broadway, New York
Blue Mountains	Nilgiri Hills	Herring Pond	Atlantic Ocean
City of the Golden Gate	San Francisco, U.S.A.	Holy Land	Palestine
City of the Golden Temple	Amritsar	Hermit Kingdom	Korea
Sick Man of Europe	Turkey	Island of Cloves	Zanzibar
Sorrow of China/Yellow River	River Hwang Ho	Island of Pearls	Bahrain
Spice Garden of India	Kerala	Key of the Mediterranean	Gibraltar
Venice of the East	Alappuzha	Lady with the Lamp	Florence Nightingale
Venice of the North	Stockholm, Sweden	Land of Cakes	Scotland
White City	Belgrade, Serbia	Land of the Kangaroo	Australia
World's Bread Basket	Prairies of N. America	Land of the Golden Pagoda	Myanmar (Burma)
World's Loneliest Island	Tristan da Cunha	Land of Lilies	Canada
City of Dreaming Spires	Oxford, U.K.	Land of Morning Calm	Korea
City of Magnificent Distances	Washington, D.C. U.S.A.	Land of the Midnight Sun	Norway
		Windy City	Chicago, U.S.A.
City of Seven Hills/Eternal City	Rome	White Man's Grave	Guinea Coast
Cockpit of Europe	Belgium	Britain of the South	New Zealand
Dark Continent	Africa	City of Palaces	Kolkata, India
Emerald Island	Ireland	Forbidden City	Lhasa, Tibet
Pink City	Jaipur	Gate of Tears	Bab-el-mandab, Jerusalem
Playground of Europe	Switzerland	Garden of India	Bangalore
Quaker City	Philadelphia	Land of Golden Fleece	Australia
Queen of the Adriatic	Venice, Italy	Land of Maple	Canada
Queen of the Arabian Sea	Kochi	Land of Five Rivers	Punjab, India

INTERNATIONAL DAYS

International Customs Day	January 26	World Meterological Day	March 23
World Leprosy day	January 30	World Health Day	April 7
International Women's Day	March 8	World Heritage Day	April 18
World Disabled Day	March 15	Earth Day	April 22
World Forestry Day	March 21	International Labour Day	May 1
International Day for the Elimination of Racial Discrimination	March 21	Press Freedom Day	May 3
		Mother's Day	May (2nd Sunday)

Day	Date	Day	Date
World Red Cross Day	May 8	International Day for the Elderly	October 1
International Day of the Family	May 15	World Animal Day	October 2
World Telecommunication Day	May 17	International Day of Non-Violence	October 2
Commonwealth Day	May 24	World Habitat Day	October 3
Anti-tobacco Day	May 31	World Animal Welfare Day	October 4
International Day of Innocent Children Victims of Aggression	June 4	World Postal Day	October 9
World Environment Day	June 5	U.N. International Day for Natural Disaster Reduction	October 13
International Day against Drug Abuse and Illicit Trafficking	June 26	World Standards Day	October 14
World Diabetes Day	June 27	World White Cane Day (guiding the blind)	October 15
World Population Day	July 11	World Food Day	October 16
World Peace Day	August 6	U.N. Day	October 24
Nagasaki Day	August 9	World Thrift Day	October 30
International Literacy Day	September 8	Africa Industrialization Day	November 20
World Ozone Day	September 16	International Day of Solidarity with Palestinian People	November 29
Alzheimer's Day	September 21	World AIDS Day	December 1
Day of the Deaf	September 26	Human Rights Day (U.N.)	December 10
World Tourism Day	September 27		

FAMOUS BOUNDARY LINES

Durand Line : This was the line demarcating the boundaries of India and Afghanistan, drawn in 1896 by Sir Mortimor Durand. Now, it is a line of demarcation between Pakistan and Afghanistan.

Hindenburg Line : During the first World War, the Germans, retreated to this line in 1917, representing the boundary between Poland and Germany.

Moginot Line : This line of fortification was constructed by France to protect its border from the German attack.

McMahon Line : This is the boundary between India and China as demarcated by Sir McMahon.

Mannerheim Line : This is the line of fortification of Russia-Finish border as drawn by General Mannerheim.

Oder Neisse Line : This is the boundary between Poland and East Germany agreed at the end of World War II.

Siegfreid Line : This is the line of fortification drawn by Germany on her border with France in World War I.

17th Parallel : It is the boundary between North Vietnam and South Vietnam.

38th Parallel : This is the line demarcating the boundary between North Korea and South Korea.

49th Parallel : This is the boundary between USA and Canada.

LANGUAGE

PRINCIPAL LANGUAGES OF THE WORLD

Language	Speakers *(million)*	Language	Speakers *(million)*
Chinese	1,197	Bengali	193
Spanish	406	Russian	122
English	335	Japanese	84
Hindi	260	Javanese	84
Arabic	223	German	84
Portuguese	202	Lahnda	83

Language	Speakers *(million)*	Language	Speakers *(million)*
Telugu	74	Vietnamese	68
Marathi	72	Korean	66
Tamil	69	Urdu	63
French	69	Italian	61

WORLDWIDE WEATHER EXTREMS, TEMPERATURE EXTREMES

Temperature extremes for any place on Earth are determined by a number of factors, including altitude, latitude and physical characteristics. For an extreme to be recorded, an observation must be made at the precise time and place of occurrence; consequently, more extreme temperatures undoubtedly have occurred.

THE HOTTEST

Area	Maximum (°F)	Place	Elevation (ft)	Date
North America	134°	Death Valley, CA, U.S. (Furnace Creek Ranch)	–179	July 10, 1913
Africa	131°	Kabili, Tunisia	125	July 7, 1931
Asia	129.2°	Tirat Tsvi, Israel	–722	June 21, 1942
Australia	123°	Oodnadatta, South Australia	367	Jan. 2, 1960
South America	120°	Rivadavia, Argentina	2,192	Dec. 11, 1905
Europe	118.4°	Athens, Greece (and Elefsina, Greece)	774	July. 10, 1977
Oceania	108°	Tuguegarao, Philippines	676	Apr. 29, 1912
Antarctica	59°	Vanda Station (New Zealand), Wright Valley	49	May 1, 1974

THE COLDEST

Area	Maximum (°F)	Place	Elevation (ft)	Date
Antarctica	–128.6°	Vostok Station (Russia)	11,220	July 21, 1983
Asia	–90°	Verkhoyansk, Russia	350	Feb. 5 & 7, 1892
	–90°	Oimekon, Russia	2,625	Feb. 6, 1933
North America	–81.4°	Snag, Yukon, Canada	2,120	Feb. 3, 1947
Europe	–72.6°	Ust-Shchugor, Russia	279	Dec. 31, 1978
South America	–27°	Sarmiento, Argentina	879	June 1, 1907
Africa	–11°	Ifrane, Morocco	5,364	Feb. 11, 1935
Australia	–9.4°	Charlotte Pass, New South Wales	5,758	June 29, 1994

RELIGIONS

MAJOR RELIGIONS AT A GLANCE

Buddhism : Founded about 525 B.C. by Gautama Buddha; practised throughout Asia.

Confucianism : Founded about 500 B.C. by Confucius; located in China and Taiwan.

Christianity : Founded about 2000 years ago by Prophet Jesus of Nazareth; located all over the world.

Hinduism : Founded about 1500 B.C. by Aryans and followed in India and Nepal.

Islam : Founded 622 A.D. by Prophet Mohammed (PBH), located from the west coast of Africa to the Philippines, western China, central Asia, India, Pakistan, Bangladesh, Malaysia and Indonesia.

Judaism : Founded about 1300 B.C. by Prophet Moses; practised worldwide, particularly in Israel & U.S.

Shintoism : Practised in Japan.

Sikhism : Founded about 1500 A.D. by Guru Nanak; practised in India.

Taoism : Founded about 6th Century B.C. by Laotze (China); practised in China and Taiwan.

Zoroastriansim : Founded by Zoratushtra practised in India.

RELIGIOUS POPULATION OF THE WORLD

Religion	Population	%
Christians	2,319,839,000	32.9
Muslims	1,609,200,900	22.8
Hindus	967,164,000	13.7
Buddhism	504,784,000	7.2
Chinese folk religionists	437,133,000	6.2
Ethnoreligionists	247,473,000	3.5
Neoreligionists	63,327,000	0.9
Sikhs	24,793,400	0.4
Jews	14,993,900	0.2
Spiritists	13,932,900	0.2
Daoists	8,543,200	0.1
Baha'is	7,550,000	0.1
Confucianists	8,194,690	0.1
Jains	5,452,600	0.1
Shintoists	2,766,200	0.0
Zoroastrians	199,800	0.0
Other religionists	1,407,000	0.0
Nonreligious	679,054,310	9.6
Atheists	136,327,000	1.9

Source: *Time Almanac 2013 Page 508-509*

FAMOUS SITES OF WORLD

Site	Location	Country
Al-aqsa	Jerusalem	Israel
Big Ben	London	UK
Brandenberg gate	Berlin	Germany
Broadway	New York	USA
Buckingham Palace	London	UK
Colossium	Rome	Italy
Downing Street	London	UK
Eiffel Tower	Paris	France
Empire State Building	New York	USA
Fleet Street	London	UK
Grand Canyon	Arizona	USA
Great Wall		China
Greenwich		UK
Hanging Garden	Babylon	Iraq
Hyde Park	London	UK
India House	London	UK
Kaaba	Mecca	Saudi Arabia
Kremlin	Moscow	Russia
Leaning Tower	Pisa	Italy
Louvre	Paris	France
Merdeka Palace	Jakarta	Indonesia
Pashupati Temple	Kathmandu	Nepal
Pentagon	Washington	USA
Potala	Lhasa	Tibet
Porcelain Tower	Nanking	China
Pyramid		Egypt
Red Square	Moscow	Russia
Scotland Yard	London	UK
Pagodas		Myanmar
Sphinx		Egypt

Site	Location	Country
Statue of Liberty	New York	USA
St. Sophia	Constantapole	Turkey
Tiannman Square	Beijing	China
Vatican		Italy
Wailing Street	Jerusalem	Israel

Site	Location	Country
Wall Street	New York	USA
Westminster Abbey	London	UK
Whilte Hall	London	UK
White House	Washington	USA

PLACES OF WORSHIP AND SCRIPTURES MIX WITH POUNDER AND FOLLOWS

Religion	Place of Worship	Scripture
Buddhism	Pagoda and Vihar	Tripitakas
Christianity	Church	Bible
Hinduism	Temple	Vedas, Geeta, Ramayana
Islam	Mosque	Holy Qur'an
Jainism	Jain Temple	Teachings of Mahavira
Judaism	Synagogue	Torah
Sikhism	Gurudwaras	Guru Granth Sahib
Zoroastrianism	Fire Temple	Zend Avesta

BRIEF INTRODUCTION OF SEVEN WONDERS OF THE WORLD

The Seven Wonders of the World were first designated by Antipater of Sidon in the second century AD. Not all classical writers list the same items as the Seven Wonders but most of them agree on the following:

1. **The Pyramids of Egypt:** From Gizeh (near Cairo) to a southern limit 96 km distant. The oldest is that of Zoser, at Saggara, built about 2700 BC. The Great Pyramid of Cheops covers more than 12 acres and was originally 146.61 metres (481 ft) in height and 230.43 × 230.43 metres (756 × 756 ft) at the base. Of all the Seven Wonders, the Pyramids alone survive.
2. **The Hanging Gardens of Babylon:** Adjoining Nebuchadnezzar's palace, 96 km south of Baghdad. Terraced gardens ranging from 23 to 91 metres (75 to 300 ft) above ground level, watered from storage tank on the highest terrace.
3. **The Tomb of Mausolus:** At Halicarnassus in Asia Minor. Built by the widowed Queen Artemisia about 350 BC. The memorial originated the term mausoleum.
4. **The Temple of Diana at Ephesus:** Ionic temple erected about 350 BC in honour of a non-Helleonic goddess who later became identified with the Greek goddess of the same name. The temple with Ionic Columns 18 metres high was destroyed by invading Goth in 262 AD.
5. **The Colossus of Rhodes:** A bronze statue of Apollo, set up about 280 BC. According to legend it stood at the harbour entrance of sea-port of Rhodes. It was destroyed during an earthquake in 224 BC.
6. **The Statue of Jupiter Olympus:** At Olympia in the plain of Ellis constructed of marble inlaid with ivory and gold by the sculptor Phidias, about 430 BC. All trace of it is lost, except for reproduction of coins.
7. **The Pharos of Alexandria:** A marble watch tower and lighthouse on the island of Pharos in the harbour of Alexandria, built by Sostratus of Cnidus during the 3rd century BC. It was destroyed by an earthquake during the 13th century.

WORLD ORGANISATIONS

THE UNITED NATIONS

Origin : Great Britain, U.S.A., Russia and China made the first draft of a new world organisation for peace in 1944 at Dumbarton Oaks, near Washington. The right to take action for maintaining peace was vested in a Security Council of eleven members. Five permanent and six temperory members. The Dumbarton Oaks plan and the Yalta interpretation on voting in the Security Council thus formed the basis of discussion at the San Francisco meeting (1945) of fifty states.

The Charter became effective on October 24, 1945, when the United Nations formally came into existence. It was decided that the seat of the organisation should be in New York.

Membership : Application to join the organisation may be made by nations which accept the obligations of the charter and which are considered able and willing to observe them. The admission of any such state to membership in the Untied Nations is effected by a decision of the General Assembly, upon the recommendation of the Security Council.

Total Members : 193 States (South Sudan) be came the 193 member of UN.

Principal Organs : Principal organs of the UN are : General Assembly, Secretariat, Security Council, Trusteeship Council, Economic and Social Council and International Court of Justice.

Headquarters : First Avenue, UN plaza, New York City, N.Y., U.S.A.

Official Languages : United Nations' official languages are six in number— English, French, Spanish, Russian, Chinese and Arabic. However, the working languages are English and French only.

Flag : The UN flag is blue in colour and emblazoned in white, in its centre is the UN symbol—a polar map of world—embraced by twin olive branches open at the top.

UN System : The bulk of the work of UN, measured in terms of money and personnel, aimed at achieving the pledge made in Article 55 are to promote higher standards of living, full employment and conditions of economic and social progress and development.

TENURE OF SECRETARY GENERAL

S. No.	Name	Secretaries General of UN
1.	Trygve Lie (Norway)	1946-53
2.	Dag Hammarskjoeld (Sweden)	1953-61
3.	U. Thant (Myanmar)	1961-71
4.	Kurt Waldheim (Austria)	1972- 81
5.	Javier Perez de Cuellar (Peru)	1982-91
6.	Dr. Boutros-Boutros Ghali (Egypt)	1992-96
7.	Dr. Kofi Annan (Ghana)	1997-2006
8.	Ban Ki-moon (South Korea)	2007-till date

SPECIFIC AGENCIES

International Monetary Fund (IMF) : The International Monetary Fund was established on 27 Dec., 1945, as an independent international organisation and began operations on 1 March, 1947. Headquarters : Washington, D.C. Offices in Paris and Geneva.

United Nations Development Programme (UNDP) : It is the world's largest agency for multilateral, technical and pre-investment cooperation. It is the funding source for most of the technical assistance provided by the Untied Nations system, and UNDP is active in almost 150 countries and territories and in virtually every economic and social sector. UNDP assistance is provided only at the request of governments and in response to their priority needs.

United Nations Educational, Scientific and Cultural Organisation (UNESCO) : A conference for the establishment of United Nations Educational, Scientific and Cultural Organisation was convened by the Government of the UK in association with the Government of France which met in London, from 1 to 16 Nov. 1945. UNESCO came into being on 4 Nov. 1946.

United Nations Children's Fund (UNICEF) : It was established in 1946 as United Nations International Children's Emergency Fund to deliver post-war relief to children. Now it concentrates assistance on development activities aimed at improving the quality of the life for children and mothers in developing countries.

World Health Organisation (WHO) : An international conference, convened by the UN Economic and Social Council, to consider the establishment of a single health organisation resulted in the adoption on 22 July, 1946 of the constitution of the WHO. Headquarters : Geneva. Offices : Alexandria, Brazzaville, Copenhagen, Manila, New Delhi, Nakajima (Japan).

International Labour Organisation (ILO) : Established in 1919 as an autonomous part of the League of Nations, it is an inter-governmental agency with a tripartite structure in which representatives of governments, employers and workers participate. In 1969, it won the Nobel Peace Prize. It has more than 150 members. Headquarters : Geneva, Switzerland.

RELIEF AGENCIES

Humanitarian relief to refugees and victims of natural and man-made disasters is also an important function of the UN system. Among the organisations involved in such relief activities are : Office of the UN Disaster Relief Coordinator (UNDRO), the Office of the UN High Commission for Refugees (UNHCR) and the Relief and Works Agency for Palestine Refugees in the Near East (UNRWA). UNRWA was created by the General Assembly in 1949 as a temporary non-political agency to provide relief to nearly 7,50,000 people who became refugees as a result of the disturbances during and after the creation of the state of Israel in the former British Mandate territory of Palestine.

WTO (GATT)

The easing of trade barriers is being successfully promoted through the operation of an international commercial treaty, the General Agreement on Tariffs and Trade. Headquarters : Geneva (Switzerland).

The Endorsement : The GATT treaty was endorsed by as many as 117 countries of the world, on December 15, 1993. On that historic day, in Geneva, the delegations from 117 countries of the world approved the consensus on GATT, the world trade treaty, aimed at opening up international markets and spurring global economic growth into twenty-first century. After seven years of tough negotiations, the last round came to a successful finale and the world famous Uruguay Round was concluded. And a declaration to the effect was made by Peter Sutherland, the chief of the world trade body.

GATT at a Glance : On April 15, 1994, India and 124 countries signed the General Agreement on Tariffs and Trade (GATT) in Marrakesh, Morocco. This historic pact creates a new multilateral trading system slashing tariffs up to 40 per cent in the biggest package of market access concessions ever negotiated.

Major Agreements : There are six major agreements running into 500 pages of Final Act and around 20,000 pages of Individual National Concessions. They include agreement on establishment of the preparatory committee for the World Trade Organisation (WTO), acceptance of the agreements, establishment of the WTO as well as pacts on trade and environment and organisational and financial consequences, following the setting up of the WTO.

WTO at Work : WTO started functioning from January, 1995. It has prepared a comprehensive set of rules and disciplines covering every aspect of world commerce, including trade in services and intellectual property protection.

OTHER INTERNATIONAL ORGANISATIONS

The Non-Aligned Movement (NAM)

The Non-Aligned Movement was born in September, 1961 with the first summit meeting of the non-aligned countries at Belgrade in Yugoslavia. It was base of the principles of 'Panch Sheel'. President Tito of Yugoslavia, Prime Minister Nehru of India and President Nasser of Egypt were the founding fathers of the movement. Among other founder members of the NAM were Archbishop Makarios of Cyprus, U Nu of Burma, President Sukarno of Indonesia, Kwame Nkrumah of Ghana, emperor Haile Sellasie of Ethiopia, and king Mahendra Bir Bikram Shah of Nepal. The basic principles of Non-Aligned Movement are to keep away, as far as possible, from the power blocs or the group of countries aligned against each other, to keep close terms of friendship with all the countries and to have friendship and cooperation with America as well as with Russia and China. The NAM meetings discuss problems of mutual interest and exchange views on issues facing the world at large.

The first meeting of NAM was attended by 25 member countries, Syria, Yemen and Yugoslavia. With the emancipation of more nations from the colonial yoke, NAM gained wide acceptance and now it has 120 members, besides guests and observers who are invited to these meetings. The NAM celebrated its Silver Jubilee at its meeting at Harare in 1986. Despite the over fourfold enlargement in its membership, the NAM has retained its basic thrust in favour of world peace, disarmament, development and freedom.

South Commission

Initially known as South-South commission, the South Commission, set up by the Non-Aligned Movement, seeks to safeguard the interests of the member countries against the discriminatory practices and policies imposed by the international financial institutions and the creditor governments. The commission's headquarter at Geneva (Switzerland) was opened on October 2, 1987.

Organisation of Islamic Countries (OIC)

The organisation was established in May, 1971, following a summit meeting of Muslim Heads of State at Rabat, Morocco in September-1969, and the Islamic Foreign Ministers' Meet in Pakistan in December, 1970. It has now 57 members. The Supreme body of the Organisation is the Conference of Heads of States, which meets every third year. It aims to promote Islamic solidarity, cooperation in various areas of national development, endeavour to eliminate racism, safeguard of holy places and to contribute towards world peace.

Organisation of Petroleum Exporting Countries (OPEC)

The Formation : A conference called at Baghdad in 1962 decided to form the OPEC. This conference was attended by the representatives of Iraq, Kuwait, Saudi Arabia (Arab Muslim States), Iran (non-Arab but Muslim State) and Venezuela (a non-Arab, non-Muslim State in far away south America). These countries at that time controlled 80 percent of the world oil trade. Membership is open to any other country having substantial net exports of crude petroleum, which has fundamentally similar interests to those of member countries. Till March, 2014 the organisation had 12 members. Headquarters : Vienna, Austria.

The Commonwealth

The 54-nation Commonwealth represents more than a fourth of the nations of the world. The idea of Commonwealth of Nations comprising Great Britain and the Dominions and other Territories in the British Empire was first accepted at the Imperial Conference of 1926. In 1931, the Statute of Westminster recognised the status of the Dominions and defined the relations of the British Crown with the Dominions. The other territories were entitled to become members of the Commonwealth on attaining full self-government. In 1947, the office of the Secretary of State for Dominions was abolished and the Secretary of Commonwealth Relations assumed charge. Headquarters : London.

The Difference : Some of the members like Canada, Australia and New Zealand recognise the Queen as the titular head of their States and have Governors-General appointed by the Queen on the recommendation of the State Cabinets. Some like India, Pakistan, Kenya and Sri Lanka, who have elected Presidents of their own as Heads of State, recognise the Queen as the Head of the Commonwealth only. Members of the Commonwealth are represented in other Commonwealth countries by diplomatic officers called High Commissioners in place of ambassadors representing non-Commonwealth countries. Commonwealth Heads of Government Meet (CHOGM) has become an important international event.

The French Community

The French Community was created in 1958, through French Constitution and modified by later amendments. It is an association of France, its overseas Dominions and Territories, six African republics (former possessions) and one Condominium (New Hebrides). France aids members in construction of roads, rail-roads etc. and in improvement of agricultural production, health and eduction. It is an organisation like the British Commonwealth. It offers to the French overseas Territories, which manifest their will to adhere to it, new institutions based on the common idea of liberty, equality and fraternity and conceived with a view of the democratic evolution. This principle was accepted and promulgated by the Constitution of the French Republic, which came into force in 1953. Independent members of the Community are : French Republic, Central African Republic, Republic of Congo, Gabon, Senegal, Chad, Madagascar and Djibouti etc.

G-8

The world's most industrialised nations call themselves as Group of Seven. They are the United States, Britain, France, Japan Italy, Canada, Germany and Russia. Russia is expelled from the group in 2014 on Ukraine issue.

G-19

It is an economic grouping of developing countries formed in Malaysia in 1990. The members are Mexico, Jamaica, Venezuela, Peru, Brazil, Argentina, Senegal, Algeria, Nigeria, Yugoslavia, Zimbabwe, Egypt, Malaysia, Indonesia, India, Kenya, Sri Lanka, Columbia and Iran.

The Group of 77

It is another Third World economic grouping. It was founded under the auspices of the UN in 1964 to defend the economic and trade interests of the developing world. It comprises developing countries from Asia, Africa and Latin America. The 'Group of 77' is an economic group to protect and defend the economic and trade interests of the developing countries.

REGIONAL ORGANISATIONS

The European Union

Formerly European Economic Community (EEC), popularly known as the Common Market, established on January 1, 1958, is a bloc of 28 adjacent West European industrial nations which, through a network of agreements, are seeking to pool their economies while retaining their separate national identities. Their ultimate goal is a complete customs union with free flow of goods, services and labour among all members. Its members are Belgium, France, Germany, Italy, Luxembourg, the Netherlands, Britain, Denmark, Ireland, Greece, Spain and Portugal. Earlier, known as the European Common Market (ECM), it was brought into existence by the Treaty of Rome on March 25, 1957, signed by six countries —France, Belgium, the Netherlands, Luxembourg, Germany and Italy. Later Britain, Ireland, Denmark and Norway signed the treaty of accession but Norway withdrew. Greece, Spain and Portugal joined later. On January 1, 1995, Austria, Finland and Sweden also became its members. 10 new members namely Cyprus, Czech Republic, Estonia, Hungary, Latvia, Lithuania, Malta, Poland, Slovakia and Slovania were admitted in EU in May, 2004. Romania and Bulgaria joined EU in January, 2007. Croatia was admitted to the European Union in 2013.

Common Currency : The members of the European Union launched a new common currency, Euro, at Brussels. However, only 11 member nations, out of a total of 15 nations, joined the venture on January 1, 1999. Till January 2015, 18 member countries of 27 European Union Countries had accepted the Euro Currency.

Guarantees : The Treaty of Rome guarantees certain rights to the citizens of all member states (e.g. the ban on economic discrimination by nationality, and equal pay for equal work, as should be between men and women) and delineates certain other areas where secondary legislation is to fill in the details.

Largest and Prosperous : EU has become the world's largest and most prosperous trading area, with a population of nearly 400 million—larger than that of any superpower. Headquarters : Brussels.

European Parliament : Composed of 638 members, it is directly elected from all the 28 member states. Headquarters : Brussels, Belgium.

The Arab League

A league of Arab States, it is the outcome of a national awakening of the Arabs, following the fall of the Ottoman Empire during the First World War. It was formally instituted on March 22, 1945. The Arab League consists of a Council, a Secretary General and a few permanent committees. The League considers itself a regional organisation within the framework of the UN, of which its Secretary General is an observer.

Member countries (22) : Algeria, Bahrain, Djibouti, Iraq, Jordan, Kuwait, Comoros, Lebanon, Libya, Egypt, Mauritania, Morocco, Oman, Palestine, Qatar, Saudi Arabia, Somalia, Sudan, Syria, Tunisia, UAE and Yemen.

Secretariat : After Iraq's invasion of Kuwait in August 1990, the venue was shifted to Cairo.

South Asian Association for Regional Cooperation (SAARC)

The first South Asian summit held in Dhaka (Bangladesh) in December, 1985, culminated in the formation of the South Asian Association for Regional Cooperation. As the 'beginning of a new dawn', the SAARC points the way towards collective self-reliance in order to overcome problems of poverty, illiteracy, malnutrition and disease in this area. SAARC has eight member States, viz, India, Bangladesh, Pakistan, Sri Lanka, Bhutan, Nepal, Maldives and Afghanistan. The Charter of SAARC provides for annual meetings of the Head of States and Governments and six monthly meetings of a Council of Ministers, which is the organisation's highest policy-making body. A permanent secretariat of SAARC has been set up at Kathmandu in Nepal.

The Association of South East Asian Nations (ASEAN)

It is a regional organisation formed by the governments of Indonesia, Malaysia, the Philippines, Singapore and Thailand, through the Bangkok Declaration which was signed by the Foreign Ministers of ASEAN countries on August 8, 1967. Brunei joined in 1984. Its aim is to accelerate economic progress and maintain the economic stability of South East Asia. Each ASEAN capital has an ASEAN National Secretariat. The central secretariat for ASEAN is located in Jakarta (Indonesia) and is headed by the Secretory General, a post that revolves among the member States in alphabetical order every 3 years. Bureau directors and other officers of the ASEAN Secretariat also remain in office for 3 years.

European Free Trade Association (EFTA)

EFTA was formed in January, 1960, as a limited version of EEC, with its main goal as the gradual reduction of customs duties and quantitative restrictions on industrial goods among members. By December 31, 1996, all tariffs and quotas had been eliminated. Its member nations are : Austria, Finland, Iceland, Norway, Sweden and Switzerland. Two founder members, the U.K. and Denmark, left EFTA on December 31, 1972 to join the European community. Headquarters : Geneva (Switzerland).

European Space Research Organisation (ESRO)

It was formally established in 1964 to promote collaboration among European States in space research and technology exclusively for peaceful purposes. The members are : Belgium, Denmark, France, Germany, Italy, the Netherlands, Spain, Sweden, Switzerland and the U.K. Austria, Ireland and Norway participated as observers. Headquarters : Paris, France.

North America Free Trade Agreement (NAFTA)

Concluded in November, 1993 and coming into effect in January, 1994, NAFTA is composed of the USA, Canada and Mexico. In this trading bloc of 360 million people, tariff is to be eliminated over a period of 15 years. The agreement deals with certain other subjects including agriculture, automobiles, financial services, textiles, and communication with time-bound targets.

WELFARE ORGANISATIONS

Amnesty International

It is a worldwide human rights organisation with headquarters in London. The organisation was established on May 28, 1961 with a newspaper appeal by the British lawyer Peter Berenson. Now it has more than 11,00,000 members in more than 150 countries with 6,000 local groups in 70 countries in Africa, the Americas, Asia, Europe and the Middle East. It won the Nobel Prize for peace in 1977. Headquarters : London.

Red Cross

International Committee of the Red Cross (ICRC), established in 1863, organises care for the victims of war and enforces various conventions on wartime practices. The ICRC, constituted with the League of Red Cross Societies, founded in 1929, has member societies in 186 countries. It is an international society for alleviating sufferings in the time of war or disaster. International Committee of Red Cross was founded on advocacy of J.H. Durant, providing for neutrality of personnel treating wounded etc. Awarded Nobel Peace Prize (1917, 1944, 1963). Headquarters : Geneva.

Scouts and Guides

Scouting, a worldwide organised movement for young people, started by an Englishman, Lieutenant General Sir Robert S. S. Baden Powell in 1907. He gave boys outdoor skills which he had illustrated well in his book explaining scouting, tracking and map-making skills. The movements' goals include encouraging good character, loyalty to God and the country, service to other people and physical and mental fitness. 'Be Prepared' is the slogan. The World Scouts Bureau is in Geneva, Switzerland.

A similar movement for girls—the Girl Guide Movement—was founded by Baden Powell and his sister Agnes in 1910.

Interpol

International Criminal Police Organisation (Interpol), formed in 1956, ensures maximum cooperation between police authorities with the strict exclusion of political, military, religious and racial matters. Interpol is a successor to the International Criminal Police Commission which was established in 1923. It acts as a clearing house for information on international criminal matters. The organisation has official police bodies in 188 countries. Headquarters : Lyons.

GEOGRAPHY

GALAXY

According to astronomers, there exist some 60-90 billion galaxies in the universe. Larger galaxies may contain up to one trillion stars while the smallest may have about a million. Our knowledge is limited to only two galaxies. One, the *Milky Way,* of which our solar system is a part and the other one, visible to naked eyes, is *Andromeda.*

Galaxies : These are huge congregations of stars that are held together by force of gravity. Our Earth and the Solar System are contained in the Galaxy called *Milky Way.*

Stars : Stars account for 98 percent of the matter in a galaxy. The stars nearest to the earth are *Proxima Centauri, Alpha Centauri, Barnard's Star, Sirius* and so on. Of these, *Sirius* is the brightest and proxima centauri is nearest.

The Planets and the Moons : Our solar system comprises the sun, the planets and their moons. It also consists of several thousand minor planets called asteroids or planetoids and a large number of comets. In order of their distance from the sun, the planets of the solar system are : Mercury, Venus, Earth, Mars, Jupiter, Saturn, Uranus and Neptune.

Sun : The sun, which is one of the stars in the *Milky Way,* is composed mainly of hydrogen. The sun consists of the Photosphere, the Chromosphere and Corona. The age of the sun is about 5 billion years. Its diameter is 13,92,000 km. It is about 149.8 million kms away from the earth and its surface is approximately 12,000 times that of the earth. Its rotation period is 25 days 9 hours and 7 minutes. Sun's rays travel at a tremendous speed of about 3,00,000 km. per second and take eight minutes to reach the earth.

Mercury : Mercury is the closest planet to the sun. It is the smallest of the eight planets orbiting the sun at an average distance of 5,79,09,100 km. Its diameter is 4,878 km. and its period of revolution is about 88 days. The planet rotates on its axis in a period of 58 days, 15 hours, 36 minutes. Being nearest to the sun, Mercury receives the greatest amount of heat from it.

Venus : Venus is the brightest of all the planets and is slightly smaller than the earth. Its diameter is 12,102 km. It is at a distance of 10,82,08,900 km from the sun. It rotates very slowly in a clockwise direction, *i.e.*, contrary to the spin of other planets and this rotational period is 244 days. It revolves round the sun in about 224 days. The picture sent by Russian probes show rocks strewn on the surface of this planet. It is known as twin planet to earth.

Mars : Mars is the first planet beyond earth. Its equatorial diameter is 6,794 km. and polar diameter 6,752 km. It is 22,79,40,500 km. away from the sun. Moving at a speed of about 25 kms. per second, Mars completes one revolution around the sun in about 687 days. It rotates on its axis in 24 hours, 37 minutes and 22 seconds, *i.e.*, almost the same period of time as taken by the earth. Picture sent back by Mariner - 9 probes in 1971-72 have shown that Mars is a world of mountains, craters and giant volcanoes. It is known as earth's son.

Jupiter : Jupiter with an equatorial diameter of 1,42,880 km, and a polar diameter of 1,33,540 km., is the largest planet of our solar system. Its outer layers are gaseous—composed of hydrogen and hydrogen compounds. Jupiter's rate of rotation is rapid and it completes one rotation in 9 hours, 55 minutes and 30 seconds. Jupiter revolves round the sun, once in about 12 years. Jupiter is said to have 67 satellites, fourteen of which have been found through earth based observations.

Saturn : Second in size after Jupiter, Saturn is about 1,42,69,78,000 kms. away from the sun. Its equatorial diameter is 1,06,900 km. It takes 10 hours and 30 minutes to complete one rotation. It revolves round the sun in 10,759.06 days (about 30 years). Saturn is less dense but colder than Jupiter. Its specific gravity is less than that of water. Until Pioneer 11 passed Saturn in September 1979, only 10 satellites of Saturn were known. Since that time, the situation is quite confused. It is now believed that Saturn has at least 60 satellites. Voyager I and II flybys would help sort out the confusion. Saturn was first discovered by Galileo.

Uranus : Uranus is believed to be similar to Saturn and Jupiter and has the same density as that of Jupiter. Its equatorial diameter is 51,400 km and polar diameter 50,300 kms, *i.e.,* nearly four times that of earth. It is at a distance of 2,87,09,91,000 km. from the sun. It rotates on its axis in 17 hours and 14 minutes and revolves round the sun in 30,707.79 days (about 84 years). It is believed that Uranus is a grim frozen world. Uranus has 27 known satellites. It was discovered by Sir William Herschel on March 13,1781.

Neptune : Neptune too is believed to be similar to Saturn and Jupiter. It has an equatorial diameter of 48,600 km. and a polar diameter of 47,500 km. It is at a distance of 4,49,70,70,000 km. away from the sun and takes 60,19,963 days (nearly 165 years) to make one revolution of the sun. The period of its rotation is 16 hours and 27 minutes. Neptune has 13 satellites.

Note: Pluto was stripped of its status as a planet on August 24, 2006.

THE EARTH

In solar system, the earth is the third nearest planet from the sun and is the fifth largest planet. It has an equatorial diameter of 12,756 kms and a polar diameter of 12,714 kms. The earth is at a distance of 14,95,97,900 kms. from the sun and orbits round the sun in elliptical at a speed of 1,07,220 km. per hour, making one revolution in 365 days, 5 hours, 48 minutes and 45.51 seconds. It completes one rotation on its axis every 23 hours, 56 minutes and 4.2 seconds. The earth is a unique planet. It is oblate rather than a true sphere. The earth is considered to be a solid, rigid mass with a dense core of magnetic, probably metallic material. It is the only planet containing ample water and air around it. The temperature on the earth is also suitable for human life.

The age of the earth is estimated to be around 4.6 billion years. Its total area is 510,100,448 sq. km and nearly five-seventh of the same is covered by water.

Dimensions of the Earth

Mass	:	5.97×10^{24} kg.
Density	:	5.517 times that of water.
	:	1,08,32,08, 840.000 cubic km.
Equatorial Circumference		40,075.03 km.
Polar or Meridian Circumference	:	40,007.89 km.
Polar Diameter	:	12,714 km.

Land and Sea Surface : The estimated total surface area of the earth is 510,100,448 sq. km. of which the sea or hydrosphere covers five-sevenths or more accurately, 70.92 per cent and the land or lithosphere the remaining two-sevenths or 29.8 percent. The mean depth of the hydrosphere is 3,554 metres.

Orbit : It is the elliptical path of earth's revolution round the sun.

Perihelion : It is the nearest point to the sun. The earth reaches its perihelion in the beginning of January.

Aphelion : It is the point in earth's or other planet's orbit which is farthest from the sun. The earth reaches its aphelion in the end of June.

Solstice : It is the date on which the sun shines vertically over a tropic. On June 21, the sun shines vertically on the Tropic of Cancer and this date is termed as summer solstice for northern hemisphere and winter solstice for the southern hemisphere. Similarly, on December 22 the sun shines vertically on the Tropic of Capricorn. Hence, this date is summer solstice for the southern hemisphere and winter solstice for the northern hemisphere.

Equinox : It means equal nights (aquas=equal; nox=night). It is the period when sun inevitably shines vertically over the equator at noon, making the duration of days and nights of the same span of the period, *i.e.*, twelve hours for a day and twelve hours for a night. March 21 and September 23, when days and nights are of equal duration throughout the globe, are called equinoxes. March 21 is called vernal equinox and September 23 is called autumnal equinox.

Where Days and Nights are Always Equal : At the equator the days and nights are equal throughout the year since the circle of illumination always divides the equator into two equal parts.

Change of Seasons : The inclination of earth's axis by 66½° and earth's revolution round the sun bring about changing seasons. The two hemispheres experience summer when they are closer to the sun and winter when farther and away from it.

Moon : Moon is the only natural satellite of the earth. It is also the nearest neighbour of the earth at a mean distance of 3,84,400 km. centre to centre, 3,76,284 km. surface to surface. Its diameter is 3,475 km. and average orbital speed is 3,680 km per hour. Earth is being orbited by the moon. Only 59 per cent of the moon's surface is directly visible from earth. The period of rotation of our moon is equal to its period of revolution around the earth. This period is 27 days, 7 hours, 43 minutes and 11.47 seconds.

THE CONTINENTS OF THE WORLD

Asia

Asia, the largest continent, extends over nearly one-third (29.5%) of the land surface of the earth. **Area:** 43,998,000 sq. km. **Population:** (2013) 4,298 million. **Chief Mountain Ranges:** Himalayas, Kunlun, Tien Shah, Altai, Tibetan Plateau. **Chief Rivers:** Ganges, Yang-tze, Yamuna, Yensei, Amur, Hwang-ho, Mekong. **Deserts:** Arabia, Thar. **Climate:** Very varied, extreme in north, monsoonal in the south and east. **Minerals:** Gold, coal, oil, iron, manganese. **Principal Countries in Asia:** India, Iran, Iraq, Israel, Jordan, Pakistan, Sri Lanka, Myanmar (Burma), Russia, China, Vietnam, Indonesia, Malaysia, Japan, Bangladesh. **Important Cities:** New Delhi, Mumbai, Tokyo, Dhaka, Beijing, Yangoon, (Rangoon), Bangkok, Colombo, Hanoi, Tashkent.

Africa

Africa, the second largest continent, bounded by Mediterranean Sea on the north, by Red Sea and Indian Ocean in east, by Atlantic Ocean in the west, adjoins Asia and isthumus of Suez. **Area:** (approx 29,807,200) sq. km (20% of the world). **Population:** (2013) 1110 million. **Principal Countries:** Egypt, Libya, Algeria, Morocco, Niger, Chad, Sudan, Ethiopia, Kenya, Somalia, Congo, Zambia, South Africa, Nigeria, Angola. Desert in north, forest in centre and lotty plateaus in the south. **Highest Mountain:** Kilimanjaro—5,895 metres. **Chief Rivers:** Nile, Congo, Niger, Zambezi. **Largest Lake:** Victoria, Great Rift valley in East Africa. **Rainfall:** Heavy near equator, almost rainless in Sahara and Kalahari, elsewhere moderate, **Agriculture:** Wine olives, wheat, esparto grass in north; cocoa, oil palm, groundnut, coffee, cotton in centre; wheat, maize, wool in south. **Minerals:** Gold, diamonds, copper. **Important Cities:** Cairo, Lusaka, Mombasa, Nairobi, Adis Ababa, Harare, Cape Town, Pretoria.

Europe

Area: (approx.) 9,699,550 sq. km (6.5%); greatest length north to south 3,860 km; breadth east to west 5,300 km. **Population:** (2013) 742 million. **Chief Mountains:** Alps, Pyrenes, Carpathians, Balkans, Apennines, Sierra Nevada, Urals, Caucasus. **Chief Rivers:** Volga, Danube, Rhine, Dnieper, Ural, Don. **Climate:** Arctic border, long cold winter; short cool summer, snow.

Chief Industries: Agriculture—cereals, fruits, sugarbeet, potato, wax, hemp, pastoral—cattle-rearing, dairying, fishing, forestry, wood, pulp, paper, iron, coal, petroleum, hydroelectric power, etc. **Principal Countries:** U.K., France, Germany, Poland, Czechoslovakia (Czech and Slovak Federative Republics), Hungary, Norway, Sweden, Portugal, Italy, Spain, Switzerland, Austria, Romania. **Important Cities:** Berne, Paris, Berlin, London, Bonn, Vienna, Munich, Prague, Warsaw, Rome, Budapest, Stockholm, Moscow, Belgrade, Madrid, Oslo.

North America

North America, northern continent of Western Hemisphere, comprising U.S.A., Canada, Central America and the Caribbean, on west high chain of mountains, lower range in east and central plains, climate varies considerably owing to wide range of latitude and altitude. **Area:** 24,235,280 sq. km (16.3%). **Population:** (2009) 534 million. **Agriculture:** Temperate and tropical products, cereals, tobacco, sugarbeet, potatoes, etc., lumbering, rich in minerals, coal, petroleum, iron, manganese, etc. **General Industries:** Ship building. Occupied formerly by Red Indians; now mainly by white races with many Negroes in south. **Important Cities:** New York, Washington D.C., San Francisco, Chicago, Mexico, Montreal, Ottawa, Jamaica.

South America

South America, southern continent of Western Hemisphere including Argentina, Bolivia, Brazil, Chile, Colombia, Ecuador, Paraguay, Peru, Uruguay, Venezuela and Guayana. **Area:** 17,820,770 sq. km (13.4%). **Population:** (2013) 406 million. **Climate:** Diverse, varying with latitude and altitude, equatorial, hot and wet, Atacama, a rainless desert on middle west coast in south temperate. **Chief Industries:** Tropical agriculture: cocoa, coffee, sugarcane, rubber, cereals. **Minerals:** Gold, silver, copper, tin, diamonds, nitrates; factory Industries developing gradually. Portuguese descent, Indians, Negroes, Mulattoes and Mestizos (mixed races). **Important Cities:** Rio de Janeiro, Salvador, Trinidad, Buenos Aires, La Paz, Bogota.

Australia

Australia is an Island continent and is a British Dominion. The Commonwealth of Australia, including the island of Tasmania, is nearly as large as Europe but has only 17.8 million inhabitants, most of whom are of British origin, but there are about 50,000 native aborigines. **Area:** 8,426,638 sq. km (6.5%). **Population:** (2009) 34.68 million. **States:** New South Wales (Cap. Sydney); Queensland (Cap. Brisbane); South Australia (Cap. Adelaide); Western Australia (Cap. Perth); Victoria (Cap. Melbourne); Tasmania (Cap. Hobart). All these capital cities are ports though Perth is served by the port of Fremantle. An area, largely uninhabited, is the Northern Territory. Its capital is Darwin and another famous town is Alice Springs. The Territory does not yet govern itself in the way other states do. Federal capital, Canberra. **Industry:** Wool, gold, iron ore, lead and zinc. One of the most important rivers is the Snowy in New South Wales and Victoria. A big new irrigation scheme is being carried out on this river and on the Murray. The first free immigrants arrived from Britain in 1793, the east coast of Australia having been discovered by Captain Cook about twenty years before. These settlers came to New South Wales which is thus the oldest state in Australia. In 1910 the six States were all united in a federation called the Commonwealth of Australia.

WINDS : REGIONWISE

Wind	Region
Blizzard	Polar region and North America
Bora	Cold dry wind from Hungary to the north of Italy
Breeze	In coastal areas
Chinook	Rocky mountains
Cyclones	Indian Ocean
Harmattan	Interior of Guinea
Hurricane	West Indies
Mistral	Cold wind from Central France
Monsoon	South Asia
Punas	Western side of the Andes
Roaring Forties	Southern Hemisphere between 40 and 50 degrees
Sirocco	From North Sahara towards Mediterranean countries
Solano	From Sahara to Iberian Peninsula
Tornado	South Asia
Trade Winds	From high pressure towards low pressure within 30 degree north and south of the equator
Typhoon	The Pacific Ocean
Westerlies	Temperate Zones
Willy-willy	North western Australia and Timor

MAJOR CITIES AT RIVER BANKS

City	River	Country	City	River	Country
Alexandria	Nile	Egypt	Karachi	Indus	Pakistan
Amsterdam	Amsel	Netherlands	Lahore	Ravi	Pakistan
Antwerp	Scheldt	Belgium	London	Thames	England
Baghdad	Tigris	Iraq	Montreal	Ottawa	Canada
Bangkok	Menam (Chao Phraya)	Thailand	Moscow	Moskva	Russia
			New York	Hudson	U.S.A.
Belgrade	Danube	Yugoslavia	Paris	Seine	France
Berlin	Spree	Germany	Quebec	St. Lawrence	Canada
Bonn	Rhine	Germany	Rome	Tiber	Italy
Budapest	Danube	Hungary	Tokyo	Sumida	Japan
Cairo	Nile	Egypt	Vienna	Danube	Austria
Canton	Canton	China	Warsaw	Vistula	Poland
Glasgow	Clyde	Scotland	Washington	Potamac	U.S.A.
Hamburg	Elbe	Germany	Yangoon	Irawady	Myanmar

MAJOR RIVERS

River	Length	River	Length
Nile (Africa)	6,690 Km.	Murray (Australia)	3,996 Km.
Amazon, Brazil (S.America)	6,570 Km.	Volga (Russia)	3,664 Km.
Mississipi (N.America)	5,970 Km.	St. Lawrence (Canada)	3,040 Km.
Yangtze (China)	5,440 Km.	Danube (Europe)	2,760 Km.
Congo (Africa)	4,640 Km.	Indus (India-Pakistan)	2,720 Km.
Huang Ho/Yellow River (China)	4,344 Km.	Brahmaputra (India)	2,688 Km.
		Ganges (India)	2,640 Km.
		Irawady (Myanmar)	2,120 Km.

RIVERS AND THEIR OUTFLOWS

River	Outflow	River	Outflow
Amazon	Atlantic Ocean	Indus	Arabian Sea
Amur	Tatar Strait	Lena	Arctic Ocean
Brahmaputra	Joins River Padma and falls in Bay of Bengal	Mississipi	Gulf of Mexico
		Missouri	Mississipi River
Colorado	Gulf of California	Niger	Gulf of Guinea
Columbia	Pacific Ocean	Nile	Mediterranean Sea
Danube	Black Sea	Orange	Atlantic Ocean
Darling	Mozambique Channel	Red Rock	Gulf of Mexico
		Salween	Gulf of Martaban
Dnieper	Black Sea	Tigris	Shatt-al-Arab
Euphrates	Shatt-al-Arab	Ural	Caspian Sea
Ganges	Bay of Bengal	Volga	Caspian Sea
Hwang Ho	Gulf of China	Yangtze Kiang	China Sea

PRINCIPAL SEAS

Sea	Average depth (metres)
Andaman Sea	865
Baltic Sea	55
Bering Sea	1,400
Black Sea	1,100
Caribbean Sea	2,400
Hudson Bay	120
Malay Sea	1,200
Mediterranean Sea	1,485
Persian Gulf	24
Red Sea	490
Sea of Japan	1,370
Sea of Okhotsk	840

WATER FALLS

Water Fall	Location	Height (metres)
Angel	Venezuela	807
Mongefossen	Norway	774
Utigard	Norway	600
Ribbon	U.S.A.	491
King George VI	Guyana	487
Yosemite	U.S.A.	435
Gavarnie	France	421
Tugela	South Africa	410
Takakkaw	Canada	365

LARGE LAKES

Name	Location	Area : Sq. mile	Depth (meters)
Caspian Sea	Russia-Iran	1,43,244	980
Lake Superior	U.S.A.–Canada	31,700	406
Victoria	Tanzania-Uganda	26,828	82
Aral	Kazakhstan	24,904	68
Michigan	U.S.A.	22,300	281
Tanganyika	Tanzania-Zaire	12,700	1,435
Baikal	Russia	12,162	1,940
Great Bear	Canada	12,096	82
Nipigon	Canada	1,872	7
Manitoba	Canada	1,799	7

MAJOR DESERTS

Name	Location	Area (sq. km.)
Sahara (Largest)	Africa	84,00,000
Australian Desert	Australia	15,50,000
Arabian Desert	Saudi Arabia, Yemen	13,00,000
Gobi Desert	Mongolia and China	10,40,000
Kalahari Desert	Botswana	5,20,000
Takla Makan	China	3,20,000
Sanoran Desert	U.S.A. and Mexico	3,10,000
Namib Desert	Namibia	2,70,000
Thar Desert	NW India and Pakistan	2,60,000
Atacama Desert	Northern Chile	1,80,000

ACTIVE VOLCANOES

Name	Location	Name	Location
Etna	Italy	Krakatau	Indonesia
Fuego	Guatemala	Lopevi	Vanuatu
Kotopaxi	Ecuador	Manam	Papua New Guinea
Kilauea	Hawaii	Mt. Cameroon	Cameroon
Kiluchevskoi	Russia	Rabaul	Papua New Guinea
		Slamet	Indonesia

LARGE ISLANDS

Name	Area in sq. km	Location
Greenland	21,75,600	Arctic Ocean
New Guinea	7,77,000	West Pacific
Borneo	7,25,545	Indian Ocean
Malagasy Republic	5,90,000	Indian Ocean
Baffin Island	4,76,065	Arctic Ocean
Sumatra	4,73,600	Indian Ocean
Honshu	2,28,000	Northwest Pacific
British Isles	2,18,041	North Atlantic
Victoria Island	2,12,197	Arctic Ocean
Ellesmere	1,96,236	Arctic Ocean
Celebes	1,89,035	Indian Ocean
New Zealand (North)	1,50,460	Southwest Pacific
Java	1,26,295	Indian Ocean
New Zealand (South)	1,14,687	Southwest Pacific
Cuba	1,14,522	Caribbean Sea
Newfoundland	1,12,300	North Atlantic
Iceland	1,03,000	North Atlantic
Ireland (including N. Ireland)	82,460	North Atlantic
Hokkaido	77,900	Northwest Pacific
Dominican Republic and Haiti	76,192	Caribbean Sea
Sakhalin	74,060	Northwest Pacific
Tasmania	67,900	Southwest Pacific
Sri Lanka	65,600	Indian Ocean

MOUNTAIN PEAKS

Name	Country	Range	Height (m)	Dt. of first ascent
Mt. Everest	Nepal-Tibet	Himalayas	8,848	May 29, 1953
K-2 (Godwin Austin)	India	Karakoram	8,611	July 31, 1954
Kanchenjunga	Nepal-India	Himalayas	8,598	May 25, 1955
Lhotse	Nepal-China	Himalayas	8,511	May 18, 1956
Makaly	Tibet-Nepal	Himalayas	8,481	May 15, 1955
Dhaulagiri-I	Nepal	Himalayas	8,172	May 13 1960
Nanga Parbat	India	Himalayas	8,124	July 03, 1953
Nanda Devi	India	Himalayas	7,817	Aug. 29, 1960

LARGE PENINSULAS

Name	Area in sq. km.
Arabia	32,50,000
Southern India	20,72,000
Alaska	15,00,000
Labrador	13,00,000
Scandinavia	8,00,300
Iberian	5,84,000

OTHER FACTS

Largest Continent	Asia
Smallest Continent	Australia
Largest Sea	South China Sea
Largest Archipelago (group of islands)	Indonesia (13,000 islands)
Longest Canal (big ship)	Suez Canal (U.A.R.)
Largest Country	Russia
Driest Place	Atacama Desert, Chile
Hottest Place	Azizia (Libya)
Rainiest Place	Mawsymam, near Cherrapunji, India
Highest Waterfall	Salto Angel Falls, Venezuela

MISCELLANEOUS INFORMATION

FAMOUS TOWNS, PLACES AND BUILDINGS

Abadan : Major oil terminal and refining centre in Iran.

Abu Simbel : In Egypt; ancient temples carved out of solid sandstone.

Adam's Bridge : Chain of sandbanks, 22 metres long, in Palk Strait.

Alaska : It is the largest US State situated near Canada. It was purchased by the USA in 1867 from Russia; Famous for mining, lumbering and pulp-milling industries; Oil resources are available here in plenty.

Alexandria : Important city and seaport of Egypt: founded by Alexander the Great; Chief centre of foreign trade; It is famous for white marble lighthouse of the island of Pharaos

Algiers : Capital city of Algeria in north Africa, renamed El Dzejair in 1972.

Amsterdam : Capital of the Netherlands; famous for diamond-cutting industry.

Angkor Vat : Famous for ruins of ancient Hindu Temples dedicated to Vishnu in Cambodia built between 800 to 1200 A.D.

Aswan High Dam: Opened in 1971, a 350 feet high dam on river Nile in Egypt.

Attock : In Pakistan on the bank of river Indus; Known for its oil wells, oil refinery.

Baikanour : Spaceship launching station (cosmodrome) in Kazakhstan.

Baku : Situated on the Caspian Sea, an oil field in Azerbaijan.

Bandung : In Indonesia, venue of Afro-Asian Conference in April, 1955.

Bangkok : Capital of Thailand; venue of Asian Games in 1966, 1970, 1978 and 1998. It is called the Venice of the East.

Beijing : Capital of China and venue of Asiad 1990;

Beijing is the new romanised spelling of Peking; name was introduced from September 1,1975.

Bethlehem : In Israel, birth place of Jesus Christ.

Big Ben : The Great Bell in Parliament Clock Tower, London.

Bikini : Northernmost a toll of Ralik group, Marshal island, in the Pacific Ocean; the site where atom bomb tests were conducted by the U.S.A. in 1946.

Buckingham Palace : In London; residence of the royal family of England.

Cape Kennedy : In Florida (USA); America's spaceship launching centre; Now known as Cape Canaveral.

Cape Trafalgar : On the coast of Spain, where the British fleet won a decisive victory over Napoleon in 1805.

Catacombs of Rome : There are the sepulchres of the early Christians and consisted of more than 40 groups of labyrinths, sometimes going down to 5 storeys below the surface of the ground.

Cenotaph : A monument in White Hall, London in memory of those who sacrificed their lives during World War I.

Chicago : Situated at the mouth of Chicago river in the U.S.A.; Second city in terms of population; Great railway centre; Biggest grain and meat market of the world.

Colombo : Capital and port of Sri Lanka; it holds very strategic importance on the ocean highway for east and west.

Colossus of Rhodes: A bronze statue of Greek sun-god Helios, erected by Charles of Kindus at the port of the city of Rhodes.

Corsica : An island in the Mediterranean Sea where Napoleon was born.

Cotopaxi : In Ecuador; it is the loftiest active volcano in the world with a height of 19,500 ft.

Detroit : The fourth largest city in U.S.A.; known as the city of motor cars.

Diego Garcia : An island in the Indian Ocean near Mauritius. The U.S.A. has set up a big naval base here. The littoral countries led by India raised protest against this step.

Disneyland : An amusement park at Anaheim, California. It was built in 1955 by Walter Elias Disney, the world famous American Cartoonist and motion-picture producer. The park encloses 170 acres of land. Each main division of the park has its own theme indicated by its name viz Fantasy land, Adventure land etc. Disneyland's unusual transportation facilities include a monorail, submarines, keel boats etc.

Eiffel Tower : A 985 feet high tower designed by Alexander Gustave Eiffel for Paris Exposition in 1889 in Paris (France), now being used as a meteorological wireless station.

Helena, St. : An isolated island in the Mediterranean Sea where Napoleon was exiled in 1815.

Fleet Street : A street in London named after the river Fleet; there are offices and printing establishments of many of the leading British newspapers and press agencies.

Fuji Yama : Extinct volcano in Japan near Tokyo; pilgrim resort; the highest peak of Japan.

Geneva : In Switzerland; venue of several international conferences; headquarters of ILO, WHO and Red Cross Society.

Great wall of China : A wall built in northern China along southern edge of Mongolian plateau to keep out invading Mongols; 1,500 miles long, from 15 to 50 feet high and 15 to 25 feet wide; its construction was completed in 3rd century.

Greenwich : Situated on the Thames river near London; Noted for its astronomical observatory; longitude conventionally calculated with Greenwich meridian either east or west.

Hagia Sophia : Church of St. Sophia at Constantinople built by Roman Emperor Justinian (531-538 A.D.).

Hague : The seat of the Government of Netherlands. International Court of Justice, a UN organ, is located here.

Hanging Gardens of Babylon : They were in the palace of King Nebuchadnezzar, 100 km south of present Baghdad.

Harappa : In Pakistan; Known for excavation of prehistoric buildings of pre-Aryan age.

Havana : Capital of Cuba, Olympic games were held here in 1952. SALT talks held in 1970-71.

Hiroshima : A flourishing Japanese town completely destroyed by the first atom bomb on August 6,1945.

Hollywood : Centre of world's biggest film industry in California, the U.S.A.

Hong Kong : A former British colony composed of a peninsula on the southeast China mainland and many islands off the coast; one of the world's finest harbours;. In 1997, the Chinese sovereignty on Hong Kong was restored.

Hyde Park : Famous place for public meetings in London.

Jakarta (Djakarta) : Capital of Indonesia, formerly known as Batavia, chief exporter of rubber and tea.

Jerusalem : Capital of Israel. Holy city for three faiths; Jews, Christians and Muslims.

Johannesburg : Gold mining centre in South Africa.

Jordell Bank Observatory : It is the locale of the world famous radio telescope near Manchester in U.K. It has played an important role in international space research.

Kaaba : The holiest place for the Muslims in Mecca, Saudi Arabia.

Karakoram Highway : It is an 800 km all-weather road linking border of China's Sinkiang province with Pakistan. The road was inaugurated on June 18, 1978, by General Zia and the Chinese Vice-Premier Keng Piao. India lodged her protest against the opening of this road as it passes through Kashmir territory.

Kilimanjaro : Volcanic mountain in north Tanzania, the highest peak in Africa (19,340 ft.).

Kimberley : Situated on the east of Kalahari desert in South Africa, the biggest diamond mining centre/market in the world.

Kremlin : Headquarters of the former Soviet Union.

Leaning Tower of Pisa : 180 ft. high, 8 storey marble tower in Pisa (Italy) built in 1154 AD.

Leeds : Centre of cotton and chemical industry in England.

Leningrad : See St. Peterburg.

London : Capital of England; one of the world's great cities; situated on river Thames; centre of communication and finance; seat of learning and has some most beautiful buildings.

Los Angeles : A port of California; the famous film industry of Hollywood is situated here; a few miles off the city is the world famous Disneyland; 1984 Olympic Games were held here.

Lop Nor : Located at Sinkiang desert in China where China's nuclear installations are located. It is also China's atomic testing ground.

Lumbini : The birth place of Gautam Buddha in Nepal.

Lusaka : The capital of Zambia; The 1970 NAM Summit was held here.

Madrid : Capital of Spain; Europe's highest capital; known for metallurgical industry, leather, textile and chemical industry; 1982 World Cup Football Championship was held here.

Mecca : Holy city of Islam; Birth place of Mohammed (PBUH); Kaaba, a place of pilgrimage for Muslims, is located here.

Mont Blanc : Alpine massif on Franco-Italian border; rises to 15,781 ft. in France, the highest point of the Alps.

Moscow : Capital of Russia; big commercial and industrial centre, fine buildings like the Kremlin, the palaces of Tsars; the venue of 1980 Olympic Games.

Nagasaki : A city and port in Japan; destroyed by atom bomb in 1945.

Nankana Sahib : In Pakistan, birth place of Guru Nanak.

Nuremberg : City of Bavaria in Germany; under Hitler, Nuremberg was the scene of the National Socialist Party Congress; in 1945-46, the first international war-criminals trials were held here.

Paris : Capital of France; Situated on the river Seine; The cultural and fashion metropolis of the world; UNESCO headquarters are located here.

Pearl Harbour : A key naval base of the U.S.A. at Oahu in Hawaii Islands. It was the scene of the Japanese air attack during World War II.

Pentagon : Headquarters of the Department of Defence in Virginia, USA; world's largest office building; construction completed on January 15, 1943.

Philadelphia : Place of historic importance, where Americans declared their independence on July 4, 1776, after framing their constitution.

Pisa : A town in Italy; famous for its leaning tower; birth place of Galileo.

Pompeii : Ruined Roman city in south Italy; situated at the foot of Mountain Vesuvius; destroyed by earthquake (63 A.D.) and buried by an eruption of Vesuvius (79 A.D.).

Porcelain Tower of Nanking : Built in the ancient capital of south China in early 15th century.

Pyramids of Egypt : Erected as royal tombs to protect the body and thereby, to preserve the spirit; Such pyramids are found only in Egypt, Great Pyramid of Khufu of Cheops at Gizeh, one of the seven wonders of the world, is the largest pyramid ever built; The pyramids date back to 2700 B.C.

Red Square : A famous open space in Moscow, near Kremlin used for political demonstrations and processions. Lenin's mausoleum and tombs of other revolutionary leaders are in Red Square.

Rhur : Famous for rich coal fields and heavy iron industry in Germany.

Rome : Capital of Italy; situated on the bank of river Tiber; Called "The Eternal City"; One of the world's outstanding historical, religious, cultural and art centres with Vatican City and St. Peters Church.

Sandhurst : Chief military training centre in England, near London.

Scotland Yard : Headquarters of the Metropolitan Police, London; As the seat of the criminal investigations department, Scotland Yard is a synonym for the force of detectives.

Sphinx : A fabulous monster represented in Egyptian art as a lion with a human head; It also figures in the art of Greece, Syria, Persia, etc; The best known example is the great Sphinx at Gizeh, Egypt, 52.6 m. long and 20.1 m. high, built around 2900-2750 B.C.

St. Helena : An island in the south Atlantic; 1,200 miles west of Africa. It became a British possession in 1673; Napoleon died here in exile in 1821.

Stockholm : Capital of Sweden, Sometimes called the 'Venice of the North'. A great manufacturing centre and an important seaport . A 35 nation disarmament conference was held here in 1984.

Stonehenge : It is a circular assemblage of huge stone in Salisbury; Placed at about 145 km southwest of London and built in 1800-1500 BC.

Stratford-upon-Avon : Birth place of Shakespeare in England.

Suez Canal : Ship canal in Egypt linking the Mediterranean and Red Seas and separating Africa from Asia; built by Ferdinand de Lesseps; nationalised by President Nasser in 1956.

St. Peterburg : Former capital of Russia founded by reformist Russian Tsar, Peter the Great, during the 18th century; After the death of Lenin, the city was renamed as Leningrad; With the dissolution of the U.S.S.R., its original name has been restored.

Taxila : A ruined city in Pakistan near Rawalpindi; ancient seat of Indian learning and a Buddhist university.

Tashkent : Capital of Uzbekistan. Tashkent Pact between India and Pakistan was signed here in January, 1966.

Texas : Second largest state of the USA; leads all the American states in cotton, cattle and petroleum production.

Trieste : An important seaport of Italy; famous for shipbuilding industry, iron works and oil refineries. In 1954, it was divided into two zones; Zone 'A' handed over to Italy and Zone 'B' handed over to Yugoslavia.

Vatican City : Sovereign papal state of about 109 acres forming an enclave near the city of Rome, Italy; The smallest independent state, it has its own railway and radio and television station; issues its own stamps and coinage; created by the Lateran Treaty (1929) between the Pope and the Italian Government.

Venezuela : Republic of South America on the Caribbean coast between Brazil and Columbia; The country is rich in minerals including iron-ore and petroleum.

Vienna : Capital of Austria; Headquarters of International Atomic Energy Agency.

Wall Street : Thoroughfare in New York; The stock exchange here has come to be used as a synonym for stock dealing in U.S.A.

Waterloo : In Belgium; On June 18,1815, Wellington defeated Napoleon here.

Wembley : Famous sports stadium in London.

White House : Official residence of the U.S. President in Washington; Oldest public building in Washington; John Adams (1800) was the first President to live here.

Wimbledon : A London suburb, famous tennis ground where International tennis matches are played.

Yellowstone National Park : A national American Reserve established in 1872; Yellowstone river flows through it; it includes more than 3,000 geysers, hot springs and very fine scenery.

PROMINENT NEWSPAPERS

Newspapers	Country	Newspapers	Country
ABC	Madrid (Spain)	Merdeka	Jakarta (Indonesia)
Al-Ahram	Cairo (Egypt)	New Statesman	London (Britain)
Daily Mirror	London (Britain)	New York Times	New York (U.S.A.)
Daily News	New York (U.S.A.)	People's Daily	Beijing (China)
Daily Telegraph	London (Britain)	Pravda	Moscow (Russia)
Dawn	Karachi (Pakistan)	Saudi Gazette	Jeddah (Saudi Arabia)
Gulf News	Dubai (U.A.E.)	The Guardian	London (Britain)
Izevestia	Moscow (Russia)	The Times	London (Britain)
Kayhan	Tehran (Iran)	The Time of India	Mumbai (India)
International Khaleej Times	Dubai (U.A.E.)	Washington Post	Washington (U.S.A.)
Le Monde	Paris (France)	Wymiuri Shimbun	Tokyo (Japan)

IMPORTANT NEWS AGENCIES

Agency	Country	Agency	Country
Agence France Presse (AFP)	France	New China News Agency (NCNA)	China
Antara	Indonesia	Palestinian News Agency (WAFA)	Palestine
Associated Press (AP)	U.S.A.	Press Trust of India (PTI)	India
Associated Press of Pakistan (APP)	Pakistan	Reuters	Britain
Australian Associated Press (AAP)	Australia	RITA (Russian Information Telegraph Agency)	Russia
Bangladesh Sanghbad Sansthan (BSS)	Bangladesh	Saudi Press Agency (SPA)	Saudi Arabia
Canadian Press (CP)	Canada	United News of India (UNI)	India
Ceteka	Czechoslovakia	United Press of America (UPA)	U.S.A.
EXTEL	Britain	Vietnam News Agency (VNA)	Vietnam
Globe News Agency	France	XINHUA	China
International News Services (INSUS)	U.S.A.		

PRINCIPAL AIRLINES

Airline	Country	Airline	Country
Aeroflot	Russia	K.L.M. Royal Dutch	Netherlands
Air India	India	Lufthansa	Germany
Air-Lanka	Sri Lanka	Northwest	U.S.A.
Air-France	France	Pakistan International (PIA)	Pakistan
Alitalia	Italy	Quantas Empire (PIA)	Australia
Ariana Afghan Airlines	Afghanistan	Royal Nepal Airlines	Nepal
British Airways	England	Sabena	Belgium
Cathay Pacific	Hongkong	Scandinavian Airlines System	Sweden
Delta	U.S.A	Swissair	Switzerland
Finnair	Finland	Thai Airways System	Thailand
Garuda Airways	Indonesia	Trans-World Airlines	U.S.A.
Japan Airlines Ltd.	Japan		

MAJOR AIRPORTS

Country	Airport
Britain	Heathrow (London)
France	Charles de Gaulle (Paris)
India	Indira Gandhi International Airport (New Delhi)
	Chhatrapati Shivaji International Airport (Mumbai)
Japan	Narita and Haneda (Tokyo)
Russia	Sheremetyevo (Moscow)
Sweden	Arlanda (Stockholm)
USA	Kennedy Air Port (New York)

SIGNS AND SYMBOLS

Sign/Symbol	Stands for
Red Triangle	Family Planning
Red Cross	Medical Aid
Red Light	Stop—Danger, Emergency
Green Light	Line Clear
Black Flag	Protest
Red Flag	Revolution
Lotus	Culture and Civilisation
Olive Branch	Peace
Dove	Peace
Pigeon	Peace
Socialist Maharaja	Air India
White Flag	Truce
Tricolour	National Flag of India
Union Jack	National Flag of U.K.
Stars & Strips (Old Glory)	National Flag of U.S.A.
Hammer & Sickle	National Flag of Russia

SEVEN WONDERS OF THE WORLD

(a) Ancient

1. The Pyramids of Egypt
2. The Hanging Gardens of Babylon
3. The Temple of Diana of Ephesus
4. The Statue of Zeus of Olympia
5. The Mausoleum at Halicarnassus
6. The Colossus of Rhodes
7. The Pharos (Light House) of Alexandria

(b) Medieval

1. The Colosseum of Rome
2. The Great Wall of China
3. The Tower of Nanking
4. The Mosque at St. Sophia
5. The Stonehenge of England
6. The Catacombs of Alexandria
7. The Leaning Tower of Pisa

(c) New

1. The Taj Mahal of Agra, India
2. The Pyramid at Chichen Itza, Mexico
3. The Machu Picchu, Peru
4. The Christ Redeemer, Rio de Janeiro, Brazil
5. The Great Wall of China
6. The Roman Colosseum, Rome
7. The Petra, Jordan

NATIONAL ANTHEMS

Bangladesh : (Amar Sonar Bangla) First Line : My golden Bengal, I love you
Canada : O Canada, Our Home and Native Land
China : March of the Volunteers
Cyprus : Ode to Freedom
Dominica : Isle of Beauty
Estonia : My Fatherland
Germany : Unity and Right and Freedom
Greece : Hymm to Freedom
Hungary : God Bless the Hungarians
Iceland : O God of our country
Japan : Kimi ga yo wa (May your Peaceful Reign Last Long)
Myanmar (Burma) : We shall Love Burma Evermore
Pakistan : Quami Tarana
Panama : Victory is Ours at Last
Russia : Slavsya (Be Great)
Saudi Arabia : Long Live Our Beloved King
Sri Lanka : Sri Lanka Matha, Apa Sri Lanka (Mother Sri Lanka, thy Sri Lanka)
Tanzania : God Bless Africa
UK : God Save the Queen
USA : The Star-Spangled Banner
Zimbabwe : Blessed be the country of Zimbabwe

IMMORTAL PAINTINGS AND SCULPTURES

Mona Lisa : It is world's most valuable painting, made by Leonardo da Vinci (1452-1519). It measures 30.5 by 20.9 inches (77 × 55 cm) and is now preserved in the Louvre. It is a portrait of a young women faintly smiling, believed to be Mona, wife of Francisco del

Giocondo of Florence or La Gioconda or mistress of Guiliamo de Medici. In 1517, it was purchased by Francis-I, the king of France, for 15.30 kg of gold.

Panorama of the Mississipi : World's largest painting made by John Banvard in 1846, showing the river in a strip, 1525 m. long and 3.65 m. wide.

Statue of Liberty : Situated on Bedloe Island in New York, it is a huge bronze statue of a woman facing the sea with a Tablet in her left hand and lighted Torch in her right hand. The Tablet bears the inscription 'July 4, 1776' the date of American independence. It is identical to a statue which still stands on the bank of river Seine in Paris. The New York version was designed by French sculptor Frederic Auguste Bartholi in 1886. It is 46 m. tall and stands on a pedestal of about similar height, making the total height as 93 m. from the ground level to the top of the torch.

THE SUPERLATIVES

(Highest/Longest/Largest/Tallest/Smallest etc.)

Airports Largest—King Fahd International Airport outside Riyadh (Saudi Arabia)
Highest—Daocheng Yading Airport, Tibet
Busiest—Harts field Jackson International Airport (Atlanta, USA)

Animals Tallest—Giraffe
Largest and Heaviest—Blue or Sulphur Bottom Whale
Largest Land Animal—African Bush Elephant
Fastest Land Animal—Cheetah

Bay Largest—Hudson Bay (northern Canada)

Bridge Highest—Near Khardungla, Ladakh at an altitude of 5600m.
Largest—Oakland Bridge, San Francisco (U.S.A.).
Busiest—Howrah Bridge on Hoogly River, Kolkata
Longest (river) —Mahatma Gandhi Setu on Ganga, Patna (5575 m.)
Longest steel arch—New River George Bridge in West Virginia U.S.A. (518.2 m.)

Building Tallest—Burj Khalifa, in Dubai.

Cathedral Largest—Cathedral Church of the Diocese of New York

Cemetery Largest—Ohlsdorf Cemetery, Hamburg, Germany

Church Largest—Beslica of St. Peter in the Vatican City, Rome

Continents Largest—Asia
Smallest—Australia

Countries Largest in Area—Russia
Smallest in Area—The Holy See

Dams Largest—Grand Coulee Dam, U.S.A. (1272 m.).
Highest—Rougunskaya, Tajikistan.

Day Longest—21 June.

Delta Largest—Sunderbans, created by The Ganges and Brahamaputra in India and Bangladesh

Desert Largest—The Sahara (north Africa)

Dome Largest—Louisiana Superdome, New Orleans, U.S.A.

Estuary Largest—Ob' in northern C.I.S.

Fountain Tallest—Fountain Hills, Arizona (the U.S.A.)

Glacier Largest—Siachen, Indo-Pak Border (75.6 Km long)

Gulf Largest—Gulf of Mexico

Hotel Largest—The Excalibur Hotel in Las Vegas Nevada (USA)
Highest—The Grand Hyatt, Shanghai (China) at 88th storey.

Island Largest—Greenland

Lakes Largest—Caspian Sea
Deepest—Lake Baikal, eastern Siberia, Russia
Largest—Freshwater-Lake Superior (North America)

Library Largest—United States Library of Congress, Washington D.C. USA

Minaret Tallest—Great Hassan II Mosque, Casablanca, Morocco
Tallest (free standing)—Qutub Minar, New Delhi (India)

Mosque Largest (Ruinous)—Al Mawiya Mosque of Mutawakkil in Smarra (Iraq)
Largest—Merdeka Mosque in Jakarta (Indonesia)

Mountains Highest Mountain Range—The Himalayas, Asia.

	Largest Mountain Range—The Andes, S. America.
	Highest Mountain Peak—Mt. Everest in the Himalayas, Nepal.
	Lowest Mountain—Bheinna Bhaile
Museums	Oldest—Ashmolean Museum, Oxford
	Largest—American Museum of Natural History, New York U.S.A
Ocean	Largest—Pacific Ocean
	Deepest—Pacific Ocean
Palace	Largest—Imperial Palace, Beijing, China
Park	Largest—National Park of Northeastern Greenland (9,72,000 sq. kms)
Peninsula	Largest—Arabia
Planets	Largest—Jupiter (1,42,984 kms Equatorial Diameter)
	Hottest—Venus
	Nearest to Sun—Mercury
	Nearest of Earth—Venus
	Brightest—Venus
Planet	Fastest—Mercury (1,72,248 km/h Revolution)
Plateau	Greatest—Tibetan Plateau in Central Asia (area 2,00,000 sq. kms)
Population	Most Populated Country—China
	Least Populated Country—The Holy See
	Most Populous City—Shanghai
	Most Densely Populated Territory—Portuguese Province of Macau.
	Most Sparsely Populated Territory-Antarctica
Post Office	Highest—Spiti valley at Hakkim in Himachal Pradesh (15,00 ft. above sea level)
Railway	Largest Railway Station—Grand Central Terminal, New York City, U.S.A. (19 hectares)
	Largest Railway Platform—Gorakhpur (Uttar Pradesh)
Religion	Oldest—Hinduism
	Largest—Christianity
River	Longest—Nile (6,690 kms long)
	Largest in volume—Amazon
Sea	Largest—South China Sea
Sea Port	Largest—Port of New York
Stadium	Starhove Stadium, Prague, Czechoslovakia
Star	Brightest—Sirius (Dog Star)
Statue	Tallest—Buddha's Statue (120 m.), Tokyo, Japan.
Straits	Largest—Tartar Straits (between Sakhalin Island and C.I.S. mainland)
	Broadest—Davis Straits (between Greenland and Baffu Island)
Structure	Tallest—Burj Khalifa (Dubai)
Telescope	Largest Reflector—Arizona, USA
	Largest—Radio Telescope at Khadod near Pune (India)
Temple	Largest—Angkor Wat in Kampuchea
Theatre	Oldest (indoor)—Teatro Olimpico, Vicenza, Italy
Tomb	Largest—First Emperor of China in Xianyang
Tower	Tallest—Tokyo Sky Tree, Japan 2080 ft
Trees	Largest—General Sharman Tree, California, U.S.A.
Tunnel	Longest (Railway)—Seikan Rail Tunnel, below the sea bed, Japan (53.85 km)
	Longest (Road)—Laerdal, Norway (24.51 km)
Volcano (Active)	Largest—Mouna Loa (Hawaii)
Wall	Longest—Great Wall of China
Waterfalls	Highest—Salto Angel Falls (Venezuela).
	Widest—Khone Falls (Laos)
Zoo	Largest—Etosha Reserve, Namibia (10 million hc.).

FIRSTS

First man in space	Yuri Gagarin (Russia)
First European invader on Indian soil	Alexander the Great
First President of U.S.A.	George Washington
First Indian in space	Rakesh Sharma
First Prime Minister of Britain	Robert Walpole
First woman Prime Minister of a country	Mrs. Bandaranaike (Sri Lanka)
First man to set foot on the moon	Neil A. Armstrong (U.S.A.)
First President of U.S.A. to visit India	D. Eisenhower
First British Prime Minister to visit India	Harold Macmillan
First Chinese pilgrim to visit India	Fahein
First European to visit China	Marco Polo
First Chairman of People's Republic of China	Mao Tse Tung
First President of Chinese Republic	Sun-yat Sen
First atom bomb dropped at	Hiroshima (Japan)
First woman in the Space	Valentina Tereshkova (U.S.S.R.)
First person to walk in the Space	Alexei Leonox (U.S.S.R.)
First and the only woman to have climbed Mt. Everest twice	Santosh Yadav (Mar 12, 1992 & May 10, 1993)
First person on Mt. Everest without Oxygen	Phu Dorjee (May 9, 1984)
First person to Climb Mt. Everest 10 times	Ang Rita (1983—1995)
First person to swim across English Channel	Mathew Webb
First woman to swim across English Channel	Gertrude Caroline Ederle
First aeroplane to fly round the world without refuelling	Voyager (Dec. 1986)
First test tube baby	Louise Brown (U.K.: 1978)
First woman President of the UN General Assembly	Vijayalakshmi Pandit (India: 1953)
First woman to reach the North Pole	Ann Bancroft (1986)
The first woman to conquer Mount Everest	Junko Tabei of Japan (May 16,1975)
The first man to climb Mount Everest	Sherpa Tenzing, (May 22, 1953)
The first Indian woman to climb Mount Everest	Bachchendri Pal
The first person to sail round the world	Magellan
The first person to reach the North Pole by overland journey	Robert Peary
The first person to reach the South Pole	Amundsen

INDIA GEOGRAPHY

Location : India is a large country; it accounts for about 2.4% of the total world area. It lies on the northern hemisphere between parallels of latitude 8°4' N and 37°6' and between meridians of longitude 68°7' E and 97°25' E. India is the seventh largest country of the world.

Dimensions:

Distance from north to south	3,214 km.
Distance from east to west	2,933 km.
Length of coastline	7,517 km.
Length of land frontier	15,200 km.
Total Area	32,87,263 Sq. km.

Boundaries : Great Himalayas stand on the northern border of India. Nepal, a small Himalayan country lies in the north. Bhutan, another small country, also lies in north east. Apart from these two, China is a large country, sharing a frontiers with India. On the western side of the northern border, Afghanistan touches Indian frontier and Pakistan shares a long border, with this country on the west of northern India. On the west of southern India is Arabian Sea. In south, lies Indian Ocean. Sri Lanka is an island country which is separated from India by the Gulf of Mannar and the Palk Strait, both being a part of the Indian Ocean. In the east is situated Bay of Bengal, which touches the southern side of the eastern frontier and also the southern part of eastern India. The rest of the eastern border, in the northern side, is shared by Myanmar (Burma) and Bangladesh which forms an enclave within India.

Extent : India, which is also officially called Bharat, is the seventh largest and the second most populous nation. It is bounded by the great Himalayas and other snowy mountains in the north. The country stretches southwards and at the Tropic of Cancer, narrows down and ends into the Indian Ocean between the Bay of Bengal on the east and the Arabian sea on the west.

Neighbours:

North : China, Nepal, Bhutan, Afghanistan
South : Sri Lanka
East : Myanmar (Burma), Bangladesh
West : Pakistan

Physical Geography : Geographically, India is divided into four physical zones.

(i) The Himalayan Range.
(ii) The Northern Plains
(iii) The Deccan Plateau
(iv) The Coastal Plains

The Himalayan Range : The Himalayas surround India, on the north, northwest and northeast. It extends about 2,400 kms, with a width, varying between 160 and 450 kms, while the height of the Himalayan mountains vary between 1,000 and 6,000 metres. The highest peak on the Indian side is K2. In the Himalayan belt lie the Kashmir valley, Kulu and Kangra areas. The foothills of the Himalayas are called Shivaliks.

The Northern Plains : The northern plains consists of the valleys of rivers, Ganga and Brahmaputra and their tributaries, with a length of about 2500 kms, and width varying between 400 and 600 kms. The plains make one-third of India's surface and are most fertile.

The Deccan Plateau : Beyond Vindhyachal mountain lies the Deccan Plateau, with an elevation, ranging between 500 and 1,300m above the sea level and a slope from west to east. It is walled by the Eastern and Western Ghats on both sides.

The Coastal Plains : The Coastal Plains are stretched along the sea shore on both sides of the Indian peninsula. The western plain comprises the Konkan and Malabar areas while the eastern plain is known as Coromandal.

The Mountains

North : The Himalayas
South : Vindhyachal, Satpura, Western Ghats, Eastern Ghats, Nilgiri
West : Aravali

The Rivers:

North : Himalayan System : Ganga, Indus and their tributaries

South : Deccan System : Narmada, Tapti, Mahanadi, Godavri, Krishna, Cauveri, Tungbhadra

The Ganga Basin : The Ganga basin, which is receiving waters from an area of about one-quarter of the total area of India, is the largest. Its boundaries are defined by the Himalayas in the north and the Vindhya mountain in the south. The Ganga has two main headwaters in the Himalayas—the Bhagirathi and the Alaknanda, the former rising from the Gangotri glacier at Gaumukh and the latter from a glacial spout of the Alkapuri glacier. A number of Himalayan rivers including the Yamuna, Ghaghra, Gomti, Gandak and Kosi join the Ganges. Yamuna which rises in the Yamnotri glacier and joins the the Ganges at Allahabad, is the westernmost river of the Ganges system. Of the rivers flowing to north from central India into the Yamuna or the Ganges, mention may be made of the Chambal, the Betwa and the Sone.

Peninsular River Basins : The Godavri river basin is the second largest in India. It covers an area of about 10 percent of the total area of India. The Brahamaputra basin in the east and the Indus basin in the west are of about the same size. The Krishna basin is the second largest in the peninsula. The basins of the Narmada in the Deccan flowing into the Arabian Sea and of the Cauveri in the far south flowing into the Bay of the Bengal are also of about the same size, though of different character and shape.

The two other river systems, though small but nevertheless agriculturally very important, are those of the Tapti in the north of Deccan and Periar in the south.

TOWNS AT RIVER BANKS

Town	River	Town	River
Agra	Yamuna	Kanpur	The Ganges
Allahabad	Confluence of the Ganges and the Yamuna	Kota	Chambal
		Kurnool	Tungbhadra
Ayodhya	Saryu	Lucknow	Gomti
Badrinath	The Ganges	Ludhiana	Sutlej
Kolkata	Hooghly	Nasik	Godavri
Cuttuck	Mahanadi	Pandharpur	Bhima
Delhi	Yamuna	Patna	The Ganges
Dibrugarh	Brahmaputra	Sambalpur	Mahanadi
Ferozepur	Satluj	Srinagar	Jhelum
Guwahati	Brahmaputra	Srirangapattam	Cauveri
Hardwar	The Ganges	Surat	Tapti
Hyderabad	Musi	Varanasi	The Ganges
Jabalpur	Narmada	Vijaywada	Krishna

RIVER, CITY AND STATE

River	City	State	River	City	State
Yamuna	Agra	Uttar Pradesh	Gomti	Lucknow	Uttar Pradesh
Sabarmati	Ahmedabad	Gujarat	Godavri	Nasik	Maharashtra
Hooghly	Kolkata	West Bengal	The Ganges	Patna	Bihar
Mahanadi	Cuttuck	Orissa	Jhelum	Srinagar	Jammu & Kashmir
Yamuna	Delhi	Delhi	Tapti	Surat	Gujarat
Brahmaputra	Guwahati	Assam	Cauveri	Tiruchirapalli	Tamil Nadu
Musi	Hyderabad	Andhra Pradesh	Krishna	Vijaywada	Andhra Pradesh

FAMOUS INDIAN PEAKS

Peak	Height in metres above Mean Sea Level		Peak	Height in metres above Mean Sea Level	
K2	8,611		Kamet	7,756	
Kanchen Junga	8,598		Saser Kangri	7,672	
Nanga Parbat	8,126		Skyang Kangri	7,544	In Pak-occupied territory
Gasher Brum	8,068	In Pak-occupied territory	Sia Kangri	7,544	In Pak-occupied territory
Broad Peak	8,047	In Pak-occupied territory	Chaukhamba (Badrinath Peak)	7,138	
Disteghil Sar	7,885	In Pak-occupied territory	Trishul West	7,138	
Masher Brum E	7,821		Nunkun	7,135	
Nanda Devi	7,817		Pauhunri	7,128	
Masher Brum W	7,806	In Pak-occupied territory	Kangto	7,090	
Rakaposhi	7,788	In Pak-occupied territory	Dunagiri	7,066	

ISLANDS

Andaman Nicobar : A cluster of 572 islands called Andaman and Nicobar is situated in the Bay of Bengal.

Lakshadweep : A cluster of 27 coral islands, with only 10 of them inhabited, is situated in the Arabian Sea, 300 kms away from Kerala coast.

CLIMATE

Seasons : India is a tropical country. The meteorological experts have recognised four seasons :

(i) Winter (December-March)
(ii) Summer (April-June)
(iii) Monsoon (July-September)
(iv) Retreating Monsoon (October-November)

Climatic Conditions : India can boast of a wide range of climatic conditions : Assam and Meghalaya have the highest rainfall, whereas Rajasthan is more or less a desert. However, Indo-Gangetic plain has an average rainfall. There is nothing like a winter season in south, while the northern hilly areas have no summer.

Coldest Region : Kargil and Dras in Ladakh (J&K) are the coldest areas in the country.

Hottest Region : Barmer in western Rajasthan is the hottest area.

Wettest Region : Cherapunji in Meghalaya is the wettest place. Mawyrnam, 10 kms away from Cherapunji receives the maximum amount of rainfall, in the world.

Driest Region : Jaisalmer in western Rajasthan is the driest place, with lowest rainfall.

Rainfall:

Regions of Heavy Rainfall : Assam, Arunachal, Meghalaya, Sikkim, northern parts of West Bengal, western Ghats and the Himalayan slopes.

Regions of Low Rainfall : Western Rajasthan, Kutch, southern Haryana, southeast Punjab and Ladakh.

CLIMATIC REGIONS

There are four broad climatic regions based on rainfall. Practically, the whole of Assam and west coast of India lying at the foot of the western Ghats and extending from the north of Mumbai to Thiruvananthapuram are the areas of very heavy rainfall. In contrast to these, the desert of Rajasthan extending to Kutch, and the high Ladakh plateau of Kashmir extending westwards to Gilgit are regions of low precipitation. In between these, there are areas of moderately high and low rainfall respectively. The former consists of a broad belt in the eastern part of the peninsula merging northward with the north Indian plains and southwards with coastal plains. The latter comprises a belt extending from the Punjab plains across the Vindhya mountains into the western part of the Deccan, widening considerably in the Mysore plateau.

Physical Characteristics : The mainland consists of four well-defined regions: *(i)* the great mountain zone; *(ii)* the Indo-Gangetic plains; *(iii)* the desert region; and *(iv)* the southern peninsula.

PEOPLE

POPULATION

Second Largest Nation : In terms of the size of population, India is the second largest country in the world, next only to China. China tops the list with 1.314 billion people. India's population constitutes nearly 17.5 percent of the total world population while her geographical area is only 2.42 per cent of the world area.

2011 CENSUS HIGHLIGHTS

Population of India—Total	:	1,21,05,69,573
Male	:	62,31,21,843
Females	:	58,74,47,730

Indian population is 17.5% of total world population.

Decadal Growth (2001-2011)	:	17.69 per cent (Males – 17.19 per cent) (Females – 18.12 per cent)
Highest Decadal Growth (State-wise)	:	Meghalaya (27.95 per cent)
Lowest Decadal Growth (State-wise)	:	Nagaland (–0.58 per cent)
Most populous State	:	Uttar Pradesh (16.5 per cent of National Population)
Density of population	:	382 persons per sq. km.
Most densely populated State	:	Bihar : 1106 per sq. km
Sex Ratio	:	943 females per 1000 males
Total Literacy Rate	:	73% (Males – 80.9%) (Females – 64.6%)
Highest Literacy (Statewise)	:	Kerala (94%)
Lowest Literacy (Statewise)	:	Bihar (61.8%)

OTHER DETAILS

(a) Population of India

1951	36,10,88,090
1961	43,92,34,771
1971	54,81,59,652
1981	68,38,10,951
1991	84,63,02,688
2001	102,70,15,247
2011	**1,21,05,69,573**

(b) Density of Population (Persons per square kilometre)

1951	113
1961	138
1971	177
1981	216
1991	267
2001	324
2011	**382**

(c) Annual Compound Rate of Growth

1941-1951	1.3 per cent
1951-1961	2.1 per cent
1961-1971	2.2 per cent
1971-1981	2.3 per cent
1981-1991	2.4 per cent
1991-2001	2.1 per cent
2001-2011	**1.69 per cent**

LANGUAGES

OFFICIAL LANGUAGE

According to Article 343 (1) of the Constitution, Hindi is the official language of the Union. But provision was also made in Article 343 (1) for continuing the use of English in official work for a period of

15 years *i.e.* up to 25th January 1965 from the date of commencement of the Constitution. Article 343 (3) empowered Parliament to provide by law for continued use of English for official purposes even after 25th January 1965. Accordingly, the official language Act, 1963 (amended in 1967) was passed for continuing the use of English in official work even after 25th January 1965.

PRINCIPAL LANGUAGES

The fact that as many as 1,652 languages and dialects are spoken in India is a proof of the country's amazing diversity. Broadly, these languages belong to the Indo-Aryan and Dravidian families of languages, though some Indo-European languages are also spoken and understood by some of the people in India.

Indo-Aryan Languages : The Indo-Aryan languages, including Hindi, Bihari, Rajasthani, Gujarati, Marathi, Bengali, Oriya, Assamese, Sanskrit, Kashmiri, Sindhi are spoken by three-fourth of India's population. Among these, Hindi alone is spoken by about 38 per cent of the Indians and understood by most of the inhabitants of northern India.

Dravidian Languages : The languages of the southern India, viz. Tamil, Telugu, Kannada and Malayalam, belong to the Dravidian family and bear little resemblance to Hindi except for some expression of Sanskrit, the language of the Hindu scriptures.

Indo-European Languages : Of the Indo-European languages, English is the most widely used one and is the common medium of instruction and learning in the institutions imparting higher education. Besides, it has emerged as the language of the elite under the British rule and continues to hold its sway in the large metropolitan cities. French and Portuguese languages are also used by some people in the erstwhile colonial territories of Pondicherry and Goa.

Austric Family : Spoken by the primitive tribes, inhabiting the hills and jungles of central and north-eastern India. The following are the Austric languages : (a) Kolor Munda group which includes Santhali; Mundari, Ho etc.; (b) Khasi in Assam; and (c) Nicobarese in Nicobar Islands.

Sino-Tibetan Family : Used by small tribes along the southern slopes of the Himalayas in north Bengal and Assam.

Major Languages : The Constitution of India recognises 22 major languages, which are specified in the Eighth Schedule of the Constitution. These are : Assamese, Bengali, Gujarati, Hindi, Kannada, Kashmiri, Konkani, Malayalam, Manipuri, Marathi, Nepali, Oriya, Punjabi, Sanskrit, Sindhi, Tamil, Telugu, Urdu, Bodo, Maithili, Santhali and Dogri. Hindi is the national and official language of India and English is an associate official language.

Linguistic States : The interstate boundaries of the Union of India were delineated on the linguistic basis with a view to bringing people, who speak the same language and the related dialects under one administration.

LANGUAGES OF THE STATES AND UNION TERRITORIES

S.No.	State	Official Language	S.No.	State	Official Language
1.	Andhra Pradesh	Telugu and Urdu	12.	Maharashtra	Marathi
2.	Asom	Assamese	13.	Karnataka	Kannada
3.	Bihar	Hindi and Urdu	14.	Nagaland	English
4.	Chhattisgarh	Hindi	15.	Odisha	Odiya
5.	Gujarat	Gujarati	16.	Punjab	Punjabi
6.	Haryana	Hindi	17.	Rajasthan	Hindi and Rajasthani
7.	Himachal Pradesh	Hindi and Pahari	18.	Tamil Nadu	Tamil
8.	Jammu and Kashmir	Urdu and Kashmiri	19.	Uttarakhand	Hindi
9.	Jharkhand	Hindi	20.	Uttar Pradesh	Hindi and Urdu
10.	Kerala	Malayalam	21.	West Bengal	Bengali
11.	Madhya Pradesh	Hindi	22.	Tripura	Bengali

S.No.	State	Official Language
23.	Manipur	Manipuri
24.	Meghalaya	Assamese and English
25.	Mizoram	Mizo and English
26.	Arunachal Pradesh	English
27.	Sikkim	Nepali and Bhutia
28.	Goa	Konkani and Marathi
29.	Telangana	Telugu, Urdu

Union Territories	Official Language
1. Andaman and Nicobar	English and Nicobarese
2. Chandigarh	Hindi and Punjabi
3. Dadra and Nagar Haveli	Gujarati
4. Delhi	Hindi, Punjabi and Urdu
5. Daman and Diu	Gujarati
6. Lakshadweep	Modified Malayalam and Mahi
7. Puducherry	Tamil and French

ART AND CULTURE

CINEMA

The first motion picture was shown in India in 1896 in Mumbai by the touring agent of a French Company. India's first cinema house was built in Kolkata in 1907.

The Beginning : Feature films found their place in India in 1912 when the first film 'Pundalik' was made by R.G. Torney and N.G. Chitre. This was followed by 'Raja Harishchandra' in 1913 by Dhundiraj Govind Phalke. The era of talkie films began in 1931, when the first talkie film 'Alam Ara' was produced by Ardsher Irani. These early films were followed by many Indian talkies which set the record of the production of 270 movies in 1931. The first coloured film in India was 'Kisan Kanya' – made in 1937 – and the first cinemascope film was 'Kagaz ke Phool' made by Guru Dutt in 1959. The first 3-D film was 'My dear Kuttichathan' (Malayalam) in 1984.

INDIAN DANCE

There are two main branches of Indian dance, namely, classical and folk. Classical dances are those which are based on ancient dance discipline and have rigid rules for presentation. Folk dances, which are also called tribal dances, are of various patterns.

The Leading Classical Dances at a Glance

Bharatnatyam : Originated in Tamil Nadu.

Kathakali : The dance-drama of Kerala.

Kathak : The principal classical dance of north India.

Kuchipudi : A dance-drama from Andhra Pradesh.

Manipuri : A delicate, lyrical style of dance from Manipur.

Odissi : A dance from Odisha.

Classical Dances

Kathak : This dance form originated in north India. It has its roots in 'Katha' meaning story. The story-tellers, who were attached to the temples in north India, narrated stories from the epic in the form of Radha and Krishna *Lilas*. With the advent of Muslim rule, it came out of the temples in the form of a sophisticated dance of the Mughal courts. Lucknow, Jaipur and Benaras became its centres. Wajid Ali Shah, the king of Lucknow patronised this dance form which drifted from a pure dance form into erotics. Binda Din Maharaj, Kalkadin, Achchhu Maharaj, Gopi Krishna and Birju Maharaj are some of the greatest exponents of Kathak.

Kuchipudi : It is a solo dance popular in Andhra Pradesh. It originated in a place called Kuchelapur. Tirtha Narayana and Siddendra Yogi evolved this style, traditionally performed by men attired like women. It has a style which corresponds with the Bhagvata Mela Natak of Tamil Nadu. Except for the emphasis on animations, it draws upon the principles of the Natya Shastra and in all other aspects, it is akin to Bharatnatyam. Vedantham Satyanarayana is the doyen of Kuchipudi. China Satyam is a renowned guru in this dance form.

Kathakali : This dance form is from Kerala which is more dramatic than narrative in form. It has its origin in the courts of the kings of Kerala and is considered to be the most scientific and elaborately defined dance form. The body gestures, head movements, eye movements and eyeball movements comprise its language. It is not a folk dance but is highly classical, though not very old. Poet Vallathol revived Kathakali in its present form.

Manipuri : Manipuri is a dance form, mostly ritualistic, popular in the Northeast. From 15th to 18th century, Vaishnavism came to be adopted and this ushered a new era in the development of this style. The ragas comprise five different types of ballets based on the Radha-Krishna-gopis theme. The other form of this dance is the Sankirtanas, usually performed by men carrying drums called Pung. It is a highly lyrical dance but lacks dramatic facial and gesture expressions.

Odissi : Odissi is a dance form developed in Orissa during second century B.C. when the king Kharvela ruled. He was himself an expert dancer. It is also based on the principles of Natya Shastra. Themes from Jayadeva's Gita Govinda, poems in the praise of Krishna, written around the 12th century, dominate the contents. First performed by women called maharis in the Jagnnath Temple and then by young boys attired as women called gopuas, Odissi is woven around the basic tribhanga pose typical of Indian sculpture. It has gained great popularity today and the credit goes to Smt. Sanjukta Panigrahi, who gave it a universal appeal. The name of Guru Kelucharan Mahapatra is at the forefront of Odissi.

Bharatnatyam : Bharatnatyam is poetry in motion. It is a solo dance originating from the temples of south India. It is based on the principles of Natya Shastra, written by the great sage, Bharata, around 4000 B.C. It is a highly traditional dance form performed to a repertory of carnatic music and comprises items such as the alarippu, varnam, padam, thillana and so on. Earlier, variedly known as Dasi Attam and Sadir, it was practised by devadasis in the south Indian temples. Its present form was evolved in Tanjore by Ponniah Pillai and brothers. Smt. Rukmani Devi gave it a new life and respectability. On par with her was T. Bala Saraswati, the queen of Bharatnatyam.

FOLK AND TRIBAL DANCES

Dance	State	Dance	State
Bidesia	Bihar, Jharkhand	Ghumar	Rajasthan
Bhangra	Punjab and Haryana (male)	Kayanga Bakayanga	Himachal Pradesh
Bihu	Assam (Asom)	Kottam	Andhra Pradesh
Chakri	Jammu and Kashmir	Lai Haroba	Manipur
Chiraw (Bamboo dance)	Mizoram	Lota	Madhya Pradesh, Chhattisgarh
Dandiya Raas	Rajasthan	Nautanki	Uttar Pradesh, Uttarakhand
Garba	Gujarat	Pandvani	Madhya Pradesh, Chhattisgarh
Chamar Gindad	Rajasthan	Tamasha	Maharashtra
Giddha	Punjab and Haryana (female)	Wangala Laho	Meghalaya

Names Associated with Music and Dance

Music (Vocal) : Begum Akhtar, Bade Gulam Ali Khan, Bhimsen Joshi, Balamurali Krishna, Pankaj Mullick, M.S. Subbulakshmi, Mallikarjuna Mansur, V.R. Patwardhan, Gangubai Hangal, V.D. Paluskar, Thyagarajan, Puranandaradasa, Omkarnatha Thakur, Jesudas, Mohammed Rafi, Lata Mangeshkar, Mukesh, Chembai Vaidyanthah Bhagavatar.

Instrumental Music : Bismillah Khan, Veena Dorai Swamy Iyengar, K.S. Manjunath, Palghat Mani Iyaer, Ravishankar, Ali Akbar Khan, Rahmat Khan, Pannalal Ghosh, Lalguid Jayaraman, R.K. Venkatarama Shastri, R.K. Surayanarayana, T. Chowdiah, R.R. Mahalingam, V.G. Jog.

Bharatnatyam : Yamini K. Krishna Murthy, U.S. Krishna Rao, Chandraprabha Devi, Komala Varadhan, P.C. Pillai, Vyjayanthi Mala, Padmini, Hema Malini.

Kathak : Birju Maharaj, Gopikrishna, Shambhu Maharaj, Sitaradevi, Damayanti Joshi.

Kathakali : Kunju Kurup, T.K. Chandi, Udaya Shankar.

MAJOR FESTIVALS

Festival	Month/Date	Areas Where Celebrated
Baisakhi	13th April	Punjab and Haryana
Basant Panchami	January/February	All over India
Buddha Jayanti	April-May	All over India
Christmas	25th December	All over India
Diwali	October/November	All over India
Dussehra	September/October	All over India
Easter	March/April	All over India
Gandhi Jayanti	2nd October	All over India
Good Friday	March/April	All over India
Guru Purb	October/November	All over India
Holi	February/March	All over India
Id-e-Milad	*	All over India
Id-ul-Fitr	*	All over India
Id-ul-Zuha	*	All over India
Independence Day	15th August	All over India
Janmashtami	August/September	All over India
Lohri	January	Punjab and Haryana
Mahavir Jayanti	March/April	All over India
Muharram	*	All over India
Nag Panchami	July/August	All over India
Navaratri	October/November	All over India
New Year's Day	1st January	All over India
Onam	August/September	Kerala
Pongal	January	Tamil Nadu and Andhra Pradesh
Raksha Bandhan	July/August	North and Western India
Ram Navami	March/April	Specially in UP
Republic Day	26th January	All over India
Shab-e-barat	*	All over India
Shivratri	February/March	All over India

Note: * These Muslim festivalls depend upon the sighting of moon, according to the lunar calendar.

SIGNIFICANT DAYS

Name of the Day	Date	Name of the Day	Date
Air Force Day	October 8	National Integration Day	October 31
Armed Forces Flag Day	December 7	National Maritime Day	April 5
Army Day	January 15	National Science Day	February 28
Children's Day	November 14	National Solidarity Day	May 13
Consumers' Day	March 15	National Sports Day	August 29
Flag Day	December 7	National Technology Day	May 11
Gandhi Jayanti	October 2	National Youth Day	January 12
Independence Day	August 15	Navy Day	December 4
Kisan's Day	December 23	Quit India Movement Day	August 8
Martyr's Day	January 30	Republic Day	January 26
		Teacher's Day	September 5

HIGH COURTS AND THEIR TERRITORIAL JURISDICTION

	Name of the High Court	Territorial Jurisdiction
1.	Allahabad	State of Uttar Pradesh
2.	Andhra Pradesh	State of Andhra Pradesh and Telangana
3.	Guwahati	States of Asom, Nagaland, Arunachal Pradesh and Mizoram.
4.	Bombay	State of Maharashtra, Union Territory of Dadra and Nagar Haveli
5.	Calcutta	State of West Bengal, Union Territory of Andaman and Nicobar Islands.
6.	Delhi	Delhi
7.	Gujarat	State of Gujarat
8.	Himachal Pradesh	State of Himachal Pradesh
9.	Jammu and Kashmir	State of Jammu and Kashmir
10.	Kerala	State of Kerala, Union Territory of Lakshadweep
11.	Madhya Pradesh	State of Madhya Pradesh
12.	Madras	State of Tamil Nadu and Union Territory of Puducherry
13.	Karnataka	State of Karnataka
14.	Orissa	State of Odisha
15.	Patna	State of Bihar
16.	Punjab & Haryana	State of Punjab and Haryana and Union Territory of Chandigarh
17.	Rajasthan	State of Rajasthan
18.	Sikkim	State of Sikkim
19.	Chhattisgarh	State of Chhattisgarh
20.	Jharkhand	State of Jharkhand
21.	Uttarakhand	State of Uttarakhand
22.	Manipur	State of Manipur
23.	Meghalaya	State of Meghalaya
24.	Tripura	State of Tripura

INDIAN CONSTITUTION

NATURE OF INDIAN CONSTITUTION

The Constitution of India provides for a Federal System of Government, though the term 'federation' has nowhere been used in the Constitution. For resolving the controversy regarding the nature of the Indian Federal System, it is desirable to understand as to what is implied by a federal System; what are its special features and how far these features are present in India.

Conclusion

The Indian Constitution outwardly possesses a federal structure, in spirit, it is unitary. The framers of the Constitution deliberately made the Centre strong in keeping with the inescapable realities of the situation.

IMPORTANT SOURCES OF THE CONSTITUTION

Source	Subject
Government of India Act, 1935	*(i)* Structural part (Administrative details). *(ii)* Union-State Relations. *(iii)* Emergency Provisions.

Source	Subject
American Constitution	*(i)* Fundamental Rights.
	(ii) Powerful Judiciary.
Irish Constitution	*(i)* Directive Principles of State Policy.
	(ii) Elected President in a Parliamentary form of Government.
British Constitution	*(i)* Cabinet Government.
	(ii) Relations between the Executive and the Legislature.
	(iii) Parliamentary Model.
Canadian Constitution	*(i)* Union-State Relations.
Australian Constitution	*(i)* Concurrent List.
	(ii) Trade and Commerce.
	(iii) Privileges of the members of Parliament and of the state Legislatures.
Constitution of German Reich.	*(i)* Emergency Provisions.

PREAMBLE TO INDIAN CONSTITUTION

The Preamble to the Indian Constitution reads thus:

"We, the people of India, having solemnly resolved to constitute India into a Sovereign, Socialist, Secular, Democratic Republic and to secure to all its citizens:

Justice, social, economic and political;

Liberty of thought, expression, belief, faith and worship;

Equality of status and of opportunity; and to promote among them all

Fraternity assuring the dignity of the individual and the unity and integrity of the Nation;

In our Constituent Assembly this twenty-sixth day of November, 1949, do hereby adopt, enact and give to ourselves this Constitution"

CITIZENSHIP

The Constitution of India provides for a single citizenship for the hole of India. It does not lay down a permanent law relating to the Indian citizenship but has left the matter entirely to legislation by Parliament. However, it lays down the classes of persons who would be deemed to be citizens of India at the commencement of the Constitution.

(1) Domicile
(2) Immigrants from Pakistan
(3) Migrants to Pakistan
(4) Residents in Foreign Countries

SALIENT FEATURES

(1) It makes India Sovereign, Socialist, Secular, Democratic Republic.
(2) It is designed to work as Federal Government in normal times and as a Unitary Government in an emergency.
(3) It establishes India as a Secular State
(4) It establishes a Parliamentary System of Government in India
(5) It introduces adult franchise and the system of Government in India
(6) India is a Union of 29 States and 7 Union Territories.
(7) It abolishes untouchability in India
(8) It guarantees Fundamental Rights to all citizens of India.
(9) It lays down Directive Principles of state Policy for the guidance of Legislature and the Executive of the country.
(10) It establishes independence of judiciary from the executive.
(11) It declares Hindi as the National language of India which would replace English as early as possible.
(12) A Union Public service Commission has been set up to make recruitment to various services.
(13) provision has been made for amending the constitution .

FUNDAMENTAL RIGHTS

Fundamental Rights are those rights which are essential for the growth of an indivjduals personality and are enjoyed by every citizen irrespective of caste, colour, creed , race and sex.

Indian Constitution guarantees the following Fundamental Rights:

(1) Right to Equality
(2) Right to Particular Freedoms
(3) Right against Exploitation
(4) Right to Freedom of religion
(5) Cultural and Educational Rights
(6) Right to Constitutional Remedies

Note: Right of Property is now a legal right under Arc. 300 A of the Constitution.

DIRECTIVE PRINCIPLES

These principles are embodied in Part IV of the Constitution. These are instructions or directives issued to the Legislature or the executive for day-to-day administration. These are based upon Irish Constitution. Some of the directive principles are:

(1) Adequate means of livelihood for all citizens.
(2) Fair distribution of wealth and material resources among all classes.
(3) Equal pay for equal work for men as well as women.
(4) To raise the standard of nutrition and standard of living of the people.
(5) To organize village panchayats and to endow them with such powers and authority as may be necessary to enable them to function as units of self-government.
(6) To secure just and humane conditions of work and maternity relief.
(7) To promote cottage industries on individual or co-operative basis in rural areas.
(8) To secure uniform code of law for all citizens throughout the territory of India.
(9) Free and compulsory education up to the age of 14 years.
(10) To safeguard and promote the educational and economic interests of the Scheduled Castes and Scheduled Tribes.
(11) To bring about the prohibition of consumption of intoxicating liquors.
(12) To organize agriculture and animal husbandry on modern and scientific lines and, in particular, prohibit slaughter of cows.
(13) To protect monuments of historical and national importance.
(14) To separate the judiciary from the executive.
(15) To promote international peace and security.
(16) Equal justice and free legal aid to economically backward classes.
(17) Participation of workers in management of organizations engaged in any industry.
(18) Protection and improvement of environment and safeguarding of forests and wildlife.

Differences between Fundamental Rights and Directive Principles

(1) Fundamental Rights are enforceable in the courts of law while Directive Principles cannot be enforced.
(2) While Fundamental Rights constitute limitations upon state action, the Directive Principles are in the nature of instructions to the Government to achieve certain ends by their decisions.
(3) Judiciary can declare any law void on the ground that it contravenes any of the Fundamental Rights, while the same is not in the case of Directive Principles.
(4) In the case of conflict between the Fundamental Rights and the Directive Principles, the former prevail.

FUNDAMENTAL DUTIES

These have been provided in Art. 51A [Part IV(A)] of the Constitution. According to these, it shall be the duty of every citizen of India:

(1) To abide by the Constitution and respect its ideals and institutions, the National Flag and the National Anthem.
(2) To cherish and follow the noble ideals which inspired our national struggle for freedom.
(3) To uphold and protect the sovereignty, unity and integrity of India.
(4) To defend the country and render national service when called upon to do so.
(5) To promote harmony and the spirit of common brotherhood against all the people of In-

dia transcending religious, linguistic and regional or sectional diversities, to renounce practices derogatory to the dignity of woman.

(6) To value and preserve the rich heritage of our composite culture.

(7) To protect and improve the natural environment including forests, lakes, rivers and wildlife, and to have compassion for living creatures.

(8) To develop the scientific temper, humanism and the spirit of inquiry and reform.

(9) To safeguard public property and to abjure violence.

(10) To strive towards excellence in all spheres of individual and collective activity so that the nation constantly rises to higher levels of endeavor and achievement.

(11) Every citizen to offer opportunities for education to his child the age of 6-14 years.

MACHINERY OF GOVERNMENT OF THE UNION THE EXECUTIVE

The Constitution provides for a parliamentary executive which consists of the President, the Vice-President and the Council of Ministers, with the Prime Minister at its head.

THE PRESIDENT

Election: The President is elected by an electoral college composed of elected members of both Houses of Parliament and elected members of State Legislative Assemblies by a system of proportional representation by means of a single transferable vote; the voting shall be by secret ballot.

Term of Office: The President holds office for a period of five years from the day on which he enters upon his office. He is eligible for re-election.

Qualifications for Election as President

(1) He should be a citizen of India. (2) He should not be less than 35 years of age. (3) He should be qualified for election as a member of Lok Sabha. (4) He should not hold any office of profit under the Government. (5) He should not be a member of either House of Parliament or State Legislature.

Salary and Allowances

The President is entitled to anofficial rent-free residence and draws a salary of Rs. 1,50,000 per month besides various allowances.

VICE-PRESIDENT

Method of Election

The Vice-President is elected by the members of both Houses of Parliament at a joint session by means of single transferable vote according to the system of proportional representation. Voting is by secret ballot.

Qualifications

(1) He must be a citizen of India. (2) He must not be less than 35 years of age. (3) He must be qualified to become a member of the Rajya Sabha. (4) He should not be holding any office of profit under the Government. (5) He should not be a member of either House of Parliament or State Legislature.

Terms of Office

The Vice-President holds office for a maximum period of five years and is eligible for re-election.

Functions

(1) The Vice-President is ex-officio Chairman of the Rajya Sabha.

(2) If there occurs any vacancy in the office of President by reason of his death, resignation or remova, then he acts as President till a new President is elected, subject to a maximum period of six months. During this period he ceases to be the Chairman of Rajya Sabha.

(3) He also acts as the President during the temporary absence of the President due to illness or any other cause.

Removal

The Vice-President can be removed from his office by a Resolution of the Rajya Sabha by a majority of its total membership and agreed to by the Lok Sabha by a simple majority.

COUNCIL OF MINISTERS

The Constitution provides for a Council of Ministers with a Prime Minister as its head to aid and advise the President in the exercise of his functions. The Prime Minister is appointed by the President.

The other Ministers are appointed by the President on the advice of the Prime Minister. The Council of Ministers is collectively responsible to the Lok Sabha under Art. 75(3) of the Constitution. The President is bound by the advice of Council of Ministers.

INDIAN PARLIAMENT

The Union Parliament consists of the President and two Houses - Lok Sabha and Rajya Sabha.

RAJYA SABHA

Composition

It consists of not more than 250 members, out of which 238 are elected and the remaining 12 nominated by the President for their special contribution to art, literature, science and social services. The elected members are chosen by the State Assemblies in accordance with the system of proportional representation by means of a single transferable vote. The allocation of seats among the States is not on the basis of equality of representation. In the case of Union Territories, members are chosen in such a manner as the Parliament by law determines. A candidate for election to the Council of States (Rajya Sabha) must be (i) a citizen of India; (ii) not less than 30 years of age; (iii) not holding any office of profit under the Government; and (iv) ordinarily a resident of the State from which he is contesting.

Duration

The Council of States is a permanent body, not subject to dissolution. The term of office for its members is six years, one-third of the members retiring after every second year.

Other Provisions

The Vice-President of India is ex-officio Chairman of the Council of States. The Council elects one of its members as Deputy Chairman, who presides over its meetings in the absence of the Vice-President. But whenever the Council is considering a Resolution for the removal of the Vice-President or the Deputy Chairman from his office, these officers shall not preside over the sitting of the House, nor can they vote on the resolution, though they are entitled to speak.

Powers and Functions

With regard to legislative powers, the authority of the Rajya Sabha is co-extensive with that of the Lok Sabha. No measure can become a law, unless it has been passed by the Rajya Sabha. It exercises control over the Union Administration by seeking information, by means of questions and supplementaries, by moving resolutions or motions of adjournment or censure. But it cannot oust the Ministry from office.

As regards the Money Bills, these cannot be introduced in the Council of States. Also when a Money Bill is passed by the Lok Sabha and transmitted to the Rajya Sabha, the latter can delay the Bill for 14 days. It cannot reject the Bill.

LOK SABHA

Composition

It consists of not more than 552 members, out of which 530 members are elected from States and not more than 20 members from the Union Territories and tribal areas. The representatives from the States are directly elected by the people on the basis of adult franchise. At present there are 543 elected members.

The representatives of the Union Territories are to be chosen in such manner as the Parliament may, by law, provide. The President can also nominate two Members to Lok Sabha to represent the Anglo-Indian community if, in his opinion, it is not adequately represented. *[Art. 331]*

A member for election to Lok Sabha must be (i) a citizen of India; (ii)not less than 25 years of age; and (iii) not holding any office of profit. The number of seats to each State is so allotted that the ratio between the members and population, as far as practicable, is the same for each State.

Tenure

Lok Sabha has a tenure of 5 years unless dissolved earlier. But while a Proclamation of Emergency under Art. 352 is in operation, this period may be extended for a period not exceeding one year at a time and not exceeding in any case beyond a period of six months after the proclamation has ceased to operate.

Disqualification of Members of Parliament

A person shall be disqualified for being chosen as, and for being, a member of either House of Parliament:

(i) if he holds any such office of profit under the Government of India or Government of State, as is declared by Parliament by law to disqualify its holder;

(ii) if he is of unsound mind and stands so declared by a competent court;

(iii) if he is an undischarged insolvent;

(iv) if he is not a citizen of India, or has voluntarily acquired citizenship of a foreign State; and

(v) if he is so disqualified by any law made by Parliament.

Powers and Functions of Parliament

(1) Its main function is to enact laws for the good government of the country. (2) It can pass a vote of No-confidence and thus dismiss the Government in power. (3) It controls the finances of the Union. (4) The members can elicit information by asking questions and supplimentaries. (5) The members can move adjournment motions and thus criticize the government. (6) It can impeach the President in case he violates the Constitution.

N.B.: Maximum Gap between two sessions of Parliament is 6 months under Art. 85(1).

THE SPEAKER

Election

The Speaker of the Lok Sabha is elected by the members of Lok Sabha by a simple majority. The term of his office is co-terminus with the life of the House itself.

Power and Functions

(1) He presides over the sitting of Lok Sabha and the joint session of Parliament. (2) He decides whether a particular Bill is a Money Bill or not and his decision is final. (3) He determines the order of the business in the House in consultation with the Leader of the House. (4) He decides about the admissibility of questions and Adjournment Motions, etc. (5) He appoints Chairmen of the Select Committees. (6) He maintains proper decorum in the House. He warns disorderly members and suspends them from sittings of the House, if any member flouts his authority.

Removal

The House of the People can remove the Speaker at any time by a resolution passed by the majority of the members of the time being. Such a resolution can be introduced in the House only after a notice has been given to that effect at least fourteen days in advance.

Powers of parliament

The privileges, powers and immunities of a House of Parliament are:

(i) that no court shall look into the validity of its proceedings;

(ii) no Officer or Member of Parliament is answerable to any court for exercise of the powers vested in him under the Constitution.

(iii) To make its own rules for regulating its procedure and business;

(iv) To regulate recruitment and conditions of service of persons appointed to the Secretariat of the House; and

(v) To punish any person for contempt of the House and breach of privileges of Members, Committees and the House.

SUPREME COURT

Appointment of judges

Every judge of the Supreme Court is appointed by the President by warrant under his hand and seal after consultation with such Judges of the Supreme Court and of the High Courts as the president may deem necessary for the purpose. In case of appointment of a judge, other than chief Justice, the Chief Justice of India is to be necessarily consulted. A Judge of the Supreme Court remains in office until he attains the age of 65 years. No person can be appointed a Judge of the Supreme Court unless (i) he is a citizen of India, (ii) has been for at least five years a Judge of High Court or has been for at least ten years an advocate of a High Court or two or more courts in succession, (iii) is in the opinion of the President a distinguished jurist.

Privileges of Judges

A Judge of the Supreme Court is entitled to such salaries as are specified in the Second Schedule. The Chief Justice get rupees 1,00,000 per month and other Judges rupees 90,000 per month. Besides, every Judge of the Supreme Court is entitled to the use of an official residence without rent. Also, every judge is entitled to such privileges and allowances and to such rights in respect of leave of absence and pension as may, from time to time, be determined by the Parliament.

Removal of Judges

A Judge of the Supreme Court can only be removed from office by an order of the president, Parliament, supported by a majority of not less than two-thirds of the members of that house present and voting. Has been presented to the President in the same session for such removal on the ground of proved misbehavior or incapacity. The parliament has been empowered to regulate the procedure for the presentation of an address and for the investigation and proof of the misbehavior or incapacity of a Judge under 124.

Composition

The Supreme Court is the highest court of justice in India. It consists of one chief justice and 30 other judges. Provision has also been madder for the appointment of ad hoc judges and even the retired judges may be at times, when the necessity arises, requested to be present.

Guardian of the Constitution

It is clear from the powers and functions of the Supreme Court that it is the ultimate interpreter of the Constitution and, as such, its guardian. The authority of the Court is further re-inforced by the provision that "the law declared by the Supreme Court shall be binding on all courts within the territory of India" (Art. 141). Further, in the exercise of its jurisdiction, the court is authorized to pass appropriate decrees or orders in the interests of complete justice in any case before it.

Independence of Judiciary

The independence and impartiality of the Supreme Court is the corner-stone of democracy. Justice is said to be blind and this must be so, especially in a democracy which professes all its citizens to be equal before law. Our Constitution ensures the independence of the Judiciary through the following measures:

(1) Though appointed by the President, a judge of the Supreme Court can only be removed after an address of each House of Parliament supported by a majority of the total membership of that House and by a majority of not less than 2/3 of the members present and voting and presented to the President on the ground of proved misbehaviour or incapacity.

(2) The salary and the conditions of service of a judge of the Supreme Court cannot be varied to his disadvantage after his appointment.

(3) After retirement, a judge of the Supreme Court cannot plead or act in any other Court or before any authority within the territory of India.

(4) The salaries, etc., of the judges and administrative expenses of the Supreme Court are chargeable on the Consolidated Fund of India and are, therefore, not votable.

HIGH COURTS

Appointment of Judges

A judge of the High Court is appointed by the Pesident by warrant under his hand and seal after consultation with the Chief Justice of India, the Governor of the State, and in the case of appointment of a judge other than Chief Justice, the Chief Justice of the High Court concerned. Provision has also been made for the attendance of the retired judges at sittings of the High Courts.

Qualifications

A person cannot be appointed a judge of a High Court unless:

(i) he is a citizen of India;

(ii) has for at least ten years held a judicial office in the territory of India; and

(iii) has for at least ten years been the advocate of a High Court or of two or more such Courts in succession.

Conditions of Services

A judge of a High Court holds office until he attains the age of 62 years. He may be removed form his office in the same manner in which a judge of the Supreme Court is removed (discussed earlier). The Chief Justice of a High Court gets a salary of Rs. 90,000 per month and any other judge Rs. 80,000 per month. Besides, every judge is entitled to such allowances and to such rights in respect of leave and pension as may from time to time be determined by the Parliamentary enactment. His allowances and other rights are not to be varied to his disadvantage after the appointment.

THE GOVERNOR

Appointment

The Governor of a State is appointed by the President. Only a citizen of India, who has completed 35 years of age, is eligible for appointment as a Governor. He need not be a resident of that State for appointment as Governor. He holds office during the pleasure of the President. Subject to this, he holds office for a period of five years. He receives a salary of Rs. 1,10,000 per month, and is entitled to certain other allowances and privileges.

Role of Governor

Ordinarily, the Governor has to act according to the wishes of the Council of Ministers. No other role can fit in well in a Parliamentary set up. It is only in the exercise of discretionary powers when he may ignore the wishes of the Ministers. Apart from the role of Governor as a Constitutional head of the State, the Constitution certainly visualizes another role on his part when he acts as the agent of the Centre. It is only, when so doing that the use of discretionary powers become relevant. When the administration of State is not carried on in accordance with the provisions of the Constitution, he is to report to the Centre. During President's Rule, he runs the administration directly with the help of the Advisers appointed by the Central Government.

STATE LEGISLATURE

In every State, the Legislature consists of the Governor and (a) in case of Andhra Pradesh, Telangana, Bihar, Maharashtra, Karnataka, U.P. and Jammu & Kashmir two Houses, namely, Legislative Council and Legislative Assembly and (b) in other States one House, viz., Legislative Assembly.

Legislative Assembly: It is a directly elected body on the basis of adult franchise. The total number of members of the Assembly shall in no case be more than 500 or less than 60. Its normal life is five years. A candidate for election to the Legislative Assembly of a State should be (i) a citizen of India; (ii) not less than 25 years of age; and (iii) not holding an office of profit under the Government.

Legislative Council

This is a permanent body. One-third of its members retire every second year. Its total members should not exceed one-third of the members of State Legislative Assembly. Its minimum strength is 40. Only Andhra Pradesh, Telangana U.P., Bihar, Maharashtra, Karnataka and Jammu & Kashmir have Legislative Councils.

DISTRIBUTION OF LEGISLATIVE POWERS BETWEEN THE UNION AND THE STATES

The Constitution of India makes a division of legislative powers between the Union and the States under Seventh Schedule. The Union Parliament has powers to make laws for the whole or any part of the territory of India, while the Legislature of a State can make laws for the State concerned. Also, like the Government of India Act, 1935, there is three-fold distribution of powers between the Union and the States:

(1) **Union List:** It includes 97 subjects over which the Union Parliament has exclusive power of Legislation such as Defence, Foreign Affairs, Banking, Currency, etc.

(2) **State List:** It comprises 66 items over which the State Legislatures have exclusive powers of Legislation, e.g., Health, Agriculture, etc.

(3) **Concurrent List:** It comprises 47 items on which the Union and the State Legislatures both can make laws, e.g., criminal law and procedure, marriages, economic planning, education, etc.

(4) **Residuary Powers:** According to Art. 248 of the Constitution, the residuary powers are vested in the Union Legislature, i.e., the Parliament have the exclusive right to make any law with regard to any matter not specified in the Concurrent or State List.

FINANCIAL RELATIONS BETWEEN THE UNION AND THE STATES

Ideally speaking, the best system of federal finance would be one which effected a clear-cut division of sources of the revenue between the Federal and the State Governments so as to make each of the parties financially independent of each other. Indian Constitution make elaborate provisions regarding the distribution of revenues between the Centre and the States. The financial relations between the Union and the States can be studied under the following heads:

(1) **Duties levied by the Union but Collected and Appropriated by the States:** Stamp duties and duties of excise on the medical and toilet preparations are levied by the Government of India, but collected and appropriated by the States within which such duties are leviable except in the Union Territories where they are collected by the Union Government. *[Art. 268]*

(2) **Taxes Levied and Collected by the Union but Assigned to the States within which they are Leviable:** (i) Succession duty in respect of property other than agriculture land; (ii) Estate duty in respect of property other than agricultural land; (iii) Terminal taxes on goods or passengers carried by railways, sea or air; (iv) Taxes on railway fares and freights; (v) Taxes on transactions in stock exchanges; (vi) Taxes on sale and purchase of newspapers, including advertisements published therein; (vii) Taxes on the sale and purchase of goods other than newspapers, where such purchase takes place in the course of inter-state trade or commerce. *[Art. 269]*

(3) **Taxes Levied and collected by the union and Distributed between the Union and the States:** Certain taxes are levied as well as collected by the Union, but their proceeds are divided between the Union and the States in a certain proportion in order to effect an equitable distribution of the financial resources. There are:
   (a) taxes on income other than agricultural income; and
   (b) excise duties as are included in the Union List, excepting medicinal and toilet preparations.

(4) **Surcharge:** The Parliament is, however, authorized to levy surcharge on the taxes mentioned at (2) above and on income-tax for the purpose of the Union.

(5) **Grants-in-Aid:** Parliament may make grants-in-aid from the Consolidated Fund of India to such States as are in need of assistance, particularly for the promotion of welfare of tribal areas, including special grant to Assam.

(6) **Loans:** The Union Government may make loan to any State or give guarantees with respect to loans raised by any States.

(7) **Previous Sanction of the President:** No Bill or amendment can be introduced or moved in either House of Parliament without the previous sanction of the President, if:
   (a) it imposes or varies any tax in which the States are interested; or
   (b) it varies the meaning of the expression "Agricultural Income" as defined in the Indian Income-Tax Act; or
   (c) it affects the principles on which money are distributed to the States; or
   (d) it imposes a surcharge on the State taxes for the purpose of the Union.

(8) According to Article 301, freedom of trade, commerce and intercourse throughout the territory of India is guaranteed, but the Parliament has the power to impose restrictions in public interest.

(9) Although taxes on income, other than agricultural income, are levied by the Union, yet the State Legislatures can levy taxes on profession, trade, etc., provided that the total amount of such taxes payable in respect of any one person should not exceed Rs. 2500 per month.

(10) Provision has been made for the constitution of a Finance Commission to recommend to the President certain measures for the distribution of financial resources between the Union and the States.

FINANCE COMMISSION

Constitution

Under Art. 280 of the Constitution, provision has been made for the Constitution of a Finance Commission within 2 years of the commencement of the Constitution and thereafter after expiration of every fifth year. It consists of a chairman and four other members appointed by the President.

Functions

It is the duty of the Commission to make recommendations to the President as to:

(i) the distribution between the Union and the States, the net proceeds of taxes, which are divisible between the Union and the States;

(ii) the principles, which should govern the grant-in-aid of revenues to the States out of the Consolidated Funds of India;

(iii) the measures needed to augment the Consolidated Fund of a State to supplement the resources of the Panchayats in the State on the basis of the recommendations made by the Finance Commission of the State;

(iv) the measures needed to augment the Consolidated Fund of a State to supplement the resources of Municipalities in the State on the basis of the Finance Commission of the State; and

(v) any other matter referred to the Commission by the President in the interest of sound Finance.

Report

The President shall cause the report of the Finance Commission with an explanatory memorandum as to the action taken thereon, to be laid before each House of Parliament.

UNION PUBLIC SERVICE COMMISSION

Constitution

The Union Public Service Commission consists of a Chairman and other members appointed by the President and they hold office for a period of 6 years from the date of their appointment.

Functions

The following are the main functions of the U.P.S.C.:

(1) To conduct examinations for appointment to the Services of the Union.

(2) If requested by two or more States, to assist those States in framing and operating the scheme of joint recruitment for services for which candidates possessing special qualifications are required.

(3) To serve all or any of the needs of a State with the approval of the President if requested by the Governor of a State.

(4) To advise the Union Government on:

(i) all matters relating to methods of recruitment to civil services and for civil posts;

(ii) the principles to be followed in making appointments to civil services and posts and in making promotions and transfers from one service to another;

(iii) suitability of candidates for such appointments, promotions or transfers;

(iv) all disciplinary matters affecting a person serving under the Government of India, including memorials or petitions relating thereto;

(v) any claim for the reimbursement of expenses incurred by a Government servant in defending legal proceedings against him for acts done in the execution of his duties;

(vi) any claim for the award of pension for injury sustained by a person while serving under the Govt. of India in a civil capacity; and

(vii) on any matter which the President may refer to the Commission.

ALL-INDIA SERVICES

Under Art. 312 of the Constitution, if the Rajya Sabha declared by resolution supported by not less than two-third of the members present and voting, that it is necessary or expedient to create an All-India Service, common to the Union and the States, Parliament may by law create such a service and regulate the recruitment and conditions of service of person appointed to any such service.

The Indian Administrative Service and Indian Police Service, which were in existence at the commencement of Constitution, are deemed to be All-India Services created by the Parliament.

The All-India Services Act was passed by Parliament in 1951 and detailed rules and regulations under the Act have since been promulgated. The recruitment to All-India Services, namely, I.A.S., I.F.S., I.P.S., etc., is made by the U.P.S.C. on the basis of a competitive examination supplemented by viva-voce test. The conditions of service of persons appointed to those services have since been regulated by an act of Parliament.

ATTORNEY-GENERAL OF INDIA

Appointment

The Attorney-General of India is appointed by the President under Article 76 of the Constitution. A person qualified to be a judge of the Supreme Court is appointed to such a post. He is the highest legal adviser to the Govt. of India and is consulted in all important cases. He also appears in the Supreme Court on behalf of the Govt. of India to conduct important cases.

Functions

The main functions of the Attorney-General are:

(i) to advise the Union Government in legal matters;

(ii) to perform such other legal duties, which may be assigned to him by the President; and

(iii) to discharge such other functions conferred on him by or under the Constitution or any other law for the time being in force.

Terms of Office

He holds office during the pleasure of the President and receives such remuneration as the President may determine.

Rights

In pursuance of his duties, the Attorney-General has the right of audience in all courts in the territory of India. He has also a right to speak or take part in proceedings in either House of Parliament or in the joint session of two Houses or any Committee of the Parliament. He cannot, however, vote.

COMPTROLLER AND AUDITOR-GENERAL

Functions

The comptroller and Auditor-general of India is appointed by the President. His main function are :

(i) to bring account the recipes and expenditure of the Union Government (except Railways, Defence Services and other ministries, the accounts of which are maintained by the departmental authorities);

(ii) to audit all expenditure from the revenues of the Union and states; and

(iii) to audit all trading manufacturing and Profit and Loss Accounts of stores and stocks, where the President may have required him to conduct such audit.

Independence of Audit

The independence of the Comptroller and Auditor-General has been sought to be ensured by the following provisions of the Constitution:

(1) Though appointed by the President, the Comptroller and Auditor-General of India can be removed from his office only after an address of each House of Parliament, supported by a majority of total membership of that House and not less than 2/3 of the members of the House present and voting, has been presented to the President on the grounds of (i) proved misbehaviour and (ii) incapacity.

(2) The salary and the conditions of service of the Comptroller and Auditor-General of India cannot be varied to his disadvantage after his appointment.

(3) He is not eligible for further appointment after his retirement, so that he may have no inducement to please the Executive of the Union or any State.

(4) The salaries, etc., of the Comptroller and Auditor-General and his staff are charged upon the Consolidated Fund of India and are thus non-votable.

(5) The reports of the Comptroller and Auditor-General relating to Accounts are submitted to the President who causes them to be laid before the Parliament.

ELECTION COMMISSION

Composition

It is a statutory body appointed under Article 324 of the Constitution. It consists of a Chief Election Commissioner and two other Election Commissioners. The Chief Election Commissioner is the Chairman of the Commission.

Functions

The main functions of the Election Commission are:

(i) to superintend, direct and control the preparation of electoral rolls for the elections;

(ii) to conduct all elections and by-elections to the Parliament and State Legislatures and elections to the offices of President and Vice-President;

(iii) to advise the President/ Governors regarding the disqualification of Members of Parliament or Members of State Legislatures; and

(iv) to examine the return of expenses filed by the candidates nominated to various elections, disqualify the defaulting candidates and their election agents and consider the representation of such of them as apply for the removal of their disqualification.

LANGUAGE

The official language of the Union is Hindi in Devnagari script and international form of Indian numerals is used for official purposes. For a period of fifteen years from the commencement of the Constitution, English was to continue for official purposes of the Union. If at the end of 15 years, Hindi was not able to replace English, Parliament could provide for the use of English for specific purposes. The Constitution also lays down that the legislature of a State may, by law, adopt any one or more of the languages for use in the State, but Hindi is to be used for all official purposes of the Union. The need for use of English in the proceedings of the Supreme Court, High Courts, etc., and in bills and enactments has been recognized.

The Official Language Act of 1967 has provided for the use of English indefinitely. It has been provided that the Centre will carry on the correspondence with non-Hindi-speaking States in English and with the Hindi-speaking States in Hindi.

Language Recognised in the Indian Constitution

According to the Eighth Schedule of the Indian Constitution, the following 22 languages have been recognized as regional languages:

(1) Assanese; (2) Bengali; (3) Gujarati; (4) Hindi; (5) Kannada; (6) Kashmiri; (7) Malayalam; (8) Marathi; (9) Oriya; (10) Punjabi; (11) Sanskrit; (12) Sindhi; (13) Tamil; (14) Telugu; (15) Urdu; (16) Gorkhali; (17) Manipuri; (18) Konkani; (19) Bodo; (20) Ogni; (21) Maithili and (22) Santhali.

The last three languages were introduced in the Constitution (71st Amendment) Bill, 1992.

ZONAL COUNCILS

Zonal Councils have been established by the States Reorganisation Act, 1956 to advise on matters of common interest to each of the five zones into which the territories of India has been divided - Northern, Southern, Eastern, Western and Central. These Zonal Councils do not owe their origin to the Constitution but to an Act of Parliament, having been introduced by the States Reorganisation Act, with a view to securing co-operation and co-ordination as between the States, the Union Territories and the Union, particularly in respect of economic and social development. If properly worked these Councils would thus foster the "federal sentiment" by resisting the separatist tendencies of linguism and provincialism. The zones covered by these councils are as under:

(i) The Central Zone, comprising the States of Uttar Pradesh, Madhya Pradesh, Uttarakhand and Chhattisgarh.

(ii) The Northern Zone, comprising the States of Haryana, Himachal Pradesh, Punjab, Rajasthan, Jammu & Kashmir and the Union Territories of Delhi and Chandigarh.

(iii) The Eastern Zone, comprising the States of Bihar, West Bengal, Orissa and Jharkhand.

(iv) The Western Zone, comprising the States of Gujarat, Maharashtra, Goa and the Union Territories of Dadra & Nagar Haveli, Daman and Diu.

(v) The Southern Zone, comprising the States of Andhra Pradesh, Karnataka, Tamil Nadu, Kerala, and the Union Territory of Pondicherry.

Besides these, there is the North Eastern Council set up in 1971, to deal with the common problems of

Assam, Meghalaya, Manipur, Nagaland, Sikkim, Tripura, Arunachal Pradesh and Mizoram.

Constitution

Each Zonal Council consists of the Chief Minister and two other Ministers of each of the States in the Zone and the Administrator in the case of a Union Territory. There is also provision for holding joint meetings of two or more Zonal Councils. The Union Home Minister has been nominated as the common Chairman of all the Zonal Councils.

Functions

The main functions of Zonal Councils are:

(a) to inquire into and advise upon disputes, which may arise among the States;

(b) to investigate and discuss subjects, in which some or all the States or Union and one or more States have common interest; and

(c) to make recommendations upon any such subject and, in particular, recommendations for better co-ordination of policy and action with respect to that subject.

Role

The Zonal Councils play multiplicity of roles in order to achieve

(i) an emotional integration of the people;

(ii) arresting the growth of acute state consciousness in the form of regionalism, linguism, etc.;

(iii) enabling the Centre and the States in economic and social matters for evolving the uniform policies;

(iv) co-operating with each other in speedy and successful execution of developmental plans; and

(v) securing some kind of political equilibrium between different regions of the country.

Importance

The importance of the Zonal Councils lies in the fact, they help to further co-ordination and integration through extra-constitutional advisory organization, without undermining the autonomy of States, thereby fostering the "federal sentiment" by resisting the separatist tendencies of linguism and provincialism.

NATIONAL FLAG

The National Flag of India consists of three horizontal bands - saffron, white and dark green with the Asoka Wheel (having 24 spokes) in dark blue colour in the centre of the white band; all strips being equal in width. It is rectangular in shape, the ratio of the length to breadth being 3:2. The emblem of the flag is an exact reproduction of the Dharma Chakra on the capitol of Asoka's pillar at Sarnath.

Symbolic Representation: According to Dr. S. Radhakrishnan, the saffron colour represents the spirit of renunciation, the white stands for truth and peace, and green signifies growth.

NATIONAL EMBLEM

The emblem of the Government of India is a reproduction of the Asoka's Pillar at Sarnath. It shows three standing lions at a base having a Dharma Chakra in the centre, a bull on the right and a horse to the left. The words "Satyameva Jayate" , taken from Mundaka Upanishad, meaning "Truth Alone Triumphs", are inscribed in Devnagari at the bottom.

MISCELLANEOUS

Public Interest Litigation (PIL)

Public Interest Litigation means that any member of the public can directly write and draw attention of the Court to some injustice being suffered by the member of the public. The PIL has its genesis in the Articles 32 and 226 of the Constitution. The impact of PIL can be seen from the degree of Court's intervention, which needless to say, is invariably based on the people's outcry for justice and quest for Fundamental Rights.

Suspension of Fundamental Rights

The Fundamental Rights guaranteed by the Constitution can be suspended during the National Emergency proclaimed by the President under Article 352. As soon as a proclamation is made, the State shall be freed from the limitations imposed by Article 19.

This means that the Legislature shall be competent to make any law and the Executive shall be at liberty to take any action, even though it contravenes or restricts the right of freedom of speech and expression, assembly, association, movement, residency, profession or occupation. The President may also by order declare that the right to move a court for the enforcement of any of Fundamental Rights shall remain suspended for the period during which the Proclamation remains in force (Article 359). This Order of the President shall, however, be laid before each House of Parliament and it will be within the competence of Parliament to disapprove of it. Articles 20-21, however, cannot be suspended by any Order under Article 359.

Lok Adalats

These were set up by Legal Services Authorities Act, 1987 as a legal forum for resolution of disputes through conciliatory methods. These Lok Adalats are the moving courts which are held in the different parts of the country for speedy disposal of the piling cases. Lok Adalat has now been given the status of a Civil Court and every award made by Lok Adalat is final and binding on all parties and no appeal lies before any court against its award. Pursuant to the decision taken at the First Annual Meet of the State Legal Services Authorities, permanent and continuous Lok Adalats are being set up in every district throughout the country. Efforts are on for establishment of separate Lok Adalat for different departments of the Governments and Public Sector Undertakings (PSUs).

Differentiate between State and National Party

State Party: To be recognized as a State Party, a party should secure at least 6 percent of total valid votes in the Parliamentary of State elections in the State or Union Territory. Alternatively, it should return at least one member to Lok Sabha for every 25 members elected from that State.

National Party: To be recognized as a National Party, a party which enjoys the status of a state party in at least four States or Union Territories would become eligible.

Significance of Article 17

Ans. Under Article 17, 'Untouchability' is abolished and its practice in any form is prohibited. The enforcement of any disability arising out of untouchability shall be an offence punishable in accordance with law.

National Literacy Mission (NLM)

It was launched in 1988. It aims at attaining functional literacy for 100 million persons in the age-group of 15-35 (including age-group 9-14 were Non-Formal education is not in operation) in a time-bound manner. The most important development has taken place under NLM is the near ascending of campaign made in adult education programme in the country.

Minorities Commission

Status: It was set up as a statutory Commission for Minorities in 1992.

Composition: It consists of a Chairman and six other members.

Functions: Its main functions are

(i) evaluation of the working of various safeguards for the minorities provided in the Constitution;

(ii) making recommendations for the effective implementation of safeguards for the protection of the interests of minorities by the Central Government or State Governments;

(iii) reviewing of implementation of policies pursued by the Union and State Governments;

(iv) looking into specific complaints regarding deprivation of rights and safeguards;

(v) making surveys and research;

(vi) suggesting appropriate and legal welfare measures in respect of any minority requiring special protection;

(vii) making periodic or special reports to the Central Government on any matter pertaining to the minorities and in particular difficulties confronted by them; and

(viii) making recommendations regarding any other matter referred to it by the Central Government.

THE GUARDS

PRESIDENTS OF INDIA

Name	Tenure
Dr. Rajendra Prasad	1950 - 1962
Dr. Sarvapalli Radhakrishnan	1962 - 1967
Dr. Zakir Husain	1967 - 1969
Varahagiri Venkata Giri	1969 - 1974
Fakhruddin Ali Ahmed	1974 - 1977
Neelam Sanjiva Reddy	1977 - 1982
Giani Zail Singh	1982 - 1987
R.Venkata Raman	1987 - 1992
Dr. Shankar Dayal Sharma	1992 - 1997
K.R. Narayanan	1997 - 2002
A.P.J. Abdul Kalam	2002 - 2007
Pratibha Patil	2007 - 2012
Pranab Mukherjee	2012 -

VICE-PRESIDENTS

Name	Tenure
Dr. Sarvapalli Radhakrishnan	1952 - 1962
Dr. Zakir Husain	1962 - 1967
Varahagiri Venkata Giri	1967 - 1969
Gopal Swarup Pathak	1969 - 1974
B.D. Jatti	1974 - 1979
Justice Mohammed Hidayatullah	1979 - 1984
R.Venkata Raman	1984 - 1987
Dr. Shankar Dayal Sharma	1987 - 1992
K.R. Narayanan	1992 - 1997
Krishan Kant	1997 - 2002
Bhairon Singh Shekhawat	2002 - 2007
Mohd. Hamid Ansari	2007 -

PRIME MINISTERS

Name	Tenure
Jawaharlal Nehru	1947 - 1964
Gulzari Lal Nanda (Acting)	1964 - 1964
Lal Bhadur Shastri	1964 - 1966
Gulzari Lal Nanda (Acting)	1966 - 1966
Indira Gandhi	1966 - 1977
Morarji Desai	1977 - 1979
Charan Singh	1979 - 1980
Indira Gandhi	1980 - 1984
Rajiv Gandhi	1984 - 1989
Vishwanath Pratap Singh	1989 - 1990
Chandra Shekhar	1990 - 1991
P.V. Narasimha Rao	1991 - 1996
Atal Behari Vajpayee	1996 - 1996
H.D. Deve Gowda	1996 - 1997
Inder Kumar Gujral	1997 - 1998
Atal Behari Vajpayee	1998 - 2004
Dr. Manmohan Singh	2004 - 2014
Narendra Modi	2014 -

CHIEF JUSTICES

Name	Tenure
Harilal J. Kania	1950 - 1951
M. Patanjali Sastri	1951 - 1954
Mehar Chand Mahajan	1954 - 1954
B.K. Mukherjee	1954 - 1956
S.R. Das	1956 - 1959
Bhuvaneshwar Prasad Sinha	1959 - 1964
P.B. Gajendragadkar	1964 - 1966
A.K. Sarkar	1966 - 1966
K. Subba Rao	1966 - 1967
K.N. Wanchoo	1967 - 1968
M. Hidayatullah	1968 - 1970
J.C. Shah	1970 - 1971
S.M. Sikri	1971 - 1973
A.N. Ray	1972 - 1977
M.H. Beg	1977 - 1978
Y.V. Chandrachud	1978 - 1985
P.N. Bhagwati	1985 - 1986
R.S. Pathak	1986 - 1989
E.S. Venkataramiah	1989 - 1989
Sabyasachi Mukerjee	1989 - 1990
Ranganath Mishra	1990 - 1991
K.N. Singh	1991 - 1991
M.H. Kania	1991 - 1992
Lalit Mohan Sharma	1992 - 1993
M.N. Venkatachaliah	1993 - 1994

Name	Tenure	Name	Tenure
A.M. Ahmadi	1994 - 1997	S. Rajendra Babu	2004 - 2004
J.S. Verma	1997 - 1998	R.C. Lahoti	2004 - 2005
M.M. Punchhi	1998 - 1998	Y.K. Sabharwal	2005 - 2007
A.S. Anand	1998 - 2001	K.G. Balakrishnan	2007 - 2010
S.P. Bharucha	2001 - 2002	S.H. Kapadia	2010 - 2013
B.N. Kirpal	2002 - 2002	P. Sathasivam	2013 - 2014
G.B. Patnayak	2002 - 2002	R.M. Lodha	2014 - 2014
V.N. Khare	2002 - 2004	H.L. Dattu	2014 -

CHIEF ELECTION COMMISSIONERS

Name	Tenure	Name	Tenure
Sukumar Sen	1950 - 1958	T.N. Seshan	1990 - 1996
K.V.K. Sundaram	1958 - 1967	M.S. Gill	1996 - 2001
S.P. Sen Verma	1967 - 1972	J. M. Lyngdoh	2001 - 2004
Dr. Nagendra Singh	1972 - 1973	T.S. Krishnamurthi	2004 - 2005
T. Swaminathan	1973 - 1977	B.B. Tandon	2005 - 2006
S.L. Shakdhar	1977 - 1982	N. Gopalaswami	2006 - 2009
R.K. Trivedi	1982 - 1985	Navin Chawla	2009 - 2010
R.K.S. Peri Sastri	1986 - 1990	Shahabuddin Yaqoob Quraishi	2010 - 2012
Mrs.V.S. Rama Devi	1990 - 1990	V.S. Sampath	2012 -

COMMANDERS-IN-CHIEF

Name	Tenure
General Sir Roy Bucher	1948- 1949
General (later Field Marshal) K.M.Cariappa	1949 - 1953
General Maharaj Rajendra Sinhji	1953 - 1955

CHIEFS OF ARMY STAFF

Name	Tenure
General Maharaja Rajendra Singhji	1955 - 1955
General V.P. Malik	1997 - 2000
General S. Padmanabhan	2000 - 2002
General N.C. Viz	2003 - 2005
General Joginder Jashwant Singh	2005 - 2007
General Deepak Kapoor	2007 - 2010
General Vijay Kumar Singh	2010 - 2012
General Bikram Singh	2012 - 2014
General Dalbir Singh Suhag	2014 -

CHIEFS OF AIR STAFF

Name	Tenure
Air Marshal Sir Thomas Elmhirst	1947 - 1950
Air Marshal Sir Ronald Lvelaw Chapnam	1950 - 1951
Air Marshal S. Mukherjee	1954 - 1960
Air Chief Marshal A.Y. Tipnis	1998 - 2001
Air Chief Marshal N. Krishna Swami	2001 - 2004
Air Chief Marshal S.P. Tyagi	2005 - 2007
Air Chief Marshal Fali H. Major	2007 - 2009
Air Chief Marshal Pradeep Vasant Naik	2009 - 2011
Air Chief Marshal Normen A. K. Brown	2011 - 2013
Air Chief Marshal Arup Raha	2013 -

CHIEFS OF NAVAL STAFF

Name	Tenure
Vice-Admiral R.D. Katari	1958 - 1962
Admiral Sushil Kumar	1998 - 2001
Admiral Madhavendra Singh	2001 - 2004
Admiral Arun Prakash	2004 - 2006
Admiral Sureesh Mehta	2006 - 2009
Admiral Nirmal Kumar Verma	2009 - 2012
Admiral D.K. Joshi	2012 - 2014
Admiral R.K. Dhowan	2014 -

FACT FILE

THE BREAKUP OF STATE-WISE LOK SABHA SEATS

State	Number of Seats	State	Number of Seats
Andhra Pradesh	25	Rajasthan	25
Arunachal Pradesh	2	Sikkim	1
Asom	14	Tamil Nadu	39
Bihar	40	Tripura	2
Goa	2	Uttar Pradesh	80
Gujarat	26	West Bengal	42
Haryana	10	Chhattisgarh	11
Himachal Pradesh	4	Jharkhand	14
Jammu and Kashmir	6	Uttarakhand	05
Karnataka	28	Telangana	17
Kerala	20	**Union Territories**	**No. of Seats**
Madhya Pradesh	29	Andaman and Nicobar	01
Maharashtra	48	Chandigarh	01
Manipur	2	Dadra and Nagar Haveli	01
Meghalaya	2	Daman and Diu	01
Mizoram	1	Delhi	07
Nagaland	1	Lakshadweep	01
Odisha	21	Puducherry	01
Punjab	13		

TOWNS, MONUMENTS, BUILDINGS AND PLACES OF INTEREST

Mt. Abu : Hill Station on the Aravali Range in Rajasthan; famous for Dilwara Jain Temples.

Agra : Historical place on the bank of Yamuna; famous for Taj Mahal.

Agha Khan Palace : In Pune, where Mahatma Gandhi with his wife Kasturba was kept interned; she died in this palace.

Ahmedabad : Industrial city of Gujarat; famous as a great cotton textile centre of India.

Ajmer : A sacred place for Muslims, famous for the Durgah of Hazrat Khwaja Moinuddin Chishti; Mayo college and a centre of Education.

Ajanta and Ellora Caves : Near Aurangabad famous for Buddhist cave temples, richly ornamented with sculptures and carved with paintings of exceptional skills.

Aliabet : First off-shore oil well, nearly 45 km from Bhavnagar in Gujarat.

Alipur : Near Kolkata, Government Mint, Zoological Garden.

Allahabad : Situated at the confluence of the Ganga, the Yamuna and the Saraswati (not visible) and a place of pilgrimage for Hindus. Kumbh fair is held here.

Amar Nath : A place of pilgrimage for Hindus, 45 km from Pahalgam, Kashmir.

Amritsar : Very old city of Punjab, founded by Guru Ram Das; a sacred place famous for Golden Temple; Jallianwala Bagh massacre occurred here on April 13, 1919; manufacturing centre of textile goods, woollen clothes etc.

Anand : Near Vadodara in Gujarat, famous for milk dairy, manufacturing Amul Butter, Amul Milk powder and other milk products.

Anand Bhawan : Residence of Pt. Motilal Nehru in Allahabad, donated to the nation.

Anandpur Sahib : A place of pilgrimage for the Sikhs in Punjab where Takht Keshgarh Sahib is located.

Ankleshwar : Oil struck here with the help of Russia and Romania. It feeds Koyali oil refineries in Gujarat.

Auroville : World's first International township near Pondicherry where people of all countries are able to live in peace and harmony irrespective of any caste and creed. It is named after saint Aurobindo Ghosh.

Ayodhya : Situated on the bank of river Saryu in Uttar Pradesh. It is the birth place of Lord Rama. A place of pilgrimage for Hindus for its famous Ram Janmbhumi Temple.

Badri Nath : Place of pilgrimage for Hindus near Gangotri Glacier.

Bengaluru : Capital of Karnataka, famous for silk manufacturing; Hindustan Aircraft Factory, Telephone Industries, Hindustan Electronics and Machine Tool Factories.

Banaras (Varanasi) : Seat of Hindu University, a holy place for the Hindus, famous for silk manufacturing and diesel locomotive engines.

Belur : Famous for a monastery founded by Swami Vivekanand and a centre of paper industry in West Bengal near Kolkata.

Bharatpur : Famous for its historic fort and Ghana Bird Sanctuary.

Bhopal : Capital city of Madhya Pradesh. It was in the news in December, 1984, when over 2,000 people died there due to leakage of poisonous gas Methyl Iso-Cynate from the Union Carbide Plant.

Bhubaneswar : Capital of Orissa, famous for Lingaraj Temple.

Bijapur (Karnataka) : Historical place, famous for Gol Gumbaj, the tomb of Mohammed Adil Shah and the ruins of palaces, mosques and tombs.

Birla Planetarium, Kolkata : India's first and world's second biggest planetarium.

Cherrapunji : In Meghalaya, the second heaviest rainfall (first Mawsynram) in the world nearly 1140.50 cm every year, occurs here.

Chandigarh : Union territory, beautiful city of modern style, capital of both Haryana and Punjab.

Chittranjan : Situated in West Bengal, famous for manufacturing of railway engines and locomotives works,.

Chittorgarh : Historical place, famous for its fortress, Victory Tower and Temple of Mirabai.

Corbett Park : A national park near Nainital in Uttarakhand.

Damanjodi : In Orissa. Located here is the Rs. 1,242 crore aluminium-cum-alumina complex, the largest in Asia.

Dandi : Located in Gujarat where Mahatma Gandhi launched Salt Satyagrah known as Dandi March in 1930.

Darjeeling : A beautiful hill station in West Bengal.

Delhi : Capital of India, seat of University, historical monuments, *i.e.,* Red Fort, Jama Masjid, the Qutub Minar, Rajghat, Shakti Sthal, Veer Bhumi, Shantivana, Vijayaghat and industrial centre of embroidery, ivory carving, earthenware and cotton manufacturing.

Dilwara Temples : Famous for Jain temples built in 11th to 13th centuries near Mount Abu in Rajasthan.

Dudhva National Park : It is a reserve forest for tigers in Uttar Pradesh.

Dum-Dum : Airport of international importance at Kolkata.

Durgapur (West Bengal) : A public sector steel plant is located here.

Dwarika : A sacred place for the Hindus in district Jamnagar, Gujarat. Lord Krishna ruled over Dwarika.

Eagle's Nest : Historic Fort at Raigarh in the Kolaba district in Maharashtra where Shivaji was crowned in 1674.

Fatehpur Sikri : Located at a distance of 33 km from Agra in U.P., it is famous for its historical buildings including Buland Darwaza, the highest gateway in India and the Durgah of Hazrat Sheikh Salim Chishti.

Gwalior : A historical place in Madhya Pradesh, famous for Tansen's tomb, Rani Laxmi Bai's chhatri, industrial centre for textiles, pottery and cement.

Haldia : In West Bengal, a port, a big oil refinery in public sector. It also has a lubricating plant and a fertilizer factory.

Halebid : Known for the famous temples built by Hoysala rulers of Dvarasamudra.

Haldighati : A place in Rajasthan near Udaipur where Maharana Pratap fought against Mughals.

Jaipur : Pink city of India, capital of Rajasthan, famous for Hawa Mahal, Jai Singh's observatory and Maharaja's palace, known for its pottery, marble embroidery and brassware works.

Jallianwala Bagh : Located in Amritsar, Punjab, was the scene of massacre of innocent Indians by General O'Dyer on April 13, 1919.

Jamshedpur : Important centre of iron and steel industry in Jharkhand, Tata Iron and Steel Factory has been set up here. National Metallurgical Institute is also located here.

Jog Falls : Located in Karnataka, these are one of the highest waterfalls in the world.

Junagarh : In Gujarat State, it is situated below the Girnar Hills, an ancient city of India, famous for temples having delicate paintings and architecture.

Kakrapara : It is the site of India's fifth atomic power plant on the banks of the Tapti about 86 km from Surat in Gujarat.

Kalpakkam : A fast breeder test reactor which went critical in October 1985 is located here in the State of Tamil Nadu.

Kanha National Park : In M.P., one of the finest places for seeing Indian swamp, deer, chital, hundreds of species of birds in this park.

Kapilvastu : An ancient kingdom of northern India and associated with Gautam Buddha.

Kaziranga : A games sanctuary in Assam.

Kedar Nath : A holy place of the Hindus in Garhwal district of Uttarakhand.

Khajuraho : In Madhya Pradesh, famous for Hindu Temples, carrying medieval sculptures.

Kodaikanal : A hill station in Tamil Nadu and famous for its Solar Physics observatory.

Konark : A town near Puri in Orissa, famous for Sun Temple called Black Pagoda.

Kovalam : Situated on the Malabar coast, 10 km from Thiruvananthapuram in Kerala has been developed as a beach resort.

Leh : A town in Ladakh (Jammu and Kashmir), ancient caravan centre for Central Asia, now developed as a military station.

Lothal : A place in Gujarat where remains of Indus Valley civilisation have been found.

Lucknow : Capital of U.P., a big military centre, known as the City of *nawabs* and gardens, known for historical monuments and tombs of sufi-saints like Shah Meena, a seat of learning and now a busy commercial centre.

Ludhiana (Punjab) : Famous for the manufacturing hosiery, cycle parts, sewing machine industry.

Chennai : A port and capital of Tamil Nadu, is the fourth largest city in India, known for cotton and leather industry, integral coach factory, a fertilizer factory, an old refinery and the headquarters of the Theosophical Society at Adyar.

Madurai (Tamil Nadu) : A centre of cotton textile, silk weaving and handloom fabrics, famous for Meenakshi Temple.

Mathura : A holy city of U.P. on the bank of river Yamuna, birth place of Lord Krishna, famous for Hindu Temples such as Temple of Dwarikadheesh and an oil refinery.

Mahabaleshwar : The principal hill station of Maharashtra.

Mahabalipuram : Located about 55 km south of Chennai and famous for its rock-cut Rath temples.

Mussoorie : A beautiful hill station in Uttarakhand.

Nagpur : A famous and historic town of Maharashtra, trading centre, textile mills and export of oranges.

Nalanda : Seat of famous ancient Nalanda University in Bihar.

Narora : It is the site of India's fourth atomic power station near Bulandshahar in Uttar Pradesh.

Nicobar : An island in Bay of Bengal; famous as a cocoa and timber producing centre.

Panipat (Haryana) : Scene of three successive important historic battles, *i.e.,* 1526, 1556, 1761. Famous for the Durgah of Hazrat Bu Ali Shah.

Panna : In M.P., famous for diamond mines.

Parasnath : A place of pilgrimage for Jains in Bihar and associated with Jain Tirthanakars.

Patliputra : An ancient historical town, now known as Patna, the capital of Bihar.

Plassey : Situated in West Bengal and the scene of famous battle between Clive and Siraj-ud-Daula in 1757 which paved the way for the British rule in India.

Pokharan : It is in Rajasthan desert, about 150 km from the Pakistan border, between Jodhpur and Jaisalmer. India's underground nuclear tests were carried out here.

Pudducherry : The first Union Territory to achieve full literacy situated on India's eastern coast and famous for Aurbindo Ashram.

Porbandar : Birth place of Mahatma Gandhi in Gujarat.

Port Blair : Capital of the Union Territory of Andaman and Nicobar Islands. A Naval air station is located here.

Pragiyotishpuram : The site of the new capital of Assam near Guwahati, known for rice production and a military centre.

Puri : In Orissa, famous for the Jagannath Temple.

Pusa : Agricultural Research Centre in Bihar and in Delhi also.

Pushkar : Famous for ancient temple of Brahma near Ajmer in Rajasthan.

Rajgir : Near Patna in Bihar, place of pilgrimage for the Buddhists.

Rameshwaram : In Tamil Nadu, a sacred place of river, Hindu pilgrimage, situated on an island in the Palk Strait, famous for a large ancient temple with long corridors.

Ranchi : A popular hill station in Jharkhand, seat of Heavy Machine Tools and the Heavy Engineering Corporation Ltd.

Ramgarh Lake : About 30 km from Jaipur, Rajasthan; a lake has been built by construction of a dam on Banganga.

Rana Pratap Sagar : Known for its atomic power station in Rajasthan.

Ranthambhor (Rajasthan) : A historical fort near Sawai Madhopur, conquered by Akbar from the Rajputs, famous for Ganesh temple inside the fort.

Rishikesh : A religious place near Haridwar on the banks of Ganga in Uttarakhand, centre of an antibiotics factory.

Sabarmati : Situated near Ahmedabad in Gujarat, famous Ashram of Mahatma Gandhi.

Sambhar Lake : A salt water lake in Rajasthan.

Sanchi : Famous for the largest *stupas* of Ashoka. It is an important Buddhist pilgrimage centre situated near Bhopal in Madhya Pradesh.

Sarnath : Situated near Varanasi in U.P., famous for Buddhist temples. Lord Buddha preached his first sermon in the Deer Park of Sarnath.

Sewagram : It is a village near Wardha where Mahatma Gandhi lived.

Shantiniketan : Also known as Vishwa Bharati, situated near Kolkata, founded by Rabindra Nath Tagore.

Shillong : Capital of Meghalaya and a beautiful hill station.

Shivpuri : Famous for a National Park and an international tourist resort 72 miles away from Gwalior in M.P.

Shimla : A clean, beautiful health resort and the capital of Himachal Pradesh. Also an important military station.

Shravanabelagola : A place of pilgrimage for Jains, having 57.5 feet high monolithic granite statue of Lord Bahubali, Gomateshwara in Karnataka.

Sivakasi : Famous for matches and cracker factories in Ramanathpuram district in Tamil Nadu.

Somnath : Famous for its temple situated in the extreme south of Kathiawar.

Srinagar : Capital of Jammu & Kashmir, situated on the bank of river Jhelum, a great tourist centre, famous for its natural scenery, gardens, fruits, springs, Dal Lake, etc. Wood work, shawl and rugs, carpet weaving, HMT watch factory etc. are the main industries.

Sriharikota : In the Vellor district on the Andhra coasts, it is the India's Satellite Launching Centre.

Taj Mahal : It is a world famous white marble mausoleum on the banks of the river Yamuna at Agra, Uttar Pradesh.

Tanjore : In Tamil Nadu, famous for a museum, temples and library. Shri Brihadeshwara temple here is known throughout the world for its massive architectural excellence.

Taxila : Known for the famous ancient Buddhist university near Rawalpindi (now in Pakistan).

Tarapore : Near Mumbai and known for Atomic Energy plant.

Thumba : India's main space centre and famous for Thumba Equatorial Rocket Launching Station, near Thiruvananthapuram in Kerala.

Tin Bigha : It is a 187 × 85 metre corridor which was leased out to Bangladesh on June 26, 1992 in tune with a 1974 agreement between India and Bangladesh. The corridor links Bangladesh mainland with its enclaves Dahagram and Angrapota inside Indian territory.

Tirupati : Famous for the Sri Venkateshwara temple in Andhra Pradesh.

Titagarh : Famous as a paper manufacturing centre in West Bengal.

Trombay : Centre of two oil refineries, Bharat Refineries, Hindustan Petroleum and two atomic reactors. It is an island of Mumbai, a fertilizer factory has also been set up here.

Triveni : In Allahabad, a confluence of the Ganges, the Yamuna and the mythical Saraswati. A famous place of pilgrimage for Hindus.

Udaipur : It is famous as the city of lakes with island palaces, tourist centre, has a cement factory and is a former princely State of Rajasthan.

Ujjain : An ancient city of India, in Madhya Pradesh, popularly known as centre of knowledge, famous for its temples, Hindu pilgrims visit this place. It was the capital of King Vikramaditya.

Vadodara : Situated in Gujarat and famous for Lakshmi Vilas Palace.

Vaishali : Situated in Bihar, it was the capital of the famous Vaishali clan during ancient times.

Victory Tower : Located in Chittor, Rajasthan, was built by Rana Kumbha to commemorate his victory.

Vishakhapatnam : Situated on the eastern coast of India in Andhra Pradesh, famous for shipbuilding industry, a fertilizer factory and an oil refinery.

Vivekanand Rock : Situated near Kanya Kumari at the Southern tip of India's coastline, it has been so named after the memory of Swami Vivekanand.

Victoria Memorial : An art gallery in Kolkata.

Vrindavan Gardens : Beautiful gardens at Bangalore, Karnataka.

Wardha : In Maharashtra, centre of cotton trade, Mahatma Gandhi lived here for several years and Wardha System of Education was evolved here.

SUPERLATIVES

Airfield—Highest : Chushul air-field in Ladakh.

Airport—Highest Altitude : Leh airport in Ladakh.

Airport—Busiest : Mumbai airports (Sahar International and Santa Cruz).

Award—Highest : Bharat Ratna.

Award for gallantry—Highest : Param Vir Chakra.

Auditorium—Largest : Sri Shanmukhananda Hall, Mumbai having a seating capacity of 3,012 persons.

Bridge Longest—Railway : Dehri on Sone; 3,065 m.

Bridge Longest—Sea : Annai Indira Gandhi Bridge, connecting Island Rameshwaram with Mandapam (Tamil Nadu), 2.34 kms.

Bridge—Biggest Cantilever : Rabindra Setu (Howrah Bridge) on Hooghly river, 457 m.

Canal—Longest : Indira Gandhi Canal in Rajasthan 959 kms long.

Chimney—Tallest : At Thermal Power Station of Tata Electric Company, Mumbai, 275 m. high.

Church—Biggest: The St. Cathedral at Old Goa.

Cinema—largest : "Thangam" in Madurai (Tamil Nadu); 3563 Seats.

City—Largest : Mumbai.

Corridor—Largest : Corridor in Ramanathaswamy temple at Remeshwaram in Tamil Nadu (1,220 m).

Dam—Largest : Hirakud Dam, Orissa 25.4 km long.

Dam—Highest : Bhakra Dam, Himachal Pradesh, 518 m high.

Delta—Largest : Sunderbans.

Desert—Biggest : Thar Desert.

Dome—Largest : Gol Gumbad, Bijapur, Karnataka 42 m diameter.

Gateway—Highest : Buland Darwaza in Fatehpur Sikri (U.P.); 53.3 m. high .

Gurudwara—Largest : Golden Temple, Amritsar.

Highway—Longest : NH-7, connecting UP to Tamil Nadu; 2,369 kms.

Lake—Largest : Lake Wular, Kashmir.

Minaret (Tower)—Tallest : Qutub Minar Delhi; 884 m high.

Mosque—Largest : Jama Masjid, Delhi, 9,292 sq. m area. Another large mosque, known as Tajul Masajid has been constructed at Bhopal.

Mountain Peak—Highest : K2 8,611 m. high. .

Museum—Largest : Indian Museum, Kolkata.

Planetarium—Largest : Birla planetarium at Kolkata.

Railway Platform—Longest : Gorakhpur (Uttar Pradesh).

Railway Station—Highest : Ghoom, Darjeeling 2,258 m high.

Rail Tunnel—Longest : Qazigund to Banihal (Jammu & Kashmir)

Rainfall—Heaviest : Mawsynram (Meghalaya).

River Bridge—Longest : Mahatma Gandhi Setu over Ganga, near Patna (Bihar).

River—Longest : The Ganges; 2,510 kms.

Road—Highest : Road at Khardungla in the Leh–Manali sector.

Road—Longest : Sher Shah Suri Marg (G.T. Road).

Route of a Daily Train—Longest : Kerala Express between New Delhi and Thiruvananthapuram (3,054 kms).

State—Smallest in Area : Goa.

State—Most Populated : Uttar Pradesh.

State—Least Populated : Sikkim.

State—Most Densely Populated : Bihar.

State—Least Densely Populated : Arunachal Pradesh.

State—Most Literate : Kerala.

State—Most Literate (women) : Kerala.

State with the Largest Area under Forest : Madhya Pradesh.

State Largest : Rajasthan.

Statue—Largest : Statue of Risabhnath (MP 84 feet).

Tallest TV Tower : Pitampura TV tower, New Delhi; 235 m. high.

Ramgarh TV tower in Jaisalmer district, on the Indo-Pakistan border to be India's tallest TV tower, touching a height of 300 metres.

Temple—Tallest : Sri Ranganathaswamy temple at Srirangam; 72 m high.

Temple—Biggest Cave : Ellora temple, Aurangabad, Maharashtra.

Tunnel—Longest (Road) : Jawahar Tunnel, Banihal Pass (Jammu and Kashmir).

Union Territory—Most Densely Populated : Delhi.

Waterfall—Highest : Gersoppa Waterfall (Jog) in Mysore: 292 m high.

Zoo—Largest : Zoological Gardens, Kolkata.

THE FIRSTS

MEN:

First to win Nobel Prize in Physics : C.V. Raman (1930)

First Cosmonaut : Sqn. Ldr. Rakesh Sharma (1984)

First to swim across the English Channel : Mihir Sen (1958)

First to conquer Mt. Everest : Sherpa Tenzing (1953)

First man to Climb Mt. Everest twice : Nawang Gombu

First Speaker, Lok Sabha : G. V. Mavalankar (1952-57)

First Deputy Speaker, Lok Sabha : Ananthasayanam Ayyangar (1952)

First President of India : Dr Rajendra Prasad (1950-62)

First British Governor General of Free India : Lord Mountbatten (1947-48)

First Viceroy of India : Lord Canning

Last Viceroy of India : Lord Mountbatten

First Field Marshal : S.H.F.J. Manekshaw (1971)

First Chief of the Air Staff : Air Marshal Sir Thomas Elmhrst (1947-50)

First Chief of the Naval Staff : Vice Admiral R. D. Katari (1958-62)

First Pilot : J. R. D. Tata (1929)

First to reach South Pole : Col. J. K. Bajaj (1989)

First to Circumnavigate : Col. T. P. S. Chowdhury (1985)

First to reach Antarctica : Lt. Ram Charan (1960)

First to win Nobel Prize : Rabindra Nath Tagore (1913 in Literature)

First and the last Indian Governor General : C. Rajagopalachari (1948-49)

First President of Indian National Congress : W. C. Bannerjee (1885)

First in the ICS : Satyendranath Tagore

First Bar-at-Law : Gnanendra Mohan Tagore (1862)

First High Court Judge : Shambhunath Pandit (Calcutta, 1863)

First Chief Justice of India : Justice Harilal Kania (1950-51)

First Indian Commander-in-Chief : Gen.(now Field Marshal) K.M. Cariappa (1949-53)

First to scale Mount Everest without Oxygen: Phu Dorjee (1984)

WOMEN:

First and the only Muslim to sit on the Delhi Throne: Razia Sultan (1236)

First to swim across the English Channel : Miss Aarti Saha (now Mrs. Aarti Gupta)

First doctor : Anandi Bai Joshi (Graduated from America in 1890's)

First to climb Everest twice : Santosh Yadav

World's youngest woman (19 years) to scale Mt. Everest : Dicky Dolma (May, 1993)

President of UN : Vijayalakshmi Pandit (1953)

First Chief Justice : Justice Leila Seth (HP, 1991)

First judge of the Supreme Court : Fatima Beevi (1989)

First advocate : Camelia Sorabji (Allahabad, 1923)

First judge : Anna Chandy (1949) District and Sessions Judge, (1959) Judge Kerala High Court.

First IPS officer : Kiran Bedi (1972)

First pilot : Prem Mathur (1947-48)

First ambassador : Vijayalakshmi Pandit (1947-49) Former USSR

First Woman Indian National Congress president : Annie Besant (1917)

First IAS officer : Anna Rajam George (1950)

First Governor of a state : Sarojini Naidu

First union minister of cabinet rank : Rajkumari Amrit Kaur

First to win Sena Medal : Bimal Devi (CRPF, 1990)

First to win Nobel Prize : Mother Teresa (1979)

First to become 'Miss World' : Reita Faria

First to win Miss Universe title : Sushmita Sen (1994)

First Speaker of a state assembly : Shanno Devi

First to scale Mount Everest : Bachendri Pal (1984)

First Woman President : Pratibha Patil (2007)

OTHER FIRSTS:

First Talkie Movie : 'Alam Ara' directed by Ardsher Irani in 1931.

First Colour Movie : 'Kisan Kanya' made in 1937.

First Technicolour Movie : 'Aan' made in 1952, directed by Mahboob Khan.

First Black and White Cinemascope Film : 'Kaagaz Ke Phool' made in 1957.

First Coloured Cinemascope Film : 'Pyar ki Pyas' made in 1961.

First Satellite : ' Aryabhat' launched in 1975. First indigenously built satellite-INSAT-2A launched in July 1992.

First Atomic Device : Exploded on May 18, 1974 at Pokharan in Rajasthan.

First Large Scale Nuclear Reactor : 'Apsara' was put into operation on August 4, 1956.

First Hydroelectric Station : Set up at Darjeeling in 1898.

First Test Tube Baby : Baby Harsha born in 1986.

First Test Tube Buffalo : At National Dairy Research Institute, Karnal, born in 1990 (first in the world also).

First Family Planning Clinic : Opened at Mumbai in 1925 (also first in the world)

First Indigenously Designed and Built Missile : 'Prithvi', launched in 1988.

First Antarctic Expedition : December 1981/January 1982, by a team headed by Dr. S. Zahoor Qasim, Department of Ocean Development.

Railway Train-First : From Mumbai to Thane, a distance of 34 kms.

First Superfast Train : Rajdhani Express between New Delhi and Howrah

First Double Decker : Sinhagarh Express between Mumbai and Pune

NICK NAMES

Lok Nayak, J. P.	Jaya Prakash Narain
Badshah Khan, Frontier Ghandhi or Red Shirt Leader	Khan Abdul Ghaffar Khan
'C.R.'	Chakravarti Rajagopalachari
Mahamana	Pt. Madan Mohan Malviya
Gurudev	Rabindranath Tagore
Grand Old Man of India	Dadabhai Nauroji
Desh Bandhu	C. R. Das
Lion of Punjab	Lala Lajpat Rai
Andhra Kesari	T. Prakasan
Pal	Bipin Chandra Pal
Lal-Bal-Pal	Lala Lajpat Rai, Bal Gangadhar Tilak, Bipin Chandra Pal
Bapu	Mahatma Gandhi

Father of the Nation	Mahatma Gandhi
Netaji	Subhash Chandra Bose
Iron Man of India	Sardar Patel
Chacha ji	Jawaharlal Nehru
T. T. K.	T. T. Krishnamachari
Tiger of Mysore	Tipu Sultan
Anna	C.N. Annadurai
Apostle of Free Trade	Richard Cobden
Bangabandhu	Seikh Mujibur Rehman
Bard of Avon	W. Shakespeare
Deenbandhu	C.F. Andrews
Desert Fox	General Rommel
Deuce	Mussolini
Enlightened one, the	Gautam Buddha
Father of English Poetry	Geaffery Chaucer
Fuehrer	Adolf Hitler
G.B.S.	George Bernard Shaw
Grand Old Man of Britain	Gladstone
Guruji	M.S. Golwalkar
Great Commoner	Pitt, the younger
Ike	D. Eisenhower
Iron Duke, The	Duke of Wellington
Kuvempu	K.V. Puttappa
J.P.	Jaya Prakash Narayan
James Bond of the South	Jayashankar (Tamil Actor)
Lady with the Lamp	Florence Nightingale
Liskwan	Pearl Buck
Little Corporal	Napoleon
Lokmanya	Bal Gangadhar Tilak
Man of Destiny	Napoleon
Maiden Queen	Elizabeth I
Man of Blood and Iron	Bismarck
Man of Peace	Lal Bahadur Shastri
Man of Orleans	Joan of Arc
Mark Twain	Samuel Clemens
M.G.R.	M.G. Ramchandran
Nightingale of India	Sarojini Naidu
Quaide Azam	Mohammad Ali Jinnah
Uncle Ho	Dr. Ho Chi Minh
Voltaire	Francais Marie Arouet de
Vizzy	Dr. Vijaya Anand, the Maharaja Kumar of Vijainagram
Wizard of the North	Sir Walter Scott
Wizard of Hockey	Dhyan Chand

TALL STRUCTURES

Structure	Height (Feet)
Shyama Prasad Mukherjee Municipality Building Delhi	336
Qutub Minar (Delhi)	288
Rajabari Tower (Bombay University)	260
Brihadeswar Temple	216
Largest Gopuram of Arunachal Temple (Tiruvannamalai)	290
Gol Gumbad (Bijapur)	198½
Gopuram of Ekambarantha Temple (Kanchipuram)	188
Charminar (Hyderabad)	186
Victoria Memorial (Kolkata)	182
Calcutta High Court	180
Taj Mahal (Agra)	178
Buland Darwaja (Fatehpur Sikri)	176
Gopuram of Meenakshi Temple (Madurai)	152
Octerloney Monument (Kolkata)	152
Puri Temple (Puri)	142
Minarets of Taj (Each)	137
Lingaraj Temple (Bhubaneshwar)	127
Tower of Victory (Chittor)	122

MUSEUMS

Salar Jung Museum, Hyderabad

Archaeological Museum, Hyderabad

Telleshwaram Museum, Hyderabad

National Museum, Delhi

National Gallery of Modern Art, Delhi

Red Fort Museum, Delhi

War Memorial Museum, Delhi

Nehru Museum, New Delhi

National Museum of Natural History, New Delhi

Transport Museum, New Delhi.

Assam State Museum, Guwahati
Archaeological Museum, Gwalior
Central Museum, Jaipur
Ajmer Museum, Ajmer
Bharatpur Museum, Bharatpur
Jodhpur Museum, Jodhpur
Victoria Hall Museum, Udaipur
Ganga Museum, Bikaner
Pratap Singh Museum, Srinagar
Municipal Museum, Allahabad
State Museum, Lucknow
Bharatiya Kala Bhavan, Varanasi
Sarnath Museum, Varanasi
Prince of Wales Museum, Mumbai
Victoria and Albert Museum, Mumbai
Baroda Museum, Vadodara
Fateh Singh Museum, Vadodara
Municipal Museum, Vadodara
Municipal Museum, Ahmedabad
Junagadh Museum, Junagarha
Bhavnagar Museum, Bhavnagar
Jamnagar Museum, Jamnagar
Waston Museum, Rajkot
Indore Museum, Indore
Bhopal Museum, Bhopal
Sanchi Museum, Sanchi
Central Museum, Nagpur
Government Museum, Chennai
Government Museum, Bangalore
Chamarajendra Art Gallery, Mysore
Indian Memorial Museum and Library, Kolkata
Victoria Memorial Hall, Kolkata
Ashutosh Museum, Kolkata
National Mist Museum, Darjeeling
Bangiya Sahitya Parishad Museum, Kolkata
Asiatic Society Museum, Kolkata
Birla Technological and Industrial Museum, Kolkata
Patna Museum, Patna
Nalanda Museum, Nalanda
Bodh Gaya Museum, Gaya
Orissa State Museum, Bhubaneshwar
Gandhi Memorial Museum, Madurai
Saraswati Mahal Library, Tanjore

LEADING NEWSPAPERS

Newspaper	City	Language
Amrit Bazar Patrika	Kolkata	English
Statesman	New Delhi/Kolkata	English
Anand Bazar Patrika	Kolkata	Bengali
Hindustan Times	New Delhi/Patna/Lucknow/Bhopal	English
Kesari	Pune	Marathi
Nai Duniya	Indore	Hindi
Bombay Smachar	Mumbai	Gujarati
Kannada Prabha	Banglore	Kannada
Hindustan	New Delhi	Hindi
Vir Arjun	New Delhi	Hindi
Tribune	Chandigarh	English, Hindi
Akali Patrika	Jalandhar	Punjabi
National Herald	New Delhi	English
Financial Express	Mumbai/Delhi	English
Aryavarta	Patna	Hindi
Indian Express	New Delhi/Mumbai/Ahmedabad/ Chandigarh/Nagpur/Pune/Vadodara	English
Aaj	Varanasi/Kanpur/Patna/Agra/Gorakhpur	Hindi

Newspaper	City	Language
Telegraph	Kolkata	English
Times of India	New Delhi/Mumbai/Ahmedabad/ Patna/Lucknow/Bangalore	English
Navbharat Times	New Delhi/Mumbai/Lucknow/Patna	Hindi
Jansatta	New Delhi/Chandigarh	Hindi
Deccan Herald	Bangalore	English
Deccan Chronicle	Hyderabad	English
Business Standard	Kolkata	English
Economic Times	Mumbai/New Delhi	English
Maharashtra Times	Mumbai	Marathi
Hindu	Chennai/Gurgaon(Haryana)	English
Dinamani	Madurai	Tamil
Matribhoomi	Khozhikode	Malayalam
Pioneer	New Delhi/Lucknow/Kanpur	English
Qaumi Awaz	New Delhi	Urdu
Awam	New Delhi	Urdu
Rashtriya Sahara	New Delhi/Lucknow	Hindi
Dainik Jagran	Kanpur/Varanasi/Agra/Meerut/Jhansi/ New Delhi/Lucknow/Gorakhpur/ Dehradun/Bareilly/Jalandhar/Patna	Hindi
Amar Ujala	Agra/Aligarh/Meerut/Kanpur/ Moradabad/Bareilly	Hindi
Punjab Kesari	New Delhi/Jalandhar	Hindi
Hind Samachar	New Delhi/Jalandhar	Urdu
The Malyala Manorma	Kozhikode	Malyalam
Rajasthan Patrika	Jaipur/Ajmer/Kota	Hindi

PROMINENT PERIODICALS

Periodical	Language	Periodical	Language
Weeklies		***Fortinghilies***	
Blitz	English	Femina	English
Malayala Manorama	Malayalam	Frontline	English
Matribhoomi	Malayalam	Madhuri	Hindi
Desh	Bengali	Sarita	Hindi
Kumudam	Tamil	Betar Jagat	Bengali
Varantari Rani	Tamil	Business World	English
Andhra Prabha Illustrated	Tamil	Jan Kalyan	Gujarati
Sudha	Kannada	***Monthlies***	
Swaraj	Marathi	Filmfare	English
Sunday	English	Manorma	Hindi
The Week	English	Yojna	English/Hindi
India Today	English, Hindi, Tamil	Nandan	Hindi
Outlook	English, Hindi	Kadambini	Hindi
Nai Duniya	Urdu	Shama	Urdu
Employment News	English, Hindi, Urdu	Aaj Kal	Hindi/Urdu

NEWS AGENCIES

There are four major news agencies.

1. Press Turst of India (PTI)........ English : Bhasha .... Hindi
2. United News of India (UNI)..... English : Varta .... Hindi
3. Samachar Bharati .... Hindi
4. Hindustan Samachar....................... Hindi

TRANSPORT

RAILWAY AT A GLANCE

Gauge	Route kms.	Running trakc kms.	Total Track kms.
Broad Gauge (1676 mm)	55,956	80,779	1,04,693
Metre Gauge (1000 mm)	6,347	6,725	7,801
Narrow Gauge (762 mm/610 mm)	2,297	2,297	2,568
Total	**64,600**	**89,801**	**1,15,062**

Zones	Headquarters
Central	Mumbai
Eastern	Kolkata
Northern	New Delhi
North Eastern	Gorakhpur
Northeast Frontier	Guwahati
Southern	Chennai
South Central	Secunderabad
South Eastern	Kolkata
Western	Mumbai
East Coast	Bhuvaneshwar
East Central	Hajipur
North Central	Allahabad
North Western	Jaipur
South Western	Hubli
West Central	Jabalpur
South East Central	Bilaspur
Kolkata Metro	Kolkata

MAJOR ROUTES

Delhi to Mumbai (Central Railway) : Starting from Delhi, it passes through Mathura, Agra, Gwalior, Jhansi, Sanchi, Stupa, Bhopal, Itarasi, Khandwa, Bhusawal, Jalgaon and Nasik road, to reach Mumbai.

Delhi to Mumbai (Western Railway) : Starting from Delhi the train goes to Mathura and then, turns towards South-west and passes through Kota, Ratlam, Vadodara and Surat to reach Mumbai.

Delhi to Mumbai (Western Railway) : From Delhi to Rewari, Alwar, Jaipur, Ajmer and Mount Abu Road to reach Ahmedabad. Then the train goes to Vadodara and Surat to reach Mumbai.

Mumbai to Chennai : After leaving Mumbai, it crosses Western Ghats and comes to Pune and then to Sholapur, Wadi, Raichur, Guntakal and Arkonam to reach Chennai.

Mumbai to Kolkata : Leaving Mumbai, it passes through Manmad, Bhusawal Akola, Nagpur, Raipur, Bilaspur, Tanakpur, Kharagpur and reaches Kolkata.

Kolkata to Chennai : Starting from Howrah, it passes through Kharagpur, Cuttuck, Bhubaneswar, Waltair, Bezwada and reaches Chennai.

Delhi to Amritsar : There are two railway routes up to Ambala Cantt, one via Saharanpur and the other via Karnal.

Delhi to Ferozpur Cantt. : From Delhi to Rohtak, Jind, Jakhal, Bhatinda, Faridkot and then to Ferozpur. Another route is via Karnal, Ambala, Patiala, Dhuri, Bhatinda and Ferozpur.

ROADWAYS

National Highways : The National Highway System is the primary road grid of the country. The construction and maintenance of the national highways is the direct responsibility of the central government. The National Highways have a total length of 79,116 kms. Though accounting for only about 2 per cent of the length of the total road network of the country, the National Highways carry nearly 40% of the total traffic.

State Highways and Major District Roads : The state highways and major district roads form the secondary road system and take care of collector and distributor functions. They are the responsibility of the state governments and are maintained through various agencies in the states and union territories.

Rural Roads : Construction and maintenance of roads in the rural areas is also the responsibility of the States and the union territories. Most of the rural roads are now being constructed under the Minimum Needs Programme, Rural Landless Employment Programme and the Command Area Development Programme. Since a number of organisations and agencies, at present, handle the road construction and maintenance, this results in duplication of efforts, lack of uniformity and imbalanced development of the rural road-network. Recently, the Government has set up a committee to examine different aspects of integrating various Rural Road Programmes. It is proposed to prepare master plans for rural roads in each district, so as to obtain an optimum network.

Border Roads : With a view to accelerating economic development and strengthening defence preparedness, through rapid and coordinated expansion and improvement of road networks in the north and north-western border areas, the Border Roads Development Board was set up in March, 1960. The development activities of the Board were expanded to many more areas and now cover Rajasthan, Jammu and Kashmir, Himachal Pradesh. Uttar Pradesh, Uttaranchal, Madhya Pradesh, Sikkim, Assam, Meghalaya, Nagaland, Tripura, Manipur, Bihar, Andaman and Nicobar Islands, Arunachal Pradesh, Mizoram and Bhutan.

Road Network : With over 46.90 lakh kms. of road length, India can boast of one of the largest road networks in the world. From a road length of about 4 lakh kms. in 1950-51, the road network has expanded eight times. Despite this impressive growth in road networks, about 36 per cent of villages in India remain without any road link while 65 per cent villages do not have all-weather roads. Less than half of the total road length has a metallic surface, most of the rural roads are non-surfaced, unmetallic or *kuchcha* roads.

SOME IMPORTANT NATIONAL HIGHWAYS

S. No.	National Highway	Route
1.	1	Delhi-Ambala-Jalandhar-Delhi-Amritsar-Indo-Pak Border
2.	1a	Jalandhar-Madhopur-Jammu-Banihal-Srinagar-Baramula-Uri
3.	1b	Batote-Doda-Kishtwar
4.	2	Delhi-Mathura-Agra-Kanpur-Allahabad-Varanasi-Mohania-Barhi-Palsit-Baidyabati Bara-Kolkata.
5.	3	Agra-Gwalior-Shivpuri-Indore-Dhule-Nasik-Thane-Mumbai
6.	4	Junction with National Highway No. 3 near Thane-Pune Belgaum-Hubli-Bangalore-Ranipet-Chennai
7.	4a	Belgaum-Anmod-Ponda-Panaji

S. No.	National Highway	Route
8.	4b	Nhava Sheva-Kalamboli-Palspe
9.	5	Junction with National Highway No. 6 near Baharagora-Cuttuck-Bhubaneshwar Vishakhapatnam-Vijayawada-Chennai
10.	5a	Junction with National Highway No. 6 near Haridaspur-Paradip Port
11.	6	Dhule-Nagpur-Rajpur-Sambalpur-Baharagora-Kolkata
12.	7	Varanasi-Mangawan-Rewa-Jabalpur-Lakhnadon Nagpur-Hyderabad-Kurnool-Bangalore-Krishnagiri-Salem-Dindigul-Madurai-Cape Comorin (Kanyakumari)
13.	7a	Palyankotta-Tuticorin Port
14.	8	Delhi-Jaipur-Udaipur-Ahmedabad-Vadodara-Mumbai
15.	8a	Ahmedabad-Limbdi-Morvi- Kandla
16.	8b	Bamanbore-Rajkot-Porbander
17.	8c	Chiloda-Gandhinagar-Sarkhej
18.	9	Pune-Sholapur-Hyderabad-Vijayawada
19.	10	Delhi-Fazilka-Indo-Pak Border
20.	11	Agra-Jaipur-Bikaner
21.	12	Jabalpur-Bhopal-Biaora-Rajgarh-Khilchipur-Aklera-Jhalawar-Kota-Bundi-Devli-Tonk-Jaipur
22.	13	Sholapur-Chitradurga
23.	15	Pathankot-Amritsar-Bhatinda-Ganganagar-Bikaner-Jaisalmer-Barmer-Samakhiali (near Kandla)
24.	17	Panvel-Mahad-Panaji-Klarwar-Mangalore-Cannanore-Calicut (Kozhikode)-Ferokh-Kuttipuram-Pudu Ponnani Chowghat-Cranganur-Junction with National Highway No. 47 near Edapally
25.	17a	Junction with National Highway No. 17 Near Cortalin-Marmugao
26.	21	Junction with National Highway No. 22 Near Chandigarh-Rajpur-Bilaspur-Mandi-Kulu-Manali
27.	22	Ambala-Kalka-Shimla-Narkanda-Rampur-China-Indo-Tibet Border near Shipkila
28.	23	Chas-Ranchi-Rourkela-Tacher, Junction with National Highway No. 42
29.	24	Delhi-Mumbai-Lucknow
30.	25	Lucknow-Kanpur-Jhansi-Shivpuri
31.	26	Jhansi-Lakhnadon
32.	27	Allahabad-Mangawan
33.	28	Junction with National Highway No. 31 near Barauni-Muzaffarpur-Pipra-Gorakhpur-Lucknow
34.	28a	Junction with National Highway No. 28 near Pipra-Sagauli-Raxaul-Indo-Nepal Border
35.	29	Gorakhpur-Ghazipur-Varanasi
36.	30	Junction with National Highway No. 2 near Mohania-Patna-Bakhtiyarpur
37.	31	Junction with National Highway No. 2 near Barhi-Bakhtiyarpur-Mokameh-Purnia-Dalkola-Siliguri-Sivok-Kuch Bihar-North Salmara-Nalbari-Charali Amingaon Junction with National Highway No. 37
38.	31a	Sivok-Gangtok

S. No.	National Highway	Route
39.	31b	North Salmara-Junction with National Highway No. 37 near Jogigopa.
40.	31c	Near Galgalia-Baghdogra-Chalsa-Nagrakata-Goyerkata-Dalgaon-Hasimara-Rajabhat-Khawa-Kochugaon-Sidili-Junction with National Highway No. 31 near Bijni
41.	32	Junction with National Highway No. 2 Near Gobindpuri-Dhanbad-Jamshedpur
42.	33	Junction with National Highway No. 2 near Barhi-Ranchi-Junction with National Highway No. 6 near Baharagora
43.	34	Junction with National Highway No. 31 near Dalkoi-Berhampore-Barasat-Kolkata
44.	35	Barasat-Bangaon-Indo-Bangladesh Border
45.	36	Nowgong-Debaka-Dimapur (Manipur Road)
46.	37	Junction with National Highway No. 31 near Goalpara-Guwahati-Jorabat-Kamargaon-Mukum Saikhoaghat
47.	37a	Kuarital-Junction with National Highway No. 52 near Tezpur
48.	38	Mukum-Ledo-Lekhapani
49.	39	Numaligarh-Imphal-Patel-Indo-Burma-Border
50.	40	Jorabat-Shillong-Indo-Bangladesh Border near Dawki
51.	41	Junction with National Highway No. 6 near Kolaghat-Haldia Port
52.	42	Junction with National Highway No. 6 near Sambalpur
53.	43	Angul-Junction with National Highway No. 5 near Cuttuck Raipur-Vizianagaram-Junction with National Highway No. 5
54.	44	Shillong-Passi Badarpur-Agartala
55.	45	Chennai-Tiruchirapalli-Dindigul
56.	45a	Link to Pondicherry (Villupuram-Pondicherry)
57.	46	Krishnagiri-Ranipet
58.	47	Salem-Coimbatore-Trichur-Ernakulam-Thiruvananthapuram-Cape Comorin (Kanyakumari)
59.	47a	Junction with National Highway No. 47-Willington Island
60.	48	Bangalore-Hassan-Mangalore
61.	49	Madurai-Dhanushkodi
62.	50	Nasik-Junction with National Highway No. 4 near Pune
63.	51	Paikan-Tura-Dalu
64.	52	Baihata Charall-Tezpur-Bander Dewa-North Lakhimpur-Pasighat-Teza-Sitapuani-Junction with National Highway No. 37 near Shailkhoaghat
65.	52a	Bander Dewa-Itanagar
66.	53	Junction with National Highway No. 44 near Badarpur-Jirighat-Imphal-Silchar
67.	54	Silchar-Aizawal-Tuipang
68.	54a	Theriat-Lunglei
69.	54b	Venus-Saddle-Saiha
70.	56	Lucknow-Varanasi
71.	NE	Ahmedabad-Vadodara

AIR TRANSPORT

Private Airlines : Now private sector also have a share in air transport as some of private airlines like Jet Airways, SpiceJet, IndiGo, Kingfisher have also come in the field. These companies offer their services for domestic air travel.

International Airports : There are 15 international airports in India. Main international airports are: Dum-Dum (Kolkata), Santa Cruz and Sahar (Mumbai), Indira Gandhi (Delhi), Meenambakkam (Chennai), Rajasansi (Amritsar) and the Thiruvananthapuram Airport.

Domestic Airports : Among the major domestic airports are the aerodromes at Ahmedabad, Agartala, Amritsar, Aurangabad, Bangalore, Bhubaneswar, Kolkata, Delhi, Guwahati, Hyderabad, Imphal, Khajuraho, Lucknow, Mangalore, Nagpur, Patna, Ranchi, Shillong, Thiruvananthapuram, Tiruchirapalli, Udaipur, Varanasi etc. Besides, there are civil enclaves in many of the aerodromes of the defence forces. The domestic aerodromes, which were earlier managed by the Civil Aviation Department of the Government of India, are now looked after by the National Airport Authority of India, which was established in 1986. The NAAI is responsible for the management, construction, maintenance, development and other operational functions at the aerodromes.

MAJOR ROUTES

- Delhi to Kolkata via Lucknow, Varanasi, Patna.
- Delhi to Kolkata via Kanpur, Allahabad, Patna.
- Delhi to Mumbai via Jaipur and Ahmedabad.
- Delhi to Mumbai via Gwalior and Indore.
- Delhi to Srinagar via Amritsar and Jammu.
- Mumbai to Kolkata.
- Mumbai to Bangalore via Pune.
- Mumbai to Chennai.
- Mumbai to Colombo via Hyderabad and Chennai.
- Chennai to Thiruvananthapuram via Bangalore, Coimbatore and Kochi.

SHIPPING

Shipping Companies : There are 136 shipping companies of which one, the Shipping Corporation of India (in which Moghul Lines Ltd. merged in June, 1986) is in the public sector and the remaining are in the private sector. The Shipping Corporation of India owns nearly half of India's total merchant fleet. The top 12 companies, including the Shipping Corporation of India, make up for 90 percent of the total shipping tonnage. Of the 136 shipping companies, 98 are engaged exclusively in coastal trade, 18 in overseas trade and the remaining (including the public sector company) carry on overseas as well as coastal trade.

MAJOR PORTS

There are 13 major ports and 200 minor working ports along the coast line of (about 7,516.6 km.) India. The major ports on the west coast of India are Mumbai, Kandla, Mormugao, New Mangalore, Kochin and Jawaharlal Nehru port at Nhava Sheva. On the east coast, the major ports are Tuticorin, Chennai, Vishakhapatnam, Paradip and Kolkata (Haldia). Port Blair becomes the 13th major port of the country.

INLAND WATER TRANSPORT

Inland water transport also plays an important role. India has about 5,200 kms of major rivers, which are navigable by merchandise craft, but only 1,700 kms are actually utilised. Important among the navigable rivers are the Ganges, Brahamaputra and their tributaries, Godavari, Krishna, Mahanadi, Narmada, Tapti and their canals, the backwaters and canals of Kerala, the Buckingham canal in Andhra Pradesh and Tamil Nadu, the Combarjua canal connecting Mandovi and Zuvari rivers in Goa and the network of tidal rivers of Sunderbans.

Waterways : The river Ganga and the river Brahamaputra are navigable by steamers and country boats. The Chief Salt Water canals which are navigable are:

- The Hugali Tidal Canal in West Bengal.
- The Orissa Coast Canal.
- The Buckingham Canal in Andhra Pradesh.
- Vedaraniyan Canal in Andhra Pradesh and Tamil Nadu.
- A channel from Calcutta to Raniganj coal-fields is provided by the Damodar Valley Project.
- The Kakrapar project provides navigable channel from the sea to Kakrapar Dam.

* The Hirakud project has made Mahanadi navigable.

DEFENCE

ARMED FORCES

The supreme command of the Armed Forces is vested in the President of India. The responsibility for national defence, however, rests with the Cabinet. All important questions, having a bearing on defence, are decided by the Cabinet Committee on Political affairs, which is presided over by the Prime Minister. The Defence Minister is responsible to Parliament for all matters concerning the Defence Services. The administrative and operational control of the Armed Forces is exercised by the Ministry of Defence and the three Services Headquarters of the Army, Navy and Air Force. The three Services—Army, Navy and Air Force-function through their respective Services Headquarters, headed by Chiefs of Staff.

ARMY

The Army is organised into seven Commands—Western, Eastern, Northern, Southern, Central, South-Western and Training—each under a General Officer Commanding-in-chief of the rank of Lieutenant General. The Commands are divided into Areas, Independent Sub-areas and Sub-areas. An Area is commanded by a General Officer of the rank of Major General and an independent Sub-area and Sub-area by a Brigadier. The Army consists of a number of services. The sanctioned strength of all ranks of the Army is over 12 lakhs. A new system of recruitment to the Indian Army has been introduced from October 1, 1981. The purpose of this system is to eliminate subjective assessment and recruit the best available talent.

Self Relient : The country is self-relient, regarding a number of weapons and is at present, manufacturing Vijayanta tanks, Shaktiman army trucks. Continuous efforts are being made to modernise the armed forces and keep them technologically updated with the latest equipment.

AIR FORCE

The Indian Air Force is organised into seven Commands : (1) Western Air Command; (2) Southwestern Air Command; (3) Central Air Command; (4) Eastern Air Command; (5) Southern Air Command; (6) Training Command; and (7) Maintenance Command. While the first five are Operational Commands, the last two are Functional Commands.

NAVY

The Navy is organised into three Naval Commands, under Flag Officers Commanding-in-chief. These are : (1) Western Naval Command, Mumbai, (2) Eastern Naval Command, Vishakhapatnam and (3) Southern Naval Command, Kochi. The Navy has two-fleets—the Western Fleet and the Eastern Fleet. The two fleets consist of the aircraft carrier INS Vikrant, one destroyer INS Rajput, a number of frigate squadrons, including some of the latest types of anti-submarine and anti-aircraft frigates, a squadron of anti-marine patrol vessels, one mine-sweeping squadron, submarines, a submarine depot ship and fast vessels, carrying surface to surface guided missiles. The recently commissioned naval air station at Port Blair, INS Utkrosh, carries out the air surveillance of far flung island territories of Andaman and Nicobar in the Bay of Bengal. The Navy has a sizeable air wing with various types of fixed wing aircraft and helicopters. Besides, there are some survey ships, two fleet tankers and a number of auxiliary crafts.

COAST GUARD

The function of Coast Guard is to protect the maritime and other interests in the maritime zones of India, covering an area of approximately 28 lakh square kilometre. It was constituted as an armed force in 1978 under the Coast Guard Act. The national maritime zones have been divided into three regions, namely Western, Eastern and Andaman and Nicobar, with regional headquarters located at Mumbai, Chennai and Port Blair respectively. Its headquarters are presently located at New Delhi and Ministry of Defence exercises administrative control over it through the Director General, Coast Guard. Its available resources are being utilised in the areas of illegal fishing, smuggling, search and rescue, anti-pollution measures etc.

TERRITORIAL ARMY

The Territorial Army, which was raised in 1949 is designed to give the youth of the country an opportunity for receiving military training in their spare time and to serve the country during the times of emergency by providing units to the regular army. All able bodied nationals of India, between the age of 18 and 35 (with age relaxation) and possessing the requisite qualifications are eligible to join the Territorial Army as officers or in other ranks. It has recently been decided to raise the upper age limits for entry into Territorial Army from 35 to 42.

NATIONAL CADET CORPS

The National Cadet Corps (NCC), which comprises of three divisions, *i.e.*, Senior, Junior and Girls, is composed of students in educational institutions and is the premier scheme of youth activities. The students are trained in handling arms, learning the basic functions of Defence Service personnel and living for short period in camps under discipline. Participation in the NCC is entirely voluntary except in two of the Indian universities, *i.e.*, Agricultural University, Hissar and University of Agricultural Sciences, Bangalore.

The Objectives : The objectives of the NCC are to stimulate interest among the youth in the defence of the country so as to build up a resource of manpower to enable the armed forces to expand rapidly. It also builds up the character of young boys and girls so that they may become disciplined citizens. A certain percentage of the total intake of candidates for commissioned ranks in the Army. Navy and Air Force is reserved for NCC cadets of the three services.

HOME GUARDS

After the Chinese invasion of India in October, 1962, the Government felt the necessity of forming this organisation so that the personnel of this organisation could relieve the state police personnel from their normal patrol or traffic duties. The functions of the Home Guards are to assist the police in maintaining integral security, to assist in case of air raids, fire fighting and epidemics and to man important services in the states.

COMMISSIONED RANKS

Army	Navy	Air Force
General	Admiral	Air Chief Marshal
Lieutenant-General	Vice-Admiral	Air Marshal
Major-General	Rear-Admiral	Air Vice-Marshal
Brigadier	Commodore	Air Commodore
Colonel	Captain	Group Captain
Lieutenant-Colonel	Commander	Wing Commander
Major	Lt. Commander	Squadron Leader
Captain	Lieutenant	Flight Lieutenant
Lieutenant	Sub-Lieutenant	Flying Officer

Highest Military Decorations of Various Countries

India	—	Param Vir Chakra
U.S.A.	—	Victory Medal
France	—	Croiv de Guerra
Belgium	—	Military Cross
Italy	—	Medal for Valour
Germany	—	Iron Cross
Japan	—	Order of the Rising Sun
Russia	—	Order of the Patriotic War
Great Britain	—	Victoria Cross

HISTORY

PRE-HISTORIC INDIA

Prehistoric man, according to the materials used in making tools and utensils has passed through four stages: (1) the Palaeolithic or old Stone Age; (2) the Neolithic or New Stone Age; (3) the Copper Age; and (4) the Iron Age.

In the Palaeolithic Age, the implements were of roughly hewn stone. Thousands of years thereafter man reached the Neolithic Age. The Stone was ground against some hard material and shaped into weapons and utensils, sharply pointed and decently executed. Gradually, man came to learn about the use of metals in the Copper Age. The next and the last stage was the Iron Age when man learnt to use iron.

The Indus Valley Civilization

On the basis of archaeological discoveries at Mohenjo-daro in Sind, India along with Egypt and Babylonia can claim to be one of the earliest sites of civilization. The site contains the ruins of an ancient city, of which seven strata, one built upon the other, have been found. The date of the upper strata has been fixed at 2500 B.C.

An Urban River Valley : It was largely an urban river valley civilization. The excavations show the existence of : *(i)* building made up of bricks, pillared halls, a series of halls and baths, long halls probably used as granaries; *(ii)* the street and roads were well-planned, well laid out with *Pucca* drains; *(iii)* crafts like tool-making, toys, pottery and jewellery had flourished; *(iv)* farming and trade were their main occupations (wheat, barley, field peas, melon seeds and cotton were grown) and *(v)* domesticated animals like dogs, cats, humped cattle, buffaloes, camels, horses and asses. The decline of this civilization was due to wars, climate, racial degeneration, violent geographical changes and the arrival of the Aryans.

THE ANCIENT PERIOD

THE ENTRY OF ARYANS

The Aryans entered India from the north and northwest and their first settlement in India was established in the Punjab region between B.C. 1500 and then, they spread eastwards and occupied the whole of northern India. In the course of time, they penetrated into South India as well. At first, there were conflicts between the invading Aryans and the natives, believed to be the Dravidians. But gradually, the two intermingled. The Aryans were pastoral people and patriarchal family was their unit.

The Tribal Set up : The tribal chief, known as the Raja, ruled on the advice of a popular assembly. The early Aryans were a strong race and their main occupations were cattle-raising and war. After settling down in India, they adopted agriculture as their principal occupation. In the beginning there were no social divisions among the Aryans. Later, they grouped the society into four divisions—*Brahmins, Kshatriyas Vaishyas and Shudras* and this developed laterly into a rigid caste-system.

COMPARISON OF THE INDUS AND VEDIC CIVILIZATIONS

In both the civilizations, people domesticated animals and were engaged in hunting. In both, men and women decorated their bodies with ornaments though there was difference in the types of ornaments. The Vedic people were warlike, raided their neighbourhood for conquest or plunder. The Indus people had no armour or weapons. The Indus civilization was urban, but the Vedic civilization was rural. The people in the Indus Valley worshipped gods—Rudra and Bhagwati (goddess). The Aryans on the other hand were polytheists who worshipped Nature-gods, preferred outdoor entertainments and used *"Som Rasa"* as an intoxicant.

THE DRAVIDIANS

In the earliest historic period the natives of India were the people called the "Dravidians" (the name applied only to a group of languages). They belonged to the Melonid Stock and once occupied the whole of India. Aryans gradually pushed them back to the South, where they preserved their old culture. They were civilized people, leading a settled life.

They knew the usage of metals. Their chief occupations were agriculture and commerce. They had a well-defined system of administration. Their structure of society was matriarchal. They worshipped snakes and the Earth. There was no caste system in their society. Dravidian languages are *Tamil, Telugu, Kannad and Malayalam.*

VEDIC LITERATURE

The whole Vedic literature, according to an an orthodox view, was revealed to a favoured few "the *rishis*" or the "seers" who uttered the hymns and was communicated down to their descendants. The word "*Ved*" means knowledge.

The *Vedas* : These are four in number—the *Rig Veda*, the *Sam Veda*, the *Yajur Veda* and the *Atharva Veda*. The *Rig Veda* is believed to be the oldest. The *Rig Veda* has a great literary merit, apart from being a philosophical treatise. The parts which constitute the *Vedas* are: (1) the *Samhitas* of the four Vedas; (2) the *Brahmins* attached to each of the Samhitas; (3) the *Aranyakas* and (4) the *Upanishads*, mostly attached to the Brahmans, but in reality forming separate and unconnected treatise.

The *Upanishadas* : The *Upanishadas* deal with spiritual topics and are mostly appended to the *Aranyakas*. These are 108 in number. The philosophy contained in the *Upanishadas* is called *Vedanta* (end of the Veda). The essence of this philosophy is "the world is God and God is my soul". This universal philosophy cuts across the frontiers of all religions.

The *Puranas* : They are 18 in number. They are a mixture of history, religion, mythology and tradition. They deal with primary creation, secondary creation, genealogies of gods and patriarchs, laws of Manu and the history of various dynasties.

The *Sutras* : The *Sutra* literature consists of manuals of instructions on various subjects. The *Sutras* are composed in the most compressed form of prose to ensure brevity and easy memorisation.

The *Jatakas* : The *Jatakas* form part of the Buddhist Tripitaka. These give accounts of some of the lives which the Buddha had lived before he attained Buddhahood in his final life as Siddhartha. In reality, however, these are merely folklore and popular stories which have been forcibly given a Buddhistic air and made to suit the Buddhist doctrines.

The Epics

There are two epics—The Ramayana and the Mahabharata, originally written in Sanskrit. These took shape before the 6th Century B.C. The epics present a pantheon of new gods in place of Vedic culture. They reflect a complex social and political set up to replace the simple life of the early Aryans.

Jainism

Jainism was founded by Vardhamana Mahavira. Essentials of Jainism are rejection of the supreme power, acceptance of *Karma* and the belief that deliverance from *Karma* is salvation which can be attained through the *Triratna* (right faith, right knowledge and right conduct).

Buddhism

Buddhism was founded by Gautama Buddha. Essentials of Buddhism are as follows: (i) *Trishna* or desire is the root cause of all sufferings and it must be eradicated through a multifold path prescribed by him (right belief, right thought, right speech, right action, right means of livelihood, right endeavour, and right meditation). Buddhism was introduced in China by Kashyapa Matanga in 67 A.D. It was under the patronage of Kanishka that Mahayana Buddhism became popular. The greatest exponent of this doctrine was Nagarjuna. This school started worshipping the Buddha in images.

Alexander's Invasion

Alexander, the great (son of King Phillip of Macedonia in Greece) crossed the river Indus in B.C. 327 as the head of a large army. After conquering small kingdoms in the northwest, he confronted Puru, ruler of one of the States between Jhelum and Chenab in Punjab. Puru was defeated in the Battle of Hydaspes (Jhelum). Alexander advanced up to Beas when his forces refused to go further. On his way back, he died at Babylon in B.C. 323. Alexander's campaign opened up four distinct routes by land and sea.

The Mauryan Empire

Chandragupta Maurya (322-298 B.C.) : In 322 B.C. he was made the king of Magadh. He came into conflict with Seleucas, the king of western Asia. As Seleucas was defeated, he handed over Berat, Kandhar, Baluchistan, Kabul and also gave his daughter in marriage to Chandragupta.

Ashoka (269-232 B.C.) : He ascended the throne in 273 B.C. Ashoka attacked and captured Kalinga in 261 B.C. and renounced war during that very year. His empire extended up to Mysore in south, Assam in east and Kandhar in the northwest. After renouncing war, he became a Buddhist and propagated "Law of Piety" or "Dharma".

The Kushans (120-162 A.D.)

Kanishka : He became a convert to Buddhism and summoned a Buddhist council at Peshawar to settle the differences among the Buddhists. He built a great stupa at Peshawar and his court was adorned by Buddhist teacher Vasumitra, the Buddhist poet and philosopher Ashvaghosha, the reputed philosopher Nagarjuna and the great authority on Ayurved, Charak. Two schools of art flourished during his time. They were: *(i)* the Gandhar school of art (which dealt with stories connected with Ashoka's life); and *(ii)* the Mathura School of art.

Gupta Dynasty (320-540 A.D.)

The rise of the Guptas is of extraordinary significance for Hinduism. The great rulers in this dynasty are : Chandra Gupta I. (2) Samudra Gupta, (335-375 A.D.). Also Known as Napoleon of India, (3) Chandra Gupta II. (375-415 A.D.) (Vikramaditya), and (4) Skanda Gupta (455-467 A.D.). The Gupta period is described as the golden period in the history of ancient India.

Harshvardhan (606-47 A.D.)

It was in 606 that Kannauj was ruled by Harshvardhan. He fought many wars to establish an empire but he was not successful. During his time, Chinese traveller Hiuen Tsang visited many provinces of India and was on friendly terms with Harsha. He left a detailed account about the famous Buddhist conference held at Kannauj.

THE MEDIEVAL PERIOD

THE ADVENT OF MUSLIMS

Mahmud Ghaznavi (999-1030) : He carried out seventeen invasions on India. His chief invasions were against the rulers of Punjab, Nagarkot and Thaneswar.

A Great Patron : Many scholars were in his court, like: *(a)* famous historian Alberuni who is also called Mohammed-bin-Ahmed (he wrote Kitab-ul-Hind (Tehkikat-i-Hind) and Alkanun-al-Masudi); *(b)* the famous poet Firdausi composed his Shahnama; and *(c)* Utbi (historian), who wrote his Tarikh-i-Yamini.

The Conquests of Mohammed Ghori

He was a great commander but he suffered defeat at the hands of Mulraj II, the Chalukya king of Anhilwara (Gujarat) in 1178 A.D. and in the first battle of Tarain in 1191 A.D. at the hands of Prithvi Raj Chauhan. But later on, he won the second battle of Tarain in 1192 A.D. He established the Muslim Empire in India and is considered to be the real founder of Muslim rule in India. Farishta, the famous historian, has greatly praised Mohammed Ghori's love for art and literature though he did not construct beautiful buildings like Mahmud Ghazni nor did he give patronage to as many scholars.

The Slave Dynasty (1206-1290 A.D.)

Qutubuddin Aibak (1206-1210) : Qutubuddin Aibak was the founder of the Slave Dynasty. He commenced the building of the Qutub Minar which was later completed by Iltutmish (1210-1236). Razia Sultan (1236-1240) and Balban were the other great rulers in this dynasty.

The Khilji Dynasty (1290-1320 A.D.)

Alauddin Khilji (1296-1316) : He was the first Muslim ruler to invade southern India. It was Alauddin Khilji, who introduced famous market regulations to maintain correct prices and also punished merchants for using false weights.

The Tughlak Dynasty (1320-1414 A.D.)

Ghyasuddin Tughlak (1320-25) was the founder of Tughlak dynasty. Mohammed Bin Tughlak (1325-1351) was the most distinguished ruler of this dynasty. He was a mixture of opposites. His transfer of capital from Delhi to Daulatabad has been described by historians as an act of madness.

Timur's Invasion

Timur invaded India in 1398. He massacred his prisoners, totalling 1,00,000 thousand in number. He plundered many a city in north India and looted wealth from Delhi and elsewhere. He did not prefere to establish an empire in India and returned.

The Lodi Dynasty (1451-1526)

Bahlol Lodi (1451-89) : He established his control over Delhi and defeated powerful Sharqi Sultan of Jaunpur and the Rajputs of Doab.

Sikander Lodi (1489-1517) : He worked impartially and delivered justice according to Islamic principles. He got land measured and re-fixed land revenue. He built Agra Fort and tomb of his father Bahlol Lodi in Delhi. He could not conquer Gwalior and Ranthambor but he successfully suppressed many Afghan chiefs.

Ibrahim Lodi (1517-1526) : He was last and incapable ruler of this dynasty. He fought the first battle of Panipat and lost it to Babar.

The Mughal Dynasty (1526-1857)

Babar (1526-30) : The founder of the Mughal empire, Babar is an interesting personality. After having been defeated like a king on the chessboard in Central Asia, Babar turned his attention towards India to take advantages of prevailing weaknesses in the country. In 1526, he defeated Ibrahim Lodi. In 1527, he defeated Rana Sangram Singh. In the Battle of Gogra, he destroyed the Afghans. As a man he was a noble person. His biography, known as the Tuzuk-e-Babri is written in chaste Turkish. The style is simple and he recorded everything in his life, including failures.

Humayun (1530-40 & 1552-56) : Humayun was not a strong ruler and he was ousted by Sher Shah. After having lost the battles at Chausa and Kannauj, he had to flee to Iran. He waited for his turn and attacked India again in 1552. He defeated the successor of Sher Shah Suri and regained control over his lost kingdom.

Sher Shah Suri (1540-45) : Sher Shah's rule is of tremendous significance because the beginnings that he made during his life were carried to their logical conclusions by Akbar. He introduced a system of survey and assessment of land. He built his own mausoleum at Sasaram – the first example of Hindu-Muslim synthesis of architecture. After five years of rule, Sher Shah died.

Akbar (1556-1605) : Akbar defeated the Afghans in the second Battle of Panipat in 1556. Then he conquered Rajputana and Chittor. Rana Pratap, the ruler of Mewar was defeated in the famous battle of Haldighati, in 1576, by a general of Akbar. Akbar introduced a very successful revenue administration with the guidance of Todarmal, a former employee of Sher Shah. Because of Akbar's personal interest in administration, every aspect of it functioned well.

Jehangir (1605-27) : After Akbar, Jehangir succeeded him. He was an easy- going and luxury oriented ruler. He is remembered for this romance with Nurjehan, who, to a great extent, dominated politics, and so, his eldest son Khurram rebelled. Mahabat Khan, a general, was also a suspect in the eyes of Nurjehan and so, he too rebelled. Jehangir is known for his exemplary justice and love for the gardens.

Shahjehan (1627-58) : During the reign of Shahjehan, there were no great military victories. The central Asian policy of Shahjehan was a failure. The annexation of Deccan Kingdoms was not complete. There was a war of succession among his sons. During his reign, India was at the peak of prosperity and the country was known as the golden bird. In fact, Shahjehan's reign is known as the golden era of medieval history. Shahjehan was a great builder. He founded Shahjehanabad (Delhi) and built the world famous Taj Mahal at Agra along with Red Fort and Jama Masjid at Delhi.

Aurangzeb (1658-1707) : Aurangzeb was a strong ruler and a great general but his reign witnessed a lot of turbulence. He devoted almost half of his time in Deccan. During Aurangzeb's rule, the Mughal empire was extended to almost whole of India and included Afghanistan also. He was intolerant towards others. He re-imposed Jazia. He alienated the sympathies of Rajputs also. These resulted in a series of wrangles. After a long rule, Aurangzeb left the vast empire without any able successor.

Shivaji : Shivaji, who founded the Maratha Kingdom was the son of Shahji who served the Bijapur state. His mother, Jijabai and teacher, Dadji Kundev enthused him with religious spirit since his childhood. Then, Shaista Khan, sent by Aurangzeb was also disgraced by him. Once he was captured and imprisoned by Aurangzeb. Luckily, he escaped, reconquered the territory and was crowned as

Chhtrapati in 1674 at Raigarh. Shivaji was not only a good soldier, but also an able administrator. He organised civil and military systems. During his time, Marathas came to be recognised as a separate entity. The war waged by Aurangzeb against them was of no use as even after Shivaji's death, Marathas maintained themselves as a military power and gave a lot of trouble to Mughal empire.

Onslaught from Northwest

Nadir Shah's Invasion (1739) : In 1739, the famous invasion of Nadir Shah occurred who entered the capital of Mughals and ordered a general massacre. He carried away with him the diamond of Kohinoor and the peacock throne of Shahjehan. However, he didn't stay in Delhi for long and handed the empire back to the Mughal ruler, Mohammed Shah.

Abdali's Attacks : Ahmed Shah Abdali also invaded India five times. In 1761, he won the famous third battle of Panipat wherein he routed the Marathas completely. This disabled the Marathas to exploit the political vacuum created by the displacement of Mughal empire and the English extended their authority over India.

THE STATES IN SOUTH INDIA

VIJAYANAGAR EMPIRE

During medieval period, a powerful Hindu state flourished in South India which was known as Vijayanagar Empire. The following dynasties ruled this empire.

Sangam Dynasty (1336-1485) : Harihar-I laid the foundation of Vijayanagar kingdom in collaboration with his brother. He extended along the sea coast to west in the areas and into the north to the river Krishna and river Cauveri in the south. The first struggle against the Bahamani Kingdom took place during his reign. Bukka-I, the other ruler sent his ambassador for diplomatic relations with China. He was mostly engaged in conflicts with the Bahamani Sultans, Mohammed-I and Mujahid, which resulted in the great ruin of Vijayanagar. Following a tolerant policy he established a feeling of unity between the followers of Jainism and Vaishnavism. Harihar-II, assumed the title of Maharajadhiraj and Rajparmeshwar. Devrai-I came in some conflict with Bahamani Sultan-Feroze Shah. He built a dam on river Tungabhadra. Devrai-II was not only a great conqueror but also a great organiser. Famous Telugu poet, Shrinath, was his court poet. His reign saw the sojourn of famous Persian poet, Abdur-Razaaq, to Vijayanagar.

Saluva Dynasty (1486-1507) : Saluva Narsingh, the first ruler of this dynasty saved the Vijayanagar from ruins and regained the entire area that was lost by his preceding rulers.

Tuluva dynasty (1507-65) : Krishnadev Rai was the most powerful ruler of Tuluva dynasty. He wrote a poem *Amuktamalyada* in Telugu. There were many learned men in his court of whom, chief one was Telugu poet Allasani Peddana. He got a new Gopura temple constructed and Gopura of Virupaksha temple repaired. He also built the city of Naglapur.

BAHAMANI EMPIRE

The important Bahamani Kingdom was founded in 1347 A.D. It owed its origin to the Muslim nobles. The Bahamani Kingdom was founded by Hasan who assumed the title of Bahaman Shah. The most important name of this dynasty is Mehmud Gawan, the Chief Minister of the state. He was famous for his military conquests and also, for introducing order and administration in the state. Soon, Bahamani Kingdom was divided into five states: Bijapur; Bidar; Barar; Golkunda; and Ahmednagar; these were later absorbed by the Mughal Empire.

ARRIVAL OF THE BRITISH

In 1600, East India Company was granted the right to trade with East Indies by Queen Elizabeth-I. By one *Sanad*, the English established a factory at Surat and later, factories at Madras and Calcutta followed. By this time, the Portuguese were a power in India. From 1505, they acquired a few areas like Goa, Daman and Dieu. But their power declined very soon as they carried sword in one hand and the Bible in the other. Albuquerque, who captured Goa was an important governor. Portuguese rule, though short-lived, was significant. The famous Saint Xavier visited India. They introduced Bangalore-type architecture, established missionary schools and translated some Indian books on medicine.

Carnatic Wars

There was a trial of strength between the French and the English in Carnatic Wars and the French were defeated due to various reasons; like Duplex, their general, was too hot headed and he could not foresee that the English too could participate in internal affairs of the princes and thus, check French domination. The home government did not help them much. They lacked resources. The French generals were of divided opinion and thus, their ambitions were foiled in the battlefields.

Battle of Plassey

The English won a victory over Siraj-ud-Daula, the *Nawab* of Bengal, at the battle of Plassey in 1757. After this, the English won the battle of Buxar in 1764 against the Mughal Emperor, the *Nawab* of Awadh and Mir Kasim, the new *Nawab* of Bengal. In 1765, the Mughal emperor granted to the English the *Diwani* of Bengal, Bihar and Orissa. The revenue administration was in the hands of the English Company while responsibility for law and order was that of the native *Nawabs*. This notorious experiment caused much harm to Bengal.

Regulating Act of 1773

The famous Regulating Act of 1773 was passed. According to this, a Governor General was appointed to look after the internal affairs from Calcutta and a provision to establish a Supreme Court was also there. The act did not work well due to unsaid things like: *(a)* to what extent the Governor General had overriding authority on Madras and Bombay; *(b)* the jurisdiction of the Supreme Court and its relations with the Supreme Council; and *(c)* that law should be administered by the Supreme Court.

Warren Hastings (1774-85) : Warren Hastings became the first Governor General in 1774. He patronised William Jones and Colebrookle who did much for modern India. He organised district administration, appointed Superintendents of Police and organised revenue administration. Hastings was notorious because of his impolitic and scandulous dealings with Chait Singh, the Begums of Awadh and Nand Kumar. He was impeached after his return to England but he was honourably acquitted later. The Act of 1781 was passed which was in favour of the Governor General and opposed to the Supreme Court.

Pitt's India Act, 1784

In 1784, Pitt's India Act was passed. By this Act, the control of the Home Government was increased as a member of the British Cabinet began to look after Indian affairs.

Lord Cornwallis (1786-93) : Lord Cornwallis introduced the famous Permanent Revenue Settlement of 1793 which brought *Zamindars* into being and created unhappiness for the peasants.

Lord Wellesley (1798-1805) : He introduced the notorious System of Subsidiary Alliance according to which foreign affairs of native states were looked after by the British Raj in return for a payment. This system ultimately led to annexation of native states.

Lord Hastings (1813-1823) : Lord Hastings completed the rout of Marathas in 1818. He was also responsible for the suppression of certain lawless elements like pindaris and the thugs.

The Role of Lord Macaulay : During his reign of Lord Bentick decided the educational fate of India through his doctrine of 1835. According to this, English became the medium of instruction. This step resulted in important consequences as Indians came into contact with the ideas and beliefs of western civilization through English language. The liberal ideas of Bentham and Mill, radical ideas of Tom Paine and Rousseau, the literary products of Shakespeare and Milton influenced the intelligentsia of the country of that time. Other important individuals were: Wiks for the history of Mysore, Tod for his annals of Rajasthan, Sleeman for suppression of *Thuggi.*

The Revolt of 1857

The people of India, right from the beginning of the British conquest never acquiesced in their political exploitation. Not a year passed without an armed resistance to British rule in one part of the country or the other. The greatest of these revolts, which shook the very foundations of the British rule, occurred in 1857. The revolt began at Meerut on 10th May 1857, with the uprising of Indian sepoys of the British armies in India. It was the result of accumulated resentment which had been growing since the beginning of British conquest, but was triggered off by the greased cartridges incident. Dalhousie, who came to India as the Governor General, annexed eight new states in the course of the eight years of his stay in office. The revolt soon spread all over northern and eastern India and in the Deccan. The rebels declared Bahadur Shah-II the nominal Mughal King, the Emperor of Hindustan. Hindus and Muslims fought shoulder to shoulder against the British. The deeds of valour of revolutionaries, like the Rani of Jhansi, Begum Hazrat Mahal, Kanwar Singh, Bakht Khan and Tantia Tope, have become proud legends and have inspired the posterity. The revolt was suppressed after bitter fighting for over a year, though peace was not restored until 1859. The British rulers followed a ruthless and indiscriminate policy of vengeance. The revolt marked a turning point in the history of India. The rule of the East India Company passed to the British Crown.

THE MODERN PERIOD

INDIA UNDER THE CROWN

Rule of the East India Company came to an end and administration was transferred to the British Crown. Secretary of state for India was appointed with a Council of fifteen members to assist him. Proclamation of Queen Victoria was issued. The first step after 1857 was the Indian Council Act of 1861. It provided that the Legislative Council should confine itself strictly to legislation.

Indian Council Act of 1892 : Indian Councils Act of 1892 was passed. It raised the number of members in Governor General's Council and also, in Provincial Legislative Councils. This recognised elections because the local bodies were given the right to nominate the members for vacant seats in the Provincial Legislative Councils.

Morley-Minto Reforms of 1909

The Morley-Minto Reforms of 1909 constituted the next stage in the growth of Indian Constitution. It increased the size of the legislatures. The principle of election was frankly accepted but the introduction of separate electorate for Muslims widened the rift between Hindus and Muslims. King George V and his consort visited India. Partition of Bengal was revoked.

Delhi Made Capital : The capital of India was transferred from Calcutta to Delhi in 1912. World War-I started in 1914.

The August Declaration : In August 1917, Montague declared that it was the intention of His Majesty's Government to introduce self-government in India by gradual stages. Then Montague-Chelmsford Reforms increased the membership of legislatures both at Centre and in the Provinces. World War I ended in 1918.

Government of India Act of 1919 : Government of India Act was passed which was largely based on Montague-Chelmsford Reforms. This act introduced double executive. Later, the Rowlatt Act was passed.

Other Events : Mahatma Gandhi launched *Satyagraha*. Jalianwala Bagh Massacre occurred (1919). Third Afghan War took place.

The Khilafat Movement

The Khilafat movement was organised by the famous Ali brothers, Mohammed Ali and Shaukat Ali, in protest against the injustice done to Turkey after the war. In fact, it became a part of the Indian national movement. The Congress leaders joined the Khilafat agitation and helped in organizing it throughout the country.

Non-cooperation Movement

In 1920, the Congress adopted the new programme of non-cooperation under the leadership of Gandhiji and Moti Lal Nehru. The aims of the non-cooperation movement were to redress the wrongs done to Punjab and Turkey and to help the attainment of Swaraj. It was to proceed in stages, beginning with the renunciation of titles, to be followed by the boycott of the legislatures, law courts and educational institutions and the campaign of non-payment of taxes. The noncooperation movement was a great success. In the elections to the legislatures, about two-thirds of voters did not vote. Educational institutions were deserted.

A New Programme of National Education : A new programme of national education was started. Such institutions as the Jamia Millia Islamia and the Kashi Vidya Peeth were established. Many Indians resigned their government jobs. Foreign clothes were burnt in bonfires. There were strikes in schools, colleges and commercial establishments all over the country at the height of the noncooperation movement and against the repressive measures of the British government.

The Congress Session : The annual session of the Congress was held at Ahmedabad in December, 1921. The Congress, under the Presidentship of Hakim Ajmal Khan decided to continue the movement until Punjab and Khilafat grievances were redressed and Swaraj was attained. Early in February, Gandhiji decided to launch a no-tax campaign in Bardoli district in Gujarat.

The Chauri Chaura Incident : In Chauri Chaura (in Uttar Pradesh) people turned violent and set fire to a police station causing the death of 22 policemen. When the news reached Gandhiji, he decided to call off the non-cooperation movement.

Stress on Hindu-Muslim Unity : The Working committee of the Congress met on 12th February 1922 and decided to concentrate on the popularisation of Charkha, the promotion of Hindu-Muslim unity and combating untouchability.

Round Table Conferences (1930, 1931 and 1932)

The Government of England summoned the First Round Table Conference in London but it was not attended by Mahatma Gandhi. Civil Disobedience Movement was started. The Second Round Table Conference was attended by Mahatma Gandhi. The Third Round Table Conference was held in 1932. At the conferences representatives of all political groups of India, representatives of the rulers of India, princely states and representatives from three political parties of England participated.

Government of India Act, 1935

For soothing the Indian people, the British government promulgated the Government of India Act on 2nd August, 1935. This act envisaged an All India Federation of Provinces and Indian States and the establishment of provincial autonomy in the federating provinces. At the centre, a central legislative assembly and a council of states were to be formed. The Indian princes were to be given disproportionately high representation in the two houses at the Centre. The provision regarding the formation of the federation never came into operation and the new constitution was introduced only in the provinces.

Cripps Mission (1942) : In 1942, the Cripps Mission was sent to satisfy the constitutional demands of the people and it proposed for Dominion Status after the war. Congress rejected the offer and started the famous "Quit India Movement" which was put down.

Bengal Famine (1943) : Bengal famine caused a heavy loss to human lives. Indian National Army was formed at Singapore by S.C. Bose in 1943.

The Wavell Plan (1944) : The Wavell Plan was put forward which conceded the essential unity of India. The plan also proposed certain changes in the Central Executive. The plan failed.

British Cabinet Mission (1946) : British Cabinet Mission came to India. An interim Government was constituted by Jawaharlal Nehru. The first session of the Constituent Assembly was held on 9th December, 1946.

The Partition (1947)

In June 1947, Lord Mountbatten declared the partition of India including the partition of Bengal, Assam and Punjab.

Indian Independence Act (1947) : In July, 1947 the British Parliament passed the Indian Independence Act, providing for the independence of two dominions. On 15th August 1947, the British Rule ended in India and two Dominions of India and Pakistan came into being. Kashmir legally acceded to India in October, 1947 and Indian troops were sent to Kashmir by air for the fist time to fight against Pakistani aggression. Lord Mountbatten was the first Governor General of free India from 15th August, 1947 to 2nd May, 1948.

NATIONAL MOVEMENT

The National Movement or the movement of independence was a part of a larger spectrum of national resurgence which covered almost all the aspects of national life—religious, social, educational, cultural and economic. While the progress in different spheres differed in degree and in kind from region to region, one common desire animated all regions—namely independence.

Origin

The origin of the national movement can be traced back to the revolt of 1857. In the summer of 1857, the masses revolted and the entire British dominion of India shook to its foundations. The British historians dubbed the revolt of 1857 as the sepoy-mutiny while the Indian historians termed it as the first war of Independence. True, it began as a mutiny of Indian soldiers against their British Commanders, but it soon changed its character and became a fight against British rule as such. However Indian nationalism was quite weak in 1857. For 23 years more, it could not succeed in finding a regular expression. The national movement really began in 1885 with the birth of the Indian National Congress. It is sometimes said that the history of the Indian National Congress is the history of Indian nationalism.

Indian National Congress

The birth of the Indian National Congress was an unprecedented phenomenon in the political history of India. It marked the entry of the newly educated middle class into national politics. This middle class, a by-product of the British Raj, was mainly composed of three classes: agricultural, industrial and professional. Each class had its own interests but a growing sense of nationality, often extolled as patriotism, united them in a common programme of action. From 1885 onwards, the Indian National Congress met every year. Its influence spread rapidly among the middle classes. Three main topics engaged its attention: (1) representative government and expansion of the number of functions of legislative councils both in the provinces and at the centre; (2) Indianisation of higher services; and (3) poverty in the country.

The Partition of Bengal

As the 19th century drew to a close—on December 30, 1899 – Lord Curzon came down to India as Viceroy. The growing ambition of Curzon was to destroy the political influence of the educated middle class, among whom the Bengali intelligentsia were most prominent. So his first attention was directed to Bengal. By a Royal proclamation of 16th October 1905, Bengal Province was reduced in size and population and a new province called East Bengal was created. The Indian National Congress, unanimously condemned the partition.

The *Swadeshi* Movement

The constitutional agitation so far pursued had not made an impact. The *Swadeshi* movement and boycott of foreign goods, became the mainstay of the freedom movement. Besides, open defiance of government order, refusal to pay taxes and *bandhs and hartals* followed one after the other. The Swadeshi movement gave a fillip to indigenous products, especially textiles.

An Aggressive Approach

Lord Minto, who succeeded Curzon, followed a judicious policy of admixture of the carrot and the stick. The 1905 session of the Congress at Benaras was in a sense, a turning point in the history of the Congress. The President, Gopalkrishna Gokhale, though a moderate himself, approved of aggressive agitation. From 1905, the Congress started functioning as a permanent organisation.

Rift Between Hindus and Muslims

The seeds of distrust and suspicion between Hindus and Muslims, which Minto had sown sprouted. The Muslims formed a political organization, tentatively named Muslim League. Communal riots on bigger scale occurred in 1907 at Comilla in Tripura district and in Jamalpur taluk of Mymensingh district. In future, these riots were to become almost a daily occurrence everywhere in British India.

Differences in Opinions

Differences of opinion regarding attitudes and policies to be adopted in the National Movement were discussed in 1907 when the Congress met at Surat. The moderates (doves) in the Congress were against the extremist programme of action lest it should strengthen the anti-Indian stances of the British public. Leaders of the extremist section wanted to "capture the Congress and make it an instrument of revolutionary action." The moderates retained control of the Congress. They met immediately after and drafted the new creed of Congress. The moderates, left alone, kept the Congress going as best they could.

The First World War

The First World War brought Britain into conflict with Turkey, whose Sultan was also the Khalifa of all the Muslims. That the Khilafat was in danger shook the passivity of the Indian Muslims and made them restive and thirsting for some sort of action. The change in leadership helped to bring the Congress and League together. With Turkey joining Germany against the allies in the first World War, loyalty of the Indian Muslims to the British crown became suspect. The Muslim newspapers, which supported Turkey, were suppressed and repression was let loose on the Muslims.

Demand for Home Rule

Annie Beasant, who had joined the Congress joined hands with Tilak in demanding Home Rule for India. With the defeat of Turkey and the abolition of the Sultanate, the Khilafat ceased to exist. This agitated all Muslims in India as the Muslims of the world had no religious head.

All India Khilafat Committee

In 1919, a conference at Lucknow, sponsored by Muslim leaders, the Ali brothers, Mohammed Ali and Shaukat Ali and Maulana Abul Kalam Azad decided to form an All India Khilafat Committee. Rowlatt Act roused the ire of all Indians, Hindus and Muslims alike. Mohammed Ali Jinnah, later to become the president of the Muslim League and the founder of Pakistan, resigned from his seat in the Council.

Massacre at Jalianwallah Bagh

Punjab saw the worst manifestation of British power. When the news of Gandhiji's arrest reached Lahore, the students took out a protest procession. The police opened fire on the un-offending processionists. Worse was the fate of Amritsar. Mounted police fired upon the crowd, killing some and wounding many. A protest meeting against this outrage was arranged at Jallianwallah Bagh on 13th April, 1919. The government, in anticipation of trouble, handed over Amritsar to the army under the command of General O'Dyer. Jallianwallah Bagh turned out to be a deadly trap. As the crowd filled the enclosure, O'Dyer and his troops appeared at the main entrance and rained bullets on the crowd. Men died in hundreds.The massacre at Jallianwallah Bagh was an act of unprovoked savagery, unequalled in history. It shook the country from end to end.

Swaraj Party

Swaraj Party, founded by C.R. Das and Moti Lal Nehru in 1923, consisted of Moderates and Liberals. They contested the 1920 elections and some of them were elected. They formed a type of opposition and succeeded in defeating many government motions and abolishing certain obnoxious acts like the Press Act of 1910.

Parliamentary Commission

In 1927, a Parliamentary Commission was appointed to look into the question of Constitutional Reforms for India and make suitable recommendations. The Commission was headed by Sir John Simon, a leading constitutional lawyer of Britain and a member of parliament. The Commission visited India in 1928. The Congress boycotted the Commission.

Satyagraha (1930)

Gandhiji decided to launch satyagraha and informed the Viceroy about his decision. His first act was to go to Dandi and make salt which was then a government monopoly. He set out on the march and reached Dandi with his followers on April 5, 1930. He walked into the sea waters and on return, took a lump of salt from the salt fields and thus violated the law.

Repressive Measures : All repressive laws were soon brought into force. The repealed Press Act of 1910 was revised. Gandhiji and many other outstanding leaders were arrested.

Gandhi-Irwin Pact (1931)

A pact was agreed upon between Mahatma Gandhi and Lord Irwin, the Viceroy. The Gandhi-Irwin pact was ratified by the Congress at its Karachi Session presided over by Vallabh Bhai Patel on March 29, 1934. The Congress had not attended the first Round Table Conference. However, the second Round Table Conference, which opened on 7th September, 1931, was distinguished by the fact that the Congress participated in it and was represented by Gandhiji as the sole delegate of the Congress.

Matters Complicated : By this time, a National Government by Ramsay Macdonald was formed in Britain. It was dominated by the Conservative party. Sir Samuel Hoare succeeded Wedgewood Benn as the Secretary of State for India while Lord Willingdon replaced Irwin as Viceroy.

The White Paper : The third Round Table Conference met in London on November 17, 1932 and continued its deliberations till December 24. After the end of the conference the British Government published a white paper which practically reproduced the recommendations of Simon Commission but added a scheme for a Federal Government if the Princely States agreed. The white paper, in due course, became the Government of India Act, 1935.

Khudai Khidmatgars

In the North-West Frontier Province, Abdul Ghaffar Khan (known as the Frontier Gandhi) raised a volunteer corps of one lakh Pathans, called the Servants of God and affiliated it to the Congress.

First Elections

The Act of 1935 provided two alternate constitutions for the Central Government. Firstly a Federal Government consisting of British provinces and Indian States, provided a majority of Indian States were willing to accede to the Federation. This never happened. Secondly, there was an alternative to work under the 1919 Act with some modifications. This alternative was finally accepted. In the elections, the Congress won with a huge majority, in the provinces of Madras, Bombay, Bihar, Central Province, United Province and Orissa. In other Provinces, Congress acquired a sizeable number of seats. In 1937, the Congress took charge of the governments in seven provinces. In the remaining four provinces—Punjab, Bengal, Assam and Sindh—non-Congress parties took office.

The Second World War

The outbreak of the second Word War, which commenced with Hitler's invasion of Poland on September 1, 1939, called for a complete change of policy on both sides—the British Indian Government and the Indian National Congress. India was declared a belligerent nation by Britain on September 3, 1939 and the British Indian administration was executed on a war footing. The war lasted for 6 years, till September 1945. The Congress asked all provincial Congress ministries to resign.

Demand for Freedom : In March 1940, at its annual session in Ramgarh, the Congress demanded complete independence and a Constituent Assembly to draft a constitution for free India. In the same month, the Muslim League at its Lahore session demanded a separate state for the Muslims of India.

Quit India Movement

In March 1942, the British Government sent Sir Stafford Cripps to India with proposals for a constitution. The Cripps' proposals were found unsatisfactory and were rejected both by the Congress and the League. In May 1942, Gandhiji called Britain to "leave India to God. If this is too much, then leave her to anarchy". In August 1942, the Congress committee considered Gandhiji's call to Britain and passed the famous 'Quit India' resolution.

Shimla Conference : In 1945, Lord Wavell, the Viceroy, announced that he was holding a conference in Shimla to consider the steps necessary to advance self-government for India in the near future. All the leaders in prison, were released. The Shimla conference (June-July 1945) turned out to be a fiasco. But by that time, (July), a Labour Government came into power in Britain. The Labour Government took serious notice of the Indian situation.

Cabinet Mission

The Labour Secretary of State for India, Lord Lawrence announced that a parliamentary commission would be visiting India to negotiate the question of India's independence. This delegation, which later became famous as the Cabinet Mission, announced its constitutional scheme which simply recognised the right of the Muslims to have a state of their own. While the Muslim League accepted the proposal, the Congress rejected it.

The Communal Riots : This was followed by riots. The great Calcutta killings of August 16-18, 1946, were the first of the riots. Then followed the killings in Punjab. The Congress, in desperation, accepted the partition of the country.

The Partition of India

Lord Mountbatten who succeeded Lord Wavell as Viceroy in March 1947, boldly announced the partition of India. The provinces, where the Muslims formed the majority were to be constituted into a separate state—Pakistan. The Indian Independence Act, passed by the British Parliament (July 1947) formalised the division of India into two fully independent states—India and Pakistan.

GLIMPSES

FOREIGN TRAVELLERS AND ENVOYS

Megasthenese : He came to India as the ambassador of Seleucas in the Court of Chandragupta Maurya. He wrote 'Indika'.

Delmachos : The Greek ambassador, who came to the court of Bindusara.

Fahien : A Chinese pilgrim, who visited India (401 - 410 A.D.) during the reign of Chandragupta II of Gupta dynasty.

Hiuen Tsang : A Chinese pilgrim who visited India (629-643 A.D.) during Harsha's rule.

Wang-Hiuen Tset : A Chinese envoy who visited India in the middle of the 9th century.

Al Masudi : A native of Baghadad who visited India in the first half of the 10th century.

Al Beruni : A noted scientists and scholar from Central Asia who lived in India for about ten years during the early part of the 11th century.

Barbosa : A Portuguese traveller, who visited Vijayanagar during the reign of Krishna Dev Rai.

Vasco-da-Gama : A Portuguese sailor who succeeded in reaching the port of Calicut (Kozhikode) by taking a round of the Cape of Good Hope in 1498.

Marco-Polo : A Venetian traveller, who visited south India, particularly the Pandya Kingdom, on his way to China (1288-93).

Ibn-e-Batutah : A resident of Tangier in north Africa (Morocco) who visited India in the first half of the 14th century and lived during the reign of Mohammed-bin-Tughlak for eight years.

Nicolo Conti : An Italian traveller, who visited Vijayanagar empire in 1420 during the reign of Dev Rai-I.

Abdur Razzaq : The Persian traveller, who had travelled widely in and outside India, visited the Vijayanagar empire during the reign of Dev Rai-II.

Nikitin : A Russian traveller, who visited the Bahmani Kingdom (1470-74) during the reign of Feroze Shah.

Nuniz : A Portuguese writer of 16th century who visited Vijayanagar empire during the reign of Achua Rai.

Paes : An Italian traveller, who spent a number of years at Krishna Dev Rai's court at Vijayanagar.

Caesar Frederic : A Venetian traveller, who visited Vijayanagar in the second half of 16th century.

Manuchi : An Italian traveller, who came to India and witnessed the reign of five Mughal emperors.

MINERAL WEALTH AT A GLANCE

(Metallic Minerals)

Mineral	Chief Producers
Bauxite	Orissa, Andhra Pradesh
Chromite	Orissa, Karnataka
Coal	Jharkhand, West Bengal
Copper	Rajasthan, Andhra Pradesh, Jharkhand
Diaspore	Uttar Pradesh, Madhya Pradesh
Gold	Karnataka, Rajasthan, West Bengal
Iron	Karnataka, Goa, Madhya Pradesh, Chhattisgarh
Lead	Rajasthan, Andhra Pradesh
Lignite	Tamil Nadu, Jammu & Kashmir
Manganese	Orissa, Karnataka
Natural Gas	Gujarat, Assam, Maharashtra, Andhra Pradesh
Petroleum	Gujarat, Assam, Maharashtra, Andhra Pradesh
Silver	Rajasthan, Jharkhand
Tungsten	Rajasthan, Karnataka
Zinc	Rajasthan, Bihar, Maharashtra

PRINCIPAL INDUSTRIAL CENTRES

City	Industries
Agra (U.P.)	Stoneware, Marble, Leather and Carpets
Ahmedabad (Gujarat)	Cotton textiles
Aligarh (U.P.)	Locks, Cutlery and dairy-industries
Alwaye (Kerala)	Fertilizers
Ambala (Haryana)	Scientific goods
Amritsar (Punjab)	Shawls, acid, carpet, woollen goods, cloth printing
Bangalore (Karnataka)	Aircraft Industry, telephone, watches.
Bareilly (U.P.)	Bamboo, wood work, match box, rubber, kattha.
Bhagalpur (Bihar)	Silk
Bhopal (M.P.)	Heavy electricals
Kolkata (West Bengal)	Jute, paper, iron and steel, pottery, leather works
Chennai (Tamil Nadu)	Cotton, leather, cigarette, sugar and iron factories, integral coach factory
Chittranjan (W.Bengal)	Electrical locomotives
Churk (U.P.)	Cement
Dalmia Nagar (Bihar)	Cement
Darjeeling (W.Bengal)	Tea, orange and cinchona
Delhi	Textiles, chemicals, electronics, sewing machines
Dhariwal (Punjab)	Woollen goods
Ferozabad (U.P.)	Glass-bangles
Guntur (Andhra)	Tobacco
Hardwar (Uttarakhand)	Heavy electricals
Jaipur (Rajasthan)	Cloth-printing, stoneware, brass and enamel work, lacquer work, ivory work, jewellery, pottery
Jalandhar (Punjab)	Surgical goods and sports articles

City	Industries
Jamshedpur (Jharkhand)	Iron and Steel works, locomotives, train-coaches
Kalol	Fertilizer (Gujarat) & many more
Kanpur (U.P.)	Sugar, cotton, woollen mills, soap, iron, leather, aircrafts, flour mills, tents.
Katni (M.P.)	Cement, lime
Kochi (Kerala)	Shipbuilding, coffee, coconut oil, rubber, coir mat
Kozikode (Kerala)	Calico, rubber and coir
Lucknow (U.P.)	Gold, silver, lac and embroidery-work
Ludhiana (Punjab)	Hosiery, cycle and sewing machines
Madurai (Tamil Nadu)	Cotton and Silk weaving
Mirzapur (U.P.)	Carpet, pottery, stoneware
Moradabad (U.P.)	Brassware, cutlery, enamel industry
Mumbai (Maharashtra)	Woollen goods, cotton manufacturing, chemicals, leather and metal wares, atomic reactor, oil refineries, fertilizers, film-industry.
Murshidabad (W.B.)	Silk in Bengal
Mysore (Karnataka)	Sandalwood, oil, silk goods, ivory and ebony work
Nagpur (Maharashtra)	Cotton mills
Nangal (Punjab)	Fertilizer
Nepanagar (M.P.)	Newsprint
Panipat (Haryana)	Handloom
Panna (M.P.)	Diamond Mining
Pimpri (Poona)	Antibiotic
Renukoot (U.P.)	Hindustan aluminium works
Rupnarainpur (W.B.)	Telephone Cable
Saharanpur (U.P.)	Cigarette and paper
Sindri (Jharkhand)	Fertilizers and chemicals
Srinagar (Kashmir)	Woollen shawls, silk, woodwork, embroidery, H.M.T. factory
Surat (Gujarat)	Silk, textile, diamond
Talcher (Orissa)	Fertilizer
Varanasi (U.P.)	Silk and brocade, brassware, Lac bangles, diesel locomotives

AGRICULTURE

Agriculture is the main occupation of Indian people, with 55 per cent of them engaged in it.

Land under Cultivation : In India, about 141.23 million hectares of land are under cultivation which makes 43% of the India's total land. India's agricultural growth rate is above 3.5%.

The Backbone : Agriculture is the backbone of India's economy; it provides direct employment to about 55 per cent of working people in the country, cuntributes nearly 14 per cent of Gross Domestic Product. It forms the basis of many premier industries of India, including cotton textile, jute and sugar industries. Being the largest source of employrnent and income to the millions of people, it provides vast markets for our industrial products. It is because of this paramount significance of agriculture in India's economy that this sector has been and continues to be, accorded a place of pride in India's plans for economic development. However, in spite of all the efforts, agriculture continues to remain, by and large, underdeveloped and backward. Some of the main features of agriculture in India are as follows.

CROPS

Agricultural crops can be broadly divided into two categories, viz., food crops and non-food crops. Foodgrains comprise cereals and pulses. Among the cereals, are included rice, wheat, *jowar, bajra,* maize etc. Pulses include gram, moong, masur, arhar etc. The non-food crops comprise a number of cash crops such as sugarcane, cotton, jute, tobacco etc. Tea coffee and rubber are included among the plantation crops. Besides these, we have the horticulture crops like fruit, vegetables, coconut, cashew etc.

Crop Categories

Crops in India can be categorised into two classes.

Subsistence Crops : Crops for individual consumption like foodgrains, (also known as ('food crops') cover nearly 75% of total cultivated land. Foodgrain production, which was only about 55 million tonnes in 1950-51, increased to 259.32 million tonnes in 2011-12.

Commercial Crops : Crops for an earning purpose (also known as 'cash crops'), like cotton, oil seeds, sugarcane, tobacco, groundnut etc. These also include 'Plantation Crops' (tea, coffee, rubber) and 'Horticulture Crops' (fruits, vegetables, coconut, cashewnut etc.) and cover nearly 25% of total cultivated area.

Crop Seasons

(*i*) Rabi (*ii*) Kharif

Land Classification

Net Area Sown	43.0%
Forest Cover	21.2%
Used for other Purposes	12.9%
Fallow Land	7.2%
Other Uncultivated Land	10.9%

Climate Favourable for Agriculture : 43 per cent of India's land surface is covered by plains, 28 percent of it is plateaus and 29 per cent comprises mountains and hills. In all, only 62 per cent of the Indian land is useable. India is a land of long growing seasons and there are very few parts where temperature stands in the way of developing agriculture.

CHIEF CROP PRODUCERS

Crop	State	Crop	State
Bajra	Gujarat, Rajasthan	Niger seed	West Bengal, Tamil Nadu
Barley	Uttar Pradesh, Rajasthan	Oil seeds	Uttar Pradesh, Bihar, Gujarat
Black Pepper	Kerala, Karnataka	Pulses	Madhya Pradesh, Maharashtra, Rajasthan
Cardamom	Karnataka, Kerala	Ragi	Karnataka, Tamil Nadu
Castor seed	Gujarat, Andhra Pradesh	Rapeseed and Mustard	Rajasthan, Uttar Pradesh
Chillies (dry)	Tamil Nadu, Andhra Pradesh	Rice	West Bengal, Punjab, Uttar Pradesh
Coffee	Karnataka, Kerala	Rubber	Kerala, Tamil Nadu, Karnataka
Coriander	Rajasthan, Andhra Pradesh	Sunflower	Karnataka, Maharashtra
Cotton	Gujarat, Maharashtra	Sesamum	Uttar Pradesh, Rajasthan
Ginger (dry)	Kerala, Himachal Pradesh	Silk Mulberry	Karnataka, Jammu and Kashmir, Assam
Gram	Rajasthan, Uttar Pradesh	Sugarcane	Uttar Pradesh, Maharashtra
Groundnut	Gujarat, Tamil Nadu	Tapioca	Kerala, Tamil Nadu
Guar Seed	Rajasthan, Haryana	Tea	Assam, Kerala
Hemp	Uttar Pradesh, Madhya Pradesh	Tobacco	Gujarat, Maharashtra, Tamil Nadu
Jowar	Maharashtra, Karnataka	Tur	Uttar Pradesh, Madhya Pradesh
Jute	West Bengal, Bihar, Assam	Wheat	Uttar Pradesh, Punjab, Haryana
Linseed	Madhya Pradesh, Uttar Pradesh		
Maize	Karnataka, Andhra Pradesh, Maharashtra		
Mesta	Andhra Pradesh, Orissa		
Millets (small)	Orissa, Uttar Pradesh		

MAJOR POWER PROJECTS

Thermal

- Badarpur Thermal Power Station: Delhi
- Bandel Thermal Power Station: West Bengal
- Barauni Thermal Power Station: Bihar
- Chandrapur Thermal Power Staiton: Uttar Pradesh
- Dadri Thermal Power Station: Uttar Pradesh
- Dhuvaran Thermal Power Station: Gujarat
- Ennore Thermal Power Station: Tamil Nadu
- Farakka Thermal Power Station: West Bengal
- Faridabad Thermal Power Station: Haryana
- Guru Nanak Thermal Power Station: Punjab
- Harduaganj Thermal Power Station: Uttar Pradesh
- Indraprastha Thermal Power Station: Delhi
- Korba Thermal Power Station: Chhatisgarh
- Koradi Thermal Power Station: Maharashtra
- Kothagudam Thermal Power Station: Andhra Pradesh
- Nagpur Thermal Power Station: Maharashtra
- Naharkatiya Thermal Power Station: Assam
- Nasik Thermal Power Station: Maharashtra
- Neyveli Thermal Power Station: Tamil Nadu
- North Gujarat Thermal Power Station:Gujarat
- Obra Thermal Power Station: Uttar Pradesh
- Panki Thermal Power Station:Uttar Pradesh
- Patratu Thermal Power Station: Jharkhand
- Ramagundam Thermal Power Station: Andhra Pradesh
- Sabarigiri Thermal Power Station: Kerala
- Santaldih Thermal Power Station: West Bengal
- Satpura Thermal Power Station: Madhya Pradesh and Rajasthan
- Singrauli Thermal Power Station: Uttar Pradesh
- Talcher Thermal Power Station: Orissa
- Trombay Thermal Power Station: Maharashtra
- Ukai Thermal Power Station: Gujarat
- Vindhyachal Thermal Power Station: Madhya Pradesh
- Kahalgaon Thermal Power Station: Bihar
- Yamunanagar Thermal Power Station: Haryana

Hydro-Electric

- Baira-Siul Hydro-electric Project: Himachal Pradesh
- Balimela Hydro-electric Project: Orissa and Andhra Pradesh
- Hirakud Hydro-electric Project: Orissa
- Idduki Hydro-electric Project: Kerala
- Kalinadi Hydro-electric Project: Karnataka
- Koyna Hydro-electric Project: Maharashtra
- Loktok Hydro-electric Project: Manipur
- Lower-Siliru Hydro-electric Project: Andhra Pradesh
- Machkund Hydro-electric Project: Andhra Pradesh & Orissa
- Maneri-Bhali Hydro-electric Project: Uttaranchal
- Mettur Hydro-electric Project: Tamil Nadu
- Rihand Hydro-electric Project: Uttar Pradesh
- Salal Hydro-electric Project: Jammu & Kashmir
- Sharavathi Hydro-electric Project: Karnataka
- Srisailam Hydro-electric Project: Andhra Pradesh
- Upper-Sileru Hydro-electric Project: Andhra Pradesh
- Yamuna Hydro-electric Project: Uttar Pradesh

Atomic

- Tarapur Atomic Power Project: Maharashtra
- Kakrapara Atomic Power Project: Gujarat
- Kalpakkam Atomic Power Project: Tamil Nadu
- Kota Atomic Power Project: Rajasthan
- Narora Atomic Power Project: Uttar Pradesh

IRRIGATION PROJECTS

Nagarjunasagar (Andhra Pradesh) : On the Krishna river near Nandikona village (about 44 kms from Hyderabad).

Tungabhadra (Joint project of Andhra Pradesh and Karnataka) : On the Tungabhadra river.

Pochampad (Andhra Pradesh) : Across Godavri river.

Gandak (Joint Project of Bihar and Uttar Pradesh): Nepal also derives irrigation and power benefits from this project.

Kosi (Bihar) : A multipurpose project which serves Bihar and Nepal.

Sone High Level Canal (Bihar) : An extension of Sone barrage project.

Kakrapara (Gujarat) : On the Tapti river near Kakrapara, in Surat district.

Ukai (Gujarat) : A multipurpose project across Tapti river near Ukal village.

Mahi (Joint project of Gujarat and Rajasthan) : A three-phase project, one across the Mahi river near Wanakbori village and the other across Mahi river near Kadana in Gujarat and Banswara district in Rajasthan.

Sabarmati (Gujarat) : A storage dam across Sabarmati river near Dhari village in Mehsana district and Wasna barrage near Ahmedabad.

Panam (Gujarat) : A gravity masonry dam across Panam river near Keldezar village in Panchmahal district.

Bhadra (Karnataka) : A multipurpose project across the river Bhadra.

Upper Krishna (Karnataka) : A project consisting of Narayanpur dam across the Krishna river and a dam at Almatti.

Ghataprabha (Karnataka) : A project across the Ghataprabha in Belgaum and Bijapur districts.

Malaprabha (Karnataka) : A dam across the Malaprabha in Belgaum district.

Tawa (Madhya Pradesh) : A project across the Tawa river, a tributary of the Narmada, in Hoshangabad district.

Chambal (Joint project of Madhya Pradesh and Rajasthan) : The project comprises Gandhi Sagar Dam, Rana Pratap Sagar Dam and Jawahar Sagar Dam.

Bhima (Maharashtra) : Comprises two dams, one on the Pawana river near Phagne in Pune district and the other across the Krishna river near Ujjaini in Sholapur district.

Kukadi Project (Maharashtra) : Five independent storage dams, *i.e.,* Yodgaon, Manik Dohi, Dimbha, Wadaj and Pimpalgaon Jog. The canal system comprises; *(i)* Kukadi left bank canal; *(ii)* Dimbha left bank canal; *(iii)* Dimbha right bank canal; *(iv)* Meena feeder; and *(v)* Meena branch.

Krishna Project (Maharashtra) : Dhom Dam near Dhom village on Krishna and Kanhar dam near Kanhar village on Varna river in Satna district.

Bhakra Nangal (Joint project of Haryana, Punjab and Rajasthan) : India's biggest multipurpose river valley project which comprises a straight gravity dam across the Sutlej at Bhakra, the Nangal dam and Nangal Hydel channel.

Beas (Joint venture of Haryana, Punjab and Rajasthan) : It consists of Beas-Sutlej Link and Beas Dam at Pong.

Thein Dam (Punjab) : The project comprises a dam across river Ravi and power plant on its left bank.

Pong Dam (Punjab) : On river Beas, it is an important hydroelectric project. The fourth unit of the dam was commissioned in March, 1979.

Rajasthan Canal (Rajasthan) : The project uses water released from Pong dam and provides irrigation facilities to the northwestern region of Rajasthan *i.e.,* a part of the Thar desert. It consists of Rajasthan feeder canal (with the first 167 kms in Punjab and Haryana and the remaining 37 kms in Rajasthan) and 445 kms Rajasthan Main Canal entirely in Rajasthan. Rajasthan Canal has been renamed as Indira Gandhi Canal.

Sharda Sahayak (Uttar Pradesh) : The project comprises a barrage across the river Ghagra, a link channel, a barrage across river Sharda and a feeder channel involving two major aquaducts over Gomti and Sai.

Ramganga (Uttar Pradesh) : A dam across Ramganga, a tributary of the Ganga river, besides reducing the intensity of floods in central and western Uttar Pradesh, it provides water for the Delhi water supply scheme.

Left Bank Ghagra Canal (Uttar Pradesh) : A link channel taking off from the left bank of Ghagra river off barrage and joining with Saryu river. There is also a barrage across Saryu.

Tehri Dam (Uttarakhand) : Earth and rock-fill dam on Bhagirathi river in Tehri district.

Madhya Ganga Canal (Uttar Pradesh) : A barrage across The Ganges in Bijnor district.

Farakka (West Bengal) : The project, comprises a barrage across the The Ganges at Farakka, a barrage at Jangipur across the Bhagirathi and a feeder channel taking off from The Ganges at Farakka and tailing into the Bhagirathi below the Jangipur barrage.

Kangsabati (West Bengal) : The project comprises dams on the Kangsabati and Kumari rivers.

Damodar Valley Project (West Bengal and Jharkhand) : A multipurpose project for the unified development of irrigation, flood control and power generation in West Bengal and Jharkhand. It comprises multipurpose dams at Konar, Tilaiya, Maithon and Panchet and also, a barrage at Durgapur.

LIVESTOCK

Cattle

India boasts of 27 good breeds of tropical cattle and 7 breeds of buffaloes. Indian cattle are well known the world over for their quality of hardiness, endurance and resistance to tropical animal diseases. Lately, the Government has paid special attention to cattle breeding and buffalo development. Presently, seven Central Cattle Breeding Farms are looking after the scientific cattle breeding programme. To make these plans a success, a scheme of special livestock breeding programme (SLBP), with clear-cut objectives, has been prepared and is being implemented successfully.

Total Heads : India has 57 per cent of the world's buffaloes. After the Green Revolution aimed at enhancing crop-production, a white revolution was initiated in states likes Punjab and Haryana to raise the milk yields of the cattle. We have 4 per cent of the world's sheep population. Further, goats in India account for 17 per cent of the world's population.

Poultry

Poultry farming and its development has been greatly encouraged and supported by the Government. Recently, broiler and egg production has registered a compound growth rate. Central poultry breeding farms at various places are looking after the poultry development.

Fifth Largest : During the year 2009-10 the egg production was about 59.84 billion and today, India is the fifth largest egg producer in the world.

Sheep Development

Sheep Development is useful for the production of wool, required for individual consumption as well as for the garment and carpet industries. Apart from sheep development, the development of goats, rams and rabbits is also being enhanced in a planned way. For this purpose, a Central Sheep Breeding Farm has been established at Hissar.

Meat Production

Meat is produced at a large and an organised scale for domestic consumption, as well as for export purposes. Presently, there are around 4,000 major slaughter houses in the country, including some sophisticated ones.

Pig Development

India, with 11.13 million pigs, has a potential in pig farming too. Presently, there are 158 pig farm units in the country, production of pigs, being largely concentrated in the northeastern states.

Dairy Development

India's milk production has increased manifold. Operation Flood, a special State programme in dairy farming and milk production, has helped a lot for a record production in this field.

Fisheries

Like poultry and dairy farming, fisheries are also an important part of the livestock based production in this country. Fish are produced for domestic consumption and for export as well. During last five decades, the fish production in the country has increased many times.

FORESTS

Forests in India cover nearly 21.05% of the total land area (Approximately 6,92,027 sq km). It makes about 2% of total forest cover in the world. As a national policy, India's target is to raise the forest area by 33.3%.

Usefulness : The forests check soil erosion on hill slopes in upper catchment areas of rivers which ultimately contributes towards the control of floods. The forests help to increase the rainfall and improve the climate. These also produce timber, woods for raw material required by industrial units and for fuel, as well.

Third in the World : India stands third as the producer of hardwood after Brazil and Indonesia.

Forests at a Glance

Largest Forest Cover	Madhya Pradesh
Maximum Land Area under Dense Forests	Arunachal Pradesh
Minimum Land Area under Forest Cover	Haryana

Total Forests : 21.05 per cent of Indian territory, that is an area of 6,92,027 sq.km. is covered under one or the other type of forests. We have tropical evergreen forests in Kerala and Assam and coniferous forests in the west Himalayas. From Madhya Pradesh to Rajasthan tropical deciduous and horny shrubs grow. Subtropical vegetation thrives in the small areas in the Himalayas. Dense forests are confined to inaccessible parts of the Himalayas, isolated eastern hills and a few pockets in Western Ghats.

WILDLIFE

Rich with tremendous diversity of climate and supportive physical conditions, India is full of fauna, numbering a little over 92,037 known species. Of these, insects constitute about 40,000, molluscs over 5,000, mammals 392, birds 1,232, reptiles 462, amphibians 312 and fish 2,641.

Big Animals

Among important Indian mammals are Lion, Tiger, Elephant, Bison, Rhinoceros, Deer, Wild Sheep, Antelope, Black Buck, Leopard and Wild Cats etc.

Birds

The birds are also in abundance; prominent among them are Peacock, Goose, Parakeets and Pigeons.

Wildlife Protection

Most of the wild animals and birds have been declared protected in India, prominent among them being Lion, Tiger, Deer and Peacock. All rare and valuable wild animals and birds are protected by a law, known as The Wildlife Protection Act-1972. The killing and trading of the protected animals and birds is banned and punishable. For the preservation of the wildlife and especially the endangered species, there are a number of national parks, sanctuaries and zoological gardens, scattered all over the country, which cover about 4.5 per cent of the total land.

WILD WEALTH

Animals	Where found
Wild Sheep and Goat	Ladakh, Western Ghats, the Himalayas, Nilgiris Punjab, Himachal Pradesh and from the base of the Himalayas to Karnataka
Deer	Kashmir, sub-Himalayan Tract, U.P., M.P., Assam and the Indo-Gangetic plain
Antelope	Punjab and south of the Himalayas
Wild Oxe and Buffalo	Tamil Nadu, Kerala, Karnataka etc.
Wolf	From the Himalayas to Peninsular India
Hyaena	All over India
Bear	All over India
Rhinoceros	Assam and West Bengal
Elephant	Western Ghats, Karnataka, Coorg, the Nilgiris, Orissa, U.P., Assam and West Bengal
Panther	Almost in all forests throughout India
Leopard	The Himalayas, Sikkim and Bhutan
Tiger	Almost throughout India
Lion	Only in the Gir forest
Snake	All over India

NATIONAL PARKS AND WILDLIFE SANCTUARIES

Bandhavgarh National Park, Shahdol (Madhya Pradesh)
Bandipur National Park, Mysore (Karnataka)
Bannarghatta National Park, Bengluru (Karnataka)
Borivili National Park, Mumbai (Maharashtra)
Chandraprabha Sanctuary, Varanasi (Uttar Pradesh)
Corbet National Park, Nainital (Uttarakhand)
Dachigam Sanctuary, Srinagar (Jammu and Kashmir)
Dudhwa National Park, Lakhimpur Kheri (Uttar Pradesh)
Eravikulam Rajmallay National Park, Idduki (Kerala)
Ghana Bird Sanctuary, Bharatpur (Rajasthan)
Ghatprabha Bird Sanctuary, Belgaum (Karnataka)
Gir National Park, Junagarh (Gujarat)
Guindy National Park, Chennai (Tamil Nadu)
Hazaribagh National Park, Hazaribagh (Jharkhand)
Jaldapara Sanctuary, Jalpaiguri (West Bengal)
Kanha National Park, Mandla (Madhya Pradesh)
Kaziranga National Park, Jorhat (Asom)
Khangchandzenda National Park, Gangtok (Sikkim)
Kutree Game Sanctuary, Bastar (Chhatisgarh)
Manas Tiger Sanctuary, Barpeta (Asom)
Melapattu Bird Sanctuary, Nellore (Andhra Pradesh)
Mudumalai Sanctuary, Nilgiris (Tamil Nadu)
Negerhole National Park, Coorg (Karnataka)
Nal Sarovar Bird Sanctuary, Ahmedabad (Gujarat)
Nawgaon National Park, Bhandara (Maharashtra)
Palamau Tiger Sanctuary, Daltenganj (Jharkhand)
Pench National Park, Nagpur (Maharashtra)
Periyar Sanctuary, Idduki (Kerala)
Ranganthitoo Bird Sanctuary, Mysore (Karnataka)
Ranthambor Tiger Sanctuary, Sawai Madhopur (Rajasthan)
Rohia National Park, Kulu (Himachal Pradesh)
Shivpur National Park, Shivpuri (Madhya Pradesh)
Similipal Tiger Sanctuary, Mayurbhanj (Orissa)
Sultanpur Lake Bird Sanctuary, Gurgaon (Haryana)
Sunderbans Tiger Sanctuary, 24 Pargana (West Bengal)
Todoba National Park, Chandrapur (Maharashtra)
Valavadar National, Park, Bhavnagar (Gujarat)

GENERAL SCIENCE

BRANCHES OF SCIENCE

Aeronautics	The Science or art of flight.
Agronomy	The Science of soil management and the production of field crops.
Anatomy	Structure of human body.
Astronomy	Study of the heavenly bodies.
Biology	The study of living things.
Botany	Science of plant life.
Chemistry	Study of elements and their laws of combination and behaviour.
Cryptography	Study of Cyphers (secret writings).
Cytogenetics	Cell Formation.
Cytology	Study of Cells.
Dermatology	Study of Skin and Skin diseases.
Entomology	Study of insects.
Ethology	Study of animal behaviour.
Exbiology	Science dealing with life or possibilities of life existing beyond the earth.
Geology	The science that deals with the physical history of the earth.
Horticulture	Art of garden cultivation.
Hydroponics	Culture of plants without soil, with the help of chemical solution containing nutrients.
Iconography	Teaching by pictures and models.
Jurisprudence	Science of law.
Limnology	The Study of lakes.
Meteorology	Science of the atmosphere and its phenomena.
Mycology	The study of fungi and fungus diseases.
Neurology	The study of the nervous system.
Numismatics	Coins and medals.
Obstetrics	Branch of medicine dealing with pregnancy.
Odontology	The scientific study of the teeth.
Ornithology	Study of birds.
Osteology	The study of the bones.
Otorhinolaryngology	The study of diseases of ear, nose and throat.
Paleobotany	The study of fossil plants.
Paleontology	The study of fossils.
Pedogogy	Education
Phrenology	The study of the faculties and qualities of minds from the shape of the skull.
Phycology	The study of algae.
Physics	The study of the properties of matter.
Physiography	The science of physical geography.
Pomology	Fruits
Psychology	The study of human and animal behaviour.
Radiology	The study of X-rays and radioactivity.
Seisomology	The study of earthquakes.
Sericulture	Silk-worm breeding.
Sociology	The study of human society.
Telepathy	Communication between minds by some means other than sensory perception.
Therapeutics	The science and art of healing.
Toxicology	The study of poisons.
Virology	The study of viruses.
Zoology	The study of animal life.

DISEASES AFFECTING HUMAN BODY

Disease	Affected part
Arthritis	Joints
Dysentery	Bowels
Cataract	Eyes
Diabetes	Pancreas
Diphtheria	Throat
Eczema	Skin
Goiter	Thyroid gland
Jaundice	Liver
Meningitis	Spinal cord
Pleurisy	Chest wall
Pneumonia	Lungs
Pyorrhoea	Gums
Rheumatism	Joints
Trachoma	Eyes
Tuberculosis	Lungs
Typhoid	Intestines in particular

INSTRUMENTS AND APPLIANCES

Altimeter is a special type of aneroid barometer, used in measuring altitudes.

Ammeter is an instrument to measure the strength of an electric current.

Anemometer is an instrument to measure the velocity and find the direction of the wind.

Audiometer is an instrument to measure difference in hearing.

Barometer is used for measuring atmospheric pressure.

Binocular is an optical instrument designed for magnified view of distant objects by both eyes simultaneously.

Calorimeter is an instrument for measuring quantities of heat.

Clinical Thermometer is a thermometer for measuring the temperature of human body.

Colorometer is an instrument for comparing intensity of colour.

Commutator is an instrument to change or reverse the direction of an electric current. Used in dynamo to convert the alternating current into direct current.

Chronometer is a clock to determine longitude of a vessel at sea.

Dynamo is a device for converting mechanical energy into electrical energy.

Dynamometer is an instrument for measuring the electrical power.

Electroscope is an instrument for detecting the presence of electric charge.

Galvanometer is an instrument for measuring electric current.

Hydrometer is an instrument for measuring the relative density of liquids.

Hydrophone is an instrument for measuring sound under water.

Hygrometer is an instrument for measuring the relative humidity of the atmosphere.

Hygroscope is an instrument to show the changes in atmospheric humidity.

Lactometer is an instrument for measuring the relative density of milk.

Magnetometer is an instrument used to compare the magnetic moments and fields.

Manometer is an instrument to measure the pressure of gases.

Mariner's Compass is an apparatus for determining direction, graduated to indicate 33 directions. The "N" point on the dial indicates north pole and the "S" point, south pole.

Micrometer is an instrument used for accurately measuring small distances or angles.

Photometer is an instrument for comparing the luminous intensity of the sources of light.

Planimeter is a mechanical integrating instrument for measuring the area of a plane surface.

Pyknometer is an instrument used to measure the density and coefficient of expansion of a liquid.

Pyrheliometer is an instrument for measuring solar radiation.

Pyrometer is an instrument for measuring high temperatures.

Quadrant is an instrument for measuring altitudes and angles in navigation and astronomy.

Quartz Clock is a highly accurate clock used in astronomical observation and other precision work.

Radio Micrometer is an instrument for measuring heat radiation.

Rain Gauge is an instrument for measuring rainfall.

Refractometer is an instrument used to measure the refractive index of a substance.

Resistance Thermometer is used for determining the electrical resistance of a conductor.

Salinometer is a type of hydrometer used to determine the concentration of salt solutions by measuring their densities.

Seismograph is an instrument used for recording the intensity and origin of earthquake shocks.

Sextant is an instrument used for the measurement of angular distances between two objects.

Spectroscope is an instrument used for spectrum analysis.

Spectrometer is a type of spectroscope so calibrated as to make it suitable for the precise measurement of refractive indices.

Spherometer is an instrument used for accurately measuring the curvature of spherical objects.

Sphygmomanometer is an apparatus for measuring blood pressure.

Spring Balance is used to measure the mass of a body. It is preferred only when quick but approximate determinations are to be carried out.

Stereoscope is an optical device to see two dimensional pictures have depth and solidity.

Stethoscope is a medical instrument for hearing and analysing the sound of heart and lungs.

Stroboscope is an instrument used for viewing the objects moving rapidly with a periodic motion and to view them as if they were at rest.

Tangent Galvanometer is an instrument for measuring the strength of direct current.

Thermometer is an instrument for measuring the temperature of a substance. It makes use of the fact that a substance expands or exhibits a change in temperature. It measures the temperature relative to two physical constants—the freezing point and the boiling point of water.

Thermoscope is used for measuring the temperature change (approximately) of the substance by noting the corresponding change in volume.

Thermostat is an automatic device for regulating constant temperatures.

Transistor is a small device which may be used to amplify currents and perform other functions usually performed by a thermionic valve.

Vernier is an adjustable scale with marking of 10 subdivisions of one-tenth of an inch or any other suitable markings for measuring small sub-divisions of scale.

Viscometer is an instrument for measuring the viscosity, *i.e.* the property of resistance of a fluid to relative motion within itself.

Voltmeter is an instrument to measure potential difference between two points.

SCIENTIFIC MEASURES

Ampere : Unit of electric current. It is approximately equal to the flow of 6.023×10^{23} electrons per second.

Atomic Weight : The weight of an atom of hydrogen is taken as a standard. The respective weights of the atoms of all other substances are expressed in terms of it. So, when it is stated that the atomic weight of iron is 56, it is meant that an atom of iron is 56 times as heavy as an atom of hydrogen.

Angstrom : The unit of wavelength of light is Angstrom. 1 Angstrom=10^{-6} cm. There is a bigger unit for measuring the wavelength of infrared light; it is called a milli-micron and is equal to 10^{-7} cm.

Bar : Bar is the unit of atmospheric pressure; one bar is equal to a pressure of 10^6 dynes per sq. cm.

Calories : It is the unit of heat. It is the amount of heat required to raise the temperature of one gram of water.

Horse Power : The practical unit of power, it is the power of an agent which can work at the rate of 550 foot pounds per second or 33,000 foot pounds per minute. 1HP=746 watts.

Joule : It is the unit of work or energy. It is equal to 10 ergs. It is the energy consumed in one second in an electrical circuit through which a current of one ampere is flowing against a potential difference of one volt.

Knot : It is a measure to find the speed of a ship.

Light Year : A light year is the distance, light travels in one mean solar year, at a speed of 1,86,000 miles per second. It is equal to 5,880,000,000,000 miles. It is used as a unit for measuring stellar distances.

Nautical Mile : A unit of distance used in navigation. A nautical mile is approximately equal to 6,080 feet.

Pressure : The pressure is expressed in pounds weight per sq. cm. The pressure of the atmosphere is expressed in millibars. One millibar = 1 dyne per sq. cm. If the pressure is very high, this is expressed in multiples of atmospheric pressure 1 atmosphere is a pressure exerted by a column of mercury, 76 cm. high at sea level and at a latitude of 45.

Quintal : Metric measure of weight; 100 kilograms=1 quintal.

Volt : It is a unit of potential difference. The difference of potential between two parts on a conducting wire carrying a constant current of 1 ampere when the power dissipated between these two points is 1 watt.

Watt : Unit of power, it is the rate of work done in joules per seconds.

ADVANCEMENTS IN SCIENCE

INDIAN SPACE RESEARCH PROGRAMME

Indian space programme is directed towards self-reliance in the usage of space science and technology for national development. Main thrust is in the areas of: *(i)* satellite communications for various national applications including telecommunication, TV broadcast and radio networking; *(ii)* resources survey and management, environmental monitoring and meteorological services through remote sensing; and *(iii)* development of indigenous satellites and launching of vehicles to achieve the above objectives.

Space Commission : For promoting a unified development and application of space science and technology for national development, Space Commission and Department of Space were created in 1972 to evolve policies and guidelines to achieve envisaged objectives. Policies framed by Space Commission are implemented through Department of Space (DoS) and Indian Space Research Organisation (ISRO). DoS is also the nodal agency charged with the responsibility of establishing National Natural Resources Management System (NNRMS). The activities of ISRO are carried out by following centres/units.

(1) Vikram Sarabhai Space Centre (VSSC), Thiruvananthapuram. (2) Indian Satellite Application Centre (ISAC), Bangalore. (3) SHAR Centre, Sriharikota (Andhra Pradesh). (4) Space Applications Centre (SAC), Ahmedabad. (5) Liquid Propulsion Systems Centre (LPSC) with its facilities at Bangalore, Thiruvananthapuram and Mahendragiri. (6) ISRO Telemetry Tracking and Command Network (ISTRAC) with its network of ground stations and Development and Educational Communication Unit (DECU), Ahmedabad. (7) Master Control Facility (MCF), Hassan (Karnataka). (8) National Remote Sensing Agency (NRSA), Secundrabad.

The headquarters of Department of Space and ISRO are located at Bangalore.

Background : Indian participation in the field of space research dates back to 1962 when an Indian National Committee for Space Research was set up under the chairmanship of Dr. Vikram A. Sarabhai.

India's practical space activity began with the establishment of the Thumba Equatorial Rocket Launching Station (TERLS) at the Vikram Sarabhai Space Centre (VSSC) in 1963. VSSC had been established a year earlier.

Scientists from the (erstwhile) U.S.S.R., France, Germany, the United Kingdom and the United States participated in the projects involving these rockets launched for meteorological, ionospheric, serenomic and astronomical studies.

Apple

Ariane Passenger Payload Experiment (APPLE) satellite was launched at 4.43 PM on June 19, 1981. The 673 kg. satellite was put into orbit by ESAs Ariane launch vehicle under ESA-ISRO joint venture along with two other satellites Meteorite - 2 (European Weather Satellite) and CAT (Ariane Technology Capsule) from Kourou in French Guyana.

Aryabhatta

India began its experimental satellite missions during the seventies and it ultimately led to the establishment of operational space systems. Aryabhatta, the first Indian satellite was launched in April 1975 by an Intercosmos Rocket of the former U.S.S.R. Aryabhatta had carried on board three scientific payloads.

Bhaskara

Aryabhatta was followed by two remote sensing satellites, Bhaskara-1 and Bhaskara-2 launched in 1979 and 1981 respectively. The Bhaskaras paved the way for further space programmes.

Rohini

India's indigenous Satellite Launch Vehicle SLV-3 blasted off from the Sriharikota range (SHAR) on May 31, 1981, on its first development flight. It lifted into orbit the 40 kg Rohini satellite 12 minutes later, travelling at a speed of 28,000 km an hour. Ninety-five minutes after the blast, the confirmation that Rohini satellite was in orbit was received from the Thiruvananthapuram ground station which said the satellite was performing satisfactorily. Rohini burned as it entered earth's orbit in August, 1981.

INSAT SYSTEM

The Indian National Satellite (INSAT) System is a great gift, the Government and the brilliant Indian scientists have given to the people of India, during last two decades of the previous century. India has achieved a lot in its endeavours in space, in these two decades.

Through 1980s, India succeeded in establishing operational space system. INSAT was commissioned in 1983 by way of multipurpose satellites. In fact INSAT system is a multipurpose operational satellite system, involving a multi-agency system for inland telecommunications, direct telecasting broadcasting, through satellites, relaying data and meteorological observations.

INSAT System is a joint venture of to Department of Space, Department of Telecommunication, Indian Meteorological Department, Doordarshan and All India Radio. However, the Department of Space has the direct responsibility for establishing and operating the INSAT System.

In 1983, first of all, INSAT-1B was commissioned successfully (Prior to it INSAT-1A was launched in 1982, but it had failed). Then consequently, INSAT 1C (1988), INSAT-1D (1990), INSAT-2A (1992), INSAT-2B (1993), INSAT-2C (1995), INAT-2D (1997) and INSAT-2E (1999) were launched. Of these all of them—with the only exception of INSAT-1C—were successful.

Impact of INSAT System: This system has brought about a revolutionary change in the field of telecommunications, weather forecasting and television expansion. In other words, it has had a tremendous impact on the above said three areas and indirectly on all other related areas, benefitting the Indian people, as whole.

India's Moon Mission: In a major blow to India's maiden mission to the moon, the Indian Space Research Organisation (ISRO) abruptly lost contact with Chandrayaan-1 at 01.30 a.m. on August 29, 2009. This means no command can be given to the spacecraft and no data, including images of the moon's surface, are being received from it. The Chandrayaan-1 mission has come to an end in ten months instead of its slated life of two years. The spacecraft had completed 312 days in orbit, making more than 3,400 orbits around the moon and sent back more than 70,000 images of the lunar surface, which provided breathtaking views of lunar mountains and craters, especially craters in the permanently shadowed areas of the moon's polar region. It also collected data on the chemical and mineral content of the moon's soil. ISRO claimed that the mission had met most of its scientific objectives.

INSAT Satellites Launched : At a Glance

INSAT-1A April 10, 1982 : Deactivated in September 1982

INSAT-1B August 30, 1983 : Completed mission life

INSAT-1C July 22, 1988 : Abandoned in November 1989

INSAT-1D June 12, 1990 : Completed mission life

INSAT-2A July 10, 1992 : Completed mission life

INSAT-2B July 23, 1993 : Completed mission life

INSAT-2C December 7, 1997 : Completed mission life

INSAT-2D June 4, 1997 : Became inoperable in October 1997

INSAT-2DT in-Orbit Procurement : Completed mission life

INSAT-2E April 3, 1999 : In service

INSAT-3A April 10, 2003 : In service

INSAT-3B March 22, 2000 : In service

INSAT-3C January 24, 2002 : In service

Kalpana-1 September 12, 2002 : In service

GSAT-2 May 8, 2003 : In service

INSAT-3E September 28, 2003 : In service

EDUSAT September 20, 2004 : In service

INSAT-4C July 10, 2006 : Not placed in orbit

INSAT-4A December 22, 2006 : In service

INSAT-4B March 12, 2007 : In service

INSAT-4CR September 2, 2007 : Placed in orbit

G-SAT-12 July 15, 2011 : Placed in Geo-Synchronous Transfer Orbit

INSAT-3D-July 26, 2013, launched by Ariane 5

GSAT-7-August 30, 2013, launched by Ariane 5

Mangalyan-Nov. 5, 2013, launched by PSLV-C-25

GSAT 14-Jan. 1, 2014, launched by GSLV-D5

Spot-7, June 30, 2014 launched by PSLVC-23.

IRNSS-1C, Oct. 16, 2014 launched by PSLV-C-26.

INDIA'S MARS ODYSSEY

The nation's prestigious interplanetary mission to Mars, 40 crore km away, got off to a flying start on November 5 when the Indian Space Research Organisation's trusty Polar Satellite Launch Vehicle (PSLV-C25) (see photo on cover) roared off the first launch pad of the spaceport at Sriharikota at 2.38 p.m. and put the Mars orbiter precisely into its earth-orbit about 44 minutes later. The ₹ 460 crore Mars

Orbiter Mission (MOM) will voyage for 300 days before it reaches the Martian orbit. The orbiter weighs about 1350 kg with five scientific instruments on board to conduct a battery of remote-sensing experiments on the availability of methane on the Red Planet, its upper atmosphere, its surface features, mineralogy and so on. The gold-coloured probe will leave Earth's sphere of influence on December 1, 2013 and is expected to enter Mar's orbit on September 24, 2014. If the mission is successful, India will be the first Asian country to reach Mars. Only the US, Russia and Europe have succeeded till now. Later on November 19, the Mangalyaan sent its first image of earth taken by the Mars Colour Camera.

ATOMIC ENERGY

The Atomic Energy Commission, set up in August, 1948, is responsible for all atomic energy activities in the country. Research and development work on the application of atomic energy is done at the Bhabha Atomic Research Centre (BARC) at Trombay, near Mumbai.

Various Research Reactors : These include (1) Apsara; (2) Cirus; (3) Zerlina; (4) Purnima; (5) Dhruva; and (6) Kamini.

Nuclear Power : Nuclear Power made its debut in this country with the commissioning of the 420 MW Tarapur atomic power station in Maharashtra in 1969.

Nuclear Explosion : India exploded her nuclear device on May 18, 1974 first, at Pokhran in the Thar desert of Rajasthan. Thus India became the sixth nuclear power in the world. India repeated the exercise, known as Pokhran-II, in 1998. This strengthened her position as an atomic power.

Nuclear Stations : Nuclear power stations in India.

(1) Tarapur Atomic Power Station in Maharashtra.
(2) Rajasthan Atomic Power Station at Rana Pratap Sagar near Kota.
(3) Kalpakkam Atomic Power Station in Tamil Nadu.
(4) Narora Atomic Power Station at Narora (U.P.)
(5) Nuclear Power Station at Kaiga.
(6) Atomic Power Station at Kakrapar, Gujarat.
(7) Atomic Power Station at Kudan Kulam, Tamil Nadu.

Atomic Minerals : (1) Uranium is found in Jharkhand, U.P., M.P. and H.P. (2) Thorium is found in Kerala, A.P., Karnataka, Tamil Nadu and Jharkhand. (3) Beryllium is found in Jharkhand, Rajasthan, M.P. and Maharashtra.

BOOKS AND AUTHOR

INDIAN AUTHORS

Books	*Authors*
Aadhe Adhure	Mohan Rakesh
Aag Ka Dariya	Qurratul-ain-Haider
A Million Mutinies now	V.S. Naipaul
A Suitable Boy	Vikram Seth
A Passage to England	Nirad C. Chaudhury
A Voice for Freedom	Nayantara Sehgal
Accession to Extinction	D.R. Manekar
Adi Granth	Guru Arjun Dev
After the Dark Night	S.M. Ali
Agni Pariksha	Acharya Tulsi
Agni Veena	Kazi Nazrul Islam
Ain-i-Akbari	Abul Fazal
Ajatshatru	Jai Shankar Prasad
Akbarnama	Abul Fazal
An Idealist View of Life	S. Radhakrishnan
Amruta Santan	Gopinath Mohanty
Anandmath	Bankim Chandra Chatterjee
Area of darkness	V.S. Naipaul
Arthashastra	Kautilya
Autobiography of an Unknown Indian	Nirad C. Chaudhury
Awara Sajday	Kaifi Azami
Baburnama	Babur
Bandicoot run	Manohar Malgaonkar
Bang-e-dara	Mohammad Iqbal
Between the lines	Kuldip Nayar
Bhagwat Gita	Ved Vyas

Books	Authors
Bharat Bharati	Maithali Sharan Gupt
Bisarjan	Rabindarnath Tagore
Broken Wing	Sarojini Naidu
Buddha Charitran	Ashvaghosha
By God's Decree	Kapil Dev
Chandalika	Rabindranath Tagore
Chemmeen	Thakazhi Sivasankara Pillai
Chidambra	Sumitranandra Pant
Chikaveera Rajendra	Masti Venkatesh Iyengar "Srinivasa"
Chitra	Rabindranath Tagore
Chitralekha	Bhagwati Charan Verma
Confessions of a Lover	Mulk Raj Anand
Conquest of Self	Mahatma Gandhi
Continent of Circe	Nirad C. Chaudhury
Coolie	Mulk Raj Anand
Crescent moon	Rabindranath Tagore
Dark Room	R.K. Narayan
Dashdwar Se Sopan Tak	Harivansh Rai Bachchan
Day in Shadow	Nayantara Sehgal
Death of a City	Amrita Pritam
Devdas	Sarat Chandra
Discovery of India	Jawahar Lal Nehru
Divine Life	Sivananda
Durgesh Nandini	Bankim Chandra Chatterjee
End of an Era	C.S. Pandit
Fatal Cart, The	C. Rajagopalachari
Fire on the Mountain	Anita Desai
Ganadevata	Tara Shankar Bandyopadhyaya
Gardener	Rabindranath Tagore
Geet Govind	Jaye Dev
Ghasiram Kotwal	Vijay Tendulkar
Gitanjali	Rabindranath Tagore
Glimpses of World History	Jawaharlal Nehru
Godan	Munshi Prem Chand
God of Small Things, The	Arundhati Roy
Golden Gate	Vikram Seth
Gora	Rabindranath Tagore
Guide, The	R.K. Narayan
Gul-e-Nagma	Raghupati Sahai "Firaq"
Harsha Charitra	Bana Bhatt
Hindu View of Life	Radhakrishnan
Hinduism	Nirad C. Chaudhury
Hitopadarsan	Narayan
Hungry Stones	Rabindranath Tagore
I am not an Island	Khwaja Ahmed Abbas
Idols	Sunil Gavaskar
I Follow the Mahatama	K.M. Munshi
India Divided	Rajendra Prasad
India Wins Freedom	Maulana Abul Kalam Azad
Indian Muslims	Mohammad Mujeeb
Indian Philosophy	S. Radhakrishnan
Indian War of Independence	V.D. Savarkar
India — A Wounded Civilization	V.S. Naipaul
India Today	R. Palme Dutt
Iyaruingam	B.K. Bhattacharya
Jnana Gangotri	Niranjana
Juhi Ki Kali	Suryakant Tripathi "Nirala"
Justice of Peace Ke Aansu	Janardan Prasad Singh
Jobs for Millions	V.V. Giri
Kadambari	Bana Bhatt
Kamasutra	S.H. Vatsyayana
Kamayani	Jai Shankar Prasad
Kapal Kundala	Bankim Chandra Chatterjee
Karpuri Manjari	Rajsekhara
Khak-i-Dil	Jan Nissar Akhtar
Kiratar Juniya	Bharavi
Last Phase, The	Pyare Lal
Life Divine	Aurobindo Ghosh
Mahabharata	Ved Vyas
Malati Madhav	Bhavabhuti
Manvini Bhavai	Pannalal Patel
Mati Matal	Gopinath Mohanty
Meghdoot	Kalidas
Mrichcha Katikam	Sudraka
Mudrarakshasa	Vishakhadatta
Mukajjiya Kanasugalu	Shivrama Karnath
Muslim Dilemma in India	M.K.A. Baig
My Experiments with truth	Mahatama Gandhi
My Music, My Life	Ravi Shankar
My Presidential Years	R. Venkataraman
My Struggle in the Woods of God	Swami Ram Tirth Realisation
My Truth	Indira Gandhi
My Years with Nehru	B.N. Mullick

Books	Authors
Naganandan	Harsha Vardhan
Naked Triangle	Balwant Gargi
Naku Thanthi	Dattatraya Ramchandra Bendre
Netaji — Dead or Alive	Samar Guha
Nisheeth	Uma Shankar Joshi
Niti-Sataka	Bhartrihari
Oddakkuzal	G. Shankar Kurup
Our India	Minoo Masani
Our Presidents	M.A. Naidu
Padmavati	Malik Mohammad Jyasi
Panchagram	Tarashankar Bandyopadhyaya
Panchatantra	Vishnu Prabhakar Sharma
Pather Panchali	Bibhuti Bhushan Bandyopadhyaya
Pavittar Pappi	Nanak Singh
Pichale Paher	Jan Nissar Akhtar
Prathama Pratishruti	Ashapuma Devi
Prem Pachisi	Munshi Prem Chand
Prison and Chocolate cake	Nayantara Sehgal
Prison Diary	Jayaprakash Narayan
Prithviraj Raso	Chandra Bardai
Raghuvamsa	Kalidas
Rajtarangini	Kalhana
Ramayana	Valmiki
Ramayana Darshanam	K.V. Puttappa
Ram Charita Manas	Tulsidas
Rangbhoomi	Munshi Prem Chand
Ranti-Tangazhi	T.S. Pillai
Ratnavali	Harsha Vardhan
Red Lape and White Cap	P.V.R. Rao
Reminiscences of the Nehru Age	M.O. Mathai
Return of Red Rose	K.A. Abbas
Ritu Samhara	Kalidas
Saket	Maithili Sharan Gupt
Sanskriti Ke Char Adhyay	Ramdhari Singh 'Dinkar'
Satyartha Prakash	Swami Dayanand
Scholar Extraordinary	Nirad C. Chaudhury
Scope of Happiness, The	Vijayalakshmi Pandit
Seven Summers	Mulk Raj Anand
Shadow from Ladakh	Bhabani Bhattacharya
Shakuntala	Kalidas
Shahnama	Firdausi

Books	Authors
Songs of India, The	Sarojini Naidu
Soze-i-Watan	Munshi Prem Chand
Sreemad Ramayana Kalpavrikshmu	Vishwenath Satyanarayana
Story of My Life, The	Morarji Desai
Subhanna	M. Venkates Iyengar
Sunny Days	Sunil Gavaskar
Sursagar	Surdas
Tapasyi-o-Tarangini	Buddhadev Bose
Thirukkural	Thiruvalluvar
The Nation's Voice	C. Rajgopalachari
The Sikhs Today	Khushwant Singh
Towards Total Revolution	Jayaprakash Narayan
Tulsi Ka Gyanbodh	Suryakant Tripathi Nirala
Two Leaves and a Bud	Mulk Raj Anand
Tyagpatra	Jainendra
Unhappy India	Lala Lajpat Rai
Untold Story	General B.M. Kaul
Urvashi	Ramdhari Singh 'Dinkar'
Uttara-Ramcharita	Bhava Bhuti
Venisamphar	Naryana Bhatt
Vinay Patrika	Tulsidas
Virangana	Maithili Sharan Gupt
Vish Vriksha	Bankim Chandra Chatterjee
War of Indian Independence	Veer Savarkar
Yama	Mahadevi Verma
Yashodara	Maithili Saran Gupt
Yayat	V.S. Khandekar
Zulfi, My Friend	Piloo Mody

FOREIGN AUTHORS

Books	Authors
A China Passage	J.K. Galbraith
A Dangerous Place	Deniel Patrick Moynihan
A Doll's House	Ibsen
A Farewell to Arms	Ernest Hemingway
A Midsummer Night's Dream	Shakespeare
A Pair of Blue Eyes	Thomas Hardy
A Passage to India	E.M. Forster
A Study of History	Amold Toynbee
A View from Delhi	Chester Bowles
A Tale of Two Cities	Charles Dickens

Book	Author
A Thousand Days	Arthur M. Schlesinger
A Week with Gandhi	Louis Fischer
A Woman of No Importance	Oscar Wilde
Adventures of Sherlock Holmes	Sir Arthur Conan Doyle
Adventures of Tom Saweyer, The S.L. Glamentes	Mark Twain
Affluent Society, The	J.K. Galbraith
Age of Reason, The	Jean Paul Sartre
Alice's Adventure in Wonderland	Lewis Corrol
All the President's Men	Carl Bernstein and Bob Woodward
All is Well that Ends Well	William Shakespeare
All Quiet on the Western Front	Erich Maria Remarque
Ambassador's Journal	J.K. Galbraith
Ambassador's Report	Chester Bowles
An Ideal Husband	Oscar Wilde
Ancient Mariner, The	Samuel Taylor Coleridge
And Quiet Flows the Don	Mikhail Sholokhov
Animal Farm, The	George Orwell
Anna Karenina	Count Leo Tolstoy
Antony and Cleopatra	William Shakespeare
Apple Cart	George Bernard Shaw
Arabian Nights	Sir Richard Burton
Arms and the Men	George Bernard Shaw
Around the World in Eighty Days	Jules Verne
Ascent of the Everest	John Hunt
Asian Drama	Gunnar Myrdal
As You Like It	Shakespeare
August 1914	Alexander Solzhanitsyn
Babbit	Sinclair Lewis
Back to methuselah	George Bernard Shaw
Beloved	Toni Morrison
Ben Hur	Lewis Wallace
Berry Patches	Yevgeny Yevtushenko
Birth and Death of the Sun	George Gamow
Bitter Sweet	Noel Coward
Blind Beauty, The	Boris Pasternak
Blue Bird	Maurice Macterlink
Born Free	Joy Adamson
Bostaan	Sheikh Saadi
Brezhnev — The Masks of Power	John Dornberg
Caesar and Cleopatra	George Bernard Shaw
Cancer Ward	Alexander Solzhenistyn
Charging	Lio Vllmaan
Cherry Orchard	Anton Chekov
Children of Gebelawi	Naquib Mahfouz
Comedy of Errors	Shakespeare
Communist Manifesto	Karl Marx
Comus	John Milton
Confessions of a Thug	Taylor
Confessions of an English Opium Eater, The	Thomas De Quincy
Confidential Clerk, The	T.S. Eliot
Crime and Punishment	Fyodor Dostoevsky
Critical Mass	William E. Burrows and Robert Windrem
Crossing the Threshold of Hope	Pope John Paul II
Crown of Wild Olive The	John Ruskin
Cosmos	Carl Sagan
Darkness at Noon	Arthur Koestler
Das Kapital	Karl Marx
David Copperfield	Charles Dickens
Days of His Grace	Eyvind Johnson
Death of a President	William Manchester
Decline and Fall of the Roman Empire	Edward Gibbon
Decline of the West	O. Spengler
Descent of Man	Charles Darwin
Deserted village	Oliver Goldsmith
Diana — The True Story	Andrew Morton
Diana Versus Charles	James Whitakar
Die Blendung	Elias Canetti
Diplomacy	Henry Kissinger
Divine Comedy	A. Dante
Dr. Jekyll and Mr. Hyde	Robert Louis Stevenson
Doctor's Dilemma	George Bernard Shaw
Don Quixote	Saavedra Miguel de Cervantes
Dr. Zhivago	Boris Pasternak
Double Helix, The	J.D. Watson
Don Quixote	Miguel De Cervantes
Dragon's Teeth	U.B. Sinclair
Dreams, roses and Fire	Eyvind Johnson
East of Adan	John Steinbeck
Emma	Jane Austen
Ends and Means	Aldous Huxley
Escape	John Forstyte

Books	Authors
Erewhon	Samuel Butler
Essays of Elia	Charles Lamb
Eye of the Storm	Patrick White
Expanding Universe	Arthur Stanley Eddington
Experiments with Untruth	Michael Anderson
Face to Face	Lesse and Lisa Bey
Facts are Facts	Khan Abdul Wali Khan
Fairie Queen	Edmund Spencer
Far From the Madding Crowd	Thomas Hardy
Farewell the Trumpets	James Morris
Father and Sons	Ivan Turgene
Faust	Goethe
First Among Equals	Jeffrey Archer
First Circle	Alexander Solzhenitsyn
For Whom the Bell Tolls	Ernest Hemingway
Freedom at Midnight	Dominique Lapierre and Larry Collins
French Revolution	Thomas Carlyle
Friends, Not Masters	Ayub Khan
Future Shock	Alan Toffler
Gathering Storm	Winston Churchill
Going after Cacciato	Tim O'Brien
Gone With the Wind	Margaret Mitchell
Good Earth	Pearl S. Bick
Grammar of Politics	Harold Joseph Laski
Great Expectations	Charles Dickens
Great Illusion, The	Normal Angell
Grey Eminence	Aldous Huxley
Gulag Archipelago	Alexander Solzhenistyn
Gulliver's Travels	Jonathan Swift
Gypsy	Pushkin
Hemlet	William Shakespeare
Happy Valley	Patrick White
Heat and Dust	Ruth Prawer Jhabwala
Henderson the Rain King	Saul Bellow
Henry Esmond	W.M. Thackeray
Hero of Our Times	Richard Hough
Hindu Civilisation	J.M. Barrie
House Divided, A	Pearl S. Buck
Huckbbery Finn	Mark Twain
Human Factor	Graham Greene
Hunchback of Notre Dame	Victor Hugo
Icoca: An Autobiography	Lec Icoca
Idylls of the King	Lord Alfred Tennyson

Books	Authors
Illiad	Homer
India We Left	Humphrey Trevelyan
Indo-Pakistan Conflict, The	Russell Brines
Inside Asia	John Gunther
Inside the Third Reich	Albert Spencer
Invisible Man, The	H.G. Wells
Isabella	John Keats
Ivanhoe	Sir Walter Scott
Jane Eyre	Charlotte Bronte
Jean Christopher	Romain Rolland
Jungle Book	Rudyard Kipling
Julius Ceaser	Williams Shakespeare
Jurassic Park	Michael Crichton
Kane and Abel	Jeffrey Archer
Ken Attendent Godot	Samuel Beckett
Kennilworth	Sir Walter Scott
Kidnapped	Robert Louis Stevenson
Kim	Rudyard Kipling
King Lear	William Shakespeare
Kipps	H.G. Wells
Kublai Khan	Samuel Taylor Coleridge
Labyrinth of Solitude, The	Octavio Paz
Lady Chatterley's Lover	D.H. Lawrence
Lajja	Teslima Nasreen
Lamps of Architecture	John Ruskin
L' Allegro	John Milton
Last Days of Pompeii	Edward George Lytton
Lead Kindly Light	Cardinal Newman
Le Contract Social	J.J. Rousseau (The Social Contract)
Les Miserables	Victor Hugo
Life of Dr. Samuel Johnson	James Boswell
Living Room	Graham Greene
Lolita	V. Nabakov
Lord of the Flies	William Golding
Lycidas	John Milton
Macbeth	William Shakespeare
Magic Mountain	Thomas mann
Major Barbara	Geroge Bernard Shaw
Man and Superman	George Bernard Shaw
Maneaters of Kumaon	Jim Corbett
Marriage and Morals	Bertrand Russell
Mein Kampf	Adolf Hitler
Memoirs of the Second World War	Churchill
Men Who Kept the Secrets	Thomas Powers

Books	*Authors*
Merchant of Venice, The	William Shakespeare
Midnight's Children	Salman Rushdie
Miser, The	Moliere
Modern Painters	John Ruskin
Mother	Maxim Gorky
Mother India	Kathereine Mayo
Mountbattan	Philip Ziegler
Mrs. Warren's Profession	George Bernard Shaw
Much Ado About Nothing	Shakespeare
Murder in the Catherdral	T.S. Elliot
My Life, Law and Other Things	M.C. Setelued
Mysterious Universe	James Jeans
Myth of Independence	Z.A. Bhutto
Naked Came the Stranger	Penelope Ashe
Nana	Emile Zola
Nine Days' Wonder	John Mansfield
Ninteen Eighty-four	George Orwell
Ninth Symphony	Li Beethovan
O' Jerusalem	Larry Collins and Dominique Lapierre
Odyssey	Homer
Of Human Bondage	W. Somerset Maugham
Oh, Calcutta	Kennelt Tynan
Oh, Le Beaux Jourrs	Samuel Beckett
Old Man and the Sea, The	Ernest Hemingway
Oliver Twist	Charles Dickens
On Contradiction	Mao Tse-tung
One Hundred Years of Solitude	Gabriel Garcia Marquez
One World	Wendell Wilkie
One Life	Christian Bernard
Only One Year	Svetlana
Origin of Species	Charles Darwin
Orion, The	Richard Henry Horne
Oscar and Lucinda	Peter Carey
Othello	William Shakespeare
Other Side of Midnight, The	Sidney Sheldon
Out of Dust	E.D. Karaka
Paddy Clarke Ha, Ha, Ha	Roddy Doyle
Pakistan Crisis	David Loshak
Pakistan: The Gathering Storm	Benazir Bhutto
Paradise Lost	John Milton
Paradise Regained	John Milton
Peter Pan	J.M. Barrie

Books	*Authors*
Pickwick Papers	Charles Dickens
Pilgrim's Progress, The	John Bunyan
Plague, The	Albert Camus
Pompei the Great	John Masefield
Possession	A.S. Byatt
Prince, The	Niccolo Machiavelli
Pride and Prejudice	Jane Austin
Principia	Issac Newton Bronte
Professor, The	Chariotte Bronte
Pygmaliun	George Bernard Shaw
Rains Came	Louis Bromfield
Rape of Bangladesh	Anthony Mascrrenhas
Razor's Edge	W. Somerset Maugham
Red Gaunlet	Walter Scott
Red Star Over China	Edger Snow
Reflections on the French Revolution	Edmund Burke
Reprieve	Jean Paul Sartre
Republic	Plato
Rivals, The	R.B. Sheridan
Robinson Crusoe	Daniel Defoe
Room at the Top	John Braine Roots
Romeo and Juliet	William Shakespeare
Roots	Alex Haley
Roses in December	M.C. Chagla
Rubaiyat-i-Omar Kyayyam	Edward Fitzgerald
Sanctuary	William Faulkner
Satanic Verses	Salman Rushdie
Scarlet Pimpernel, The	Baroness Orczy
Seven Lamps of Architecture	John Ruskin
Sense and Sensibility	Jane Austen
Shame	Salman Rushdie
Shape of Things to Come	H.G. Wells
She Stoops to Conquer	Oliver Goldsmith
Silent Woman	Ben Johnson
Sohrab and Rustam	Matthew Arnold
Sons and Lovers	D.H. Lawrence
Sound and the Fury, The	William Faulkner
Spirit of the Age	William Hazlitt
Spy Catcher	Peter Wright
St. Joan	G.B. Shaw
Strangers and Brothers Omnibus	C.P. Snow
Surviving Doomsday	Buice Sibley
Tales from Shakespeare	Charles Lamb

Books	Authors
Talisman	Sir Walter Scott
Tarzon of the Apes	Edgar Rice Burroughs
Tempest, The	William Shakespeare
Tess of the D'Urbervilles	Thomas Hardy
Testament of Beauty	Robert Bridges
Thank You, Jeeves	P.G. Wodehouse
The Adventures of Angie March	Saul Bellow
The Affluent Society	J.K. Galbraith
The Interpretors	Wole Soyinka
The God That Failed	Arthur Koestler
The Great Depression of 1990	Ravi Batra
The Mousetop	Agatha Christie
The Old Devils	Kingsley Amiss
The Pursuit of Love	Nancy Mitford
The Unknown Man	Carrol
Three Musketeers	Alexander Dumas
Thus Spake Zarathustra	Friedrich Wilhelm Nietzsche
Time Machine	H.G. Wells
To Light a Candle	Welthy Fisher
The Light that Failed	Rudyard Kipling
Tom Jones	Henry Fielding
Travels With a Donkey	Robert Louis Stevenson
Treasure Island, The	Robert Louis Stevenson
Trial of Jesus	John Masefield
Triumph, The	John Kenneth Galbraith
Tropic of Cancer	Henry Miller
Trumpet Major, The	Thomas Hardy
Twelfth Night	William Shakespeare
The Rape of the Lock	Alexander Pope
The Conqueror	P.G. Woodhouse
The Code	P.G. Woodhouse
Ulysees	James Joyce
Uncle Tom's Cabin	Harriet B. Stowe
Universe Around Us, The	James Jeans
Unto this Last	John Ruskin
Upturned soil, The	Mikhail Sholokhov
Utopia	Thomas Moore
Valley of Dolls	Jacqueline Susann
Viceroy's Journal	Penderel Moon
Vikar of Wakefield	Oliver Goldsmith
Waiting for Godot	Thomas Becket
Wake-up India	Annie Besant
War and Peace	Leo Tolstoy
Waste Land, The	T.S. Eliot
Way of All Flesh	Samuel Butler
Wealth of Nations, The	Adam Smith
Wilhelm Meister	J.W. Von Goethe
Witness to An Era	Frank Moraes
Wuthering Heights	Emily Bronte

LATEST BOOKS AND AUTHORS

Books	Authors
Assam—A Valley Divided	Shekhar Singh
My Life Struggle	Khan Abdul Gaffar Khan
Asking for Trouble	Amreek Singh
Sandy Storms	Sandeep Patil
Runs in Ruins	Sunil Gavaskar
Storm Over the Sutlej—Akali Politics	A.M. Narang
Reflection on our Time	P.N. Haksar
Secular Perception in Sikh Faith	K.M. Duggal
Basanti	Bhishma Sahani
Rich Like Us	Nayantara Sehgal
The Heritage of Sikhs	Harbans Singh
Hinduism	Nirad C. Chaudhari
Bliss was in that Dawn	Minoo Masani
Netaji and Gandhi	Shashi Ahluwalia
Survivors	Randheer Khare
Alone in the Multitude	Amrita Pritam
Swami and Friends	R.K. Narain
Destination Man	S.K. Day
Terrorism in India	Shaileshwar Jha
Struggle For Change	K.B. Lal
The Indian Epics Retold	R.K. Narain
Indian Drama	Chelapati Rao
The Last Hero	Mihir Bose
You cannot Please every one	Kavita Sarkar
Mrs. Gandhi's Second Regime	Arun Shourie
The Emerging Developing Countries	P.G. Salve
The Morarji Papers	Arun Gandhi
The Lord of the Flies	William Goldings
Agnigarbha	Amrit Lal Nagar
World Power	Jonathan Steel
M.N. Roy—The Man	J.B.H. Wadia

Book	Author
We the People	Nani Palkiwala
The Islamic Bomb	Steave Baseman & Herber Cronsne
Portrait of a Lady	Henry James
My India	S. Nihal Singh
View from the U.N.	U. Thant
Inside Third World	V. Harrison
India's Nuclear Status	Dhirendra Sharma
Indian Womens' Battle for Freedom	Kamala Devi Chattopadhyaya
Indian Cinema	Feeroz Rangoonwala
Cricket My Style	Kapil Dev
Sunny Days	Sunil Gavaskar
By God's Decree	The Autobiography of Kapil Dev
The Famished Road	Ben Okri
Scarlett	Alexandra Ripley
Freedom from Fear	Aung San Suu Kyi
The Power and the Glory	Graham Green
Against the Grain	Boris Yeltsin
My Childhood Days	Taslima Nasreen
Myth of Mahatma	Michael Edwards
The City of Joy	Dominique Lapierre
God of Small Things	Arundhati Rai
The Tin Drum	Guentar Grass
Development as Freedom	Amartya Sen
Disgrace	J.M. Coetzee
Speed Post	Shobha De
My Century	Guentar Grass
A New World	Amit Chaudhury
Interpreter of Maladies	Jhumpa Lahiri
Soul Mountain	Gao Xingjian
The Brief History of Time	Stephen Hawking
The Transparent Mind	Ingram Smith
The True History of the Kelly Gang	Peter Carey
Bradman's Best	Rolland Perry

Book	Author
Living History	Hillary Rodham Clinton
Business at the Speed of Thought	Bill Gates
The Impressionist	Hari Kunzru
Ignited Minds	Dr. A.P.J. Abdul Kalam
Wings of Fire	Dr. A.P.J. Abdul Kalam
Life of Pi	Yann Martel
Long Walk to Freedom	Nelson Mandela
The Writer and the World	V.N. Naipaul
Two Lives	Vikram Seth
The Great Indian Dawn	Malay Chaudhury and Arindam Chaudhury
The Namesake	Jhumpa Lahiri
Vernon God Little	D.B.C. Pierre
India First	K.R. Malkani
Why America Slept	Gerald Posner
Straight From the Heart	Kapil Dev
Modern Jihad	Lonetta Napoleoni
The Roaring Nineties : Seeds of Destruction	Joseph Stiglitz
Burial at Sea	Khushwant Singh
Wall at Wagah—India-Pakistan Relationship	Kuldip Nayar
Understanding Partition	Yuvraj Krishan
Being Indian	Pawan Varma
My Life	Bill Clinton
Too Many with Little—The Challenges for India's Development Paradigm	George B. Asaf
Adam's Curse	Bryan Sykes
Byline	M.J. Akbar
The Hungary Tide	Amitav Ghosh
My Country : My Life	L.K. Advani
The White Tiger	Arvind Adiga
Jinnah–India–Partition Independence	Jaswant Singh

FAMOUS AUTHORS IN DIFFERENT LANGUAGES

English : William Shakespeare, John Milton, Chaucer, Spenser, Lord Byron, P.B. Shelley, John Keats, Francis Bacon, T.S. Eliot, Cecil Dlay Lewis, Alduous Huxley, W.B. Yeats, Bunyan, Dryden, Dr. Johnson, Alexander pope, Robert Browning, Charles Lamb, Charles Dickens, Thomas Hardy, W.M. Thackeray, George Eliot, Alfred Tennyson, Robert Bridges, George Bernard Shaw, D.H. Lawrence, Oliver Goldsmith, Sheridan, Walter Scott, William Wordsworth, S.T. Coleridge, Henry Fielding, Somerset Maugham.

French : Imile Zola, Gustave Flaubert, Moliere, Proudhon, Jean Paul Sartre, Le Sage, Victor Hugo, Alexander Dumas, Balzac.
German : Goethe, Hoffman, Lessing, Schelling, Schaupenhuer, Heinrich Heine, Guenter Grass.
Russian : Tolstoy, Mikhail Solokhov, Turgenev, Dostoevsky, Maxim Gorky, Techov, Alexander Salzhenitsyn, Boris Pasternak.
Greek : Homer, Aesop, Aristophanes, Euripedes, Herodotus, Hesoid, Theocritus, Xenophon, Aeschylus, Sophocles.
Latin : Dante, Boccacio, Terence, Virgil, Ovid, Horace, Seneca.
Persian : Ghalib, Umar Khyyam, Abul Fazal, Amir Khusro, Faiz, Firdausi, Mohd. Iqbal Saddi.
Spanish : Juan Valera, Lope De Vega, Cervantes.
Norwegian: John Bojer, Ibsen.

FAMOUS CHARACTERS AND THEIR CREATORS

Adam : Milton
Alice : Lewis Carroll
Ancient Mariner : Coleridge
Ariel : William Shakespeare
Antonio : William Shakespeare
Anna Karenina : Leo Tolstoy
Bassomio : William Shakespeare
Bertie Wooster : P.G. Wodehouse
Brutus : William Shakespeare
Beatrix : Thackery
Beatrice : William Shakespeare
Christian : John Bunyan
Cordelia : William Shakespeare
Cleopatra : William Shakespeare
Clare : Thomas Hardy
Claudius : William Shakespeare
David Copperfield : Charles Dickens
Dushyanta : Kalidas
Don Quixote : Cervantes
Eliza Doolittle : George Bernard Shaw
Estella : Charles Dickens
Faust : J.W. Von Goethe
Gora : Rabindranath Tagore
Hamlet : William Shakespeare
Hyde : R.L. Stevenson
Hercule Poirot : Agatha Christie
Hawkins : R.L. Stevenson
Hector : Homer
Ivanhoe : Sir Walter Scott
Iago : William Shakespeare
James Bond : Ian Fleming
Juliet : William Shakespeare
Jessica : William Shakespeare
Jean Valjin : Victor Hugo
Jacques : William Shakespeare
Jeeves : P.G. Wodehouse
King Arthur : Tennyson
Kim : Rudyard Kipling
Long John Silver : R.L. Stevenson
Macbeth : William Shakespeare
Micawber : Charles Dickens
Miranda : William Shakespeare
Mephistopheles : J.W. Von Goethe
Mellors : D.H. Lawrence
Malaprop : Sheridian
Oliver Twist : Charles Dickens
Peggotty : Charles Dickens
Priyangbada : Kalidas
Portia : William Shakespeare
Pip : Charles Dickens
Perry Mason : Erle Stanley Gardner
Pickwick : Charles Dickens
Rip Van Winkle : Washington Irving
Sam Weller : Charles Dickens
Surpanakha : Valmiki
Shylock : William Shakespeare
Sherlock Halmes : Arthur Conan Doyle
Shakuntala : Kalidas
Sancho Panza : Cervantes Saavedra
Tess : Thomas Hardy
Watson : Arthur Conan Doyle
Zhivago : Boris Pasternak

GREATEST POETS

Language	Poet
Hindi	Tulsidas
Sanskrit	Kalidas
Bengali	Rabindra Nath Tagore
Urdu	Mirza Ghalib
Persian	Sheikh Saadi
Latin	Virgil
Greek	Homer
English	Shakespeare
German	Goethe
Italian	Dante
French	Sully Proudhone
Punjabi	Waris Shah

FAMOUS PERSONALITIES

WORLD PERSONALITIES

Aesop (6th Century BC): A traditional Greek author who wrote fables about animals with human traits.

Alfred, the Great (849-899): Famous king of the West Saxons in the South of England. Noted for his zeal for learning and scholarship. He made a compilation of laws and did the translation of some important Latin works into English.

Alexander, the Great (356-323 BC): King of Macedonia; one of the mightiest generals. Invaded India in 326 BC; died at Babylon on his way back to Greece.

Amundsen, Capt R (1872-1928): A great Norwegian explorer---first to reach South Pole on December 14, 1911.

Arafat, Yasser (1929-2004): (Mohammed Abdul-Raouf Arafat al-Oudwaal-Husseini) Palestinian President; Leader of PLO from 1968-2004; Shared Nobel peace Prize '94.

Archimedes (287-212 BC): Famous Greek scientist, mathematician and inventor. He invented a number of machines and discovered many laws, the most important among which are laws of floating bodies and value of pie.

Aristotle (384-322 BC): A Greek Philosopher and political thinker, a tutor to Alexander the Great, author of Poetics, Politics and Ethics.

Armstrong, Neil (1930-2012): A US astronaut and the first human being to set his foot on the moon on July 20, 1969.

Ataturk, Kemal (1881-1938): The first President of the modern Turkish State (1923-38) he helped to found. He repulsed the Greek invasion of Anatolia (1922) exiled the Sultan, proclaimed a republic and modernized Turkey's economy.

Attlee, Clement Richard (1883-1967): British Statesman and Great Britain's Prime Minister (1945-51). It was during his tenure that India, Ceylon and Burma were granted independence.

Bach, Johann Sebastian (1685-1750): Founder of modern music was born in Germany. He was the greatest musical genius of all time. He perfected hundreds of instrumental and vocal compositions.

Baden Powell (1857-1941): He founded the Boy Scouts in 1908. It was so popular that Scouts became a world-wide organisation. Also in 1910 he and his sister founded the Girl Guides (Girl Scouts).

Beethoven, Ludwig Van (1770-1827): German Composer considered as one of the world's greatest composers and musicians. He wrote many memorable symphonies: Appassionata (Sonata), Fidelio (Opera), Eroica.

Begin, Menachem (1904-1992): Former PM of Israel, a giant of the reborn Jewish State, who signed the historic Camp David peace accord with Egypt and shared the 1978 Nobel Peace Prize with Egypt's President Anwar Sadat.

Bismark, Prince Otto (1815-1898): Great German Statesman, was called the 'Man of Blood and Iron', and 'Iron Chancellor'; unified Germany which was merely a number of states around Prussia and Austria. The First chancellor of unified Germany. Quarelled with William II, the new Emperor, and resigned in 1890.

Braille, Louis (1809-1852): French teacher of the blind; and inventor of the dot system of writing and reading for the blind, now known as Braille system.

Brandt, Willy (1913-1992): The former West German Chancellor. Died at the age of 78 after a long battle with cancer. He carried out *Ostpolitik,* a policy to have normal relations with eastern Europe. He joined the Social Democrat Party (SDP) at the age of 16 in the turbulent final years of the doomed Weimer Republic, engineered the detente between East & West Germany, for which he was acclaimed Nobel Peace laureate in 1971.

Cabot, John (1455-1498): An Italian born navigator who discovered the coast of North America, the New Foundland in 1497.

Caesar, Julius (102-44 BC): Roman General and Statesman and the greatest among the conquerers of the world; invaded Britain twice; was assassinated by Brutus, a noble friend of his.

Castro, Fidel (1927----): A revolutionary leader of Cuba who overthrew the Cuban dictator Fulgencio Batista and became President of the country in 1959. He brought about many social and economic reforms. He was President till January, 2008.

Caxton, William (1422-1491): The English printer to have set-up the first English printing press in London.

Chaplin, Charlie (Sir Charles Spencer) (1889-1977): Born in London, a reputed king of comedians, settled in Switzerland, recipient of Lenin Peace Prize in 1954. His leading films were the Gold Rush, Limelight, Modern Times, The Great Dictator, City Lights etc.

Charlemagne (742-814): Charlemagne or Charles the Great, was king of the Franks and founder of the Holy Roman Empire. He was a patron of scholars and a supporter of learning.

Charles De-Gaulle (1890-1970): Deadly opponent of Communist bloc, provi-sional President when France was made free; became Prime Minister in 1958, Constitution was redrafted and passed, elected President of 5th Republic of France, strongest man of France after Napoleon but in 1969 he was succeed-ed by Pompidou as President, died in October 1970. He wrote 'The Army of the Future.'

Chou-En-Lai (1898-1976): Chinese Revolutionary Statesman, administrator & diplomat and Prime Minister of China from 1942 till death. He visited India, signed Panchshila Treaty with Nehru, but his country invaded India in 1962 when he was PM.

Churchill, Winston (1874-1965): A British Statesman, Prime Minister, soldier and author. He was member of Parliament from 1900-1965. Saved England during World War II when he was Prime Minister and Minister of Defence 1940-45. Nobel Prize winner for literature in 1953. Author of the 'Gathering Storm.'

Clive, Robert (1725-1774): Twice governor of Bengal and the real founder of the British rule in India. He was a great soldier and his greatest victory was at Plassey, near Calcutta.

Columbus, Christopher (1451-1506): Italian navigator and explorer who dis-covered America in 1492.

Confucius or K'ung Fu-tse (551-478 BC): A Chinese saint and philosopher; founded the great religion of Confucianism. He appealed to reason and taught love and respect of one's fellows.

Cook, James (1728-1779): An English sailor and explorer who undertook many sea voyages and discovered Sandwich Islands (Hawaiian).

Copernicus, Nicolaus (1473-1543): A Polish astronomer, he was the first person to put forth evidence that the earth and other planets revolve around the sun (1543).

Cuellar, Javier Perez de (1920----): The Peruvian diplomat and recipient of Nehru Award for International Understanding 1987, who had been Secretary General of the UN for 10 years, relinquished his office on January 1, 1992.

Curie, Marie (1867-1934): Polish born French physicist who with her husband Pierre Curie discovered radioactivity and the Curies (the wife and the hus-band) shared the 1903 Nobel Prize for Physics. In 1911 Madam Curie received the Nobel Prize in Chemistry for discovery of radium.

Darwin, Charles Robert (1809-1882): A renowned experimental biologist and scientist, changed the entire concept of human origin. He wrote, 'Origin of Species' in 1859 and 'Descent of Man' in 1871; in the former he explained his theory of Natural Selection or Evolution.

Disney, Walter Elias (1901-1966): American film cartoonist, creator of Mickey Mouse and Donald Duck.

Edison, Thomas Alva (1847-1931): American inventor of the transmitter and receiver for the telegraph system, the phonograph and the incandescent lamp.

Eiffel, Alexander Gustave (1832-1923): French engineer who built Eiffel Tower.

Einstein, Albert (1879-1955): World famous German-American physicist, born in Germany but driven by Nazis in 1933; propounder of the famous 'Theory of Relativity.' Won Nobel Prize in 1921 for Physics for his investigations of the photoelectric effect.

Eliot, T S (1888-1965): American-born leading lyric poet of England in the 20th century. Recipient of Nobel Prize for Literature in 1948. His famous works are 'Waste Land', 'Confidential Clerk', 'The Cocktail Party', 'FourQuarters' etc.

Euclid (About 300 BC): A Greek mathematician, who is called the Father of Geometry.

Fahrenheit Gabriel Daniel (1686-1736): German physicist who introduced the mercury thermometer.

Firdausi (940-1020): A great Persian poet and author of the 'Shah Namah', Persia's national epic.

Fleming, Sir Alexander (1881-1955): Scottish bacteriologist and discoverer of penicillin (1928).

Franklin, Benjamin (1706-1790): American scientist who invented lightening conductor.

Freud, Sigmund (1856-1939): Born of Jewish parents, migrated to London in 1938 when Nazis occupied Vienna. His chief works include, 'The Psycho-pathology of everyday Life', 'The Interpretation of Dreams.'

Froebel, Friedrich (1782-1852): A German educator noted as the founder of the Kindergarten system of education.

Gagarin, Yuri (1934-1968): The first Russian Cosmonaut, who orbited the earth in Vostok-I on April 12, 1961 safely. Honoured with the highest Soviet award, died in an aircrash on March 25, 1968.

Galileo, Galilei (1564-1642): Italian scientist and astronomer. He improved the telescope; first man to see the satellites of Jupiter.

Gama, Vasco-Da (1469-1524): The famous Portuguese sailor who discovered the sea-route to India via Cape of Good Hope in 1498 AD.

Garibaldi, Giuseppe (1807-1882): Italian patriot and general who was one of the makers of modern Italy.

Ghali, Boutros (1922----): Former Deputy PM of Egypt was the Secretary General of the UN from 1992-96.

Goldsmith, Oliver (1730-1774): An Anglo-Irish man of letters whose best known works are 'The Vicar of Wakefield', 'She Stoops to Conquer' and 'The Deserted Village.'

Gorbachev, Mikhail (1931----): Recipient of 1990 Nobel Peace Prize. The first and the last Executive President of the now disintegrated USSR, resigned on December 25, 1991. One of the pivotal leaders of the 20th century, he helped end cold war and became a victim of his reforms.

Gutenberg, Johann (1400-1468): German inventor, who invented printing with movable types cast in moulds.

Hammarskjold, Dag, M (1905-1961): A Swedish diplomat, Secretary General of UNO (1953-1961), played an important role in bringing East and West closer; while on a peace mission on Congo, he died in a plane-crash in Sept 1961. He was honoured with Nobel Peace Prize posthumously in 1961.

Hannes Alfven (1908-1995): Great Swedish scientist, shared the Nobel Prize for Physics 1970, Hannes Alfven rejected the 'Big Bang' theory and pro-pounded the view that in the beginning was plasma.

Herodotus (485-425 BC): The first of the ancient Greek historians, called the 'father of history'.

Hill, Sir Rowland (1795-1879): Originator of the penny pound system.

Hillary, Sir Edmund Percival (1919-2008): A New Zealand mountaineer, who along with Tenzing Norgay, a sherpa from Nepal, became the first man to reach the top of the Mount Everest in 1953.

Hippocrates (430 BC): Greek physician, called the 'father of medicine'.

Hirohito (1901-1989): Emperor of Japan and an able Statesman who guided the destiny of his country for 62 years including the Second World War.

Hitler, Adolf (1889-1945): Leader of the Nazi Party, rose to be the dictator, founder and leader of the National Socialism in Germany. He started the World War II in 1939, and dreamt of world conquest but his forces were driven back by the Allied Forces, he took poison and died. Author of 'Mein Kampf' (My Struggle).

Ho-Chi-Minh (1890-1969): North Vietnamese revolutionary leader and President of North Vietnam (1954-69), advocate of Vietnamese unification. He became a legend in his life time.

Homer: Great Epic poet of Greece who wrote 'The Iliad' and 'The Odyssey.' Believed to have lived in 900 BC.

Hume, Allan Octavian (1829-1912): A British who entered the Indian Civil Service in 1849. Founder of the Indian National Congress in 1885.

Ibn Battuta (1304-1377): The greatest Arab traveller who spent about 25 years travelling in Africa, Middle East, Persia, India and the Far East. He visited India during the reign of Sultan Mohammad-bin-Tuglak (1325-51).

Jefferson, Thomas (1743-1826): He wrote most of the Declaration of Independence and was the third President of the US.

Jenner, Edward (1749-1823): An English Physician, who discovered vaccination to produce immunity from small pox.

Joan of Arc (1412-1431): Called 'Maid of Orleans', she inspired the French to drive the English out of Orleans. She was burnt alive as a heretic.

Keller, Helen Adams (1880-1968): A deaf and blind American lady who dedicated her whole life to the cause of the handicapped. 'The Story of My Life' is her famous autobiography.

Kennedy, John F (1917-1963): The most popular and youngest 35th President of the USA, (1961-63), established better relations with Russia, sponsored Civil Rights Bill, signed partial nuclear Test Ban Treaty. He was assassinated on November 22, 1963.

Kepler, Johannes (1571-1630): German astronomer who gave the laws of planetary motion.

Khrushchev, Nikita (1894-1971): Famous Soviet Statesman who gained power after the death of Stalin (1953) as the head of the state; under him Russia became less of a police state and he followed the policy of co-existence with the West.

King, Dr Martin Luther Jr. (1929-1968): American Negro leader of non-violence; called American Gandhi---fought for the Civil Rights, recipient of Nobel Prize for Peace in 1964 and was assassinated by a white on April 4, 1968.

Lao Tzu (c 604-518 BC): Chinese Philosopher, founded Taoism---an ancient religion. He was the author of 'Tao-te-ching', one of the sacred books of China.

Laski, Harold (1893-1950): A distinguished economist and writer. He was British political scientist, a prominent member of the Labour Party; author of 'A Grammar of Politics', 'Democracy in Crisis' etc.

Lenin, Vladimir Ilyich (1870-1924): Russian revolutionary, and the leader of Russian Revolution in 1917; made the country free from the rule of Czars, assumed dictatorial powers from 1917 to 1924.

Lesseps, Ferdinand (1805-1894): French Engineer who built the Suez Canal in 1869.

Lincoln, Abraham (1809-1865): Famous American Statesman and the 16th President of USA. A great advocate of democracy; he abolished slavery and was assasinated in 1865.

Louis XVI (1754-1793): French emperor during whose regime French Revolu-tion started in 1789. Louis attempted to escape but was caught and guillotined in 1793.

Luther, Martin (1483-1546): Leader of the Reformation in Germany and also the founder of the Lutherian Church.

Machiavelli, Niccolo (1469-1527): A famous Italian Statesman and political theorist. His master work is 'The Prince.'

Magellan, Ferdinand (1480-1521): Portuguese navigator, who completed the first voyage around the world and discovered the Strait of Magellan (1520).

Mandela, Nelson R (1918–2013): Recipient of Nobel Peace Prize 1993, Bharat Ratna, 1990 and the Jawaharlal Nehru Award for International Understanding 1979; he became the first democratically elected black President of the Republic of South Africa on May 10, 1994. He was set free in February 1990 after spending long 27 years in jail.

Mao Tse-Tung (1893-1976): Chairman and founder of the Communist Party of the Chinese People's Republic. He was opposed to disarmament and advocat-ed war. He started Chinese Cultural Revolution in 1967. Author of "Great Leap Forward" and "Communes."

Marconi Guglielmo (1874-1937): Italian inventor who developed the use of radio waves for communication.

Marx, Karl (1818-1883): German philosopher and Economist and socialist, founder of Modern Communist Theory, advocated the cause of the Labour classes, author of 'Das Capital' and 'Communist Manifesto.' Communism is based on his teachings.

Menuhin, Yehudi (1916-1999): World famous violinist and composer, born in New York, visited India in 1952 and 1964. He was awarded Nehru Award for International Understanding in 1968.

Michelangelo (1475-1564): Celebrated Italian painter and sculptor. One of the greatest masters of the Italian Renaissance.

Mitterand, Francois (1916-96): French socialist and President of Fifth Republic.

Mohammed Sahib (570-632): An Arabian prophet and founder of Islam. He was born in Mecca, and the Koran, Islam's sacred book, contains his teachings.

Montessori, Maria (1870-1952): Italian educationist, known for her system of Education for children called Montessori Method. She was the first woman to take a medical degree from Rome University.

Mother Teresa (1910-1997): The 87-year-old Albanian born nun, who has dedicated herself to the service of the destitutes in Calcutta. She was honoured with Nobel Peace Prize in 1979 and Bharat Ratna in 1980.

Mozart, W Amadeus (1756-1791): An Austrian composer and one of the outstanding masters of the classical period composers.

Mussolini, Benito (1883-1945): Founder of the Fascist Party, dictator of Italy (1935-43), was defeated in 1943 in the World War II, shot dead by his partisans in 1945.

Myrdal, Gunnar (1898-1987): A Swedish economist and sociologist and author of 'An American Dilemma' was co-recipient of the 1974 Nobel Prize for Economics and Nehru Award for International Understanding in 1981.

Napier, John (1550-1617): Scottish mathematician who invented logarithms.

Napoleon I, Bonaparte (1769-1821): Born in Corsica, overthrew French government in 1799 and established his dictatorship. A plebiscite confirmed his life-long consulship and another in 1804 gave him the title of 'Emperor'. In 1815 was defeated by the Duke of Wellington, exiled to St Helena where he died.

Nasser, Col Gamal Abdel (1918-70): President of Egypt (1956-70), one of the founders of non-alignment, a great leader of the Arab World. Nationalised Suez Canal in 1956, constructed Aswan Dam with Russian help, defeated at the hand of Israel in 1967, wrote 'Egyptian Liberation', died in September 1970.

Nero (37-68 AD): The infamous Roman emperor whose cruelty and instability led to a revolt. Nero committed suicide.

Newton, Sir Isaac (1642-1726): The most famous physicist and mathematician of modern times and author of 'The Theory of Gravitation'.

Nightingale, Florence (1820-1910): Famous hospital reformer, worked as nurse, served the British soldiers in the Crimean War of 1854; known as the Lady with the Lamp.

Nobel, Alfred Bernhard (1833-1896): Swedish inventor of dynamite. He left his fortune for establishment of Nobel Foundation and this fund is used to award Nobel Prizes since 1901.

Nostradamus or Michel De Notre Dame (1503-1566): French astrologer known for prophecies.

Nyerere, Julius Kambarage (1922-1999): He led Tanganyika to independence in 1961 and united it with Zanzibar forming Tanzania (1964) to become its first President. A leader of the Non-Alignment Movement he was honoured with the Nehru Award for International Understanding in 1973.

Paine, Thomas (1737-1809): An English born writer and radical. His famous works are 'The Rights of Man' and 'The Age of Man'.

Peary, Robert Edwin (1856-1920): US Arctic explorer who discovered the North Pole in 1909.

Picasso, Pablo Ruiz (1881-1973): Spanish painter, founded Cubist School of Painting.

Pasteur, Louis (1822-95): A famous French chemist, known for pasteurisation, made researches on fermentation that led to the development of bacteriology, and those on infectious diseases led to the growth of the science of immunology; made vaccinations against hydrophobia and cholera etc.

Pitman, Sir Issac (1813-1897): Inventor of a system of phonographic shorthand.

Plato (427-347 BC): A pupil of Socrates and a great philosopher of the world. His famous works are 'Republic' and 'Laws'.

Pythagoras (582-500 BC): A great Greek philosopher and mathematician, specially interested in astronomy and geometry. He propounded the theory that the basis of the universe is number and originated the idea of hormony of the spheres (planets).

Quisling, Vidkun Abraham (1887-1945): A Norwegian who sided with German invaders of Norway in 1940. After the collapse of Germany, Quisling was convicted of treason and shot dead. His name has become synonymous with traitor.

Rockfeller, J D (1839-1937): Born of poor parents in New York but rose to the world's richest man of his times; a great philanthropist, oil king of USA; founded Rockfeller Foundation in 1913.

Rommel, Field Marshall (1891-1944): The ablest German General, fought war in North Africa and West Europe; called Desert Fox. He committed suicide.

Roosevelt, Franklin Delano (1882-1945): First American to become President twice; until his death very popular and successful Statesman; founder member of UNO; met the economic crisis 1933 with the policy of New Deal.

Ross, Ronald (1857-1932): British physician who discovered the malaria parasite.

Rousseau, Jean Jacques (1717-1778): Swiss born French writer, philosopher and political theorist and author of 'The Social Contract'.

Russel, Bertrand (1872-1970): A great English philosopher, essayist and mathematician, visited many countries, opposed to arms race and nuclear testing, he was called a spoilt genius due to his critical works; won Nobel Prize for Literature in 1950. Wrote 'Marriage and Morals', 'History of Western Philosophy,' etc.

Salk, Jonas (1915-1995): Scientist who developed a successful vaccine against polio.

Sartre, Jean Paul (1905-1980): French philosopher, novelist and playwright, famous exponent of existentialism. In 1964 he refused the Nobel Prize for literature.

Shakespeare, William (1564-1616): The most famous English poet and dramatist and one of the giants of the world literature. Some of his plays are— 'Hamlet', 'Othalo', 'Henry VI'.

Shaw, George Bernard (1856-1950): An Irish dramatist and critic whose major writings are— 'Pygmalion' and 'St Joan'. He was awarded the 1925 Nobel Prize in literature.

Socrates (469-399 BC): An eminent scholar and distinguished thinker of Greece; charged for corrupting the youth of the country; forced to die by taking hemlock; Plato was his disciple. He is said to be the originator of idealistic philosophy.

Stalin, Joseph V (1879-1953): Outstanding Statesman of USSR after Lenin; took leading part in 1917 Russian revolution. Introduced Five-Year Plans in 1929 to build a new modern Russia; ousted Trotsky who was opposing his plan of socialistic pattern and industrialisation.

Stephenson, George (1781-1848): English engineer and inventor of locomotive engine.

Sun Yat Sen (1867-1925): Provisional President of the Chinese Republic; founded the Chinese Nationalist Party called Kuomintang in 1894, consolidated China, played active role in the Revolution of 1911.

Thant, U (1909-1974): Born in Burma, Buddhist by religion, an outstanding Statesman, Secretary General of UNO from 1961-1971, handled very tact-fully the international problems like the Cuba issue etc; recipient of Nehru Award for International Understanding in 1965.

Tito, Marshall (Josip Broz) (1892-1980): A Great dominating leader and life President of Yugoslavia from 1953*. Visited India in 1954 and approved *Panchshila,* a pillar of the non-aligned movement; hosted 1961 Belgrade conference; won 1971 Nehru Award for International Understanding. He opposed Soviet domination in Eastern Europe. Died on May 4, 1980 just three days before his 88th birthday.

Tolstoy, Count Leo (1828-1910): Russian Saint, holds high honour for his literary views based on morality. Author of 'War and Peace', 'Anna Karenina', 'Resurrection' etc.

Turgenev, Ivan Sergeyevich (1818-1883): A great Russian writer who wrote of peasant and country life. His greatest novel is 'Fathers and Sons'.

Vinci, Leonardo Da (1452-1519): Italian sculptor, painter, architect, musician, engineer and scientist. He was the supreme example of renaissance. His famous paintings are 'Monalisa', 'Last Supper' etc.

Virgil (70-19 BC): Roman epic poet and author of 'The Aeneid'.

Voltaire, F M (1694-1778): French philosopher and writer, a social reformer too, waged war against religious bigotry, author of 'Candide', 'Essay on Manners', 'Irene', etc.

Washington, George (1732-1799): First President of USA, called Father of the Nation, led the American war of Independence (1775-83).

Wilson, Woodrow (1856-1924): President of USA (1913-21) put his 14 points for peace after world war I; founder of the League of Nations; he was awarded Nobel Prize for Peace in 1919.

Zoroaster (6th century BC): Persian founder of the Parsee religion.

INDIAN PERSONALITIES

Abul Fazal (1561-1602): One of the nine jewels in Akbar's court and a great scholar of Persian. He wrote 'Ain-e-Akbari'.

Acharya, J B Kriplani (1888-1982): Staunch Gandhian and leading freedom fighter; became President of Indian National Congress 1946-47, left Congress in 1951, formed a new party PSP headed by himself till Dec 1954; was elected as Member of Parliament in 1967; wrote a book 'Gandhian Way and a Non-violent Revolution'. He was considered the 'Bhisham Pitamah' of Indian Politics.

Akbar (Reign 1556-1605): A great Mughal emperor in India and famous for his reforms in the land revenue administration. He founded a new religion Din-e-Ilahi.

Akhtar, Begum (1910-1974): Known as 'Ghazal Queen of India.' Akhtar Begum died in October 1974. She was honoured with Padma Bhushan in 1975 posthumously.

Ambedkar, Dr B R (1891-1956): A prominent nationalist leader, a famous constitutionalist and a crusader for social justice. As Chairman of the Drafting Committee, he played a leading part in framing of the Indian Constitution. He was Law Minister from (1947-1951). Author of 'Castes of India', 'Thoughts on Pakistan', etc. He was honoured with 'Bharat Ratna' (posthumously) in 1990.

Azad, Chandra Shekhar (1906-1931): Indian revolutionary, died fighting a lone battle with police.

Azad, Maulana Abul Kalam (1888-1958): Indian Congress politician born at Mecca and educated at Al Azhar University, Cairo; he became prominent during Civil Disobedience Movement; founded and edited nationalist papers; was interned and imprisoned several times; was Congress President when India became independent; Education Minister of India (1947-58). He was posthumously honoured with Bharat Ratna in 1992.

Babar (1483-1530): As a soldier of fortune, he founded the Mughal dynasty in India in 1526 when he won the battle of Panipat.

Banabhatta (606-647): A famous Sanskrit poet in the court of Emperor Harshvardhan. His famous works are 'Kadambari' and 'Harsh Charit'.

Banerjee, Surendranath (1848-1925): A great Indian patriot and a powerful leader of the anti-partition movement in Bengal during the British rule. He was elected President of the Indian National Congress (1895).

Banerjee, Woomesh Chandra (1844-1906): He was the first President of the Indian National Congress (1885).

Besant, Mrs Annie (1847-1933): First lady President of Indian National Congress in 1917; founder of the Theosophical Society; took active part in the Home Rule Movement.

Bhabha, Dr Homi Jehangir (1909-66): Eminent Indian scientist; first Chairman of the Atomic Energy Commission, Former Director of Tata Institute of Fundamental Research; pace setter of nuclear India; died in a plane crash on January 24, 1966. Published papers on cosmic rays and quantum theory. Attended 'Atom for Peace' conference at Geneva, 1955.

Bharati, Subramania (1881-1921): A philosopher, patriot and journalist and a powerful poet of Tamil, whose birth-centenary year was observed in 1981.

Bhaskaracharya: The author of famous 'Sidhanta Shiromani', Bhaskaracharya was a great Indian mathematician and astronomer of the 12th century.

Bhatnagar, S S (1894-1955): A prominent scientist; was director general of Indian Council of Scientific Research, established a chain of science laboratories in India.

Bhatta, Arya (476-520): A great Indian mathematician and astronomer of the Gupta Age. He pointed out the importance of zero and laid foundations of Algebra. He propounded the theory of rotation of the earth. After his name India's first satellite was launched on April 19, 1975.

Bhatt, Kumaril: He was a great Hindu saint in the 8th century.

Bhave, Acharya Vinoba (1895-1982): Distinguished Scholar of Gandhian Philosophy, active participation in Civil Disobedience Movements, Sarvodaya leader. He started *Bhoodan*, *Shramdan* and *Gramdan* movements for the cause of needy and landless, recipient of Magsaysay Award and Bharat Ratna (posthumously) (1983). He lived in 'Pavnar Ashram'.

Bose, J C (1858-1937): An eminent Indian physicist. Founder of Bose Research Institute, Kolkata; invented crescograph for measuring plant growth.

Bose, Subhash Chandra (1897-1945): Formidable nationalist leader and a great patriot, founder of Azad Hind Fouj; known as Netaji. He was elected President of Indian National Congress (1939); was put under house arrest in 1941, but escaped, went to Germany via Afghanistan and Turkey. He reached Japan and Singapore, organised Indian National Army, but he is reported to have died in an air crash in 1945. He was posthumously honoured with Bharat Ratna in 1992.

Buddha, Gautam (563-483 BC): Born at Lumbini as a prince to Shuddodhana, the king of Kapilavastu, Gautam Buddha was the founder of Buddhism. He attained enlightenment under a *Bodhi* tree in Bodh Gaya in Bihar.

Chaitanya (1445-1533): Born at Nadia in Bengal and a pioneer of Bhakti movement, Chaitanya was a devotee of Lord Krishna.

Chand, Dhyan (1905-79): Indian hockey wizard, won Olympic gold 1928, 1932 and 1936.

Chandragupta II (Vikramaditya) (Reign 375-413): A great conqueror and a great emperor whose period is known as the golden period of Hindu India. Chinese pilgrim Fahien visited India during his reign.

Chatterjee, Bankim Chandra (1838-1894): Distinguished Bengali novelist and author of 'Anand Math' and composer of '*Bande Mataram.*'

Chauhan, Prithviraj: A great Rajput ruler of Delhi, who defeated Mohammed Ghori in 1191 but lost to him in 1192 and was killed.

Das, Chitaranjan (1870-1925): A famous advocate, journalist and freedom fighter, Chitaranjan Das worked with Lala Lajpat Rai and Motilal Nehru. He was one of the founders of the Swaraj Party.

Dadabhai Naoroji (1825-1911): A great nationalist of India; President of Indian National Congress (1886, 1893, 1906) and the first Indian to become a Member of the British House of Commons; popularly known as 'Grand Old Man of India.'

Daya Nand Saraswati (1824-83): Founder of Arya Samaj; Great Hindu refor-mer of the 19th century. Stressed the need to wipe out untouchability, purdah-pratha and other religious superstitions prevalent in the then Hindu Society.

Desai, Morarji R. (1896-1995): India's tallest freedom fighter, staunch Gandhian, seniormost politician and the Prime Minister of India (Nov. 77--July 79). He died on April 10, 1995.

Dhanvantri: A renowned physician in the reign of Chandragupta Vikramaditya in the 4th century.

Gandhi, M K (1869-1948): The greatest Indian personality after Buddha; known as the 'Father of the Nation'; Born at Porbander (Kathiawar) on Oct 2; studied Law in England, led Satyagraha movement in South Africa, started non-cooperation movement and civil disobedience movement, preached truth and non-violence; was arrested several times in the struggle for freedom; fought for Hindu-Muslim Unity, and abolition of untouchability; widely respected in the entire world; author of 'My Experiments with Truth'. He was shot dead by Nathu Ram Godse on January 30, 1948.

Gandhi, Rajiv (1944-1991): The eldest son of Mrs. Indira Gandhi, the first woman Prime Minister of India and the grand-son of Pt. Jawaharlal Nehru, the first Prime Minister of India. Became the youngest Prime Minister of the country after the death of his mother in 1984. In 1989 elections he lost the power. Assassinated at Perambudur near Chennai on May 21, 1991 during mid-term elections campaign. Awarded 'Bharat Ratna' posthumously in 1991.

Gandhi, Smt Indira (1917-1984): Daughter of late Pt Jawaharlal Nehru; educated at Oxford. An active worker of Congress, she became President of Congress in 1959, Minister of Information and Broadcasting (1964-65), and Prime Minister of India (Jan 24, 1966 to March 23, 1977); honoured with Bharat Ratna in 1971; declared Emergency on June 26, 1975 and was defeated in 1977 General Elections but in the mid-term poll January 1980, Mrs Gandhi again came to power as PM and remained in that position till her assassination in October 1984.

Ghalib, Mirza Asadullah Khan (1796-1868): A renowned Urdu poet. Compilation of his poems—Diwan-e-Ghalib.

Ghori, Mohammad: He become the founder of the Muslim rule in India in 1192 when he defeated Prithviraj Chauhan in the battle of Tarain.

Ghosh, Aurobindo (1872-1950): A revolutionary philosopher and a yogi, Aurobindo founded the famous Pondicherry Ashram. His famous works are—Divine Life and Essays on Gita.

Giri, V V (1894-1980): A great labour leader and the fourth President of India, Mr Giri was honoured with Bharat Ratna in 1975.

Gokhale, G K (1866-1915): A Great nationalist and patriot; political guru of Mahatma Gandhi; founded the Servants of India Society. Gokhale was the greatest parliamentarian known to India. He was President of Indian National Congress in 1905.

Harshvardhana (Reign 606-647): The last great Hindu ruler of northern India; he embraced Buddhism. Chinese traveller Hiuen Tsang visited India during his reign.

Hussain, Dr Zakir (1897-1969): A great educationist, statesman and philosopher, Vice-Chancellor of Aligarh Muslim University (1948-56), great exponent and author of Basic Education, proposed Wardha scheme of education, Vice-President of India (1962-67) and elected President of India (1967-69), died on May 3, 1969; received Bharat Ratna in 1963.

Jaya Prakash Narain (1901-79): A great revolutionary socialist leader, a true Gandhian in thoughts and actions he was General Secretary of the Congress (1930-32); formed Congress Socialist Party. This great Sarvodaya leader, was a member of the peace mission for conducting talks with rebel Nagas; persuaded dacoits of Chambal ravines to surrender. He gave a call for the Total Revolution; worked as an inspiring force in the formation of Janata Party in 1977.

Jayadeva (12th century): Famous poet; his work is Gita Govinda.

Jinnah, Mohemmed Ali (1876-1948): A prominent Muslim leader and zealous advocate of two-nation theory. He was the first Governor-General of Pakistan. He was for many years, President of All India Muslim League.

Kabir: An Indian saint and poet of Nirguna Bhakti in the fourteenth century. He believed in the unity of God. Beejak and Sakhi are his famous collection of poems.

Kalhana: Author of 'Rajatarangini'; a great historian of Kashmir in the 11th century.

Kalidasa: A renowned Sanskrit poet and dramatist of the 4th century. His works include Raghuvansha, Shakuntala, Kumar Sambhava, Meghduta. He is called the Shakespeare of India. He lived during the reign of Vikramaditya.

Kanishka (2nd C. AD): A great Kushan ruler of India, who patronised Buddhism and was promoter of art and literature.

Karve, D.K. (1858-1962): Indian social worker who championed the cause of widow marriage and women's education.

Kautilya (Chanakya): Vishnugupta Chanakya was the Prime Minister of Chandragupta Maurya (3rd

& 4th century BC), the founder of the Mauryan dynasty. He is the author of Arthashastra, a great treatise on statecraft.

Khan, Abdul Ghaffar Khan (1890-1987): Red shirt leader and popularly known as Frontier Gandhi, Abdul Ghaffar Khan, was a close associate of Mahatma Gandhi. He was honoured with Nehru Award for International Understanding in 1967 and Bharat Ratna in 1987.

Khusro, Amir (1253-1325): A scholar, saint, poet and a master of music, Amir Khusro adorned the courts of Khiljis and Tughlaks.

Kumbha, Rana (1431-1469): Himself a scholar and a patron of learning, Rana Kumbha was a great ruler of Mewar who built *Vijaya Stambha* (Victory Tower) in Chittor, Rajasthan.

Lakshmibai, Rani of Jhansi (1828-58): She took active part in the first war of independence 1857. Died in battle.

Lala Lajpat Rai (1865-1928): A valiant freedom fighter, powerful writer, great orator and dominant Congress leader known as *Sher-e-Punjab*, exiled by the British Govt. for political activities; among the founder of DAV College, Lahore; founded the Servants of People Society in 1924; died of fatal lathi blows of the police during the demonstration against Simon Commission in 1928; editor of Bande Mataram.

Lohia, Dr Ram Manohar (1910-1967): A distinguished social leader who actively participated in the freedom struggle; imprisoned several times; a great parliamentarian and a mighty orator; founder of Socialist Party; he vehemently opposed the continuance of English in India.

Mahavira (540-468 BC): An apostle of non-violence and preacher of penance and self-mortification, Mahavira was the founder of Jainism.

Malaviya, Pt Madan Mohan (1861-1946): A great nationalist and zealous freedom fighter; a leading lawyer, founder of the Banaras Hindu University and served as its Vice-Chancellor for several years; represented India in Round Table Conference. He was elected twice (1909, 1918) as the President of Indian National Congress.

Manu: A great philosopher and the ancient law-giver of India. His famous work is Manu Smiriti.

Mavalankar, G.V. (1888-1956): First Speaker of the Lok Sabha of Indian Republic.

Mukherji, Dr Shyama Prasad (1901-1953): Founder of Jana Sangh, Central Minister of Industries and Supplies (1947-50); expired while in detention in Srinagar Jail; a renowned political thinker and fearless parliamentarian.

Muni, Acharya Sushil Kumar (-1994): He was the founder President of World Fellowship of Religions and International Mahavir Jain Mission.

Nagarjuna: A renowned chemist during 7th and 8th century and author of Ras Ratnakar.

Naidu, Mrs Sarojini (1870-1948): Gifted poetess and impressive orator; actively participated in the freedom struggle; President Indian National Congress, 1925; Governor of Uttar Pradesh, author of the 'Songs of India', 'Bird of Time', 'The Broken Wings' and 'The Golden Threshold.'

Nanak, Guru (1469-1538): Born in Nankana Sahib, a great Indian saint and philosopher, Guru Nanak was the founder of Sikhism.

Narendra Dev, Acharya (1889-1956): A great Indian leader and socialist thinker.

Nehru, Jawahar Lal (1889-1964): Politician and Statesman of world repute; a fluent speaker and an ardent patriot; participated actively in freedom movement; imprisoned several times; President of Congress in 1929, 1930, 1952-53; Prime Minister of India from 1947-1964. Author of 'Discovery of India,' 'Glimpses of World History,' 'An Autobiography.' His policy of co-existence and non-alignment had won him worldwide fame; author of the doctrine of *Panchsheel* and a great champion of world peace; he was opposed to regional pacts, colonialism and nuclear armaments; died on May 27, 1964.

Norgay, Tenzing (1914-1986): An ace mountaineer, who with Edmund Hillary was first Indian to climb Mount Everest.

Panini (5th Century BC): A great scholar of Sanskrit and a distinguished grammarian and an authority on the subject. His work is 'Ashtadhayi', a famous book on Sanskrit grammar.

Paramhansa, Ramakrishna (1836-1886): He was a great saint and guru of Swami Vivekanand. Ramakrishna Mission has been founded after his name.

Patel, Sardar Vallabhbhai (1875-1950): Called 'Iron Man of India', unification of princely states was the stupendous task that won him glory and fame. Actively joined several Congress movements for freedom; imprisoned a number of times; President Indian National Congress, 1931; Deputy Prime Minister and Minister of Home Affairs, Information and Broadcasting (1947-50); died on December 14, 1950. He was honoured with Bharat Ratna (posthumously) in 1991.

Phule, Jyotiram G. (Mahatma Phule) (1827-1890): A pioneer in social reform and founded *Satya Shodhak Samaj* for creating social awakening.

Pratap, Rana (Reign 1572-1597): The brave ruler of Mewar, who carried on incessant war against the Mughals.

Premchand, Munshi (1880-1937): A great story-writer and novelist, his famous books are Godaan, Gaban, Rang Bhumi, Prem Pachisi.

Pulkesin II (Reign 608-642): A famous Chalukya ruler of south India who defeated Harshavardhana.

Radhakrishnan, Dr S (1888-1975): An eminent philosopher of international fame, and a great author, President of India (1962-67). Vice-Chancellor, Banaras Hindu University (1939-48); Indian Ambassador to USSR; Vice-President and Chairman of Rajya Sabha (1952-62). Templeton Foundation prize winner 1974 and honoured with Bharat Ratna 1954.

Rajagopalachari, Chakravarti (1879-1972): A shrewd politician, statesman and a good administrator. He is called the Chanakya of Modern India. First and last Indian Governor-General of free India, President of the Congress, (1932-34, 1939-46); Chief Minister of Madras (1937-39 and 1952-54). He started a new political party Swatantra Party. He was opposed to the introduction of Hindi Language in the South. He was also called grand-old man of Tamil Nadu and was honoured with Bharat Ratna 1954.

Dr Rajendra Prasad (1884-1963): First President of the Indian Republic (1950-62). He was an active member of the youth movement in Bihar. In 1917, he joined Congress and took active part in non-cooperation movement in 1920, President of Congress (1932-34, 1939, 1946). Minister for Food and Agriculture in 1947. President of the Indian Constituent Assembly (1946-1949), author of 'India Divided'; honoured with Bharat Ratna (1962) and died on Feb 28, 1963.

Raja Rammohan Roy (1772-1833): A great political and social reformer of India in 19th century, helped William Bentinck in the abolition of Sati system and other social evils; founder of *Brahma Samaj*; great scholar of Sanskrit and Persian.

Raman, C V (1880-1970): A scientist of world repute; National Professor of Physics. Inventor of 'Raman Effect', Nobel Prize winner in 1929; member, Academy of Philosophy of Sciences at Brussels; honoured with Bharat Ratna (1954).

Ramanujacharya: A religious teacher of Vishishtadvaita philosophy in the 12th century, founder of *Rama Bhakti*. He revived Hinduism to restore its glory.

Ramanuja Srinivasa (1887-1920): One of the greatest mathematician of India.

Ray, Satyajit (1921-1992): Veteran film maker and recipient of Bharat Ratna (1992) and Special Oscar; Died in Calcutta on April 23, 1992.

Raya, Krishnadeva (Reign 1509-1529): He was a great ruler of the Vijayanagar Empire and a great scholar and patron of learning.

Razia Sultana (Reign 1236-40): Daughter of Sultan Iltutmish and the first and the only muslim lady to rule from Delhi.

Roerich, Devika Rani (1908-1994): Recipient of prestigious Dada Saheb Phalke Award and earlier honoured with Padma Shri, she was the first lady of the Indian silver screen, the last surviving link between the 'silent' and the 'talkies' era.

Samudragupta (Reign 335-375): A valiant conqueror, an able administrator, scholar, poet and master of music, Samudragupta is known as 'Indian Napolean.'

Sanga (Sangram Singh), Rana (Reign 1509-1527): A distinguished brave ruler of Mewar who lost to Babar in 1527 at the battle of Khanwa.

Sarabhai, Dr Vikram (1919-1971): Chairman of India's Atomic Energy Commission, and Indian Space Research Organisation; was awarded Padma Bhushan in 1966. His greatest achievement is founding of Equatorial-Rocket Launching Station at Thumba.

Savarkar, V D (1883-1966): An ardent Indian nationalist and freedom fighter. He was sentenced to transportation for life in the Nasik Conspiracy Case. He remained President of Hindu Maha Sabha for a long time. His famous book is 'Indian War of Independence.'

Shahjehan (Reign 1627-1658): A great Mughal ruler whose reign is called 'Golden Age' of Muslim rule in India. He built Taj Mahal at Agra and Red Fort and Jama Masjid in Delhi.

Shankaracharya: A great scholar and philosopher, zealous preacher of Hinduism in the 8th century. He held religious debates with Buddhists and Jains and converted them to Hinduism.

Shastri, Lal Bahadur (1904-1966): Born in a humble family he rose to be the Prime Minister of India, a zealous and hard Congress worker; very simple in living but honest and high in thinking. He resigned from the Railway Ministry when there was a serious railway accident; after Nehru he became the Prime Minister of India. He won a great name and fame during the Indo-Pak War (1965). He signed the Tashkent Pact with President Ayub Khan; died on January 10, 1966. He was awarded Bharat Ratna posthumously (1966).

Shivaji (1627-80): Son of Shahji Bhonsle, a valiant fighter and patriot. He was the last great Hindu king who succeeded in establishing *Hindu Swarajya*. He made Marathas a strong nation; fought successfully many battles against Aurangzeb.

Subramanyam Chandrasekhar (1910-1995): Winner of 1983 Physics Nobel Prize for his studies regarding structure and evolution of stars. He died on August 21, 1995.

Surdas: A great saint and a poet of Krishna Bhakti and author of *Sur Sagar*.

Suri, Shershah (Reign 1540-45): A famous and powerful Afghan ruler who drove the Mughals out of India. A very efficient administrator, he built the Grand Trunk Road.

Syed, Ahmad Khan (1815-1898): A great Muslim educationist and reformer in the 19th century and founder of the Aligarh Muslim University.

Tagore, Dr Rabindra Nath (1861-1941): Won Nobel Prize for literature in 1913; one of the greatest lyric poets and a writer of short stories, novels and dramas. He founded the International University at Shanti Niketan in Bengal; Gitanjali, Gora, Chitra, Post Office are some of his famous works.

Tansen (1506-1589): Celebrated musician and one of the nine jewels in Akbar's court.

Tata, JRD (1904-1993): Popularly known JRD, he was the doyen of the Indian industry and father of the Indian Civil Aviation. Honoured with Bharat Ratna, the highest civilian award, he contributed a lot to the promotion of science in the country.

Thiruvalluvar (1st century): The greatest ever Tamil poet, who wrote *Thirukural.*

Tilak, Bal Gangadhar (1856-1920): A great nationalist leader and a prolific scholar of Sanskrit, author of several books; imprisoned a number of times in the independence movement; organised the extremist section among the congress men; started Home Rule League in 1916.

Tipu Sultan (1750-1799): Sultan of Mysore who fought valiantly against the British.

Todar Mal (16th Century): Revenue Minister of Akbar who efficiently implemented important land revenue reforms.

Tope, Tantya (1814-1859): A prominent patriot, who joined Nana Sahib and Rani of Jhansi in the first war of India's independence in 1857. He was captured and hanged by the English in 1859.

Tughlaq, Mohammad-Bin (Reign 1325-1351): A famous sultan of Delhi, known for his imaginary schemes and undue haste in their implementation.

Tuka Ram: A religious reformer and saint of Maharashtra, he was contemporary of Shivaji.

Tulsidas (1532-1623): A great Hindu saint, devotee of Rama and author of *Rama Charit Manas*.

Upadhyaya, Din Dayal (1917-1968): He was considered to be a great inspiring force behind the Bharatiya Jan Sangh, he worked as the General Secretary of the Party for 14 years and was President at the time of his murder in train on Feb 11, 1968. He was a silent but enthusiastic worker and a zealous builder of the Party.

Valmiki (800 BC): A great saint and celebrated poet (Adi-kavi) of Sanskrit in the ancient India. He wrote *Ramayana* in Sanskrit.

Varahamihir (505-587): A distinguished astronomer, mathematician & philosopher who adorned the court of King Vikramaditya of Ujjaini.

Ved Vyas: A great saint and Sanskrit scholar of ancient India who wrote *Mahabharata* and *Bhagwat-Gita*.

Vidyasagar, Ishwar Chandra (1820-91): Great Indian scholar and reformer who fought for widow's re-marriage, higher education for women and against child marriage.

Vivekananda, Swami (1863-1902): A great propagator of Vedantic Philosophy, founder of Ramakrishna Mission at Belur (West Bengal); an eminent scholar of dynamic energy and inspiring personality, he left an indelible print on the minds of people both at home and abroad.

Visvesvarayya, Sri M (1861-1963): A great philanthropist and engineer. Chief Engineer Mysore State (1909); Chairman, Indian Economic Committee and President All India Manufacturers Organisation (1941). Awarded Bharat Ratna in 1955.

Zafar, Bahadur Shah (1775-1862): The last Mughal ruler in India and a renowned Urdu poet, Bahadur Shah took part in the first war of Indian Independence in 1857. He was arrested, put in jail in Rangoon where he died in 1862.

FAMOUS ARTISTS

Name	Field of Activity
Abanindranath Tagore	Painter
Abdul Halim Zafar Khan	Sitar
Ahmad Jan Thirkuwa	Tabla
Akhtar Begum	Ghazal
Albert Schewitzer (Germany)	Musician, Composer
Ali Akbar Khan	Sarod
Allauddin Khan	Sarod
Amjad Ali Khan	Sarod
Amrita Shergil	Painter
Angelico Era (Italy)	Painter
Arpita Singh	Painter
Asad Ali Khan	Veena
Auguste Rodin (France)	Sculptor
Badal Sarkar	Dramatist
Bade Ghulam Ali Khan	Musician
Bala Saraswathi	Dance (Bharat Natyam)
Name	Field of Activity
Birju Maharaj	Dance (Kathak)
Bismillah Khan	Shahnai
Damayanti Joshi	Dance (Kathak)
David Wilkie (Scotland)	Painter
Durga Das	Dance (Kathak)
Edouard Vuillard (France)	Painter
Edvard Grieg (Norway)	Composer and Musician
Fats Waller (USA)	Piano
Fra Angelico (Italy)	Painter
Francisco de Zurbaran (Spain)	Painter
Frederic Chopin (Poland)	Musician
Gajanan Rao Joshi	Violin
Ganga Devi	Painter (Madhubani)
Ghulam Ali	Ghazal
Giuseppe Verdi (Italy)	Musician
Gopi Krishna	Dance (Kathak, Bharat Natyam)
Heitor Villa Lobos (Brazil)	Composer
Hirabai Barodekar	Classical Vocalist
Hugo Wolf (Austria)	Composer
Indrani Rahman	Dance (Bharat Natyam)
Jacob Epstein (USA)	Sculptor
Jaheeruddin Dagar	Musician (Dhrupad)
Jan Steen (Dutch)	Painter
Joseph Haydin (Austria)	Composer
Joshua Reynolds (England)	Painter
Keshava Shankar Pillai	Cartoonist
Kishan Maharaj	Tabla
Krishna Rao Shankar Pandit	Musician
Leonardo Da Vinci (Italy)	Painter/Sculptor
Lorenzo Ghiberti (Italy)	Sculptor
Luca della Robbia (Italy)	Sculptor
Ludwig Van Bethoven (Austria)	Composer
Mehndi Hasan	Ghazal
M F Hussain	Painter
Michelangelo Bounarroti (Italy)	Painter, Sculptor
Mrinalini Sarabhai	Dance (Bharat Natyam)
Name	Field of Activity
M S Subbulakshmi	Classical Vocal Music
Naina Devi	Hindustani Classical
Nanda Lal Bose	Painter
Nazir Aminuddin Dagar	Musician (Dhrupad)
Nikhil Banerjee	Sitar

Name	Field of Activity
Onkarnath Thakur	Musician
Paderewski, Jan (Poland)	Piano
Pandit Nikhil Ghosh	Tabla
Panna Lal Ghosh	Flute
Paolo Uccello (Italy)	Painter
Paul Cezanne (France)	Painter
Peter Ilyrich Tchaikovsky (Russia)	Composer
Peter Paul Rubens (England)	Painter
Phidias (Greece)	Sculptor
Picasso (Spain)	Painter
Rais Khan	Sitar
Ram Gopal	Dance (Kathakali)
Ram Kumar	Painter
Raphael, Sanzio (Italy)	Painter
Ravi Shankar	Sitar
Rita Devi	Dance (Manipuri)
Rodin Auguste (France)	Sculptor
Rukmini Devi	Dance (Bharat Natyam)
R K Laxman	Cartoonist
Sadiq Ali Khan	Veena
Satish Gujral	Painter
Shafat Ahmad Khan	Tabla
Shambhu Maharaj	Dance (Kathak)
Siddheswari Devi	Musician
Sitara Devi	Dance (Kathak)
Sonal Mansingh	Dance (Bharat Natyam)
Stevie Wonder (USA)	Composer and Singer
Sudhir Dhar	Cartoonist
Sudhir Tailang	Cartoonist
Syvatoslov Roerich (Russia)	Painter
Tansen	Musician
Name	Field of Activity
T R Mahalingam	Flute
Uday Shankar	Dance (Bharat Natyam)
Ustad Vilayat Khan	Sitar
Van Ryn Rembrandt (Dutch)	Painter
Vishwa Mohan Bhatt	Guitarist
Walt Disney (USA)	Cartoonist
W A Mozart (Austria)	Composer
Wang Wei (China)	Painter
Whitneny Houston	Female pop vocalist
William Hogarth (England)	Painter
Yamini Krishnamurthi	Dance (Bharat Natyam)
Yehudi Menuhin (USA)	Violin

ABBREVIATIONS

A

AAFI : Amateur Athletics Federation of India

ABC : Audit Bureau of Circulation; American Broadcasting Company; Australian Broadcasting Company

ABM : Anti Ballistic Missiles

AC : Alternating Current; Ashok Chakra; Ante Christum (Before Christ)

AD : Anno Domini (After Death)

ADB : Asian Development Bank

AEC : Atomic Energy Commission

AF : Audio Frequency

AFC : Asian Football Confederation

AICC : All India Congress Committee

AID : Agency for International Development

AIDS : Acquired Immune Deficiency Syndrome

AIIMS : All India Institute of Medical Sciences

AJT : Advanced Jet Trainer

AM : Ante Meridian (before noon)

ASI : Archaeological Survey of India

ASLV : Augmented Satellite Launch Vehicle

ASSOCHAM : Associated Chamber of Commerce and Industry

AVARD : Association of Voluntary Agencies for Rural Development

AVC : Army Veterinary Corps

AVSM : Ati Vishisht Seva Medal

AWACS : Airborne Warning and Control System

B

BARC : Bhabha Atomic Research Centre
BBC : British Broadcasting Corporation
BCCI : Board of Control for Cricket in India
BCG : Bacillus Calamette Guerin (preventive vaccine for tuberculosis)
BHU : Banaras Hindu University
BIS : Bureau of Indian Standards; British Information Service; Bank of International Settlements
BSF : Border Security Force
BSS : Bharat Sewak Samaj; British Standard Specifications

C

CAPART : Council for Advancement of People's Action and Rural Technology
CARD : Centre for Astronomical Research and Development
CARE : Cooperation for American Relief Everywhere
CAS : Chief of the Air Staff.
CAT : Centre for Advanced Technology
CAZRI : Central Arid Zone Research Institute
CBI : Central Bureau of Investigation
CBSE : Central Board of Secondary Education
CEC : Chief Election Commissioner; Chief Executive Councillor
CHOGM : Commonwealth Heads of Government Meeting
CIA : Central Intelligence Agency (U.S.A)
CID : Criminal Investigation Department
CIET : Central Institute of Educational Technology
CISF : Central Industrial Security Force
COD : Cash on Delivery; Central Ordnance Depot.
COFEPOSA : Conservation of Foreign Exchange and Prevention of Smuggling Act
CPC : Civil Procedure Code
CPI : Communist Party of India
CPI (M) : Communist Party of India (Marxist)
CRR : Cash Reserve Ratio
CST : Central Sales Tax
CTBT : Comprehensive Test Ban Treaty

D

DAE : Department of Atomic Energy
DDT : Dichloro Diphenyl Trichloro-ethane (insecticide)
DG : Director General, Dei Gratia (By the Grace of God)
DMK : Dravida Munnetra Kazhagam
DNA : De-oxyribonucleio acid
DRDO : Defence Research and Development Organisation

E

ECG : Electrocardiogram
EFTA : European Free Trade Association
ERDA : Energy Research and Development Administration
ESA : European Space Agency
ESCAP : Economic and Social Commission for Asia and the Pacific
ESI : Employees State Insurance
EVM : Electronic Voting Machine
EWS : Economically Weaker Sections

F

FAO : Food and Agriculture Organisation (United Nations)
FBI : Federal Bureau of Investigation (of U.S.A)
FCI : Food Corporation of India
FDI : Foreign Direct Investment
FERA : Foreign Exchange Regulation Act
FICCI : Federation of Indian Chambers of Commerce and Industry
FIDE : Federation Internationale d'Echees (International Chess Federation)

G

GATT : General Agreement on Tariff and Trade
GDP : Gross Domestic Product
GIC : General Insurance Corporation
GMT : Greenwich Mean Time
GNP : Gross National Product
GPF : General Provident Fund; Gandhi Peace Foundation

GRP : Government Railway Police
GSI : Geological Survey of India
GSLV : Geosynchoronous Satellite Launch Vehicle

H

HAL : Hindustan Aeronautics Limited
HMT : Hindustan Machine Tools; Head Micro Telephone
HUDCO : Housing and Urban Development Corporation

I

IADF : International Agricultural Development Fund
IAEC : Indian Atomic Energy Commission
IAS : Indian Administrative Service
IATA : International Air Transport Association
IBRD : International Bank for Reconstruction and Development (World Bank)
ICAR : Indian Council of Agricultural Research
ICC : International Chamber of Commerce; International Control Commission; International Cricket Conference
ICICI : Industrial Credit and Investment Corporation of India
ICJ : International Court of Justice
ICW : International Council of Women
IDA : International Development Agency
IDBI : Industrial Development Bank of India
IEA : International Energy Agency
IFFI : International Film Festival of India
IFS : Indian Foreign Service; Indian Forest Service
IGNOU : Indira Gandhi National Open University
IIT : Indian Institute of Technology
ILO : International Labour Organisation
IMF : International Monetary Fund
INA : Iraqi News Agency
INSAT : Indian National Satellite
INTERPOL : International Criminal Police Organisation
IOC : International Olympic Committee ; Indian Oil Corporation
IRDP : Integrated Rural Development Programme
ISD : International Subscriber Dialling
ISI : Inter Services Intelligence (of Pakistan)
ISO : International Standardisation Organisation
ISRO : Indian Space Research Organisation

J

JMM : Jharkhand Mukti Morcha
JNU : Jawahar Lal Nehru University
JRY : Jawahar Rozgar Yojana

K

KANU : Kenya African National Union
KG : Kindergarten
KMT : Kuomintang (Nationalist Party of Taiwan)

L

LASER : Light Amplification by Stimulated Emission of Radiation
LCA : Light Combat Aircraft
LDC : Least Development Countries; Lower Division Clerk
LIC : Life Insurance Corporation
LPG : Liquified Petroleum Gas
LSD : Dextro-lysergic acid diethylamide (hallucinogen)

M

MBA : Master of Business Administration
MBBS : Bachelor of Medicine and Bachelor of surgery
MCA : Monetary Compensatory Account; Master of Computer Application
MCC : Marylebone Cricket Club; Missile Control Centre
MLA : Member of Legislative Assembly
MLC : Member of Legislative Council
MRTPC : Monopolies and Restrictive Trade Practices Commission

N

NABARD : National Bank of Agricultural and Rural Development
NAFTA : North American Free Trade Agreement
NAM : Non-Aligned Movement
NASA : National Aeronautics and Space Administration (U.S.A.)
NATO : North Atlantic Treaty Organisation
NBT : National Book Trust
NCERT : National Council of Educational Research and Training
NCR : National Capital Region
NFDC : National Film Development Corporation
NID : National Institute of Designs (Ahmedabad)
NIDC : National Industrial Development Corporation
NIFT : National Institute of Fashion Technology
NIIT : National Institute of Information Technology
NPT : Non-Proliferation Treaty
NRI : Non-Resident Indian
NRSA : National Remote Sensing Agency
NSA : National Security Act; National Security Agency (of U.S.)
NSG : National Security Guards
NSS : National Service Scheme
NTPC : National Thermal Power Corporation

O

OAPEC : Organisation of Arab Petroleum Exporting Countries
OAS : Organisation of American States
OAU : Organisation of African Unity
OECD : Organisation of Economic Cooperation And Development
OIC : Organisation of Islamic Countries
OIL : Oil India Limited
ONGC : Oil and Natural Gas Commission
OPEC : Organisation of Petroleum Exporting Countries

P

PBX : Private Branch Exchange (telephone)
PCI : Press Council of India
PIB : Press Information Bureau
PIN-Code : Postal Index Number Code
PSLV : Polar Satellite Launch Vehicle
PTBT : Partial Test Ban Treaty
PTI : Press Trust of India
PVC : Param Vir Chakra
PVSM : Param Vishisht Seva Medal
PWD : Public Works Department

R

RADAR : Radio Detecting and Ranging
RAF : Royal Air Force (U.K.); Rapid Action Force
RAW : Research and Analysis Wing
RBI : Reserve Bank of India
RCC : Reinforced Cement Concrete
RSS : Rashtriya Swayamsewak Sangh
RSVP : Respondez sil vous plait (please reply)

S

SAARC : South Asian Association for Regional Cooperation
SAIL : Steel Authority of India Limited
SALT : Strategic Arms Limitation Treaty
SEATO : South East Asia Treaty Organisation
SEBI : Securities and Exchange Board of India
SEWA : Self-Employed Women's Association
SGPC : Shiromani Gurdwara Prabandhak Committee
SIDBI : Small Industries Development Bank of India
SITE : Satellite Instruction Television Experiment
SLV : Satellite Launch Vehicle
SPCA : Society for the Prevention of Cruelty to Animals
SPG : Special Protection Group
SSB : Services Selection Board
STD : Subscriber Trunk Dialling (telephone)

T

TNT : Tri nitro toluene (explosive)
TTBT : Threshold Test Ban Treaty
TTE : Travelling Ticket Examiner
TWA : Trans-World Airlines (U.S.A.)

U

UAE : United Arab Emirates
UAR : United Arab Republic
UFO : Unidentified Flying Object
UGC : University Grants Commission
UN : United Nations
UNCTAD : United Nations Conference on Trade and Development
UNDP : United Nations Development Programme
UNEP : United Nations Environment Programme
UNESCO : United Nations Educational, Scientific and Cultural Organisation
UNHCR : United Nations High Commission for Refugees
UNI : United News of India
UNICEF : United Nations International Children's Emergency Fund
UNIDO : United Nations Industrial Development Organisation
UNIIOG : United Nations Iraq-Iran Observer Group
UPC : Under Postal Certificate
UPSC : Union Public Serviced Commission
UPU : Universal Postal Union
USA : United States of America
USSR : Union of Soviet Socialist Republic (now dissolved)
UTI : Unit Trust of India

V

VAT : Value Added Tax
VSSC : Vikram Sarabhai Space Centre

W

WFP : World Food Programme
WFTU : World Federation of Trade Unions
WHO : World Health Organisation
WTO : World Trade Organisation; World Tourism Organisation
WWFN : World Wide Fund for Nature

Y

YMCA : Young Men's Christian Association
YWCA : Young Women's Christian Association

INDIAN STATES : AT A GLANCE

ANDHRA PRADESH

Area : 1,60,229 sq. km.
Capital : Hyderabad
Formation Day : 1st November, 1956
Population : 4,93,86,799
Male : 2,47,38,068
Female : 2,46,48,731
Sex Ratio : 996 females (per 1000 males)
Density of Population : 308 persons per sq. km.
Literacy : 67.04%
No. of M.P. : 25
No. of Rajya Sabha's Members : 11
No. of Districts : 13 — Ananthapur, Chittoor, Cuddapah, East Godavari, Guntur, Hyderabad, Krishna, Kurnool, Nellore, Prakasam, Srikakulam, Visakhapatnam, Vizianagaram, West Godavari.

Principal Languages : Telugu and Urdu

Principal Religions : Hindus : 89.14%, Muslims: 8.91%, Christians : 1.83%, Sikhs : 0.03%, Buddhist: 0.03%; Jains : 0.04%; Others : 0.02% (2001)

Agriculture and Horticulture : Rice, Jowar, Maize, Sugarcane, Tobacco, Banana, Cashew-nuts

Airport : Hyderabad, Tirupathi, Visakhapatnam, Vijayawada

Industries : Machine Tools, Synthetic drugs, Pharmaceuticals, Heavy electrical machinery, Ships, Fertilizers, Electronic equipment, Aeronautical parts, Cement, Chemicals, Asbestos, Cement products and Glass.

Minerals : Chrysolite Asbestos, Copper, Manganese, Mica, Coal and Lime-Stone

High Court : Hyderabad

Festivals : Yugadi, Sankranti, Vinayak Chaturthi

Tourist Places : Hyderabad, Secunderabad, Mangalagiri, Tirumala-Tirupathi, Ahobilam, Anakapalle, Bhadrachalam, Himayat Sagar, Usman Sagar, Kolleroo, Rajmandi, Visakhapatnam Yadagiri Gutta, Parwal, Waltair, Nagarjun Sagar, Machilipatnam, Kailasnath Kona, Kuchipudi.

ARUNACHAL PRADESH

Area : 83,743 sq. km.

Capital : Itanagar

Formation Day : 20th January, 1972

Population : 13,83,727

Male : 7,13,912

Female : 6,69,815

Sex Ratio : 938 females (per 1000 males)

Density of Population : 17 persons per sq. km.

Literacy : 65.4% (Males : 72.6%; Females : 57.7%)

No. of M. P. : 2

No. of Rajya Sabha's Members : 1

No. of Districts : 16— Changlang, Dibang Valley, Lower Dibang Valley, Anjaw, East Kameng, East Siang, Upper Siang, Lohit, Lower Subansiri, Papum pare, Tawang, Tirap, Upper Subansiri,West Kameng, West Siang, Kurung Kumey.

Principal Languages : Nyishi, Monpa, Miji, Aka, Sherdukpen, Apatani, Jageri, Hillmiri, Adi Gallong, Digaru, Mishmi, Idu Mishmi, Miju Mishmi, Khampti, Nocte, Tangsa and Wanchu.

Principal Religions : Hindus : 37.04%, Muslims: 1.38%, Christians : 10.29%, Sikhs : 0.14%, Buddhists: 12.88%, Jains : 0.01%, Others : 38.26%. (2001)

Agriculture and Horticulture : Rice, Potato, Apple, Orange.

Roads : 330 km National Highways.
Metalled : 2,328 km.
Unmetalled : 1,380 km.

Railway : 25 km.

Industries : Forest based cottage industries.

Minerals : Coal, Dolomite.

Electrified Villages : 72%.

High Court : The State comes under the jurisdiction of Guwahati High Court.

Festivals : Lossar, Khan, Nwokum, Orankum, Garkuo, Boriboot, Dree, Si-Donyi, Mopin, Solung, Sangken, Ren Auraha, Chalo Lokoo,Onjile and Bhol.

Time for Tourism : October to May.

Tourist Places : Bomdila, Tawang, Along, Itanagar, Malinithan, Bhishmaknagar, Changlang, Vijay Nagar, Parsuram Kund, Pasighat.

ASOM

Area : 78,438 sq. km.

Capital : Dispur.

Population : 3,12,05,576.

Male : 1,59,39,443.

Female : 1,52,66,133.

Sex Ratio : 958 females (per 1000 males).

Density of Population : 398 persons per sq. km.

Literacy : 72.2%

No. of M.P. : 14

No. of Rajya Sabha's Members : 7

No. of Districts : 27 — Barpeta, Cachar, Darrang, Dhubri, Dibrugarh, Goalpara, Jorhat, Kamrup Metro, Kamrup, Chirang, Baksa, Udalguri, Karbi-Anglong, Karimganj, Kokrajhar, Lakhimpur, Nagaon, Shibsagar, Sonitpur, Nalbari, Pragjyotishpur, Golaghat, Dhemaji, Tinsukia, Hailakandi, Bongaigaon, Morigaon.

Principal Language : Assamese.

Principal Religions : Hindus : 67.13%, Muslims: 28.43%, Christians : 3.32%, Sikhs : 0.07%, Buddhists : 0.29%, Jains : 0.09%, Others : 0.67% (2001)

Agriculture and Horticulture : Tea, rice, orange and lemon.

Total Length of Roads : 37,515 km.

National Highways (metalled) : 2,836 km.

Railway : 2,284 km

Airports : 6 — Guwahati, Tejpur, Dibrugarh, Lakhimpur, Silchar and Jorhat.

Industries : Tea, Sugar, Paper, Petroleum, Plywood and cottage industries.

Minerals : Coal, Lime-stone, Dolomite and Natural Gas.

Electrified Villages : 68%

High Court : Guwahati

Climate : Summer Season : 35ºC to 18ºC
Winter Season : 26ºC to 7ºC

Monsoon : June to September

Festivals : Bihu, Batho, Khairepooja, Gobara, Baisatak

Tourist Places : Shibsagar, Tejpur, Haflong, Chandubi Lake, Hajo, Barpeta, Dispur, Guwahati, Dibrugarh, Majuli, Kaziranga, Silchar, Suwalkuchi, Digboi, Manas, Darrang, Dobaka, Orang, Batadrav

BIHAR

Area : 94,163 sq. km.

Capital : Patna

Formation Day : 1st November, 1956

Population : 10,40,99,452

Male : 5,42,78,157

Female : 4,98,21,295

Sex Ratio : 918 females per 1000 males

Density of Population : 1,106 person per sq. km.

Literacy : 61.8%

No. of M.P. : 40

No. of Rajya Sabha's Members : 16

No. of Districts : 38 — Patna, Nalanda, Rohtas, Kaimoor (Bhabhua), Bhojpur, Buxar, Gaya, Jahanabad, Nawada, Aurangabad, Saran, Siwan, Gopalganj, Muzaffarpur, Sitamarhi, Sheohar, West Champaran, East Champaran, Vaishali, Darbhanga, Madhubani, Samastipur, Saharsa, Supaul, Madhepura, Purnea, Araria, Kishanganj, Katihar, Bhagalpur, Banka, Munger, Lakhisarai, Shekhpura, Jamui, Khagaria, Begusarai, Arwal.

Principal Languages : Hindi, Urdu, Maithili

Principal Religions : Hindus : 82.42%; Muslims: 19.18%; Christians: 0.98%; Sikhs : 0.09/%; Jains : 0.03%; Others : 1.67% (2001)

Agriculture and Horticulture : Paddy, Wheat, Maize, Pulses, Sugarcane, Potato, Tobacco, Oilseed, Mango, Black-plum, Jack-fruit.

Roads : National Highway : 3,734.38 km
State Highways : 3,989 km

Railways : 5,108 km

Airports : Gaya, Patna, Muzaffarpur, Raxaul, Bhagalpur

Industries : 13 sugarmill in the private sectors and 15 in the public sectors, Distilleries, Tanning and leather finishing industries and 3 large Jute mills at Katihar and Samastipur

High Court : Patna

Climate : Summer Season : 47ºC to 20ºC
Winter Season : 28ºC to 4ºC

Festivals : Chhath, Durgapuja, Deepawali, Sonepur Cattle Fair, Holi

Tourist Places : Bodh Gaya, Patna, Vaishali, Nalanda, Pawapuri, Bihar Sharif, Sonepur, Munger, Gaya, Sasaram, Dehri-on-Sone

CHHATTISGARH

Area : 1,37,898 sq. km.

Capital : Raipur

Formation Day : 1st November, 2000

Population : 2,55,45,198

Male : 1,28,32,895

Female : 1,27,12,303

Sex Ratio : 991 females per 1000 males

Density of Population : 189 persons per sq. km.

Literacy : 70.3%

No. of M.P. : 11

No. of Rajya Sabha's Members : 5

Districts : 18— Bastar, Bilaspur, Bijapur, Dhantewada (South Bastar), Dhamatari, Durg, Janjgir-Champa, Jashpur, Kanker (North Bastar), Kawardha, Koriya, Mahasamund, Narayanpur, Raigarh, Raipur, Rajnandgaon, Sarguja and Korba.

Principal Languages : Hindi

Principal Religions : Hindus : 92.80%; Muslims: 4.26%; Christians : 0.65%; Sikhs : 0.24%; Buddhists: 0.33%; Jains : 0.74%; Others : 0.28% (2001)

Agriculture and Horticulture : Paddy, Wheat, Pulses, Mango, Banana

Total Length of Roads : 31,803 km.

Roads : National Highways : 2,226 km
State Roads : 5,240 km
District Roads : 10,539 km
Village Roads : 13,798 km

Railways : 1,053 km (approximate)

Airports : Raipur and Bilaspur

Industries : Aluminium, Steel, Paper, Silk, Cement, Energy projects.

Minerals : Coal, Diamond, Iron, Manganese.

High Court : Bilaspur

Climate : Summer Season : 48ºC to 22ºC
Winter Season : 25ºC to 3ºC

Monsoon : June to September

Festivals : Pola, Nawakhoi, Govardhan Pooja, Holi, Deepawali, Mahashivaratri, Festival of Tribals

Tourist Places : Raipur Mahanagar, Bhilai, Korba, Malhar, Khallari, Kharaud, Rajim, Amarkantak, Bhoramdeva, Sinhawa

GOA

Area : 3,702 sq. km.

Capital : Panaji

Formation Day : May 30, 1987
Population : 14,58,545
Male : 7,39,140
Female : 7,19,405
Sex Ratio : 973 females per 1000 males
Density of Population : 394 persons per sq. km.
Literacy : 88.7%
No. of M.P. : 2
No. of Rajya Sabha's Member : 1
No. of Districts : 2 — North Goa, South Goa
Principal Languages : Konkani, Marathi

Principal Religions : Hindus : 64.68%; Muslims 5.25%; Christians : 29.86%; Sikhs : 0.09%; Buddhists : 0.02%; Jains : 0.04%; Others : 0.06% (2001)

Agriculture and Horticulture : Rice, Pulse, Ragi, Coconut, Cashew-nut, Betel-nut, Pine-apple, Mango and Banana.

Roads : National Highways : 264 km
State Highways : 279.4 km
Other Roads : 4501.18 km
Railways : 79 km
Airports : Dabolim

Industries : Workshop, Bakery, Printing Press, Wood Saw Mill, Mozaic tiles, Soap and Furniture.

Minerals : Iron-ores, Manganese, Ferro-manganese, Bauxite, Chalk etc.

Electrified Villages : hundred per cent
High Court : Mumbai
Climate : Oceasanic : 32ºC to 21ºC
Monsoon : June to October
Festivals : Christmas and New Year

Tourist Places : Dona Pola, Panaji, Velha (old) Goa, Dudhsagar, Chandreshwar Bhootnath, Agoda, Harvalem, Mormugao, Mapuka, Vasco-da-Gama, Vagatore, Bicholim

GUJARAT

Area : 1,96,024 sq. km.
Capital : Gandhinagar
Formation Day : 1st May, 1966
Population : 6,04,39,692
Male : 3,14,91,260
Female : 2,89,48,432
Sex Ratio : 919 females per 1000 males
Density of Population : 308 persons per sq. km.
Literacy : 78.0%
No. of M.P. : 26
No. of Rajya Sabha's Member : 11

No. of Districts : 26 — Ahmedabad, Amreli, Anand, Banaskantha, Bharuch, Bhavnagar, Dahod, Gandhinagar, Jamnagar, Junagarh, Kachchh, Kheda, Mehsana, Patan, Panchmahal, Rajkot, Sabarkantha, Surat, Surendranagar, Valsad, NavSari, Vadodara, Dang, Porbandar, Tapi and Narmada.

Principal Languages : Gujarati, Marathi, Hindi and Sindhi.

Principal Religions : Hindus : 89.48%; Muslims: 8.73%; Christians : 0.44%; Sikhs : 0.08%; Buddhists: 0.03%; Jains : 1.197%; Others : 0.02% (2001)

Agriculture and Horticulture : Cotton, Tobacco, Groundnuts, Paddy, Wheat, Bajra, Sugarcane, Mango, Banana etc.

Roads : National Highways : 1,425 km
State Highways : 73,937 km
Total length of Roads : 77,000 km
Railways : 5,550 km

Airports : Ahmedabad, Vadodara, Bhavnagar, Bhuj, Surat, Jamnagar, Kandla, Keshod, Porbandar, Rajkot.

Industries : Textiles, Chemicals and Petro-chemicals, Pharmaceuticals, Dyes, Fertilizers, Cement, Dairy, Sugar, Engineering, Salt and Vegetable, Ghee etc.

Minerals : Lime-Stone, Oil, Natural Gas, Fluorite, Lignite.

Electrified Villages : 99.5%
High Court : Ahmedabad
Climate : Summer Season : 41ºC to 27ºC
Winter Season : 29ºC to 14ºC
Monsoon : June to September.

Festivals : Navratri, Makar Sakranti, Dangi Durbar, Bhavnath fair, Shamlaji fair etc.

Tourist Places : Ahmedabad, Ambaji, Dwarka, Gandhinagar, Lothal, Somnath, Gir Forest, Jamnagar, Bhuj, Anand, Girnar, Palitana, Nal Sarovar, Velavadar, Rajkot, Porbandar, Vadodara, Pawagarh, Kandla, Surat.

HARYANA

Area : 44,212 sq. km.
Capital : Chandigarh
Formation Day : 1st November, 1966
Population : 2,53,51,462
Male : 1,34,94,734

Female : 1,18,56,728

Sex Ratio : 879 females per 1000 males

Density of Population : 573 persons per sq. km.

Literacy : 75.6%

No. of M.P. : 10

No. of Rajya Sabha's Member : 5

Districts : 21 — Ambala, Bhiwani, Faridabad, Fatehabad, Gurgaon, Hisar, Jhajjar, Jind, Kaithal, Karnal, Kurukshetra, Mahendragarh, Panchkula, Panipat, Rewari, Rohtak, Sirsa, Sonepat, Yamunanagar, Mewat, Palwal.

Principal Languages : Hindi and Punjabi.

Principal Religions : Hindus : 89.2%; Muslims : 4.64%; Christians : 0.10%; Sikhs : 5.81%; Buddhists: 0.01%; Jains : 0.21%; Others : 2.02% (2001)

Agriculture and Horticulture : Rice, Wheat, Sugarcane, Barley, Cotton, Jowar, Bajra, Oilseed, Pulses etc.

Roads : ***Total Length*** : 35,303 km

Railways : 1250 km (appr.)

Airports : Chandigarh, Hisar, Karnal, Pinjore, Narnaul and Bhiwani.

Industries : Cars, Motorcycles, Tractors, Cycles, Dairy, Paper, Sugar and Textiles.

Minerals : Iron, Lime-Stone, Marble, Sulphur, China-clay.

Electrified Villages : Hundred per cent

High Court : Chandigarh

Climate : Summer Season : 46ºC to 35ºC
Winter Season : 14ºC to 2ºC

Tourist Places : Hissar, Jhajjar, Sultanpur, Ambala, Kalesar, Bhiwani, Faridabad, Kurukshetra, Panipat, Surajkund, Hansi

HIMACHAL PRADESH

Area : 55,673 sq. km.

Capital : Shimla

Formation Day : 1st November, 1956

Population : 68,64,602

Male : 34,81,873

Female : 33,82,729

Sex Ratio : 972 females per 1000 males

Density of Population : 123 persons per sq. km.

Literacy : 82.8%

No. of M.P. : 4

No. of Rajya Sabha's Member : 3

Districts : 12 — Bilaspur, Chamba, Hamirpur, Kangra, Kinnaur, Kullu, Lahaul & Spiti, Mandi, Shimla, Shirmaur, Solan, Una.

Principal Languages : Hindi, Pahari, Punjabi.

Principal Religions : Hindus : 95.90%; Muslims: 1.72%; Christians : 0.09: Sikhs : 1.01%; Buddhists : 1.24%; Jains 0.02%; Others : 0.02% (2001)

Agriculture & Horticulture : Apple, Potato, Orange, Ginger, Citron, Chilgoza (fruits of the Pine tree).

Roads : Total length of roads in the State : 33,171 km.

Railways : 210 km (appr.)

Airports : Bhuntar (Kullu Valley), Jubbarhatti (Shimla), Geggal (Kangra).

Industries : Fertilizers, Cement, Electronics, Wine, Handicrafts, Looms, Tea, Cottage Industries.

Minerals : Lime-Stone, Rock-Salt, Gypsum, Silica-Sand, Barytes.

Electrified Villages : Hundred per cent.

High Court : Shimla

Climate : Summer Season : 33ºC to 14ºC
Winter Season : 15ºC to 0ºC

Festivals : Minja Mela, Jwalamukhi Mela, Kullu Dussehra.

Tourist Places : Dharmashala, Kullu, Manali, Chamba, Shimla, Dalhousie, Kalpa, Chail, Kasouli, Renuka, Solan, Masobra, Baijnath.

JAMMU & KASHMIR

Area : 2,22,236 sq. km. (The areas occupied by Pakistan and China are also included)

Capital : Srinagar (Summer) and Jammu (Winter)

Formation Day : 26th October, 1947

Population : 1,25,41,320 (The population of Pakistan and China occupied areas not included)

Male : 66,40,662

Female : 59,00,640

Sex Ratio : 889 females per 1000 males

Density of Population : 124 persons per sq. km.

Literacy : 67.2%

No. of M.P. : 6

No. of Rajya Sabha's Member : 4

Districts : 22 — Anantnag, Badgam, Baramula, Doda, Jammu, Kargil, Kathua, Kupwara, Leh, Pulwama, Poonch, Rajouri, Srinagar, Udhampur, Bandipur, Kulagram, Gandherbal, Sopor, Samba, Kistwad, Riyasi and Ramban.

Principal Languages : Urdu, Kashmiri, Dogri, Gujri, Punjabi, Balti, Dadri, Pahari and Ladakhi.

Principal Religions : Hindus : 32.24%; Muslims: 64.19%; Christians: 0.14%; Sikhs : 2.23%; Buddhists : 1.17%; Jains : 0.03% (2001)

Agriculture and Horticulture : Saffron, Rice, Wheat, Jowar, Bajra, Fruit and Flower.

Roads : Total length of Roads : 27,778 km

Railways : 77 km.

Airports : Srinagar, Leh and Jammu.

Industries : Engraving on wood, making of carpets and shawls, embroidery, silk industries, looms and handicrafts.

Minerals : Iron ores, Copper, Zinc, Bauxite, Silver, Chalk, Lime-Stone, Lignite, Coal.

Electrified Villages : More than 96%.

High Court : Srinagar and Jammu.

Climate : Jammu — Summer Season : 35ºC
Winter Season : 20ºC
Srinagar — Summer Season : 30ºC
Winter Season : Below 0ºC

Festivals : Janmashtami, Dussehra, Deepawli, Holi, Shivaratri, Id, Bakrid, Muharram.

Tourist Places : Amarnath, Srinagar, Charar-e-Sharief, Wular Lake, Dachigam, Jammu, Kargil, Gangabal, Batoti, Kokemarg, Speetok Gompa, Vaishno Devi, Leh

JHARKHAND

Area : 79,714 sq. km.

Capital : Ranchi

Formation Day : 15th November, 2000

Population : 3,29,88,134

Male : 1,69,30,315

Female : 1,60,57,819

Sex Ratio : 949 females per 1000 males

Density of Population : 414 persons per sq. km.

Literacy : 64.4%

No. of M.P. : 14

No. of Rajya Sabha's Members : 6

Districts : 24 — Bokaro, Chatra, Dhanbad, Deoghar, Dumka, Garhwa, Giridih, Godda, Gumla, Hazaribagh, Lohardaga, Pakur, Palamau, East Singhbhum, West Singhbum, Sahibganj, Kodarma, Ranchi, Latehar, Jamtara, Saraikela Kharsawan, Simdega, Ramgarh and Khunti.

Principal Languages : Hindi, Urdu, Santhali.

Principal Religions : Hindus : 82.42%; Muslim : 14.18%; Christians : 0.98%; Sikhs : 0.09%; Jains : 0.03%; Others : 1.67% (2001)

Agriculture and Horticulture : Rice, Jowar, Bajra, Oilseed, Wheat, Mango, Guava, Jack-fruit etc.

Roads : Total length of Roads : 4,311 km.
National Highways : 1,500 km
State Highways : 2711 km

Airports : Ranchi and Jamshedpur.

Industries : The State though backward yet very rich in minerals and dotted with heavy industries along with the natural wealth of forests. The major industries are— TISCO, TELCO, Bokaro Steel Plant, Hindustan Copper Limited, Usha Industries, Hindustan Zinc Ltd., Bihar Sponge Iron Limited, Uranium Corporation of India etc.

Minerals : Coal, Mica, Iron, Manganese, Gold, Silver, Uranium, Copper, Bauxite, Lime-stone etc.

High Court : Ranchi

Climate : Summer Season : 48ºC to 20ºC
Winter Season : 28ºC to 5ºC

Festivals : Durgapooja, Holi, Deepawali and various Adivasis' festivals.

Tourist Places : Ranchi, Parasnath, Dhanbad, Dumka, Rajmahal, Hazaribagh, Madhupur, Jamshedpur, Kodarma, Netarhat, Jharia

KARNATAKA

Area : 1,91,791 sq. km.

Capital : Bengaluru

Formation Day : 1st November, 1956

Population : 6,10,95,297

Male : 3,09,66,657

Female : 3,01,28,640

Sex Ratio : 973 females per 1000 males

Density of Population : 319 persons per sq. km.

Literacy : 75.4%

No. of M.P. : 28

No. of Rajya Sabha's Members : 12

Districts : 30 — Bagalkot, Bengaluru, Bengaluru Rural, Belgaum, Bellary, Bidar, Bijapur, Chikmagalur, Chitradurga, Chamarajnagar, Devanagere, Dakshina Kannada, Dharwad, Gulbarga, Hassan, Haveri, Kodagu, Kolar, Mandya, Mysore, Raichur, Shimoga, Tumkur, Udupi, Uttara Kannada, Koppal, Gadag, Ramanagara, Chikkabellapura and Yadgir.

Principal Language : Kannada

Principal Religions : Hindus : 85.45%; Muslims: 11.64%; Christians: 1.91%; Sikhs : 0.02%; Buddhists : 0.16%; Jains : 0.73%; Others : 0.09% (2001)

Agriculture and Horticulture : Cashew-nut, Coconut, Coffee, Tobacco, Banana, Jack-fruit, Mango, Tea etc.

Roads : Total length of Roads : 2,15,849 km.

Railways : 3,270 km.

Airports : Bangalore, Belgau Manga re, Hubli.

Industries : Karnataka is one of the leading industrialised State in the country. There are several big factories in th public, joint as well as private sector. Aircrafts, Te equipments, Machine tools, Earth movers, Ele uipmen heels and Axles of Railways, Ferr , Electric motors, Engines an are produce in Karnataka. A whole r ods are produc the small and medium tri In the h crafts sector, silk is the most pro sandal oil and agarbattis are als quantity.

Minerals : Gold, Lime-Stone, R nese, Chromite, Granite and China-

Electrified Villages : hundred pe

High Court : Bangalore

Climate : Summer Season : 35°C to 26

Winter Season : 25°C to 14°C

Monsoon : June to October

Festivals : Mysore Dussehra, Yugadi, Sankranti.

Tourist Places : Shravanbelagola, Mysore, Bangalore, Bandipur, Aihole, Halebid, Udupi, Srirangapatnam, Chamarajnagar, Belgaum, Gokaran, Gulbarga Dandeli, Krishnaraja Sagar, Kollur, Madikeri, Jog Falls, Sringeri, Ranganathittoo, Nagerhole, Gokak, Nandi Hills, Raichur, Bijapur, Badami, Talkaveri, Tungabhadra, Shivasamudram, Kolar.

KERALA

Area : 38,863 sq. km.

Capital : Thiruvananthapuram

Formation Year : 1951

Population : 3,34,06,061

Male : 1,60,27,412

Female : 1,73,78,649

Sex Ratio : 1,084 females per 1000 males

Density of Population : 860 persons per sq. km.

Literacy : 94%

No. of M.P. : 20

No. of Rajya Sabha's Members : 9

Districts : 14 — Allapuzha, Ernakulam, Idukki, Kannur, Kasaragode, Kollam, Kottayam, Kozhikode, Malappuram, Palakkad, Pathanamthitta, Thiruvananthapuram, Thrissur, Wayanad.

Principal Language : Malayalam.

Principal Religions : Hindus : 57.28%; Muslims: 23.33%; Christians: 19.32%; Sikhs : 0.01%; Jains : 0.01%, Others : 0.05% (2001)

Agriculture and Horticulture : Coconut, Rubber, Betel-nut, Cardamom, Cashew-nut, Sugarcane, Black-pepper, Spices, Banana, Pineapple, Mango etc.

Roads : Total length of Roads : 31811.6 km (in which the length of National Highway 1,542 km is included)

ays : 1,257 km

rts : Thiruvananthapuram, Kochi,

s : Oil refinery at Cochin, Fertilizer and ctories. Aluminium extraction plant, Ma- ant, Rare earth extraction plant, Titanium plants, Electronic equipments, Soaps and and Rubber factories, Traditional factories e: Handloom, Cashew, Coir and Handicrafts.

Minerals : Ilmenite, Rutile, Monozite, Zircon, Clay and Quartz sand minerals from which rare metals are extracted. Thorium used in radio-activity is also found.

High Court : Ernakulam.

Climate : Temperature : 35°C to 21°C

Monsoon : June to September/October.

Festivals : Onam, Mahashivaratri, Id, Bakrid, Ramzan, Muharram, Vishoo etc.

Tourist Places : Kovalam, Thiruvananthapuram, Kaladi, Alwaye, Pathanamthitta, Kasargod, Thrissur, Alleppey, Calicut (Kozhikode), Saberimalai, Warkallai, Quilon, Sultan ki-Betari, Thekkadi, Kodungalur, Pyramid

MADHYA PRADESH

Area : 3,08,000 sq. km.

Capital : Bhopal

Formation Day : 1st November, 1956

Population : 7,26,26,809
Male : 3,76,12,306
Female : 3,50,14,503
Sex Ratio : 931 females per 1000 males
Density of Population : 236 persons per sq. km.
Literacy : 69.3%
No. of M.P. : 29
No. of Rajya Sabha's Members : 11

Districts : 51 — Balaghat, Betul, Bhind, Bhopal, Badrani, Chhatarpur, Chhindwara, Damoh, Dindori, Datia, Dewas, Dhar, Katni, Khandwa (East Nimar), Guna, Gwalior, Harda, Hoshangabad, Indore, Jabalpur, Jhabua, Mandla, Mandsaur, Morena, Narsingpur, Neemach, Panna, Raisen, Rajgarh, Ratlam, Rewa, Sagar, Satana, Sehore, Seoni, Shahdol, Shajapur, Shayopur, Shivpuri, Sidhi, Tikamgarh, Ujjain, Vidisha, West Nimar, Umaria, Agar, Ashok Nagar, Burhanpur, Anooppur, Alirajpur and Singrauli.

Principal Language : Hindi

Principal Religions : Hindus : 92.80%; Muslims 4.26%; Christians : 0.65%; Sikhs : 0.24%; Buddhists: 0.33%; Jains : 0.74%; Others : 0.28% (2001)

Agriculture and Horticulture : Paddy, Wheat, Jowar, Barley, Opium, Soyabean, Oilseed, Pulses, Saal, Sagaun, Spices and Catechu.

Roads : National Highways : 4,709 km
State Highways : 10,501 km
Total length of Roads : 58,423 km

Railways : 4,800 km (approx.)

Airports : Bhopal, Gwalior, Jabalpur, Khajuraho, Indore.

Industries : Iron & Steel, Paper, Silk, Aluminium, Cement, Chemicals, Heavy electrical mahinery plant at Bhopal, Pulp plant at Nepanagar, Bank note press at Dewas, Alkaloid factory at Neemuch etc.

Minerals : Coal, Bauxite,Dolomite, Diamond, Lime-Stone, Iron (raw)

High Court : Jabalpur (with benches at Gwalior and Indore).

Climate : Summer Season : 48°C to 22°C
Winter Season : 23°C to 4°C

Festivals : Bhageria, Holi, Deepawali, Dussehra, Basant Panchami, Shivaratri, Ramanavami.

Tourist Places: Amarkantak, Khajuraho, Onkareshwar, Bawangaja, Ujjain, Mandasaur Fort,Chanderi Fort, Gwalior Fort, Udaigiri, Mandu, Chanderi, Bhopal, Bandhawgarh, Maheshwar, Shivpuri, Vidisha.

MAHARASHTRA

Area : 3,07,713 sq. km.
Capital : Mumbai
Formation Day : 1st May, 1960
Population : 11,23,74,333
Male : 5,82,43,056
Female : 5,41,31,277
Sex Ratio : 929 females per 1000 males
Density of Population : 365 persons per sq. km.
Literacy : 82.3%
No. of M.P. : 48
No. of Rajya Sabha's Member : 19

Districts : 35 — Ahmednagar, Akola, Amravati, Aurangabad, Bhandara, Beed, Mumbai City, Mumbai (Suburban), Buldhana, Chandrapur, Dhule, Gadchiroli, Gondiya, Hingoli, Jalgaon, Jalna, Kolhapur, Latur, Nagpur, Nanded, Nasik, Osmanabad, Parbhani, Pune, Raigad, Ratnagiri, Sangli, Satara, Sindhudurg, Sholapur, Thane, Wardha, Yavatmal, Nandurbar, Washim.

Principal Languages : Marathi, Hindi, Urdu and Gujarati.

Principal Religions : Hindus : 81.12%; Muslims: 9.67%; Christians : 1.12%; Sikhs : 0.2%; Buddhists: 6.39%; Jains : 1.22%; Others : 0.27% (2001)

Agriculture and Horticulture : Rice, Wheat, Jowar, Bajra, Pulses, Forest products etc.

Roads : National Highways : 4,376 km
State Highways : 34,157 km
Major District Roads : 50,256 km
Other District Roads : 46,817 km
Village Roads : 1,06,601 km
Total length of roads in the State : 2.43 Lakh km

Railways : 5,983 km

Airports : The major airports are — Mumbai, Aurangabad, Pune, Nagpur and Nasik.

Industries : The large industries include textiles, ginning and pressing silk, rayon, synthetic fabrics and vegetable products. Mumbai is the centre of the most of the textiles mills. The new industrial centre of Maharashtra are in Nasik, Aurangabad, Nagpur, Roha, Tarapur and Ahmednagar. Maharashtra is also a major sugar producing State. Nitrogenous fertilisers, Super-phosphate, Petro-chemicals, Drugs and Pharmaceuticals and photographic chemicals are the important chemical industries. Emergence of oil-fields at Mumbai High and Bassein North and the new fertiliser unit at Thal-Vaishet near Alibag have given further boost to petro-chemical industry. Marine industries and fish processing units in the coastal area of the State have also been developed. The state leads in motion picture industries and in sophisticated elecronic equipments. A number of defence and public sector industries are located in the State.

Minerals : Raw-Iron, Coal, Bauxite, Manganese, Salt and Lime-Stone.

Electrified Villages : Hundred per cent.

High Court : Mumbai

Climate : Summer Season : 39ºC to 22ºC
Winter Season : 34ºC to 12ºC

Festivals : Ganesh Pooja, Gokulashtami, Mahashivaratri, Holi and Deepawali.

Tourist Places : Ellora Elephanta, Mumbai, Ajanta, Amravati, Aurangabad, Kolhapur, Wardha, Shirdi, Pune, Nagpur, Satara, Paithad, Nasik, Raigarh

MANIPUR

Area : 22,327 sq. km.

Capital : Imphal

Formation Day : 21st January, 1972

Population : 25,70,390

Male : 12,90,171

Female : 12,80,219

Sex Ratio : 992 females per 1000 males

Density of Population : 115 persons per sq. km.

Literacy : 79.2%

No. of M.P. : 2

No. of Rajya Sabha's Member : 1

Districts : 9 — Bishnupur, Chandel, Churachandpur, Imphal East, Imphal West, Senapati, Tamenglong, Thoubal, Ukhrul.

Principal Languages : Manipuri, Gorkha, Bengali, Thado, Mao etc.

Principal Religions : Hindus : 57.67%; Muslims 7.2%, Christians : 34.11%; Sikhs : 0.07%; Buddhists: 0.04%; Jains : 0.07%; Others : 0.77%. (2001)

Agriculture and Horticulture : Sugarcane, Rice, Jowar, Bajra, Forest products.

Roads : National Highways : 957 km
State Highways : 839 km
District Roads : 1,946 km
Total length of Roads : 12,618 km

Airports : Imphal

Industries : Manipur lacks good infrastructure facilities and it is industrially backward State. There is no large scale industry in Manipur. Handloom weaving is the largest single cottage industry. Other cottage industries are sericulture, bamboo and cane articles, carpentry, blacksmithy, leather goods, edible oil crushing, rice milling, gur and khandsari.

Minerals : Salt.

High Court : Imphal.

Climate : Summer Season : 29ºC to 14ºC
Winter Season : 25ºC to 7ºC

Festivals : Dol-Jatra, Rath-Jatra, Moirang Thangjig Laiharaoba, Laiharaoba, Raslila, Idul-Joha, Idul-Fitr, Christmas etc.

Tourist Places : Imphal, Moirang, Churachandpur, Ukhrul, Langthabal, Kaina, Loktak, Kangchup

MEGHALAYA

Area : 22,429 sq. km.

Capital : Shillong

Formation Day : 21st January, 1972

Population : 29,66,889

Male : 14,91,832

Female : 14,75,057

Sex Ratio : 989 females per 1000 males

Density of Population : 132 persons per sq. km.

Literacy : 74.4%

No. of M.P. : 2

No. of Rajya Sabha's Member : 1

Districts — 7 : East Garo Hills, East Khasi Hills, Jaintia Hills, West Garo Hills, West Khasi Hills, Ri-Bhoi, South Garo Hills.

Principal Languages : Khasi, Garo, Jaintia, English.

Principal Religions : Hindus: 14.67%; Muslims: 3.46%; Christians : 64.58%; Sikhs : 0.15%; Buddhists : 0.16%; Jains : 0.02%; Others : 16.96% (2001)

Agriculture and Horticulture : Rice, Potato, Jowar, Bajra, Forest-products, Fruit etc.

Roads : National Highways : 606 km
Total length of metalled and unmetalled Roads : 7,977.98 km

Railways : The State is not connected by railway network.

Airports : Umroi (It is located at the distance of 35 km from Shillong)

Industries : Industrial production in Meghalaya is not large. A few cement plant and some middle scale industries co-exist with several small scale industries. Forests, however provide employment to a large number and add to the State's economy.

Minerals : Coal, Sillimanite, Limestone, Dolomite, Fireclay, Felspar, Quartz, Glass sand and Light coloured sand stone.

High Court : Shillong.

Climate : Summer Season : 25°C to 15°C
Winter Season : 16°C to 4°C

Festivals : Ko Pomblang Nongkrem, Shad Sukmynsiem, Behdieng Khalem and Wangala.

Tourist Places : Shillong, Cherrapunjee, Mawsynram, Mawphyang, Tura, Jowai

MIZORAM

Area : 21,081 sq. km.

Capital : Aizawl

Formation Day : 20th February, 1987

Population : 10,97,206

Male : 5,55,339

Female : 5,41,867

Sex Ratio : 976 females per 1000 males

Density of Population : 52 persons per sq. km.

Literacy : 91.3%

No. of M.P. : 1

No. of Rajya Sabha's Member : 1

Districts : 9 — Aizawl, Lunglei, Chhimtuipui, Lawngtlai, Champhai, Kolasib, Mamit, Saiha, Serchhip.

Principal Languages : Mizo and English.

Principal Religions : Hindus : 5.05%, Muslims : 0.66%; Christians : 85.73%; Sikhs : .04%; Buddhists: 7.83%; Others : 6.9% (2001)

Agriculture and Horticulture : Forest products, Fruit, Rice, Potato and Sugarcane.

Roads : National Highways : 54 km
Total length of Roads : 6,349.60 km

Airports : Lengpun

Industries : Mizoram has no major industry. The cottage industries comprise of handloom and handicrafts. In the small scale sector are the rice milling, oil and flour milling, mechanised bamboo workshops, saw milling, brick making and furniture workshops.

High Court : Mizoram comes under the Jurisdiction of Guwahati High Court and has a bench at Aizawl.

Climate : Summer Season : 18°C to 29°C
Winter Season : 11°C to 24°C

Festivals : Chapchar Kut, Mim Kut and Pawl Kut.

Tourist Places : Aizawl, Champhai, Wantawng Fall, Tamdil

NAGALAND

Area : 16,579 sq. km.

Capital : Kohima

Formation Day : 1st December, 1963

Population : 19,78,502

Male : 10,24,649

Female : 9,53,853

Sex Ratio : 931 females per 1000 males

Density of Population : 119 persons per sq. km.

Literacy : 79.6%

No. of M.P. : 1

No. of Rajya Sabha's Member : 1

Districts : 11 — Kohima, Mokokchung, Mon, Phek, Tuensang, Wokha, Zunheboto, Dimapur, Kiphire, Longleng, Peren.

Principal Languages : Ao, Chang, Chakhesang, Sangtam, Konyak, Angami, Sema and Lotha.

Principal Religions : Hindus : 10.12%, Muslims: 1.71% Christians : 70.20%; Sikhs : 0.60%; Buddhists : 0.05%; Jains : 0.10%; Others : 0.49% (2001)

Agriculture and Horticulture : Rice, Jowar, Bajra, Sugarcane, Forest products.

Roads : National Highways : 113 km
Total length of Roads : 23,466 km

Railways : 9 km

Airports : Dimapur

Industries : Plywood industry, Handloom and sericulture are the important cottage industries.

Minerals : Clay, Coal, Glass, Limestone and Sand are the minerals found in Nagaland.

Electrified Villages : 96%

High Court : Nagaland comes under the jurisdiction of Guwahati High Court which has a circuit bench at Kohima.

Festivals : Sekrenyi, Moatsu, Tuluni and Tokhu Emong.

Tourist Places : Wokha, Kohima, Itanki, Dimapur

ODISHA

Area : 1,55,707 sq. km.
Capital : Bhubaneshwar
Formation Day : 1st January, 1949
Population : 4,19,74,218
Male : 2,12,12,136
Female : 2,07,62,082
Sex Ratio : 979 females (per 1000 males)
Density of Population : 270 persons per sq. km.
Literacy : 72.9%
No. of M.P. : 21
No. of Rajya Sabha's Members : 10
No. of Districts : 30 — Angul, Balasore, Bolangir, Bhadrak, Bargarh, Cuttack, Dhenkanal, Ganjam, Gajapati, Jagatsinghpur, Jajpur, Keonjhar, Kalahandi, Koraput, Kendrapara, Khurda, Mayurbhanj, Malkangiri, Nawarangpur, Nayagarh, Nawapara, Puri, Kandhamal, Rayagada, Sambalpur, Sundergarh, Sonepur, Boudh, Deogarh, Jharsuguda
Principal Languages : Odiya, Bengali and Hindi
Principal Religions : Hindus : 94.67%; Muslims: 1.834%; Christians: 2.10%; Sikhs : .05%; Buddhists: 0.03%, Jains : 0.02%; Others : 1.30% (2001)
Agriculture and Horticulture : Rice, Sugarcane, Coconut, Forest product, Linseed, Jute etc.
Roads : National Highways : 3,592 km
State Highways : 3,675 km
State Express Highways : 18 km
Major District Roads : 3984 km
Other District Roads : 6564 km
Rural Roads : 20,314 km
Railways : 2,339 km
Airport : Bhubaneshwar
Industries : Iron, Steel, Paper, Sugarcane, Fertilizers, Cement, Aluminium
Minerals : Coal, Graphite, Bauxite, Limestone, Manganese and Salt
Electrified Villages : 73%
High Court : Bhubaneshwar
Climate : Summer Season : 49ºC to 27ºC
Winter Season : 16ºC to 5ºC
Monsoon : July to October
Festivals : Holi, Deepawali and Puri Ratha Yatra
Tourist Places : Bhubaneswar, Puri, Konark, Chilka Lake, Nandan Kanan, Dhauli, Bolangir, Rourkela, Gupteshwar, Kapilash, Paradeep, Taptapani, Tikarpra (Badrama), Kiching, Ratnagiri, Cuttack, Brahmapur, Haripur, Hirakud, Dhauli, Udayagiri, Jaipur, Similipal

PUNJAB

Area : 50,362 sq. km.
Capital : Chandigarh
Formation Day : 1st November, 1956
Population : 2,77,43,338
Male : 1,46,39,465
Female : 1,31,03,873
Sex Ratio : 895 females per 1000 males
Density of Population : 551 persons per sq. km.
Literacy : 75.8%
No. of M.P. : 13
No. of Rajya Sabha's Members : 7
Districts : 22 — Amritsar, Bhatinda, Faridkot, Fatehgarh Sahib, Ferozpur, Gurdaspur, Hoshiarpur, Jalandhar, Kapurthala, Ludhiana, Mansa, Moga, Muktsar, Patiala, Rupnagar, Sangrur, Tarantaran, S.A.S. Nagar, S.B.S. Nagar, Barnala, Pathankot, Fazilka.
Principal Languages : Punjabi, Hindi
Principal Religions : Hindus : 34.46%; Muslims: 1.18%; Christians : 1.11%; Sikhs : 62.95%; Buddhists : 0.12%; Jains : 0.10%; Others : 0.08% (2001)
Agriculture and Horticulture : Rice, Wheat, Maize, Pulse, Gram, Mushroom, Chilli, Potato
Roads : National Highways : 1,739 km
State Highways : 1,485 km
Major and Other District Roads : 6,888 km
Total length of Roads : 67,370 km
Railways : 3726.06 km
Airports : Chandigarh, Amritsar, Patiala, Ludhiana.
Industries : Punjab's industrial development is mainly based on small scale units. These produce sewing machines, hand tools, machine tools, hosiery, knitwear, textiles,woollen garments, sugar, vegetable oils, processed food, nuts and bolts and electronic items. Large factories producing fertilisers, textiles and railway wagons also exist in the State. An oil refinery is being set up.
Mineral : Limestone.
Electrified Villages : Hundred per cent.
High Court : Punjab and Haryana have a common High Court at Chandigarh.
Climate : Summer Season : 45ºC to 35ºC
Winter Season : 14ºC to 0ºC
Festivals : Holi, Diwali, Dussehra, Baisakhi, Hola Mohalla, Basant, Maghi Mela and birthdays of Sikh Gurus.

Tourist Places : Anandpur, Amritsar, Tarantaran, Jalandhar, Nangal, Ludhiana, Sarhind, Patiala, Sangrur, Ramtirtha

RAJASTHAN

Area : 3,42,239 sq. km.
Capital : Jaipur
Formation Day : 1st November, 1956
Population : 6,85,48,437
Male : 3,55,50,997
Female : 3,29,97,440
Sex Ratio : 928 females per 1000 males
Density of Population : 200 persons per sq. km.
Literacy : 66.1%
No. of M.P. : 25
No. of Rajya Sabha's Member : 10

Districts : 33 — Ajmer, Alwar, Banswara, Barmer, Bharatpur, Bhilwara, Bikaner, Bundi, Chittorgarh, Churu, Dholpur, Dungarpur, Ganganagar, Jaipur, Jaisalmer, Jalore, Jhalawar, Jhunjhunu, Jodhpur, Kota, Nagaur, Pali, Sawai Madhopur, Sikar, Sirohi, Tonk, Udaipur, Dausa, Baran, Rajsamand, Hanumangarh, Karoli and Pratapgarh.

Principal Languages : Hindi, Rajasthani

Principal Religions : Hindus : 89.08%; Muslims: 8.01%; Christians : 0.11%; Sikhs : 1.48%; Buddhists: 0.01%; Jains : 1.28%; Others : 0.03% (2001)

Agriculture and Horticulture : Rice, Barley, Jowart, Bajra, Maize, Gram, Wheat, Oilseed, Cotton, Pulses, Tobacco.

Roads : Total length of Roads : 1,90,000 km
Railways : 5,784 km
Airports : Jaipur, Jodhpur and Udaipur.

Industries : Textiles, Woollens, Sugar, Cement, Glass, Sodium plant, Oxygen, Vegetable dyes, Pesticides, Zinc, Fertilisers, RailwayWagons, Ball-bearing, Water and Electricity metre, Sulphuric Acid,Television sets, Synthetic yarn and Insulating bricks, Precious and Semi-precious stones, Caustic soda, Calcium Carbide, Nylon and Tyres etc.

Minerals : Copper, Manganese, Iron-ores, Tungston, Mica, Gypsum, Silver, Asbestos, Garnet, Emerald, Felspar, Salt, Rock Phosphate, Marble and Red-stone, Zinc etc.

Electrified Villages : 91%
High Court : Jodhpur
Climate : Summer Season : 45ºC to 17ºC
Winter Season : 32ºC to 7ºC

Festivals : Holi, Deepawali, Vijayadashami, Muharram, Christmas, Kartik Purnima, Urs of Ajmer Sharief.

Tourist Places : Jaisalmer, Ajmer, Jodhpur, Bikaner, Udaipur, Mount Abu, Pushkar, Jaipur, Bharatpur, Chittorgarh, Jaisamand, Sanganer

SIKKIM

Area : 7,096 sq. km.
Capital : Gangtok
Formation Day : 26th April, 1975
Population : 6,10,577
Male : 3,23,070
Female : 2,87,507
Sex Ratio : 890 females per 1000 males
Density of Population : 86 persons per sq. km.
Literacy : 81.4%
No. of M.P. : 1
No. of Rajya Sabha's Member : 1

Districts : 4 — East District, North District, South District, West District.

Principal Languages : Nepali, Bhutia, Lepcha, Limbu.

Principal Religions : Hindus : 68.37%; Muslims: 0.95%; Christians : 3.30%; Sikhs : 0.09%; Buddhists: 27.5%; Jains : 0.01%; Others : 1.03% (2001)

Agriculture and Horticulture : Maize, Rice, Wheat, Ginger, Orange and big Cardamom.

Roads : National Highways : 41 km
Total length of Roads : 3672.32 km

Railways : Nearest railway station of the State is - Siliguri (114 km), Jalpaiguri (125 km)

Airports : There is no airport in the State. Bagdogra airport in west Bengal which caters the need of the state is 124 km from Gangtok.

High Court : Gangtok

Festivals : Maghe Sakranti, Durga Pooja, Laxmi Pooja and Chaite Dasai are celebrated by the Nepali community. Pang Lhabsol, Losoong and Losar are celebrated by the Bhutia community. Namsoong and Tendong Hlo Rum Faat is celebrated by the Lepcha community.

Tourist Places : Gangtok, Rumtek, Yuksam, Pemayantse, Lachung

TAMIL NADU

Area : 1,30,058 sq. km.
Capital : Chennai
Formation Day : 1947
Population : 7,21,47,030
Male : 3,61,37,975
Female : 3,60,09,055
Sex Ratio : 996 females per 1000 males
Density of Population : 555 persons per sq. km.
Literacy : 80.1%
No. of M.P. : 39
No. of Rajya Sabha's Member : 18

Districts : 32 — Chennai, Kancheepuram, Thiruvallur, Vellore, Tiruvannamalai, Cuddalore, Villupuram, Salem, Namakkal, Dharmapuri, Pudukottai, Erode, The Nilgiris, Coimbatore, Tiruchirapalli, Karur, Perambalur, Thanjavur, Nagapattinam, Thiruvarur, Madurai, Theni, Dindigul, Ramanathapuram, Sivagangai, Virudhunagar, Tirunelveli, Toothukudi, Kanyakumari, Ariyalur, Krishnagiri and Tiruppur.

Principal Languages : Tamil, Kannada, Malayalam, Telugu.

Principal Religions : Hindus : 88.67%; Muslims: 5.47%; Christians : 5.69%; Sikhs : 0.01%; Jains : 0.12%; Others : 0.04% (2001)

Agriculture and Horticulture : Rice, Bajra, Maize, Cotton, Groundnut, Banana, Mango, Cashewnuts, Coconut.

Roads : Total length of Roads : 62,017 km
Railways : 3,761 km

Airports : Chennai, Madurai, Tiruchirapalli, Coimbatore, Salem.

Industries : Textiles, Fertilizers, Paper product, Printing, Engines, Automobiles and ancillaries, Railway wagon and coaches, Cement, Sugar and Electrical machinery.

Minerals : Mica, Salt, Bauxite, Limestone, Magnesite, Quartz, Felspar.

High Court : Chennai
Climate : Temperature : 43ºC to 18ºC

Festivals : Pongal, Chithirai, Adipperukku, Mamallapuram, Navaratri etc.

Tourist Places : Sriperambdur, Oraville, Coimbatore, Kancheepuram, Rameshwaram, Trichirapalli, Madurai, Chennai, Tanjavur, Vedanthangal, Pulicut, Tiruvannamalai

TELANGANA

Area : 1,14,840 sq. km.
Population : 3,51,93,978
Density (persons per sq km) : 310
Literacy rate : 67.2% (males 75.6%; females : 58.77%).
Capital : Hyderabad
No. of Districts : 10

Legislature : Bicameral, the Legislative Assembly has 119 seats and the Legislative Council has 40 seats.

Judicature : High Court at Hyderabad

Principal Languages : Telugu (76%), Urdu (12%) and Others (12%)

Districts : Adilabad, Karimnagar, Nizamabad, Medak, Khammam, Mahaboobnagar, Warangal, Ranga Reddy, Nalgonda and Hyderabad

Minerals : Coal, Singareni, Limestone, Bauxite and Mica. Kothagudem, Jammikunta, Palwancha are main industrial towns.

Telangana has three national parks—Kasu Brahmanada Reddy National Park (Hyderabad district) and Mahavira Harina Vanasthali National Park and Mrugavani National Park (both in Ranga Reddy district).

Mahatma Gandhi Bus Station (M.G.B.S) in Hyderabad is one of the largest bus stands in Asia.

Secunderabad and Hyderabad are the main divisions of South Central Railway that fall in the State.

TRIPURA

Area : 10,491.69 sq. km.
Capital : Agartala
Formation Year : 1956
Population : 36,73,917
Male : 18,74,376
Female : 17,99,541
Sex Ratio : 960 females per 1000 males
Density of Population : 350 persons per sq. km.
Literacy : 87.2%
No. of M.P. : 2
No. of Rajya Sabha's Member : 1

Districts : 8 — North Tripura, South Tripura, West Tripura, Dhalai, Khowai, Gomti, Unakoti and Sipahijala.

Principal Languages : Bengali, Kakborak and Manipuri.

Principal Religions : Hindus : 86.5%; Muslims : 7.13%; Christians : 1.68%; Sikhs : 0.03%; Buddhists: 4.65%; Jains : 0.01% (2001)

Agriculture and Horticulture : Paddy, Wheat, Potato, Sugarcane, Oilseed and Forest product.

Roads : State Highways : 689 km
Major District Roads : 90 km
Other District Roads : 1,218 km
Total Length of Roads : 1,997 km

Railways : 64 km

Airports : Agartala

Industries : Handlooms, Handicrafts and Cottage industries.

Electrified Villages : 95%

High Court : Agartala

Climate : Summer Season : 35ºC to 24ºC
Winter Season : 27ºC to 13ºC

Festivals : Makar-Sakranti, Holi, Hozagiri festival, Mansa Mangal festival, Christmas and Budha Purnima.

Tourist Places : Agartala, Old Agartala, Udaipur, Melaghat, Belonia, Sepahijala, Radhakishorepur

UTTAR PRADESH

Area : 2,40,928 sq. km.

Capital : Lucknow

Formation Day : 1st November, 1956

Population : 19,98,12,341

Male : 10,44,80,510

Female : 9,53,31,831

Sex Ratio : 912 females per 1000 males

Density of Population : 829 persons per sq. km.

Literacy : 67.7%

No. of M.P. : 80

No. of Rajya Sabha's Members : 31

Districts : 75 — Agra, Aligarh, Etah, Firozabad, Mainpuri, Mathura, Hathras, Azamgarh, Ballia, Mau, Kaushambi, Fatehpur, Pratapgarh, Allahabad, ...akoot, Badaun, Bareilly, Pilibhit, Shahjahanpur, ...mbedkar Nagar, Bahraich, Barabanki, ... Gorakhpur, Deoria, Kushinagar, ... Hamirpur, Jalaun, Lalitpur, ... (Nagar), Kanpur (Dehat), ...now, Hardoi, Lakhimpur ...nao, Bulandshahar, Meerut, Ghaziabad, Gautam Buddha Nagar, Moradabad, Bijnor, Rampur, Jyotiba Phule Nagar, Saharanpur, Muzaffarnagar, Varanasi, Jaunpur, Chandauli, Ghazipur, Sant Ravidas Nagar, Mirzapur, Sonbhadra, Basti, Balarampur, Shravasti, Siddharth Nagar, Bagpat, Kannauj, Orraiya, Sant Kabir Nagar, Kanshiram Nagar, Chattrapti Sahuji Maharaj Nagar, Prabudh Nagar, Panchseel Nagar and Bhim Nagar.

Principal Languages : Hindi and Urdu.

Principal Religions : Hindus : 81.74%; Muslims: 17.33%; Christians: 0.14%; Sikhs : 0.45%; Buddhists : 0.16%; Jains : 0.13%; Others : 0.02% (2001)

Agriculture and Horticulture : Wheat, Paddy, Sugarcane, Pulse, Oilseed, Mango, Guava, Banana.

Roads : National Highways : 3,820 km
State Highways : 8,391 km
Other District Roads : 1,19,726 km
Total Roads : 1,46,728 km

Airports : Lucknow, Kanpur, Agra, Gorakhpur, Varanasi, Allahabad, Jhansi, Bareilly, Hindon, Sarsawa (Saharanpur) and Fursatganj (Rae-Bareli).

Industries : Sugar, Leather, Wine, Paper, Glass, Handicrafts, Edible oils, Chemicals etc.

Minerals : Lime, Copper, Uranium, Dolomite, Coal, Marble, Fire-clay, Bauxite etc.

High Court : Allahabad.

Climate : Summer Season : 45ºC to 11ºC
Winter Season : 32ºC to 2ºC

Monsoon : June to September.

Festivals : Holi, Deepawali, Dussehra, Janmashtami and Kumbha fair.

Tourist Places : Ayodhya, Agra, Varanasi, Allahabad, Sikandara, Chitrakoot, Fatehpur Sikri, Garh Mukteshwar, Aligarh, Deoband, Kanpur, Lucknow, Gola Gokarnanath, Magahar, Chandraprabha, Mathura, Mukteshwar, Badaun, Nemisharanya, Sarnath, Shravasti, Kushinagar, Gorakhpur, Rajapur, Bareilly

UTTARAKHAND

Area : 53,484 sq. km.

Capital : Dehradun

Formation Day : 9th November, 2000

Population : 1,00,86,292

Male : 51,37,773

Female : 49,48,519

Sex Ratio : 963 females per 1000 males

D... of Population : 189 persons per sq. km.

Lite... ...8%

No. of M.P. : 5

Rajya Sabha's Members

Districts : 21 — Uttarkashi, Chamoli, Rudra Prayag, Tehri Garhwal, Dehradun, Pauri Garhwal, Pithoragarh, Champawat, Almorah, Bageshwar, Nainital, Udham Singh Nagar, Haridwar.

New Districts : Yamunotri, Kotdwar, Didihat, Ranikhet.

Principal Languages : Hindi, Garhwali and Kumaoni.

Principal Religions : Hindus : 96.74%; Muslims: 2.33%; Christians : 0.14%; Sikhs : 0.45%; Buddhists: 0.16%; Jains : 0.13%; Others : 0.02% (2001)

Agriculture and Horticulture : Forest products, Wheat, Paddy, Jowar, Oilseed etc.

Principal Source of Income : Tourism.

Roads : Total length of Roads : 33,914 km

Electrified Villages : 75.30%

High Court : Nainital

Climate : Summer Season : 38ºC to 10ºC
Winter Season : 25ºC to 0ºC

Monsoon : July to September.

Festivals : Kumbha and Half Kumbha, Nandadevi fair, Baisakhi (Uttarkashi), Holi, Deepawali, Dussehra, Janmashtami etc.

Tourist Places : Badrinath, Dehradun, Kedarnath, Almorah, Valley of Flowers, Corbett National Park, Haridwar, Chakrata, Mussourie, Nainital, Rajajee, Rishikesh, Uttarkashi, Gangotri, Yamunotri, Jogeshwar, Champawat, Bhairo Ghati, Lansdowne, Ranikhet, Lakhamandal, Haldwani, Pant Nagar

WEST BENGAL

Area : 88,752 sq. km.

Capital : Kolkata

Formation Day : 1st November, 19

Population : 9,12,76,115

Male : 4,68,09,027

Female : 4,44,67,088

Sex Ratio : 950 females per 1000 males

Density of Population : 1,028 persons per sq. km.

Literacy : 76.3%

No. of M.P. : 42

No. of Rajya Sabha's Members : 16

Districts : 19 — Bankura, Bardhaman, Birbhum, Kolkata, Darjeeling, Howrah, Hooghly, Jalpaiguri, Cooch Behar, Malda, Paschim Medinipur, Murshidabad, Nadia, North 24 Parganas, South 24 Parganas, Purulia, North Dinajpur, South Dinajpur and Purb Medinipur

Principal Languages : Bengali and Hindi

Principal Religions : Hindus : 74.72%; Muslims : 23.61%; Christians: 0.56%; Sikhs : 0.08%; Buddhists : 0.30%; Jains : 0.05%; Others : 0.68% (2001)

Agriculture and Horticulture : Rice, Sugarcane, Tea, Betel-leaves, Jute, Pulses, Oilseeds and Forest products.

Roads : National Highways : 1,898 km
State Highways : 3,533 km
P.W.D. Roads : 12,565 km
District Roads : 42,479 km
Total length of Roads : 91,970 km

Railways : 4,561.93 km

Airports : Dum Dum is international airport, Balurghat, Coochbehar, Malda, Bagdogra, Panagarh, Behala, Barrackpore and Kalaikunda.

Industries : Coal, Paper, Jute, Pharmaceuticals, Tea, Leather, Automatic machineries, Heavy and Light Engineering etc.

Minerals : The State is rich in mineral resources. Coal, China-clay and Dolomite are the three most important minerals available in the State. Other minerals are Rock Phosphate, Fire clay, Limestone, Copper, Iron, Silica,Quartz, Manganese and Sandstone.

High Court : Kolkata

Climate : Summer Season : 40ºC to 24ºC
Winter Season : 26ºC to 7ºC

Festivals : Durgapooja, Kali pooja, Basant Panchami, Laxmi pooja, Shivaratri, Deepawali, Holi, Janmashtami, Id.

Tourist Places : Darjeeling, Kolkata, Dakshineshwar, Belur, Sachel, Kangsabati, Jaldapara, Shanti Niketan, Murshidabad

UNION TERRITORIES

A... AN & NICOBAR ISLANDS

... km.

... ir

Forma... ...7

Populatio...

Male : 2,02,8...

Female : 1,77,710

Sex Ratio : 876 females per 1000 males

Density of Population : 46 persons per sq. km.

Literacy : 86.6%

No. of M.P. : 1

No. of Rajya Sabha's Member : — None

Districts : 3 — South Andaman, North & Middle Andaman and Nicobar.

Principal Languages : Hindi, Nicobarese, English, Bengali, Tamil, Malayalam, Telugu.

Principal Religions : Hindus : 67.53%; Muslims: 7.61%; Christians : 23.95%; Sikhs : 0.47%; Buddhists : 0.11%; Jains : 0.01%; Others : 3.1% (2001)

Agriculture and Horticulture : Mango, Orange, Banana, Papaya, Pineapple, Rice, Rubber etc.

Roads : Metalled : 552 km
Unmetalled : 36 km
Other Roads : 13 km

Airports : Port Blair

Industries : There are 1,833 registered small scale, village and handicrafts units. Two units are export oriented in the line of fish processing activity. There are also shell and wood based handicraft units. There are four medium sized industrial units. SSI units are engaged in the production of Polythene bags, PVC conduit pipes and fittings, paints and varnishes, fibre glass and mini flour mills, soft drinks and beverages etc.

Electrified Villages : Hundred per cent.

High Court : The Union Territory comes under the jurisdiction of Kolkata.

Climate : Summer Season : 33ºC to 22ºC
Winter Season : 31ºC to 20ºC

Festivals : Onam, Kalipooja, Pongal and Sankranti.

Tourist Places : Port Blair, Andaman & Nicobar Islands, Ross Island, Little Andaman

CHANDIGARH

Area : 114 sq. km.

Capital : Chandigarh

Formation Day : 1st November, 1966

Population : 10,55,450

Male : 580,663

Female : 4,74,787

Sex Ratio : 818 females per 1000 males

Density of Population : 9,258 persons per sq. km.

Literacy : 86.0%

No. of M.P. : 1

No. of Rajya Sabha's Member : — None

Principal Languages : Hindi, Punjabi.

Principal Religions : Hindus : 75.84%; Muslims: 2.72%; Christians : 0.78%; Sikhs : 20.29%; Buddhists : 0.11% (2001)

Agriculture and Horticulture : Wheat, Maize, Vegetables, Fodder, Paddy.

Roads : Total length of Roads : National Highways which go through Chandigarh is 15.275 km

Industries : Heavy and Medium sized industries and Cottage industries.

High Court : Chandigarh

Festivals : Baisakhi, Holi, Rakshabandhan, Deepawali.

Tourist Places : The main tourist spots are : Bougainvilla garden, Deer park, International Dolls Museum, Leisure valley, Log Hut (Khudda Alisher), Museum and Art gallery, National gallery of portraits, Panjab University Campus, Nek Chand's Rock Garden, Shanti Kunj, Smriti-Upavan, Sukhna Lake, Terraced Garden, Topiary Park, Zakir Rose Garden.

DADRA AND NAGAR HAVELI

Area : 491 sq. km.

Capital : Silvassa

Formation Day : 11th August, 1961

Population : 3,43,709

Male : 1,93,760

Female : 1,49,949

Sex Ratio : 774 females per 1000 males

Density of Population : 700 persons per sq. km.

Literacy : 76.2%

District : 1 — Silvassa

Principal Languages : Hindi, English, Gujarati, Marathi.

Principal Religions : Hindus : 95.48%, Muslims: 2.41%, Christians : 1.5%; Sikhs : 0.01%; Buddhists: 0.15%; Jains : 0.38%; Others : 0.06% (2001)

Agriculture and Horticulture : Paddy, Jowar, Mango, Banana and Chiku etc.

Roads : Metalled : 570 km
Unmetalled : 65 km
Total length of Roads : 635 km

Airports : The nearest airport is Mumbai.

Industries : There are no major industries in Dadra and Nagar Haveli. The medium scale industries manufacture automobile parts, spectacle frames, cotton and art silk fabrics, nylon filaments, foam product, detergent powder, soap, biscuits, chemical engineering goods, candles, fruit juice, wrist watches etc.

Electrified Villages : Hundred per cent.

High Court : The Union Territory comes under the jurisdiction of Mumbai High Court.

Festivals : Diwali, Diwaso, Rakshabandhan, Bhawada, Kalipooja.

Tourist Places : The important tourist places are: Silvassa, Van Vihar Udhyan on Khanvel river, Van Ganga and Vandhara Gardens on Damanganga river, Bai Udyan, Tad Keshwara temple on Sakartod river at Brindaban, Adivasi cultural museum.

DAMAN AND DIU

Area : 112 sq. km.

Capital : Daman

Formation Day : 30th May, 1961

Population : 2,43,247

Male : 1,50,301

Female : 92,946

Sex Ratio : 618 females per 1000 males

Density of Population : 2,191 persons per sq. km.

Literacy : 87.1%

No. of M.P. : 1

No. of Rajya Sabha's Member : — None

No. of Districts : 2 — Daman, Diu

Principal Languages : Gujarati

Principal Religions : Hindus : 87.76%; Muslims : 8.91%; Sikhs : 0.1%; Jains : 0.21%; Others : 0.13% (2001)

Agriculture and Horticulture : Paddy, Ragi, Bajra, Sugarcane, Mango.

Roads : 191 km in Daman and 78 km in Diu.

Airports : There are airports both in Daman and Diu.

Industries : There are 1,600 small scale and medium scale industries in Daman and Diu.

Electrified Villages : Hundred per cent.

High Court : Mumbai

Festivals : Holi, Makar Sankranti, Navaratri.

Tourist Places : Daman, Diu

DELHI

Area : 1,483 sq. km.

Capital : Delhi

Formation Day : 1st November, 1956

Population : 1,67,87,941

Male : 89,87,326

Female : 78,00,615

Sex Ratio : 868 females per 1000 males

Density of Population : 11,320 persons per sq. km.

Literacy : 86.2%

No. of M.P. : 7

No. of Rajya Sabha's Members : 3

Districts : 11 — North-West, North, North-East, East, New Delhi, Central, West, South-West, South, South East, Shahdara.

Principal Languages : Hindi, Punjabi, Urdu and English.

Principal Religions : Hindus : 83.67%; Muslims: 9.44%; Christians : 0.88%; Sikhs : 4.84%; Buddhists: 0.15%; Jains : 1.00%; Others 0.02% (2001)

Agriculture and Horticulture : Wheat, Bajra, Jowar, Maize etc.

Roads : Total length of Roads : 32,663 km (including the lengths of 5 National Highways).

Metro : 190 km (approx.)

Airports : There are three airports in Delhi. They are — Indira Gandhi International Airport for international flights, Palam Airport for national air services and Safdarjung Airport for training purposes.

Industries : Televisions, Tape-recorders, Light engineering machines and automobile parts, Sports goods, Bicycles and PVC goods including footwear, textiles, fertilizers, medicines, hosiery, leather goods, softwares etc.

Electrified Villages : Hundred per cent.

High Court : Delhi.

Climate : Summer Season : 45ºC to 35ºC
Winter Season : 20ºC to 7ºC

Festivals : Independence Day, Republic Day, Phool-walo-ki-sair, Dussehra, Deepawali, Holi, Id, Muharram, Navaratri etc.

Tourist Places : Buddha Jayanti Partk, Chandni Chowk, Connaught Place, Gurdwara Bangla Sahib, Gurdwara Rakabganj, Gurdwara Sis Ganj, Hauz Khas, Humayun's Tomb, India Gate, Jama Masjid, Jantar Mantar, Lal Quila (Red Fort), Lodhi Tomb, Lotus Temple, Mahalakshi Mandir (Birla Mandir), Mughal Garden, National Museum, Nehru Memorial Museum, Parliament House, Purana Quila, Rabindra Rangshala, Rajghat (Mahatma Gandhi's Samadhi), Rashtrapati Bhawan, Qutab Minar, Vijayghat and Zoo etc.

LAKSHADWEEP

Area : 32 sq. km.

Capital : Kavaratti

Formation Day : 1956

Population : 64,473

Male : 33,123

Female : 31,350

Sex Ratio : 947 females per 1000 males

Density of Population : 2,149 persons per sq. km.

Literacy : 91.8%

No. of M.P. : 1

No. of Rajya Sabha's Member : — None

District : 1 — Kavaratti.

Principal Languages : Malayalam.

Principal Religions : Hindus : 3.66%; Muslims: 95.47%; Christians : 0.8% (2001)

Agriculture and Horticulture : Coconut and fruits.

Industries : Coconut, Fish product, Date product.

Minerals : Carbonate, Phosphate, Calcium.

High Court : The Union Territory comes under the jurisdiction of Kerala High Court.

Festivals : Onam, Vishu, Id, Muharram.

Tourist Places : Agatti, Amini, Andrott, Bangaram, Bitra Cheriyam, Chetlat, Kadmat, Kalpeni, Kavaratti (Headquarters' Town), Kiltan, Minicoy, Suheli, Tinakara, Valiyakara.

PUDUCHERRY

Area : 479 sq. km.

Capital : Puducherry

Formation Day : 28th May, 1956

Population : 1,247,953

Male : 6,12,511

Female : 6,35,442

Sex Ratio : 1,037 females per 1000 males

Density of Population : 2,547 persons per sq. km.

Literacy : 85.8%

No. of M.P. : 1

No. of Rajya Sabha's Member : 1

Districts : 4 — Karaikal, Mahe, Puducherry, Yanam.

Principal Languages : Tamil, French, English, Malayalam and Telugu.

Principal Religions : Hindus : 86.16%, Muslims: 6.54%; Christians : 7.23%; Buddhists : 0.01%; Jains: 0.06% (2001)

Agriculture and Horticulture : Jowar, Bajra, Cotton, Sugarcane, Paddy, Oilseeds etc.

Roads : Total length of Roads : 677.525 km

Railways : 47 km (approx.)

Airports : Nearest airport is Chennai which 160 km away from Pondicherry.

Industries : Textiles, Wine, Small industries, Paper and electric equipments.

Electrified Villages : Hundred per cent.

High Court : Madras

Climate : As Tamil Nadu.

Festivals : Pongal and Masi Magham.

Tourist Places : Karaikal (former French Colony), Mahe (former French dependency), Pondicherry (former French colony famous for Auroville), Beach, Bharathiar and Bharathidasan Memorials, Boat Club at Chunnambar river, Botanical Garden, French Institute, Government square, Joan of Arc, Manakula Vinayanagar Temple, Pondicherry Museum, Sacred Heart of Jesus Church, Sri Aurobindo Ashram, Yanam (former French enclave).

HONOURS AND AWARDS

INTERNATIONAL

Nobel Prize

The most prestigious award in the world is supported by the Nobel Foundation. This award was set up in 1900 under the will to Alfred Bernhard Nobel (1833-96). Alfred Nobel was an unmarried, Swedish scientist and chemical engineer who discovered Nitroglycerin ($C_3H_5N_3O_9$) and its use in the manufacture of dynamite. The interest accrued on the fortune left by him is divided annually among the persons who have made outstanding contribution in science, literature, peace and economics. Swedes found out about the prizes only after his death in 1896. When they read his will in which he had donated the annual income from his fortune to support the awards. In his will he ordered that 'the most worthy shall receive the prize, whether he is Scandinavian or not. This led to his criticism as being unpatriotic for not reserving the prizes only for Swedes. Even his relatives, in a futile bid, contested the will for three years.

Anyone proposing himself for Nobel Prize is ruled out of consideration. The recommendations have to come from outside. The Noble Prizes are presented annually on December 10, the death anniversary of the founder and the festival day of the Foundation. Originally it was awarded for works in five disciplines. The prize for Economics was instituted in 1967 by Sverigs Riksbank, Swedish Bank, in celebration of its 300th anniversary and was awarded for the first time in 1969, It is called Nobel Memorial Prize in Economics.

Nobel Foundation's Prize Awarding Bodies

(i) The Royal Swedish Academy of Sciences, awards the Nobel prize in Physics and Chemistry.

(ii) The Nobel Assembly of Karolinska Chirugical Institute. Sweden, awards the Nobel Prize in Medicine and Physiology.

(iii) The Swedish Academy awards the Prize in Literature.

(iv) The Committee of the Norwegian Parliament awards the Prize for Peace.

(v) The Bank of Sweden awards the Nobel Prize in Economics.

Value of the Nobel Prize The amount of each prize varies with the income from the fund. The value of noble prize was 150,782 Swedish crown in 1901. No Noble prize was awarded for 1940, 1941 & 1942; prizes for literature were not awarded for 1914, 1918, 1943.

Maximum Nobel Prizes: US citizens have won outright as well as shared the maximum number of Nobel Prizes. Individually the only person to have two Nobel Prizes in different subjects: Dr Linus Carl Pauling, Professor of Chemistry at California. He received the Nobel Prize for Chemistry in 1954 and the peace prize in 1962.

First Couple to Receive the Nobel Prize: [illegible] Marie Curie shared the 1903 Nobel [illegible] with her husband Pierre Curie, [illegible] the Prize for Chemistry in 19[illegible]

Three Nobel Prizes: Th[illegible]ational Committee of the Red Cross was awarded the Nobel Prize for Peace three times: 1917, 1944 and 1963.

TWICE RECIPIENTS OF THE NOBEL PRIZE	
Different Subjects	
Madame Curie Sklodowska	Physics (1903)
Madame Curie Sklodowska	Chemistry (1911)
Linus Pauling	Chemistry (1954)
Linus Pauling	Peace (1962)
Same Subjects	
John Bardeen	Physics (1965)
John Bardeen	Physics (1972)
Frederic Sanger	Chemistry (1958)
Frederic Sanger	Chemistry (1980)

First Woman to Receive the Nobel Prize: Madame Curie Sklodowska—Physics (1903)

First Indian to Receive the Nobel Prize: Rabindranath Tagore was awarded Prize for literature in 1913 for his love lyrics 'Gitanjali'.

First Indian Woman to Receive the Nobel Prize: Mother Teresa won the Nobel Prize for Peace in 1979.

INDIAN NOBEL LAUREATES

Name	Field	Year
Rabindranath Tagore	Literature	1913
Dr C.V. Raman	Physics	1930
Dr Hargobind Khorana	Medicine	1968
Mother Teresa	Peace	1979
Dr S. Chandrasekhar	Physics	1983
Dr. Amartya Sen	Economics	1998
Sir V.S. Naipaul	Literature	2001
Dr. V. Ramakrishnan	Chemistry	2009
Kailash Satyarthi	Peace	2014

MAJOR AWARDS AND PRIZE

PULITZER PRIZE

Instituted in 1970 and named after the US publisher Joseph Pulitzer (1847-1911). It is conferred annually in the United States for accomplishment in journalism, literature and music under the management to the Pulitzer Prize Board at Columbia University.

RAMON MAGSAYSAY AWARD

Instituted in 1957, named after Ramon Magsaysay, President of the Philippines, who died in an air crash in 1957. He became world renowned figure in the 1950's for his land reform programme to defuse communist insurgency. The award is given annually on August 31st, the birth anniversary of Magsaysay, for outstanding contributions to Public Service, Community Leadership, Journalism, Literature and Creative Arts and International Understanding. It is equivalent to the Nobel Prize in Asia. It may also be awarded to organisations/ institutions and non-Asians working for the benefit of Asia. It is considered to be Asian equivalent to Nobel Prize.

MAN BOOKER PRIZE

Instituted in 1968, it is the highest literary award set up by the Booker Company and the British Publishers Association along the lines of the Pultizer Prize, of USA. The Booker Prize has only been shared in 1974 and 1992. Since 2002, it has been known as the **'Man Booker Prize'**, reflecting the sponsorship by an investment company, the Man Group plc.

JAWAHARLAL NEHRU AWARD FOR INTERNATIONAL UNDERSTANDING

Instituted in 1965, the Government of India in the memory of Jawaharlal Nehru. This award is given annually to persons for outstanding contributions to the promotion of international understanding, goodwill and friendship among the people of world. The award is administered by the Indian Council of Cultural Relations.

RIGHT LIVELIHOOD AWARD

Instituted in 1980, by Jakob Von Uexkull, a Swedish-German writer and philatetic expert after selling his stamp collection. This award is known as the 'Alternative Nobel Prize'. The Pro-ecology Right Livelihood Society, based in Britain's Isle of Man, but with a staff in Stockholm, awards this prize annually for practical and exemplary solutions to real problems of today.

UNESCO INTERNATIONAL LITERACY PRIZES

One of UNESCO's main missions is to recognize education as a human right. The organization has placed special emphasis on the education of women, because they comprise two-thirds of the world's 885 million adults with low or no literacy skills. Girls make up the majority of the more than 130 million children without access to primary schooling.

The prize giving ceremony take place each year during a special ceremony on International Literacy Day, September 8.

UNESCO'S ASIA-PACIFIC HERITAGE AWARDS

Unesco's Asia-Pacific Heritage Awards for Culture Heritage Conservation recognise the efforts and contributions of individuals and organisations within the private sector, including private-public partnerships, who have successfully restored and conserved structures and buildings of heritage value in the Asia-Pacific region.

FAO'S CERES MEDAL

The FAO awards the Ceres Medal, named after the Roman goddess of agriculture, to distinguished women who have fought against poverty. Previous recipients from South Asia include the late Indian Prime Minister Indira Gandhi, the late Mother Teresa and the Prime Minister of Bangladesh Sheikh Hasina.

OSCAR AWARDS

The annual Oscar presentation has been held since 1929. After three-quarters of a century of recognizing excellence in cinema achievement, the annual presentation of the Oscars has become the Academy of Motion Picture Arts and Sciences' most famous activity.

KALINGA AWARD

The award given for popularisation of science is an international award conferred annually by the United

Nations Educational, Scientific and Cultural Organisation (UNESCO) to a person with a distinguished career of service in the interpretation of science and research to the public. The award was instituted in 1952 at the initiative of Mr Biju Patnaik the founder of the Kalinga Foundation Trust in Orissa.

UNITED NATIONS POPULATION AWARD

This award is given annually to individuals and institutions for their outstanding work in the field of population and in the improvement of health and welfare of individuals.

THE DAVID COHEN BRITISH LITERATURE PRIZE IN ENGLISH LITERATURE

In 1993, the Cohen prize is administered by the Arts Council. It is unusual in that the general public is invited to nominate prize winners. It is awarded every year. The funds are provided by the David Cohen Family Charitable Trust and the Art Council. It recognizes lifetime achievement. V. S. Naipaul was the winner of the first award in 1993.

COMMONWEALTH WRITERS PRIZE

Since 1987 the Commonwealth Writers Prize has been awarded by the Commonwealth Foundation to "reward and encourage the upsurge of new Commonwealth fiction, and to ensure that works of merit reach a wider audience outside their own country." In each region a best book and a best first book are chosen: these comprise the overall shortlist.

THE ORANGE PRIZE FOR FICTION

Announced in 1994 and first awarded in 1996, the Orange Prize is unique in being limited to women authors.

SYDNEY PEACE PRIZE

The Sydney Peace Prize is the only International Peace Prize awarded in Australia. This Prize has global significance in terms of the support and recognition given to leaders for peace.

GOLDMAN ENVIRONMENTAL PRIZE

The Goldman Environmental prize is the world's largest prize program honouring grass roots environmentalists and is known as the noble prize for environment. Awards are given to activists in six regions-Africa, Asia, Europe, Island Nation, North America and South/ Central America.

INTERNATIONAL SIMON BOLIVAR PRIZE

The purpose of the International Simon Bolivar Prize is stated in its statutes as being to reward activity of outstanding merit which, in accordance with the ideals of Simon Bolivar, has contributed to the freedom, independence and dignity of people.

UNESCO EISENSTEIN MEDAL

The medal, bearing the likeness and signature of world cinema giant Sergei Eisenstein is awarded to deserving individuals from the world of cinematography for their contribution a dialogue among peoples, according to UNESCO.

WORLD FOOD PRIZE

The Prize recognizes contributions in any field involved in the world food supply — food and agriculture science and technology, manufacturing, marketing, nutrition, economics, poverty alleviation, political leadership and the social sciences.

The prize was created in 1986 by Nobel Peace Prize Laureate Norman Borlaug and since 1990 has been sponsored by business man and Philanthropist John Ruan.

GRAMMY AWARDS

The GRAMMY Foundation was established in 1989 to cultivate an awareness, appreciation and advancement of the contribution of recorded music American culture from the and technical legends of the past to the still unimagined musical breakthroughs of the future generations of the music professionals. The GRAMMY Foundation works in partnership with its founder, the Recording Academy, to bring national attention to important issues such as the value and impact of music and arts education and the urgency of preserving our rich cultural legacy.

MISS UNIVERSE TITLE HOLDERS

Name	Year	Country
Sushmita Sen	1994	India
Chelsi Smith	1995	USA
Alicia Machado	1996	Venezuela
Brook Lee	1997	USA
Wendy Fitzwilliam	1998	Trinidad & Tobago
Mpule Kwelagobe	1999	Botswana
Lara Dutta	2000	India
Denise M. Quinones	2001	Puerto Rico
Justine Pasek	2002	Panama
Amelia Vega Polanco	2003	Dominican Rep.
Jennifer Hawkins	2004	Australia
Natalie Glebova	2005	Canada
Zuleyka Rivera Mendoza	2006	Puerto Rico
Riyo Mori	2007	Japan
Dayana Mendoza	2008	Venezuela
Stefania Fernandez	2009	Venezuela
Ximena Navarrek	2010	Mexico
Laila Lopez	2011	Angola
Olivia Culpo	2012	USA
Gabriela Isler	2013	Russia

MISS WORLD TITLE HOLDERS

Name	Year	Country
Aishwarya Rai	1994	India
Jacqueline Maria Aguilera Morcano	1995	Venezuela
Irene Skliva	1996	Greece
Diana Hayden	1997	India
Linor Abargil	1998	Israel
Yukta Mookhey	1999	India
Priyanka Chopra	2000	India
Agbani Darego	2001	Nigeria
Azra Akin	2002	Turkey
Rosanna Davison	2003	Ireland
Maria Julia Mantilla Garcia	2004	Peru
Unnur Birna Vilhjalmsdottier	2005	Iceland
Tatana Kucharova	2006	Czech Republic
Zhang Zilin	2007	China
Ksenya Sukhinova	2008	Russia
Kaiani Aldorino	2009	Gibraltar
Alexandria Mills	2010	USA
Ivian Sarcos	2011	Venzuela
Wen Xia Yu	2012	China
Megan Young	2013	Philippines
Rolena Strauss	2014	South Africa

NATIONAL

CIVILIAN AWARDS

Bharatratna

Bharat Ratna is the highest national award given for exceptional work for advancement of art, literature and science, sports or in recognition of public service of the highest order.

RECIPIENTS OF BHARAT RATNA	
C. Rajagopalachari (1878-1972)	1954
Dr. Sarvepalli Radhakrishnan (1888-1975)	1954
Dr. C.V. Raman (1888-1970)	1954
Dr. Bhagwan Das (1869-1958)	1955
Dr. M.Visvesvaraya (1861-1962)	1955
Jawaharlal Nehru (1889-1964)	1955
Govind Ballabh Pant (1887-1961)	1957
Dr. Dhondo Keshav Karve (1858-1962)	1958
Dr. Bidhan Chandra Roy (1882-1962)	1961
Purushottam Das Tandon (1882-1962)	1961
Dr. Rajendra Prasad (1884-1963)	1962
Dr. Zakir Hussain (1897-1969)	1963
Dr. Pandurang Vaman Kane (1880-1972)	1963
Lal Bahadur Shastri (1904-1966) (Posthumous)	1966
Indira Gandhi (1917-1984)	1971
Varahagiri Venkatagiri (1884-1980)	1975
Kumaraswami Kamraj (1903-1975) (Posthumous)	1976
Mother Teresa (1910-1997)	1980
Acharya Vinobha Bhave (1895-1982)	1983
Khan Abdul Ghaffar Khan (1890-1988)	1987
Marudu Gopalan Ramachandran (1917-1987) (Posthumous)	1988
Dr. Bhim Rao Ramji Ambedkar (1891-1956) (Posthumous)	1990
Dr. Nelson Rolihlahla Mandela (1918-)	1990
Rajiv Gandhi (1944-1991) (Posthumous)	1991
Sardar Val1abhbhai Patel (1875-1950)	
Morarji Ranchhodji Desai (1896-1995)	1991
Maulana Abul Kalam Azad (1888-1958) (Posthumous)	1992
Jahangir Ratanji Dadabhai (J.R.D) Tata (1904-1993)	1992
Satyajit Ray (1922-1992)	1992

Aruna Asaf Ali (1909-1996) (Posthumous)	1997
Gulzari Lal Nanda (1898-1997) (Posthumous)	1997
Dr. Avul Pakir Jainulabdeen Abdul Kalam (1931-)	1997
Madurai Shanmukhavadivu (M.S.) Subbalakshmi (1916-)	1998
Chidambaram Subramaniam (1910-2000)	1998
Loknayak Jayaprakash Narayan (1902-1979) (Posthumous)	1999
Professor Amartya Sen (1933-)	1999
Lokpriya Gopinath Bordoloi (1890-1950) (posthumous)	1999
Pandit Ravi Shankar (1920-)	1999
Lata Mangeshkar (1929-)	2001
Ustad Bissmillah Khan (1916-2006)	2001
Pt. Bhimsen Joshi (1922-2011)	2008
C.N.R. Rao (1934-)	2013
Sachin Tendulkar (1973-)	2013
Madan Mohan Malaviya (1861-1946) (posthumous)	2014
Atal Behari Vajpayee (1924-)	2014

Feature : The decoration is in the form of a Peepal leaf, 2 in. long, 1-1/8 in. in width and 1/2 in. thick, toned in bronze. On the obverse side is embossed a replica of the sun, below which the words 'Bharat Ratna' are embossed in Hindi. On the reverse are the State Emblem and a motto in Hindi. The Emblem, the sun and rim are made of platinum.

Padma Awards

Padma Awards fall next in line after the Bharat Ratna as national awards. They were also discontinued in 1977 along with the Bharat Ratna and revived again in 1980. There are three Padma awards, viz.

(i) ***Padma Vibhushan*** is the second highest national award, given for exceptional and distinguished service in any field including services rendered by government employees.

(ii) ***Padma Bhushan*** is the third highest national award given for distinguished service in any field.

(iii) ***Padma Shri*** It is the fourth highest award given for distinguished service in any field.

Gallantry Awards

Param Vir Chakra : The Param Vir Chakra is the highest decoration of valour awarded for most conspicuous bravery, or some act of valour (in self-sacrifice, in the presence of the enemy, whether on land, at sea or in the air. The medal is made of bronze.

Mahavir Chakra : Mahavir Chakra is the second highest gallantry award for acts of conspicuous gallantry in the presence of the enemy whether on land. at sea or in the air. The medal is made of standard silver.

Vir Chakra : Vir Chakra is awarded for acts of gallantry in the presence of enemy, whether on land, at sea or in the air. The medal is made of standard silver.

Ashok Chakra : is awarded for most conspicuous bravery or some act of daring or pre-eminent valour or self-sacrifice in the face of the enemy. The medal is made of gold gilt.

Kirti Chakra : is awarded for conspicuous gallantry, otherwise than in the face of the enemy. The medal is made of standard silver.

Jamnalal Bajaj AWARDS

In 1976, the Jamnalal Bajaj Foundation was established for promoting Gandhian constructive programmes and assisting constructive workers who devoted themselves to the national cause. The foundation has instituted four annual awards each carrying a cash prize of Rs. 500,000/- for its equivalent in foreign currency a citation and a trophy. The awards are intended to recognise outstanding contribution in -

- Constructive work
- Application of science and technology for rural development
- Upliftment and welfare of women and children and/or Gandhian constructive work by women workers
- Promotion of Gandhian values outside India by individuals other than Indian citizens

Dada Saheb Phalke Award

Instituted in 1970 the Dada Saheb Phalke Award is awarded by the Government of India for outstanding contribution to the cause of cinema. The award is named after Dhundiraj Govind Phalke, the father of Indian cinema, who made India's first feature film ***Raja Harishchandra*** in 1913.

The award comprises a Swarna Kamal, a cash prize of Rs. 10 lakh and a shawl.

The award was first given to Devika Rani in 1969 who became the first lady recipient of the award.

Prithviraj Kapoor was the first to be honoured posthumously with the Dada Saheb Phalke Award.

LIST OF DADA SAHEB PHALKE AWARDEES

Year	Winner	Occupation
1969	Devika Rani	Actress
1970	B. N. Sircar	Producer
1971	Prithviraj Kapoor	actor (posthumous)
1972	Pankaj Mullick	Composer (music director)
1973	Ruby Myers (Sulochana)	Actress
1974	B. N. Reddy	Director
1975	Dhirendranath Ganguly	Actor, director
1976	Kanan Devi	Actress
1977	Nitin Bose	Cinematographer, director, writer,
1978	Rai Chand Boral	Composer, director
1979	Sohrab Modi	Actor, director, producer
1980	P. Jairaj	Actor, director
1981	Naushad Ali	Composer (music director)
1982	L. V. Prasad	Actor, director, producer
1983	Durga Khote	Actress
1984	Satyajit Ray	Director
1985	V. Shantaram	Actor, director, producer
1986	B. Nagi Reddy	Producer
1987	Raj Kapoor	Actor, director
1988	Ashok Kumar	Actor
1989	Lata Mangeshkar	Singer
1990	A. Nageswara Rao	Actor
1991	Bhalji Pendharkar	Director, producer, writer
1992	Bhupen Hazarika	Composer (music director)
1993	Majrooh Sultanpuri	Lyricist
1994	Dilip Kumar	Actor
1995	Dr. Rajkumar	Actor
1996	Sivaji Ganesan	Actor
1997	Pradeep	Lyricist
1998	B.R. Chopra	Director, producer
1999	Hrishikesh Mukherjee	Director
2000	Asha Bhonsle	Singer
2001	Yash Chopra	Director, producer
2002	Dev Anand	Actor, director, producer
2003	Mrinal Sen	Director
2004	Adoor Gopalakrishnan	Director
2005	Shyam Benegal	Director
2006	Tapan Sinha	Director
2007	Manna Dey	Singer
2008	V.K. Murthy	Cinematoegrapher
2009	Daggubati Ramanaidu	Producer
2010	K. Balachander	Director, Producer
2011	Soumitra Chatterjee	Actor
2012	Pran	Actor
2013	Gulzar	Lyricist

GOLDEN PEACOCK AWARDS

These awards have been instituted by the Institute of Directors in 1991 have given boost to Indian Industry. One can fairly assert that India's manufacturing success today is to a great measure due to the learning experience provided by the self assessment model on which the Golden Peacock Award is based. The Golden Peacock Awards are now considered as the holy grail of corporate excellence and its guidelines provide a checklist for improvement and self assessment in areas of quality, Innovation, training, governance, environment management and corporate social responsibility.

All institutions whether public, private, non-profit, government, business, manufacturing and service sector are eligible to apply. Leadership Awards are determined through nomination. They provide not only worldwide recognition and prestige but also a competitive advantage in driving business in this tumultuous world under Golden Peacock Award models. The Awards are bestowed annually and are designed to encourage total improvement in each sector of our business.

RAJIV GANDHI KHEL RATNA AWARD

It was launched in the year 1991-92 with the objective of honouring sports persons to enhance their dignity and place of honour in society. Under this, an amount of Rs. 7.5 lakhs is given as award for the most spectacular and outstanding performance in the field of sports by an individual sports person or a team.

ARJUNA AWARD

Instituted in 1961 this award is given to a sportsman who has displayed outstanding performance for three years (prior to the year of award) both at national and international levels.

The award comprises a cheque of Rs. 5.00 lakhs a small statue of the great archer from the epic Mahabharata and a citation.

DRONACHARYA AWARD

Instituted in 1985 the award was named after Dronacharya—the legendary guru of the epic age of Mahabharata who taught archery and sports to Kauravas and Pandavas.

The award comprises a cheque of Rs. 5.00 lakhs a plaque, a blazer and a citation.

DHYANCHAND AWARD

The objective of Dhyan Chand Award is to honour those Sports persons who have contributed to sports by their performance and continue to contribute to promotion of sports even after retirement from their active sporting career. This award carries an amount of Rs. 5.00 lakhs.

MAULANA KALAM AZAD TROPHY

This Trophy is awarded annually to the University which has given the best and all round performance in sports activities during the year of the award. The winner receives a replica of the Trophy and cash award of Rs. 2.00 lakhs which is to be utilized for acquiring sports equipments.

TENZING NORGAY NATIONAL ADVENTURE AWARD

These awards are given to recognize the contribution and performance in the field of adventure sports in air, water and on land. One award is given for lifetime achievement in the field of adventure sports. This is the first time that these awards are being conferred by the President of India. These awards have now been equated with the Arjuna Awards in all respects.

SAHITYA AKADEMI AWARD

It is awarded for outstanding literary works and comprises a cash prize of Rs. 1,00,000 in each of the 22 languages mentioned in the Eighth schedule of the Constitution that it supports and a copper plaque.

HARI OM ASHRAM AWARD

Administered by the University Grant Commission (UGC) out of an endowment created with the funds of the Hari Om Ashram, Nadiad (Gujarat) to honour professors in various disciplines.

SHANTI SWAROOP BHATNAGAR PRIZES

The Shanti Swaroop Bhatnagar (SSB) Prizes are awarded annually by the Council of Scientific & Industrial Research (CSIR) to outstanding Indian research workers in seven disciplines of science and technology. The SSB Prizes are awarded to scientists for their outstanding scientific contributions made primarily in India during last 5 years preceding the year of the award are eligible for the Prize.

SHAHEED NIYOGI MEMORIAL AWARD

The award was instituted in 1998 to recognise the contribution of journalists in upholding the legacy of Shanker Guha Niyogi, the firebrand trade union leader and social activist from Chhattisgarh who was murdered on September 28, 1991 by the industrial mafia.

SARASWATI SAMMAN

The award is given by K.K. Birla Foundation to an outstanding author for his literary work in any Indian language mentioned in the Eighth Schedule of the Constitution and published during the last 10 years.

CHAMELI DEVI AWARD

Endowed by Ms. Laxmi Jain in the memory of her mother, Chameli Devi Jain, the award goes to a woman journalist on the basis of excellence in terms of writing style, content as well as social concerns.

LALITKALA AKADEMI RATNA

It is an honour for the fine-arts in India, in the field of visual arts.

PRIME MINISTER'S SHRAM AWARDS

The objective of the Prime Minister's Shram Awards is to recognize the outstanding contributions made by workmen as defined in the Industrial Dispute Act,

1947 in organizations both in public and private sector and who have distinguished record of performance, devotion to duty of a high order, specific contribution in the field of productivity, proven innovative abilities, presence of mind and exceptional courage and also to the workmen who have made supreme sacrifice of laying down their lives in the conscientious discharge of their duties.

JNANPITH AWARD
Field: Literature
Instituted in: 1965

Awarded to outstanding authors of creative literature in any of the Indian languages recognised by the Constitution of India. It was sponsored by the Bharatiya Jnanpith a culturo-literary society founded in 1944 by Shanti Prasad Jain, an eminent industrialist.

SPORTS

THE OLYMPICS

The Olympic Games are the oldest and biggest series of athletic competition in the world.

Ancient Olympic Games: The origin of the ancient Olympic Games is shrouded in mystery. The first historical mention of the Game was in 776 B.C. Iphites (King of Elis) in collaboration with Cleosthenes (King of Pisa) and Lycurgus (King of Sparta) is reported to have promoted or initiated the Games at Olympia. The Olympiad celebrated that year was considered as the first and was used to date subsequent historic events. The old Olympiads were held after every four years and the Greeks measured the time in terms of the Games started on the first new moon after the summer solstice, around mid-July/August.

Modern Olympic Games: The revival of the Games was undertaken by Baron Pierre de Coubertin, a French nobleman, a brilliant educator and a practical dreamer. The Games were revived after nearly 1500 years. Baron Pierre de Coubertin was born in a family of Italian origin which had settled in France. On November 25. 1892, during a conference at Sorbonne about 'history of physical exercise', he pronounced the famous six words in public: 'The Restoration of the Olympic Games'. Coubertin wanted Paris to be the site of the First Modern Olympics and he proposed that the same should be started in the year 1900. But it was decided that the Games be started in the year 1896 itself. Venue of the First Modern Olympics was Athens (Greece). The first Modern Olympic Games were held in 1896.

Olympic Torch: The Olympic flame symbolises the continuity between the ancient and modem Olympics. The Olympic flame was lighted for the first time in 1928 at the Amsterdam stadium and since then the practice has continued.

The torch used to kindle the flame is first lit by the sun's rays at the shrine of Zeus (Greece). It is then carried overland by a relay of runners to the site of the games and placed in a bowl where it burns during the period of the Games.

The Olympic Torch Relay: The practice of Torch Relay from Olympia (Greece) to the venue of the Games was first introduced by German Olympic Committee for the Berlin Games in 1936 and, has since become part of the Olympic games.

Olympic Mascot: It was introduced in 1972 at the 20th Olympics Games held at Munich and since then an Olympic Mascot is selected for a particular year and venue. The following have been the Mascot so far:

YEAR	MASCOT	VENUE
1972	Waldi (Dachshund)	Munich
1976	Amik (Beaver)	Montreal
1980	Misha (Bear)	Moscow
1984	Sam (Eagle)	Los Angeles

1988	Hodon (Cub Tiger)	Seoul
1992	Cobi (Spain)	Barcelona
1996	lzzy (Space Creature)	Atlanta
2000	Ollie, Syd and Mille (a bird, a platypuss, and a hedge hog)	Sydney
2004	Phevos and Athena (Two brother & sister inspired by Greek dolls)	Athens
2008	The Fuwa consisting of five figures; Beibei, Jing Jing, Huan Huan, Ying ying and Nini	Beijing
2012	Wenlock and Mandeville	London

Olympic Awards and Certificates: Originally meat of the sacrificed animal was offered as prizes to the winners, which was subsequently replaced by a crown of olive branches. However, in modern Olympics, winners are awarded medals and certificates. There are three medals for the first three top positions.

I Prize	Gold Medal
II Prize	Silver Medal
III Prize	Bronze Medal

For the fourth, fifth, sixth, seventh and eighth positions only certificates are given.

Medals: The medal is about 60 mm in diameter and 3 mm in thickness. The Gold and Silver medals are both made of 92.5% pure silver. However the Gold medal is plated with 6 gm, of pure gold. The third position medal is made of bronze.

OLYMPIC GAMES (1896-2012) : AT A GLANCE

S.No.	Year	Place and Host	Countries securing first, second and third positions
1.	1896	Athens, Greece	USA, Greece, Germany
2.	1900	Paris, France	France, USA, UK
3.	1904	St. Louis, United States	USA, Cuba, Germany
4.	1908	London, United Kingdom	UK, USA, Sweden
5.	1912	Stockholm, Sweden	USA, Sweden, UK
6.	1916	Berlin, Germany	Abandoned due to World War-I
7.	1920	Antwerp, Belgium	USA, Sweden, UK
8.	1924	Paris, France	USA, Finland, France
9.	1928	Amsterdam, Netherlands	USA, Germany, Finland
10.	1932	Los Angeles, United States	USA, Italy, France
11.	1936	Berlin, Germany	Germany, USA, Hungary
12.	1940	Helsinki, Finland	Abandoned due to World War-II
13.	1944	London, United Kingdom	Abandoned due to World War-II
14.	1948	London, United Kingdom	USA, Sweden, France
15.	1952	Helsinki, Finland	USA, USSR, Hungary
16.	1956	Melbourne, Australia	USSR, USA, Australia
17.	1960	Rome, Italy	USSR, USA, Italy
18.	1964	Tokyo, Japan	USA, USSR, Japan
19.	1968	Mexico City, Mexico	USA, USSR, Japan
20.	1972	Munich, West Germany	USSR, USA, East Germany
21.	1976	Montreal, Canada	USSR, East Germany, USA

22.	1980	Moscow, Russia	USSR, East Germany, Bulgaria
23.	1984	Los Angeles, United States	USA, Rumania, West Germany
24.	1988	Seoul, South Korea	USSR, East Germany, USA
25.	1992	Barcelona, Spain	CIS, USA, Germany
26.	1996	Atlanta, United States	USA, Russia, Germany
27.	2000	Sydney, Australia	USA; Russia, Germany
28.	2004	Athens, Greece	USA. China, Russia
29.	2008	Beijing, China	China, USA, Russia
30.	2012	London, United Kingdom	USA, China, UK
31.	2016	Rio de Janeiro, Brazil	Scheduled
32.	2020	Tokyo, Japan	Scheduled

INDIA IN THE OLYMPICS

This chart comprises of only those olympics where India could manage to win at least one medal.

Year	Gold	Discipline	Silver	Discipline	Bronze	Discipline
1900			2	Athletics		
1928	1	Hockey				
1932	1	Hockey				
1936	1	Hockey				
1948	1	Hockey				
1952	1	Hockey			1	Wrestling
1956	1	Hockey				
1960			1	Hockey		
1964	1	Hockey				
1968					1	Hockey
1972					1	Hockey
1980	1	Hockey				
1996					1	Tennis
2000					1	Weight Lifting
2004			1	Shooting		
2008	1	Shooting			2	1 Wrestling 1 Boxing
2012			2	Shooting, Wrestling one each	4	Shooting, Wrestling, Boxing and Badminton one each

WINTER OLYMPIC GAMES

Winter Olympic Games were started in the year A.D. 1924. The first Games were held at Chamonix (France). The Winter Games are numbered in rotation as they are held. The programme at the winter games includes ice hockey, figure skating, speed skating, alpine skating. skiing, etc. Like the Summer Games, the winners of Winter Games are also awarded gold, silver and bronze medals. The XIX Winter Olympic Games were held in February 8, 2002 at Salt Lake City Utah (U.S.A.). It saw the expansion of the Olympic programme to 78 events including the return of Skeleton and the introduction of women's bobsleigh. Athletes from a record 18 nations earned gold medals.

VENUES OF WINTER OLYMPIC GAMES

Year	Venue
1924	Chamonix, France
1928	St. Moritz, Switzerland
1932	Lake Placid, New York
1936	Garmisch-Parten Kirchen, Germany
1948	St Mortiz

1952	Oslo, Norway
1956	Cortina d' Ampezze, Italy
1960	Squaw Valley, California
1964	Innsbruck, Austria
1968	Grenoble, France
1972	Sapporo, Japan
1976	Innsbruck, Austria
1980	Lake Placid, New York
1984	Sarajevo, Yugoslavia
1988	Calgary, Alberta
1992	Albertville, France
1994	Lillehammer, Norway
1998	Nagono, Japan
2002	Salt Lake City, USA
2006	Turin, Italy
2010	Vancouver, Canada
2014	Sochi, Russia
2018	Pyeongelang South Korea

Fundamental Principles at Olympic Games

(i) There is no distinction based on caste, colour, creed in the Olympic family.

(ii) All competitors have to be amateurs.

(iii) To create worldwide amity, feelings of brotherhood and fairplay.

Games Declared Open: The Games are declared open by the head of the State (of the host nation).

ASIAN GAMES

HISTORY

The idea of the Asian Games was first conceived by Prof. G.D. Sondhi. The suggestion for holding the Asian Games was first made in a conference of Asian countries held in New Delhi in 1947 and Jawaharlal Nehru suggested that it be called 'Asian Games'. The first Asian Games were held at New Delhi in March 1951. Since then Asian Games are held after every four years.

VENUES OF ASIAN GAMES

Year	Venue
1951	New Delhi, India
1954	Manila, Philippines
1958	Tokyo, Japan.
1962	Jakarta, Indonesia
1966	Bangkok,Thailand
1970	Bangkok, Thailand
1974	Tehran, Iran
1978	Bangkok, Thailand
1982	New Delhi, India
1986	Seoul, South Korea
1990	Beijing, China
1994	Hiroshima, Japan
1998	Bangkok, Thailand
2002	Busan (formerly-Pusan), South Korea
2006	Doha, Qatar
2010	Guangzhou, China
2014	Incheon, S. Korea
2018	Jakarta (Indonesia Scheduled)

MOTTO, EMBLEM AND TORCH OF ASIAN GAMES

The AGF adopted 'Ever Onward' given by Pt Jawaharlal Nehru as the motto of the Asian Games. The Emblem is a bright full rising sun with interlocking rings. The Maharaja of Patiala (Yadvendra Singh) presented a Torch and a flag for the first Asian Games and since then they have been carried from country to country.

First Asian Games The first Asian Games were held in 1951 at the National stadium, New Delhi, and was inaugurated by Dr Rajendra Prasad (first President of India). About 489 participants from 11 different nations participated in the Games.

Nations Which Participated in the First Asian Games Afghanistan. Burma, India, Indonesia, Iran, Japan, Nepal, Philippines, Singapore, Sri Lanka and Thailand.

Sports Played in the First Asian Games Athletics, swimming, diving and waterpolo, cycling, weightlifting, football and basketball.

COMMONWEALTH GAMES

The Commonwealth Games are a festival of sports of the Commonwealth countries. The games are held once in four years but only in between the Olympic years. When the games first began, in 1930, only 11 countries participated. The Games were originally known as the British Empire Games. These have undergone a change of name and expanded into a major multiracial and cultural event.

VENUES OF COMMONWEALTH GAMES

Year	Venue
1930	Hamilton, Canada
1934	London, England
1938	Sydney, Australia
1942-46	Games were not held
1950	Auckland, New Zealand
1954	Vancouver, Canada
1958	Cardiff, Wales
1962	Perth, Australia
1966	Kingston, Jamaica
1970	Edinburgh, Scotland
1974	Christchurch, New Zealand
1978	Edmonton, Canada
1982	Brisbane, Australia
1986	Edinburgh, Scotland
1990	Auckland, New Zealand
1994	Victoria, Canada
1998	Kuala Lumpur, Malaysia
2002	Manchester, England
2006	Melbourne, Australia
2010	New Delhi, India
2014	Glasgow, Scotland
2018	Gold Coast (Australia)

WORLD CUP FOOTBALL

The Federation International de Football Association (FIFA) was founded in Paris by representatives of seven countries Belgium, Denmark, France, Netherlands, Spain, Sweden and Switzerland on May 21, 1904. On 28th May 1928, the FIFA decided to stage a world championship of football and Uruguay was finally chosen as the host country in 1929. The original world cup trophy bore Frenchman Jules Rimet's name since. It was he who had proposed the tournament. The trophy was awarded to Brazil permanently in 1970 when it became the first country to win the world cup thrice. A new trophy called the 'FIFA World Cup' was put up for competition. Since 1930, only eight teams have been able to win the trophy.

HISTORY OF FOOTBALL WORLD CUP

Year	Host	Winner	Runner-up
1930	Uruguay	Uruguay	Argentina
1934	Italy	Italy	Czechoslovakia
1938	France	Italy	Hungary
1950	Brazil	Uruguay	Brazil
1954	Switzerland	West Germany	Hungary
1958	Sweden	Brazil	Sweden
1962	Chile	Brazil	Czechoslovakia
1966	England	England	West Germany
1970	Mexico	Brazil	Italy
1974	West Germany	West Germany	Netherlands
1978	Argentina	Argentina	Netherlands
1982	Spain	Italy	West Germany
1986	Mexico	Argentina	West Germany
1990	Italy	West Germany	Argentina
1994	United States	Brazil	Italy
1998	France	France	Brazil
2002	South Korea and Japan	Brazil	Germany
2006	Germany	Italy	France
2010	South Africa	Spain	Netherlands
2014	Brazil	Germany	Argentina
2018	Russia	Scheduled	
2022	Qatar	Scheduled	

HOCKEY WORLD CUP

The concept for an international hockey competition at the world level originated in a joint proposal made by India and Pakistan at an International Hockey Federation FIH Council meeting on March 30,1969. The first world cup was held in Barcelona (Spain) in 1971. From 1978 onwards, the tournament has been held once in four years. India has won the tournament only once in 1975.

HOCKEY WORLD CUP AT A GLANCE

Year	Host	Winner	Runner-up
1971	Spain	Pakistan	Spain
1973	The Netherlands	The Netherlands	India
1975	Malaysia	India	Pakistan
1978	Argentina	Pakistan	The Netherlands
1982	India	Pakistan	West Germany
1986	England	Australia	England
1990	Pakistan	The Netherlands	Pakistan
1994	Australia	Pakistan	The Netherlands
1998	The Netherlands	The Netherlands	Spain
2002	Malaysia	Germany	Australia
2006	Germany	Germany	Australia
2010	India	Australia	Germany
2014	The Hague Netherlands	Australia	The Netherlands

SOUTH ASIAN FEDERATION (SAG) GAMES

The SAF games was first held in 1984 at Kathmandu, Nepal. The seven participating countries are India, Pakistan, Sri Lanka, Bangladesh, Nepal, Bhutan and

Maldives. The motto of SAG games is 'Peace, Prosperity and Progress.

Year	Venus	Ranking Ist/IInd/IIIrd
1984	Kathmandu (Nepal)	India/Sri Lanka/Pakistan
1985	Dhaka (Bangladesh)	India/Pakistan/ Bangladesh
1989	Calcutta (India)	India/Pakistan/Sri Lanka
1989	Islamabad (Pakistan)	India/Pakistan/Sri Lanka
1991	Colombo (Sri Lanka)	India/Sri Lanka/Pakistan
1993	Dhaka (Bangladesh)	India/Pakistan/Sri Lanka
1995	Chennai (India)	India/Sri Lanka/Pakistan
1999	Kathmandu (Nepal)	India/Nepal/Sri Lanka
2004	Islamabad (Pakistan)	India/Pakistan/Sri Lanka
2006	Colombo (Sri Lanka)	India/Pakistan/Sri Lanka
2010	Dhaka (Bangladesh)	India/Pakistan/ Bangladesh
2013	New Delhi (India)	
2014	Kathmandu (Nepal)	Scheduled

WORLD CUP CRICKET HISTORY

Year	Venue	Winner/Runner
1975	U.K.	West Indies beat Australia
1979	U.K.	West Indies beat England
1983	U.K.	India beat West Indies
1987	India & Pakistan	Australia beat England
1992	Australia	Pakistan beat England
1996	India, Sri Lanka	Sri Lanka beat Australia
1999	U.K.	Australia beat Pakistan
2003	South Africa	Australia beat India
2007	West Indies	Australia beat Sri Lanka
2011	India, Sri Lanka, Bangladesh	India beat Sri Lanka
2015	Australia, New Zealand	(to be held)
2019	England	(to be held)

TERMINOLOGY

Athletics: Alley, Apron, Baton, Bend, Blind pass, Box, Circle, Clearance, Crossbar, Heats, False start, Flop style, Foul, Hurdles, Lane, Lap, Decathlon, Heptathlon, Marathon, Pentathlon, Scratch, Shot put, Sprint, Starting blocks, Steeplechase, Straddle, Stride, Tie, Zone

Badminton: Ace, Alley, Backhand, Block, Carry, Checking the Smash, Court, Cross-court, Double hit, Drop shot, Fault, Forehand, Frame, Game point, Kill, Lob, Love, Net, Racket, Rally, Serve, Short Serve, Shuttle (also called bird), Side-out, Underhand

Baseball: Arm thrower, Around the horn, Balk, Ball, Ball hawk, Base open, Base runner, Bat, Batter, Battery, Blank, Block, Bobble, Catcher, Cocked arm, Cross fire, Downer, Home, Hot corner, Infield fly, Keystone sack, Let up, Peg, Pinch hitter, Poppy, Punch, Rubber, Run-up, Sinker, Slider, Three foot lines

Basketball: Back-door, Bang-board, Bank bank shot, Baseball pass, Bounce pass, Charge, Chest pass, Corner players, Cut, Dead ball, Double foul, Dribble, Fake, Field goal, Foul, Free throw, Goal, Held ball, Jump ball, Pivot, Rebound, Restraining circles, T, Technical foul, Throw-in

Billiards and Snooker: Angle, Around the table, Balk, Ball, Break, Bridge, Cannon, Cue, Cue ball, Coup, Follow, Hazard, Inning, Miss, Nurse, Pocket, Pot, Pyramid, Red ball, Rests, Run, Set-up, Short, Swing, Table

Bowling: Apple, Approach, Average, Baby split, Bias, Big five, Big four, Box, Break, Bucket, Bumper, Cutter, Dive, Double, Drive, Dutchman, Floater, Grip, Groove, Handicap, Headpin, Honey, Lane, Lead, Leave, Maples, Nose hit, Mother-in-law, Pick, Pins, Pocket, Port, Sleeper, Splash, Turkey

Boxing: Apron, Attack, Back-pedal, Backhand punch, Blocking, Bolo, Bout, Butt, Chop, Combination, Cut, Dive, Elbowing, First blood, Floor, Full count, Gloves, Heeling, Holding, Hook, Jab, Mouthpiece, Punch, Ring, Scoring, Second, Spar, Warning

The boxing among the amateurs is always arranged among the boxers of almost same weights. Accordingly various categories have been made — Light flyweight (upto 48 kg), Fly-weight (upto 51 kg), Bantam-weight (upto 54 kg), Feather weight (upto 57 kg), Light weight (upto 60 kg), Light-welter weight (upto 63.5 kg), Welter-weight (upto 67 kg), Light-middle weight (upto 71 kg), Middle weight (upto 75 kg), Light heavy weight (upto 81 kg), Heavy weight (upto 100 kg), Super heavy weight (above 100 kg)

Cricket: All-rounder, Ashes, Backfoot, Bails, Ball, Bat, Batting, Batsman, Beamer, Bouncer, Boundary, Bowler, Bowling crease, Byes, Caught and bowled,

Call, Catch, Caught behind, Century, Cheeky single, Chinaman, Checker, Clean bowled, Cover, Cover-point, Cross bat, Cut, Cutters, Dead ball, Extras, Fast medium, Follow-on, Front foot, Full toss, Glance, Googly, Guard, Gully, Half Volley, Hat trick, Hit-wicket, Hook, In-swinger, Late cut, Leg break, Leg side, Maiden, Mid off, Mid on, Mid wicket, Night watchman, Point, Off-drive, Opener, Over, Overthrow, Over the wicket, Pitch, Pull, Round the wicket, Square cut, Square-leg, Sweep, Toss, Umpire, Wicket keeper, Yorker

Cycling: Ankling, Break, Bunch, Handicap, Honk, Madison relay, Musette, Pursuit

Golf: Ace, Address, Air shot, Apron, Away, Ball mark, Birdie, Bogey, Bye, Chip, Club, Cup, Drive, Eagle, Fluff, Halved, Handicap, Hazard, Hole, Honour, Hook, Jigger, Lie, Par, Pin, Pitch, Putt, Run, Slice, Stance, Swing, Tee, Wedge

Hockey: Backpass, Bully, Carrying the ball, Centre forward, Charging, Corner, D, Defender, Dribbling, Flick, Forward, Foul, Free hit, Fullbacks, Goal, Halves, Hit, Hooking, Intercepting, Long corner, Obstruction, Off-side Penalty Corner or Short Penalty stroke, Push, Reverse Stick, Scoop, Sixteen yard hit, Stick, Striking circle, Tackling, Through pass, Trapping, Twenty-five-yard line, Undercutting

Rowing: Aweigh all, Beat, Bow, Canvass, Catch, Coxswain or cox, Double, Eight, Paddle, Puddle, Recovery, Rigging, Row, Sculls, Single, Slide, Sweep, Swivel

Rugby: Blocking back, Button-hook, Centre, Clipping, Cross bar, cut back, Dead ball line, Drop kick, Fade, Fair catch, Flanker, Flat pass, Fumble, Goal, Huddle, Kick-off, Looping line, Off-side, Pack, Punt, Pushing the passer, Safety man, Screen pass, Slugging, Tackle, Throw-in, Time out, Trap, Try

Shooting: Air gun, Barrel, Bore diameter, Bull, Calibre, Canting, Drag, Firearm, Grip, Long rifle, Muzzle velocity, Rifle, Sighters, Snap, Stock

Soccer: Bicycle kick, Body swerve, Box or the penalty area, Carrying, Chesting, Clearing, Corner kick, Corner flags, Cross, Cross over, D, Direct free kick, Dive, Double Foul, Dribble, Drop ball, Extra-time, Finishing, Flank, Foul, Goal kick, Goal posts, Goals, Half-volley, Hat trick, Heading, Indirect free kick, Interception, Kickoff, Linesman, Linkman, Lob, Marking, Nutmeg, Obstruction, Off-side, Pass, Penalty spot, Reverse pass, Scissor kick, Shadow marking, Sidelines, Striker, Sweeper, Tackle, Throw-in, Tripping, Winger, Yellow card

Squash: Angle, Board court, Cut line, Drive, Foot fault, Half court line, Hammer, Hand in, Kill, Nick, Penalty point, Rally, Service box, Set, Short line, Volley, Wells

Swimming: Backstroke, Butterfly, Breast stroke, Castle, Crawl, False start, Freestyle, Kicking, Leg, Medley relay, Pool, Touch

Table Tennis: Ace, Backhand shot, Blade, Block shot, Deuce, Drop shot, Game, Grip, Rally, Service, Smash, Topspin

Tennis: Ace, Advantage, Back-court, Backhand, Ball boy or ball girl, Break, Bye, Centre line, Chip, Chop, Court, Dead, Deuce, Double fault, Down-the-line, Drop shot, Drop volley, Error, Face or a racket, Fault, Fore court, Frame, Game, Game point, Ground stroke, Let, Line ball, Lob, Love, Match point, Net, Net ball, Overhead smash, Passing shot, Rally, Retire, Return, Serve, Service, Set, Set point, Short ball, Smash, Stroke, Toss, Underhand, Volley

Volleyball: Ace, Add on, Backline, Block, Body foul, Carrying the ball, Chest pass, Cover, Cross-court shot, Deuce, Dig, Double hit, Foot fault, Game point, Kill, Held ball, Multiple touches, Net, Over-net, Point, Power serve, Serve, Set, Sideout, Smash, Spiker, Time-out, Volley

Wrestling: Ankle and leg drive, Body lock, Body press, Bridge, Cobra twist, Craddle, Cross buttock, Default, Elimination, Fall or Pin, Freestyle, Full nelson, Greeco Roman, Head-hold, Mat, Neutral position, Passivity, Penalty points, Round, Slam, Stalemate, Stranglehold, Sumo, Three points, Two points

Number of Players each side in different team games

- ✦ Baseball — Nine
- ✦ Polo — Four
- ✦ Basketball — Five
- ✦ Rugby — Fifteen
- ✦ Cricket — Eleven
- ✦ Soccer — Eleven
- ✦ Hockey — Eleven
- ✦ Volleyball — Six

In Badminton, Tennis, Table Tennis, one player on each side plays single matches and two players in each side play doubles.

IMPORTANT DIMENSIONS IN SPORTS

- ✦ Badminton Court: 20 ft x 44 ft (doubles); 17 ft × 44 ft (singles)
- ✦ Baseball: The distance between adjoining bases is 90 ft and 127 ft 33/8" among the diagonal bases. The distance between the circles of pitcher and baller is 60½ ft.
- ✦ Basketball Court: 85 ft × 46 ft
- ✦ Billiard Table: 12 ft × 6½ inch
- ✦ Boxing ring: 20 ft square
- ✦ Cricket: Wickets are 22 yard apart. Ball is about 9 cms in diameter and weighs 5½ to 53/4 ounces
- ✦ Diving: Springboards are 1 m and 3 m above the water level
- ✦ Handball court: 126 to 147 ft long and 60 to 73 ft wide
- ✦ Hockey ground: 100 yds × 55 yds
- ✦ Ice hockey ground: 184 to 200 ft long and 85-98 ft wide
- ✦ Rowing: The length of boats for Single Sculls is 27 ft, Double Sculls is 34 ft, Coxed pair is 35 ft, Coxless four is 44 ft, Coxed four is 45 ft and eight is 62 ft
- ✦ Rugby ground: Oval shaped, with maximum length 150 to 200 yds and maximum width 120 to 170 yds
- ✦ Soccer ground: 100 to 130 yds long and 50 to 100 yds wide
- ✦ Squash court: 32 ft × 21 ft. Cut line is at 6 ft and the tin at 19 inches
- ✦ Swimming pool: 50 m long
- ✦ Table Tennis: Table is 9 ft × 5 ft. The net's height is 6 inches
- ✦ Tennis Court: 78 ft × 27 ft for Singles and 78 ft × 36 ft for Doubles
- ✦ Volleyball court: 18 m × 9 m
- ✦ Marathon race: 26 miles 385 yards

FAMOUS CUPS AND TROPHIES — WORLD

American Cup	Yacht racing
Ashes	Cricket (England Vs Australia)
Canada Cup	Golf (World Championship)
Colombo Cup	Soccer
Champions trophy	Hockey (Men) (top six teams in the world)
Corbillon Cup	Table Tennis (Women) — World Cup
Davis Cup	Lawn Tennis (Men)
Derby	Horse Racing (England)
Indira Gandhi Gold Cup	Hockey (Women) (India)
Jules Rimet Cup	Soccer — World Cup (Men)
King's cup	Air races (England)
Merdeka	Soccer (Men) (Malaysia)
Prince of Wales Cup	Golf (England)
Rothman's Cup	Cricket
Ryder Cup	Golf (England)
Swaythling Cup	World Table Tennis (Men)
Thomas Cup	World Badminton (Men)
Tunku Abdul Rahman Cup	Badminton
Uber Cup	World Badminton (Women)
Walker Cup	Golf (England)
Wightman Cup	Lawn Tennis (Women)
Wimbledon	Lawn Tennis (England)

CUPS AND TROPHIES — INDIA

Aga Khan Cup	Hockey (Mumbai)
All-India Maharaja Ranjit Singh Gold Cup	Hockey
All India Guru Nanak Championship	Hockey (Women)
Barna Bellack Cup	Table Tennis (Men)
Beighton Cup	Hockey (Men)
Mumbai Gold Cup	Hockey
Burdwan Trophy	Weightlifting
C K Naidu Trophy	Cricket
DCM Trophy	Football
Dhyan Chand Trophy	Hockey
Dr B C Roy Trophy	National Junior Football
Duleep Trophy	Cricket
Durand Cup	Football
Ezra Cup	Polo
IFA Shield	Football
Irani Cup	Cricket
Deodhar Trophy	Cricket
Jayalakshmi Cup	National Women Table Tennis

Kuppuswamy Naidu Trophy	Hockey
Lady Ratan Tata Trophy	Hockey
Maulana Azad Trophy	Inter University Games
Murugappa Gold Cup	Hockey
National League	Football
Nehru Trophy	Hockey
Obaidullah Gold Cup	Hockey
Radha Mohan Cup	Polo
Rajkumari Challenge Cup	Junior Girls Table Tennis
Ramanujam Trophy	Junior Boys Table Tennis
Ramnivas Ruia Challenge Gold Trophy	Bridge
Rangaswami Cup	National Men's Hockey
Ranji Trophy	National Men's Cricket
Rohinton Baria Trophy	Inter-University Cricket
Rovers Cup	Football
Santosh Trophy	Nation Men's Football
Subroto Cup	Inter-School Football
Vizzy Trophy	Cricket
Wellington Trophy	Rowing

PLACES ASSOCIATED WITH SPORTS

Place	**Sports**
Aintree	Horse-racing (England)
Blackheath	Rugby football (England)
Brooklyn	Baseball (USA)
Cheapuk Ground	Cricket (Chennai)
Donchester	Horse-racing (England)
Eden Gardens	Cricket (Kolkata)
Epsom	Derby horse-racing (England)
Forest Hills	Tennis (USA)
Henley	Boat race (England)
Hurlingham	Polo (England)
Leeds	
Lords	Cricket (England)
Oval	
Madison Square Garden	Boxing (England)
Wimbledon	Tennis (England)
Yankee Stadium	Boxing (USA)

STADIA IN VARIOUS CITIES OF INDIA

Delhi: Ambedkar Stadium, Ferozshah Kotla Stadium, Jawaharlal Nehru Stadium, Indira Gandhi Indoor Stadium, Shivaji Stadium, National Stadium.

Mumbai: Brabourne Stadium, Wankhede Stadium.

Kolkata: Eden Gardens, Salt Lake Stadium, Ranjit Stadium, Subhas Sarovar.

Chennai: Nehru Stadium, Chidambaram Stadium, Chepauk.

Cuttack: Barabati Stadium.

Kanpur: Green Park.

Jamshedpur: Keenan Stadium.

Nagpur: Vidarbha CA Ground

Jaipur: Swai Mansingh Stadium

Gwalior: Roop Singh Stadium

Pune: Nehru Stadium

Baroda: Moti Bagh Stadium

Patna: Moin-ul-Haq Stadium

Hyderabad: Lal Bahadur Stadium

Patiala: Yaduvindra Stadium.

Bangalore: Chinnaswami Stadium.

Siliguri: Kanchenjunga Stadium.

Faridabad: Mayur Stadium.

Vishakhapatnam: Indira Priyadarshini Stadium.